OF
LOVE
AND
WARS

ALSO BY TERESA DE KERPELY

Fiction
A Crown for Ashes
The Burning Jewel
A Kiss from Aphrodite
Arabesque
Fugue

Nonfiction
Black Nightshade

OF LOVE AND WARS

Theresa de Kerpely

STEIN AND DAY/*Publishers*/New York

Acknowledgments

I wish to thank my friend Professor István Anhalt for his kindness in permitting me to quote from Pater Antal's letter to him. I also wish to thank my daughter Nina Selby for giving me access to her 1944 diary.

First published in 1984
Copyright © 1984 by Theresa de Kerpely
All rights reserved, Stein and Day, Incorporated
Designed by Louis A. Ditizio
Printed in the United States of America
STEIN AND DAY/*Publishers*
Scarborough House
Briarcliff Manor, N.Y. 10510

Library of Congress Cataloging in Publication Data

Kerpely, Theresa de, 1898–
    Of love and wars.

    1. Kerpely, Theresa de, 1898– —Biography.
2. Authors, American—20th century—Biography.   I. Title.
PS3561.E63Z472   1984   813'.54 [B]   83-40584
ISBN 0-8128-2967-0

CONTENTS

The Birth Experience

1

A Bunch of Spring Flowers

*T*HE birth of my four children was a cumulative experience, of which each successive pregnancy and labor emphasized a different aspect, and brought me to a new level of awareness. Far from being a series of isolated events, they were closely linked, and added up to a psychological whole of immense importance in the development of the person that, for better or worse, I am still in the process of becoming.

My earliest memories of the birth experience lie at the bottom of a sea sixty years deep. But as I bring them up to the surface one by one, the light I see them by is the light of the present. And in fleshing them out, struggling to recover lost details, recall half-forgotten names, clean away the accretions of time, I inevitably make use of the insights and knowledge that time has bestowed on me. And all along, under the surface, the subtle, unconscious process of reshaping, selecting, discarding has been at work.

A decision that everyone who sets out to write an autobiography has to make is whether to stick to a simple black-and-white record of documented facts, or to give equal credence to the complex, multicolored images supplied by the living memory. My decision, as a teller of tales, is a foregone conclusion.

It is March 1918. A teen-age "war bride," I am living with my parents in a little seaside town in the south of England while my husband is away fighting on a front so remote that home leave is out of the question.

My husband. I find myself using the proud possessive on every possible occasion. But a more precise word would be *bridegroom,*

3

for an interrupted honeymoon is all the married life we have had—and all we may ever have. The war has overturned the old values, the middle-class conventions—time to get to know each other, time to buy a trousseau, to furnish a new home, to establish future security. There is no time for anything now, and no predictable future to be secured. The night of love, with or without a ring, is an opportunity to be grasped at all costs, for the chances are ninety-to-one that it won't ever come again. And if it results in a child, so much the better; after this war, there won't be any young men left alive to give the young women of England their children.

I long for my absent bridegroom with all the ardor of newly awakened sex. Cut off from its natural outlet while still in full flame, it is burning me up. I have no idea how to cope with it—infidelity is unthinkable—and no one to talk with about it. Sex has never been a topic of conversation between me and my mother. And for the past three years, there has been no conversation at all between me and my father, whose speech, if not his mind, has been badly blurred by a stroke. Anyway, I am convinced that my parents know less about love than I do, and very much less about sex.

My longing for my husband is not only physical. I miss him in other ways, too—untried ways. I have, in his absence, furnished him with a halo that he has not yet had a chance to earn.

Eight-and-a-half-months pregnant, and beset by most of the miseries in the book, which no one has seen fit to explain to me, I have been forced back, willy-nilly, into dependency on my mother. Every morning after breakfast, we walk together along the seafront and into the town to do the daily errands. The morning sickness I thought I had got rid of has come back to plague me in my ninth month, and my mother says the best cure for that, and for everything else I have to endure, is plenty of exercise in the open air. I would much rather sit on a bench in the pale March sunshine and watch the waves roll in, but my mother urges me on. "Walking is good for you, darling. It improves the circulation—it will help your swollen ankles."

But nothing my mother can say or do is of any help to me in my present state of mind. There is only one cure, I think, for my ills of body and soul: the return of my husband. It's a thought that I usually keep to myself, but today I am unusually edgy, and I tell my mother ungratefully, that it would all be quite easy to bear if my husband were with me.

Her dry rejoinder takes me aback. "As a matter of fact, it's probably just as well that your husband is not with you now."

"What on earth do you mean?"

"It's a difficult time for a husband."

"But he wants more than anything in the world to be with me now! He says so in every letter!"

"No doubt he does—he's in love with you. All the same, . . ."

Catching sight of myself in a store window, I realize what she may mean. But I refuse to believe that my altered appearance would make him love me less . . . or would it? Another look, and I'm not so sure.

"All the same . . . what?"

My mother changes direction. "At a time like this, darling, a man is only in the way."

"Oh? Was Daddy in the way when you were having me?"

"Your father is a very exceptional man, darling."

Outmaneuvered, I sulk.

On our way home along the seafront, we stop by the four-sided shelter where my invalid father is sitting in his wheelchair with his back to the wind and the sea. Our wartime lodger, Mr. Fitch-Keane, is with him. Taking my father out for an airing makes Mr. Fitch-Keane feel useful. There is no place for him in this war. But although he seems old to me, it is ill health, rather than age, that keeps him from "doing his bit" in an active way. His wife is doing hers as an ambulance driver in France; his son was killed in the early months of the war. Left alone in a house much too big for one man, he offered his empty rooms to his country. They proved more acceptable than his services. Before the ensuing invasion of Belgian refugees, he fled, with his books, to the attic. A quarrelsome, ungrateful lot, his guests pursued him with constant complaints and demands, until finally he gave up, left them in full possession, and became a refugee himself—in my parents' house.

In his deerstalker cap and his Inverness cape, he looks like Sherlock Holmes. He has the same lanky build and the same droopy mustache. He is reading the morning paper aloud to my father, who listens with an expression of intense concentration, as if trying to understand a foreign language.

Upon seeing my mother and me, Mr. Fitch-Keane puts the

newspaper down and rises to his feet. He has old-fashioned manners, and an old-fashioned way of talking. "And how is our brave little lady today?" he inquires.

"Very well, thank you, Mr. Fitch-Keane. Well enough to take you on at chess again this evening."

The ends of his mustache twitch with the ghost of a smile. Every afternoon between tea and supper, I play chess with him, in the belief that I am doing him a kindness. And maybe I am, in a roundabout way. If so, the kindness is mutual; he could mate me blindfolded every time, but he sometimes allows me to win; and he always pretends I have given him a hard game.

Coal is rationed, like everything else, and very soon after our frugal supper, we let the sitting room fire go out, and retire to our unheated bedrooms, hugging our stone hot-water bottles.

Alone in my chilly double bed, propped up with pillows, the soles of my feet, braced against the side wall of my hot-water bottle, too hot, and my hands, outside the covers, icy cold, I begin my nightly ritual of communication with my husband.

The first step is to reread some of his letters to me. I skip over the passionate bits—dwelling on them leads only to frustration—and concentrate on the passages in which he describes, as far as the censor will allow, his day-to-day life as a soldier on active service; its alternating extremes of boredom and excitement, dull discomfort and mortal danger; its comedy and its agony.

Jotted down on stray pieces of paper at odd, and often precarious, moments, these letters have an immediacy that is at variance with the length of time they take to reach me. Seaborne, they arrive in batches—if an enemy submarine doesn't interfere—at irregular intervals of from four to seven weeks. And the only assurance I have that my husband is still alive when I get them is not hearing anything to the contrary from the War Office; a minute-to-minute assurance that creates its own fever of anxiety.

My letters take just as long to reach him, and the lapse of time between call and response has the same effect that distance has on a cry for help.

The help I need from him, and what every letter brings me, is a transfusion of something that he possesses in abundance, and of which I have a great deal less than I thought I had—courage.

For the benefit of everyone around me, including my parents, I wear the good-mannered, "made in England" mask of the plucky little war bride and mother-to-be keeping a stiff upper lip. But inside I am scared to death. Afraid of losing my husband, afraid of losing my baby, afraid of having my baby—terribly afraid of the unknown, untalked about experience of childbirth.

This fear is rooted in a deadly combination of imagination and ignorance, brought about by the absurd reticence of all those on whom I depend for information. My mother, my doctor, and even the seemingly no-nonsense nurse midwife who will see me through my confinement are still hidebound by Victorian prudery when it comes to the reproductive organs, and wrap up their workings in impenetrable euphemisms. My twenty-two-year-old husband knows even less about childbirth than I do. His fantasies and mine are equally unrealistic, but while I am preoccupied with the unpredictable tunnel I have to go through to become a mother, he is dazzled by the prospect of his fatherhood at the other end of it. And in writing to him I try not to dim this brightness with my own fears, or even by complaining about my bodily ills—so petty compared with his hardships and dangers.

My letters are my earliest efforts at imaginative writing; an attempt to do something more than recount the events of my day; to convey the humor or pathos underlying a banal encounter, or the emotional impact on me of a storm or a sunset, in addition to a vivid physical description of it.

Tonight, my creative energy is at a low ebb. I reread what I have written and don't think much of it. But I shall send it just the same, and exactly as it is; that is part of the ritual. At the bottom of the last page, separate from the rest of the letter, I print the words *I love you*, and underline them. They are talismanic; sent out into the dark every night like a child's prayer, in the hope that against all reason they possess the power to save and protect. Now I kiss the letter, put it into its envelope, address it, stamp it—all ready to be mailed in the morning except that it's still unsealed. The ritual demands that the line of communication should remain symbolically open until the last possible moment.

On the table beside my bed is a calendar. Before I screw the cap on my fountain pen, I put a strike through the day that is almost at an end. Now, if the doctor's calculations are correct, I have sixteen more days of waiting—or respite—before I go into the tunnel. Two days before that, just to be on the safe side, the nurse midwife will arrive. The little room next to mine has been prepared for her. The doctor, whose home is a couple of miles away, will be on call. We don't have a telephone, but our druggist, who lives over his pharmacy in the town, has offered to let us use his phone in case of emergency. "But if it's in the middle of the night," he warns my mother, "you may have a job waking me. Once I'm asleep, I sleep heavy."

In having my baby at home, I am doing the usual thing. Generally speaking, only women with no proper home, or those who have reason to fear complications, go to a lying-in hospital—at least in this little backwater. And at this stage of the war, there are very few hospital beds available. The same goes for physicians. The young ones, the pioneers of new methods, have all volunteered for the army medical corps, leaving only a handful of old-fashioned family doctors to take care of the civilian population. Mine is an elderly man who was just about to retire when war broke out, and is keeping up his practice only as a patriotic duty. He has brought a good many babies into the world in his time, and discourages fuss. "For a healthy woman," he says, "having a baby is as easy as falling off a log."

He has seen me twice and examined me once, which was quite enough for me. Spread-eagled and defenseless, my outraged body resisted this horrible new experience in the only way left to it; every muscle tensed and closed against the probing fingers. "Come, come, young lady, let go, loosen up! I'm not going to hurt you, but I've got to get in there!" Precisely. That, not the fear of being hurt, was the cause of my resistance; what I couldn't bear was the foreign invasion of territory consecrated to love.

Restored to a more dignified position, but still feeling outraged, I managed to ask him whether he had found anything wrong with me. "Not a thing! Not a thing! Just live a normal life, and it will all go like clockwork." I ventured a timid complaint about heartburn, morning sickness, and a few other disagreeable symptoms, and was told not to fuss about trifles.

When the nurse-midwife came, in my seventh month, to give me what she called "the once-over," I catalogued all my complaints for her, hoping for sympathy, and getting only philosophy, "You can't have the sweets without the bitters, dearie." But she readily answered a question that the doctor wouldn't even listen to. "It's a boy, dearie, mark my words! Only boys set up high like that—lords of creation even before they're born, bless 'em."

On her list of necessary purchases was a rubber sheet for the bed. "Why do I need this? Am I going to revert to infancy?"

"I should hope not!"

"Then what is it for?"

"It's for when the waters break, dearie."

For when the waters break. . . . I found the phrase so poetical that I didn't want to spoil it by discussing its literal meaning. Never precisely explained, it lingers in my mind like a vaguely troubling prophecy. How shall I know when the waters are going to break . . . and will they, perhaps, drown me?

It is past eleven o'clock. Time to go to sleep—if I can. First, I get up and go to the bathroom, which is next to the room in which Mr. Fitch-Keane is breathing in long-drawn rasping snores, as though his lungs are rusty. No sound comes from my parents' room. My mother has finished her nightly reading aloud to my father, and both are fast asleep. Two people with absolute faith in God, and the watch He keeps over us all. The peculiar isolation of being awake when everyone else in the house is asleep, which usually gives me a sense of freedom and power, fills me tonight with an overwhelming loneliness.

The bathroom looking glass, old enough not to flatter, confirms my misgivings of the morning and forces me to admit to myself that my pasty complexion, my lusterless hair, the dark circles under my eyes, and the formidable barrier of my swollen belly are enough to put off the most loving husband.

This glimpse of a hard reality obscured until now by the haze of romantic love, sends through me a shiver of apprehension. I become aware of a new kind of loneliness, the isolation of being trapped in an unsightly body. And now, for the first time since my marriage, I want my mother, like any frightened child. But after my implicit denial that very morning of her ability to help and console me, I am ashamed to knock on her door now and tell her that I need her. I am tempted to awaken her and attract her attention by the indirect means of pulling the chain of the tank above the toilet, which makes so much noise that we don't pull it during the night unless absolutely necessary. But that would awaken my father and Mr. Fitch-Keane as well, which wouldn't be fair—just on account of a fit of depression. I tiptoe back to my room, feeling miserable but righteous.

There is no light switch beside my bed, the overhead bulb in its milky glass globe is controlled by a switch near the door. Before I turn it off for the night, I set a little wax night-light, about half the size of a votive candle, at the bottom of my washbasin. Its tiny flame is invisible as long as the overhead light is on, but as soon as I turn it off, the night-light develops a sinister power out of all proportion to its size—just as it used to do in my childhood. From the depths of its pink china crater, it transmogrifies the room; casts enormous, fluttery shadows on walls and ceiling, turns the bulky Victorian wardrobe into a monster, lets loose the baleful monkey that chatters and grins on the other side of the looking glass.

Getting to sleep is a matter of physical weariness overcoming physical discomfort. Tonight, the weight of the child is almost insupportable, and its restlessness defeats every change of position. It seems to be pressing against my belly on all sides, as though in a desperate attempt to get out.

I wish it would get out. I want to be rid of it. I resent its merciless takeover. I want to possess my own body again.

Sleep, when it finally comes, is riddled with evil dreams. The night-light shadows come down from the walls and ceiling and flap around me like ravens. The wardrobe threatens to crush me. The monkey leaps up on the bed and attacks me with grinning teeth. The child inside me heaves like an earthquake, shatters the walls of its prison, and overpowers me.

I wake up gasping for breath and fighting off my quilt as if it were alive. My throat is very dry. I empty the glass of water beside my bed and get up for more. I am sweating profusely, yet the room is colder now than it was when I went to sleep. A sea wind has sprung up, making the windows rattle and blowing draftily in through the chinks in their ill-fitting frames. I can

hear the exciting roar of an incoming tide. I slip behind the
curtains—lined with black cotton to keep the light from showing
—and look out across the strip of wasteland that separates the
road from the beach. But I can't see the water. I can't see anything. The blackout is total, without moon or stars to relieve it.
Just the sort of night for an air raid, though up to now there
haven't been any raids on this stretch of coast. Farther down the
road, which tails off into sand dunes, are a few other small houses
like ours. We don't know the people who live in them; we are all
enclosed in our own private zones of darkness. I wonder what it
would be like, what would happen, if a zeppelin actually were to
appear in the overcast sky. Would the shock of it serve to unlock
the doors between each little blacked-out cell?

It is two o'clock in the morning.

I get back into bed and try to ease the weight of my body by
taking a pillow from under my head and putting it under the base
of my spine. The shift of balance helps. The cold air by the window
has chilled me, and the warmth of my down quilt, stifling before,
is now deliciously comforting. Mind and body relax together. I
feel the approach of sleep and the lovely sensation of surrendering
to it, of slowly, slowly, going under. . . .

The monkey springs. It catches me around the middle with the
grip of a steel vise. I am too frightened to move or even to cry out.

When it lets go, the relief is instantaneous, the freedom from
pain total, and I realize that the same thing must have happened
before, more than once, perhaps, while I was still asleep; that my
nightmares were the symbols of a physical reality.

Now I am not ashamed to go to my mother and tell her that I
need her. I knock softly, so as not to awaken my father. She opens
the door at once. She is still half asleep. "What is it?"

"A perfectly awful pain."

"Where?"

"All around here—back and front. Do you think it's the baby
coming . . . so soon?"

"It could be. Whatever it is, I must call the doctor. Go back to
bed, and I'll get dressed."

I must look as terrified as I feel. My mother puts her arms
around me. "There's nothing to be afraid of, darling. Even if it is
the baby coming, nothing will happen yet—these are only the

first pains. Don't resist them, go with them, and after a while you'll get used to them. Now, get back into bed and keep warm— you're shivering."

In less than ten minutes, she looks into my room, all ready to go out. "Daddy wants to come in and keep you company while I'm gone—would you like that?"

"Oh, yes!"

My father comes shuffling in on my mother's arm. She settles him into an easy chair beside the empty fireplace, tucks a plaid around his knees and a shawl around his shoulders.

He says thickly, "Fitchkeane."

"Should I tell him?"

My father nods emphatically. My mother's eyes question me.

I want all the moral support I can get. "Yes, Mummie, tell him—he'll be hurt if you don't."

While my mother is talking to Mr. Fitch-Keane, another pain grips me. This time I cry out. My mother comes running and holds my hand while the pain lasts, and it doesn't seem quite as bad as it was before. "I wish you didn't have to leave me, Mummie."

"So do I . . . but I must."

"Couldn't Mr. Fitch-Keane go instead?"

"I'd rather speak to the doctor myself. I won't be long. I can get to the pharmacy and back in half an hour, if I walk fast."

My father looks worried. "Takecare," he says all in one word. "Dark."

I hear the front door close behind her with a sinking sense of abandonment. This panic fear of being left is something altogether new; as a rule, when I'm not feeling well I want above everything else to be left alone. Now, I welcome even my father's mute presence in the room. At the head and foot of my old-fashioned bedstead are bars and crossbars of polished brass. From where I lie, I can see my father's face between them, like a portrait framed in gilt. Detached from the rest of him, like the separately reproduced detail of a large painting, his slightly lopsided face is amazingly eloquent. It tells me what his tongue cannot say, and never could say, even before his stroke; how dearly he loves me. My mother has often told me that whenever I got sick as a child, my father would get sick too, out of sympathy.

But I never really believed that, until this moment. I get out of bed and crouch on the floor beside him, my head against his knees.

A timid knock on the half-open door, an apologetic cough. "It's Fitch-Keane. . . . Is there anything I can do?"

"I don't think so—but do come in."

"Please excuse my informal attire."

His informal attire is as modest as a monk's habit, but more elegant: a camel's hair dressing gown that covers all but the cuffs of his striped pajama legs, soft morocco slippers that reveal no more than an inch or two of bare ankle, and a paisley silk scarf that conceals his collarless neck up to his Adam's apple. Compared to this, my appearance is almost indecent; naked feet, loose, tangled hair, a nightgown missing a top button, and a wrapper that doesn't quite meet across my bulging stomach. I suppress a hysterical giggle and an urge to hug the immaculate Mr. Fitch-Keane for restoring my sense of humor, too long mislaid.

"I think I'll get back to bed."

Mr. Fitch-Keane offers me his arm and conducts me to my bedside as though to a dinner table.

"Fire," says my father.

"Fire?"

"Cold."

"Oh, *I* see . . . you'd like me to get a fire going! Of course, of course . . . with pleasure."

"A fire would be lovely, if you really don't mind. Mr. Fitch-Keane."

"Just tell me where to find the makings."

"You'll find sticks and newspaper in the kitchen, next to the range. There's probably a scuttleful of coal there too."

I feel I ought to help him. I am perfectly capable of moving about between pains. But I can't get over a fear that something might happen without warning—just what I don't know, but I feel more secure in bed.

Mr. Fitch-Keane builds a tidy pyramid of sticks around a pile of crushed newspaper, boy scout fashion, dots the whole structure with pieces of coal small enough to catch fire easily, then sets a match to it. The paper flames up, the dry sticks start to crackle, the first coal catches, and the room is filled with smoke.

"Damper," says my father.

"Damp?"

Choking with laughter and smoke, I manage to say, "He means the damper's closed. You can push it open with the poker."

Mr. Fitch-Keane pokes blindly into the chimney and almost falls into the grate when the damper flies suddenly open and releases a torrent of soot that puts the fire out and covers his beautiful camel's hair robe with a fine black bloom.

His ruined elegance makes me feel guilty. But I can't control my laughter. I have to escape for a moment. "I'll fetch a brush and dustpan. . . ."

"No, no! *Please* don't move!"

I am up and out of the room before he can stop me. The mops and brooms are kept in a closet just along the passage. A fallen broom handle trips me up as I reach for a dustpan hanging on the wall, and I come down heavily, knocking over a bucket.

"Oh my God!"

Can it really be Mr. Fitch-Keane saying that, and in such a tone? I am helped to my feet, gently propelled along the passage and into my room, laid gingerly on my bed like a parcel marked *Fragile,* and carefully covered with my down quilt. "All right now?"

"Yes, thank you, Mr. Fitch-Keane." I would like to apologize to him for being such a nuisance, but the effort is too great.

I lie very still, hoping that everything *is* all right. My father utters indistinct, anxious-sounding monosyllables. Mr. Fitch-Keane moves about the room quietly, doing this and that. Pains come and go. The intervals between them seem to be getting longer instead of shorter, as if the baby is growing tired. But that may be an illusion. I am growing very tired myself. Letting myself go with the rhythmic rise and fall of the pains, I am drifting in and out of a semi-sleep that confuses my sense of time, and the wavering light of the fire, now brightly burning, is sweetly hypnotic.

"Kettleon," says my father.

Too lethargic to speak, I leave Mr. Fitch-Keane to translate this as best he can. He does very well. He brings in the big kitchen kettle with the curved spout and plants it amid the flaming, illicit coals of that wickedly extravagant fire. Very soon, licked on all sides by the flames, it begins to sing. The hot-water is meant for the doctor's use, I realize that, but the kettle sings of tea. Mr. Fitch-Keane, who hears the same song, brews a whole potful. If it weren't for my pains, and the relentless approach of their climax, it would be quite cozy.

The strong tea pulls me together and helps me to think more clearly. I look at the clock. My mother has been gone for more than two hours. What can have happened? Have my father's fears come true—has she fallen and hurt herself, has she never got to the pharmacy? I fight down a rising panic. Scraps of information come into my head, and I grasp at whatever reassurance they offer: *With a first baby labor is always slow.... You can judge how it's getting on by the nature of the pains. ... When the final stage sets in they undergo a change, and the waters break.*

That reminds me that I haven't put the rubber sheeting over the mattress. But I don't feel capable now of remaking the bed without help, and I can hardly ask Mr. Fitch-Keane to help me with something like that. Oh Mummie! Mummie! Where are you? Why don't you come?

Without any warning, the waters break. "Mr. Fitch-Keane! Will you please give me a towel—they're in that drawer. . . ."

He brings me a big soft towel, very quickly, as though he has guessed what it's for. As soon as his back is turned, I shove it under me. I feel sick and rather giddy, as if I am going to faint. Suddenly I hear myself scream. Then the pain rushes into my lungs like water, stopping my breath. The pain is inside me and all around me at the same time. It picks me up and smashes me down like a match-stick raft beached by a giant breaker. . . .

When I come to my senses I find myself clinging with all my might to Mr. Fitch-Keane's hand.

He is saying something. His voice seems to come from a distance. From somewhere high up, where the waves that are drowning me can't get at him. "When my wife was in labor with our son, I remember it very distinctly, she held onto the bedrail... like this . . . may I?" He gently frees his hand from my grasp and places my sweating palms around the cold brass bed-rail. "She found it a great help. . . ."

But I need a different kind of help, and my eyes fill with tears because Mr. Fitch-Keane has taken his hand away.

The waves of pain mount. The bed-rail becomes the rope thrown from a lifeboat. Mr. Fitch-Keane's voice comes closer. "That's right . . . Hold on . . . Hold on. . . ." Now his hand, which I thought I had lost, is pressed against the small of my back, pushing against my pain, keeping my spine from breaking in two as my body is picked up and thrown down by the storm, picked up and thrown down, over and over and over. . . . "Hold on! Hold on! Now rest . . . rest. . . ." My body responds to these orders on its own. I am not in charge any longer.

I lie in momentary peace in the trough of a wave, waiting. But the wave fails to mount. It's as if the spring that controls the storm has suddenly snapped. My hands let go of the bed-rail. My arms drop to my sides. "She's falling asleep. . . ." Mr. Fitch-Keane's voice is so distant now I can scarcely hear it. The hand at the base of my spine is withdrawn. Bruised and exhausted, I float all alone on the sea wrack.

I become aware of movement around me, excitement, voices, hands. Are they pulling my drowned body out of the sea?
"Will everyone please leave the room."
"One moment, Doctor, I want her to know that I'm here."
"Mummie!"
Doctor and nurse bend over me, feeling, pressing, probing my inert body, and talking to one another in terms I don't understand.
They pull me up to a sitting position, swing my legs over the side of the bed, and set my feet on the floor. "We've got to get things moving again, young lady."
So I'm going to be rewound like a run-down clockwork toy.
"Now, dearie, we'll walk up and down the room for a bit and see if that livens things up."
It does. Afraid that the child will drop out of me onto the floor at any moment, I beg them to let me lie down. But they keep me upright. "Push . . . Pull . . . Push . . . Breathe in . . . Breathe out. . . ." They are like relentless drill sergeants. "Bear down . . . Harder, harder, harder. . . ."
I am stretched to bursting point. It is almost beyond endurance.

Then everything comes to a halt, as it did before. The nurse helps me onto the bed and sponges my face with cold water. She and the doctor once again murmur together in cryptic medical terms. I grab the nurse's hand, "What's the matter? What's going to happen?"

"Everything's all right, dearie. You'll have your baby very soon now. Doctor's going to help you."

I feel the cold touch of metal, a gradual, blessed easing, then a sudden, gigantic relief. I can't see what's going on, I am lying with my head lower than the rest of me, and I don't have the strength to raise it. I hear the sound of a slap, but no cry. I am seized by a terrible fear. Doctor and nurse move away from my bed. More slaps, and a splashing of water. At last it comes, the cry that is like nothing else in the world. But so weak, so dreadfully weak. . . . "Nurse! Nurse!" "Just a minute, dearie." The cry is repeated, more strongly, becomes an enraged howl. Only now am I told that I have a son.

The nurse brings him over to me, wrapped in a towel. "Isn't he beautiful?"

He is wizened and purple, like an angry old man. Not beautiful at all. Just a miracle.

Cleaned up, washed, powdered with scented talcum, I am carefully placed on a Turkish towel folded in half lengthwise. "What's this for?" "You'll soon see, dearie." It is wound around my middle, pulled tight, wound again, pulled tight with all the nurse's quite considerable strength, and secured with half a dozen large safety pins. When I complain that I can't breathe, she says, "You want to get your flat tummy back, don't you? You want that handsome husband of yours to fall in love with you all over again when he comes home, don't you?"

The baby has been trussed with a strip of flannel in much the same way, but for different reasons. "We don't want our belly button to stick out, do we, lovey?" He is placed in my arms now and introduced to my breast.

"Nurse, there's something I want to know. As soon as he was born you slapped him—I heard you."

"That's right. We slap newborn babies to start them crying."

"But he didn't cry. Why not? What was wrong?"

"Now, dearie, let's not worry our heads about what's over and done with."

"*What was wrong?* I demand to be told! I'm sick of being treated like a child or an idiot!"

"All right, all right! Calm down or you'll give the baby colic! If you must know, he was born with the cord, the umbilical cord, wound around his neck, so he couldn't breathe."

"And you were afraid he wasn't ever going to breathe, weren't you?

"Just for a moment, yes."

"So he really is a miracle."

"Of course he is! Every perfect baby that comes into the world is a miracle. You'd know that if you'd seen what I've seen in my time."

Her tone suggests a rich vein of fascinating information to be tapped, if only I go about it in the right way.

She goes off now to unpack her things and drink a cup of tea, leaving me alone with my miracle. Spent, but happy, I lie thinking of nothing; content in that special state of bliss that follows relief from extreme pain—as if, in the final analysis, all grief and unrest have their origins in the body. My son falls asleep at my breast. I lay him carefully down beside me on the vacant side of the big bed.

My mother comes in to adore. She has just been into the town to send a telegram to my husband in care of the War Office. There is a subtle change in her manner to me—or is the change in me, in my perception of her? Whichever way it is, I feel for the first time that she and I are on equal terms; that in giving birth, I have come of age. But the sense of having achieved a new status doesn't lessen my reserve. I tell her nothing of what I went through during her absence; it is she who tells me, rather apologetically, what happened to her.

First of all, she explains, the walk into the town took much longer in the blackout than it did during the day. And when she finally got to the pharmacy, she couldn't arouse the druggist. "I banged and banged on the door, and I rang the bell over and over again—I could hear it jangling—but that man slept through everything!"

"He said he was a sound sleeper."

"He must be deaf as well, or do you think he drinks?"

"More likely he mixes a sleeping draught for himself."

"Well, you can imagine how desperate I felt. I didn't know where to turn—at three o'clock in the morning with the whole town blacked-out and dead as a doornail."

"You would have found somebody to help you at the police station."

"The *police station!* But I've no idea where it is! I've never been arrested, darling!"

"Neither have I, Mummie. But I know it's on Hill Street. Anyway, what did you do?"

"I decided to waste no more time, but simply to walk the two miles, or whatever it is—it felt more like three—to the doctor's house. And when I got there, he was out! *Out!* Delivering some other woman's baby! I could have wept. Well... I did weep a little. The doctor's wife was very sympathetic. She got hold of him on the phone, and he said he was almost ready to leave, and would pick up the nurse on his way home and drive us both back here in his pony trap. Thank God we arrived when we did."

"How's Daddy? Was he dreadfully upset?"

"Upset! He might just as well have been having the baby himself, and I'm sure he wished he could have had it for you. I made him go to bed, but he didn't sleep; he refused even to close his eyes until he knew that you and the baby were all right. He's asleep now. He'll come in to see you later. And Mr. Fitch-Keane would like to 'pay his respects,' as he puts it, whenever you feel up to seeing him. Daddy said he was very helpful last night."

"Yes. He was. I'll see him now, if he'd like to come in for a moment."

He comes in on tiptoe, with a bunch of spring flowers in his hand. I feel very shy, and so, I think, does he. Last night's abandonment of decorum stands between us now like a guilty secret. I have no experience in handling a situation like this. But Mr. Fitch-Keane handles it for me with an exaggerated old-world courtesy, which before last night would have made me want to laugh, but which now brings a lump to my throat.

"I would like to offer you my congratulations on the birth of your son."

"Thank you, Mr. Fitch-Keane."

"And my sincere admiration. You passed, if I may be permitted to say so, a very trying ordeal with flying colors."

I would like to say, *So did you*, but I feel it would only embarrass him. "You are very kind, Mr. Fitch-Keane."

He stands looking down at me and my sleeping son, now soft and pink as a peony bud, as if he is not quite sure where he is, or who we are, or for whom he has brought the flowers.

2

A Celebration of Friendship

*I*F the birth of my first child was primarily a matter of coming to grips with the frightening independence of my own body, the birth of my second marked the first stage of a long voyage of emotional and psychological discovery that began with my husband's return from the war.

He was demobilized, with a Military Cross and the rank of captain, when his son was sixteen months old.

He and I had not seen each other for two years; during which time we had each constructed an idealized image of the other, based on a courtship compressed by the war into three or four love-dazed encounters and a few precarious weekends of married life in a hotel room near his camp, from which at any moment could come a message that might take him away from me forever.

The two years following our reunion were, for both of us, a struggle to come to terms with reality. His problem was that of the soldier who comes home at the end of a long war to find himself hopelessly out of tune with his former life; a spiritual changeling. Mine was the problem of getting to know the stranger to whom I was married. And of learning to live with him in a world as alien and indifferent to me as it now was to him; the London world of the rich and famous, of the writers and artists and politicians who crowded around my husband's beautiful, brilliant mother—who was, ironically, the only member of his family who did not dismiss me as an utterly insignificant country mouse.

In choosing the Foreign Service as a career, my husband was

seduced by the combination of security and escape that it offered. For me, who had never been farther from home than Scotland, the prospect of foreign travel was wildly exciting. And I had an idea that it might be less painful to be an alien in a strange land than to feel like an alien in one's own.

The strange land I envisioned was a long way off, bathed in continual sunshine and drenched with the perfume of lemons. The actuality turned out to be just across the Channel, bathed in gray mist, and drenched in cold rain for most of the year—the Netherlands.

Our first home there—not counting the pension where we learned to eat cheese on slices of gingerbread for breakfast—was on the main floor of a once-magnificent merchant's house in Old Rotterdam, the Rotterdam that was bombed out of existence in World War II. They told us at the consulate that the quarter was unsuitable for a British official to reside in. Formerly a citadel to which only the wealthiest foreigner could have gained admittance, it was now considered too disreputable even for an impecunious junior vice-consul. But that in itself was a recommendation as far as my husband was concerned; he detested middle-class respectability and was always trying to cure me of mine, as if it were a bad habit.

He heard about the vacant apartment from a maverick member of the consular corps, the Russian consul, an aristocrat by birth and a bohemian by nature, who lived, undeterred by convention, in a part of town that had never been considered anything but disreputable. My husband took to him at once, and the liking was mutual. Each recognized in the other a kindred spirit. As for me, I was fascinated by a personality that I believed to have been invented by Dostoevski and never expected to encounter in real life. Emotional, generous, melancholy, at once childlike and subtle, religious and libertine, this unlikely individual soon became our best friend. Although he was older than we were, he was still a young man, probably in his mid-thirties. But for me, his age was as irrelevant as the age of a rare species of bird. His name was Fersen. Baron Fersen.

His position as Russian consul was anomalous and exceedingly uncomfortable. Appointed to the post some years earlier by the tsarist regime, he was not officially recognized by the Bolsheviks, but neither was he replaced. Unpaid, living on a tiny private income, he continued to look after the welfare of his compatriots, whether settled, long-time residents of the city, refugees from the revolution, or stranded seamen. And in the eyes of all these people, badly shaken by the events in their own country, Baron Fersen was irreplaceable; a sort of "little father."

I met him for the first time when he came to pick us up at our pension to take us to see the dwelling that British officialdom disapproved of. What impressed me most about him then was the ease with which he made friends with my little son, whose experience with his father, as a stranger who had entered his life too late to be anything but an invader, had made him wary of men in general. He must have sensed the child in Fersen and the deep understanding of children that seems to be part of the Russian makeup, for he trotted happily to the streetcar stop hand in hand with this man he had never seen before, and insisted on sitting beside him on the trip downtown. My husband was clearly upset, and I knew that only his liking for Fersen kept him from indulging in the sarcasm with which he usually tried to disguise hurt feelings.

His failure to win his son's confidence and affection was the chief reason why I was once again pregnant. He wanted another chance, a child who would be as much his as mine from the very beginning. And he hoped it would be a daughter.

We got off the tram at the corner of a wide, but lifeless, street and walked a little way along it. The forlorn dignity of departed glory gave it a melancholy air. The upper floors of its ancient dwellings still retained their lovely façades, but on the ground level, where the grand front doors used to be, were poor little neighborhood shops; a bakery, a shoemaker's, a tavern, a shop that sold horsemeat—"One eats that here," Fersen told us in French, which he spoke fluently, "and it's not bad."

He stopped, facing a house on the other side of the street with two large first-floor windows jutting out over the sidewalk. "There you are," he said, "that's the house, and those are the windows of the apartment." Below them were no shops, but no front door either, only a bricked-up archway and a row of small windows masked with lace curtains. The entrance, Fersen told us, was on the other side of the building.

Still hand in hand with my son, he led us into a narrow, cobble-stoned back street, whose name, on a sign affixed to a lamp post, was Houttuin, which he translated literally as Woodgarden, "A pretty name, *hein?*"

Whatever the origin of the pretty name may have been, no trace remained of the rustic peace it suggested. The Houttuin's present charm lay in its gutter vitality. It had the peculiar behind-the-scenes authenticity that distinguishes backs from fronts, and the eloquent blend of odors that leave you in no doubt as to which side you are on. In this Dutch alley, the aroma was made up of coffee, chocolate, baking bread, frying fish, garbage, and the astringent, ammoniac smell of a stable—whose source was not far to seek. Almost blocking the street were two strapping cart horses har-nessed to a dray being loaded with mammoth cheeses that were being rolled down a ramp from the warehouse, like so many spare wheels.

From beyond this obstruction came three boys on bicycles, all dressed alike in dark blue jackets with red knitted caps and mufflers. One after another, they swerved to the right to avoid the horses and then to the left to avoid us, gaily describing figures of eight. My son clapped his hands, "Circus!"

"No, my small one," said Fersen, whose English was a literal translation from French, "those are the messengers of the land-lord."

The landlord, a burly, red-bearded man wearing a white coat like a doctor's, was awaiting us at the open door of his business premises on the ground floor of his house; the headquarters of the De Groote Messenger Service, of which he was the proud, the inordi-nately proud, commander in chief.

"Mynheer De Groote," said Fersen, who obviously knew his man, "is of more importance to the population of this city than the postmaster himself—especially to the ladies. How can one trust a *billet doux* to a postman who may deliver it at exactly the wrong moment?"

The landlord smiled, ostensibly at the compliment, but a twin-kle in his small, flesh-buried eyes suggested that he had delivered a good many *billets doux* for Fersen at exactly the right moments. Among his consular colleagues, Fersen had the reputation for being a bit of a womanizer, and my husband had been jokingly advised to keep an eye on me. But he needed no warning to do that; his eye was never off me.

Without mentioning the reason for our visit, Fersen drew our attention to the fleet of shining bicycles standing, or rather, hanging at the ready so that if one should come back with a flat tire, there would always be another to take its place. Taking Fersen's cue, we asked questions, and marveled politely at the efficiency of Mynheer De Groote's organization. The lads reported for work in shifts, in numbers suited to the demand at different times of the day, but their commander took pride in the fact that whatever the hour there was always someone available to pick up and deliver an urgent message or a bottle of needed medicine.

When Mynheer De Groote was not busy dispatching his messengers, he was busy taking care of his property. It seemed there was nothing that he could not repair expertly for himself, from a leaky roof to a piece of antique furniture, of which there were two examples in his workshop; a seventeenth century chest that was being refinished after something had been spilled on it and an equally ancient wooden cradle with an obstinate creak in its rockers.

Only after all this had been explained and applauded did Fersen say, casually, "Mynheer Consul is looking for a furnished apartment for his family. . . ."

The landlord now reversed the official position by scrutinizing us as if he wasn't at all sure that we would be suitable tenants for his precious apartment. Finally he said, "It is possible that I have what Mynheer Consul is looking for." But when my husband inquired about the rent, he shrugged. "The rent is not important, Mynheer."

My husband said, "It's important to me." But the landlord chose not to understand. The mixture of Dutch, English, and French in which our three-sided conversation was carried on left plenty of room for intentional misunderstanding.

The business premises were connected with the rest of the house by an inside door, which led into a hallway with a staircase in the middle and a door at each end. The one at the Houttuin end was the entrance for all the occupants of the house. The one at the other end was, Fersen said, that of the ground floor apartment, whose small, lace-curtained windows we had seen from the outside. I assumed it was where the landlord himself lived.

He led us up the uncarpeted wooden stairway to the first landing, where he unlocked a small but heavy door. With an expansive gesture, he ushered us into one of those interiors, half-glimpsed and half-imagined behind the portraits or the still-life studies of laden tables, done by the old Dutch painters.

What I took away with me that day was not the sharply detailed picture that I recall now, but a general impression and a revelation of national character that was verified by closer acquaintance. The special characteristics of the Dutch people—their domestic pride, their fanatical cleanliness, their moral austerity coupled with physical self-indulgence, even their secret licentious dreams—were all manifested in Mynheer De Groote's treasured apartment, together with a physical phenomenon peculiar to Dutch interiors, the luminosity of objects, which acts as an antidote to the gloom of the weather outside.

The apartment, which covered the entire first floor of the house, was divided into two distinct areas; the converted, in which a cluster of small rooms had been made over into bathroom, kitchen, pantry, and a room for a live-in maid; and the unconverted, in which the past had been left intact. We were shown this first.

A wide corridor, whose floor was so highly polished that it reflected all the other luminosities—of polished wood paneling, mirrors, and the diamond panes of a stained glass window, ran the length of the building, rising with three shallow steps to the double-winged doors of the room with the jutting windows.

All my life I have assessed the liveability of a room in proportion to the scope of its view of the world outside, and these particular windows seemed to promise a glimpse of the unknown. Deeply embrasured, with folding inside shutters and cushioned window seats, they had heavy looped-back curtains of crimson velvet, which could enclose anyone sitting there like the curtains in back of a box at the theater.

It was not yet four o'clock in the afternoon, but the sky was overcast, and the lights were beginning to go on in the little shops on the other side of the street and in some of the upper windows, setting in motion the strange allure of other people's lives. The landlord switched on the lights in the room behind me. Turning back into it, I sensed in advance the enclosure of long winter evenings to come and a vague apprehension. Two anachronistic overstuffed easy chairs faced each other from either side of the stove, a potbellied iron monster with a red mica face, and I could see my pregnant self sitting there tranquilly reading or sewing. But I couldn't see my husband sitting tranquilly opposite me.

The bulky modern armchairs, though they didn't go with the rest of the room, were legitimate concessions to comfort on the part of the landlord. But how could a man with such a strong sense of the past and so much pride in its preservation conceal the rude beauty of an ancient refectory table with a red plush table-cloth? I did him an injustice. The cloth was there to conceal hideous scars, deep wounds made by knives or swords, records of human passion that his sense of the past would not allow him to eliminate.

Except for the table, the various shining surfaces diffused their luminosity unhindered. A tall oak dresser mirrored the burnished pewter arranged on its shelves. A huge cupboard, dark and forbidding as an up-ended coffin, returned the red glow of the stove's mica face. And the floorboards reflected everything, dark and light, like a clear pool.

The bathroom and kitchen were modern, with a big gas geyser to heat the bathwater, and a little one over the kitchen sink to heat the dishwater, and intimidatingly clean. I wasn't sure whether I could live up to such a standard.

Adjoining the bathroom was what Fersen called an "English sleeping room." Airy, but austere, it suggested woolen nightcaps and red flannel nightshirts.

"But we can't do with fewer than two bedrooms!"

"Do not disturb yourselves," Fersen said, "a surprise awaits you."

My husband brightened. He loved surprises of any kind, and if they didn't occur in the natural order of events he expected me to provide them.

A section of paneled wall in the corridor turned out to be a door, worked by a secret spring like those of the priests' hideouts in the country houses of Catholic noblemen in Elizabethan England, when the celebration of the Mass was proscribed.

But behind this hidden door no such holy rite was in progress. Quite the contrary.

At the landlord's sweeping gesture of invitation, we stepped straight into a pagan dream. The voluptuous secret dream of a long dead Dutch merchant. A painted world peopled with nymphs and satyrs, frenzied maenads and grape-stained acolytes of an obscene vine-garlanded god; a world with only one season— the season of lust.

We stood there stunned. A pair of naked bacchantes laughed down at us from the ceiling, suspending between them a golden chandelier like a tempting cluster of grapes. Below it, deep in the lush green and rose of an Aubusson carpet, stood an elegant eighteenth century table surrounded by little gilt chairs. Nothing else. No windows, only a latticed air vent high up on one wall. Nothing to spoil the alfresco illusion. Whoever dined here would be a participant, willing or no, in the bacchanalian revels.

My son sat down on the Aubusson carpet and gazed in innocent wonder at the goings-on around him.

"If we do take this place," my husband said, "the first thing we'll do is give a dinner in here and invite the CG."

Fersen laughed. The excessive starchiness of the British consul general was made fun of by his colleagues as well as by his subordinates. But I didn't want to embarrass him or do anything that he would consider in poor taste, which was just the sort of conventional attitude that my husband wanted to cure me of.

"Don't look like that," he said. "It may give the old boy a bit of a shock, but behind that stiff shirt of his he'll love it."

"Naturally," said Fersen. "Under the shirt is a man, after all."

Mynheer De Groote laid his large hairy hand on a ripe pomegranate, and the whole tree moved back, extending the sylvan scene to the room beyond. A much smaller room, almost entirely filled by a built-in bed; a feather-pillowed alcove with green velvet hangings to conceal the all too solid flesh of mortal lovers from the mocking eyes of the mythical beings around them.

"*Voilà!* The Dutch sleeping room!" Fersen said. "A pretty surprise, *hein*? Nice dreams!"

My husband and I exchanged glances, and Mynheer De Groote smiled.

The rent he asked was absurdly low. We signed a year's lease there and then, over a glass of schnapps, and moved in a week later.

I was less than three months pregnant, but the canny, concupiscent eyes of Mynheer De Groote must have perceived what I thought was still imperceptible, for the wooden cradle, its rockers now smoothly silent, had been placed, with a fine sense of fitness, beside the bed in the "English sleeping room."

The consul general was spared the shock of our bacchanalian dining room, thanks to the problems involved in giving a formal dinner party. For one thing, we didn't have enough place settings—war weddings like ours went unblessed by the usual rain of household equipment; for another, I had no experience in formal entertaining, and the two models offered me thus far, one by the CG himself and the other by the burgomaster, were so wildly beyond our range that I couldn't even begin to imitate them. At the burgomaster's dinner, with no one else present but members of his family, more than a dozen full courses had been served, with a different wine for each one. Later, I learned from Fersen how to be acceptably bohemian. And a young Dutch woman of great spiritual beauty demonstrated to me the dignity of absolute simplicity. But it was a long time before I acquired sufficient self-assurance to cut loose from convention in either direction.

I was not unresourceful in coping with practical problems; in fact, I was rather ingenious. But in this new life, every difficulty I encountered was made twice as hard to surmount by that all-pervasive obstacle known as the language barrier.

At that time, the British Consular Service had three divisions; one for the Far East, one for the Levant, and one for the rest of the world—a grab bag of mixed plums and lemons appropriately designated The General Service. A career officer in this last was expected to speak at least two European languages fluently; but he would almost invariably be posted to those countries whose language he did not speak. Whether this was designed to extend his scope or merely to keep him from getting too friendly with the natives is uncertain, but it did make life difficult; though not so much for the consul, who usually had a bilingual secretary to help him, as for the consul's wife, who had to go it alone and unaided on all the domestic fronts. Fronts that would inexorably move on to a new country, like those of a conquering army, as soon as each successive barrier had been overcome.

In the pension, where we stayed for six weeks, the evening meal was served at about five-thirty, which seemed more like teatime and left us with a long, awkward stretch of time to fill in before we went to bed. As newcomers, still on the outside of the various social cliques of the British colony, we had nowhere to go in the evenings but the cinema, which proved unexpectedly useful. The movies were, of course, silent, with captions in Dutch, and by matching caption to action night after night in an effort to grasp the story, we automatically acquired some knowledge of the language, though most of the dialog was out of the wrong phrase book to be of much help to me; passionate endearments and threats of murder were equally dangerous when it came to buying a tender roast or making my instructions understood by the buxom, but sulky wench the landlord had engaged as our maid.

It didn't take me long to find out that where women were concerned big was beautiful for Mynheer De Groote, and the more soft rolls of fat, the better. But his wife's austere bones were innocent of any such sensual cushioning. Had he married her for her money—had the grand old house been her dowry? Or was his love of large ladies a postmarital development brought about by sleeping with a ramrod?

Small and slight, I enjoyed immunity from the landlord's roving fancy at the price of his general disapproval. I had only one thing going for me: my pregnancy. In his opinion the production of children was a wife's first duty, and in this, too, his own wife had failed. They had been married ten years, and she had given him only one child, a little girl as skinny as herself.

The De Grootes didn't live in the ground floor apartment as I had supposed. They occupied the floor above ours, under the roof. Soon after we moved in, Mevrouw De Groote sent me a little note written in English—no doubt at her husband's dictation, inviting me to take tea with her in the early afternoon and to bring my little son with me. But I went up alone, while he was having his nap, which gave me a valid excuse for not staying too long.

Their living room, with small attic windows and sloping ceilings, was polished beyond belief. *Immaculate* is too passive a word to describe it. For once the sun was shining, and everything in the room caught and refracted the light; even the trills of a pair of canaries in a cage by a window seemed to sparkle, like scintillas of light transmuted into sound. It represented, I realize now, the sublimation of a woman's frustrated passion; the transference of a burning unrequited love to inanimate objects, conferring on them a counterfeit glow of life.

Mevrouw De Groote spoke almost no English, but her nine-year-old daughter was learning it in school, and with her help and a few edited extracts from my cinematic phrase book, we managed to carry on a halting conversation. I have long forgotten what we talked about, but I remember very clearly the way my hostess looked and acted and the startling change that came over her when her husband joined us.

She was a very tall woman, erect and angular, with straight brown hair strained back from her face into a tight bun, which gave her the look of a severe, middle-aged schoolmarm, though she was not yet thirty. Her fashionable, fitted dress of some dark woolen material, with high neck and long sleeves, accentuated the angularity of her flat-chested body. It was as if, having realized that her naturally slender figure would never please her husband, she had decided to make it as displeasing to him as possible. Once again, this is a retrospective insight; at the time, all I saw was a woman who could have been beautiful in her own way, but wasn't.

She received me with exaggerated formality and paid me the delicate compliment of serving English tea, with sugar and cream, and imported Scotch shortbread. Her pigtailed daughter sat on a stool between us like a little Miss Muffet and did her best to act as translator. Together with their surroundings, into which they fitted as perfectly as actors fit into a stage setting, mother and child presented what seemed to me, a foreigner, a flawless picture of serene Dutch domesticity.

Then Mynheer De Groote came in, like the wicked sorcerer in a fairy tale whose very entrance is enough to blight the festivities, and the flawless scene was reduced in an instant to cardboard and scrim, and the hostess turned into a trembling menial caught masquerading as the lady of the house.

After bowing to me, Mynheer De Groote issued a curt order in

Dutch, and his wife left the room, followed by her daughter. A moment or two later, she came back, alone, with a bottle of schnapps and two small glasses on a tray, which she put down without a word beside her lord and master. Ignoring her completely, he filled one of the glasses and offered it to me. I refused it, and he took it for himself, inquiring between sips how we were getting along—was my little boy well, was the maid satisfactory, was there anything I needed? Meanwhile, his wife stood silently in the background, like a servant awaiting further orders.

His extreme politeness to me only made his rudeness to her more insufferable—implicating me, somehow, in her humiliation. How dared he put me in such a position! I was furious, but for his wife's sake, I had to make my escape gracefully.

One of those odd silences, said to be the passing of an angel, now descended on the room. Even the canaries stopped singing. The only continuing sound was the heartbeat-soft tick of an old grandfather clock. Then it, too, caught its breath with a little whirr, as if the heart were about to break, and chimed three melancholy strokes. I had been given the cue for my departure. My son, I said, would be waking up now and wondering where I was.

Mynheer De Groote, who said he had to get back to his business, came away with me. As he went on down the stairs after leaving me at my door, a door on the ground floor opened, and I heard a woman's voice say very softly, "Dirk. . . ."

But I heard it only with my ears; my mind was already on my son, who was calling me, and on getting him up and out before the sun disappeared.

When we came back from our walk, about half an hour later, I opened the outside door just in time to see the landlord coming out of the ground floor apartment. In the doorway, stuffing the aperture like a bunched-up, multicolored eiderdown, was a woman clad in a flowered wrapper. As my son ran ahead of me to the stairs, she exclaimed in French, "Oh! What an adorable child!" and came forward, forcing De Groote to introduce us.

So this was the occupant of the apartment most accessible to the landlord.

About thirty years old, blonde, and blowsily pretty for all her surplus fat, she was, she explained volubly in French, a Belgian. But her husband was Dutch. A sea captain, master of a cargo

boat, whose voyages took him away, *hélas*, for months at a time...
it was hard, sometimes, not to have a man about the house... but
Monsieur De Groote was a good landlord, always ready to help....
The look on the landlord's face must have made her realize the
ambiguity of what she was saying, for she hastily added something about a broken sewing machine that he had just put right
for her.

I excused myself and went upstairs feeling slightly sick.

One day, soon after that, she ambushed me in the hallway and
invited me in to see her apartment and have a cup of coffee. I said,
untruthfully, that I was sorry, but I didn't have the time just then.
Her face fell. "I quite understand," she said, not without dignity,
"another day, perhaps." But she never suggested it again. She had
understood—had probably known in her heart even before she
asked—that I would never have the time, that I had no intention
of ever setting foot in her apartment. But I wished I could tell her
that I wasn't condemning her—whose husband was always away
at sea, if indeed he existed at all, but her lover, whose wife was
always at home, under the same roof. I felt equally sorry for both
women, but I had to put myself squarely on the side of the
wronged wife and mother. As a wife and mother myself I couldn't
do otherwise. All the same, every time I encountered the Belgian
woman in the hallway, I had a twinge of conscience.

When Mynheer De Groote had asked me if I was satisfied with
the maid, I had answered in the affirmative, without suspecting,
as I should have, that he had asked her the same question about
me.

Her round, rosy face had been growing steadily longer and
sulkier, and I couldn't imagine why. She was well paid, well
treated in every way, and hard-worked only by her own passion
for cleaning, which far exceeded my requirements. I took care of
the shopping, the cooking, and my son. She had every evening off
and any baby-sitting she did for us was counted as overtime. Why
then was she so glum? She certainly wasn't sick; she was bursting
with energy, and she ate like a horse. Was the landlord annoying
her? She was just his type.

She had been with us for almost a month before I discovered
that I was the culprit.

One evening when my husband came home, he was button-holed by the landlord, who wanted a word with him. The word, as he repeated it to me afterward with a mixture of amusement and indignation—"Damn the fellow's impertinence!"—was to the effect that he should pay more attention to his household. A young wife like me needed a husband's guidance. The maid was very upset. She was used to working for ladies with more experience. She was trying her best to keep the place looking nice, but I bought all the wrong cleaning materials and not half enough of them. I also bought the wrong kind of food and not half enough of that either, and I didn't seem to know how many times a day a healthy person had to eat—I was starving her. And myself as well, by the looks of me. A lady in my condition, if he might be permitted to say so, should be eating for two.

"And what did you say to all that?"

"Not what I felt like saying. We can't afford to move now that we've signed a year's lease, and anyway we'll never find another apartment like this one."

"But you did defend me, didn't you?"

"One doesn't *defend* one's wife to one's landlord. I simply told him that the running of the household was entirely in your hands, and if the maid wasn't satisfied she could leave. As for your diet, that was for your doctor to prescribe. By the way, just out of curiosity, what *do* you give the girl to eat?"

"Everything that we have ourselves and three times as much of it as I give you."

Next day, I gave the girl her notice. I wasn't going to put up with being complained about to Mynheer De Groote.

Someone in the consulate found us a replacement. A German-speaking woman with the additional advantage that she didn't want to live in, which would give us the extra room we would need when the baby was born. Her papers described her as the German-born wife of a Dutch citizen. Thirty-five years of age. No children. Her references described her as reliable, clean, honest, and a good worker. Her name was Ilse Koch. But to me, she was always Frau Koch. I had to balance in some way the embarrassment of being addressed as *Gnadige Frau* by a woman who looked old enough to be my mother.

Pale, drab, thin to the point of emaciation, with a way of lowering her head whenever anyone was speaking to her, Frau Koch was anything but the landlord's type. When I introduced her to him as our new maid, he looked at her with unconcealed disgust, as if she were some repulsive spidery-legged insect. Perhaps he saw in her, as I did, a terrible caricature of his own neglected and bullied wife.

The barrier between me and Frau Koch was not linguistic—I knew German—but emotional, if such a word can be used with regard to such a distant relationship, and it took the form of an almost invincible wall of silence. She never spoke unless she was spoken to, never uttered the smallest complaint, never gave an opinion on anything, never volunteered an iota of information about herself or the life she went home to every evening.

She would appear in the morning at eight sharp, not a minute later, and leave in the evening at five sharp, not a minute earlier, and she never missed a day. This clockwork regularity, which governed all her actions—she had the German genius for organization—combined with her taciturnity and apparent absence of all feeling, made her seem inhuman; a robot. Used as I was to the garrulous, grumbling, lazy, but warmhearted British variety of daily help, Frau Koch's faultless mechanism chilled me. Yet it gave me a sense of security. I was convinced that no matter what happened, Frau Koch would fulfill her daily ritual of arrival, performance, and departure as unfailingly, and almost as unnoticeably, as the winter sun. Though like the sun, there was no way of detaining her, or, once she had left, of getting her back before the appointed hour. With our live-in maid, we had lost our built-in baby-sitter.

But the disadvantage of not being free to go out in the evening whenever we felt like it was compensated for by the freedom to do as we pleased in our own home, unwatched and uncriticized. It was only then that we were able to fully enjoy our secret garden of earthly delights.

Our gambols seemed to us rather naughty—if they hadn't we wouldn't have enjoyed them half so much—but not immoral; true love, we thought, sanctified everything, and marriage made it legal into the bargain. This point of view was in direct opposition to the middle-class morality of our time, which condemned all variations of the sex act between husband and wife as defiling the sanctity of marriage, and an insult to a good woman.

My husband and I had read and digested Vandervelde's book, *Ideal Marriage*—then considered very daring, and gone on to other, considerably more exotic manuals of instruction on how to vary one's sex life without committing adultery. For these exercises, the bacchanalian rooms provided a stimulating background. But even if advancing pregnancy had not interfered with their performance, we were both too imaginative and too intellectually oriented to be satisfied with purely physical diversions, however novel and acrobatic. We also used the painted rooms as stage settings.

A surprise that never failed to delight my husband was to come home in the evening and find me dressed up as a character in a play. He would immediately respond in the role of the male protagonist. If he came back from the consulate in a bad temper, it soon put him into a good one to find Desdemona, or Portia, or someone equally improbable all ready to serve up oysters on the half-shell with a bottle of sparkling Rhine wine (we couldn't afford champagne) in the company of the nymphs and satyrs. And he had no difficulty in making the instant transition from tired official to ardent Shakespearean lover; he had understudied most of them as a neophyte member of Ben Greet's Shakespearean Company, before the war changed the whole direction of his life.

On the surface, these charades were spontaneous and lighthearted. But they had a dark underside. Subconsciously motivated, they had the same double-edged effect as that produced by haunting the vicinity of a lost love. They helped to keep at bay the black cloud of depression that was always hovering near, threatening to close in on our most joyous moments, like thunder in summer, and at the same time they perpetuated at least one of its contributory causes. Acting was my husband's great talent, his art; which, but for the war, his marriage to me, and our incontinent parenthood, would have been his career. And it should have been, regardless. The decision against it was as much his as mine. We were both too young to know that the artist who abandons his art in favor of security does so at his peril; that talent frustrated remains in the blood like a subtle poison—slow, but deadly. Fifteen years later, when my husband was close to his premature death from a heart ailment, a wise and gentle Jewish doctor, himself approaching annihilation, defined his condition more truly than anyone else—as a sickness of the soul.

On the Feast of the Epiphany, Fersen invited us to dinner at his house. "A very small party," he said, "just for my very good friends."

My husband said, "Black tie?" And I hoped the answer would be yes. I had a new evening dress that I wanted a chance to wear while I could still get into it.

"No," Fersen said, "no black tie. For most of us, Russian blouse. For you, *mon vieux*, whatever you like."

This offered a tempting opportunity that my husband found hard to forgo, but he had to agree with me that we didn't know Fersen well enough yet to indulge in a masquerade. So we went to his party with no disguises to save us from our embarrassment when the lavish smorgasbord we had stuffed ourselves with, believing it to be the whole meal, turned out to be only the hors d'oeuvres.

Fersen lived in a decrepit little house squeezed in between two taller ones—which seemed to be holding it up, on an ill-lit, cloak-and-dagger alley. All I ever saw of this dwelling was the ground floor; two small, scantily furnished rooms that opened into each other, with a glimpse of a rather disorderly kitchen beyond. The attic above them was occupied by a Russian couple who kept house for Fersen in return for their board and lodging. The man's name was Timofei, and although I cannot recall the face of a single guest at that party, I remember Timofei clearly. I encountered his type again, years later, among the soldiers of the Red Army, recognized it, and, with good reason, disliked it every bit as much as I had instinctively disliked Timofei on sight. A loutish peasant with cunning eyes and an insolent manner, he gave the impression of having invaded Fersen's home and taken it over as ruthlessly as his counterparts in the Red Army were later to invade and take over mine. His wife, or girl friend, has left no image in my memory. I may never have seen her. Pregnant, and close to her time, she had doubtless been ordered by him to stay in the kitchen on pain of a beating.

Perhaps because of this cuckoo couple, we were seldom invited to Fersen's house. But our friendship with him was not dependent on hospitality or even on frequent meetings. It simply *existed*, as if it were a family relationship, or one of those friendships formed in childhood that survive without any artificial nourishment. The strangest part of it was, that although my husband and I were as dissimilar in temperament as we could possibly be, and Fersen was as Slavic as we were British, he was like a brother to us both.

My husband saw more of him than I did. They attended the same official functions, and they would sometimes have lunch together, or play a game of chess at a marble-topped table in a coffeehouse. But from time to time, he would drop in unexpectedly on a Saturday afternoon and drag all three of us out for a walk through the oldest parts of the city, or down to the docks to show my son the seagoing ships and teach him how to tell their nationality by the colors banding their bulky funnels.

It was in this relatively carefree early period of my pregnancy that we acquired another unconventional friend. His name was Bernard Canter. He came to the consulate with a query concerning some business he had with an art dealer in London and aroused my husband's interest with his witty, derisive comments on that bastion of conservative art, the Royal Academy. It was near closing time. They left the consulate together and went to a nearby coffeehouse to continue their conversation. My husband came home afterward in a state of mental euphoria. "I've just met an amazing man," he said. "He's an avant-garde painter, a critic, a playwright, and tremendously well-informed on all sorts of subjects. I'm sure you'll like him—anyway, I've asked him to tea on Sunday."

A brilliant, eclectic European Jew, Canter was, for me, just as exotic a type as that son of Dostoevski and Holy Mother Russia, Baron Fersen, and his personality was equally complex and fascinating. At opposite poles in almost every respect, these two complicated beings had one characteristic in common; an inward quality that I sensed without being able to give it a name, because it was not yet part of my intellectual experience, but which drew me to them, different though they were, and evoked in my still undeveloped mind stirrings of a future philosophy of life. The Dutch Jew and the Russian nobleman were both mystics.

Quite apart from this hidden magnet, which affected me but not my husband—whose nature was romantic rather than mystical—Canter's multifaceted charm was enough in itself to turn our heads, and the trouble he took to dazzle us with it was flattering. But puzzling; we were modest enough to admit that. And even now, I am not sure just what it was that made him seek our company, why he talked so freely to us—strangers, foreigners, years younger than himself even in chronological age, and mere children when measured against his ancient heritage of wisdom. Perhaps it was just on account of these differences. Perhaps he found us refreshing. Perhaps he thought we were still teachable.

Our apartment delighted him. But he asked me, rather curiously, whether I didn't find it embarrassing to live in that sort of neighborhood. Not quite sure what he meant by that, I said, "No, not at all," and he said, "Bravo!"

He took to dropping in on us almost every Sunday afternoon, to drink hot chocolate—he didn't like tea and he never touched alcohol—and discourse on art, literature, philosophy, the theater, the play he was writing, music, and whatever else had been occupying his mind during the week. Unlike Fersen, whose tolerance extended even to those who injured him, and who never said a cruel thing about anyone, Canter was intolerant—especially of stupidity, and like many witty conversationalists he was verbally malicious.

His connection with the theater was charged with emotion. He had been stormily married to a well-known actress, from whom he was divorced. But the law had not severed the psychological bonds of their love-hate relationship. He couldn't help talking about her, and it seemed that she couldn't help talking about him. According to him, not content with ruining him materially, she was now determined to ruin him professionally as well and was going about slandering him in public. Apparently he thought that talking against her to us was justifiable, like confiding in a doctor or a priest. Not that we were capable of advising him—we were still learning how to be married to each other—but we

listened, though not without a certain uneasiness, and simply by
listening we helped him, I think, to achieve a sort of catharsis.

One Sunday in March, when he had known us for about eight
weeks—I was already five months pregnant and looked it—he
was telling us about his ex-wife's latest attempt to discredit him,
when he suddenly stopped short and stared at me. "You are going
to have a child!" he said, as if he had only just realized my
condition.

"Yes," said my husband, "in July. And this time it's going to be a
daughter."

"Forgive me," he said. "I have been terribly wrong to inject all
this poison into your lives."

Privately, we agreed with him, and our silence now must have
told him so. He looked very distressed. "It is not that I don't have
the antidote," he said. "I do. It is always at hand. But there are
times when I don't want to use it. Times when I have to spit out my
venom on someone else. Can you understand that, my young
friend?" He was looking now at my husband, not at me.

"You're damn right I can," my husband said.

"In that case," Canter told him, "you should learn the value of
your particular antidote."

There was a moment or two of silence. What my husband had
said was disturbing because it was true. Canter seemed to be
trying to make up his mind about something. He got up. "Come.
Put on your coats, there's a cold wind where we're going, and
come with me. I have something to show you."

My son, playing with building blocks on the floor but listening
at the same time, looked up anxiously.

"You too, little boy. You like motorcars, yes?"

My son, who was shy of Canter, who took very little notice of
him, nodded his head without speaking. His face fell when we all
got into a tram instead of into a motorcar, but I couldn't tell him
what Canter had meant because I had no idea where he was
taking us. I didn't even know where he lived. With all his talka-
tiveness, he was as secretive about his home life as Frau Koch was
about hers.

The tram brought us down to the river, to an out of the way inlet
where barges were moored at a wharf bordered with doddering
houses in the last stages of a neglected old age. Bright colored

washing strung out on the decks of the barges flapped in a cold wind from the sea, and the cries of barge children at play were out-shrilled by the cries of sea gulls at war over patches of floating garbage.

The whole scene was so alien to Canter's sophisticated personality that I couldn't believe this was where he lived. He must, I thought, be taking us to visit some wise recluse who had learned how to defang the inner serpent. We entered one of the dilapidated houses and climbed up a flight of rickety stairs to the top floor, where Canter opened the door without knocking and invited us to go in.

Although I went there again many times, the clearest image my memory has retained is that first impression, an image so sharp and essential that no conscious effort of recall can add anything to it. What I see is a single attic room bare to the point of nudity, yet containing all the qualities of a home, including the intangibles. The surfaces are scrubbed but not polished. Roughly white-washed walls diffuse the pallid March light without refracting it. There is nothing to mirror the yellow and blue of tulips in a delft bowl. The only luminosities are a couple of copper pans on a high shelf and the golden hair of the woman who is reaching up for one of them. She stands there forever in the same pose in the center of the picture in my mind's eye; a Dutch painter's madonna of the home; the sleeves of her blue dress rolled up above her elbows and a big white apron tied around her waist.

"I have brought my English friends to see you," Canter said, addressing her by what I took to be a Dutch diminutive of Maria—the name by which I remember her, but which may or may not have been her real name. With the formal manners of the period, and of English people in particular, I never addressed her as anything but Mevrouw, or Madame.

Canter introduced her as his "good angel," as if the word "wife" had become contaminated in his eyes, and perhaps the whole concept of marriage as well. Later he told us that he and his "angel" were married, but he wanted to keep it secret to protect her from the spite of his "devil"—by which he may have meant his ex-wife or the devil in himself. Or an unholy alliance of both.

The similarities and contrasts between this attic home and its inhabitants and the De Grootes's gave me a through-the-looking-glass feeling. One scene was very like the other in form and structure, but all the essentials were reversed. It was as if a dramatist had written two different plays about the same basic situation. In the one, the woman is shriveled, reduced to a nothing, by the presence of her husband. In the other, the man is transformed, even transfigured, in the presence of his wife.

All Canter's undeniable intellectual arrogance, all his conscious wizardry, all his malice, the whole complex mask that we thought was his real face, fell away from him in the presence of his "angel," like accumulated impurities in a white-hot flame. Which is a strange metaphor for that serene and tender young woman to call up in my mind. But not inapt. She had an aura of such limpid clarity that no impurities could survive for long within the sphere of its influence.

It is very difficult to describe anyone whose magic comes from within. And Maria was magical to an extent that her physical appearance, charming though it was, could not entirely account for.

She was not, strictly speaking, beautiful, or even pretty. She was, to use a biblical expression, comely. She came from Frisia, in the north of Holland, and her long face with its high forehead reminded one of the female saints in Dutch and Flemish stained glass windows. She had the milk and roses complexion seen most often in Holland and in Ireland, as if it owed its freshness to the constant mist and rain of their common climate. Her well-proportioned body, tall and slender, but rounded, suggested health and vigor and the potential for lavish maternity.

But Maria Canter was a childless madonna. Her husband confided to mine that he could not give her a child. So all her maternal tenderness was lavished on this man twenty years older than herself, and alien to her in almost every respect.

Looking back, our unquestioning acceptance of this union of two people so different from each other in so many important ways, seems incredibly naive. Perhaps it was that their love for each other was so tremendous that it made everything else seem irrelevant. In any case, we never made any attempt to unravel the strands of this extraordinary relationship. Canter was proudly Jewish. Maria was quite obviously Aryan, and had been brought up, as I was, in the protestant Christian tradition. Now, she joined her husband in observing all the traditional Jewish feasts and holy days, including, very strictly, the Sabbath. Had she converted? We never inquired. Not even when we asked her to be our daughter's godmother, and she accepted.

At the time, our reasons for taking this odd step were obscure—not fully understood by either of us. But I realize now that we had a two-fold motivation: a desire (particularly on my part) to admit her, if only by a side door, into the realm of motherhood, and a hope that she might, through her participation in the baptism, endow our child with some of the spiritual strength and serenity that we lacked.

But to go back to that Sunday afternoon when we met her for the first time. She welcomed us as her husband's friends with the simplicity and sincerity that were her hallmark, and served us with the hot chocolate beloved by her husband, and the gingerbread cookies beloved by the entire Dutch nation. In the middle of eating his, my son, who hadn't uttered a sound since he entered the house, said in a small, unhappy voice, as though musing on the unreliability of grown-ups, "Motorcars."

"But of course!" Canter said, delighted. "There they are, little boy! Look! Over there—on the walls."

The walls at one end of the room were covered with roughly framed pictures; mostly pastels, too pale and indistinct for their subjects to be identifiable at a distance—though they didn't look like motorcars. But when we were close enough to perceive them clearly, my memory photographed them in the same sharp detail as Maria reaching up for the copper pan, which she used to make the hot chocolate, and the blue bowl of yellow tulips on the scrubbed table. They were, I suppose, technically classifiable as pointilliste, in that they were composed entirely of minute dots. But it was a futuristic pointillism, a prophecy of the jet age in terms of a cosmic sandstorm. As for the motorcars, they were barely visible; little patches of darker dots that symbolized the genesis of a speed and power still in the realm of science fiction. Eccentric, a little crazy, Canter's obsession with speed seemed to us then at odds with his love for a woman who was the embodiment of stillness and serenity. We had yet to learn that the greater the velocity of the imagination, the greater the need for a fixed star.

My three-year-old son understood Canter's pictures better than we did. For the rest of the afternoon he was happily absorbed in spotting the man-made motor in the eye of every storm.

Many of the important events of my life, good and bad, have happened in March; a month whose approach fills me, even now, with a mixture of apprehension and expectation. In that March of 1921, I was anticipating a pleasure, a two-week visit from my parents. My father's doctor had thought a change of scene would be good for him. We were planning to give them the English sleeping room, which had twin beds, and squeeze ourselves into the Dutch wall bed; although with me in my present condition it would be a tight fit, and its surroundings tantalizingly, perhaps even dangerously, aphrodisiac. We were not sure how long we could safely go on making love, or how frequently, and we were then both too shy to ask the doctor. We thought of ourselves as a modern couple, but we still had reticences undreamed of today.

I was devising all sorts of extra comforts for the austere English room, when my mother wrote that my father had caught a chill and their visit would have to be postponed. I was amazed at the depth of my disappointment. Having my mother visit me in my home was a very different thing from living with her, *force majeure*, in hers. I was dying to show off my ability to run a household, to get along in a foreign country, to make interesting friends. But that was not all. Deep down there was a touch of homesickness, of loneliness for my own family, which I didn't want to admit even to myself, because it seemed disloyal to my husband.

On the twenty-second of March, and the fourth anniversary of the day on which he asked me to marry him, he surprised me by coming home in the middle of the day.

I was lying down with a book, taking the daily siesta recommended by my doctor; my son was having his nap; Frau Koch was maintaining her role of noiseless, nonstop cleaning machine. It couldn't have been more tranquil. My husband came into the room very quietly, and, seeing that I was awake, he presented me with a bunch of lilies of the valley—the flowers associated with our courtship.

I was so happy with this token of remembrance that I threw my arms around his neck and showered him with little kisses of delight. He returned my kisses tenderly, but gravely, and I felt slightly dashed. He took both my hands in his. "Dearest little wife . . . I love you more than anything or anyone in the world. . . ." Then, plunging suddenly into icy water and taking me with him, "I have some bad news to tell you. Your father died this morning."

It was my first personal loss, and it stunned me. Of my four grandparents, two had died long before I was born and the others while I was still a baby. Many of the boys with whom I had danced and played tennis as a young girl had been killed in the war, and I had grieved over them; but all I had lost by their deaths were dreams—the romantic dreams of adolescence. My parents were the underpinnings of my life. And I wasn't ready yet to do without them.

Tears didn't come easily to me. But I wept now. I recalled my father's face as I saw it framed by the brass bars of my bedstead the night my son was born, and I wept for what I had failed to do and failed to be while I had the chance.

My husband said, "You loved him very much, didn't you? When *my* father dies you won't catch me shedding any tears for him."

I said, *"He* loved *me* very much . . ." and in saying it I recalled something I had read, but not understood at the time, about the awesome responsibility of being loved.

My father's death accelerated the inevitable inward-turning of the last months of pregnancy. Birth and death became linked in my mind. And between them they affected my relationship with my husband; adding another dimension to the progressive influence of my pregnancy on it. Moodiness had been his prerogative; keeping it at bay had been mine. Which was not unreasonable. Four years of fighting in a war was enough in itself to make a man moody, and the war was not the only battlefield in my husband's life; my family relationships were idyllic compared to his. But the physical vitality and the nervous energy I had drawn on to combat his moods of depression were now being used up by the baby. Emotionally I was in need of more patience than he possessed, and the kind of understanding—a female understanding—that was not in his power to give.

Circumstances were forcing me to realize that our love for each other was born of the attraction of opposites.

My sheltered, solitary childhood and introverted adolescence had made me hungry for life—or what I imagined life to be; and the intense warmth of my husband's personality, with its strong emotional extremes, offered me something I had missed, and lifted me out of myself. But pregnancy, that most private of all experiences, was steadily drawing me inward again; and my natural traits, nurtured and developed by my upbringing, reasserted themselves; to show me very clearly that my married life would be an unending balancing trick in which either one of us could destroy the other merely by taking too deep a breath.

At a more immediate level, the shadows glimpsed in the old bathroom mirror at home began to materialize. There were times when my husband would get up in the middle of the night and go out for a walk; or he would say that he felt like reading and would go to the other bedroom so as not to keep me awake. And I was never quite sure whether it was because he wanted me more often than he thought was good for me and the child, or whether he was finding me increasingly unattractive physically. If I had asked him outright, he would have told me. He always gave direct answers. But I didn't ask, precisely for that reason.

I became self-conscious about my increasing size, and I thought I detected embarrassment on my husband's part when we went out together. So although we had found a baby-sitter, a spinsterish Englishwoman who was trying unsuccessfully to make a living teaching in the Berlitz School, I preferred to spend my evenings at home, which often meant spending them alone. There were times, however, when my husband was content to stay quietly at home in the evening. He would read a play aloud to me while I sewed, or we would make a little music together. He was learning to play the cello, and I would accompany his instrument, or my own singing, on a tinkling antique spinet that De Groote had procured for us—there was nothing De Groote couldn't procure if he had a mind to. And occasionally Fersen, who had lent us a book of Russian folk tunes, would come and sing them for us. But these were rare moments of tranquillity on mostly restless waters.

Usually, around nine o'clock, my husband would say, "I think I'll go over to the Institute for a bit. Do you mind?" And I would say with a mixture of chagrin and relief that of course I didn't mind.

The Institute was a home away from home for British seamen, run by a couple of social workers under the overall direction of the British chaplain—a celibate Anglican priest with a strong social sense, and enthusiastically supported by my husband. His particular bailiwick in the consulate was the shipping office, and he knew how much trouble a British seaman could get himself into in a foreign port between voyages.

While he was at the Institute playing pool, darts, and checkers and exchanging yarns with the seamen, and through that, reliving an aspect of army life that he missed—the easy comradeship among all sorts and conditions of men—I would install myself on one of the deeply embrasured window seats in our living room, draw the velvet curtains close behind me so as not to be seen against a lighted background, and watch the sleepy street start to purr with nocturnal animal life.

Immediately opposite my window was a break in the row of houses flush with the sidewalk; it may have been the opening of an alleyway, or it may have been the entrance to some building set farther back—I don't remember. But it was an unlit recess that served to shelter activities unsuitable for the open street, even that one. In the rather low-roofed house whose wall enclosed the recess on one side, there was a small casement window on the same level as my little box at the theater, and below it was a door which must have opened onto a stairway that led straight up to the room with the window. The casement curtains were kept closed all the time, but after dark a faint light would show behind them, like that of a kerosene lamp or a candle.

What intrigued me about this particular window was that after dark a white handkerchief was to be seen, at irregular intervals, dangling from the sill. An obvious signal; though for whom, or for what purpose, I didn't immediately guess. After a

while, however, I noticed that the presence or absence of the
handkerchief coincided with the comings and goings of men
through the door below.

One evening, preparing supper, I found I had run out of some
necessary ingredient, and I went to get it at one of the little
neighborhood stores. When I opened the door with its jangling
bell, the storekeeper, who was talking and laughing in a very
friendly way with a woman customer, broke off abruptly and
handed her her packages as if anxious to get rid of her. She looked
like a Toulouse-Lautrec model. As she brushed past me on her
way out, she gave my belly a pat and made a remark in a dialect
that was unintelligible to me. The storekeeper, who knew me,
said in the Rotterdam Dutch I was used to, "Don't mind her,
Mevrouw, she doesn't mean any harm."

As I left the store, I saw her go in at the door I watched every
night. So that was the mysterious owner of the white handkerchief! I had imagined a pale *Dame aux Camélias*, or a young girl
betrayed by a faithless lover, or a penniless orphan reduced to
prostitution to keep herself alive; and now, the whole romantic
bag of tricks was blown sky-high by a heavy, healthy, red-faced,
good-natured creature with fat legs squeezed into high-buttoned
boots, and a hoarse voice like a man's.

She made sin seem clownish.

I began to recognize her kind. Once, two of them, younger and
prettier than she was, came strolling along together. At the
recess, they stopped, looked up and down the street, then, stepping into the shadow, lifted up their voluminous petticoats, squatted down side by side, and relieved themselves on the cobble-
stones. A man came out of the hospitable door, waved to them,
laughed, and said something over his shoulder that made them
shriek. Many a time I would see a man and a girl go into the
shadow together and after a few minutes emerge, adjusting their
clothes, and go their separate ways. There were other shady
activities, unconnected with sex; but it was the women who interested me. I watched them closely night after night, and I perceived a certain hierarchy among them. I realized that the
Toulousé-Lautrec lady was of higher status than her sisters who
worked the streets. She had her own decent place and a steady
clientèle, who came to her like patients to a doctor when she let

them know she was ready to see them. She was the kind one reads about in nineteenth-century French novels; the hard-working professional who saves up to buy a little place in the country to retire to when the clients don't come anymore, and keep chickens.

I kept my discoveries to myself. My interest in prostitution would have shocked my husband at this stage of our marriage. Because of my inexperience, my ignorance of the world, when he first knew me, he felt responsible for my loss of innocence and thought that whatever I needed to learn about the seamy side of life should be told me by him. The idea that I should want to investigate it on my own would have lowered me in his eyes, destroyed his idealistic image of me. In the end, I was the greater realist.

As for my "box at the theater," I was as secretive about that as I had been about a similar one in my childhood, when my father was pastor of a poor parish in a mill-town, where we lived among the workers, in one of a row of identical houses on one of a dreary maze of identical streets. The house back to back with ours was inhabited by a family much too large for it, and every night, when I was supposed to be asleep, I would creep behind the curtains of my back bedroom window and watch with burning interest the life lived by other children of my own age behind the lighted, unshaded windows of what seemed like another world. And in trying to discover for myself the meaning of what I saw, through those and other windows, I developed intuitive powers far in advance of my rational understanding.

One evening, my husband came back from the Seamen's Institute unexpectedly early and couldn't find me. The anguished note in his voice as he went from room to room calling me made my heart thud with joy, and I stayed where I was for as long as I dared. When, finally, I emerged from behind the curtains, he burst into tears.

He understood why I hadn't come out sooner. But he didn't understand what I was doing there in the first place. "It's all very well to sit by the window in daytime," he said, "but if passersby see you there at night they might get the wrong idea—particularly in this neighborhood." Which was something that had never occurred to me; I had thought of myself as watching the inhabitants of the jungle, not as being watched by them and sized up as a possible prey.

In the early spring, Timofei's woman gave birth to a sickly, premature baby, and home life became intolerable, even for the easy-going and infinitely patient Fersen. "You cannot imagine," he said, "how one suffers since the birth of that child! Such a dear little child. But so unhappy. It cries and cries. And its mother, too, is unhappy. She, too, cries and cries. And Timofei beats her because he, too, is unhappy."

"And what about you?" my husband asked.

"I am not unhappy—only fatigued. I have a great need for sleep. But I cannot obtain it in my house, so I go to look for it in the house of some good friends in The Hague."

"But it's monstrous that you should be driven out of your own home by those parasites! If I were in your place I'd tell them to shut up or get out."

"They have nowhere to go, poor things."

As it turned out, they did have somewhere to go, and Fersen's absence provided them with the means of getting there. He came back from The Hague to a peaceful house. No more cries. No more quarrels. And no more possessions. Not even a mattress to sleep on. Only a pile of pawn tickets.

All Fersen said was, "It was good of Timofei to think of leaving me the pawn tickets. It will make getting my things back much easier."

In our household, too, there was an "incident"—minor, but still disturbing.

I happened to go into the kitchen one afternoon, when Frau Koch had just left for the day, and found a brown paper bag on the table—the sort of little bag in which British charladies carry away "perks," sometimes legitimate, sometimes not. In this one there were no illegitimate perks, but something more puzzling; all Frau Koch's meals for the day, carefully packed in her own little containers. She had eaten nothing of the food she had been given but one end of the pumpernickel loaf I bought especially for her.

I was wondering what to make of this, when she came back.

"Excuse me, *Gnadige Frau*, I beg pardon for disturbing you, but I have forgotten something."

When she realized that I knew what that something was, a peculiar expression came into her pale eyes, an abject look, as if she were ready to fall on her knees and beg me not to stop her from taking it. It was the first time she had ever betrayed any kind of human feeling, and it shocked me. I handed the bag to her. "You are perfectly free to take your meals home if you want to," I told her, "but I don't like the idea of your working all day on an empty stomach."

"I eat some bread, and I drink some coffee with milk. That is enough."

So she was living on dry bread and coffee and taking the rest of her food home as a regular thing. Why? With anyone else I would not have hesitated to ask. But questioning Frau Koch was like knocking on the lid of a closed coffin. I tried a shot in the dark. "I see. You're starving yourself for the sake of someone else."

She didn't deny it. She hung her head like a child caught redhanded in some wrongdoing. I pressed my advantage. "But suppose that I refuse to allow you to starve yourself? Suppose I insist that from now on you should eat all your meals here, instead of taking them home?"

There was a long silence. At last she said, mumbling half under her breath, as if making a shameful admission, "I would not be allowed to work for the *Herrshaften* any longer."

"Who would stop you?"

"*Mein mann.*"

My husband. These two little words held so much significance for me that the way in which they were uttered by other married women told me volumes. And below the flat surface of Frau Koch's toneless voice I perceived an abyss of hatred and fear that made me shudder.

From a practical standpoint, there was only one thing I could do to help her—without losing her. And that was to stretch my housekeeping money to cover some extra food for her to eat while she was at work that her husband need never know about. Whether as a result of this nourishment, or of having been treated with humanity, she began to show signs of being a creature of flesh and blood; there were even times when I thought I detected a

ghost of a smile on her dry lips. But her silences held, and I made
no further effort to penetrate them. Perhaps I was afraid of what
I might discover.

Then, on a Friday morning less than two weeks before my baby
was due, what had once been unthinkable happened; Frau Koch
failed to turn up.

On Sunday, a hulking brute of a man, who told us in bad
German that he was Frau Koch's husband, came to collect her
wages. He brought no message from his wife, either written or
verbal. He simply said, "She won't be coming anymore."

"Why not? Is she sick? Has she had an accident?" He met our
questions with surly silence. My husband told him sharply to
answer when he was spoken to. He said again, "She won't be
coming anymore. That's all." My husband asked him for some
identification. He produced his taxi driver's license. We told him
to wait outside on the landing.

"What a thug!" my husband said.

"Must we give him the money?"

"I'm afraid so. But we can make him sign a receipt, just in case
he's here without her knowledge."

We never saw her again or heard from her, and I couldn't shake
off a haunting vision of her lying in the mud at the bottom of the
river, like a bit of worn-out machinery dumped by an owner who
couldn't make it work anymore.

Whatever her fate, her unexplained disappearance from our
lives was profoundly upsetting. Added to the inevitable feeling
that I was in some way responsible for it, was the urgent problem
of finding someone to replace her before the baby came.

I had been relying on her to keep everything running smoothly
during my confinement. Not that she would have stayed on after
her usual time, but she would have made it as easy as possible for
my husband to take over from her every evening. Even so, the
prospect was alarming to him; he was not a domesticated man.
And now the possibility that he might have to take over altogether threw him into a panic, and he sent a telegram to my
mother. She was planning to come to us on a long visit, but not
until after the baby was born. Although she had never said so in so
many words, I knew that she wanted me to have the experience of
relying solely on my husband up to the last possible moment. And

I, too, wanted it that way. I saw it as an essential test of our relationship, which the presence of my mother would nullify.

As my time drew closer, he had become more attentive, but also more nervous and moody. He would rush home the minute the consulate closed and refrain from going out again after supper. But his controlled restlessness chafed me as much as it chafed him.

Canter, who missed nothing, sent his angel to see me. She found me in tears; overwhelmed by what seemed to be unsurmountable problems, which other well-meaning visitors had only aggravated by adding the need for concealment. But proud though I was, I had no desire to conceal anything from Maria. And within a couple of hours she had brought order out of chaos both in my soul and in my kitchen. Next day she found me a replacement for Frau Koch.

I was to have my baby at home. The doctor would be responsible for the delivery, and a visiting nurse, who would assist him, would come to see me and "fix me up" twice a day for a week. After which time the doctor, who was young and favored early mobility after labor, expected me to be up and about.

My mother came over in time for the birth, as my husband wanted. One of his Institute friends, the captain of a small cargo boat plying regularly between England and Holland, had agreed to bring her over in the single passenger cabin of his antiquated little tub, which had pitched and tossed like a cockleshell all the way. By the time it docked in Rotterdam, my poor mother was so prostrate with seasickness that she had to be carried ashore.

She looked ten years older than when I had last seen her, just before we left England, and not only as a result of the journey. The change went deeper than that. The loss of my father had somehow wilted her. Small and slender, she had always had an air of fragility, but like many a fine-stemmed flower, she could bend with the wind without breaking. Now, that tensile strength, on which I had unconsciously relied, was no longer there. I almost wished that she hadn't come. And I think she must sometimes have wished the same thing. She was out of place in this foreign land—and I mean not only the country of Holland, but the foreign land of my married life. To one member of the family, however, her coming gave unalloyed happiness: my son, who had been almost as close to her as he was to me for the first eighteen months of his life.

My first pains began very quietly at five o'clock in the morning a day or two earlier than expected. My husband, who was much more nervous and excited than I was, wanted to awaken my mother immediately, but I asked him not to. He insisted, however, on calling the doctor. We had no telephone in the apartment, but De Groote had one in his workshop and had told my husband where to find the key if he needed to call the doctor during the night. Phone calls in those days were a slow and often maddening process, carried on through an operator who seemed to be permanently tangled up in some other line. It took my husband twenty minutes to reach the doctor, who asked a few questions, predicted smooth sailing for several hours, and promised that he and the nurse would be with me in plenty of time.

Reassured, my husband made tea and toast, which we shared. Experience made me confident. I was not afraid, now that I had some idea of what to expect when, and of how to cope with it. And now that the moment of real need had come, my husband was showing me the tenderness and consideration I had dreamed of when we were separated but had almost despaired of ever getting.

He lay down beside me on the bed, holding me in his arms, helping me rise and fall with the rhythm of the waves, which was slow and untroubled, like a deep swell. The final storm, I thought, must still be a long way off. . . .

It took me by surprise. It's swiftness and violence left me gasping for breath, unable even to scream.

My husband told me afterward that while he was trying in vain to get hold of the telephone operator, the first little messenger boy showed up for the early shift and was instantly dispatched to the doctor's house, which he reached, to De Groote's delight, long before the telephone operator got the call through.

But my daughter wasn't waiting for anyone. By the time the doctor arrived, she had already come into the world unaided and after a labor of not much more than two hours. Which I thought was a good omen for her future. I knew enough about the world now to realize the value of independence, not to mention speed and efficiency.

Later in the day, Fersen brought me a bunch of red roses. He lightly touched my daughter's porcelain cheek to see if she was real. "What a marvel!" he said. But I wasn't sure whether he meant the marvel of her miniature perfection or the peacefulness of her sleep.

Her christening, arranged by my husband without consulting my mother, in case she should object, was characteristically unconventional. It took place on a British cargo boat—the same one that brought my mother to Holland—in symbolic affirmation of nationality. The ceremony was performed with a portable font by the British chaplain, for whom it symbolized the baptism of the cargo boat as well, and by extension, all British cargo boats.

Only one godfather being needed for a girl, my husband assumed the responsibility, which made her his child twice over. My mother and Maria were the two godmothers. But it was Maria who held the infant in her arms and made the baptismal responses, repeating them haltingly after the priest, like an English lesson only half-understood. Fersen, hand in hand with my wide-eyed son, stood next to me, devoutly crossing himself in the left-handed Russian manner. Canter, the equally devout Jew, stood in the background, along with the Berlitz teacher, who wept all the time for reasons unknown to me then, and the ship's Captain, a Presbyterian Scot, who invited us all to his cabin afterward to drink my daughter's health in good Scotch whisky.

My father, I thought, would have been delighted and amused by the whole thing. My mother, more conservative and lacking a sense of humor, would have offered numerous objections if my husband had given her an opportunity. But she accepted the *fait accompli* with melancholy resignation; as part of my general apostasy.

Today, the word "ecumenical" would be used to describe my daughter's christening. For us, it was simply a celebration of friendship.

Mannie

AUGUST, 1922

*T*HE scene has changed. We are still in the Netherlands, but we have left the faded grandeur of the old house in the city, the fabulous painted rooms, the windows on the night world, for a pokey little modern bungalow on a side street in Scheveningen. A third pregnancy, started fewer than six months after the birth of my daughter—the result of a misplaced faith in the contraceptive effects of breastfeeding—has lowered my physical vitality, and the doctor has recommended sea air and sea bathing for both me and my son, who is a rather frail child.

My mother survived my father for less than a year. Thirteen years older than he was, she had been, I was told by those who knew her before I was born, almost literally transfigured by love. The pale rose withering in the bud had been brought by love to full bloom on the verge of winter. And the magic had not been ephemeral. It had given her the power to transcend, for as long as my father lived, the difference in age between them that had made my birth almost a miracle. But the moment he was gone, she became the old woman she really was; frail, tired, and mortally ill.

Now, with both of them gone, I too feel a loss of power; though its source went unrecognized while I still had it. Deprived of the spiritual strength that flowed from my parents' unselfish love, both for me and for each other, I find myself less and less able to help my husband fight off his black fits of depression. Indeed, I feel more bereft than I would have thought possible four years ago—when all I wanted, and all I thought I needed, was my husband's return from the war.

His problems are not only personal. Professionally, he has recently suffered a bitter disillusionment that has shaken his confidence in himself and in human nature generally. A man he both liked and trusted, a middle-aged consular clerk who taught him the ropes when he first arrived, in the way that an old army sergeant sometimes teaches a very young officer, took advantage of his trust and his lack of experience to doctor the books ingeniously and embezzle a large sum of money, for which my husband, as the career officer in charge, is being held responsible. And even if the money is eventually refunded, that won't erase the blot on my husband's career.

Altogether—physically, emotionally, financially—we are at a very low ebb.

The spinsterish Berlitz teacher, whose name is Doris, has come to live in our house as a mother's helper. She is no more efficient at that than she is at teaching English. But she means well, and the arrangement helps her to survive.

Now that we know each other better, she has confided in me. Thirty-five years old, she has relinquished all hope of achieving the goal that the girls of her generation were taught to strive for without being given the least idea of what it entailed—marriage. Until she entered our household, Doris had no notion of what it really meant to live with a man and have his children, and she got a few surprises. But she did know what it meant to be rejected. The only man who had ever asked her to marry him, and to whom she was briefly engaged, had jilted her without explanation; leaving her bewildered and humiliated and turning her overnight into an old maid.

She tried, in telling me about it, to excuse his behavior—and soothe her own bruised ego—by attributing it to all sorts of absurdly romantic reasons. But I think the true reason was absurdly unromantic, and that plain moral cowardice was to blame for the way things turned out.

Doris, poor girl, suffered from one of those antisocial afflictions that "even your best friends won't tell you about"—as the ads put it. Before she came to live with us we were only occasionally aware of it, usually as the aftermath of an evening's baby-sitting;

a vaguely oniony odor that haunted the folds of the velvet curtains like last week's cigar or the previous winter's mothballs. But when she moved in, it moved in with her. Inescapable, it soon became intolerable.

My husband said, "If *you* don't tell her about it, *I* will."

Deodorants are not yet a universal commodity. But there is one good product on the market which I have sent to me from England, and one day I showed it to Doris and asked her whether she would like me to order some for her, too.

"Oh dear no," she said, "I'm lucky, I don't need anything like that. I've always found plain soap and water quite enough."

I stared at her, speechless.

The implication of my silence took a few painful moments to sink in. Then her sallow face suddenly crimsoned, her short-sighted eyes filled with tears, and she rushed from the room. We have never mentioned the matter again. There hasn't been any need to. She has never mentioned her broken engagement again, either. Has she put two and two together? The idea that a vital relationship can be ruined by something so trivial is rather frightening. But I'm sure that given enough self-deception on one side and timidity on the other, it could happen only too easily. It takes moral courage to broach such a delicate personal matter to someone you don't want to hurt, and where women are concerned, most men are moral cowards. My husband is an exception. He wields his moral courage like a sword, and it can be devastating.

It is a warm Friday evening in August, milky blue and windless—unusual weather for this gray coast—and the esplanade is packed with weekenders out to enjoy it while it lasts. I am taking the children to meet their father, who comes back from Rotterdam every day on the six o'clock train. My daughter, plump and jolly, sits up perkily in her stroller watching the passersby and finding them very amusing. My son trots alongside; interested, observant, but not in the least amused. He is a solemn little boy at all times; already convinced that life is a serious matter.

For me, life gets more and more serious every day, and I only wish I could take a holiday from it. Now, in the eighth month of a pregnancy I resent because it's taking place at the wrong time, I feel hopelessly trapped. Everything wearies me, and it doesn't take much to make me cry. The doctor says I'm "run down." But it feels more like being wound up to the point where the spring is ready to snap. My emotions are so brittle and so intense that they clash with one another; as now, for example, when the wide expanse of merging sea and sky offers balm to my nerves and creates an illusion of freedom, while the idle, vacationing crowd exacerbates my sense of captivity.

The railway station is a small open terminal for electric trains, not very far from the esplanade. From the street, on the other side of a fence smothered in climbing roses, I can see the train come in and the passengers getting off. My husband appears just behind a girl in an emerald green dress. I notice her only because of its color. She is unknown to me. But she and my husband seem to know each other quite well. They walk along the platform together laughing and talking like old acquaintances. As they wait together at the bottleneck of the ticket barrier, she looks up into his face and puts her hand on his arm. The easy familiarity of the gesture detonates a dormant explosive in me. I turn and leave the vicinity of the station as fast as I can, pushing the stroller along at a furious pace in the opposite direction to home. My son can barely keep up with me, but he doesn't complain. He is used to explosions of one sort or another. I am upset beyond all reason—I know that, but I can't help it. I do have enough sense, however, not to confront my husband until I have cooled down.

Gradually, the soft voice of the sea on the sand and the gentle touch of the mild evening breeze on my hot face restore my precarious control, and I turn around and go home.

My husband is sitting out in the backyard having a drink and reading the evening paper, which he usually reads on the train. His manner is aggrieved. "Where on earth have you been? It's almost seven o'clock, and Doris says the roast you left in the oven is getting all dried up."

"Doris doesn't know what she's talking about."

"Well, where were you? I looked for you at the station, but there was no sign of you."

"I was waiting by the fence when the train came in. Then I saw you with that girl. So I left."

"What girl?"

"Don't pretend. You know perfectly well who I mean."

"If you mean the girl who was walking down the platform with me, I ran into her by pure chance. She's an English girl here on holiday. She was in the consulate this morning, asking about something, and she recognized me on the train, that's all."

"She didn't act like a chance acquaintance. She grabbed your arm as if she'd known you for ages."

"Maybe she was hoping I'd ask her to go out with me—and trying to give me a little encouragement."

"Didn't you tell her you were married?"

"The occasion didn't arise. But she'd have found out soon enough if you hadn't turned tail and left the station in a stupid fit of jealousy—*absolutely* unwarranted, let me tell you."

I know he is speaking the truth. I know I have no reason, as yet, to be jealous of any other woman, either physically or emotionally. I know that I alone have his love. But the jealousy I feel is at once more trivial and more comprehensive. I am envious of the light step, the slender body, the ability to move about freely, the generally carefree state, the possibility of adventure that this girl, or any footloose unmarried girl, represents. And I see the obvious pleasure, however innocent and momentary, that my husband took in her company as a straw in the wind.

On Saturday night, at about ten o'clock, when I am beginning to feel sleepy, my husband shows signs of restlessness. "How would you like to go over to the *Kurhaus* for a bit and watch the floor show? We can sit in one of those alcoves at the side where no one will notice you."

I am more than ever self-conscious about my shape since the wife of the French Consul told me that in Holland it was not considered *convenable* for a visibly pregnant woman of good social position to be seen at public functions. So I put on a long, soft-falling evening dress that disguises my figure, and over it a still more concealing cloak. The open dances held in the *Kurhaus* ballroom on Saturday evenings are dress-up affairs, though anyone may attend them who can afford the price of a ticket—and has the right clothes.

We arrive just in time for the floor show; a pair of exotic ballroom dancers whose performance of the tango is almost

unbearably sensual. Their incredibly lithe bodies coil and uncoil
around each other like mating serpents. The female partner in
particular exudes sensuality. No one could look like that, I think,
and dance like that, and not have lovers. I wish I could ask her
how she manages not to get pregnant.

Refreshments have to be fetched from the bar on the other side
of the dance floor. When the show is over, my husband goes off to
get lemonade for me and a whisky for himself. On his way, he
stops at a table to speak to someone—it is the girl of the green
dress, only now she is wearing a red one. The band strikes up a fox
trot. The couple the girl is with get up and dance together. Then
she and my husband take to the floor. I tell myself he is only being
polite, he had to ask her, he couldn't just leave her sitting there all
by herself. But when the music stops, instead of returning her to
her table he claps with everyone else for an encore, and off they go
again.

I am too wrought up to react sensibly. I can't endure my impo-
tence, my maddening inability to challenge this free young
woman on her own terms. I am a better dancer than she is and a
good deal prettier, and probably younger—I'm only twenty-three
and she looks nearer thirty—but I'm caught, trapped, blown up,
slowed down, turned into a cow ... Oh God! I'm going to cry, and
the people at the next table are watching me, damn them! I must
get away before I make a complete fool of myself.

In my haste, I drop my handbag. Stooping to pick it up brings
on a feeling of faintness and dizziness. In the lobby, the man who
took our tickets when we came in looks surprised to see me
leaving alone, and the doorman asks if I want him to call a cab.
No. "No thank you, I'm just going out for a breath of fresh air."

But once outside, alone in my trailing evening clothes on the
all-but-deserted esplanade, I wish I were safely ensconced in a
cab. An elderly man walking a poodle on a leash stops while it
lifts a leg, and lifts his hat to me. I have never seen him before.
Farther on, a younger man smoking under a streetlight says,
"Good evening," and holds out a silver cigarette case. I walk past
him quickly. Still dizzy, as if I had drunk too much—though I
haven't had anything to drink—I long to sit down on one of the
unoccupied benches facing the sea. But I daren't. Just ahead of
me, a man and a woman—he broad-shouldered and she broad-

beamed—are ambling along, nuzzling each other as they go like a pair of amorous carthorses yoked together. There is something simple about them, something bucolic, that gives me a sense of protection. I keep close behind them. When they turn down some steps to the beach, I follow. They don't look round; they are totally absorbed in each other. I miss the bottom step, and my right foot sinks unexpectedly deep into soft dry sand. I grasp the rail just in time to preserve my balance. I mustn't collapse here. I must find a more sheltered spot—over there, perhaps, where the beach chairs are stacked . . . But the going is heavy. The loose sand sucks in my high heels at every step and tries to pull off my shoes. I stumble and fall. The sand gives under my weight like a sack of beans, and I think, as the blood flows away from my brain, how lovely it feels to be safely in bed.

Something cold and wet on my face startles me back into consciousness. It's a dog's nose. At my sudden movement, the dog growls. It is sharply called to heel by its master, who takes me, no doubt, for a vagrant—or merely a pile of seaweed.

I tell myself I must get up and go before they come back. But a terrible lethargy holds me down; the sort of inertia that keeps the legendary lost mountaineer fatally bedded in the snow.

It's a still, clear night. The tide, one of those seasonal full-moon tides that drag the sea in and out to its farthest limits, is now at its lowest ebb, leaving a runneled expanse of wet sand that glistens gunmetal gray in a long path of moonlight. A few yards from where I am lying is the halved-beehive silhouette of a single, wicker beach chair. It emits an odd sound, as if it were groaning in pain. Then it tips over backward. Four sturdy legs fly up in the air as two bodies joined in the middle turn head over heels out of the beehive onto the yielding sand and carry on to a finish.

The man wastes no time in breaking away. He pulls up his trousers, buttons up his jacket, and sets the fallen beach chair upright. The woman stays flat on her back with her skirt halfway up to her neck and her thighs apart. The man says, "Come on! Get up! What are you waiting for?"

She gets up slowly, without speaking; pulls down her skirt, smoothes down her hair, goes close up to the man, slaps his face—bing bang on each cheek—and gallops coquettishly off to the water's edge.

The man is in no hurry to follow her. First, he lights up a cigarette. Then he strolls past me to the seawall and urinates in a leisurely way against it. I lie as still as the pile of seaweed he probably takes me for, while he buttons up his fly and saunters off, whistling, to where the woman is waiting.

When their bulky silhouettes merge, I pull myself to my feet and go warily back up the steps to the esplanade. The turn into my street is only a couple of hundred yards distant, not far by day, but now, in the middle of the night, it seems like as many miles. A seedy looking man sidles up to me, making an obscene gesture, then turns away with a crude Dutch word for pregnancy. I cross the road, thinking I'll be less exposed on the sidewalk lined with houses. But I attract the attention of two men standing outside the door of a small hotel, talking rather loudly. They are probably tipsy. They whistle at me as I pass and make vulgar noises. Then I hear their footsteps behind me. I can tell they are following me by the way they quicken their pace when I quicken mine. It is like being stalked by two animals sure of their prey and only waiting for the right moment to pounce. When I've turned my corner, I start to run. This gives me a slight edge on them, and I duck into our house just in time to slam the door in their faces. They shout something through the locked door that I don't understand and go away laughing. I stand trembling in the hallway; for the first time I have an idea of what it must feel like to belong to the world on the other side of the window.

The house is completely quiet. No one stirs. The children are sound sleepers, and Doris has learned to ignore slamming doors. My husband's evening clothes lie in a heap on the bedroom floor, along with his patent-leather shoes. He must have come straight home as soon as he discovered that I had left the *Kurhaus,* and failing to find me here, changed his clothes in a hurry and rushed out again to search for me. The scattered garments are eloquent of his desperate anxiety. But I feel no contrition. He has made me suffer in the same way over and over again, getting up in the middle of the night to go swimming in the sea, and not coming back for hours.

All the same, I know I've behaved like a fool. And I fear the possible consequences. I undress and get into bed, and lie there praying that nothing will happen to the baby.

I have left the light on so that when my husband comes back he will see from the corner of the street that I'm home. At this moment, I both love him and hate him. I am still furious with him. But I listen eagerly for the sound of his footsteps. They approach at a run. The front door is slammed again.

"Thank God! Oh! *Thank God!*"

Now, I have only to hold out my arms. But, perversely, I don't do it, and within a few seconds we are quarreling. Fiercely. Savagely. Stabbing each other where it hurts most, with the terrible accuracy of intimates.

On Sunday mornings, Doris takes care of the children's breakfast, which allows us to sleep late and, on this particular Sunday, gives us the time and the privacy in which to achieve reconciliation.

The sweetness of making up after a quarrel is undeniable, but not unalloyed. I would always rather the quarrel had never taken place, and although it was I who provoked it last night, that was an exception. My husband, more volatile than I am, quick to fight and quick to forgive and forget, expects other people to be the same.

As soon as he awakens, he puts out a tentative hand. "Love me now?"

"I never stop loving you, even when I hate you."

He buries his face in my hair. "I'm sorry ... I'm sorry ... I didn't mean a word of what I said last night—did you?"

"No. Of course I didn't."

"So let's forgive each other for being a pair of bloody fools, shall we?"

"I wonder what it is that makes one say things that one doesn't mean a word of. . . ."

"I'm damned if I know."

We neither of us know much about psychology. But I am more analytical than he is, more interested in people, and what makes them tick. And I promise myself that as soon as I have the time to do some serious reading, that's what I'll study first.

Now he wants to know where I was and what I was doing during the interval between leaving the *Kurhaus* and coming home. I tell him about the beach, and the dog that took me for God

only knows what garbage, and the lovers who fell head over heels
out of the beehive onto the sand without ever coming apart. "Quite
an accomplishment, that," he says, "like something out of the
Decameron."

I don't mention the men who tried to pick me up or the two
drunks who followed me home. That would only make him angry.
Angry that anyone should dare to molest me and angry with me
for making it possible.

Before we get up, we make tender love, not so much out of
desire as to seal the peace between us. I am so unwieldy now that
making love is no longer a graceful act, and I have an idea that
our coupling, sweet as it is to us, would seem to an onlooker no less
grotesque than that of the pair I have just been making fun of.

In the afternoon, we all go for a picnic on the beach. The nimbus
of reconciliation sheds its beneficent light over everyone. The
children behave like angels. My daughter sits on the sand with
me at the water's edge, withdrawing her fat little feet with a
joyous squeal at each touch of a wave. My son is gently encouraged to swim out of his depth with his hands on his father's
shoulders, and a small seed of trust is sown. Even Doris, who
hates cold water, is so beguiled by the sunny mood of the afternoon that she lifts her skirt to her calves and gingerly wades in
two inches of foam. After tea, a sand castle is built, and cricket is
practiced with a soft rubber ball. Going home, my daughter rides
on her father's shoulders while my son runs in and out of the
water singing a song he has made up himself.

Tired, we all go to bed early. We kiss the children goodnight
and wish them happy dreams. To Doris, who thinks she is coming
down with a cold from putting her feet in the water, I give two
aspirins.

"Poor old Doris," my husband says. "A man, that's what she
needs. Aren't you glad you've got me?"

It is two o'clock in the afternoon on Monday, and all seems to be
well. The children are having their naps. Doris, who teaches her
genteel brand of English to a handful of private pupils, is busy
preparing tomorrow's lesson, and I am taking the afternoon rest
insisted upon by my doctor. I am reading an instructive, but
deadly sentimental book on planned parenthood by Dr. Marie

Stopes and making up my mind to go over to London for a few
days after my baby is born and get fitted up with one of her
contraceptive devices. I must not—I *will* not get pregnant again.
At least, not for a long time. When I was first married, I envisioned the ideal family as two boys and two girls. But spaced out,
with intervals of two or three years between each. The fate of my
mother's beautiful eldest sister was an object lesson for me. She
had died, worn out, in her twenties, after giving birth to half a
dozen children in quick succession. But I realize now that I am no
more in command of my own body than she was. And it is this
power that Dr. Marie Stopes seems to be offering me.

I put down the book and pick up a pencil and paper to make a
list of things that still have to be bought for the new baby, due in
about six weeks. A bassinet is one of them. There is no antique
cradle in this little house. Tomorrow, I think, I'll take the tram to
The Hague and buy a plain wicker cradle and trim it myself.
Once again, I am to have the baby at home. My doctor, who has
ten children of his own, has put me in touch with the elderly
nurse-midwife who brought them all into the world. She is semi-
retired now; she takes only a few special cases to please the doctor,
who says I am lucky to be one of them. She will live in and stay for
a week after the birth. And according to the doctor, she won't
expect to be waited on hand and foot, as nurses usually do; she will
look after herself—and everyone else as well. She is a big, bustling old countrywoman, who speaks only Dutch and treats me
as if I were her own daughter. Which is just what I need. But my
husband is not at all sure that he wants to be treated as a son-in-
law by a bossy old peasant who thinks that our whole bohemian
way of life is *vreselijk*, a Dutch word meaning "terrible," which
she applies impartially to sins, misfortunes, foreigners, and her
own rheumatism.

The inconvenient little house is not at all what she is accustomed to finding on her job; most of her clients live in large,
comfortable homes, but she is, as the doctor told us she would be,
undemanding and prepared to put up with any unavoidable
discomfort. Doris, however, has an old-fashioned sense of *noblesse
oblige* and has offered to give up her own room and move in with
the children for as long as the nurse is with us. As for my husband,
he has his orders; for as long as she is in charge of a mother and

baby, the old despot says, the husband loses his rights. He says, "We'll see about that," but he has agreed, *force majeure*, to sleep on a couch in the living room, which is separated from the bedroom only by glass folding doors—a symbolical rather than an actual barrier.

Now, the daily maid taps on the pane. I can see her plump silhouette through the semitransparent curtains. "I'm ready to leave, Mevrouw. My work is all done."

It is three o'clock. Time to get up and go out for a walk with the children.

The sharp pain that shoots through the lower part of my back as I get off the bed is so unexpected and so short-lived that I mistake it for a muscular twinge caused by an awkward movement. But its recurrence a few minutes later tells me the truth, and with alarming force. I call Doris and ask her to go to the nearest pharmacy and phone the doctor from there—we still have no private phone—and tell him I'm not feeling well and would like him to come as soon as he can. I don't want to frighten Doris by being too urgent, but I think I'm going to need him very soon. I hastily get out the rubber sheeting and remake the bed in the way successive nurses have taught me to do it. Further preparations are cut short by overwhelming contractions that force me to lie down. My son calls, "Mummie! Can I get up now?" "Yes . . . but play quietly . . . Mummie isn't well. . . ." It is all I can do not to scream. But I mustn't frighten him. I stuff the sheet in my mouth. Doris comes in to say that the doctor is out on his rounds but they'll try to get ahold of him. Gasping, I tell her to go back and call an emergency number given me by the doctor and tell them to send someone immediately. She runs from the room and out of the house like a scared rabbit. I am scared myself. This is no ordinary storm—it's a hurricane, and it's moving unbelievably fast. If the clock hasn't stopped, it's barely a quarter of four . . . Oh! Oh! It's coming . . . it's coming. . . .

The front door opens and shuts, "Doris! Doris! Help me!" She runs in, stops dead, screams, and rushes away. The baby is lying between my legs on the soaked bed. It has to be slapped . . . made to breathe, to cry . . . the cord must be cut . . . I try to raise myself up. Immediately everything turns, and I fall back into an abyss.

Now I hear an unknown voice speaking Dutch. Now I feel a

hand on my wrist. Now the doctor's familiar voice says "Mevrouw ... Mevrouw ..." very close to my ear. I open my eyes and meet his round blue ones, anxiously gazing down at me. Black garments rustle around the room like crows' wings. They belong to a nun. I'm too tired even to wonder why she is there. My lids are so heavy they close again of their own accord.

Next time I open my eyes, the doctor has gone, and so have the black wings. My husband is there, looking silently down at a bureau drawer placed across two chairs. The expression on his face is one of pity and sadness. So my baby never breathed ... the drawer is an improvised coffin. ... Then a sudden feeble complaint issues from it—oh blessed sound! My husband says softly, "Poor little bugger ..." and the nurse comes bustling in. She elbows my husband aside and picks up the wailing morsel, clucking and crooning and calling it something that sounds like *Mannikin.* I start to cry, and my husband, who thought I was sleeping, runs to my side. But after one kiss, he is again pushed away by the old nurse, who lays in my arms a bundle small as a doll. "Less than five pounds," she says, *"vreselijk!"*

Now a feeding ritual starts that will go on all night. My new son is too weak to suck for more than a few seconds at a time. But every two minutes or so, she makes him try again, helping him out by squeezing my nipple between her broad fingers and squirting the liquid into the tiny mouth. When she thinks he has swallowed enough to keep him alive for the next half hour, she lays him back in his drawer. "Poor little *mannikin* ... poor little mite, with only a drawer in which to lay his head. *Vreselijk!*"

She says it so often that we nickname her Old Terrible. Realizing that the term is somehow related to her, she asks what it means. Rather nervously, I explain. She laughs. She is not in the least offended, in fact, I think she's a bit flattered. Her Dutch name for the baby is translated by us as Mannie and is destined to cling to him all through his early childhood.

As he gains a little in strength, the nursing times are changed to once every hour; then to once every hour during the day with two screaming three-hour intervals during the night, when Old Terrible takes him into her room so that I can get some sleep. One night, she brings him to nurse and finds my husband lying beside me, chastely outside the cover. *"Vreselijk!"* she says, sending him back to the living room couch. I protest. "But I like having him here! He's not doing any harm!" "He's young," she says, "and the young don't know what they are doing."

Tyrannical as Old Terrible sometimes is, she is indispensable. There is no question now of her leaving at the end of a week; Mannie will need expert care for a month, at least, and left to myself, I don't think I'd have the heart to carry out the spartan regimen prescribed for him by the doctor, which is that of a tuberculosis sanatorium in the mountains. He has to stay out in the open air all day, rain or shine. At night, or in freezing weather—for the treatment won't end with the summer—he must sleep or play bundled up by a wide-open window. And I must feed him myself for as long as I have any milk. The salt sea air and his mother's milk will save little Mannie, the doctor says, and because he has ten healthy children of his own, I believe him. Old Terrible, who adores the doctor, obeys him to the letter; she even insists that I nurse Mannie out-of-doors. A proceeding that embarrasses everyone. The maid clearly thinks it undignified. Doris averts her eyes and calls my son indoors. Even my husband is annoyed by it, though I'm not quite sure why. But he only has to put up with it on the weekends.

As Mannie's hold on his life gets stronger day by day, so does Old Terrible's hold over ours; between them, she and my tiny son have drastically altered its rhythm. She intimidates us all, even my husband. Yet her sway is benign. Doris has never been so efficient, the children never so obedient, the house never so clean, and the meals never so punctual as now. But during the week, my husband has taken to eating all of his at a Rotterdam café. He leaves by an earlier train and comes home by a later one, thus avoiding most of Old Terrible's irksome restrictions; such as no smoking anywhere within breathing distance of Mannie, and no upsetting of me, no exciting me, even pleasurably. I am sacrosanct, like a Hindu cow; but only on account of my life-giving milk; in the interests of which all sorts of peculiar foods have been added to my diet, and most of the things I like cut out of it. I may drink beer, which I detest, but no wine, no coffee, and no real tea—just a pale concoction of herbs. Meanwhile, Old Terrible keeps up her strength with a thick black essence of tannin. Her enamel teapot stands simmering on the stove all day long, stewing the last drop of poison out of the tea leaves, which she then puts to various uses, such as fertilizing the house plants and telling fortunes.

I am worried and, at the same time, relieved by my husband's altered schedule; worried that it may turn into a habit and relieved, for the moment, because it saves friction. Old Terrible retires to her own room before he gets back, and so does Doris, and the quiet hours I have with him before I go to sleep are unusually happy. Deprivation of privacy has had the effect of enhancing its value. Where before, too much time alone with me when I was inactive made my husband restless, now, he values every moment.

Quietly, reasonably, we review our relationship and discuss the emotional causes behind Mannie's premature birth. For both of us, marriage is for life. But we are both beginning to realize that despite our deep love and our strong physical need for each other, we are in many ways incompatible. And we both take for granted that most, if not all of the adjusting will have to be done by me. I have been reared in the tradition that it is a wife's duty to make her husband happy—even to the extent of finding her own happiness solely in his. My mother regarded women who were not prepared to subordinate their lives to their husbands (provided they were what she called "good husbands") as selfish and destructive. Those few women who had proved incontestably that their personal accomplishments were of equal or superior value, were considered exceptions to the rule, and justified only by God-given genius. They were, so to speak, the chosen. I have no God-given genius, no claim to be "chosen," but I do have a burning desire for self-expression and a fear that it's going to be quenched. But I don't mention this to my husband, or to anyone.

Old Terrible knows a lot about married life and what it means for most women. The stories she tells are Gothic tales. She never names the protagonists. She always begins in the same way, "I once had a patient . . ." and goes on to reveal the secret hells enclosed by the four walls of the large and comfortable homes that have been the theater of her activities for the past forty years. Only the home of the blue-eyed, apple-cheeked doctor is without any evil secret. Struggle, yes. Sickness, yes. Sorrow, yes. But no infidelity, no hatred, no cruelty. As for his ten blue-eyed, apple-cheeked children, she is justly proud of her role in their birth and survival, which she sees as nothing less than that of an essential collaborator in the work of the Lord.

When Mannie was two months old, we left the summer cottage in which he was born and moved to a semidetached villa farther away from the sea, but larger, and more suitable for the winter. At first, we had turned it down, when the real estate agent had told us that its owner, who lived in The Hague, liked to keep it free for his own use during July and August. We didn't want to have to move again before we left the country for a new post. But the owner, it seemed, was very particular in the matter of tenants, and if getting the right people meant giving a year-round lease, he might agree to forgo his summer vacation for once.

He showed us the villa himself. It was furnished in a stiff, bourgeois style with no frills, but it contained an object of more importance to us than any amount of luxury—an excellent upright grand piano. And just as our reaction to the secret painted rooms in the Rotterdam apartment had tipped the scales in our favor with De Groote, so now our delighted reaction to the piano won us the year's lease we wanted from this very different, but equally choosey, house owner.

Like De Groote, he was a big man with a beard. But there the resemblance ended. His was a type that I had learned to recognize as Jewish; though not yet as specifically Sephardic and aristocratic. Tall, and powerfully built, he looked like an ancient Hebrew king; with a noble forehead, heavy-lidded, opaque brown eyes under arched black brows, a long, straight nose, rather fleshy, and a singularly sweet smile. De Groote had been the quintessential landlord; a man whose property was his whole treasure. But this Hebrew king was the quintessential father, whose treasure lay in the burgeoning lives and talents of his offspring. For some capricious reason, my memory refuses to yield up his name, while presenting everything else about him—his magnificent appearance, benignly patriarchal bearing, and deep, authoritative voice—with the utmost clarity.

An accomplished amateur musician, he could play several instruments, but his love was the double bass; a full, but restrained musical voice that expressed him perfectly. He and his family of five sons and one daughter made up a chamber music group that was unlike any other in my rather limited experience; I had yet to discover the music-making families of European Jewry, in which music, religion, and family piety were so closely intertwined that they formed an indissoluble trinity, a mystical union of immense virtue.

On hearing that my husband was taking lessons from the cellist Johan Ydo, a great artist and a teacher of infinite patience and skill, and that I could play the piano and sing, our musician landlord offered to bring his family orchestra out to the villa to make music both for us, and, overestimating our abilities, with us.

They came and played for us on more than one dream-like occasion. But the memory of them is contained in a single, powerful image, which, when I summon it up, transports me backward in time to a world I know only through art and the poetry of the Bible. I perceive in the sculptured faces of the five young men bent over their instruments, engrossed in the music they are playing and ennobled by it, archetypes of the young David bent over his harp, singing for his friend Jonathan.

The girl, the only daughter, is the youngest. Fifteen or sixteen years old, with her dark hair in two long braids, she sits at the piano, rapt, her hands poised over the keyboard like small white birds poised for flight. As I watch the rhythms of the music racing like wind-driven clouds across her expressive face, I recognize her. She is one of the "chosen"; a possessor of God-given genius.

When we left Holland, she slowly drifted down to the bottom of my mind, where she lay undisturbed and unsullied for half a century. Then, as if aware that her time had come, she rose to the surface without being consciously summoned, to fulfill her tragic destiny as the "lost girl" in my novel, *Fugue.*

If this account of our sojourn in Holland were fiction, this is where I would end it. But real life doesn't lend itself to such tidy shaping. It leaves ragged edges.

Roughly superimposed on the image of a romantic musical experience is another, and vastly different, combination of sight and sound; an image of excruciating pain. The image of Mannie at fourteen months old, pierced through and through by arrows; imploring help with uncomprehending eyes; beating his tortured head over and over against the padded sides of his crib like a maniac butting the walls of a padded cell. And all to the sound of heartrending screams; high-pitched, inhuman screams of pure agony.

Old Terrible comes to offer help. "*Vreselijk!* Oh! *Vreselijk!* Poor little Mannikin tossed about on the devil's pitchforks!"

To me, the doctor guardedly speaks of infection, of an inflammation attacking the membranes of the brain. To my husband, he says simply, "Meningitis." He comes to see Mannie every few hours to administer medication, an unidentified gray powder. My husband stays at home. We are all burning up together in Mannie's undeserved hell.

We take turns in watching over him. On the fourth or fifth night—I am not sure which, I have lost all sense of time—I take over from my husband at two o'clock in the morning. It seems to me that the intervals between the onslaughts of pain and screaming are growing longer. Does this mean he is getting better? Or is it a sign of exhaustion, of the body losing its resistance? I catch myself dozing off, and what jerks me back into wakefulness is not the onset of sound, but the depth of the silence.

Mannie's pain-racked body is still, completely still for the first time since his illness started. His cavernous, black-ringed eyes are closed. But his pulse still beats. It is sleep, not death. Not this time.

4

A Case of Champagne

*D*o you remember, Mother, telling me on a journey from London to Bucharest, when I was six years old, that life was hell for a women?

So writes my eldest son more than fifty years later. I don't recall having actually said those words that made so deep an impression on him, but that particular journey was enough to wring the truth out of any woman.

Early in 1924, my husband was transferred to Rumania, to take charge of the vice-consulate in Bucharest. For him, this was a small but reassuring step-up on a long professional ladder. For me, it was more like a flying leap out of a settling fog and into a new stream of air, with a hint of glitter in the distance.

My husband conceded the glitter, but was not dazzled by it. Five years earlier, on his return to England after the war and before being demobilized, he was temporarily appointed by the War Office as a king's messenger; one of a special corps of couriers who carried the diplomatic pouch, known then as "the bag," to and from the newly re-established British missions all over Europe, one of which was in Bucharest. Later, king's messengers were attached to the Foreign Office; they were highly privileged persons who traveled only in first-class *wagons-lits* on trains like the Orient Express. But the first postwar trips, which took weeks instead of days, were made on a succession of limping, battle-scarred local trains in third-class coaches with wooden seats, no heat, very little light, and so many seatless passengers sleeping upright or slumped over their bundles in the corridors that it seemed a sin for one man, even a king's messenger, to take up a whole compartment. But those were his orders.

On arriving in Bucharest at about four o'clock one morning, after more than a week on a train that had been held up several times in the middle of nowhere while damaged rails were repaired, all my husband wanted was a hot bath and a few hours sleep in a comfortable bed before reporting to the legation. But the one and only hotel was out of hot water and swarming with bedbugs; disadvantages that the management tried to make up for Rumanian style. "Those damn girls," he told me when he got home, "were just as big a nuisance as the bedbugs. They refused to believe they weren't wanted—they kept knocking on my door and lowering their rates."

Invited to lunch at the legation, he had said he could accept only if a hot bath was thrown in. The chargé d'affaires had a sense of humor, and a prelunch bath was provided. Over lunch, the political and economic situations in the country were discussed, but when the men were alone with their brandy and cigars, the talk turned to the foibles of Bucharest society. "Foppish men who wear corsets, and incredibly beautiful women who don't. Hospitable. Unhygienic. Decadent. Brilliant. Corrupt. Amoral. Charming. By Jove, yes! Ab-so-lutely charming!" A collection of paradoxes, which added up to a kinder and truer verdict than that of the irreverent Frenchman whose three-line epigram on Rumania—*Les fleurs sans odeur. Les hommes sans honneur. Les femmes sans pudeur*—sacrificed fairness to wit and seriously libeled the flowers.

My husband's fading impressions of that brief visit to Bucharest as a king's messenger were confirmed and revived by a letter from the vice-consul he was now going to replace and whose apartment we were hoping to take over. He wrote that he couldn't recommend it. It was inconvenient, damp, overrun with assorted pests, and outrageously expensive. He was damn glad to be getting out of it and, to be honest, out of Bucharest altogether. The life there wasn't at all his cup of tea; in fact, it was more like bad champagne. But some Britishers seemed to enjoy getting tight on it, and it would certainly be a change for us after dear old respectable Holland. However, he strongly advised my husband to come first by himself and send for me and the children only when he had found a decent place for us to live... "Which I warn you won't be easy, because, my dear fellow, British standards of decency simply don't apply in this country."

All the more reason, I thought, why I should be there to choose between greater and lesser evils. And, incidentally, to protect my husband from those incredibly beautiful women who didn't wear corsets—or anything else—under their Paris dresses.

But there were deeper reasons than that why I didn't want my husband to go without me. Our unexpectedly long separation when we were first married, followed so closely by his absences as a king's messenger that they were virtually a continuation of it, had left me with an almost pathological fear of parting from him again.

Now, we ended up making what everyone thought was a sensible compromise. We would go together to Bucharest, but leave the children in England until we had found a suitable home, when I would return to fetch them. Doris undertook to remain with them until then, and one of my husband's numerous aunts, who lived in a Wiltshire village, found rooms for them in a cottage near her with an elderly couple—retired family retainers, who liked children and could be relied on to feed them well and make them generally comfortable. The aunt, of course, would keep a watchful eye.

The only missing element in all this was maternal love.

During our three-year sojourn in Holland, I had only once been away from the children and then for just a few days, and I didn't fully realize what this indefinite parting would cost both me and them until the moment came to say goodbye. My daughter and little Mannie were still too young to understand that I wouldn't be back next day. But my eldest son understood, and his look of silent reproach almost stopped me from going. But the cab was at the door, and my husband kept calling, "Come on! Come on! We'll miss the boat train!"

I cried all the way to Dover. But crossing the channel, the misery of seasickness blotted out the misery of the heart, and as soon as we were settled in our *wagon-lit* on the Orient Express, I lay down on my bunk and fell into the deep sleep of emotional and physical exhaustion.

Awakening in the morning to a new and sunny landscape unfolding, and my husband humming a happy tune as he dressed, and the dining car attendant knocking on the doors announcing the first breakfast, I felt as if I were off on a long-delayed second honeymoon.

The outgoing vice consul had booked a room for us at the second-best hotel, instead of at the Athénée Palace, where most foreigners stayed. "You can always eat there," he said, "and make use of the bar and the lounge by day. But at night . . . Well, one bedbug's as good as another, so why choose the most expensive?"

I was eager to start house hunting. But it wasn't the organized undertaking that I expected. There were no real estate agents to consult, no reliable ads to follow up; it was all done by word of mouth in a closed circuit of foreigners likely to pay high rentals. The moment we heard of a place that might suit us, we would rush out to see it. But there would always be something wrong, and it was usually the same thing. Despite a veneer of French culture, Bucharest at that time was still a semi-oriental city, with hardly any modern buildings. Dilapidated old houses, large and small, jostled one another in picturesque disorder on narrow, muddy streets. Barricaded with iron grilles against the outside world, they were designed to protect the privacy of the family as a whole, but not of its individual members. The rooms would be strung together with communicating doors, but would have no separate entrances, and the only bathroom would open out of the last room on the string, with no other means of access. For a British family brought up to regard personal privacy as a God-given right, this was an impossible arrangement. And the servants' quarters horrified us. Their so-called bedrooms were nothing but windowless holes opening off the kitchen and barely big enough to contain a narrow cot. Somewhere in back there would be a smelly toilet, or outhouse, but servants were expected to wash themselves in the kitchen sink and go out to the public baths once a week.

"I absolutely refuse," my husband said, "to treat my domestics like animals." But it looked as if the only alternative would be not to have any domestics, which was unthinkable for people in our position and would have brought a stiff reprimand down on our heads from the Foreign Office. Besides, the conditions were such that to do without help would have been a practical impossibility.

We were getting desperate when someone said, "What about the American Baptist missionaries?"

Missionaries in Rumania, with its myriad Christian churches and dignified black-robed priests? How odd! Twice a year in my father's church, the collection had gone to the Foreign Missions, which I envisaged as a corps of devoted but foolhardy Christians who thought it their duty to teach cannibals not to eat one another. In my husband's opinion, they were a set of interfering busybodies who deserved to be eaten themselves.

"Well," he said now, "what about them?"

Within ten minutes of asking that ironical question, he was on the telephone talking to a missionary for the first time in his life, and being exceedingly polite.

The American voice at the other end of the line belonged to the woman who headed a group of a dozen men and women dedicated to a sterner form of Christian conduct than that enjoined by the lenient Orthodox priests. Now, after two years of discouraging labor in an unfruitful field, they were going back to the States. But before they could leave, they had to dispose of the remaining three years of a five-year lease on the makeshift, but spacious, apartment—actually the whole top floor of an office building— which had served as their headquarters and as housing for the single women in the group.

Although I eventually met them all, the woman with whom we first spoke over the phone and later transacted business, is the only one I can still see clearly and the only one whose name I remember—no doubt because she fitted it so perfectly. It was Button. Sister Button to her group, Miss Button to us, Jane Button on documents, she was the living personification of those flat, bone buttons used on plain, durable garments, like work-men's trousers. There was nothing about her that could rub off, chip, or tarnish, and I could not imagine anyone less likely to succeed in luring the warm and wayward Rumanians out of their gilded churches and into a chilly river.

As devoutly as Miss Button must have been hoping that we would take over the lease of the apartment, she showed us around it with an air of condescension, as if we were lucky beyond our deserts to be offered an opportunity of living in such a presanctified atmosphere.

The former business premises had, like the Rumanian people, resisted conversion. But for all its original sins the apartment possessed the one great virtue that we had despaired of ever finding: a separate entrance to each room, of which there were five, all exactly alike, and each with its own glass-paned double doors opening into the large rectangular hall that was used by the group for prayer meetings. A sixth room had been partitioned to make a bathroom—almost entirely filled by the tub and the wood-burning water heater—and a kitchen—almost entirely filled by a huge wood-burning range. Unlike most of the kitchens we had seen, it was scrupulously tidy and clean. "Our two servants come from a Swabian enclave in Transylvania," Miss Button told us. "They are both out now, if you care to see their room."

Airy and light, it was identical with the missionary ladies' own bedrooms and provided with exactly the same items of primitive, functional furniture; painted wooden chest and wardrobe, straight chairs to match, tautly made-up cots, and beside each a small rectangular peasant rug. Here, indeed, was democracy.

"In the States," Miss Button told us with pride, "the household help is accommodated with dignity. And we like to think of our headquarters as representative of the best aspects of American life."

"Hear hear!" said my husband.

Before she could make any more democratic speeches, the phone rang. While she took the call, my husband whispered to me, "Ask her where the bog is."

Translating, I asked her where the *lavatory* was.

"If you mean the toilet facilities," she said, "there are two of them and they are out on the landing. It is not very convenient. But we have been trained to endure worse hardships than that when in the field."

Finding us eager to take over the apartment despite this inconvenience, Miss Button shrewdly imposed the condition that we take over the furniture as well. "I suppose we could use it until we get something else?" my husband said, appealing to me as an expert disguiser of junk.

I wanted to say, *No.* To call Miss Button's bluff. And later I wished that I had. Very soon after we moved in, we had to throw the cots out. But not all their insect inhabitants went with them; a contingent was left behind to propagate their species in the box springs of our nice new beds. Was it possible that the upright Sister Button had knowingly palmed them off on us? My husband thought she had. He ridiculed my suggestion that she might have been insensible to their bites, like the holy men of India who can walk barefoot on sharp nails without feeling them.

We signed the lease in March, but it was not until May that the missionaries finally sailed for the States and we took triumphant possession of their vacated headquarters—blissfully unaware of its bloodthirsty occupying army of bedbugs, and the huge, black, Kafkaesque cockroaches that invaded the kitchen every night.

Next day, disillusioned, itchy, surrounded by crates and cartons in our comfortless new abode, and confronted by the task of transforming it into a home, I felt as though I were literally sobering up from a prolonged high on the bad champagne mentioned by the previous vice-consul; coming painfully to my senses after four months of semi-intoxication, during which, among other follies, I had once again managed to get pregnant.

Britishers who permanently succumbed to this insidious intoxicant were referred to by their stronger-minded compatriots as "Rumanianized"—a contemptuous term which covered a multitude of sins, but which I could never hear without a twinge of conscience; we had come so close to succumbing ourselves. We had each been susceptible to its lure for different reasons. In my case, circumstances—the war, my father's illness, my early marriage and pregnancy—had denied me the scamper in the grass between one hegemony and another that is youth's prerogative. Belatedly presented by a new set of circumstances with an enticing but subtly poisonous imitation of what I thought I had missed forever, I had found it irresistible. In my husband's case, it had been a deliberate decision to try a form of drug which earlier he had condemned in the "bright young people" of London, including his own two sisters, as making a mockery of the war, of the slaughter of a whole generation of young men, and trivializing the anguish of those who had, like him, miraculously survived.

Not since the ten days of compassionate leave granted to him for our honeymoon, had he and I been alone together as we were during those first months in Bucharest. Without the children, without a home to run, with nothing to do but accept invitations to the dance, I was thrust into a role I had envied but never been free to play; that of mistress and companion, rather than wife and mother, and I discovered not only that it wasn't as easy as I had imagined, but also that it wasn't what my husband really wanted.

At the time he met me on a weekend in Devon, he had been in England for several months, recovering from a wound, and was just about ready to be sent back to the fighting in France. During his convalescence, he had made the acquaintance of a beautiful and wealthy young girl who was very attracted to him, and whose parents would have welcomed him as a son-in-law. His sudden marriage to me, a little country mouse with no money, no social position, no glamour, astounded everyone who knew him. Some of them asked him outright what on earth he saw in me.

He saw, I think now, a safe harbor, from which he could come and go with the tides of his restless nature, which craved freedom, but feared solitude. And the ties that curtailed my freedom to come and go with him—even metaphorically, were precisely what bound him to me and gave our ill-assorted marriage its stability.

As for the "pleasure drug," it provided no lasting relief from his deep depressions, only an added problem. The attention I got from Rumanian men, attracted by my "English-rose" type of looks, and perhaps by my English reserve as well, aroused in him the sexual jealousy and possessiveness that hitherto had been almost entirely on my side. This dangerous flame, once ignited, continued to burn him up for the rest of his life, with very little fuel but that of his own imagination.

By the time the apartment was ready for the children, the hot weather was approaching, and we were advised to keep them in England until it was over. My doctor thought it would be better for me, too, to be out of Bucharest in the summer. Once again I was emotionally torn. But this time the decision was clear-cut.

And the fact that I would be the one to go away, while my husband's duties obliged him to stay behind, gave me a sense of power and made me less apprehensive about parting with him. Besides, I was longing to see the children again.

In mid-June I left for England on the Orient Express, four months pregnant, in spite of using Dr. Stopes' new-fangled device, and feeling ten years older in sophistication than when I had traveled eastward on that same train five months earlier.

I had a sleeping compartment to myself, and I spent most of my time lying down, trying to keep at bay a horrible mixture of morning and motion sickness. At the frontier stations, at Budapest, at Vienna—wherever the train stopped for any length of time and the passengers were allowed to get off—I would cautiously descend from my *wagon-lit* and walk up and down on the platform, absorbing the smells and sounds peculiar to each stop. At the borders, in the middle of open country, it might be the cackle of geese or the fragrance of lime trees in flower; in the great glass-domed depots, clouded with steam, of the capital cities, it would be the composite but highly individual odor that enables one to identify a particular city even in the dark; and its composite voice, whose inflections alone are enough to establish nationality.

From London, where I stayed overnight, I sent a telegram to Doris telling her by what train to expect me in Wiltshire next day. But there was no one at the station to meet me, and I had to hire a cab to take me to the village.

The cottage in which the children were staying had a large garden surrounded by a yew hedge. Through the wicket gate I could see my eldest son aimlessly poking about by himself. When I called his name, he turned and came to meet me, but hesitantly, as if I were a stranger. He allowed himself to be hugged with the same polite reluctance.

"Where are the others?"

"Upstairs."

"And Doris?"

"She's gone."

The woman of the cottage came bustling out. "Oh Madam! I'm that glad to see you! What with Miss Doris gone, and your auntie away, and all. . . ."

"When did Miss Doris leave?"

"First thing this morning, Madam. She packed her bags last night, when she got your telegram."

"I don't understand . . . Was she ill?"

"Not that I know of, Madam. She was just . . . nervous like."

"But why did she leave before I got here?"

"I'm sure I couldn't say, Madam."

"I know why," said my son. "I know because she told me."

"What did she tell you?"

"She said she didn't want to see you, Mother. I think," he added in his solemn, grown-up way, "she was afraid you would be cross."

And I was cross—very cross indeed. The change the children had undergone in barely five months was incredible; particularly the two little ones. Although they had grown both in stature and in beauty, they were pitiful. Apparently healthy, they were nonetheless starvelings, deprived of something just as important as food, and shamefully neglected. Never again, I thought. In future we would all stay together no matter what.

My chubby toddler of a daughter had changed to a graceful little girl; her curly chestnut hair fell half-way down her back in a matted, tangled mane. Wearing nothing but a torn nightie with all its buttons missing, she looked like a waif, a lovely lost child stolen away from a good home by gypsies and dressed in old rags. While my eldest son stood aloof, reserving judgment, she and Mannie, bright-eyed and elfin, clung to me, begging me not to leave them. "Stay wiv' us! Stay wiv' us!" They kept saying it over and over, all the time, like an incantation, until, as the days went by, and every morning when they woke up they found me still there, they gradually regained their lost sense of security. But I don't think my eldest son wholly regained his, then or ever.

Thanks to the good, country meals provided by the woman of the cottage—fresh fruit and vegetables from the garden, home-baked bread, chickens and eggs and milk from a neighboring farm—they had stayed well. But their healthy appearance had blinded the aunt, on whose watchful eye we had depended, to everything else. Unused to small children and lacking maternal instincts, she had failed to perceive how neglected they were, much less how unhappy.

She had noticed that Doris seemed depressed and, ascribing it to boredom, had tried to involve her in some of the village activities. She never suspected what the woman of the cottage had been afraid to tell her; that Doris spent most of the day in bed crying, while the two younger children stayed imprisoned in their room, untended, for hours at a stretch, and my eldest son wandered about alone.

Their clothes, whole new outfits lovingly made by me for their stay in England, were no longer fit to wear; nothing had been washed, cleaned, or mended. Shoes had gone unrepaired, and Mannie, who had grown out of his, was running barefoot. What had Doris done with the money we had sent her to provide for all these needs?

My husband was furious. "I only hope," he wrote, "that one fine day she will turn up at some British consulate asking for help, as she did at Rotterdam, and find *me* there!" But when he understood that she had cracked up under a strain she was not equipped to bear, he said, "Poor bitch.... We should never have given her so much responsibility."

For me, that summer in the country—peaceful, monotonous, sometimes wearisome, was a period of growth and recognitions. I was back in the landscape of my young girlhood, with its yews and herbaceous borders and swallows at evening. Sitting in the parlor of the cottage after the children had gone to bed, writing to my husband by the light of an oil lamp, the only sounds the occasional bark of a dog and the chirp of crickets, I felt like a revenant in a world of which I had once been an inhabitant.

From this detached vantage point I could see my past and present lives in clear perspective, and I perceived myself to be in danger of being destroyed by forces in my life that should not have been in opposition, yet were; my love for my husband and my love for my children, their need of me and his need of me, and an aching need of my own that neither my husband nor my children could satisfy. If spiritual strength begins with the perception of one's weaknesses, then whatever degree of it I have since developed took root in me during that interlude of suspended action, which besides enabling me to see clearly into myself, allowed me to watch undisturbed the unfolding personalities of my two younger children, and to recover some of the closeness that had once existed between me and my firstborn.

The most endearing of the three, at that point in their lives, was Mannie. Open and loving, but small and fragile, he was a risk-laden mixture of vulnerability and trustfulness. Luckily for him, his sister, so near him in age, was made of tougher material and would eventually provoke in him the aggressiveness necessary for survival. My eldest, at six, had already discovered and sharpened his own special weapons; passive resistance, and a clever, manipulative mind. All three were beautiful, intelligent, and full of promise. But in writing to their father about them I was careful not to rhapsodize. My letters to him were in every respect less open than those I had written him while he was away at the war. I had learned how easy it is, and how dangerous, to endow a distant correspondant with perfect understanding; a painful lesson that all writers, whether of letters or of books, have to learn sooner or later.

My husband's letters to me, on the other hand, were more open, though less romantic, than those he had written from the front when we were first married. I had become the intimate friend to whom he confided everything, and he took my perfect understanding for granted.

On the whole his reports of his daily existence as a grass widower were reassuring. He had a lot to do in the consulate—his assistants were taking their vacations one after another, keeping him shorthanded—and at home he was being well cared for by the Button-trained mother and daughter who had stayed on to keep house for us. The heat was "bloody awful," but even that had its compensations; it had caused the wife of the chargé d'affaires to go home to England for the whole summer, and knowing my husband to be a fine horseman, she had put her two mounts at his disposal during her absence. He had his dark times, during which he drank too much. And he had his temptations; in fact, as I very well knew, he was surrounded by them. But in every letter he said, "I am waiting for you. I really want only you. Do you still want me?" And such was the pact of honesty we had made that I knew he was speaking the truth. As for me, I did still want him and no one else, and in any case I was surrounded by a total absence of temptations.

At the beginning of September he wrote, "It's cooling off now, thank God. I'm making arrangements for you and the children to leave England on the fifteenth and to travel on the same train as the king's messenger—it's not anyone you know, he's new on the job; but he's a very likable chap, an Irishman, and he says he'll be delighted to keep an eye on you and the children. He's young and unmarried, and when I told him that you were expecting in November he looked a bit startled. But secretly, I think, he rather likes the idea of a bit of knight-errantry—looking after that bloody bag can get awfully boring."

The journey might not have been so difficult if it hadn't started badly and if I had been as mentally prepared to cope with the worst as I usually was. But my long stay in the somnolent countryside, with its rustic routine of leisurely morning rambles and lazy, lukewarm afternoons in a deck chair, reading or sewing and watching the children play, of falling asleep with the swallows and waking up at cockcrow (which had been our accustomed bedtime in Bucharest), had tranquilized me into forgetting, or ignoring, all the lessons of past experience.

The aunt had agreed to come up to London with us, stay with us overnight in a hotel, and take care of the children for me while I did some errands and kept an appointment with my husband's department chief at the Foreign Office—which I didn't look forward to on account of my all too visible seven-month pregnancy. Junior officers in the Service were not expected to have large families; they were too expensive to move around the world.

Then, almost at the last minute, the aunt said she couldn't come, and I had to appeal to my husband's mother for help. Warmhearted and impractical, she offered to put us up in the tiny flat that she shared with his grandmother. It was a night of acute discomfort for us all. I was allotted one side of the old lady's double bed. Her asthmatic breathing kept me awake all night, and the lack of sleep brought on a fatal combination of morning sickness and nervous anxiety, which rushing around London on buses and tube trains did nothing to help. I had some bad moments in the Foreign Office, when I thought I was going to be sick on the desk of the high official who was looking at me quizzically with an odd mixture of disapproval and pity in his eyes. But I managed to get through the interview safely, without disgracing myself any more than I already had, by being pregnant in the first place. I took a taxi back to my mother-in-law's flat, collected the children and the luggage, and got to Victoria just in time to catch the boat train.

I was so blinded by migraine that I could hardly see the young king's messenger (K.M. from now on), who was holding seats for us on the crowded train, but he sounded nervous; he must have seen on my face the wild look of someone who is hanging on for dear life against an untimely physical collapse, and realized what he might be in for. The two other passengers in our compartment, both middle-aged men, gave us one disgusted look and retired behind their newspapers. The children were still too interested in everything they saw out of the train windows to be naughty, so I closed my eyes and strove to control my nausea, pretending to be asleep when the K.M. looked in to see if I wanted tea.

At Dover, the fresh sea breeze pulled me together. The K.M., whom I saw now to have lively blue eyes and a jolly Irish smile, made all the jollier by a rakishly upturned black mustache, settled us all into deck chairs and went off to the bar for a drink.

The breeze that had pulled me together pulled me very quickly to pieces again as soon as the boat was out of the harbor. When the K.M. came back to see how we were doing, he found me clinging onto the deck rail vomiting over the side, with my hat gone out to sea along with my hairpins and my long hair flying in the wind. All I had eaten that day, which wasn't much, had already come up, but I couldn't stop retching—in great convulsive spasms that shook my whole body.

The K.M. said "You can't go on like this.... Allow me to take you below, there's a cabin there where you might be able to lie down."

I didn't want to go below. The fresh air, I thought, was my only hope. But the young K.M. was my only friend on board, and I didn't want to embarrass him, so I let him steer me down the companionway to a cabin filled with other seasick females. An attendant wedged me into a bunk with two big pillows, which she called "two sailors," one on each side of me, and washed my face with a

wet cloth. Then a man appeared, a passenger I had seen on the
deck, and said he was a doctor. He gave me a pill, which I brought
up at once. Then he gave me another, dissolved in a spoonful of
water, and told me to breathe deeply. It worked, and I fell into a
half-doze, which lasted until we reached Calais.

The stewardess set me on my feet. "Better now she's stopped,
eh? The young gentleman said to wait for him."

Where were the children? Had they been with the K.M. all this
time, or were they cooped up in a special vomitorium for the very
young? The other women in mine had all gone on deck, and I was
beginning to feel abandoned when the K.M. came running down
the companionway with his precious pouch under his arm, tipped
the stewardess, and hurried me up the steps to the crowded deck,
where the children were waiting huddled together in a corner
and looking bedraggled and frightened.

"Customs?"

"All taken care of. Come on, children, keep close, we don't want
to lose you."

The train was waiting by the quay. The K.M. handed first me
and then the three children up the two steep steps of the *wagon-lit*
to a disdainful attendant, who looked as if he would love to tell us
that we were on the wrong train. Fellow passengers, pushing past
us in the corridor, stared at us with the same air of insulting
disbelief. "Here you are," said the K.M. cheerfully, "number 10,
right next door to me."

The privacy of the two-bunk sleeper, complete with washroom,
was immensely inviting. Before the journey was over it would
seem like a grimy prison, but now, all spit and polish and clean
white linen, it was balm to my seasick soul.

Looking pleased with himself at having got us thus far, the
K.M. said, "Well . . . I expect you'd like to be left in peace now. But
if there's anything I . . ." At that moment, my eldest son, who
hadn't uttered a single word since we got off the boat, said
solemnly, "I think I'm going to be sick."

The K.M. pushed him into the washroom. On the wall facing
the door was a long mirror, that explained with a single graphic
image the peculiar look on the faces of everyone who saw us. The
small boy throwing up in the washbasin; the mother, myself,
pale-faced, big-bellied, disheveled, a vomit stain on the front of

my jacket; the two bedraggled little ones clinging to my skirt; and the elegantly dressed young diplomat playing the role of pater-familias—all reflected against the background of a first-class sleeper on the Orient Express, made such an incongruous picture that I burst out laughing. "That's right," said the K.M. "there's a funny side to everything, isn't there?"

I managed to get the children safely tucked in for the night—the two little boys in one bunk and my daughter with me in the other—before the train started to move and brought my nausea back. I lay down without undressing and tried, as the train gathered speed, to control with deep breathing the convulsive dry heaves that were so exhausting and might, I thought, be danger-ous. What if I should suddenly feel the warning pangs that had heralded Mannie's forty-five minute dash into existence? I would have to tell the K.M. what was happening. How terribly embar-rassing that would be for him! I prayed that it wouldn't happen; but if it did, I knew that he wouldn't turn tail, as Doris had, and leave me to my fate. He would page the train for a doctor, that's what he would to. And this conviction of the K.M.'s common sense allayed some of my anxiety, and I managed to sleep a little.

In the morning, my eldest son did his best to take care of the two little ones; washing their faces, putting them on their potties, feeding them on the biscuits and fruit I had brought with me, and cocoa and buns from the dining car. All day he tried to stop the poor little things from disturbing me. Still unable to keep any-thing down for more than a few minutes, I was getting weaker and weaker. Never, before or since, has a journey seemed so interminable. From time to time the K.M. would look in to ask how I was and would find me prostrate, and I would assure him that I was all right—I just felt better lying down. In the middle of the day he took the children to the dining car for a meal, and when-ever the train stopped at a station he would help them down to the platform to stretch their restless little legs, while I would take advantage of the absence of motion to freshen myself up and gather my strength for the re-commencement of the movement and the misery. By the time we reached Vienna, I felt so ill that for two pins I would have leaned out of the window and appealed to one of the women passengers standing around on the platform to come and help me. There was nothing much anyone could do—short of stopping the train, but I desperately needed the understanding and moral support of another woman. I soon came to my senses. Just below my window, the K.M. was talking with the elegant young woman who occupied the compartment on the other side of mine, and I heard him telling her that the mother of the three children he was shepherding was having "a pretty rough time of it." And I felt her look of total indifference to my state like a slap in the face.

When I emerged from the washroom, where I hid until the train left the station, my son said, "You've been crying, Mummie. . . ." and the two little ones echoed him, throwing their arms around my neck in an effort to comfort me.

It may have been then that I told him that life was hell for a woman. But what I didn't say, or even perhaps fully realize at the time, was that it was made all the harder to bear by the callousness of the women of my generation toward one another, which was the result of the cutthroat competition on the postwar marriage market.

At Budapest, where we arrived late at night, I decided to venture a little walk up and down the platform on my own. The children were asleep, and the K.M. probably thought I was asleep, too, so it was easy to avoid him.

This romantic, nineteenth-century railway station, whose indescribable native odor and resounding voice that resembled no other, destined to become, years later, the distinctive odor and sound of my home, was the gateway to Eastern Europe, and as such made me feel that I was almost at the end of my journey. It was good to be up and moving, but I felt very groggy—groggy and brittle, as if I might topple over and break into little pieces at any moment. After about five minutes, I thought it wiser to get back on the train. The K.M. was standing by the door of the *wagon-lit* with a group of other passengers, including the young woman whose indifference to my state had so distressed me in Vienna. They were all buying cups of coffee from a vendor. On seeing me, the K.M. exclaimed joyfully, "Splendid! I'm so glad to see you're feeling better!" Then he introduced me to the elegant young woman as her next door neighbor on the train. "Oh, really?" she said, and immediately turned to someone else. A wave of pure hatred rose up in me and extended beyond the young woman to a marcelled, middle aged one who pushed past me so carelessly that she almost knocked me over. Only the presence of the K.M. kept me from telling her to look where she was going. "Here," he said, handing me the cup of hot coffee he had just got from the vendor, "drink this, it will buck you up."

I drank it, expecting it to disgrace me by coming up immediately, but too angry to care what happened. Miraculously, it stayed down, and I began to feel much better. "You see!" the K.M. said happily, "It *has* bucked you up!"

My husband would have said that what bucked me up in the first place was getting angry. He believed in the curative power of anger, especially righteous anger. Musing on this as I lay in my bunk, free of nausea for the first time in days, I was amazed at how often my husband's most unpopular theories were proved right in the event.

In the late afternoon of the following day we reached the outskirts of Bucharest, and I was feeling the mingled relief and trepidation that accompanies every arrival at a longed-for destination. I had tried my best to make myself and the children presentable. I had opened a suitcase and got out some clean clothes, but our faces and hands were still grimy with soot—the water in the washroom had long given out and so had my eau de cologne.

While the children were running excitedly up and down the corridor, the K.M. sat down for a moment in my compartment. "I'm afraid," he said, echoing his own phrase, "that you've been having a pretty rough time of it, and I have felt rather helpless. No experience, you know. No children of my own. No wife... until I've finished with king's messengering. My fiancée didn't like the idea of my being constantly away after our marriage."

"She's right," I said. "I know ... I've been through it."

"Have you? Have you really, now? I had no idea that your husband had been a K.M."

"A K.M. and before that a soldier—away for two years with no home leave."

"I just missed the war," he said. "Too young."

"You can thank your lucky stars for that, and so can your fiancée."

"She said that once herself. I wish you could meet her, you'd love her—and she would love you."

I knew this was an afterthought, but I didn't mind. I just hoped that she would love him.

The train was slowing down and rolling into the station, and I still hadn't thanked him for all his knight-errantry. In those days I found it difficult to say thank you; no doubt it was a holdover from childhood, when saying thank you seems like an admission of one's dependence on grown-ups, and what they choose or don't choose to give. But that didn't apply now; I was the grown-up and he the generous child. I felt like throwing my arms around him, but since that was out of the question, I smiled at him and said, "Consider yourself hugged," and to my astonishment he blushed.

My husband, bronzed and handsome, was waiting on the platform. He made me feel shy and acutely conscious of the bulk I had acquired since he last saw me. After kissing us all, he held out his hand to the K.M. and said, "Thanks, old chap." And because this seemed inadequate, I contributed what I hoped was an extra-warm smile.

Apparently it impressed my husband that way. In the droshky going home, he said, "You were quite taken with that young man, weren't you?"

"He was kind," I said, "when nobody else cared if I lived or died. I was sick all the time, nonstop, and he saw to it that the children didn't fall into the sea or out of the train. He even took them to the dining car and fed them."

"It was miles and miles and miles . . ." my daughter said, "through lots and lots of doors. . . ."

"And holes with dragons in them," said Mannie, always dramatic.

His brother disapproved of exaggeration. "Not *dragons*—wheels."

"He took us for walks," my daughter went on dreamily.

"*Long* walks," said Mannie, "in great big caves!"

"Little walks in stations," corrected his brother, adding after a moment's thought, "He was a very nice man."

A familiar shadow passed over his father's face. "It sounds as if he had thoroughly spoiled you," he said.

The stairwell of our building, with its dirty whitewashed walls, iron handrails, and crumbling steps, seemed both drearier and steeper than I remembered. At each turn in the stair I had to stop and rest, and the thought of climbing it every day, and perhaps several times a day, dismayed me. Why on earth had we chosen to ignore such a major disadvantage—what had possessed us? The apartment answered the question; sunlit and airy, and charmingly decorated if I did say so myself, it was worth every step of the dreary climb. I hoped that the snobs of the British colony would feel the same way when they came to call on us in our new home for the first time.

The two servants had heard us coming up the stairs and were at the door to greet us—in typical Rumanian fashion despite their Swabian roots, kissing our hands, and showering compliments and endearments on the children. The daughter, Antonia, had volunteered to help me with the children until after my confinement, and she took them away now for baths and supper.

My husband went with me into the bedroom and kissed me with all the pent-up passion of the long summer without me. "My God!" he said at last, "how I've longed for this!"

I too had longed for it. But to carry it to a successful conclusion I would have to overcome a continuing nausea that my husband obviously thought had stopped with the train.

Hoping that sex would prove as curative as anger, I lay down and allowed my husband to gently take off my garments one by one, kissing each part of me as he uncovered it. But this delicate, unhurried approach led to a climax so swift and shattering that I almost lost consciousness under its impact.

The anticlimax was equally devastating; an object lesson in just how inconvenient it could be to have the "toilet facility" out on the landing with two locked doors between me and it.

On the expected day in November, my fourth child, a daughter, was born just before midnight. And the still depths of her midnight temperament were foreshadowed by the moderate pace and measured accelerations of her entry into the world. The violent storms that had overwhelmed me at the birth of my two sons, and even of my first daughter at the final moment, had been replaced by a strong but quiet tide, like a powerful ground swell that mounts relentlessly, but with an undisturbed surface, to high-water mark. Lying awake in bed after it was all over, I saw it as symbolic; the bodily equivalent—or possibly the result—of a spiritual capitulation, a final acceptance of motherhood, with all its obligations and limitations.

It was two o'clock in the morning; the midwife had gone home, the baby was asleep in her cradle beside my bed, my husband was asleep in the next room—I could hear his even breathing through the open communicating door—and across the hall were the children, still whispering to one another about the new arrival. A private circle of human love. No matter what the eventual price of it might be, it gave me at that moment, which I think was a moment of illumination, a sense of completion; as if all the component parts of my present life had finally come together and filled up the gaps left by the disappearances of the past.

Along with this state of mind came a curious bodily sensation, a floating, drifting feeling. . . . And a growing physical intuition of rapids ahead. Then a hot internal rush, like the breaking of the waters, and I knew that I was drowning.

Before going under I uttered a cry for help, and my husband heard it. "His prompt action saved your life, Madame," the doctor told me later. My husband said, "I just used my common sense." He had shoved a chair under the mattress at the foot of my bed, which raised my legs high enough to temporarily stop the flowing away of my lifeblood. To the midwife he was a hero. "A husband in a thousand, *Cucoana*! And I know husbands!"

But a few days later he fell from his pedestal. She saw him leaving the apartment all dressed up for the evening. "Where is the consul going?" she asked.

"To a dinner dance at the British Club."

"When *Cucoana* is still in childbed! What a scandal! No Rumanian husband would dream of doing such a thing."

I knew just as well as she did what Rumanian husbands dreamed of—and did, when their wives were being confined. But I didn't know the language well enough to tell her why my husband's code of behavior was better than theirs, and that anyway showing up at a British Club function was one of his duties.

Privately, I wished that he hadn't gone off to his duty quite so willingly, and I shed a few tears of self-pity.

Sheer physical weakness often brought tears to my eyes when I was alone, but I tried to conceal it when visitors came; and I don't know which were the most tiring, the cheery British, for whom reserve was synonymous with good manners, and who avoided all reference to my health, or the emotional, inquisitive Rumanians, who asked intimate questions and thoroughly enjoyed commiserating.

One evening, around five o'clock, when I was already exhausted, a Rumanian acquaintance, a wealthy businessman with British interests, turned up in the expectation of finding my husband already at home—or so he said. Kissing my hand, and holding it for a moment in his, he looked at me intently. "Madame," he said, "you are like a lovely flower on a hot summer day—exquisite! But ever so slightly drooping. I think, chère Madame, that you need what you English describe as a 'pick-me-up.'"

At that moment my husband came in, and I marveled at how deftly my gallant friend changed the subject.

Next day, his chauffeur delivered a case of champagne, tactfully addressed to my husband, with a note for us both, congratulating us on the birth of our daughter.

"It's his own make," said my husband. "He's the biggest wine exporter in the country. Shall we crack a bottle now?"

"I don't know if I . . . Won't it make the baby drunk?"

"Not the little drop that you'll drink."

Sipping his fourth glass of my pick-me-up, he said, "It's not in the same class as the French . . . but it's not at all bad." Then, after a silence, "I wonder just what it is that fellow wants."

BOOK TWO

The War Experience

1

Going Toward the Sun

*A*STROLOGERS have told me that my horoscope is dominated by Mars in mid-heaven. Whether or not that has anything to do with it, war has been a dominant factor in my life and the lives of my children. World War I governed my adolescence and my first marriage. World War II, and my physical involvement in it, besides radically changing my values, gave me the impetus to write my first novel. And it was the intolerable aftermath of war that brought me to live in America and made an American of me.

I started this autobiography with the birth of my first child, rather than with my own birth, for two reasons. I have written elsewhere about the first eighteen years of my life; and here I want to tell of my life as a woman and the experiences that contributed to my development as a woman and a writer.

But between the end of what I have called "the birth experience," and the early stages of my own rebirth by way of another war, lies an undersea chasm ten years wide that yields up only the images and echoes of madness. The contortions and cries of an unstoppable descent into hell. They have nothing to do with the essential reality of my love for my first husband, or of his for me. They reflect only the contagious bitterness of that "sickness of the soul" diagnosed by the doomed Jewish doctor.

Those were the dark ages of my life, and when they finally came to an end, I emerged from them with my own soul darkened, my belief in friendship—or even ordinary human compassion—badly shaken, and my own value as a person in doubt.

Half insane from prolonged lack of sleep and unremitting stress, I was incapable of giving my deeply involved teen-age children the emotional support they needed; I was, rather, tacitly demanding it from them. Before I could function properly as a mother, I had to have a period of rest, solitude, and complete freedom from responsibility, and I knew no better way of achieving it than to take a sea voyage.

My youngest daughter, then eleven years of age, was at a boarding school, and her sister and two brothers, who were old enough to take care of themselves for a couple of weeks, agreed, though reluctantly, to my booking a round-trip passage on a small freighter plying to and from the Canary Islands.

It was late November; London was bleak and foggy, and so was the Atlantic, but at least I was going toward the sun. For the first forty-eight hours of the voyage out I stayed in my cabin, sleeping. But not peacefully. I kept dreaming that my husband was lying beside me, still suffering, still tormented in mind and body. I would think I heard him cry out in anguish and rage, and I would start up, trembling, only to find myself alone, with no voices to be heard save those of the crew on the deck above, and no movement in the cabin save for the engine's internal throb and the sigh and creak of timbers, as the sturdy little ship rode a mounting sea.

The storm she ran into was so severe that it upset the stomach of every living creature on board. One of them was a boa constrictor, being shipped to some snake fancier in Madeira. The sight of its undigested dinner of live rabbit coming up like a jet of water distending the coils of a garden hose was too much for the motherly stewardess, who told me about it while she tried to anchor my suitcase, which was sliding madly from one side of the cabin to the other. "It's downright cruelty to animals," she said. "It ought to be reported to the authorities."

Whether she was commiserating with the boa constrictor or with its dinner was not clear, but the grotesque image conjured up by her story made me laugh for the first time in months. I wondered if the rabbit had come up alive, but I didn't dare ask, for fear she should think me cruel.

On the other side of the storm were the calm and sunlit waters I was seeking. I dressed and went up on deck. There were only half-a-dozen passengers on board, and they had already got acquainted and were playing deck games. I ensconced myself in as distant a corner as possible. I had learned the hard lesson that unhappiness and misfortune are isolating, and my bitter experience of that cruel isolation, coupled with the fear that in some subtle way I was marked with the double stigmata of past affliction and present grief, made me wary of laying myself open to further rejection. Besides, I no longer wanted what hadn't been given me when I needed it. All I wanted now was peace, anonymity, and safety from chance wounds. And the beauty of being at sea was that it provided all three, and more; the ocean's ceaseless change kept the senses occupied and soothed, while under the surface the mind could proceed undisturbed with its work of healing itself.

To stave off meeting other people as long as I could, I decided to miss lunch and ask for soup and a sandwich on deck. Later on in the afternoon I must have fallen asleep, for I didn't hear anyone coming until it was too late to pick up the book I had let drop and take shelter behind it. The intruders, one of the ship's officers with a blonde girl, were obviously seeking a secluded spot for themselves. As they went by, the officer sketched a salute in the air and said, "Nice weather!" The girl just gave me a wide, rather toothy smile. And then, astonishingly, she winked at me, and I, astonishing myself, winked back.

At dinner, the passengers sat with the ship's officers at one long table. The blonde girl and I were the only women on board. She was placed directly opposite me, and for me the recollection of that absurd wink, absurdly returned, had the effect of linking us under the table, so to speak, like a slightly embarrassing private joke.

She was attractive rather than pretty, with a naturalness of manner that didn't quite go with her beauty-shop surface and the *outré* chic of her clothes. In fact, nothing about her quite went with anything else. Her candid blue eyes were fringed by lashes too black and too long to be true, and wildly at odds with her corn-gold hair. Her dazzling, toothpaste smile, on the other hand, was rendered disarmingly sincere by the rabbity prominence of her teeth. Even her brassy flirtation with every male in sight, from the ship's venerable captain down to the dining steward's teen-age assistant, seemed like a comic act. She was known, predictably, as "Blondie."

The officer with whom I had seen her on deck was the ship's doctor; an overworked hospital intern who had got away from it all for a couple of weeks by signing on for the round trip.

After dinner, Blondie, with whom I had exchanged no more than a few words across the dining table, stressed the surreptitious link between us by tucking her arm chummily into the crook of my elbow and saying in a whisper, "Doc wants us both to join him in his cabin now for a spot of brandy."

"That's very kind of him, but I don't . . ."

"Oh, you needn't drink brandy if you don't want to—he has crème de menthe as well."

"I was going to say that I don't think I'll come. He wants you, not me. I would only spoil the party."

"But he *does* want you!"

"Then why didn't he ask me himself?"

"Because he didn't want to have to ask the others as well. He asked *me* privately to ask *you* privately."

"But why on earth should he want to ask me?"

"Because *I* asked him to ask you, and he wants to please me."

I laughed in spite of myself. "All right. I'll come."

"That's better—a spot of Doc's brandy is just what you need."

"You're a funny girl," I said.

"That's what my gentleman friend keeps saying. He thinks I'm a caution. He says nobody else in the world could make him laugh like I can."

She was right about the brandy. It was just what I needed. It loosened me up and gave me the courage to ask her why she had winked at me when she didn't even know who I was.

"I just wanted to cheer you up . . . you looked so sad."

Before the voyage was half over I was thinking what a pity it was that there were no more court jesters. Modern rulers, I thought, should revive them. We would all benefit.

Blondie's gentleman friend turned out to be a Jewish film director, who had sent her on this trip to recover from an illness, and who eventually married her; though only when she agreed, absolving herself, no doubt, with a secret flourish of cap and bells, to convert to Judaism and get married in a synagogue.

But long before that happened, she introduced him to us as her gentleman friend, and he became our friend too. It was largely thanks to him that my younger son, "Mannie" (Eldon from now on), got important roles in two motion pictures; *The Mill on the Floss*, in which James Mason starred as John Tulliver, and Eldon played him as a boy, and *Big Fella*, in which he was a kidnapped child, rescued and befriended by a stevedore and his wife, played by Paul Robeson and Elizabeth Welch, both of whom Eldon grew to love and admire while working with them.

Eldon, who had inherited his father's talent, was attending the Conti School, at which many of London's best child actors were trained. My eldest son, Peter, was at London University, majoring in—or, as the British say, *reading*—German literature; and my eldest daughter, Genevra, was a student at the Royal Academy of Music. All three were living with me in the rather cramped Battersea Park flat in which my husband had died, and which, for me at least, was haunted. Nina was there only during her school holidays.

Those years in London after my husband's death were relatively peaceful. But a vital influence had gone out of our lives, and we missed it, as one misses any powerful activating force—whether for good or ill. Instead of *re*acting, as we had in the past, we were now obliged to *act*. I say "we," when perhaps I should only say "I," but I think this sense of the responsibility of freedom was shared by my children, particularly the two elder ones. There was something else, however, which they could not share, and that made them very uneasy. I had fallen in love with a foreigner, a Hungarian thirteen years my senior. And I was not only in love, but I knew without any doubt that with this man I could find the peace in which I could find myself. In short, I wanted to marry him and live with him for the rest of my days. Something that appeared, from every point of view, to be impossible. Yet, in some cobwebby corner of my subconscious, I knew it was going to happen.

This man whom I loved and needed so much was a musician, the finest Hungarian cellist of his generation, which was that of his friends Béla Bartók and Zoltán Kodály—whose sonata for solo cello was written for him and dedicated to him. His name was Eugene de Kerpely—Kerpely Jenö in Hungarian. In my novel, *Arabesque,* he appears as the cellist *B.* An initial that our American friends who knew him as K. wondered at, since it seemed to have no basis. But my love-name for him throughout our life together began with a *B.* In private, I called this tall, dignified artist with the courtly manners of a gentle prince, by the ludicrous name of *Bink,* or *Binkie.*

He called me *Tercsi,* which is short for *Teréz,* the Hungarian version of Theresa, and more often, the tenderer, *Tercsikém*—my *Tercsi.*

During what I suppose might be called our courtship, circumstances kept us apart, except for an occasional brief meeting at some place where he was playing—one of which was Warsaw, where we stayed for a few days; and where happiness sensitized me to such a degree that the impressions of Poland I gained then were so vivid that forty years later I was able to conjure them up for my novel, *Fugue.* But our relationship was based on an affinity strong enough to survive indefinite separations.

My imaginative writing at that time was confined to lyrical poetry, for which I had more feeling than talent; and whatever merit my lyrics had was thanks to my musical ear. I would enclose them with my letters to my musician, who responded by setting a number of them to music in a highly sophisticated and contemporary idiom that offset their romanticism and conferred on them a distinction they did not possess in their own right. Composing was something he did purely for pleasure; but such was his artistic integrity, and his uncompromising rejection of the second rate, that I knew I could take his setting of my little poems as an indication that, for all their faults, they were not entirely worthless.

One morning, when we were all at breakfast together, the postman brought a letter from him, and I put it aside to read when I was alone. It was a warm, sunny morning, of the kind you have to catch on the wing in London, and I took my letter, still unopened, to Green Park, and sat down to read it there under the trees.

It contained a stunning surprise. What we had both believed to be an insuperable obstacle on his side had been overcome; *And so, dearest Tercsikém, will you marry me?*

As I took in the full implication of those words, the bright future they opened up, the promise of renewal, I was overcome by the immensity of the gift I was being offered by a power that I had been taught to call *God*, and now called *Fate*; the grace of a second chance.

When I got back to the flat in the afternoon, I found my son Peter there, studying, as was his habit, to a gentle jazz program on the radio. I turned it off, which was the only way of getting his attention, and told him my news. He listened in silence. Then he said quietly, as though reminding me of something that might have escaped me, "But marrying him will mean leaving us."

It was not a protest. It was not even a reproach. It was simply a statement of what was, to him, a desolating fact. And it brought me face to face with the moral choice I would have to make, even if all the practical problems could be solved.

Those relatives who had stuck by me through my dark ages, and a few friends I had made since, were all, with the exception of Blondie, against my marriage to my Hungarian musician. Not only because it would mean leaving England and losing my British citizenship (according to an unfair law which has since been repealed), but because they mistrusted all foreigners and lumped together all artists—actors, musicians, painters—as an unreliable lot. And this one was divorced into the bargain, with a family of his own to support, and in consequence would have even less to live on than I had. How could I contemplate taking such a step? Surely I wanted some security after all I had been through? My wish to remarry was understandable—after all, I was still in my thirties and quite attractive—but why in heaven's name couldn't I choose a good solid Englishman?

I was thinking in terms of a different kind of security; a security of the spirit that this man, and this man only, could give me. My children, who knew him, liked him, and later grew to love him, understood that, even though they resented it. Their difficult adolescence had matured them in a very deep sense, and although the disruption of our newly established life in England and the consequent loss of their new-found sense of stability were profoundly upsetting to them, I think they realized better than most young people of their age that a mother is also a woman. And that I, still a young woman, needed love and companionship of a kind they couldn't give me or even compensate me for, if I renounced it for their sake.

I, for my part, realized that a parent's self-sacrifice can be double-edged; a form of blackmail. And in any case, with the best will in the world, a martyr is an uncomfortable person to live with.

All the same, what with the conflicting emotions aroused in me by my children's mute resignation to what each—for different reasons—would have preferred not to happen, and the warnings and lectures of my relatives and friends, my decision to go my own way and marry my musician was not arrived at easily. But my instinct for self-preservation—the preservation, that is, of an emergent self hitherto suppressed—won out over everything else, and in the fall of 1937, two years after my first husband's death, I became the wife of Eugene de Kerpely.

We were married very quietly in London. The brief ceremony at the Battersea registrar's office, with the pianist Louis Kentner as one of the witnesses, was followed by formalities at the Hungarian Embassy, from whose portals I emerged a Hungarian citizen by marriage and no longer entitled to the privileges that were, in fact, my birthright. I felt a little frightened by the loss of the lion's protection, but more than a little proud of having put love above safety.

K. and I (from now on I shall refer to my second husband as K.) left for Hungary with our heads stuffed full of dreams, of which only one was destined to be fulfilled; ironically, the very one which, statistically, was the least likely to come true—the dream of undying love.

We arrived in Budapest just in time for the start of the concert season and the opening of the fall semester at the Lizst Ferenc Academy of Music, where K. was a professor. We rented a tiny house, like a doll's house, with miniature wrought-iron balconies overlooking a steep cobbled street in Buda, for three months. The street and the little square at the end of it resembled the stage setting for some village opera. And as if to complete the romantic illusion, a little old woman who looked like a family retainer in a nobleman's household, came to keep house for us. Actually, this was her first venture into domestic service; and it had been carefully considered. As the impecunious widow of a fashionable, but spendthrift French hairdresser, which she proudly regarded as a link with French culture, she wanted to work only for people she could count on to treat her with due respect. Looking back, I realize that her choice of us was a compliment.

I have forgotten her married name, but her first name was Ilona, and her age entitled her to be called Ilona *néni*—Aunt Ilona. A splendid cook, sometimes crotchety, but always devoted, she took motherly care of us for about four years, when the aches and pains of old age obliged her to give up working. When she left us, she gave me a pair of her late husband's scissors as a keepsake. They were the best pair of scissors I ever owned. I preserved them all through the war and brought them with me to America, only to lose them here on one of my many moves.

Our three-month stay in the funny little stage-set house, pampered and overfed by Ilona *néni*, and experiencing for the first time since we had known each other the joy of an openly shared life, was a prolonged honeymoon. A period of grace, of *solitude à deux*, in which love and work, love and art, love and all the outside interests that impinge on a marriage, had a chance to mingle and unify in advance of the added complications of family living.

Every morning at seven o'clock, K. would get up, play a couple of scales on his cello, then put it into its canvas bag and go off to Pest to rehearse with the other members of the Waldbauer-Kerpely String Quartet, as he had done every day for twenty-eight years—ever since the quartet was first founded to perform the works of Béla Bartók. When a concert was in preparation, there were afternoon and evening rehearsals as well, some of which I was invited to attend, but the unfailing session every morning was, like K.'s unfailing daily practice of his cello—even when traveling on a train, the equivalent of an athlete's morning mile.

At about two o'clock in the afternoon we would sit down to dinner; Ilona's daily masterpiece, in which the finest traditional Hungarian cooking would be unexpectedly enlivened by exotic touches of what I can only call French Impressionism. After bringing it to the table, the old woman would stand by the door, her gnarled hands neatly folded over the absurd little parlor-maid's apron she put on to serve dinner, and await our verdict.

Too long a silence on our part would banish that particular dish from the menu; too faint praise would postpone its repetition until it was specially requested. Ilona *néni* wanted only rave reviews.

After the masterly meal we would take a siesta, drifting in and out of sleep with the comings and goings of passersby on the cobbles under our low-hung Juliet balconies. At about four, if there were no afternoon rehearsal, we would go out for a walk, exploring the lovely residential districts of Buda with the long-range aim of deciding where we would most like to live and then finding an unfurnished villa there to lease for as long as our dream of building one for ourselves took to materialize. On overcast days, we would walk through the city in search of antiques and end up in a coffeehouse, where almost everyone who came in would give K. a greeting.

In the evenings, as the season developed, there would be concerts to give or to attend, opera, theater, movies, and sometimes an evening spent at the Artists' Club, which was frequented more by painters and actors than by musicians, but where K. knew, or was known to, all the members. Wherever we went, in whatever company we found ourselves, our linked arms and clasped hands were an open proclamation of love at which no one sneered; neither then in Budapest when we were newly married, nor, more than a decade later, in America, when we still felt the same and expressed our love for each other in the same way.

No one ever sneered at K. Just what it was about this gentle, genuinely modest man that commanded so much respect is hard to define. I think, perhaps, it was that he had somehow become one with the great music to which he had devoted his life.

Although K.'s circle of acquaintances was immensely wide, he had only a few close friends, and they were, with one or two exceptions, either musicians or in some way involved with music. There could be no real communication between him and a wholly unmusical person. Music was the element in which he lived and had his being; and at first, amateur that I was, I was daunted by it, believing that before I could enter it with him I would have to master it. In time I came to realize that what was required of me was not mastery, but humility. As soon as this became clear to me, I gave up my untalented efforts to make music and learned how to listen.

For K., all beauty, whether spiritual or material, of language or of color, of nature or art, had a musical context. He translated everything into sound, and in all sounds he could discern some music; which explains, perhaps, why even in his old age he could embrace the most contemporary and experimental compositions, as he had embraced the works of Béla Bartók when he was young. He would say, "There are only two kinds of music; good and bad." And he had an unfailing ear for which was which. Even in genres outside his own sphere, such as folk music, jazz, and ragtime.

His broad but uncompromising judgment profoundly influenced my attitude, not only to music, but to all the other arts as well. Through his eyes I perceived the worthlessness of the dilettantism that I, as a young girl growing up in Edwardian England, had been taught to regard as "accomplishment." It was not that he despised amateurs, he was always happy to make music with gifted amateurs, but they were not dilettantes; like the brilliant artistic director of the Budapest Opera, Gustav Oláh, an excellent amateur pianist with whom K. often played at private gatherings, they were all experts in something else; true "amateurs" of music, in the sense of devotees, lovers, and occasional practicants of an art for the sheer pleasure of it.

K. wanted me to discover what my real talent was, among the assorted arts and crafts in which I had dabbled; and on the strength of a few true notes in my lyric verse, he believed it might lie in the translation of my strong musical feeling into the written word. I knew I would never be a poet, but I thought that I might one day succeed in expressing my ideas in some form of prose writing. And I promised myself that whether I succeeded or not, I would give it all I had; I would not be a dilettante.

Just before Christmas, we gave up our honeymoon home. We had found a villa and leased it for three years. Ilona *néni*, who had decided to remain with us, went to stay with a relative while K. and I went back to London for a couple of weeks to wind up my affairs.

Except for the touch of melancholy that accompanies the breakup of any home, even one in which one has not been happy, we were none of us sorry to leave the sad Battersea flat and its haunted ambiance. The three older children, Peter, Genevra, and Eldon, aged respectively nineteen, sixteen, and fifteen, were resettled in student-type quarters in London and would spend their vacations with us in Budapest. Nina, who was thirteen and wanted to study art, would live with us there all the time.

As a "bride," I was entitled to take with me into Hungary a fairly large amount of household goods and personal possessions duty-free; so K. and I did a little shopping. Among the objects we acquired was a Bechstein grand piano, secondhand, but in excellent condition, chosen with the help of Louis Kentner. We also took with us some lovely oriental rugs and rolls of beautiful and sturdy English material to make into curtains.

At the beginning of the new year—1938—with a new life ahead of me, I left England with a light heart, knowing that I would see my daughter and two sons in the spring. I had no premonition that I would not return for more than ten years, and then only for a two-day stopover on my way to America; where I would remain for a further twenty-four years before I was able, or willing, to revisit the land of my birth, from which I had felt estranged ever since the day when I walked out of the Hungarian Embassy stripped of my rights, and continued to feel estranged even after they had been belatedly restored to me at the end of the war.

2

The Villa on the Kelenhegyi út

*I*T was only when I began to write that I fully realized the inseparability, in both my memory and my imagination, of places and events; of emotional experiences and their physical settings. Fiction sometimes dramatizes a situation by linking it to surroundings or climactic conditions that echo it; in real life, it seems to me, the opposite is more often the case. Terrible tragedies unfold in idyllic surroundings, and intense happiness overtakes one in the midst of desolation. Rare are the occasions when inner joy is matched by the outward scene. One of the few places in which I experienced this combination of felicities—and the state of bliss it produces—was the villa on the Kelenhegyi út.

It was too small for us, its water pipes were insufficiently protected from the cold and were always bursting, it was more than a mile away from the nearest tram stop—and we were carless—but it was utterly enchanting. We fell in love with it even before we saw it, the approach to it was enough to enthrall us; with its suggestion of the mysterious and the hidden. Tall gates of wrought iron, kept locked, stood at the top of a sloping snow-covered driveway that seemed to lead only to a garden; but a slight curve at the end of the drive concealed a little shuttered house of the kind that children and lovers, who have a lot in common, imagine themselves living in.

Built on the southern slope of the Gellért Hill, fifty yards below the much larger home of its owner, it commanded a wide view of the industrial island of Csepel, and the steel gray ribbon of the

Danube flowing through the flatlands on its way to the Black Sea. Yet, camouflaged from below by the trees in its own and other gardens, and concealed from the road above by its owner's house and grounds, it was as secluded as a sylvan retreat.

The Kelenhegyi út was a dignified residential road that wound its easy-going way up the long sloping back of the rocky-faced Gellért Hill. It was lined with villas, some of them very grand, surrounded by large gardens and orchards. Slanting steeply upward between these fenced-in estates was a rustic footpath, used as a short cut by children late for school or cooks returning heavy-laden from the market. It was deep in snow when we first discovered it, but it lessened the distance between our villa and the tram stop by half a mile, so whatever the weather, we used it. And in spring it became an elysian way; fragrant with cherry and peach blossom, lilacs and syringa, and, during the month of May, frequented by nightingales, to whose golden song we would listen with awe, as to some celestial choir, when we came home late at night after a concert.

Spring brought a perfumed cloudburst of blossom to the terraced garden of our villa as well, and cascades of violets, paperwhite narcissus, and lilies of the valley. But long before the outdoors had been transformed by nature, the interior of our villa had been transformed by me; or, to put it more accurately, the combination of its specifically Hungarian character with my English taste had resulted in the same kind of synthesis, on an aesthetic level, as that exemplified in the relationship between me and K., in which neither of us dominated, but each complemented the other.

In addition to the furnishings I had brought with me from England, were some lovely antiques found in Budapest; a Biedermeier dining table with matching chairs and two credenzas of burl walnut, exquisitely inlaid; an elegant writing table for K. to work at when writing down his compositions and transcriptions in his fine, flowing script; an escritoire full of tiny drawers and pigeonholes for me; and a hand-made cabinet specially designed to hold K.'s collection of cello music, with a separate compartment for each composer.

Choosing and arranging all these things afforded me the most intense pleasure. For the first time in my life I was establishing my own ambiance with the expectation of remaining in it for as long as I lived. For even when we moved into a place of our own, as we hoped to do eventually, it would involve no discarding, only further delightful acquisition. The days of perpetual, arbitrary moves were, I thought, gone forever.

The Hungarian character of the long, low living room and adjoining dining room was manifest in the roughly whitewashed walls and ceilings, the curlicued wrought-iron grilles protecting the inward-opening casement windows, the polished parquet floors, and the tile stove built into the wall between the two rooms, filling them both, in winter, with the live, aromatic warmth radiated by glowing cedarwood ashes.

But the deep source of the villa's life, its heartbeat, was the old Italian cello, the color of dark sherry, that stood modestly in the corner next to its polished ebony partner, the grand piano. The room in which those two instruments lived and sang was itself a form of music—a form of harmonics; the thousand and one nuances of color in the oriental rugs found answering tones all around them, in the cushions and curtains, the pictures, the ornaments; even, though more by chance than design, in the fresh-cut flowers that Ilona *néni* brought back for me from the market every morning, so that I could decorate the house without despoiling the garden. And the curlicued wrought-iron grilles, themselves an echo of the gate that enclosed our Eden, were re-echoed over and over by the black sconces on the white walls.

The image that first presents itself when I call up memories of this room is one of K. bent over his cello playing the Rachmaninoff sonata for cello and piano with the pianist (and magician) Otto Herz. The lighting is subdued, coming mainly from the wall sconces, and the little group of listeners is shadowy. But in the curve of the piano, within the circle of light cast by a standing lamp that illumines the music racks of both players, are my two daughters, sitting on the floor with their full skirts spread out around them and their long hair flowing loose down their backs. As they listen with bent heads to the lovely, romantic *Andante* movement, they look like two young girls in a Sargent painting.

Years—no, a whole eternity—later, I ran across Otto Herz in

California, and his first question was, "How are your two beautiful daughters? I have never forgotten them . . . sitting on
the floor by the piano, graceful as flowers, and so unconventional!"

As, indeed, they were. In prewar Hungarian society well-bred
young ladies did not sit on the floor at parties any more than their
mothers went out into the street without hats and gloves. At the
time of our marriage, the hatless craze had just taken over in
London, but not in Budapest, where no lady, and no respectable
peasant woman, either, would be seen in the street with uncovered head. I disliked hats, they were unbecoming to me, but I
wore them, and gloves as well, to please K. I couldn't do anything
that might hurt or embarrass a man who was so considerate of me
as K. was, then and always.

When there is no friction in a marriage, and particularly when
it is not a young marriage, other people are apt to conclude that it
must be more or less platonic in nature; since a powerful sexual
attraction is, by definition, a passion, and one strong passion
tends to beget others. But the relationship between me and K.,
though free of all conflict, was far from being platonic. Its calm
was that of great depth and an even balance of physical and
spiritual elements. Sex was the concomitant of our affinity,
rather than its source, which lay infinitely deeper—even perhaps,
in an earlier incarnation. In our present lives, we had both, in our
separate pasts, known the extremes of passion and exhausted the
delights of experimentation. K.'s experience had been wider than
mine, but mine had been concentrated; and we had arrived, each
in our own way, at the same interpretation of the word *love*, as
an unarmed physical and emotional closeness combined with a
mutual artistic and intellectual understanding and support.

Paradoxically, in the final analysis, it was out of the stresses of
war—of two wars, the emotional aftereffects of the first and the
dangers and deprivations of the second—that this calm and beautifully balanced relationship between me and my musician developed and came to full flower.

I was K.'s third wife and, as he often told me, his last love. In his
first, brief, marriage, all the love had been on his side, and various
external factors, including the political upheaval of 1918–19,

contributed in bringing it to an end. His second marriage, entered into on the rebound, turned out to be a fundamentally incompatible union, which lasted for sixteen stormy years only because of his love for his children—two daughters, who adored and depended on him for their emotional security. Not that their mother did not love them, but hers was a wild and unpredictable nature, by turns fiercely loving and fiercely hating; to live with her was like being caught in a never-ending series of electrical storms, with brief, deceptive glimpses of blue sky in between. She was, however, a good-hearted woman, and except for an occasional fit of jealousy or paranoia, she put no obstacles between the two girls and their father or between them and me—once K. and I were legally married. She and I progressed fairly quickly from a state of armed truce to diplomatic relations, and finally to outright friendly ones as the larger issues of war wiped out trivial animosities.

My youngest step-daughter, Judit, was a physically delicate little girl of about twelve when I first knew her; gentle, affectionate, and preternaturally melancholy; she had grown into a beautiful, languid, and still very frail young woman, an actress with a touch of *La Traviata* about her, when I saw her for the last time, on our departure for America in the fall of 1948. She passionately wanted to come with us, but that was an impossibility.

The story of her life from then on is pure grand opera.

She falls in love with a married man and remains devoted to him—in the background of his life—for twenty years, when the opportunity finally comes for them to go off together. It is fraught with risk, and even danger, but it is their last and only hope of achieving happiness. Fate, as always in grand opera, is jealous; it grants her only the briefest of idylls before Death appears on the scene and takes her lover away from her forever. Still loving, still faithful, she stays on alone in the mountain village to which they fled, far from her home, and places fresh flowers on his grave every day.

The life of the elder daughter, Mária, has not been any easier than her sister's. Only less operatic. She takes after her father in that she accepts the vicissitudes of the human condition without complaint. I was able to get closer to her than to her sister because of her excellent knowledge of English. We were friends right from the start, and we are still friends, despite a physical separation of more than thirty years. When she was still a young girl, she called me Theresa *néni*, and addressed me in the polite third person. Now, in her letters, she calls me *Tercsikém* (my Tercsi), just as her father did, and signs herself, *Your ever-loving Steppie.*

The complex web of family relationships whose center was the villa in the Kelenhegyi út was all the more fragile because six of the eight highly individual personalities involved were still in a state of emergence from a painful childhood and adolescence. It was K. who kept this delicate structure from falling to pieces; not by anything he said, simply by being himself. Even his cello students learned more from him by osmosis, or emulation, than by technical instruction. When one of them could not master a difficult passage, he would demonstrate how it should be done by playing it on his own cello—over and over if necessary, he was patience itself—but with very little verbal explanation. Which was probably why he enjoyed teaching only advanced students, and talented ones at that.

The remarkable thing was that a man so gentle and so silent should have had so much effect on his surroundings. Much later, I was told by some of our intimates who survived the war and the Holocaust, that what made them feel happy and at ease in the villa on the Kelenhegyi út—which was not so much a place as an environment—was its aura of spiritual as well as musical harmony, and the total absence of political controversy, or of professional gossip and criticism. It was not that these topics of conversation were consciously banned by K., they just died in his presence.

But I must not paint too solemn a portrait of my very human musician. Music was his religion, but, just as many a devout Catholic enjoys a game of bingo or even a day at the races, K., who had been quite a gambler in his youth, loved card games of all kinds. He also loved crossword puzzles, the comic strips, and good science fiction. None of which, however, prevented him from reading serious works of literature in four languages: Hungarian, English, German, and French.

Not all our gatherings at the villa were devoted to the making of serious music. There were parties for the young people, with dancing to the phonograph, and bridge tournaments for their elders—at which the first violinist of the quartet, Imre Wald-bauer, was usually the all-round winner. And Otto Herz, the pianist magician, would, if he was in the right mood, dazzle us all with his sleight of hand and his incredibly brilliant and baffling tricks with cards and numbers. On summer evenings, we would eat outside on the terrace, and in the dusky garden, the "children" would play *murder*, and other scary or titillating games.

Among the young people who came to the villa were two young men who were destined to be closely involved with us both during and after the war experience. Named respectively Paul and István they were bewitched respectively (but not simultaneously, they entered our lives at a remove of almost two years) by my daughter Nina and her older sister, Genevra.

Paul was the son of a highly respected government official, and he and his family were well known to K. as music lovers and friends of the quartet. They lived on the Gellért Hill, not far from us, which made social contacts between us easy.

When I first made Paul's acquaintance, he must have been about nineteen years old; a charming young man, whose pleasantly sophisticated manners masked an unexpectedly austere set of values. He believed in, and practiced, such old-fashioned virtues as loyalty, honor, unselfishness, and respect for his elders—a trait that recommended him to the mothers of marriageable daughters, who kept a collective eye on him. But to no avail. Witchcraft and war intervened.

The other young man, István, was known to K. as a talented student of composition at the Lizst Ferenc Academy, where K. was known to him as a revered artist and professor. But the impetus for his first diffident social visit to the villa was provided by my eighteen-year-old daughter, Genevra, who had enchanted him when he met and danced with her at the Academy Ball, which was held at the Gellért Hotel.

He has told me since that although he spoke with her for the first time at the ball, he had seen both her and her sister before that, at a concert; sitting with me and K. in the Director's box in the concert hall of the Academy—a privileged location that bestowed on its two unknown occupants an aura of unattainability, as well as of mystery. "I had no idea who they were," he said.

"They were obviously not Hungarians, and to me they looked like angels. I never expected to encounter them, as creatures of flesh and blood, in the ballroom of the Gellért Hotel. It was like a miracle."

His formal call on us came very soon after that enchanted evening. I can still see him sitting up ramrod-straight in his chair; extremely polite, extremely shy, and almost totally silent. It was not, I felt sure, the silence of nothing to say; it was, rather, the emotion-charged silence of someone who is afraid of saying too much. This silence persisted through several subsequent visits—at least in the presence of K. and myself. Aside from that, he gave the impression of being happy to be there with us, even when Genevra was absent.

He was then, I believe, twenty years old; tall, upstanding, and a little armored in his movements and manner. His most striking feature was his high, intellectual forehead; a "noble brow," which caused us, among ourselves, to nickname him *Beethoven*. His heavy-lidded dark eyes held the age-old sadness of the Jewish race, but his smile, a subtle smile that played around his lips even when they were closed, balanced the melancholy strain with a sharp note of ironic humor.

Having introduced them, I shall now leave Paul and István to form, each in his own way, the bonds of friendship and affection that will draw us all together in time of danger.

At the start of this chapter, I said that life at the villa was a rare example of inner joy matched by outward circumstances—but to what degree were these glorified by the light of that inner joy?

I had lived in equally enchanting locations, in softer climates, in greater physical comfort. But in all these situations, one essential element had been missing; peace.

The physical circumstances in which I found that missing element for the first time since my childhood, when I had taken it for granted or mistaken it for dullness, were primitive by present-day American standards. Aside from electric light, indoor plumbing, and, theoretically, running water (all taken for granted and undervalued, like the peace of my childhood), there were no modern amenities, let alone labor-saving devices. Hungary was still at the tail end of an era when the work of the human hand was more highly prized than that done by a machine. The most desirable shoes were handmade to the customer's own requirements, suits and dresses likewise, and the finest furniture as well. The makers of musical instruments held a position only one rung below the musicians who played them.

On a humbler level, the personal skills that were brought to bear on domestic tasks made day-to-day living an art in itself. There was craftsmanship, in more senses than one, in Ilona *néni*'s wise choice of the raw, and frequently live, materials for a meal—not to mention the skinning, plucking, and gutting of them—and art in its final preparation. There was skill in keeping the milk sweet and the butter solid on hot summer days, when the only refrigeration was an ancient icebox that might or might not be supplied with a couple of blocks of half melted ice around noon, according to how soon the itinerant vendor's stock turned to water. There was skill in filling the tile stoves with exactly the right amount of logs for a given winter's day, and letting them burn down to exactly the right point before closing the airtight doors. The stoves themselves were examples of fine craftsmanship; specifically designed for the rooms they were destined to heat and built up there by their designer, tile by tile, their degree of efficiency dependent on that intangible quality that distinguishes good music from bad music.

The woman who came in once every two weeks to do the "big wash" was skilled in her own arduous way; capable of producing a snowy wash without any mechanical aid or chemical detergents. Clothes and household linen would be boiled with a handful of soda in a brick copper, scrubbed by hand on a washboard with yellow soap, rinsed in huge tubs with a bag of blue in the water, and hung out to dry on the line, where in summer the sun would help. But in winter the wet clothes would freeze in grotesque shapes, thaw, and freeze again, acquiring with each thaw a faint film of woodsmoke from the air. The laundry was given a week to dry, then the same woman would come in to iron it; faultlessly pressing it all, from straightforward bed sheets to trickily pointed shirt collars, with the same huge irons filled with glowing charcoal.

On "big wash" days, Ilona *néni* would bring vast supplies of food from the market, to keep up the strength of the big washerwoman.

We had engaged a young country girl to help Ilona *néni*, and between them they took care of all the other household chores, including the yearly "big cleaning." But I was not idle. I assisted in the seasonal undertakings; the boiling and bottling of the juice from a bushel of ripe tomatoes, the preserving of fruit and vegetables for the winter, the conversion of the huge, rosy apricots from our own trees into jam, and the long, slow, sugarless simmering of ripe damson plums into a naturally sweet *lekvár*—or plum butter. And I did all the gardening; keeping the weeds down, pruning fruit trees and dusting grapevines against mildew, growing zinnias and roses and radishes, and watering them all every day by hand—I acquired my first sprinkler in California.

In fall and spring I worked with my sewing machine—an old woman-powered treadle—to turn out, in a professional manner that fooled everyone, the suits and dresses I designed for myself and my daughters. I derived less creative satisfaction from turning the worn collars and cuffs of K.'s shirts, but doing it made me feel very tender toward him.

Another occupation was trying to learn Hungarian, an extremely difficult language with no helpful similarities to any other language I knew. An experienced teacher came once a week to give me a private lesson. The rules of pronunciation were logical and easy to master, but the complicated grammar and syntax, the cases, the endless suffixes, defeated me. Between lessons I struggled unsuccessfully with pages of written "exercises," and confirmed once and for all my innate inability to learn any language from a grammar book. My teacher became impatient with my mistakes, and I with her pedantry. So I gave up the lessons and fell back on my old haphazard method of learning by ear, by association of sound and action, of sound and object. The end result was an ungrammatical speech that the polite Hungarians tried not to laugh at openly, but an osmotic understanding of what was being said to me and around me. And something more; my ear assimilated the rhythms, stresses, and inflections that my tongue could not properly reproduce, and linked them up with the national music and spirit—which, in K.'s opinion, amounted to the same thing.

Even with all these activities and the entertaining of friends, the tempo of life was so unhurried that I still had plenty of time in which to read, write (mostly poems and long discursive letters to Peter), and listen to K. playing the cello—but I listened to that all the time, whatever else I was doing.

It was through this marvelous inner and outer tranquillity that I entered, or was for the first time conscious of entering, into that fecund state of mind in which the subconscious is liberated and the imagination breaks away from reality and functions on its own.

In the summer of 1938, before coming to Budapest for the "long vacation," my son Peter, who wanted to see something of the country whose literature he was studying, went on a walking tour in Germany and took his brother Eldon with him. They came back enchanted with the scenery and thoroughly disenchanted with everything else. They had stayed in youth hostels, where Peter's idiomatic knowledge of German had enabled him to get some horrifying insights into the Nazi mentality; partly from direct and not very friendly conversations with Hitler Youth, and partly from overheard ones, which were even more illuminating.

The climax of that summer, when we were all together in our new home for the first time, was not the visit of an old friend of Peter's, an American boy with whom he had gone to school in Belgium years earlier, joyful as that reunion was, but an event which happened to coincide with it, but which was, in itself, wholly extrinsic to our personal happiness; though it had an unexpectedly powerful impact on me; the first of many that would combine, more than a decade later, to bring me to an important decision.

The event was the Eucharistic Congress. Held in Budapest in late August of 1938, at the time of the great national and religious Feast of St. Stephen, it remains in my memory as an image of light juxtaposed with an image of darkness, like the two halves of the moon at the mid-point of a total eclipse.

On that fine, warm evening in August, full of the sound of bells and jubilation, we strolled—laughing and talking and reminiscing with our young American friend—from our side of the Gellért Hill to the other to watch a religious ceremonial in which none of us was qualified to participate in a strictly religious sense except K.'s two daughters, who had been raised by their mother in the Catholic faith. The rest of us approached it respectfully, as we did the magnificently sung High Masses that we sometimes attended in the cathedral, as an aesthetically moving experience, from which I, for one, imagined myself to be spiritually detached. K., who belonged to no church, did not make this distinction. For him, as for his persona, the cellist B. in my novel *Arabesque*, all great music was holy.

The scene photographed on my mind has a magical as well as a mystical quality. And the magic has its black side; symbolized by the night river, the dark stream that bears on its breast the ship of the Church, in whose light-bejeweled prow the white-clad papal legate stands with arms outstretched in benediction. It is Cardinal Pacelli, soon to become Pope Pius XII.

Tonight, this dark stream, which during his reign as pope will reflect the fires of hell and bear swollen corpses on its breast, reflects the fires of faith: hundreds of flaming torches held aloft by the Catholic youth of the city; garlands of living light wreathing both banks of the river. Close to the water on the flat Pest side are the floodlit Gothic towers of the Parliament building, and behind it the dome of the cathedral. On the opposite side, the folded hills of Buda are splashed with masses of light; the Citadel, not far from where we stand on the Gellért Hill, the spired, mosaic-tiled Matthias Church on the Vár, the gleaming white turrets and steps of the Fisherman's Bastion; all are floodlit. The bridges are glittering strings of golden beads flung from one bank to the other and stretched taut.

K. and I stand together on the edge of a deep cleft in the face of the hill. His arm is around me, holding me close to his side. "You are so small," he says, "one little push from the crowd and I could lose you."

As the papal ship moves slowly by, with its choir of strong male voices exalting the Queen of Heaven, a great collective sigh, like a wordless prayer, goes up from the watching crowds, and I feel a strange, private movement of my heart. K., sensitive to my every vibration, presses my hand and draws me closer.

I ask myself later, what was it that moved me so? It must have been something more than the sight, however splendid, of a prince of the Church in semi-royal progression along the river Danube, like Cardinal Wolsey along the river Thames. What, then, was it?

Very soon, after only a few months, this image of light was joined by the image of darkness that clings to it still.

That winter, I went with K. to Berlin, where he gave a recital. We had planned to stay on for a few days after the concert so that I could see something of the city, which I was visiting for the first time. But it was the wrong time. As far as I was concerned, whatever physical and cultural attractions Berlin may still have possessed in that last winter before the war were totally eclipsed by the spiritual darkness that reigned there. The seal of the Prince of Darkness was omnipresent; on the windows of stores and cafés, in the voices of passersby, in the rapid glance before lids were lowered or eyes averted.

I said to K., "Take me home. Let us never come here again as long as Hitler is in power."

We kept this resolve, at the cost of considerable inconvenience to the quartet. As a gesture of repudiation of a particular form of evil, it established our position for the future; but it saved us no anguish. It was only a matter of time until the same evil would make its appearance in our own city—and there would be no running away from it.

A holiday in Italy in the summer of 1939, though flooded with sunlight and joy, brought home to us—forced upon our conscious-ness—the imminent possibility of war. In every city we visited, from Venice to Naples, the medieval peace was disturbed by shrill screams of warning in the form of posters and signs point-ing the way to the nearest air-raid shelters.

Peter and Nina accompanied us on what was to be our last trip away from Hungary for nine years. Eldon was prevented from coming by a film studio commitment, and Genevra was already in Italy, studying music in Florence on the sound principle that it is easier to learn from strangers than from friends of the family. But quite aside from that, true to the promise of her speedy and self-sufficient entry into the world, she was now eager to prove her ability to live in it on her own.

As it turned out, on this particular trip Peter and Nina made ideal traveling companions, both for us and for each other. Despite, or perhaps because of, the seven years difference in their ages, they were close friends. Between the subtle but still rather insecure Peter and his strong-minded sister Genevra, there was constant sparring, and between him and his loving but slightly cocky young brother lay the irritating fact that Eldon was already self-supporting and not always as tactful about it as he might have been. But in his elder-brotherly relationship with the fourteen-year-old Nina, there was a Svengali quality, which was soothing to his ego and stimulated the natural teacher in him. Nina, already passionately interested not only in art and architecture, but in a wide range of intellectual subjects, from German poetry in the original to Jungian psychology, was gratifyingly responsive to her brother's efforts to develop her mind. They had their flare-ups, or, rather, their moody silences; and there were times when he found her disconcertingly resistant to his molding—but that was a challenge that Peter, whose chosen tilting ground was the mind, thoroughly enjoyed.

Before going to Rome, which was the last place on our itinerary and would be the most demanding, we decided to spend a few days of *dolce far niente* on the island of Capri. And it was there that I experienced one of the rarest and most marvelous sensations in life; a sensation of intense joy that involves the entire person—mind, heart, and body. I mean the full consciousness at a given moment of being absolutely and actively happy. It is not something you tell yourself, but something that your whole being suddenly and forcefully tells you; and while it lasts, while the gift of awareness is with you, gravity ceases to exist, and you rise to the weightless level of ecstasy.

This happened to me on the island of Capri.

It was early evening. Peter and Nina had gone off somewhere by themselves, and K. and I were strolling arm in arm along an unfrequented cliff path overlooking the sea when I had my epiphany. It was not to be communicated in words. Although it seemed as if my feet were no longer touching the ground, I walked calmly on without speaking. It was K. who broke the silence. He said, "I never imagined it was possible to be as happy as I am with you, Tercsikém."

When we got back to Budapest early in August, Eldon was awaiting us at the villa, being treated like a young lord by Ilona *néni*, who adored him.

We celebrated the seventeenth anniversary of his reckless leap into a naughty world with an unbelievably rich *Dobos torte*, pridefully produced by Ilona *néni*, and a gathering of young people to help eat it. Aside from that, the dog days of August 1939 were passed in deliciously idle family tranquillity, sustained by an unspoken resolve on the part of us all not to let it be disrupted by the distant thunder rumbling on the Western horizon.

On the day the news came of Hitler's invasion of Poland, I got a call from the British consul, who was also a personal friend. He said, "You had better get those two boys of yours out of here immediately. I'm swamped with work, but if they bring me their passports today, I'll do my best to settle any visa problems they may have and get them onto a train tomorrow."

"Tomorrow! Do you really think it's that urgent?"

"I do. At any moment now, the war between England and Germany will be on, and you have only to look at the map to see how that will affect getting back to England by train from here."

"But . . . it's such an important decision . . . we have to talk it over. . . ."

"Talk it over! Surely you realize that there is only one course of action open to them?"

What I realized as he was speaking was how much the arbitrary cancellation of my British citizenship had disaffected me. I said, "I wish I could be certain of that—it would make things easier."

There was a moment of silence. Then he said pompously, "The right course of action is seldom easy, my dear Madame de Kerpely."

A background murmur of voices suddenly became louder—someone must have opened the door between the outer office and the consul's inner sanctum. I heard him say, "Just a minute," then, to me, "I must ring off now. Let me know when you come to your . . . decision."

When you come to your senses was what he had almost said; only his code of politeness to a lady had stopped him. He was a kind-

hearted man, and my inside knowledge of the trials and tribulations of consuls made me doubly appreciative of his concern for us
at a time when he was being besieged by panicky British subjects,
and proportionately guilty about my lukewarm response. The
trouble was that he didn't know enough about me to realize the
complexities of my situation, and even if he had, he lacked the
imagination to put himself in the shoes of someone whose position
was so different from his own. He had no sons—no children at
all—and no conflicting ties or loyalties. His wife was British-
born, and he had only one possible alternative with regard to her;
whether or not to send her home now, of his own accord, or wait
for instructions from the Foreign Office.

Before talking things over with Peter and Eldon, I had to
clarify my own thinking. At twenty-one and seventeen respectively, both were old enough to decide for themselves whether to
go or stay; but at the same time, they were still young enough to be
swayed by my opinion and by their love for me. Which put the
ultimate responsibility on my shoulders.

What would their father say if we could ask him? At the age of
nineteen he had taken the precipitate patriotic action that the
consul would have approved, and had bitterly regretted it.
Nevertheless, he would, I felt sure, expect his sons to do the same
thing. The time had not yet come when a young man could, with
honor, keep out of his country's wars, or even try to avoid them.
But the situation that Peter and Eldon were in now differed from
their father's in 1914 in one important respect. When World War
I broke out, their father had been in the U.S.A. touring with
George Arliss's company in the play *Disraeli*, and showing so
much talent that Arliss himself did all he could to dissuade him
from taking the next boat to almost certain death in the trenches.
There was no good reason, the older man had told him, for such
rashness; he was in a friendly, neutral country, from which he
could freely depart at any time, and he would do well to stay there
until the situation in Europe became clearer.

And there, of course, lay the crucial difference.

A look at the map made clear both the difficulty of getting back
to England, with Austria already annexed by Hitler, and Italy on
the verge of becoming his ally, and the difficulty that Hungary

would have in preserving her neutrality. And in any event, her geographical position was such that she could prove a dangerous trap for two young Englishmen who, even (and perhaps especially) if they got out of it safely at the end of the war, would be suspected of having walked into it on purpose to avoid fighting for their country.

For myself, the choice was simple; come hell or high water I would never leave K. My daughters (Genevra had already arrived from Italy) had decided to stay with me, for the time being at any rate; and even if they were trapped, interment was the worst that could happen to them—or so we thought. From a moral standpoint, surely no one could seriously impugn the patriotism of two young girls who elected to stay with their mother in a country that was still uninvolved at the time.

I went up to Peter's room, where he and Eldon were discussing the news and what it might mean to them personally, and told them what the consul had said. As I spoke, I had the strange feeling of delivering some sort of death blow—to myself as well as to them.

Peter asked at once, "What do *you* think we ought to do, Mother?" And when I hesitated, his deep-set blue eyes went cloudy. Ever since he was a very small boy this curious, veiled look in his eyes had been a sign, often the only sign, that he was hurt.

Then Eldon said, "I don't see any reason why *I* shouldn't stay on for a bit and see what happens."

"While I rush back to England tomorrow and enlist. Thank you very much."

"That's what Father did in the last war."

"Yes. And spent the rest of his life wishing he hadn't—and making us wish he hadn't."

I said, "Don't quarrel . . . please. I can't bear it." And Peter, twisting my meaning, said, "Neither can we bear it, Mother."

I recall only the gist of what we said in that final, fateful discussion among the three of us. But I remember exactly how I felt, how they looked, and the pain and apprehension that circulated among us like icy currents of air.

Facing me, sitting, as though for solidarity, side by side on the edge of the divan bed in their summer garb of shorts and open-necked shirts, these "men" who would soon be called upon to kill other men looked pitifully young and vulnerable.

Peter, extremely slight in build, with thick blond hair parted on one side, a serious expression, and a subdued, watchful manner—the result of years of deliberate self-effacement in the presence of his father—could have passed for eighteen.

Eldon, though more assertive, looked just as little-boyish as he did in his twelve-year-old roles on the screen. He was as different from his brother in temperament as he was in appearance; mercurial and emotional where Peter was stoical and reserved. His hair and brows were as dark as Peter's were fair, but they both had blue eyes; Peter's sometimes piercing, sometimes veiled, usually critical; Eldon's bright, sparkling, mischievous, sometimes furious, usually smiling. But behind all the charm and the genuine charisma, lay an inherited streak of profound melancholy; a heritage shared by his brother, who was better equipped to cope with it.

I pointed out to Eldon that to spend his year of respite from the army with us in Hungary would be to cut short his acting career, as well as to risk getting trapped. I thought he should go on a visit to America, where his father's uncle, the playwright Charles Rann Kennedy, and his actress wife, could help him to make the most of his year of respite.

Peter could not count on any respite. For him the only foreseeable choice lay between two equally bad risks; one weighed down more heavily on the side of physical destruction, and the other on the side of moral destruction.

Perceiving that I was torn in two, he embarked on his own method of resolving the dilemma; he brilliantly marshaled the arguments for and against each side; then lapsed into silence, like a judge preparing to sum up the arguments he has just heard. But I knew what his silence meant. He was giving his inner voice a chance to speak.

Of Peter's and Eldon's departure next day, I retain a single, indelible image: the desolate air of an intimate room abandoned; still bearing the imprint of its beloved occupants, still strewn with the touching bits and pieces of an everyday life brutally interrupted and never to be resumed.

As for the echoes, reinforced on another hill, on another continent, they repeat themselves; echo back and forth from the walls of abandoned rooms, as the occupants quietly slip away, one after another.

Going Toward the Vortex

I

A T first, and for long enough to create a false sense of security, the undertow of moral corruption, of Nazism, in Hungary, remained so far below the surface that her inexorable movement toward destruction was almost imperceptible. And we, along with many others in far greater danger than we were, allowed ourselves to hope that she might, after all, be able to save herself and her people—a false hope treacherously sustained by her long-drawn-out official neutrality.

In the villa on the Kelenhegyi út, the departure of Peter and Eldon marked the end of an idyll. To the abstract sadness, the "sweet sorrow" of music in a minor key that touches the emotions but leaves the heart unscathed, was added now—for the first time, an undertone of true sadness; a personal undertone soon to be overwhelmed by the ever more piercing notes of a universal sorrow that I had not yet lived long enough to accept as an ineradicable element of the all-embracing music of life and death.

The parting with my two sons on the eve of a long war was, in a very profound sense, a final rupture. But some of my immediate fears and anxieties concerning them were allayed when, after an anguishing period of silence, letters from England began to arrive. To be in touch once more was in itself a reassurance.

Back in London, after a journey across Europe that recalled, with its discomforts and delays, his father's king's-messenger trips in the aftermath of the last war, Peter had duly reported for service in the British armed forces. But when he informed the interviewing officer that he was close to getting a degree in German language and literature from London University, he was told to get on with it and come back when he had it in hand; men of his skills were needed in Army Intelligence.

A few weeks later, Eldon left for America on a visit to his great-uncle, and very soon after his arrival in New York he joined the cast of the Longacre Theater production of John van Druten's play *Leave Her to Heaven*, in which Ruth Chatterton had the principal role, as Madge, the accused woman; and the part of her young son, David, was assigned to Eldon. By an ironic coincidence, of which Eldon was unaware, Ruth Chatterton had been his father's first great love when he, like Eldon now, was a neophyte actor still in his teens, and she, though not much older, was already a rising star and light years beyond his reach. But uncommonly kind. "She broke my heart and mended it again all in one evening," he had told me, recalling her compassionate response to his absurd proposal of marriage.

As the theater of war expanded, the lines of communication closed, one after another. When the mail ceased, an uncle of mine in London, a man with some influence, managed to get an occasional cryptic message to me through the International Red Cross. Then even that avenue was cut off. The last message I got before the final silence descended consisted of three short sentences: *Both boys well. Peter intelligently employed India. Eldon enjoying Canadian air.*

It was not hard to guess what that meant, and it troubled me. But it was only when the British began to bomb Budapest that I felt its full significance.

It was during the first winter of the war, when life in Budapest had not yet undergone any outward change, that Genevra and István first met at the Academy Ball. "She looked like a queen," he told me, when the silence barrier had been overcome.

First an angel, then a queen; the language was that of a very young man in love. The maternal viewpoint was more realistic. But I knew what he meant. Though only five feet two inches tall, and slender and straight as a boy, Genevra did have a queenly air. It lay in her bearing; in the haughty tilt of her head, in her level, blue gaze, in her cool English voice with its slightly arrogant timbre, and her cool English manner, which concealed a volcanic temper—ready to erupt on the slightest provocation—and an equally volatile sense of humor. Your luck depended on which you happened to provoke first.

On the night of the Academy Ball, she was looking especially lovely in one of my creations; a formal evening dress of soft blue satin, its low neckline edged with delicately tinted silk flowers that blended with the rose and ivory of her skin. But her only crown was her hair, brushed upward from her forehead, and jeweled with coppery lights.

Her sister's good looks were of quite a different order. Nina resembled a nymph rather than a queen. She had classical features, an hourglass figure, a shy manner, and a low, soft voice that was more seductive than she knew. (I once heard someone describe her as a mixture of Marlene Dietrich and Greta Garbo.) But under this deceptively feminine exterior lay a strongly feminist personality, and the combination could be disconcerting.

She attended an art school in Pest, too far from our Buda villa for her to come home for the midday break. But the British consul and his wife, who lived just around the corner from the school, invited her to take lunch with them. "It will give my wife something to do," the consul said, brushing aside my polite, demur "brighten up her day for her."

The consul's wife was a rather sad woman; an accomplished pianist who had given up her dream of a concert career in favor of marriage. When her husband was not present, she would talk animatedly about music, art, and literature. But in his company, she was mute; and in hers, he became morose. I could well imagine the gloom when they were alone together in their own, childless home, and the welcome ray of light that Nina's presence would provide.

It began by generating sparks. The consul, a middle-aged neo-Victorian husband with a successfully subdued wife, was not used to having his opinions challenged by a woman, let alone by a sixteen-year-old girl. But Nina challenged them fearlessly, and what was worse, logically.

First shocked, then annoyed, then intrigued, he ended by succumbing to the feminine charm that had misled him in the first place, and conceding her mental equality; but as an exception, a young genius by no means representative of the "weaker sex" in general. He said to me once with a sigh, "I'd give anything in the world to have a daughter like Nina." Which was less than the whole truth. He had, though he would never have admitted it, not even I suspect to himself, fallen in love with his ray of light, sparks and all.

Nina was generally liked by her fellow students, but she kept her relationships with most of them on a superficial level. Her standards for intimacy were exacting: the acid test was mental, and, in the widest sense of the word, moral. Like many idealistic young people, Nina was at the best of times intolerant of the foolish and the frivolous. But in the light of what was happening in the world now, and all around her, she regarded foolishness and frivolity as immoral.

Aside from Paul, who was part of her life, though physically absent most of the time, serving with his regiment, she had only two close friends among her contemporaries. Both were Jewish. One was a strong-minded and rather overwhelming girl of about her own age, named Agnés. The other was a Rumanian-born painter named Péter, a somber, intense young man, a few years older than she was. More of an intellectual than most painters, he shared Nina's love of literature, and delighted her with his Hoffmanesque imagination. And there were other, more subtle bonds between them; one being their common birthplace, which Nina perceived as a powerful subliminal influence on her early childhood; the other, his first name, Péter. Though distinguished by its accent and pronunciation from its English equivalent, it linked him, at least in her subconscious mind, with her absent elder brother.

Before very long, she would have to say goodbye to this Péter, too. As the deadly poison of Nazism seeped into Hungary, the young men were winnowed into two groups; both were earmarked for danger and death, but to one was given a vestige of hope and the possibility of honor, and to the other only ignominy.

When diplomatic relations were broken off between the United Kingdom and Hungary, in the spring of 1941, our friend the British consul made a last effort to persuade me to do "the right thing" as he perceived it.

The British diplomatic personnel and a few other qualified

individuals were to leave Budapest on a special train that would start them off on a complicated journey back to England that was destined to last a whole year. He could get my two daughters on that train, the consul said, if only I would consent to let them go. He might even be able to get me on it, in a pinch.

I said, "Once and for all, I am staying here with my husband. But my daughters are perfectly free to choose for themselves. Obviously, I don't want to lose them. But I won't stand in their way."

He knew that. But he wanted, poor man, to be able to blame me in his heart of hearts if Nina chose to stay. Which she did. Transplanted at the turning-point age of thirteen, she had put down roots.

Genevra, now almost twenty years old, was at an important crossroad in her life, and the problem of which direction to take when the outcome of one was just as unpredictable as the other was compounded by the complexity of her temperament, as well as by the divisive circumstances.

Her physical home, the haven to which, under normal conditions, she could always return "between flights," so to speak, was with me and K. in Hungary. But England was her spiritual home, and she felt, I think, a semipatriotic, semifilial duty to participate in its defense, as her father had done before her. On the other hand, she had already formed ties of friendship and love in Hungary, of which the strongest at that particular time was her relationship with István. It was an intense relationship with no foreseeable future; fraught from the start with difficulties, obstacles—tangible and intangible, and potential danger, by which Genevra had characteristically refused to be daunted; and, for those very reasons, of profound symbolic significance to them both.

Pretty sure that the consul would get her on that train back to England even if she showed up only as it was about to pull out of the station, she delayed making a decision until the last possible moment; when fate made it for her, by immobilizing her with acute appendicitis.

Our three-year lease of the villa on the Kelenhegyi út had expired in December 1940, and the owner, an elderly woman, had declined to renew it on the trumped-up excuse that she would shortly be needing it for a member of her family. She agreed, however, to let us rent it on a month-to-month basis until we could find a suitable place to move into. Her true reason for wanting to get rid of us was obvious, and it brought home to me the ambiguity of my position. She may or may not have been pro-German. But she saw which way the wind was blowing, and she was afraid; already a prey to that demoralizing, unspecified fear that is felt, I believe, by even the bravest person under the threat, or the fact, of foreign military occupation or internal political tyranny.

At the time, having not yet experienced any of this personally, I thought our landlady's attitude rather despicable. But I was worried by the realization that my British origin, which had been an asset in her eyes when we first rented her villa, was now seen by her as a drawback, and even a threat to her safety. If other houseowners felt the same way, we could end up with nowhere to go.

But our diminished desirability as tenants was not the only problem. The situation had changed radically since we sallied forth every afternoon to choose a home for ourselves in a preferred spot. At the outset of the war between England and Germany, many Hungarians who had been residing in Western Europe for one reason or another had come back home, to occupy dwellings that a couple of years earlier had been for rent. We desperately wanted to stay on the Gellért Hill, but we combed its slopes in vain. A second coice was the district close to the Vár, where our little honeymoon house was located, but we found nothing there either. We ended by abandoning all preferences. Anywhere in Buda would do, providing it was not too far by public transport from the Academy of Music and Nina's art school. A temptingly beautiful and inexpensive villa on the Svábhegy had to be turned down because of its inaccessibility.

In all this, good luck was with us, but so heavily disguised as its opposite that we recognized it only in retrospect.

Our landlady was getting more disagreeable by the month, and I was beginning to develop a persecution complex, when the last-minute salvation, which is my particular form of good luck, arrived, and the Miracle of the Baptist Missionaries was enacted all over again. K. learned, from a chance remark made in his hearing, of a friend of a friend's unexpected departure from Budapest, leaving his attorney to find someone to take over the lease of his rented villa on the Rózsadomb.

Off we went to see it, hope renewed. The Rózsadomb—Mount of Roses—is a relatively low hill at the northern end of Buda, overlooking the Margaret Island and the long, three-spanned bridge connecting it with both sides of the river, which is very wide at that point.

The villa turned out to be very conveniently situated on a short, countrified street, less than a five-minute walk from where the bus that ran up and down the hill every hour stopped to catch its breath.

The unpretentious three-story house was set in about a quarter of an acre of garden surrounded by a ten-foot-high, chain-link fence. The moment I saw it I knew we were going to live in it. It was not a question of love at first sight, as it had been with the Kelenhegyi út villa; it was, rather, a sense of predestination; a feeling of having been patiently awaited while we ran about frantically looking in all the wrong directions—like children playing a game of hide-the-thimble. Once discovered, it fell into our hands with the greatest of ease. The only concern of the attorney in charge of the transaction was to get the lease off his client's hands, and the landlord was either absent or indifferent as to where the rent came from, so long as it was paid.

It lacked the romantic charm of the villa on the Kelenhegyi út, but it was larger, and, surprisingly, less expensive. This may have been because its status as a gentleman's private residence, with its own "housemaster," or janitor, had been diminished by the renting out of the housemaster's quarters as a separate apartment. For me, this ground-floor apartment, with its threat to our privacy, was the one flaw in an otherwise marvelous find. Another failure on my part to recognize good luck.

We moved to the Rózsadomb at the end of July, while the two girls were away in the country visiting some distant cousins of K.'s. Dismantling the home I had so joyously constructed within the four whitewashed walls of the villa on the Kelenhegyi út was a melancholy experience, and I hoped, uncharitably, that its echoes of music and friendship and parting would haunt and disturb the new occupants—a young Hungarian nobleman and his wife, to whom our perfidious landlady turned it over the day after we left. Later in the war, this young man died a hero's death, but by then there was no villa left for his gallant spirit to haunt, only a pile of rubble.

Faced once again with the all-too-familiar problem of how to make the furnishings of one house fit another of quite different proportions, and this time without spending money—for the war had put me into severe financial difficulties, I reacted in accordance with what my son Peter teasingly called "Mother's Doctrine of Active Acceptance," and I called "making the best of things." My painfully acquired adaptability to changes beyond my control reasserted itself, acting with tonic effect, and I soon realized that whatever our new home lacked in romantic charm was amply made up for by its more practical virtues.

A house without secrets—light, airy, and spacious—its straightforward geography played such an important role as it, and we with it, fell successively into the hands of defenders, occupiers, liberators, and miscellaneous marauders, that a clear description of it is called for.

Set well back from the road and partially concealed by fruit trees—cherry and apricot, peach and plum—it was adequately guarded from all ordinary intruders by its ten-foot fence and locked gates. On one side of the house was a garage, and above it a terrace, or deck, with a sweeping semicircular view from the high hills on the northwest to the Parliament building on the east bank of the Danube. On the other side of the house was the main entrance. It opened into a rectangular hall with a wide rectangular stairway leading up to the landing of the main floor, from which an identical stairway led up to an identical landing on the top floor. Above that was an attic, reached by a ladder and a trap door. And another trap door led from the attic to the sloping mansard roof.

On the main floor were three lofty reception rooms with large casement windows facing the road and the morning sun. The central room had double folding doors with glass panes opening onto the landing, and the same type of doors connected it with the rooms on its right and left, both of which, unlike the communicating rooms in Rumanian houses, had separate entrances. The room on the left, which was the largest of the three, also had French doors opening onto the terrace over the garage. When all the doors were folded back for entertaining, the effect was palatial—but we had precious few opportunities to take advantage of that. On one side of this first landing were the kitchen premises, and on the other was a bathroom.

The three rooms on the top floor were smaller, with lower ceilings and smaller windows. Over the kitchen was a maid's room with two windows, and on the opposite side of the landing, were another, smaller room and a second bathroom.

The ground floor apartment, which had its own entrance and strip of garden in back of the house, was compressed into less than two-thirds of the upstairs floor space. It had three communicating front rooms like ours, but—and this is an important detail—only one entrance, from the narrow hallway into the first room. A bathroom and separate toilet, both so small you could barely turn around in them, and a kitchen not much bigger, with a closet-sized maid's room opening off it, completed a cramped dwelling that we, as a "family" of nine adults and two babies, were destined to share for weeks with a floating population of friends, helpers, fugitives, bombed-out neighbors, and as many of our Red Army liberators as were able to squeeze in without squeezing us out; which, to their eternal credit, they never attempted to do. There were times when as many as forty of us slept side-by-side in its bullet-pocked, windowless shelter.

In the summer of 1941, it was tenanted by one of those couples that provide the basic elements of French triangular comedy. The husband; middle-aged, doting, dull; overworked during the day and sleepy after supper. The wife; years younger than her husband, handsome, sexy, bored; underworked during the day and not a bit sleepy after supper.

I encountered her for the first time on the day we moved in; a process she watched from her open living room window—as she would, I felt sure, watch our future comings and goings; taking just as much interest in our visitors as she was obviously taking now in our belongings.

We exchanged civilities. Hungarian women tended to be effusive with other women of the same social standing, and on the whole I preferred their show of warmth, however superficial, to

the casual rudeness of the average upper-class Englishwoman.
But the downstairs tenant—I shall call her Mrs. A.—overdid it,
and I was tempted to indulge in a little casual English rudeness
myself. But I couldn't afford to antagonize her. So I gave her a
noncommittal smile and made a mental note that she must be
kept at a distance.

When I mentioned this to K., he said, "Well, yes . . . we must not
let her become a nuisance—but are you not glad that she likes
English people?"

What was happening to me? Had I already succumbed, without
realizing it, to the virus of fear and suspicion?

As a general rule, I refused invitations to mid-morning coffee,
but when Mrs. A. asked me in a few mornings later, I accepted;
partly to show her that I was not unfriendly, and partly out of
curiosity. I thought I might find in her surroundings a clue to the
real woman under the smiling mask that I couldn't quite believe
in.

Mrs. A.'s decor did nothing to help me appraise her true character. On the contrary, it confused things. Overcrowded with
spindly antiques, prim, uncomfortable needlepoint chairs, "occasional" tables, and useless knickknacks, yet well supplied with
books—they covered a whole wall from floor to ceiling—the
apartment seemed to embody the soul of some cultured but finicky spinster; with no room left over for Mrs. A.'s opulent physical
presence. But in common with many big women, Mrs. A. had
long, shapely legs with finely turned ankles, and she pranced
around her obstacle-strewn parlor like a high-stepping mare in a
school of dressage delicately picking her way around the artificial barriers placed in her path by the trainer.

And the image that invariably comes up when I try to recall her
visually is that of an elegant, satiny mare, in the guise of a big
blonde woman, curvetting down the road on her way to some
rendezvous in the city. It is always around noon. Is she going to
lunch at a Danube café? With her husband? With a lover? Who
knows. But certainly not alone. One doesn't dress up like that to
lunch alone.

As to her baffling interior, she seemed to be unaware of any
incongruity between its nature and hers. And no finicky spinster
could have kept it in better order, or shown it off more proudly

than she did. For the first time in years, I thought of Mevrouw De Groote's luminous room in the old Houttuin house. Was I looking now at a variant of the same phenomenon—a variant involving atonement?

In mid-August, Mrs. A. and her inconspicuous husband went off to Lake Balaton for their summer vacation, which left us with the happy feeling of being on vacation in our own home.

But Ilona *néni*'s departure around the same time left us feeling rather lost. We had come to rely on her semimaternal concern for our physical well-being. When she came in to say goodbye, with tears in her eyes, she told me in what corner of the attic she had placed the traditional bread and salt that would keep us from want as long as we were under that roof; then she solemnly presented me with her late husband's scissors, as with some precious talisman to protect us from dangers beyond the scope of the bread and salt.

Ever since I was made, at the age of eight, to memorize the dates of the kings and queens of England in order of their reigns, I have had a built-in resistance to memorizing dates of any kind. For me, they dim the vivid colors of history and impart a deadly dryness to any narrative in which they appear too frequently, and I wish I could keep them out of this story of my life—which may be why I omitted to mention that in June, 1941, when we were preoccupied with finding a place to live, Hungary declared war on Russia. Despite the importance of Hungary's first step into the war, it remained more or less academic in the eyes of the general public. Everyone knew that, for the moment at least, the Russians had more important things to do than attack Hungary, which certainly wasn't going to gratuitously attack Russia. As a result of this attitude, civil defense remained theoretical. Pamphlets were circulated telling people how to behave in an air raid, how to cope with a firebomb, how much water to store in their bathtubs; but it was rather like being told how to survive in a jungle one has no intention of visiting. A few public bomb shelters were established in different parts of the city—none of them near us—and now and again the air-raid sirens were briefly tested, but no blackout was in force, and any diminution of city lights was in the

interests of economy rather than safety. In fact, the immediate
consequences of going to war with Russia were nothing like as
grave as those of remaining on good terms with Germany.

During the last half of August, K. and I found ourselves completely alone together for the first time since our honeymoon four
years earlier; and now, with the Academy of Music in recess and
the quartet rehearsals in dog-day suspension, our peace was
uninterrupted by outside demands. Except for the presence in
the kitchen of Ilona *néni*'s younger helper, Mariska, who was still
working for us, we had the entire building to ourselves, and we
took advantage of that to baptize it with a magic infinitely more
powerful and protective than that of the bread and salt in the attic
and the symbolic sword of the French hairdresser's scissors.

That year, Saint Stephen's Day was celebrated with all the cus-
tomary pageantry, but more in the spirit of a feast day than a
festival—though not as unobtrusively as it should have been. K.
and I, sitting out on our terrace in the dark, were shocked to see
fireworks light up the sky, and the sudden bursts of explosive
sound sent premonitory shivers down my spine. The natural
acoustics of the Rózsadomb in those days, when it was still only
sparsely built up, were extraordinary; as amplifying and stereo-
phonic as those of a present-day concert hall. From our terrace,
we could hear with the utmost clarity all the little sounds of a city
awake later than usual and a populace trying desperately to
prolong a day of escape into past history.

K. and I were already thinking about tomorrow, and as often
happened with us, we thought of the same things at the same
time. I was wondering whether the girls really would come back
from the country next day; their visit had already been prolonged
by more than a week—no doubt at the instigation of Károly, the
young owner of the estate, though the suggestion had, like the
original invitation, come from his aunts, two very "correct" ladies
whose presence in the rambling old country house provided the
necessary chaperonage. Was Károly, twenty-seven years of age
and unmarried, simply enjoying the summer companionship of
two pretty girls, or was he seriously interested in one of them? If
so, I had a feeling it might be Genevra.

These thoughts were still in my mind, unspoken, when K. said,
"The other day, when I went into town to get a new A string, I ran

across István, and he asked me when we expected Genevra back. Have you any idea how things are between them?"

"Changed. I don't know exactly what's happened, but I think they have given up an impossible dream."

"Poor István...." It was not said lightly, but with great sadness and a compassion that extended far beyond István's immediate unhappiness or disappointment, and embraced a host of others who were, like him, being pulled by irresistible currents into a vortex from which they had little or no chance of emerging alive.

A church clock down by the river tolled midnight, while a shrill duet of demand and refusal went on at the garden gate, where Mariska was saying good night to her young man of the moment. A moment that was clearly at an end. Mariska was refusal personified.

Her acidulated tones cut into our somber mood and made us laugh. Directed against an over-amorous suitor, her shrewish tongue was amusing. But when, as the war reduced the supply of suitors, she used it against us, it led to her departure for more suitable employment in a munitions factory.

Our top-floor bedroom was on the northeast corner of the house and had an extra window at the side, just above the terrace. The unscreened casements were all wide open when we went up to bed, but the room was still very warm; it took a long time to cool off after a hot day. We left the casements open and lay down in the dark, so as not to attract mosquitoes. The city was finally falling asleep. Aside from the clang of a tram on its last run and the distant rumble of a train, the only sounds came from close by; the fretful cry of a young child, a sudden squawk from our neighbor's hen roost, and a couple of menacing barks in return from our miniature Schnauzer, Shivvy—a recent acquisition, still puppyish, endearing, and full of original sin. "One of these days," I said, "that little devil will find a way of getting at those chickens." But K. was already asleep.

I was getting drowsy myself, yet I didn't want to succumb to sleep too quickly; I wanted to prolong a particular state of awareness; the peculiar intimacy of the middle of the night and the sense of its inviolability.

An illusion ripped to pieces by the first howl of the air-raid sirens.

I yelled to K. through the ever-increasing din, "What a bloody awful time to choose for a test!" And K. said, "It sounds to me as if it might be the real thing."

We went to the side window, which had the most open view, to see what was happening. The sirens' frenzied howling drowned out the approach of two small planes that seemed to appear out of nowhere, flying very fast in our direction and very low. They had barely roared overhead when I saw their cargo falling. The explosions took away our breath. K. put his arm around my shoulders and rushed me down the stairs. Through the tall staircase window we could see the crisscross of searchlight beams sweeping the sky. A second burst of explosions came from much farther away. Then all the lights in the city went out.

Next morning, the newspapers said that the war with Russia had begun.

Within the space of a few minutes, the Russians had taught little Hungary a lesson. It was learned at the cost of at least three innocent lives—two children and their nursemaid in a villa only a few yards from ours—and one church. There were those who said, in a whisper, that the planes were not Russian, but German; that the raid was a warning rather than a lesson. Whichever it was, it taught me something about the nature of fear.

Going back over the incident in my mind, trying to remember and analyze my split-second feelings as the enemy passed directly overhead and I saw death missing me by a hairbreadth, I could not recall any feeling of fear. Yet I was by no means a fearless person. I was constantly having to overcome fears that other people didn't seem to have. The greatest of these was the fear of losing K. Of something happening to him. Of having to go on living without him. And this, I believed, was why I had felt no fear at that moment of extreme physical danger; I was unafraid because K. was so close to me that whatever happened would happen to us both at the same time. The truth of this theory was borne out over and over again, as physical danger became a chronic condition of our lives, and sometimes we would be close together during a shelling and sometimes not—when my fear was always redoubled. But there were other factors involved. As I grew more familiar with danger in varying forms and degrees, I found that the closer it came the less frightened I was; and its imminence not only numbed fear, it simultaneously generated a high pitch of excitement, exaltation, and, where a human antagonist was involved, blind fury.

The wildcat raid was followed by a period of quiescence that nobody trusted. But, precarious though it was, it created a last-minute opportunity to seize on whatever individual happiness fate might offer. And fate was offering my daughter Genevra what was destined to be the love of her life.

She and Károly were contemplating marriage. But a marriage between a member of the Hungarian landed gentry and a penniless foreigner, who was dangerously close to becoming an enemy alien into the bargain, presented problems that I, in the light of my own romantic marriages, found it difficult to evaluate—let alone solve.

They were the problems inherent in the structure of a feudal, hierarchical society. The Hungarian gentry, with their family coats of arms and minor titles, were the equivalent of the knights and esquires of Old England. Ideally, they married into the same social class, but in any case a bride was expected to bring with her a dowry in some form—land, money, valuables, and a sizable trousseau of household linens as well as personal clothing.

Poor Genevra had neither dowry nor trousseau and no way of obtaining them. The money she earned by giving private lessons in English was negligible, and the war had cut me off from the source of my income—such as it was. The only valuable gifts I had to give her were two family heirlooms; a twenty-four carat gold cross and chain, and a Brussels lace wedding veil.

My daughter's background, however, was all that could be desired by any Hungarian gentleman. Her family tree was loaded down on both sides with British ornaments to their country; bemedaled heroes, venerable churchmen, cabinet ministers, minor titles—including a baronet, and even, in a left-handed way, a king; one of the more disreputable of the monarchs whose dates I had memorized. This did something to mitigate the embarrassment I felt with regard to the financial position.

But what would have been an insurmountable obstacle to a marriage in which love was incidental, was pushed aside by Károly, for whom love was all, and who fully understood the predicament I was in. A church wedding was planned for late December, when his father and stepmother—his own mother was dead—could be there. Neither Károly nor Genevra was religious, but church weddings were traditional in both families, and I wanted my daughter to have what I had been cheated out of by the First World War: a white wedding, with all the symbolism and ceremony that goes with it—not to mention a few wedding presents.

Armed with a monetary loan from the bridegroom—to be repaid in the nebulous future time known as "after the war"—I went in search of materials for the white wedding gown and the semblance of a trousseau for the bride whose face was, for the moment, her only fortune. Textiles were getting scarce—like every other commodity—and the remaining imported fabrics were kept hidden under the counter, to be offered to special customers only, at black market prices. But small though my borrowed resources were, I had set my heart on a fine silk velvet for the once-in-a-lifetime wedding garment that I had designed myself, and that represented an unfulfilled dream of my own youth, and I didn't care how much I paid for it, or how many hours I put into the sewing of it.

On the fourth of December, when the wedding was still more than three weeks away, a good friend of Károly's, a military man who knew what was going on, came to him and said, "If you really want to marry that English girl, you had better do it immediately."

Károly took the hint, and next morning he and Genevra went through the civil ceremony that legally made them man and wife and turned Genevra into a Hungarian citizen. They were only just in time. On the following day, England declared war on Hungary.

The day after that was Pearl Harbor. And five days later, Hungary entered a state of war with the United States of America.

These events put me and my daughters into a position that can only be described as schizophrenic. And in the sense that both K. and his young cousin Károly loved their homeland as passionately as they hated the fascist cause she was being relentlessly pressured into espousing, their position too was schizophrenic. I could imagine what my son Peter would say; I could hear him saying it, see his little ironic smile, "Well, Mother dear, putting that doctrine of yours into practice now is going to be a bit of a strain, isn't it?"

Genevra's wedding stands out in my memory as an important event for two reasons. It was not only the first wedding in my immediate family, but as things turned out, it was the only one in which I was ever able to participate; and it took place at a black moment in history, in defiance of inimical circumstances that could only change for the worse. In short, it was a challenge to fate.

Yet the images that come up in my mind as I write about it now are fragmentary and almost irrelevant.

I have no recollection whatever of the church ceremony, which was held in the evening. What I see is the snow that made getting to and from the church almost impossible. Snow piled up in drifts that reach to the top of our ten-foot fence. Snow steadily falling in great fluffy flakes.

Behind this snow scene, as though on the inside flap of a Christmas card, is the image of a lighted interior. My fabric-strewn sewing room. I am sitting there hurriedly sewing on the last of twenty tiny buttons—ten to each sleeve—that fasten the tight, elbow-high cuffs of Genevra's medieval wedding dress; a tiresome little task that I have characteristically put off until the last minute. Genevra, shivering in her slip, is getting frantic—the snow will make us late anyway. Nina, ready and waiting to clasp the gold cross and chain around her sister's neck, and drape the Brussels lace veil with its orange-blossom wreath over her chestnut hair, looks on with an air of affectionate amusement. "Dearest Mama," she says, at once ironic and tender, "Dearest Mama, you are incorrigible!"

Looking back now, I think how right she was. In this respect, I haven't changed one bit; when the time comes for me to die I shall probably keep the undertaker waiting while I put the last stitches in my shroud.

The next image to emerge is one of our candle-lit dining room after the wedding supper—a strictly family supper, at which the pastor of the church is the only outsider. Through a golden haze of

Tokay, I see the bride and bridegroom posing shyly for their picture against the apple green folds of the carefully drawn window curtains. They are looking at each other, and in that look there is something that tells me the pact they have just made, before a God whose existence they doubt, will, like the pact between me and K., never be broken. No matter what becomes of us all.

II

On New Year's Eve, we opened the door to let in the year 1942 with very little hope that it would bring with it anything but trouble.

Surprisingly, it brought us no air raids, despite the fact that Hungary was at war with three nations. The systematic bombing of Budapest by British and American planes began only in 1944. But the Saint Stephen's Day lesson had given the authorities a salutary jolt. Antiaircraft positions were better manned, blackouts were enforced, district air wardens were appointed, rules for public behavior during air raids were issued. All of which kept us in a state of perpetual expectation rather than preparedness. How can one be prepared for what one cannot imagine?

In the absence of the active hostilities we expected, the passive conditions of a country at war took over. Rationing, food lines, shortages of all kinds, disappearances. The *Nyilas*—the Hungarian Arrow-Cross Party—began to take monstrous form, evoking the worst in everyone, tapping the subterranean springs of anti-Jewish feeling, and exploiting them; supporting the multiplication of those instruments of slow strangulation known as the Jew Laws—the unrecognized precursors of the mandatory ghettos, the yellow stars, the inconceivable death camps.

Categories were established. To keep out of the wrong ones, a Hungarian citizen had to produce proof of pure ancestry, which meant having four Aryan grandparents. This was a problem for me and Genevra, one we had never dreamed we would have to face. We had generations of Aryan grandparents, but no way of proving it. Whatever documents existed were in London, buried in the files of the national archive of births, marriages and deaths known as Somerset House, and as inaccessible to us as the moon.

Luckily we were not dealing with fanatical Nazis, but with

ordinary Hungarian officials whose hearts were not in the witch-hunt, and whose sympathies were pro-British. Seeing that the required legal proofs were obviously unattainable, they agreed, after a little face-saving argument, to accept circumstantial evidence in support of my sworn statement; such as the important-looking parchment certificate of my father's ordination as an Anglican priest, and a photograph of my grandfather, who was a Canon in the Church of Ireland, wearing his clerical clothes.

The period of uncertainty was short, but while it lasted, I knew fear of a kind I had never known before.

At the end of August, Genevra had a son. Like my own eldest son, after whom he was named, he came unexpectedly early. The country doctor came late, and the nurse didn't come at all. Károly's account of his son's birth sounded like a digest of my own past history.

K. and I took the next train down to the country. Károly, who met us at the station, looked relieved to see me, but a trifle dismayed to see K. and his cello as well; with the household at sixes and sevens a nonfunctional guest would only add to the confusion. But I would not part with K., even for a few days, and K. would not part with his cello. After packing us with some ingenuity into his small car (K. had long legs and his cello needed a whole seat to itself), Károly drove us uncomfortably fast along several bumpy miles of dirt road to the old country house, known as *Dombiratos*, that was now my daughter's home.

Situated south of Budapest near the Rumanian border, the estate of Dombiratos was just what I imagined the country estates in Tolstoy's novels to have been like—the sort of place in which Konstantin Levin tried to get over his love for Kitty Shcherbatsky. Indeed, there was something of Tolstoy's Levin in Károly. Not in his appearance—unlike the big, clumsy Levin, Károly was a relatively small man with the neat-but-sturdy build of a Highland pony—but in his character. A practical man when it came to managing his estate and the now-valuable sugar beet it produced, he was by temperament an artist and a dreamer; and getting a degree in agricultural science had done nothing to alter his ultimate goal in life, which was not agriculture, but art.

K. and I visited Dombiratos on two separate occasions, which have swum together in my memory to create a series of overlapping sensory images.

In one of these, K. is playing his morning scales in a large, bright bedroom, whose open casements let in with the fresh early morning air an orchestral obligato of country sounds and a lovely, compound fragrance of new mown grass and honeysuckle. On the other side of the room, reflected in a slightly blackened mirror, I see myself, naked to the waist, bending over a large china basin washing my face and neck in warm water brought to me from the kitchen in a can. Beyond my reflection in the wash-stand mirror is K.'s. He is looking across at me and smiling as he plays the last in a series of warm-up scales. Now he sets his instrument carefully down, hooks the bow over one of its pegs, and walks over to me. I feel the affectionate pressure of his big hands on my bony shoulders, and the light touch of his lips on my soapy nape. My response to this *tendresse* is to keep absolutely still. It is a moment of perfect, wordless communication. Then K. goes back to his cello and starts to play the first movement of a Beethoven sonata.

In connection with that scene, I remember wanting to lie down and sleep instead of getting dressed. I had spent a wakeful night in another room with the new baby, who was in a constant state of hunger, being too weak to suck properly.

Now—it must be later in the morning on the same day—comes a tender image of Genevra, with her baby beside her. Asleep, with her cloud of Pre-Raphaelite hair spread out over the pillow, she looks more serene than she ever looks when awake. The baby's puckered little face is serene too—for the moment. But he is so tiny, so alarmingly fragile. I think of Mannie tucked up in his bureau drawer. *Poor little bugger*, his father says faintly out of the past, and is overwhelmed by another, more gutteral echo, that seems to reach into the future, *Vreselijk, oh, vreselijk. . . .*

I leave mother and child at rest in their darkened room and go in search of K. The whole house is in twilight. In this part of Hungary the summers are very hot, and the only way to keep a house moderately cool is to keep the windows closed and shuttered until the sun goes down. I find K. in the library, reading in the half-dark. I tell him he will ruin his eyesight. He smiles and goes on reading. He is very comfortable. He is used to shuttered windows in summer, and puts up with my British mania for light and air at all costs only to please me. I say he is in the "library," but except for the formal dining room, what I recollect is not a set of rooms with specific functions, but an interior vista that reflects at every turn the accumulated good taste of generations, yet gives an impression of simplicity rather than of luxury.

What, I wonder, will it look like fifty years from now? What will my daughter bring to it, what impression will the vigorous taste of her generation leave on this twilit scene?

One final image presents itself; it resembles the frontispiece of a turn of the century novel. The time must be late afternoon. The air is still warm, but the sun has dipped down on the other side of the low-roofed, wide-winged house. On a terrace with a stone balustrade (was the balustrade really there, or have I invented it?), is a group of aunts and uncles, and maybe a cousin or two. Both men and women are dressed in summery clothes, but they give an impression of Edwardian elegance and formality—the men, for example, are wearing the jackets of their light suits, and collars and ties. The same formality governs their manners, and imparts to their conversation a certain Jamesian civility. Uppermost in everyone's mind is the war, the general darkening of the world, and of Hungary in particular. But these people believe, as does K., that no matter how much of the Hungary that they love is destroyed, or taken from them, its art will survive, and remain theirs. So their talk is not only of war, and approaching Nemesis, but of immortality in the form of painting and poetry and the music of Bartók and Kodály.

Sitting on the edge of the balustrade, talking to K., is a handsome, bearded uncle of about the same height as K. but much more powerfully built. He is a man of property, and an artist, a painter of landscapes, and also a sculptor in wood. He looks as though he himself had been carved by God from the trunk of one of those towering trees used by the Vikings to make their ships with the curved prows. Together, he and K. stand out from those around them, not only by virtue of their height and their generally idiosyncratic appearance, but by a shared quality of indestructible dignity.

Graham Greene, in his autobiography, *A Sort of Life*, says of the forgotten individuals in a writer's past, "If one day they find their way into a book, it should be without our connivance and so disguised that we don't recognize them when we see them again."

Now, conjuring up from my own past that summer scene on the terrace of a house that no longer exists, I realize that the bearded uncle I am consciously recalling for the first time in almost forty years found his way, disguised as God in the form of a benevolent landlord, and wholly without my connivance, into a short story called *Ocean in the Desert* that I wrote as a tribute to K. at the time of his death in California.

While K. and I were at Dombiratos, we had the feeling that time had been temporarily suspended. Back in Budapest the opposite was the case; the movement toward the vortex was gathering speed. Friends, fellow musicians, students, were disappearing from the scene one after another. K.'s master class was decimated.

These departures took place at short notice, or no notice at all. One of K.'s most gifted students, given no time to say goodbye to his parents, who lived in the country, brought his two indispensable possessions, his cello and his good winter coat, to us for safekeeping against his return. The possibility of a planned "no return" was still, despite terrible rumors, in the realm of the unthinkable. K. put the cello next to his own second instrument in a corner of our bedroom. The winter coat I packed away in what was known as "Mother's big box," a huge, zinc-lined, double-locked storage box bought twenty years earlier from the Army and Navy Stores to meet the exigencies of consular life. Mothproof and damp-proof, it would turn out to be looter-proof as well.

At the end of September, Nina's friend, Péter, was sent to a labor camp. A couple of months later István was sent to one. Paul was away serving with his regiment, and Nina drew closer to her friend Agnés. But in Agnés's family, too, the seeds of terror were germinating.

In the midst of all this, we had a stroke of good fortune—the kind that shows itself gradually, like those little bits of paper that unfold into flowers when you put them in water.

It came to us by way of K.'s ex-wife, Yoyo—a nickname acquired when she made the yo-yo fad into a personal fetish, and now part of her personality. I don't remember ever hearing her called anything else.

My relationship with Yoyo had now reached the state of détente. But from time to time détente would be rocked by tornadoes that blew up from nowhere, and I would be darkly suspected of alienating her daughters' affections—or trying to. A good deal of this was pure drama. She came from a thespian background. Her brother was a well-known actor, and before her marriage to K., she had aspired to be an actress herself. But she was hopelessly eclipsed by her mother, Mariska Vizáry, one of the most respected actresses in the National Theater, who was also famous for her cooking, and the author of a classic Hungarian cookbook.

This rather formidable old lady lived in a comfortable townhouse apartment in Pest; looked after by a housekeeper who was expected to produce meals that equaled, but never presumed to rival, those she would cook herself when not busy in the theater. But any meal served at her table, any luscious torte offered to teatime guests, was, so to speak, presented over her signature, whether or not she had actually prepared it with her own hands.

According to Yoyo, her mother's present housekeeper, Marcsa *néni*, was absolutely first class, but the two women didn't get along, and Yoyo suspected the trouble to be that Marcsa *néni* was too skilled a cook in her own right to enjoy "ghosting."

I had heard good things about Marcsa *néni* from my stepdaughters, but I had never seen her. K. and I had only once been invited to visit his ex-mother-in-law, and that was a matter of protocol—with a pinch of curiosity thrown in. As a devout Catholic, she disapproved of K.'s divorce and remarriage, but as a woman of the world she could not ignore the woman in whose home her two granddaughters would spend every Sunday—after Mass. She did, however, make me feel as if I were the envoy from a barely noticeable country presenting my credentials to an empress.

Yoyo, who was wildly unbusinesslike, still sought K.'s advice in practical matters and in everything that concerned their two daughters. (Not that he was a practical man; most of the advice he gave her came from me in the first place.) She seldom, if ever, followed it, but it was useful to her in counterbalancing pressures from her own family, particularly her overwhelming mother. But most of all, I think, she wanted to be able to say that she and K. were still good friends, despite my machinations.

Whenever she telephoned, which was often, K. would listen patiently to her never-ending list of grievances, anxieties, or paranoiac accusations, and give her compassionate reassurance. He was sometimes stern, but he never lost his temper or spoke impatiently. When he was finally able to put the phone down, he would say, "Poor Yoyo."

Less sympathetic, I would say, "What is it now?" to which his usual reply was, "Nothing new."

But one morning there was something new. Yoyo wanted to talk to me.

Since her English was as faulty as my Hungarian, we communicated in German, a language of which neither of us knew enough to be able to laugh at each other's mistakes. Now, I picked up the phone with an inward sigh. In Yoyo's case, wanting to talk to me usually meant wanting something from me.

"Good morning, Yoyo, how are you?"

"Not so good. And you?"

"Oh . . . pretty good."

"God be praised. Listen! How would you like to have one of the best cooks in Budapest? Marcsa *néni* is looking for a job. She and my mother have had enough of each other. What do you say— shall I send her up to see you?"

I said it wouldn't be any use. We couldn't afford her, and anyway, what good would it be to have one of the best cooks in Budapest when there was nothing for her to cook? What we needed was someone to go out and forage for food in the country, someone who didn't mind standing for hours in line for a couple of ounces of meat, someone who was willing to turn her hand to anything—and the girl who was working for us now met those criteria.

I was wasting my breath. When I stopped to catch it, Yoyo said, "I'll send her up to see you this afternoon—good?"

Ilona *néni*'s place had never been adequately filled. The present incumbent, a warm-hearted, willing girl named Margit was one of the nicest. Unfortunately, she was perpetually getting herself either into the pregnant state, or, more alarmingly, out of it. These were reasonable grounds for dismissal, but I had tolerated them for the sake of her many good qualities—much as one tolerates a natural propensity for the tiles in a faithful and industrious mouser—and to use them now as an excuse to get rid of her didn't seem fair. Tempted, I blamed the tempter, and thought for the thousandth time, why can't Yoyo leave us alone?

The woman who came to see me that afternoon was far from the stereotype of a cook. Neatly dressed in a good cloth coat and wearing a hat, she looked at first glance like a middle-class housewife. Divested of these insignia—which were damp from the rain, she was unclassifiable; an individual with a strong personality all her own and some striking contradictions in her physical appearance.

I judged her to be about the same age as myself, in her early forties. Her build was sturdier than mine, her body thicker—not with fat, but with hard-worked muscle—and her broad, capable hands were those of a peasant. But her face, fine-boned, with beautifully chiseled features, was so aristocratic that the ancient custom of the *droit de seigneur* sprang spontaneously to mind as a possible explanation. I would find out later that wherever the strain of nobility came from, it was more than skin deep; it affected her whole being.

Her manner was respectful but not in the least subservient. Her clear gray eyes met mine on equal terms; automatically changing the nature of our meeting; turning an interview into a woman-to-woman encounter. Small wonder, I thought, that she and the old autocrat of the theater didn't get along.

I found that with her I could speak my faulty Hungarian without self-consciousness. We understood each other remarkably well, both linguistically and otherwise. Essentially, we were both looking for the same thing; a form of friendship; a mutual bond of loyalty on which we could both rely in a time of general disintegration. I knew intuitively that I would find it with this woman; but why she, as a deeply religious Catholic, should expect to form such a bond with a family that practiced no religion at all was a mystery to me. I had never heard of the mitigating factor of invincible ignorance.

She was willing to accept whatever wages we could afford. Money, she said, was of no real value at such a time—a prophetic statement in the light of what was to come. Her only concern was that she should be free to attend Mass regularly.

Genevra settled the problem of what to do about Margit.

In the winter following the birth of their son, Károly, who, like
Paul, was a reserve officer in the Hungarian army, was called up
to serve on the staff of his regimental headquarters in Budapest.
Where, thanks to his excellent knowledge of English and to a
government that remained pro-British in spite of being at war
with England, he was assigned the job of monitoring the BBC
news broadcasts.

At first, Genevra and her baby had stayed down at Dombiratos.
But after a while, without Károly as a catalyst, life with the aunts
and uncles became irksome. And having her husband so near and
yet so far was an added frustration, not to mention a new baby on
the way. So she and little Peter joined Károly in Budapest. They
had found a place to live; now they needed a maid.

"I will take your Margit," Genevra said, "on one condition,
Mother. Next time she gets pregnant, she must either get married or get out."

She got married. I gave her as a wedding present an object she
had coveted all the time she was with me. It had been a gift to
me—one of those gifts you are happy to pass on. An ornate china
fruit bowl on a long stem upheld by cupids, it was totally useless,
and much too fragile to survive the daily bombardments for long.
But to Margit, it was beautiful, and a symbol of the respectability
she had at last attained—thanks to Genevra's ultimatum, which
had helped to galvanize a reluctant bridegroom.

But gratitude did not prevent the feckless Margit from getting
Genevra and Károly into serious trouble with the authorities at a
time when the authorities were themselves afraid of getting into
trouble with their Nazi masters.

The incident involved Károly's job of monitoring the BBC news
broadcasts.

In Budapest, during the last years of the war—that is, for as
long as there was any electric power—the ordinary household
radio set played an important role in everyone's life, and a very
special one in ours. It was invaluable as an early warning—the
only early warning—of threatened air raids and was supposed to
be tuned in to the Budapest radio station at all hours of the day
and night. For us, it offered the only available antidote to the
noxious Nazi propaganda that polluted the Hungarian airwaves
—and not by choice of the Hungarian people. The usual radio set

of those days could pick up distant signals; with only a little fiddling, we could tune in, more or less clearly, to a number of European stations, including the forbidden BBC. But not without risk. The owners of radios were known, theoretically at least, to the government—which levied a yearly tax on each set owned, making it possible to identify the culprit should the voice of the BBC be heard issuing from a given building; and there was no shortage of officious individuals to report having heard it.

At the time, we regarded the BBC as a fountain of pure Truth. In retrospect, and in the light of subsequent wars observed impartially from the outside, it is clear there is no such thing as a source of pure truth in a war. All we achieved by listening in to the BBC news was a balance between conflicting propaganda. But equally important to us, psychologically, were the mingled amusement and inspiration we derived from a daily half-hour series depicting the wartime trials and tribulations of an average lower middle-class British family in London, called, I think, *The Smiths*. Little people of immense courage, who set us a daily example of how to cope with a war and keep one's sense of humor.

Nominally controlled by the Hungarian government, the Budapest Radio was virtually controlled by the Nazis from the moment the Germans took over the city in the spring of 1944; which made tuning in to the BBC positively dangerous, and by the same token rendered Károly's monitoring job too risky to maintain.

It was at this critical point that Margit, who had not failed to notice how often her employers' radio was tuned in to a foreign station, became suspicious, and "denounced" them to the police, who thought they were spies, and took the precaution of putting them both under house arrest. A search of Károly's car produced what seemed to be damning evidence: a map of the city with all the most recently bombed areas carefully circled and a list of foreign words, which they took to be a code, penciled on the margin. In fact, it was merely a shopping list, jotted down by Genevra on the edge of the map for want of a piece of paper. The noting of the bomb sites was, of course, connected with Károly's military duties. But how could a simple policeman know that?

The house arrest lasted for two days and nights, during which they were closely guarded by two resident policemen, one of whom even watched over their conjugal slumbers. Luckily, they were ordinary Hungarian policemen, and had nothing to do with the SS. They were a good-natured pair, with a simple-minded sense of humor that Genevra made the most of, and very soon the guards and the guarded were laughing together—though the laughter, on one side at least, was exceedingly nervous.

When the suspects were cleared of suspicion, and the house arrest was lifted, the policemen seemed quite sorry to leave, but Genevra had a hard time concealing her delight at getting rid of them. Somehow she managed to bid them a friendly goodbye, and got in return good wishes and good advice. "Next time you tune in to the BBC," one of them said to her with a wink, "don't forget to turn the volume down."

After this incident, the official monitoring of the BBC newscasts was abolished, and Károly got orders for active service with his regiment.

Along with the cold hell of the Nazi takeover came the hot hell of the allied bombings, in which I learned what it felt like to be under attack by my own countrymen, and quite possibly by my own flesh and blood. This dichotomy extended, on a less personal level, to the greater part of the population, which would gladly have welcomed the assailants as allies and defenders.

By the time the long-expected big bombings began, strict rules for public procedure during air raids had been formulated, and anyone who disobeyed them was liable to arrest.

At the first howl of the sirens, all the traffic in the city was supposed to come to a halt. Trams would disgorge their passengers, and everyone out on the streets would make for the nearest public shelter as fast as possible and stay there until the "all clear."

For those at home, the radio would provide an earlier warning, allowing enough time for a little preparation—getting dressed, collecting a few belongings, turning off the gas—before taking refuge in one's own or a neighbor's cellar.

Our villa had no cellar. But the much smaller house of our next door neighbor—the same people whose chickens tempted the hunter in Shivvy, with bad results—did have one, and because it was the only one available in the immediate vicinity, its owner was appointed the Airwarden. Anyone less reassuring could not be imagined, or any house less welcoming; it's inhabitants might have been characters in a play by Eugene O'Neill. Stonyfaced, they kept themselves to themselves. There were four of them; the Airwarden, and head of the house—a petty functionary of some kind; his old mother, decrepit and ill-tempered; his melancholy, downtrodden sister, who was said to be married to a Jew, though no one had ever seen him or knew where he was; and an idiot girl, whose relationship to the others was never explained. When the weather was fine, this unfortunate creature would sit all day on the steps of the house, or wander about the yard, peering through our fence, gibbering unintelligible words, and making strange weaving motions with her hands.

The cellar, used in normal times to store fuel and winter vegetables, consisted of one medium-sized, dirt-floored compartment, and three or four much smaller ones. Cold, damp, smelly, ill-lit, and airless, it felt more like a deathtrap than a shelter.

My recollection of the first time we used it—of the first of the big Allied air raids—is still clear and sharp. I remember just how I felt. The tingle of excitement in my veins. The flutter of apprehension at the pit of my stomach. The unreality of what was happening while it was happening; and when it was over, the startling incompatibility of the heavenly day and the hellish rain that had come from the cloudless sky.

It is about ten o'clock on a brilliantly sunny morning. It must be a holiday of some sort, a religious feast day, perhaps, for Marcsa has gone to Mass, and Nina and K. are both at home when the music on the radio suddenly stops, and a voice says, "*Vigyázz! Vigyázz!*—Attention! Attention! Enemy planes approaching the frontier. Enemy planes approaching the frontier."

This is followed by a dead silence. We listen to it intently, as if we feared that the next message might not be audible.

When it comes, it comes like a shout. "Attention! Attention! Enemy planes approaching Budapest! Enemy planes approaching Budapest!"

Another dead silence. K. puts his cello into its hard traveling

case, and stuffs cigarettes, glasses, and a book into his pockets.
Nina puts on her knapsack. I grab the suitcase I keep ready
packed.

"Attention! Attention! Enemy planes attack Budapest. Enemy
planes. . . ." The last words are lost in the howl of the air-raid
sirens. We run downstairs, turn off the gas and electricity at the
main, and sprint across the garden and through the special gate
in the fence to the next-door cellar. The Airwarden is standing at
the top of the stairs, counting heads. He is displeased with us. We
haven't been prompt enough—Mr. and Mrs. A. came over immediately after the second warning. And where is Marcsa *néni*?

The cellar is packed. There is nowhere for the men to sit down,
and the ceiling is so low that tall men, like K., risk bumping their
heads. Two hard benches set against the walls are occupied by the
women and children. One woman tells her little girl to get up and
give the professor her seat. K. refuses it with a smile—though I'm
sure he would love to sit down. His legs have been hurting him
lately; he has to do so much walking every day now that the buses
have stopped running, and the trams are so crowded that it's next
to impossible for a man carrying a cello, and God knows what
else, to board one. Mrs. A. makes room beside her for me. "There's
room for Nina, too," she says, "you are both so thin." But Nina
prefers to stand at the bottom of the stairs—as close as she can get
to the only exit from this potential grave.

The controlled wail of the sirens dies away, and an eerie stillness takes its place—a silence so heavy it makes me feel buried
alive.

Suddenly, Nina runs up the stairs. I go after her. "Nina! Nina!
What is it?" "Nothing. I just need some air, that's all." "But
Nina . . . ! Oh, all right, but only for a second."

We stand on the threshold, half in and half out of the open door,
taking deep breaths of the still, sweet air. Into its stillness comes a
faint sound, like bees swarming. It comes from what looks like a
flock of silver-gray geese flying high overhead in perfect V-
shaped formation and at a tremendous speed. I gaze up at them—
my mind refuses to recognize them for what they are. K's voice,
unusually stern, brings me to my senses. "Come in at once," he
says, "and you too, Nina." It's the first time he has ever given
either of us an order.

Nina says, "It's not any safer down there than it is up here." She is probably right. But bombs are not the only danger for me and Nina. We are natural targets for those who hope to keep themselves out of trouble by "denouncing" other people.

We have barely got to the bottom of the stairs when pandemonium breaks out above and around us; there are antiaircraft guns within fifty yards of us, and the peculiar acoustics of the hill make every exploding bomb sound as if it were on our own doorstep. The uproar increases the sense of danger; in fact, it is more unnerving than the danger itself. Yet... only a short while back, I found the silence equally unnerving. Are there normal levels of sound and silence at which, like the normal temperature of the body, they go unnoticed? And if so, is that an advantage or a disadvantage? I would like to ask Nina what she thinks, but there's too much noise; we wouldn't be able to hear one another speak.

When we emerge once more into the sunlight, about forty-five minutes later, we are pleased but amazed to find our villa, and all the surrounding villas, intact. Down by the river are clouds of dust and smoke, and a dull red glow hangs over the island of Csepel, where most of the factories are.

In retrospect, I realize that this distancing of my initiatory experience was a grace. It depersonalized what could well have been a devastating psychological blow, splitting me in two emotionally, even if I survived it physically.

Constant repetition eventually blunted some of the nervous excitement of the big bombing raids, even though they became more and more savagely and indiscriminately destructive the closer we got to the vortex.

But one of these intensive attacks contained for me a revelation of sorts; a new perception of beauty as something that exists on its own, independent of good and evil.

The occasion was the first time that I was caught out of doors by a major night bombing, and what's more, on the open summit of our hill, with a wide view over the targeted city. It was a clear night, with stars but no moon—an ideal night for a raid. K. and I were on our way home from a friend's house when the sirens went off, and within a few seconds the serene starlight that faintly outlined the dark masses of Buda and Pest and the curve of the river between them, was violently overpowered by a dazzling burst of terrestial fireworks—rockets, searchlights, flares, and strange, blue-white suns called Stalin candles.

The magnificence of the scene overcame fear, and I stopped, with the destroyers already flying overhead, and made a reluctant K. stop with me, to marvel at the fantastic visual beauty of the prologue to destruction.

Its epilogue was just as infernally beautiful. When we emerged more than an hour later from the cellar, which we had reached just as the bombs began to fall, the whole city seemed to be aflame. Some of the fires were close enough for their heat to be felt, and the grain spouting high in the air from a burning granary down by the river fell back like a fiery hail on the roof of our house—still miraculously untouched.

My description of that raid in my first novel was criticized as too lyrical—which it was—and my young heroine's reaction as unbelievable (*No one stops in the path of an oncoming tornado to admire its awesomeness!*). This puzzled me, for I hadn't invented it. I had yet to learn how much more difficult it is for a writer to make a bizarre truth believable than a bizarre fiction.

One other air-raid night is imprinted on my memory like a poem—an elegy.

In the spring of 1944, when it was still possible to scrape together from various sources—most of them illegal—enough food to entertain a few guests, K. and I were invited to dinner by some very old friends of his who lived in the beautiful district of Buda poetically named *Hüvösvölgy*—Cool Valley. Their villa was at the far end of it, and several miles distant from the Rózsadomb.

The guest of honor was the old Countess Hubay, widow of the Hungarian violinist, Jenö Hubay.

As a brilliant figure in the musical life of Hungary, Jenö Hubay had been closely bound up with K.'s own musical life from its beginnings, and also with that of another invited guest, K.'s younger colleague and good friend, the violinist Ede Zathurezcky, who came to pick us up in his car. This was a treat in itself. There had never been very many private cars on the streets of Budapest, and at this stage of the war they were a rarity, soon to disappear altogether—either commandeered by the military or inoperable for lack of gasoline. As the present director of the Lizst Ferenc Academy, Zathurezcky was one of the lucky few to still have the use of a car, and a small weekly ration of gas for "official purposes." But it wasn't enough to take him to and from the academy every day, so he saved it up for emergencies, or special occasions like this one, and took a tram to the academy—as long as there were any trams running.

In the car with us was another musician guest; the pianist, György Faragó, a young prodigy still in his twenties, for whom Jenö Hubay was more a legend than a memory. A legend, however, that he, along with K., Zathurezcky, and many others, helped the old Countess to nourish and perpetuate. Thanks to them, the Hubay palace, the family's dignified town house in Buda, where the master's study was enshrined, was no silent mausoleum, but echoed with living music—as it had during his lifetime. After his death, in 1937, his widow established an ongoing series of chamber concerts in the music room of the palace, at which most of the musicians among whom he had lived and worked performed in his memory.

Invitations to these reverential Sunday afternoon concerts, with their top-flight performing artists and the cream of Budapest society sitting on little gilt chairs, Royalty in the front row, were eagerly sought after. They had all the prestige and exclusiveness of similar, if more grandiose, events in my past . . . a musicale in the Royal Palace at Bucharest with Queen Marie of Rumania welcoming her guests in a garment of flame-colored chiffon that billowed around her majestic form like the tongues of magical fire around Brünnhilde . . . a glittering reception in a Venetian palazzo, with royal guests of honor and the Don Cossack choir singing in the courtyard after supper . . . but with one important difference: the dual nature of their elitism, which my altered perspective made very clear to me. Countess Hubay was an aristocrat in her own right; but as the widow and celebrant of a man who belonged only to the aristocracy of art, she could not very well set a higher value on quarterings than on artistry. So she placed them both on the same exalted level—at least as far as these memorial concerts were concerned.

Royalty, however, had its own unassailable position at the top.

A position occupied with grace by the genial Archduke Charles and his beautiful, perpetually pregnant duchess, Anna, who endeared herself to K. by never allowing her pregnancy, however advanced, to keep her away from a concert. But sometimes a graceless female relative came with her instead of the archduke, and then the unassailability of royalty presented a problem. This unattractive member of the Hapsburg family had only one passion—food. Nothing was safe from her lust for food. If the petits fours destined for the reception after a concert were not kept out of sight, she would sneak out while the audience was applauding and devour whole traysful of them in advance, and nobody dared say a word.

There were endless funny stories going the rounds about this greedy duchess and the consternation she caused both in palaces and pastry shops—where her depredations would be charged to the archducal account, which took its time over paying. I laughed with everyone else at these often cruel jokes. But their victim would have the last laugh.

Now, on the way to the little party in honor of Countess Hubay, the three musicians, K., Zathurezcky, and Faragó, talked only of food, and I joined them in dreaming up impossible delicacies and in making extravagant guesses about what there would be for dinner. An ironic indication of how defenseless we were against the subtle assaults of slow starvation. We had reached the stage of prolonged undernourishment when the body is chronically hungry, and the mind obsessively preoccupied with food and how to get it.

All the necessities of life, from food to fuel and soap to shoes, were rationed. But being entitled to them was one thing, and actually getting them was another. Coupons piled up unredeemed as supplies dwindled, until finally there was nothing left to be given out, and the people went unwashed, unshod, cold, and in tatters—both literally and figuratively—to banquet on the flesh of Red Army horses left dead in the streets after a day's fighting.

In the months leading up to this total breakdown in survival conditions, a few basic items of food were obtainable from the peasants who produced them and were wily enough to outwit nosy officialdom. But trips to the country were difficult and dangerous. The slow and unpunctual trains were packed to over-flowing, and the overflow had to ride on the roof, exposed to whatever kind of rain might fall from the treacherous skies. Marcsa *néni* undertook several such expeditions to get food for us from her village. But what she brought back was too precious to eat there and then; it had to be salted away for the leaner times that we knew were bound to come—though the grim reality of them was beyond our imagining.

As an example of memory's capriciousness, despite all our talk in the car about what we hoped to be given for dinner (K., I remember, was wishing for roast goose, and Zathurezcky for Wiener schnitzel), I have not the slightest recollection of what was actually served. I can see the table and the people sitting around it, but no food. It is like a dinner party in a play, where the actors merely go through the motions of eating and drinking.

I can only suppose that the meal was so satisfying that, like anything else that temporarily stills a bodily craving, it set mind and memory free to deal with other things more worthy of remembrance. They were many. But they all add up to the single, inevitable image of light juxtaposed with darkness, and all the more brilliant on that account.

Most of the other guests are already there when we arrive, and the company—about a dozen people including ourselves—is dominated by the striking personalities of two very different women.

One is, of course, the guest of honor, old Countess Hubay. Small, slender, simply dressed in black with touches of white at neck and wrists, with a pleasant, intelligent face, but no claim to past or present beauty, she is not physically imposing. Nor does she monopolize the conversation. But she has that nebulous quality, distinction. And she manages quietly to convey the impression of being above the rest of us; of being, as the widow of a great artist, at least half way up Parnassus.

The other, much younger woman, is an artist in her own right; the brilliant and beautiful actress, Gizi Bajor.

Gizi is worried because her husband, a well-known physician, is late. She professes to be concerned only on account of her hostess, who insists on waiting dinner for him. But I see a deeper anxiety in her eyes. I have never met her husband, or seen them together, but I am sure that she feels the same way about him as I do about K., and my heart warms to her.

When the doctor finally phones to say that he is unavoidably detained at his clinic, and will join the party later in the evening, his wife's enormous relief goes unnoticed in the general delight of the famished company at not having to wait any longer for their dinner.

When we are all seated at the table, except for our host, who remains standing at the head of it, there is a funny little hush, as if a cue had been given for a moment of silent prayer. Then our host says, his tone half-serious, half-joking, "Before I sit down, I think I had better ask if anyone feels uneasy about being thirteen at table."

Everyone laughs and begs him to sit down. But the laughter is uneasy, and I think how irrational it is to be upset by a mere superstition when we face quite calmly the daily danger of being wiped out by a bomb. Do we all have the same delusion—of the charmed life that can only be destroyed by supernatural decree? Is that the secret behind all bravery in the face of danger?

I catch a little ironical smile on the pale lips of the old countess, as if she finds any uneasiness on the part of the other guests presumptuous, as well as ridiculous, in view of *her* presence at the table.

Sitting next to her is the youngest person present; the golden boy, György Faragó, or Györy, as his friends call him. Women of all ages like Györy, and the Countess Hubay is no exception. She says something to him in a low voice. He smiles, then frowns and shakes his head. Perhaps she is wittily asserting her claim to be Death's first choice. And embarrassing him; as the old always do embarrass the young when they speak of death.

After dinner there is music. A spontaneous, unrehearsed tribute to the dead violinist, whose spirit seems to be hovering over the musicians, telling them what to play—pieces of his own composition, pieces he frequently performed, pieces he particularly loved—and making Zathureczky nervous. ("I felt," he confesses to us later, "as if the old man were there at my elbow, watching every note—and criticizing.")

Across the room from me, Gizi and the countess are sitting close enough to one another to be, so to speak, in the same frame, and the picture they compose suggests a Victorian painting entitled *Full Bloom and Withering*. The juxtaposition of Gizi's glowing beauty and the old lady's faded parchment is almost obscene—an unintentional effect often produced by the homilies of Victorian painters. But in terms of color and composition the double portrait is charming, and fits in with the melancholy yet voluptuous music of the Chopin nocturne that Györy is playing.

Now, in the arch of the doorway behind the two women, Gizi's husband appears and stands quietly listening with his eyes on his wife's graceful shoulders and bent head. As the last notes of the nocturne are dying away, he goes quietly to her and, without saying a word, takes her hand and holds it in his for a long moment, so electric with love that the sweet shock of it must surely be felt by everyone in the room, as it is by me.

Now the party breaks up and regroups. The doctor is asked "Have you eaten?"—a question that eventually becomes a regular form of greeting—and the countess says it is time for her to go home. Some of the other guests leave with her, and the circle becomes more intimate. Wine is served. Glass in hand, Zathureczky sits down beside me and K.

"I played badly tonight. Especially the Tartini. . . . Tell me Jenökém, was it very bad?"

K. smiles. He has known Zathureczky for a long time. "You played two wrong notes," he says. "Aside from that, it was excellent."

"*Two* wrong notes? How is it possible...? But otherwise it was all right, *hein*?"

"You *know* it was," K. says.

Zathurezcky's basic insecurity affects every aspect of his life. He confides in me, after a fashion; that is, he will seek me out at a party, just as he seeks K. out after a concert in search of reassurance, to tell me that he is depressed, or unwell, or beset by unspecified problems regarding his love life. Privately, I am convinced that he has only one problem—a doting mama. *Doting. Domineering. Demanding.* These words are only too often synonymous. So whenever I get an opportunity, I do my best to bolster the defenses of this unsuspecting victim of too much maternal love. He says, with an air of mild surprise, "After talking with you, dear Madame de Kerpely, I always feel so much better!"

Now he and K. start discussing the loss of all their advanced students either to the army or some other form of slave labor, and I wonder how Györy, who is still so young, has managed to escape any sort of conscription. But such questions are better left unasked.

After greeting Gizi's husband, and saying goodbye to the countess, Györy has drifted back to his seat at the piano, as if that were his natural place, his home, his safety. He is rumored to be having an affair with a charming and sophisticated woman rather older than himself. But the look on his face as his hands wander lovingly over the keyboard, improvising, or playing isolated phrases of some piece that he is in the process of memorizing, betrays a passion more profound than the love of women and a dangerous rival for any woman who loves him, because it is essentially narcissistic—though I don't think Györy is conscious of that; he is too genuinely modest. He has never allowed his early success, his winning of an international piano competition while still in his teens, to go to his head; he knows how much he can still improve, which is why K. likes him and believes in his future. Yet there are moments when Györy's youthful face seems as drawn and weary as that of an old man whose future is already behind him.

As though he senses that I am observing him, he looks up at me and asks, "What shall I play? What would you like to hear?"

My answer, like so many others of greater importance, is lost in the howl of sirens. They take us by surprise, and our hostess apologizes for having turned off the radio.

"Never mind that," says our host, "the question is now, do we or don't we go down to the cellar? Actually, I think we are just as safe here on the ground floor as we would be a few steps down—and much more comfortable."

We all agree with that. But even if we didn't, we would no more admit it than we would have admitted to being uneasy at sitting thirteen at table.

The dying away of the sirens is succeeded by the usual eerie silence, which falls on the room and everyone in it like a spell.

Only Györy is able to break it. Still sitting at the piano, his question to me unanswered, he decides for himself what to play. And his furious attack on Chopin's *Revolutionary étude* coincides with the first shattering burst of antiaircraft fire.

Explosion follows explosion. The lights go out. Györy goes on playing in the dark. His hands leap from one étude to another, to a polonaise, to the preludes, to the scherzos, and on, with scarcely a pause, to the Beethoven sonatas—the *Appassionata*, the *Moonlight*, the *Waldstein*. ... Everything Györy has ever learned comes rushing back to him now as though for one great last performance, and flows through his passionate fingertips to the loving, responsive keys.

The raid is a long one. The planes must have come in successive waves. It is three o'clock in the morning when the all-clear finally sounds. Now candles are lighted, and Györy, looking half-dazed, staggers from the piano to a sofa and lies down, his face pale and covered with sweat.

Our host opens a bottle of brandy, and coffee is brought in from the kitchen. Perked up, K. and I and Zathurezcky decide to go home while the going is still good. Györy is persuaded to remain where he is.

It is the darkest hour of a very dark night, with no moon or stars to replace the extinguished street lamps. We are in a heavily wooded valley, from which nothing can be seen of the damage done by the bombing. Fearful of being held up by fires or rubble on the main *Körút*, Zathurezcky takes unfrequented back roads, all pitch dark, and illumined for only a few feet ahead by the lights of the car, which the wartime regulations have shaded and dimmed almost out of existence.

I have no idea where we are when the air-raid sirens go off again—and I doubt that Zathurezcky knows either. He mutters one of those complicated Hungarian oaths that have to do with the Mother of God. K.'s one-word expletive is only mildly blasphemous by comparison. I say simply, "Hell!" Which Zathurezcky seems to find very funny, coming from me.

"Well," he says, "what do you think—shall we stop as we are supposed to do, and sit in a ditch until the all-clear? Or shall we go on and hope for the best?"

We none of us want to spend the next hour sitting in a ditch. So Zathurezcky switches the lights off—mandatory during an air raid—and we go on in a darkness so thick it is like a blindfold.

The side of the road seems to have a magnetic attraction for Zathurezcky —or for his car, which seems to be in control of itself. We zigzag along for about a mile, missing hedges and tree trunks by inches, and end up sitting out the raid in the car in a ditch.

There is an epilogue to that evening's experience. There is also a footnote.

Of the thirteen persons who sat down together at the dinner table that night, those Death chose to take before their time were the two whose stars were in the ascendant: Győry and Gizi.

A few months after the Germans took control of the city, Győry disappeared. We were told in confidence by one of his close friends that he had been picked up by the Gestapo and taken to their headquarters for questioning. About what? No one knew. The Gestapo headquarters were set up in a couple of commandeered villas on the Svábhegy, one of which, I discovered later, was the same beautiful villa whose inaccessibility had, luckily, kept us from leasing it when we were, again luckily, forced to leave the Gellért Hill.

The next thing we heard was that Győry was sick, and then, in a lowered voice, that during the questioning by the Gestapo he had been severely beaten. Where was he now—at home? But that was a question we should have known better than to ask. Wherever he was, he did not stay there for long. Within a few days, he was in his grave.

The story of Gizi's death, and that of her husband, reached me in a series of echoes relayed by many different voices. A "love-death," with all the dark grandeur of Greek tragedy, it has not displaced my last, vivid image of her at the shining peak of her life. It has, rather, by giving it an added dimension, completed it.

And now for the footnote. After the war, K. and I went to see an excellent Russian movie called *The Cranes Are Flying*. Its climax was a scene in an attic studio, in some Russian city, of a young musician playing the piano all through an air raid. As we left the cinema, K. said, "Didn't that remind you of the night when poor Győry played for us?" The scene in the movie was more dramatic, and more immediately linked with death, than the actual experience we both remembered. But in essence, it was the same. A sobering reminder that everything we live through has already been lived through by somebody else.

The closer we got to the inevitable Nazi takeover, the more distrustful I became of everyone but our closest friends and family. As the evil power of the *Nyilas*—the Hungarian Nazi party—increased, so did the danger of betraying one's self by a careless word or action, and of being denounced by others in the hope of saving their own skins.

It was in this atmosphere of general suspicion that K. was given a proof of trust that was both gratifying and disturbing.

One day, when he came home from a quartet rehearsal, he was in a peculiar mood. I knew that something had happened, from the quality of his silence and the number of cigarettes he smoked, one after another.

I said, "Did anything bad happen?"

"Not exactly. I ran into an old school friend of mine just as I was leaving the academy—in fact, I think he was waiting for me."

"Who was it?"

"That funny Catholic priest I told you about—the one who's always getting into trouble of some sort."

"What did he want?"

"He wants us to join the underground. He wants to use our villa as one of a chain of hideaways for Allied prisoners of war who are being helped to escape by way of Hungary."

"What did you say?"

"I said I would talk it over with you."

I saw in his eyes an almost boyish eagerness, which astounded me.

"You *want* to do it, don't you?"

"Don't *you*?"

I said, "Oh my God," or something like that, and began to cry. I hardly ever cried, and it shocked K. He put his arms around me and kissed me and said, "Don't cry, Tercsikém. Of course, we won't do it if you don't want to."

"That's what's so awful," I said. "I *do* want to, but I think it would be sheer insanity. You know we can't trust the A.'s... or the

Airwarden—they both know exactly who comes to see us, and when, and any stranger would arouse suspicion. And there are other people—Sybil, for instance; she's always dropping in, and she's sharp, she'd soon smell a rat."

"But Sybil's English!"

"She's a Nazi just the same. And as for her husband, I wouldn't trust him further than I could throw him."

I was all the more vehement in my arguments against taking what really was an appalling risk that might well land us in front of a firing squad, because I had to justify in myself what I recognized as exactly the same primitive instinct for self-preservation that I had seen destroy all sense of honor in others.

Neither K. nor I slept much that night. In the morning K. said, "You are right—we are not in a position to do it. . . ."

But I could see how much he disliked the idea of telling that to his friend, who, whatever else he might be—and he had the reputation of being not only a firebrand but a rascal, too, whose cassock concealed a multitude of sins—was a brave man and a true patriot, and believed K. to be the same.

I took a deep breath, and said, "Don't refuse him. Just tell him exactly how we are placed and leave the decision up to him."

He decided against using our villa—not out of concern for our safety, but for that of the escapees. It was a sensible decision, and it let us off the hook. But it left us both with a sense of regret as well as relief; a sense of having failed, somehow, to pass a test.

That winter, the shortage of fuel obliged us to close up the rooms on the main floor and live entirely in the three smaller rooms above them, which could be kept reasonably warm with one small iron stove set in the middle room. Only Marcsa *néni* slept downstairs, next to the kitchen, where she could draw some warmth from the wood-burning range. (We had a gas stove, but the gas, though not officially rationed, came on only sporadically, and then at very low pressure.)

And that winter, our little dog, Shivvy, driven by hunger, committed the crime that cost him his life. He managed to clamber over our ten-foot fence, get inside the wire enclosure of the Airwarden's hen roost, and kill five of the six chickens that constituted the family's insurance against starvation. They were irreplaceable and worth their weight in gold, which made mone-

tary compensation out of the question. All we could do to appease
the enraged Airwarden (his sister was more understanding, but
he never listened to her), was to have poor Shivvy put to sleep
before he did any more damage. Not that he would have lived
very long anyway; in a besieged city, the dogs are the first to die.

<h1 style="text-align:center">III</h1>

Although K. came from a large family, only one of his siblings,
a widowed sister with two unmarried daughters and very little
money, lived in Budapest. Having observed at close quarters her
brother's protracted unhappiness with the tempestuous Yoyo—
who had almost succeeded in ruining his career as an artist—she
strongly approved of his divorce and thought that his marriage to
me was the best thing that had ever happened to him. An attitude
that endeared her to me.

Her first name was Metty, and her younger daughter was named
Metty after her. Mother and daughter were known as Big Metty
and Little Metty respectively, and, with sublime disregard for
the elder daughter, whose name was Gili, the family was referred
to collectively as The Mettys.

The Mettys inhabited a modest apartment in an unfashionable
district in Pest. All three worked for their living; the mother in
the home, and the two girls in offices. The elder, Gili, was in her
middle twenties; quiet, unassuming, and unlikely ever to find a
husband—given the absence of a dowry and no particular beauty
or talent to make up for it. She was one of those people who truly
deserve to be happy, yet who often get passed over by happiness
because they are too self-effacing.

Her younger sister, Little Metty, then about nineteen years old,
was equally self-effacing, but she happened to be a beauty; a true
Hungarian beauty, with slanting doe eyes under finely arched
black brows, high cheekbones, a dazzlingly sweet smile, and a
downy ripe peach complexion, and had her modest bearing been
assumed it might well have enhanced these charms, instead of
subtly veiling them. There was something sad about this alliance
of unusual physical beauty and sweetness of nature with extreme
self-deprecation. And sadder still, in K.'s opinion and mine, was
this sensitive creature's tacit engagement to marry a man who

saw in her self-effacement, her lack of self-confidence, one of the most essential qualities of a "good wife." As a middle-aged civil servant, he offered her a certain amount of material security, but not self-fulfillment. Unlikely ever to rise above the level of his own mediocrity, he would keep her tied down to it with him. But her mother said, "She could do worse—at least he will be kind to her."

In the last, rumor-laden months before the Nazi takeover, this man—I shall call him Árpád—proved useful as a barometer of the changeable political climate. Like many trusted underlings, Árpád knew a great deal more about what was going on than his superiors actually told him; and about them, and the measure of their resistance or connivance. And what he knew he told Little Metty, who passed it on to her mother, who passed it on to us.

One morning in March, one of those delirious early spring mornings in Buda, when the sun is hot, the wind is cold, and the air smells of hope and melting snow and the first almond blossom, Big Metty called up just as K. was leaving for his daily quartet rehearsal. I heard him say, "*Na*, what is it?"

Her reply was brief.

K. said, "Good. Good. Thank you. See you soon."

He put the phone down rather slowly. "Árpád says that bad weather is on the way and advises us not to go out. But if everyone turns up for rehearsal except me, Papa will be furious."

Papa was our nickname for Imre Waldbauer.

"Don't worry, he will have heard the same forecast by now."

Bad weather was on the way all right—in fact, it was there already; it had sneaked up on us during the night in the form of SS men concealed in river barges. Within a couple of hours of Metty's call, the Government Ministries had all been "peacefully" taken over at gun point, and the Hungarian people had been robbed of what little independence they had left.

That night, I found out what the "voice of doom" sounds like. I lay awake listening to it, hour after hour after hour. The voice of doom is the rumble of enemy tanks through the streets of your home town.

Now, Hungarian passivity—the last refuge of the powerless— was replaced by the swift and ruthless action of unchallenged Nazi power; terrible to watch, because of its victims' blindness;

their failure, or their refusal, to see the death's head behind the civilized mask.

Some such half-naive, half-willful blindness regarding the Nazi's true nature afflicted my English friend, Sybil D.—the young woman whose frequent visits combined with her pro-German sentiments had represented a threat when the question of our sheltering Allied escapees had come up. In Nina's diary for 1944, some pages of which have survived, she refers to Sybil D. as a "lonely, lost, Teutonically biased Englishwoman of good breeding. . . ."

Lonely and lost Sybil certainly was, which was why we accepted her—up to a point. But she was not a victim of the Nazi takeover. She was, rather, a beneficiary of it—as a result of her husband's opportunism. He did not hope, as his wife plaintively did, that the Germans would win the war. He didn't much care who won it, so long as he didn't lose it. In Nina's diary entry for November 30—the day on which she and I and K. celebrated our three birthdays, which all occurred within the same week—she says:

The D.s, to whom we haven't been very nice because of their German connections, were jolly sweet. They brought us all presents, stuff for dresses, cigarettes, and coffee—enough for two cups each.

And we, God forgive us, drank the coffee, smoked the cigarettes, and made up the fabric into dresses—knowing perfectly well where it all came from. So much for principles.

We had kept the D.'s at a distance ever since the Nazi takeover, when they had made a rather underhanded attempt to draw us into their "Teutonic" circle. Sybil had asked us in for a cup of real coffee, given her by some "good friends." They turned out to be two high-ranking German army officers, who had been invited to drink it with us.

Their presence in Sybil's living room took us by surprise, and threw me into a panic. My inward recoil from the hands extended to me by these smiling enemies was so strong that I thought they could not fail to notice it—especially as the hand I forced myself to extend to them was limp and cold and fugitive as a piece of seaweed—but if they did, they did not show it. K. became suddenly formal; matching their stiff little bows with an even stiffer little bow of his own, and keeping his hands at his sides as if that was the proper thing to do.

The two officers were genial and hearty, but their conversation made me uncomfortable, and I had a feeling that it was designed to do just that. They told disrespectful jokes about Hitler, and scandalous ones about Göring, at which it was risky to laugh and equally risky not to. K. listened with a faint, noncommittal smile and said nothing—silence was so natural to him that he could preserve it without giving offense, even when it was, in fact, hostile. But I was the one who was being tested. As an Englishwoman, I was more vulnerable than K. My reaction to these German officers, and their slyly provocative remarks, could either keep me out of, or put me into, an internment camp, and I was desperately searching my mind for suitable ambiguities when, to my surprise and relief, K. broke his silence. "I understand," he said, "that your führer is a great lover of music."

"But of course! Music is the language of the gods, *nicht wahr?*"

Although the "language of the gods" was to prove a useful Esperanto with more than one foreign invader, as a subject of conversation its power to stave off the unpleasant was limited; and it was not very long before this particular pair of music-loving monsters were speaking the language of devils.

It appeared that one of them, a staff colonel, was in charge of a special operation designed to, as he put it, "Rid Buda of its vermin."

This appalling phrase, with its unmistakable meaning, turned my stomach, an effect that must have been equally unmistakable, for the screw was turned a bit further. Looking straight at me with his cold blue eyes, the colonel said, "You can rest assured, *Gnadige frau*, that this work will be carried out with the utmost speed and efficiency. In a few weeks, this beautiful hill of yours will smell only of the roses that give it its name."

The speed and efficiency with which the German Nazis carried out their terrible work of eliminating the Budapest Jews is now history. And for most people, history is something that happened to somebody else, and long enough ago to be contemplated with a certain amount of detachment. But for those who, like me, were there when this particular infamy was happening, trapped in the inglorious position of impotent witnesses, it remains embedded in the soul; a permanent wound, unhealable because unforgivable.

Absolute power simplifies crime. The step-by-step process of genocide in the city of Budapest was absurdly simple, and the executioner's men were disarmingly polite.

The elderly Jewish couple who had lived all their married life in the villa across the road from ours, were politely informed that their home had been commandeered by the military, but that they would be comfortably relocated in Pest for as long as it should be necessary. True, they were only allowed to take with them what they could load on a small handcart, but their household possessions were inventoried, and the inventory was countersigned by the officer in charge, who assured them that no harm would come either to their things or their home—provided, of course, that it wasn't destroyed by a bomb. Well . . . that was a risk we all had to face. . . . What they worried about was their garden, with some recently planted rose trees that needed regular watering. I promised to take care of that for them—if possible—and we watched them go slowly down the road, pushing their pathetic little handcart, with no expectation of ever seeing them again.

"Relocation" was stage one of the well-organized journey toward annihilation. It meant being packed—often as many as fifteen or sixteen persons to one small room—into clusters of yellow-starred houses; improvised ghettos in which they could be kept under control, and easily rounded up for their eventual transportation to the death camps. In the meantime, every effort was made to induce death on site, so to speak, either from overcrowding, undernourishment, or unattended illness. To this end, ukases were issued almost daily denying Jews one basic right after another—even the right to a daily ration of whatever food was available, and the right to leave the ghetto to seek for other sustenance, or for needed medication.

Yet, which seemed illogical, non-Jews were allowed to visit their Jewish friends in the starred houses, if they cared to take the risk, and even to bring them food. It was the sort of risk that Nina took on principle—she would, for instance, cross a street for the express purpose of speaking with a yellow-starred acquaintance, when most people did the reverse. So when she heard that her friend Agnés had been moved from her beautiful family home to a starred house, she went to see her there and found her, together with her nearest female relatives who had been relocated with her, grieving, not for their own miserable condition, but for their menfolk. Before the relocation, Agnés's father and his four brothers had been taken away by the Gestapo, imprisoned, interrogated, beaten up, and finally, when the desired information was not forthcoming, shot.

But the first member of our family to see the unmasked face of horror with her own eyes was not Nina, who had mentally armed herself against shock before entering the ghetto, but my still very vulnerable stepdaughter, Mária. And it shattered her. She could hardly bring herself to speak of it even to her father, her beloved *Apuka*, whom she loved and trusted more than anyone else in the world. But, haltingly, it came out. On her way to work, rather earlier in the morning than usual, she was traversing the fringes of the old Jewish quarter around the synagogue, a ghetto in the traditional sense of the word; which was now packed to bursting point with relocated Jews from all over the city, when from one of its tortuous streets emerged a large, open, horse-drawn cart, or farm wagon, piled high with what she thought, at first glance, were the carcasses of animals. But they were not animals. They were human bodies. Dead, naked, people . . . "Oh *Apuka* . . . *Apuka* . . ."

Later in the year, she saw something else on her way to work one morning; five hanged men, dangling from the branches of the trees on the *Szabadság tér*—Freedom Square. "I asked a policeman who they were, what crime they had committed, and he said, *They were Communists.*"

If I have said very little thus far about my stepdaughters, it is not because they were unimportant to me, but because they lived with their mother; which made their full integration into our family life impossible for as long as they were young enough to be under her capricious and paranoiac authority.

Later, when they were old enough to go their own way, the conditions of war drove a wedge of physical danger between their household in Pest and ours in Buda, and increased the emotional pressure put on them by their mother. With the start of the big bombings, Yoyo had ample justification for keeping the girls as close to home as possible, and by the fall of 1944, crossing the river, whether over the mined bridges, or on board the exposed, slow-moving pontoon ferry, was an extremely hazardous undertaking: and by mid-winter, the blowing up of the bridges had effectively cut off civilian communication between Buda and Pest for months to come.

But in 1945, after the siege, Mária will make her way across the river and over the mountains of rubble to what remained of our villa, and find a home there. At which point she, and her sister, too, will take their proper places in this story as my "Hungarian family."

In the course of the cruel, Nazi-dominated summer and early fall of 1944, the aspect of time and events changed from lineal and serial to circular and simultaneous. We were swirling around on the edge of the vortex, drawn closer and closer to its core with every centripetal revolution. And the resulting distortion of our perceptions makes it difficult now to establish the chronology of what happened to us and to those around us, during that period.

We still clung to the illusion that we were at least partially in control of our destiny. But Károly's life, and with it, of course. Genevra's, was profoundly affected by two events over which he had no control whatever. As I mentioned earlier, when Károly's staff job of radio monitoring was abolished, he was reassigned for active service with his regiment. But while he was in training, he became seriously ill, and was found to be suffering from a bone disease that made active service, and, for the time being, any military service out of the question. The disease was eventually cured, but by disabling him when it did, it almost certainly saved his life. The other event irrevocably changed it. In the third week of August, he, Genevra, and their two children (a daughter, Elizabeth, had been born in January of the same year) went by train to Dombiratos, with the idea of celebrating little Peter's second birthday in the house in which he was born, on the country estate that, under other circumstances, would eventually have been his. They had planned to stay for a couple of weeks, but they had to leave precipitately after only two days, when the Russians crossed the nearby Rumanian border and advanced on Dombiratos. The short train journey back to Budapest turned into a fourteen-hour nightmare, with the line being constantly bombed. They never saw Dombiratos again. It became a battlefield. The old house was burned to the ground during the fighting, and after the war the land was confiscated by the government.

This left them rootless. They had no home of their own in the city, and at the moment, not even a rented apartment of their own; they were living, at uncomfortably close quarters for all concerned, in the home of a friend to whose half-Jewish wife their presence afforded some slight protection. This was a case of genuine mutual assistance between friends. On a less commendable level, the ubiquitous chameleons were once more changing color. As it became clear that the Germans were losing the war, British connections were once again regarded as an asset, and when, early in November, Nina was issued an official "letter of protection" by the Swiss consulate (where the interests of British subjects were being taken care of by a beleaguered lady named Miss Berényi), our stock went up to the point where perfect strangers were willing to take us in if we had to leave the Rózsadomb—something that I was determined not to do unless we were officially evacuated.

In October, when the Germans were preparing to defend Budapest against the advancing Russians, and a whiff of defeat was already perceptible through the smoke of Nazi propaganda, we had an odd, and oddly disturbing encounter that haunts me still, like a never finished tale.

I was working in the vegetable garden I had made out of the front lawn, gathering in the last greenish tomatoes, and digging up the beets, when someone hailed me from the gate. It was a man I had never seen before, and didn't much like the look of—he was altogether too well-clad and well-shod. At this stage of the war, only black marketeers or agents of the Gestapo went around looking like that; honest people were shabby and down at heel.

The man asked me in Hungarian whether "the professor" was at home. Wary, I replied in Hungarian that I really didn't know, but I would find out.

"Tell him," the man said, "that an old friend of his wants to see him," and gave me a name that I have irretrievably forgotten, but rather than call him Mr. X., I shall christen him *Jancsi.*

Leaving him standing outside the locked gate, I went into the house to give K. his message. K. repeated his name twice—amazed and incredulous. "Jancsi X.! Is it possible? I haven't seen him or heard of him for more than thirty years!"

I watched from the window while K. went down to the gate. As soon as he appeared, the man waiting outside cried, "*Servus,* Jënokém!"

K.'s "*Servus,* Jancsi!" was less enthusiastic; a little wary, but not unwelcoming. He unlocked the gate, and the man immediately embraced him as if he were a long-lost brother, and once again, K.'s response was reserved. He brought the visitor into the house and introduced him to me as an old schoolmate. He spoke perfect English, with a BBC accent, and except for an occasional lapse into Hungarian between the two men, our conversation was carried on in English. It was a peculiar, almost wholly one-sided conversation; consisting of a brief, and no doubt intentionally vague, account of his life since he and K. had last seen each other. A little self-deprecatory, it would have been a sort of apologia, except that it didn't ring quite true. But perhaps that was in itself a form of apologia—a tacit admission of activities too ignoble to speak of with a man of K.'s integrity. In any case, he was an expatriate; still a Hungarian citizen, but a permanent resident in Germany, where he was "in business." He had married a German woman, younger than himself, and they had one child, a little boy. Now, his unidentified business had brought him on a visit to Budapest, and he and his wife and son were staying in a furnished villa not very far from ours—one of the few villas in the vicinity that had escaped bomb damage. "Imagine my surprise and delight," he said, "when I found out that my old friend Kerpely Jenö was living on the same street!"

I didn't believe that. I felt sure that he knew all about us, and wanted something from us . . . but *what*? K. must have felt the same disbelief, for he said, with a touch of dryness. "Over the years I have played very often in Germany, both alone and with the Quartet."

"I know that, Jenökém. I read the press notices of your concerts. Your Berlin recital in 1938 was very well received."

"Were you there?"

"I was in Berlin, but not at the concert—as I recall, the house was sold out."

"But why didn't you get in touch with me?" K. said, "I would gladly have given you tickets."

K. had put this embarrassing question in such a way that our evasive visitor could have side-stepped if it I hadn't put my oar in. "Yes," I said, "why didn't you do that? You missed a wonderful concert."

"Perhaps," he said with a short laugh, "I was afraid of becoming homesick."

I thought that might well be the truth. But there was something about him that made everything he said sound phony—and most of all a seemingly careless reference to "that lunatic Hitler and all his criminal gang," which aroused in me the same feelings of uneasiness as the German officers' jokes about Hitler and Göring.

Very soon after throwing this out and getting no reaction from us one way or the other, he looked at his watch and said abruptly, "I have to go. What about coming to see us tomorrow? A good English high tea at five o'clock in the afternoon—how does that sound to you?"

It sounded uncommonly tempting. It was also impossible to refuse. And not only because of old times.

I teased K. about his peculiar school friends, and the manner in which they were coming home to roost, so to speak. I said, "I can understand your having been friends with that Underground priest, but not with this crook."

"I never was friends with him," K. said, "we were simply classmates—and only for one year, because after that I gave up studying law and went to Paris to play the cello."

It was a sad reflection of the general erosion of trust, that the motives for renewing an old acquaintance, not to mention magnifying it into an old friendship, should be automatically suspect.

On the following day we arrived at the stroke of five to partake of what we believed to be a bribe—though its purpose was obscure.

Jancsi's German wife, a pale angular woman with frizzy yellow hair and a pointed nose, received us; fluttering and apologetic, both for her husband's absence and her own inability to speak anything but German. I shall call her Hilde.

The room she ushered us into was extremely untidy, but whether the disorder was due to the original occupants of the villa—who were unknown to us—having left it, or been kicked out of it at short notice, or whether all the stuff lying about belonged to the present squatters, was impossible to judge. The general state of disorganization did not, however, affect the hospitality. The "high tea" set out on the dining room table presented a picture of almost obscene luxury. Ham. Gooseliver paté. White rolls. Butter. Jam. Pastries. An unbelievable sight, which would haunt my dreams night after night during the siege.

"Please... Please be seated. Please... My husband would not wish that you should wait for him. Serve yourselves, please... A little ham? A little paté? And some of this good sweet butter.... And how do you take your tea—with milk or with rum?"

K. chose rum, and I chose milk. At that moment Jancsi came in, obviously pleased to see us seated at table. "Good! Good! I'm sorry to be late—but other people's clocks don't always agree with mine."

He immediately established English as the language for the occasion, regardless of the fact that his wife understood not a word of what was being said. This offended my sense of good manners. During a pause in the conversation, I said—though it went against the grain, "Why don't we all speak German, so that your wife can join in?"

"As you wish. But it isn't necessary—my wife has nothing to say."

I could think of nothing, on the spur of the moment, to say to her, except to tell her how good her pastries were. But the way her face lit up at this trifling gesture of politeness gave me an unexpected pang. Suddenly, I saw her not as a female Nazi, sister to monsters, but simply as a bewildered German hausfrau struggling to maintain a few pathetic vestiges of middle-class culture amid the wreckage of her world.

I asked about her son, and she said he was playing upstairs—would I like to go up and see him?

Her husband, overhearing, said rather curtly, "Bring the boy down."

He was about seven years old; with his father's dark Hungarian coloring and his mother's anxious eyes and air of intimidation. At his father's injunction, he solemnly shook hands with me and with K., and answered the rather silly questions that one asks other people's children. This little domestic scene was interrupted by the phone. Jancsi picked it up. *"Ja. Ja. Sofort."*

"I have to go," he said. "Those damned clocks again. But that's no reason for you to leave. Hilde! Fresh tea."

We stayed on, partly out of politeness to her, and partly, I must admit, because we were still hungry.

All of a sudden, with not the slightest warning, Hilde burst into tears. "What will become of us? What will become of us?"

Her little son ran to her and kissed her, "Mutti, Mutti, don't cry!"

Dabbing at her eyes, she said, "Please, please excuse me . . . Please, I am so ashamed."

The little boy must have told his father about his "Mutti's" emotional breakdown, for Jancsi came next day to apologize for her behavior. "The poor thing is hysterical," he said. "Coming up from the air shelter to find nothing left of her home—nothing left of the whole block, was too big a shock for her weak nerves to take."

For about a week we saw nothing of them. Then Jancsi turned up one morning at about eight o'clock to say that they were leaving; going back to Germany on an army truck while it was still possible to get through the Russian lines, which were daily drawing tighter.

We wished them luck. "Are you leaving right away?"

"In about an hour," he said. "As a matter of fact, I hoped you might come and have breakfast with us—just a little farewell party before we go."

We hesitated. Then he said, disingenuously (but it worked), "Poor Hilde is beside herself."

This time, the disorder was chaotic, the food was piled up anyhow on the bare table, and Hilde was in tears. Over it all hung the marvelous aroma of good coffee. "Have some," Jancsi said, "it's the real thing, not that ersatz muck." Hilde filled two cups for us, adding her own salt tears to the rich brew.

Her husband said, "I may as well be frank with you, Jenökém—there is no time now for beating about the bush. I didn't invite you here just to kiss us goodbye. I have a favor to ask of you. You see that box?"

It was a wooden locker with his name painted on it in black.

"Yes. What is in it?"

"The only things of value we possess—two oriental rugs. They represent our entire capital. Will you take care of them for us until after the war?"

K. left decisions of that sort up to me, and Hilde must have divined this from the look he and I exchanged, for she fell, meta-phorically speaking, down on her knees before me. "Please, Frau von Kerpely, please... I beg of you, I beseech you to keep them for us! Please... They are all we have in the world! *Please....*"

"Be quiet!" her husband said.

But it was the note of utter despair in Hilde's voice that won me over.

We would not take the box, not only because of what else it might contain, but for fear that the name painted on it might implicate us by association with activities of which we knew nothing. Even keeping the rugs was a risk—without knowing how or where Jancsi had obtained them.

We never saw or heard of him again. He and his pathetic little family had passed in and out of our lives without explanation, leaving only two shabby oriental rugs as evidence of their passing.

After the siege, when Genevra and her family found a couple of habitable rooms in a nearby villa, the larger of the two rugs—which survived, along with our own, all manner of acts of God and of war—came in useful to cover a huge hole in the hardwood floor of the livingroom, where bivouacking Russian soldiers had made a fire to warm themselves by.

It was around the time (some time in October 1944) of Jancsi's precipitate departure in a German army truck, when avenues of escape from the city were still open, that the great debate began—and not only in our family, but in homes all over the city—as to whether it would be safer to go or stay, whether or not the city would be defended, and if so, how would the surviving civilians fare with the conquerors? No one doubted that ultimately Budapest would fall into the hands of the Russians. And rumors regarding the behavior of the Russians ran the whole gamut; from comradely compassion to a savagery rivaling that of Genghis Khan.

Nina's diary for the last two months of 1944 conveys the confusion and uncertainty of our lives on the extreme edge of the vortex more vividly than any retrospective narrative possibly could; though, like all purely personal records, it leaves a lot unexplained.

One of the conditions it takes for granted is the accumulation of minor lacks, which, though each is relatively small in itself, add up to a large emptiness. As 1944 drew to a close, we had less and less of everything; from the basic material necessities, such as food, heat, light, and water, to the material luxuries, such as sugar, soap, cigarettes, warm baths, and toilet paper, to the wherewithal for mental and emotional solace and distraction, such as writing paper for me and Nina, music paper for K., and new stamps for his collection, and for all of us, including Marcsa *néni*, good books to read. More and more confined as stores, schools, libraries, offices, and institutions closed down, and the city became a beleaguered fortress, we had fewer and fewer available ways of making that confinement—so strongly laced with danger—bearable. It was an ongoing object lesson for not taking anything for granted, even a needle and thread or a piece of paper and a pencil.

Most of the people, other than members of the family, referred to by Nina in her diary were her personal friends. Some were former fellow students at the art school, others, like Dr. Gere, were optimists who were taking English conversation lessons from her in the hope of its coming in useful after the war. The man she calls "my Frenchman" was an original character from whom she was taking conversation lessons in French, in the interests of keeping him going. According to his own rather bizarre story, he was formerly the manager of a shop in Paris, who somehow found himself a prisoner in a camp somewhere in

Greece, from which he escaped, to end up loosely—very loosely—interned in Budapest for the duration. He occasionally stayed on after his session with Nina to play a rubber of bridge, and, needless to say, get something to eat—even if it was only a watery bean soup. He gave us a lot of useful advice on what to do during a shelling—"For of course you are going to be shelled, *chère Madame*"—how to judge the destination of a shell by its sound, and how to choose the right moment to come up from the shelter and "do your little cooking."

Then she mentions a man named Rubányi, a young opera conductor who lived with his wife on the other side of our street. He belonged to some sort of volunteer corps, and had a machine gun at his disposal. Lively and talkative, he would pop in from time to time to see K., amuse or horrify us with the latest rumors, and cheer us up with nips of corrosive army schnapps and cigarettes of the *caporal* variety, that only K. had the fortitude to smoke.

Even Nina, who smoked a pipe, choked on Rubányi's army cigarettes.

Nina's pipe smoking contrasted almost comically with her delicately feminine appearance; moreover, as her diary demonstrates, it gave her less actual pleasure than she wanted people to believe. It was, I think, largely a symbolic gesture, which in normal times might have looked like a pose but that now, when she—like most of the young women in Budapest—stood in mortal fear of being raped wholesale by the Russians, served to reinforce the masculine elements in her nature. It would, she hoped, help to create an impression of toughness. How far this hope was realized, can, perhaps, be measured against the fact that "kind Mr. Garay," the official at the Aliens Office, where she had to report every week, referred to her as "The sweet young lady."

In the same diary entry in which she first mentions Rubányi, she reports the visit of a young man named Ruszkay. A fellow student of Nina's at the art school, Ruszkay was one of the admirable young Hungarians who had the courage to involve themselves politically against Fascism. He also played an active role in helping the Jews. Although their deepest feelings were engaged elsewhere (Ruszkay's were centered on the daughter of a distinguished Jewish family), Nina and Ruszkay liked and admired each other, played chess together, and generally enjoyed each other's company.

The first surviving entry in Nina's 1944 diary is dated October 28; and begins with a typically British understatement:

The general outlook for B.P. is rather depressing. The Russians are drawing nearer. We can hear the boom of guns. The Germans are building gun emplacements here on the Buda hills. There are rumors that the bridges are mined, and that waterworks, power stations, and gasworks will be blown up when the Russians enter the city. Furthermore, it is said that the government will evacuate Budapest, and that some of the population will be persuaded to do so, too. We are staying. The problem is, whether in Buda or in Pest.

I have prepared myself for rough living. My waterproof toboggan suit. Eldon's shoes. Wool socks. A pullover. Two shirts. Two pairs of pants. Warm gloves. My blue blanket. And then there's my attaché case filled with valuable odds and ends, and a package of books: Plato, Joad, Rilke, Tolstoy, Mazareel's *Book of Hours*—given me by Papa W., a book on chess, a book of practical knowledge, Shakespeare's sonnets, and the two Peters' poems and letters. The whole caboodle to be strapped on my back.

I also have a very sharp dagger.

SUN., OCT. 29
Today, we had to resort five times to the next-door cellar, because of raids by the Russian *zavaro repülés* [nuisance planes]. No warning alarm is given, and the Russians seem to drop their bombs at random.

Many people were killed today, according to our washerwoman. Her husband witnessed one of the bombings. He saw a missile fall in the midst of a small crowd that had gathered to watch a drama involving German soldiers who had just shot a man and were taking his corpse away. The bomb exploded on the spectators, and the washerwoman thought it served them jolly well right.

MON., OCT. 30
Another day full of alarms. No bombs, thank goodness. Family all right.

I went to report myself to the officials [at the Aliens Office]. They were quite friendly. However, it's been decided that I'm to take refuge with the Swiss. There are well-founded rumors that people living on the Buda hills will be evacuated. Mother passionately doesn't want to go. There are bedbugs in the three-room flat we've been offered [by Yoyo] in Pest. And evacuating would mean losing all our possessions, but for our immediate personal belongings. There is no transport. We'd have to hire a handcart and push it ourselves.

WED., NOV. 1

This has been a beautiful day. Fresh and lovely. Mother and I picked chrysanthemums. Dark purple single ones and mauve and white double ones. The sky has been an intense blue, the sun golden, and the leaves, which are falling, falling everywhere, are yellow, russet red, brown, and green. The scene recalls to me a Pisarro painting.

THURS., NOV. 2

"Die schlacht an Budapest hat begonnen." [The battle for Budapest has begun.]

So it was announced on the Budapest Radio. We think it has indeed begun. For the first time we can clearly hear the great guns of the ever-nearing front. . . . It seems that the German and Hungarian commanders are disagreeing as to how B.P. is to be defended. The Germans favor house-to-house fighting. That will spell ruin for our city, and for the people. Dreadful thought. . . . Mrs. W. came to us in some alarm today. She is of German origin, and her husband is a soldier. She is seriously contemplating suicide with her little boy—by way of the gas oven. Genevra says she's prepared to shoot herself and her two babies. All very bleak. I am prepared to die calmly.

I tried to get into the Swiss consulate today, but in vain. A huge, panicky, squabbling crowd of people outside, many of them Jewish, wanting letters of protection—as, indeed, I do. We need protection. My papers have also to be in Russian. The Swiss seem to be very disorganized.

FRI., NOV. 3

Again a ghastly crowd pushing and surging in front of the Swiss Legation.

I had endured it for about two and a half hours and was beginning to give up the fight to get into the building when Makaris [a student friend] turned up. With cheek and boldness he went up to the exasperated policeman and said that he worked in the legation, and that I was his wife, and demanded that we be let in immediately. And we were! Without being asked for verification! Makaris is an extraordinary boy. He is Jewish. He has an Egyptian passport. He is a painter, an intellectual, a producer of false papers when needed, and also, so Agnés tells me, a scoundrel! He is twenty years old and very handsome. He accompanied me home. He advised us to leave Buda—it *is* going to be defended, and the Russians are only twenty miles away. I passed his opinion on to Mother, who is now in a crisis of indecision. We have all got headaches, which have been exacerbated by the dropping of two nuisance bombs next door, and by the accompanying machine-gun fire. Three factors have made us decide to remain where we are: Yoyo has gone back on her promise to clear out of her flat and go to stay with her mother; there is no adequate transport available; and, finally, Károly and Genevra, who first telephoned, and then came to see us, advised us *not* to leave Buda, as they had heard from reliable sources that Buda was *not* going to be defended. They also told us that the now completely militarized Red Cross are leaving, that the Swiss have decided not to take in the British because they are not neutrals, and that German and Hungarian troops are pouring over the Margaret Bridge, apparently heading for the northwest—that is, Esztergom. And they said that if it should become necessary at any time for us to leave the Rózsadomb, they know of two places where the owners would take us in for the sake of our letter of protection. I go to get that important item tomorrow.

My Frenchman didn't appear today, although we owe him some money.

SAT., NOV. 4

Again at the Swiss. Some difficulty getting in as I lack a British passport. Mother was admitted on the strength of her age, her respectable looks, and her passport. She sent down Miss Berényi, who ordered the police to let me through. As a result, we now have the letter of protection, but not, as yet, our Russian papers. We are to get them on Monday—we hope.

Something happened today which shook our nerves. The Margaret Bridge blew up at two o'clock in the afternoon—the time of its greatest traffic flow. Mother and I had walked across it less than an hour before; Rubányi, only ten minutes before. And Mr. A. had a really narrow squeak; he was on the Number 6 tram on the Buda span when the Pest span went up. At home, we heard the explosions and saw a cloud of smoke and dust arising from behind the Gul Baba Hill, which obscures our view of the bridge.

Ruszkay came in the afternoon and reported on what he had seen. He said it was terrible; bodies entangled in the wrecked girders, or floating in the river—from which people were fishing them out to lay them in rows on the embankment; the Number 98 tram half-suspended in the water, two of its trailers submerged.

We have decided not to cross by any of the bridges in the future, but to take the ferry instead. Mr. A. said that the panic-stricken people on the Buda side started cursing the Germans, accusing them of being responsible for the accident. They were seen wiring up the bridge. We saw them ourselves when we crossed. Perhaps it was sabotage. Nothing has been said about the catastrophe either on the radio or in the evening papers.

MON., NOV. 6

It's been a very sunny day. Mother and I crossed the river by pontoon ferry [a raft] and we got a view of the wrecked bridge. When we were in mid-stream the *kis riadó* [early air-raid warning] sounded. We felt very nervous.

No papers for me at the Swiss consulate. The girl responsible for the Russian part of the document was not in—but a good-looking Jugo-Slav boy was there! I also went to report at the Aliens Office, and was told by kind Mr. Garay that they were leaving B.P. and I would not have to report any more. I shall rather miss the old boy. In the afternoon Ruszkay came. He is worried about his friend Judit. We played chess and he beat me to a frazzle. My Frenchman also turned up and got his week's pay. Agnés has written. She is all right, but finds living at such close quarters with her relatives rather nerve-racking. This morning Rubányi came to see Jenö *báci* [K.], and told him that telephone communication with the Russian-occupied towns of Szeged and Kolozsvár has not been broken off—he was able to speak with a friend of his in Kolozsvár, who told him that the Russians were behaving well. But being in need of clothing, they have commandeered all clothes, leaving each individual only a coat and dress—or the equivalent—and one change of underwear. Food stores were also being called in, and communal kitchens set up. Well—that's okay with us so long as we remain bodily undamaged. There is a rumor that Szálasi is negotiating a peace with the Russians. Rubányi says he is leaving the Rózsadomb. So are the A.'s, and the air warden and his family. That will leave us and the housemaster over the way as the only residents on our street.

The electric light is getting weak and inclined to go out for short periods.

WED., NOV. 8

Went to the Swiss and got my papers at last, with the special aid of a sweet secretary who also gave me an acid drop, or a *savanyu* (sour), as she called it—"Will you have a sour?" I have got to like Miss Berényi better than I did at first. She said she had a frightful amount of clients and would eventually end up in the loony bin. I agreed. I visited Dr. Gere, and we said a sweet goodbye to one another, assuring one another that as rascals we would certainly survive what was to come. He looked tired, however. He lost his best friend in the Margaret Bridge disaster.

I returned home by boat. It was terribly crowded, and took over an hour to cross the river. But although the boat is slow, it's better than the pontoon ferry, on which we are at the mercy of the nuisance bombers, and the crowd of passengers always in a state of tension.

THURS., NOV. 9

I write in panic. A dreadful thing has happened. I have lost my papers.
Who will find them? "I will," says Mother.

LATER.

She has just found them! Mother *always* finds *everything*.

The guns are booming. Mother and Jenö *báci* are playing "patience,"
as they usually do after supper—he is not too happy; no students, no
stamps, fewer and fewer cigarettes, only bad novels to read—and I am
cleaning my pipe. The meerschaum, which is my favorite. I'm coming
to the end of my tobacco, though. I hope that Rubányi will cough some
up, as he promised. He let me try out his machine gun today. It's got
quite a kickback. I fired at random and it made him nervous.

Marcsa has had a day of it, standing in queues morning and afternoon, chasing after a bottle of *Pálinka* [schnapps] intended to cheer us
up during the coming battle, and looking for nonexistent transport.
[For a sack of potatoes allotted to each professor in the Academy of
Music.] Today she brought her nephew back with her. He was called
up this morning, and immediately discharged. So now he's at a loose
end. Marcsa is being awfully good. She has prepared bags of highly
toasted bread pieces, and put away pieces of goose in fat.

FRI., NOV. 10

The guns are going strong this afternoon. Mother says they've been
going on like that all night. I didn't hear them. I slept splendidly. This
morning I went along with Marcsa and her nephew to lug back the
potatoes left for us at the academy. The weather is lousy; sleet and
wind. We arrived back sopping, after having dragged seventy kilos—
all the way from Pest. The boy took a load of thirty kilos, Marcsa
twenty-three, and I, seventeen. Jenö *báci* brought back five kilos in his
music satchel. We are all dead beat. There is a lack of matches and
we've been making filibus spills. Each one of us has his patent, which
he considers superior to the rest. I'm thinking of making more candles
by way of the dipping process.

A big Hurrah! Jenö *báci's* sister Metty has produced five one-pound
tins of preserved goose liver!

I've started on my last box of tobacco. Very sad.

A Hungarian commander has surrendered to the Russians. This is
significant.

My countrymen are being bombed by the V2—poor devils. However, the Germans will pay for it, and dearly.

SAT., NOV. 11

I slept like a top. Stayed in bed nice and late, read and dreamed.

It was a beautiful day, today. Mother and I dug in the rose trees in the garden—the earth being wet and soft. We found a walnut and ate half each. Hungry after digging—not that I did much, but I'm out of practice, I went to the kitchen and had a treat, a piece of the whitish bread that Marcsa's nephew brought from the country, toasted—it had to be, it was a week old—and spread with pork fat and cold roast pork gravy. The mixture melted splendidly on the bread and softened it. With every mouthful, I became increasingly conscious of a glorious well-being only rarely experienced. Man must be fed healthily. While I was enjoying a bath this evening the electricity went out. It doesn't look like it's coming back. Genevra says there was an explosion, and that most of the lights in Buda are out.

SUN., NOV. 12

The guns were silent last night and today. I read Péter's copy of *Marius the Epicurean*, and was enchanted by it. The book deals with mental states that I find actual. It proposes a philosophy common to youth, which stresses an awareness of the shortness of life, and the necessity of appreciating life through the senses with excellent good taste. He calls it *Cyrenaicism*.

I went to see Sybil D., who has just had her baby. A lonely, lost, Teutonically biased Englishwoman of good breeding. Somewhere Lytton Strachey writes that it doesn't suit the English to go Teutonic. That's true.

We have no electricity and very few candles. We all have headaches. The Mettys were here and were very gloomy about the future. Letters of protection, they told us, will not help us with the "plebs." We will starve to death. Or, if we survive, we will be transported and have to work like slaves. Furthermore, eventually there will be an Anglo-Russian war. The Mettys think they will flee to the frontier in the hope of getting into Austria. They said, too, that they saw sad lines of Jews today, getting ready to march from Pest to Buda. Where are they taking them? Is Agnés safe?

MON., NOV. 13

I went over to Pest. First to the *Váci utca*, in search of a German-Russian phrase book, and then to the academy, to pick up and haul back the last deadly load of potatoes. The Russian phrase book I tracked down eventually in the third book shop, after having embarrassed the owners of two others. At the academy, I waited an hour and a half for Marcsa *néni*, but she didn't turn up, and the 16 kilos of potatoes were put into a sack and brought home by me. I am very, very tired.

We had two alarms, one before I went out, and the other while I was out. There were also a lot of nuisance bombers flying around. There's a pontoon bridge now on the Pest side of the Margaret Bridge. I saw a crowd of Jews in procession there. Mostly old people and children, carrying their possessions and looking very sad. All of them were marked with yellow stars. They were being herded by *Nyilas* soldiers and policemen.

Still no electric light, and only a few candles left. Our chances of acquiring any more are slender. It's going to be grim if the retreating army blows up the power station.

TUES., NOV. 14

Garay rang up yesterday to say that "the sweet young lady"—meaning me—had to go and report to the police after all. I trotted along. Found Garay out, but not many co-aliens about, so the business went quickly. In Buda, I saw Jewish labor camp conscripts with their bundles marching along in a straggling line. I thought of Péter.

Mother and Marcsa *néni* had a very busy morning packing away valuables. Mother is going to hide some of her jewelry in a cavity in the wall. In the afternoon Marcsa *néni* went to Köbánya [a suburb] for our sugar ration. But it took her three hours to get there instead of the usual hour and a half, and two and a half hours to get back—without any sugar. The shop owner from whom she was to buy it was stuck in a town depot since morning and was not back even by 6:00 P.M.

It seems likely that we *are* going to starve.

WED., NOV. 15

We all froze this morning, and we have only one wee stove. The electric light is working again, however.

Mother's a bit edgy. It's my fault, I fear. In the afternoon I went over to Genevra's. It was raining cats and dogs, so I balanced Jenö *báci*'s music satchel on my head and astonished passersby. G.'s babies are sweet. Bözsi is the pet, with her beautiful blue eyes, black-lashed, and her well-shaped brows. Peter is a bit of a rascal, but I love him, and anyway, he's my godson. G. and Károly came back with me to have supper with us. The rain had stopped. The stars were out. But we heard the guns at the front and saw their flashes, like distant lightning. G. and Károly told us favorable stories about the Russians, and very sad ones about the Jews. We drank some good Burgundy at supper, brought by Károly, but Genevra coughed it up.

THURS., NOV. 16

Continual air-raid warnings. Electricity going on and off. I put off my pupil, Tamás—via his sighing mother, with relief. He's an earnest student, but stodgy.

Had a smoke of my strong English tobacco. It laid me low for two hours. Horrible feeling, being pipe sick!

We heard from Papa Waldbauer that he only narrowly got away with his life from the Margaret Bridge accident. He was actually *on* the tram that went down. But he jumped off it after the first explosion, and reached the Margaret Island just before the next span was demolished. The friend he was with got stuck in the tram, but was hauled out later by a rescue ship. He had only a leg broken. Some people got away with no more than a Danube bath, some lost their overcoats, and some died horribly.

I hear that in town stockings and leather shoes are being given out without tickets. There are terrible queues, even in front of the littlest shops, and the police are very irritable with crowds.

SAT., NOV. 18

Paul turned up out of the blue! He looks fit. Nothing has physically changed in him but the look in his eyes. They seem darker. His manner is nervous and slightly sullen. He's all heavy-booted soldier now. It's understandable. Ruszkay put me off today. I was cool, but rather pleased that he didn't come. The guns are going hard at it this evening. We're expecting a major Russian offensive.

SUN., NOV. 19

Paul came again this morning. For his sake I was up and finished—person and room—by 9:30. He brought glorious golden yellow chrysanthemums and a box of cigarettes. I'm being a doggess in not giving them to Jenö *báci*—but he's settling down to his meager ration. Mother produced a schnapps and some almonds for us, which we demolished happily, and followed up with a Camel cigarette given to Paul by the Turkish ambassador. I gave Paul two books, *Macbeth*, and *Wuthering Heights*. He left early this afternoon, as he has to be back in his barracks at Veszprém by 7:00 A.M. tomorrow. He told us that the Hungarian army is in pieces—the soldiers want to go home. And that the Russians are encircling B.P. and will later shell and bomb the city intensively before making a decisive attempt to take it. Paul's family are going to stay put on the Gellért Hill.

MON., NOV. 20

Six shells fell on B.P. yesterday. I reported at the Aliens Office (I think Garay is getting a little keen on me), and I persuaded a stationer to let me have two pen nibs and a couple of spiral-backed pocket exercise books. Today I got home at one o'clock, long before Jenö *báci*, as I promised I would do. Mother was scolding me yesterday for being lazy, getting up late, going out late, and consequently coming back home late, and putting everyone into a state. Mother *likes* getting up early. I find it makes more sense to stay in bed than get up to a freezing room.

It was very foggy and cold outside. I met the air warden's sister on my way up the hill. She was cordial, in spite of our late Shivvy's uncompensated slaughter of her chickens.

Marcsa has had a devil of a day. She has a bad cold and no winter clothes. She sent them to her nieces in the summer and now she can't get them back. She wears Mother's fur coat now when she goes to queue—it's queueing, not shopping anymore. Yesterday I went with her to get the bread.

TUES., NOV. 21

The dense fog we have had for the last few days has disappeared. It's brilliantly clear. We can see for miles around. The city seems reborn. Dark, low clouds are racing across the skies. An icy wind is hurtling the remaining leaves along, and shaking the windows. I love the town in this rhapsodic mood!

My pupil Tamás [a sixteen-year-old boy] turned up and we read some shocking bits out of Shakespeare—we've got to the lovers' quarrel in *Dream*—it was rather fun. He says he is going to stay in Hungary, whatever happens—he, too, is prepared to adapt himself to circumstances.

THURS., NOV. 23

Yoyos have no firewood, or, rather, what they have is too large to fit into their stove, and Yoyo has asked for some of ours, which is smaller. Mother gave them some, but she is cross, "Yoyo should hack up her own damn wood in these hard and impossible times!" Tempers are frayed. We are all eyeing one another with hostility. The W.C. is playing us up for the third night running.

FRI., NOV. 24

It's my birthday. Mother came into my room this morning while I was still in bed pursuing my dreams. She gave me her Indian necklace, which was given to her when she was a child by her Aunt Alice. It's made of turquoise and gold, beautifully fashioned. It's very old. Mother told me that her Uncle Lorie went into a trance over it once, and reported seeing a beautiful woman standing on the deck of a ship wearing the necklace. Perhaps he foresaw the immense amount of traveling Mother would do. I am very happy with it. It will be a treasure—a symbol from the land of Buddha. Paul sent me some red roses, via his mother. So love was sent to me, too. What more could I want?

The Mettys have fled to Lake Balaton. A woman told Marcsa, however, that *her* mother had written to warn her *not* to flee to the Balaton, because the Russians were coming up that way—via Pécs.

Marcsa got some useful items today: three candles, some sweets, and some soup cubes.

I have taken to wearing a blanket, toga-fashion. And I've vowed not to pull any more of my eyelashes out.

SAT., NOV. 25

I investigated that wretched W.C. this morning, and tied it up with a piece of string. It will have to be untied every time we use it.

The guns are booming away heavily again. The Russians have occupied half of Csepel. G. and Károly dropped in this morning, but I caught only a glimpse of them. They came to borrow the billy for Peter, who has broken his glass one—now irreplaceable.

I studied philosophy all day. I find I cannot accept Christianity, the personal God or *Bakhti*. I believe in values; Truth, Goodness, Beauty, and Humanity. Buddhism, Stoicism, even Epicureanism hold something for me.

SUN., NOV. 26

Woke up to find that we had an unexpected guest. István had come at midnight! He slept in the little room next to mine. He is now an escapee, and has had many adventures. A priest helped him through the last one, and tomorrow he is going to take asylum in a monastery. He looks very well, though he's wearing a filthy shirt and stolen army pants and boots.

Mr. A.'s brother and sister-in-law called in to see us this afternoon. I remained in my room, but I heard what was said in the next room through the connecting doors. Unpleasant stories were told; with the result that Mother became concerned again about hiding places. *I* am not going to hide. I'm a coward. I intend to rely on my letter of protection, and last, if need be, my knife.

Marcsa *néni* gave me a baked apple today, and a cup of coffee; and Jenö *báci* gave me a Stamboul—which was friendly. I was in clover.

MON., NOV. 27

Today, while I was out reporting at the Aliens' Office, a group of German soldiers walked into the house and commandeered the rooms on the main floor, which we are not at present using. Mother was naturally very worried. Food and the best furniture had to be moved upstairs. The German soldiers also noted our scanty fuel supply. When they left, they wrote in chalk on the gate that our rooms had been requisitioned. All very, very worrying.

The guns are going strong. Near the Aliens' Office, in the south of Pest facing Csepel, barbed wire defenses have been put up in the streets and along the embankment. Also, big new gun emplacements are being sited in the streets.

TUES., NOV. 28

Tamás telephoned to inform me in a healthy voice that he had a severe cold and could not leave his bed to come to his lesson. I was happy to be spared. Peterkins was here in the morning. He's a jolly little fellow, and we adore him. He laughs a lot and holds long discourses in a language of his own. We played hide and seek uproariously around the front door and corner of the house. I have at last found an aerial point for my radio—after four years! Jenö *báci* gave me a silver cello string from which I took the wire and fixed it to the W.C. All very successful. My radio is now much louder and clearer.

WED., NOV. 29

Last night and throughout the day the sound of guns. Windows and floors shook. It is a peculiar feeling to know that the front is only ten kilometers away, and advancing, and with it violence and death. Our instinct to live is strong; there are possibilities, dreams, problems, and plans that I wish very much to follow up. Fundamentally, I like my body, and the circumstances into which it was born. Yet I may have to leave it.

Today is Mother's birthday. I gave her a photograph, and a promise to clean her bathroom for her every day for a year. Jenö *báci* gave her some eau de cologne, and G. will give her a present tomorrow, when we celebrate our triple birthday feast.

The D.'s, to whom we have not been very nice because of their German connections, were jolly sweet. They gave each of us a present, stuff for dresses, cigarettes, and coffee—enough for two cups each.

Tomorrow (Churchill's seventieth birthday!) I am going to help Marcsa make the birthday cake—with prewar materials!

WED., DEC. 6

I have been reading Rilke, and I found that he had written a couple of Russian poems, which I tried to translate. Yesterday, I read Shakespeare's *Passionate Pilgrim* and Keats's *Endymion* before settling into sleep. I had beautiful, happy dreams, and woke up reluctantly. The Russians have crossed the Danube south of Budapest.

Today, our Teutonic guests arrived. We didn't much like the looks of them. They demanded, and got, three mattresses and two beds from us. There are five of them; one officer and four men. They are setting up a sort of office. They are going to heat for themselves, using the central heating and providing—decently—their own coke. We lent them some for today, which they say they will return tomorrow. I have not ventured downstairs all day. Paul was here. He doesn't want to leave Hungary with his regiment and is thinking how to avoid doing so.

THURS., DEC. 7

Two alarms today. We went to the air warden's cellar. His garden is in a mess, what with lorries and armored cars and bivouacs. It looks as if the Germans are setting up a gun emplacement there—we ardently hope not! The soldiers, though, are a civil lot—that is, they leave us alone and make no remarks. The air warden, however, complains that they are making his house very dirty. Our lot are behaving well. They are not as haughty as they were when they first came.

Mari was here today. We tried to persuade her to remain with us, but in vain. She took ten kilos of firewood with her. She had a hell of a time getting it home—it took her three hours of walking. Paul also came.

FRI., DEC. 8

None of us slept much last night. The city was shelled by the Russians. I heard the shells whining before they exploded. One narrowly missed us. The house it got burst into flames. There was much shooting as well as the sounds of explosions. I heard our sentry marching up and down the street in front of the house. It was our first battle night. Tonight it seems certain that we are in for another. The battle has been going on all day.

Our "guests" are behaving well. But I am nervous of them. The A.'s *are* going, and they are leaving us their food supplies. They hope that we will be able to take care of their flat.

Paul was here. He is worried both for himself and for his family— already in Russian hands. Pest is encircled. Buda immediately threatened from the north and the south.

The member of Paul's family who was already in Russian hands was his sister, who was staying with the family of her future husband on their country estate south of Budapest. His parents and younger brother were still in their villa on the Gellért Hill—not far from our former home on the Kelenhegyi út, which was now the scene of heavy fighting, and soon to fall into Russian hands.

4

The Vortex

I

HE guns of our first battle night silenced Nina's diary
for the time being.

I kept no diary, then or ever. The complete records of
my life have been preserved only in my memory—the safest of all
storehouses for that most private of all earthly possessions. In the
spring of 1945, however, when my experiences of the Siege and
the Liberation were fresh in my mind, I wrote some of them down
in the form of a letter addressed to my two sons, who were, I
hoped, still alive. And it confirms the first image of the siege of
Budapest that my unaided memory yields up. It is a long shot; a
broad, semicircular view in which we seem to see the twentieth
century and the Middle Ages meet; in the foreground a shrieking
hell of modern warfare, and in the encircling distance the eve of
Agincourt. An eve prolonged almost beyond endurance, as far as
we were concerned.

Terrifying as it was to be shelled—and it made me feel as if I
were physically naked under a hail of stones from all sides, the
realization that the final stage of the battle for Budapest had
begun was exhilarating. But we did not foresee how long the
Nazis, who entrenched themselves in the ancient catacombs
under the Vár, would hold out, nor had we any idea of the inex-
haustibility of Russian patience.

Like a sleepy but confident predator waiting with half-closed
eyes for its natural prey to emerge from den or burrow in search
of food, the Russians, encamped on the slopes surrounding Buda,

awaited the moment of the kill and prepared for it with carefully timed barrages, of which they were completely in control. The defenders, short of ammunition, short of men, short of everything, could only respond, and that feebly. Between these barrages, in which bombs, shells, rockets, mortars, Stalin Organs, and machine gun and rifle bullets were rained on us all at once, were periods of quiet—usually at night—when, if the weather was fine, we could see the friendly glow of innumerable Russian camp fires, and even hear the Russian soldiers singing their sad-sounding folk songs.

But both the high-intensity barrages, and the reassuring voices of our future liberators singing in the intervals, came a little later, after Christmas, when the German soldiers billeted on us had gone, and been replaced by forty young Hungarian conscripts, who had also gone—to their deaths.

On December the eighth, which is the date of Nina's last entry in her diary until Christmas Eve, we were living on the top floor of the villa, and trying our best to be at once conciliatory and invisible to the enemy in residence on the main floor. We spoke German with them, and, when they were within earshot, Hungarian among ourselves. I don't think they ever knew that Nina and I were British. They behaved, as Nina remarked, "decently," though their manner to us was arrogant. I was more uneasy with the crowd of unfamiliar officers and men who tramped in and out all day long to the office that "our" captain had established in one of the rooms. Every time I had to push past them to reach our own floor, I felt I was running some sort of gauntlet. They belonged to a *Wehrmacht* unit that seemed to be resting up behind the lines after heavy fighting at the front. But the "front" was getting closer every day, and they left suddenly, without completing the big gun emplacement they were setting up in the next door garden. Before they left, they gave Marcsa *néni*, who was a mother figure to them, as she was to everyone, three hard black loaves of army bread as a parting gift, because she had told them she was hungry.

Nina's diary fails to mention a sixth man, who arrived after the others; a sergeant with varicose veins from which he was suffering agonies. When Marcsa told me that the captain had given up his bed to this sergeant and slept on the bare floor himself, that act of compassion, combined with the gift of the loaves, enabled me to see the Germans as individuals. They were still "the enemy" but, as with Jancsi's unhappy German wife, I now perceived them as ordinary human beings who had somehow got mixed up with monsters through no fault of their own.

When the A.'s, horrified by what they had heard about the Russians from their refugee relatives, decided to flee Budapest, Genevra and Károly, who wanted to get away from living conditions in which they were increasingly uneasy, took over their apartment. With it they inherited two valuable assets; the food supplies, including three live chickens, that the A.'s couldn't take with them, and a husky Ruthenian peasant girl who had come to Budapest with her refugee employers but refused to go any farther. Her name was Oléna.

Genevra brought with her a young girl of a very different type; a budding ballet dancer, sensitive and timid, who had somehow got separated from her own family and was staying with Károly and Genevra and helping with the children. Her name was Edit.

Oléna, who was from the Ukrainian border, had strong Russian sympathies, and looked forward to the day when the hated Germans would be replaced by the soldiers of the "brave Red Army." But Edit was fearful of them—with reason.

In fairness to the A.'s it must be said that although their unspoken opinions and undeclared sympathies were opposed to ours on almost every count, they never made any "trouble" for us. But we probably owed that more to their self-serving prudence than to any active good will toward us. Unlike the shameless chameleons, they kept in apparent harmony with the constantly changing conditions by displaying no colors at all.

The one positive good turn they did us was to vacate their apartment; but that was dictated by what they saw as necessity, and it was decidedly in their interest to have it occupied in their absence by people with letters of protection. When they and their relatives departed, taking with them only what they could carry, Mrs. A., tearful and obviously shaken, for once, to the depths of her frivolous soul, said it meant a lot to her to know that all her pretty things would be well cared for—as though she now expected to find her apartment exactly as she had left it, when, and if, she returned.

It meant a lot to us to have Károly and Genevra and their children under the same roof with us. It gave us a feeling of solidarity, as well as the comforting illusion of greater safety for all in being together. K.'s only regret was that his own daughters could not be there with us, too.

István's unexpected midnight appearance at our gate two years, almost to the day, after he had been sent away to a labor camp, was a more dramatic and meaningful event than Nina's casual mention of it might suggest. Yet her casual note is in itself revealing; not of unconcern, but of conversion to the "doctrine of active acceptance" that my son Peter had teased me about—which time had proved to be a workable philosophy for survival.

In those times, midnight visitors boded no good. So when István identified himself in the darkness, our amazement was equalled by our relief.

He said, "Can I stay here tonight?" and we said, "Yes, of course—if you don't mind sleeping in an unheated room." This last must have sounded ironic to a man on the run whose only need was to be among friends in the relative safety of general warfare, as opposed to specific man hunting.

The fact that he had managed to escape, or desert, from a labor company (which, though made up of unarmed Jewish conscripts, was paramilitary), was enough in itself to provoke a whole host of questions. But he was too exhausted to answer them, and cold and wet into the bargain. We tried to warm him up from the inside with some of the precious *pálinka* that gave us Dutch Courage at bad moments; and Marcsa *néni* unobtrusively heated two bricks in the still-warm ashes of our one-and-only-stove, wrapped them in flannel, and put them in his bed. Finding them there, he has told me since, touched him almost to tears.

Lying in bed in our own cold room, seeking warmth and reassurance from each other as the Russian shells passed moaning over our heads to explode somewhere in town, K. and I talked over this new situation that had so unexpectedly presented itself for acceptance, and I wondered why István, finding himself homeless and an outlaw in his own city, should have sought refuge with us rather than with anyone else. To have gone to his old home, where his mother, stepfather, and grandmother were living in the precarious safety afforded by Swedish protection, would, of

course, have been fatal—both for him and them. But surely we
were not the only non-Jewish friends on whom he could rely?

However that may have been, he had put his trust in us, thereby
forging a new link between himself and us; a reciprocal bond of
friendship with me and K., above and beyond his romantic devotion to my daughter.

The "stolen military pants and boots" referred to by Nina
allowed us to pass him off as a cousin of K.'s on short leave from
the front, but if they really were "stolen," István was not the thief.
They had been provided for him—as an aid to escape—by a
Catholic priest, who should have come by them honestly. Though
in wartime, honesty becomes relative, and frequently irrelevant
as well.

It was this most recent episode of István's saga that he
recounted to us next day. His adventures of the preceding two
years came out only later, and bit by bit; tales told in the dark to
while away the long, eerie nights of the siege, and distract our
minds from the noise of battle.

Luck had been with him for several weeks, and was still with
him, when he and the labor company he was assigned to arrived
at the end of November in the little town of Esztergom on the
banks of the Danube north of Budapest. Now, his good luck lay in
the fact that the Hungarian officer in charge of the company did
not want to take it on into Austria, and eventually Germany,
any more than the Jewish conscripts wanted to go there. And in
István's mind, reluctance was rapidly hardening into resistance.

Approaching Esztergom, the company had encountered
another convoy on its reluctant way to the Austrian border. It was
a pitiful procession of Jews from Budapest, women and children,
the sick and the old, staggering and stumbling through the mud,
herded and harried along by *Nyilas* soldiers to meet their deaths
in a concentration camp, if not on the road.

In this heartrending sight, István had perceived both a possible
foreshadowing of his own parents' destiny and a warning not to
let himself in for the same fate, without making an effort to
escape it.

At Esztergom, the company was billeted in a stable, presumably for one night only. But the officer in charge finagled a longer
stay, in the hope of somehow managing to keep both himself and

the company in Hungary. This delay gave István his chance. He had found out that a large building in the vicinity of the stable was the monastery and college of the Salesian Fathers, and it was well known that the Catholic Church was active in helping Jews to avoid deportation. Which is to say that humble priests and nuns were willing to risk their lives to do for individual Jews what Pope Pius XII, who as Cardinal Pacelli had sailed down the Danube in princely splendor six years earlier, was not willing to risk his political balance to do for the whole threatened race.

Under cover of a blackout reinforced by a heavily overcast night sky, István slipped out of the stable yard and along a couple of deserted back alleys to the monastery, where his knock was answered by a Brother, who admitted him immediately.

Now he was faced with explaining why he was there, what he wanted, who he was, and making them take his word for it all, for he had no credentials, no "papers" to back up his statements, nothing to prove that he wasn't an *agent provocateur* sent by the *Nyilas* to catch the good Fathers out in illegally harboring Jews. Accustomed by now to dealing with problems as they appeared, he dealt with this one by asking to see the Father who played the organ in the church, thinking that a fellow musician would be both sympathetic to his plight and relatively easy to convince of his genuineness, which turned out to be the case. But the sympathetic young Music Father didn't have the authority to help him, and went to consult his Superior, leaving István alone for an anguishing half-hour of uncertainty before coming back with an older priest who asked a number of probing questions. Apparently satisfied with the answers he got, he agreed to help István to escape.

He was given a set of papers identifying him as a member of a youth organization called the *Levantes*, one of their uniform caps to wear, and the famous pants and boots. The Music Father was instructed to take him to the railway station, buy him a ticket for Budapest, and see him safely onto the local train that would, with luck, leave within the next hour or so—which was the nearest anyone could come to determining the arrival or departure of any train.

During the long wait for this one, István and his escort, hemmed in on a station bench by potential danger in the form of

other passengers, chatted nervously; desperately searching for
subjects that would not arouse suspicion. Then István chanced to
ask the right question, and the Music Father waxed eloquent on
the subject of the Salesian Order and its founder, St. John
Bosco—who believed that education was a valuable adjunct to
holiness. By the time the train came in, István knew all about this
enterprising saint, and he also knew that the Order had two
institutions in Budapest; the motherhouse, in Pest, presided over
by the provincial—head of the whole Order in Hungary, and a
smaller monastery and school in Óbuda, an old part of Buda north
of the Rózsadomb.

"And so . . . ," István said, after telling us this story over a
breakfast of ersatz coffee and sour rye bread with a scraping of
Big Metty's precious preserved goose liver on it for a special treat,
"And so . . . here I am."

After breakfast, he got in touch indirectly with his mother, who
managed, Heaven only knows how, to obtain one of the coveted
Swiss letters of protection for him. She took the heroic risk of
bringing it up to him herself; walking all the way from the center
of Pest to the Rózsadomb without wearing the mandatory yellow
star on her coat—a dangerously serious offense. But it was clear
to him, and to us, that even with the Swiss letter of protection, his
papers were not convincing enough to allow him, a young man of
military age, to remain with us for any length of time without
endangering us all. So next day he went off to Óbuda, to try his
luck once again with the Salesians.

He left none too soon. He had been gone only a couple of hours
when the German billeting officers descended on us.

About a week before Christmas, K. and I had to go over to Pest
to get some official papers—updated identity cards, or something
of that kind, and it turned out to be the last time that we would
cross the river before the bridges were blown up by the retreating
German army.

Never before or since have I experienced anything like the
appalling sense of inescapable doom that overwhelmed me that
day in the tortured city of Budapest; on the verge of falling to the
Russians, but still being stubbornly defended by the Nazis; sacrificed by them in a useless effort to delay the equally inevitable fall

of Vienna. Its aspect was ravaged and without hope, like the fact of a mortally sick person who has entered the death zone and knows it. Death's dark signature sprawled across the whole scene: the skeletons of bombed buildings tottering in their rubble, shops either boarded up or deserted and empty of goods, barbed wire entanglements and tank traps like miniature pyramids blocking the main thoroughfares, long stretches of road mined, huge gunpits all along the river front, sullen lines of over-age, under-age, or otherwise unfit men called up for fighting in Germany trudging along ankle-deep in half-frozen slush with torn shoes on their feet and no coats on their backs to keep out the icy wind and driving sleet; German soldiers everywhere—open military cars rushing by with horribly wounded men in them covered in blood. And over it all the constant thunder of guns and the intermittant scream of small planes swooping like hawks out of the snow-laden sky, machine-gunning at random.

We had crossed the river to Pest on the pontoon ferry. Coming back, we chose the slightly lesser risk of walking over the suspension bridge; now wreathed from end to end with strings of high explosives where the glittering golden beads of light used to be.

The Rózsadomb, now clearly inside the defense line, was, for the moment, less chaotic than the city, but its atmosphere was equally desolate and threatening. Big guns were positioned at various points on the crest of the hill, less than a hundred yards away from our house. Two German mine-throwers set up in the next garden were a blunt warning of what we might expect in the way of house-to-house fighting.

Our immediate vicinity was now almost devoid of civilian residents. But civilians had not been officially evacuated, and a few others beside ourselves had chosen to remain. Among them were the D.'s—which seemed rather odd in view of their openly proclaimed Nazi affiliation, and the Airwarden, who, having found no welcome anywhere else for his grim household, had made a civic virtue of necessity.

And then, in the villa whose garden backed on ours, there was a Czech baron, whose snobbish baroness thought herself socially superior to us, but changed her tune when it came to saving her two teen-age daughters from the Russians.

We, and all these people, kept very close to home, or whatever semi-ruin represented home, leaving it only to stand in line for bread. By then, visitors were a rarity—especially from other parts of the city. K.'s daughter, Mari, came to see us once or twice before the bridges went up, and Paul, who was in command of a platoon stationed elsewhere in Buda, came to see Nina whenever he could, which was sometimes in the middle of the night—when every moving shadow was a potential target for nervous members of Rubányi's volunteer defense corps. Our only regular visitor was Rubányi himself—dear good-natured man, whistling snatches of operas that he had conducted, and offering us nips from his last bottle of schnapps and drags on one of his few remaining—unsmokable—cigarettes. Army supplies were running as low as ours.

Given this isolation, I was very surprised to see, as I drew the blackout curtain over my window before putting on a light, a tall figure in the unmistakable garb of a Catholic priest walking up our street in the rapidly falling dusk of one of the shortest days in the year. Where could he be going at this dangerous hour—and for what reason? To my amazement, he stopped at our gate.

It was István, and this time he had come to stay.

Now, according to his flawless papers, complete with photograph, he had been metamorphosed into a certain Father X . . . Only the family, and its two honorary members, Marcsa *néni* and Paul, were aware of his true identity. The two girls, Edit and Oléna, were told, as were Rubányi, the Airwarden, and Sybil D. (when she came to heap coals of fire on our heads in the form of tidbits for Christmas—of suspect origin), that he was a refugee priest from the provinces and a distant relative of K.'s. A fiction so readily believed that it would lead him into difficulties of an unexpected nature.

After listening to his account of the most recent episode in the history of what might be termed his "Salesian connection," it was clear to me, though not yet, I think, to him, that he had once again forged the peculiar reciprocal bond that exists between the helper and the helped when both are sincere.

He told us that when he went to try his luck at the Salesian monastery in Óbuda, he found it in a state of extreme confusion, besieged by people like himself seeking help of some kind. It was hours before his turn came to speak with one of the Fathers, who told him that they couldn't possibly take him in there—they already had a "full house." But he wasn't refused help. "I tell you what I'll do," the good Father said. "I'll send you to our mother-house in Rákospalota—to Pater Antal, our Provincial."

Rákospalota was a district on the southeastern outskirts of Pest. It was still possible to get there by tram—at least from the other side of the river. But even in normal times, the trip was long and complicated. Now it was doubly so, and dangerous as well, especially at night, when all risks were increased, including that of being challenged, questioned, and possibly arrested by the Germans or the *Nyilas*.

It was already past nine o'clock, and István's dismay at the idea of undertaking such a trip at such a late hour must have been visible on his face, for the good Father told him not to worry; someone who knew the way would go with him—a seminarian.

"I realize now what an incredibly kind thing that was for him to do. And what a tremendous risk it was for the young seminarian to take for a total stranger. . . ."

But what impressed István most of all was the fearlessness of the mild-mannered, student priest. Throughout the hazardous journey he remained perfectly calm—even when a gang of *Nyilas* soldiers boarded the tram and started harrassing the passengers. That happened near the end of the trip, and István was afraid that the *Nyilas* would get off at the last stop with them; but luckily they got off one stop sooner—at a barracks.

His imperturbable escort went with him into the monastery and up to the second floor to the office of the Provincial. It was almost midnight. The seminarian knocked on the office door and announced their arrival. A little man in a black cassock looked out, and said that István should wait, he was busy with someone else. The seminarian, his mission accomplished, said goodbye and left. After about twenty minutes, which István spent nervously pacing the corridor, a very tall man emerged from the office and rushed off down the stairs clutching his long coat tightly around him "Almost as if he had nothing on under it."

A minute or two later the little priest opened the door and asked István to come in and sit down.

"For a moment I wasn't quite sure who he was—he seemed too simple and unassuming to be the Provincial. But he said, 'I am

Pater Antal. And now, my son, tell me. . . .' He was so friendly, so fatherly. He called me 'my son,' and 'my dear son,' as if he had known me all my life—and I had the feeling that he knew all about me without my having to tell him anything."

He must have been used to sizing people up quickly and accurately. Without waiting for István to finish his story, he asked him to try on a cassock that was lying over the back of a chair. It fitted him well—except that it was a little too long, and Father Antal remarked that its owner was an exceptionally tall man. Which explained why the tall priest had been clutching his coat around him so desperately—his cassock had been commandeered by his Superior.

That night, István slept in the guest room on the ground floor. It seemed to him to be alarmingly accessible, but the lay brother who took him there told him to sleep in peace.

He slept there in peace for two nights. Then Father Antal found a safer place for him, in an ordinary cell with a Polish refugee priest. This Pole didn't speak a word of Hungarian, or any other language that István knew except Latin, of which he had acquired a smattering at high school. "He was such a funny man! He called me *Father*—he had no idea that I wasn't the genuine article. And between that and my bad Latin, our attempts to communicate were hilarious. In the end, I just had to tell him the truth about myself. . . ."

Father Antal saw to it that István was provided with a set of watertight papers and the requisite garments to go with his new identity of refugee priest displaced by the fighting, who, like his Polish cellmate, was temporarily domiciled at the monastery; precautions that saved him from the *Nyilas* dragnet when the monastery was raided.

Apparently the *Nyilas* had suspected Father Antal not only of illegally harboring Jews, but also of being involved in the Underground Resistance movement. They searched the whole place from top to bottom and found about fifty Jews—old people—hidden in the cellars, and other damning evidence of anti-*Nyilas* activities. Father Antal was arrested and taken off to prison.

His "second in command," the Father Assistant Director, an excitable, nervous man, was utterly distraught over Father Antal's arrest. And he had good reason to be. If something wasn't done very quickly to get him out of jail, the Provincial, regarded by all who lived and worked under him as a living—if somewhat unusual—saint, would become a martyred one. And the only hope of saving him lay in the intervention of the papal nuncio on his behalf before his jailers had time to do some irreparable harm to his frail body—if not to put him in front of a firing squad. But the papal legation was miles away, in Buda . . . and the lines of communication had been cut . . . Someone would have to take a message . . . but everyone going in or out of the monastery now was liable to be searched. . . .

István, who knew that he had to leave—for everyone's sake including his own, was thinking as he listened to all this that he was the logical messenger.

He was given a letter to deliver, which seemed rather illogical in view of the risk of being searched, though on reflection he realized that without it his story might not be believed. He concealed it under his cassock and put his identity papers in his outer coat pocket, from where he could readily produce them if challenged. To his surprise, none of the *Nyilas* soldiers who saw him leaving the monastery stopped him; and all through the long, perilous walk across the besieged city—which took hours—his luck held. But the high-ranking cleric to whom he finally delivered his urgent message, said it wasn't *luck* that had brought him safely through, it was Divine Providence.

Between then and the end of the year, although István spent every night in our house, he came and went by day to an International Red Cross home for children in the vicinity, where he signed up as a religious instructor—for the record. But the director was privy to his secret and assigned him more suitable duties—such as teaching the children to sing. By New Year's, however, all such activities had come to a stop.

We held the traditional Christmas Eve celebration early in the evening with Genevra and her family in the downstairs flat. Paul had brought us a little fir tree that he had cut down himself, and we sat around it by candlelight, exchanging homemade gifts, and opening little surprise presents brought for us by István—though heaven knows how or where he managed to obtain them. If he felt any sadness, or strangeness, in celebrating this intimate family festival in the company of Genevra and Károly, and the unmistakable aura of married happiness that surrounded them, he did not show it. He had become, almost overnight, an honorary member of the family.

Later in the evening, when the children had gone to bed, the unpredictable electricity came on, and the radio surprised us by broadcasting Christmas songs instead of the usual raucous Nazi propaganda. There was even a lull in the Russian offensive. But during the night, this illusion of Christmas peace was shattered by the most terrifying barrage that we had yet experienced, and Nina was moved to write once again in her diary.

MONDAY, DECEMBER 25
Strange Christmas! Last night we became "the front." Shells, mortars, bullets, whistle and explode around us all the time. At two o'clock in the morning, Paul turned up in my room—Marcsa had let him in. He told me that the Russians were between the Jánoshegy and the Svábhegy [two high hills to the north and south of us]. He stayed for an hour with me, lying by my side, and then went to sleep for two hours in an armchair in the sitting room. At five he came in and bid me goodbye. He had, he said, to get his "boys" to safety.

The shelling reached its climax at midday. Lots of shells fell on the Rózsadomb—two quite near to us. We had our Christmas dinner in the downstairs flat with G. and family.... The battle is so bad tonight that we've all decided to sleep downstairs with them.

For our Christmas dinner we had killed the three scrawny chickens the A.'s had bequeathed us. We had nothing to feed them with, so we thought they might as well feed us before a shell got them. Plucked, they were like skinny crows. Not much of a feast for nine ravenous adults and two pitifully undernourished children. But even one mouthful of chicken stew was a rare treat—not to be tasted again for almost a year. With it went a few of the Music Academy's potatoes—one for each of us, and, for the children, a handful of brussels sprouts, bravely gathered by Genevra from my front-lawn vegetable patch, while I concocted an imitation "Christmas Pudding," whose only merit was that it was sweet.

This unusual meal was cooked and eaten in fear and trembling, and that is no figure of speech, but the literal truth. Marcsa's hands trembled so badly that she almost dropped the dish of precious stew, and we all ducked when a mortar shell exploded in the road just outside the gate. Only little Peter was unafraid, clapping his hands and saying "Bomba! Bomba!"

Next day, when we were back again in the upper part of the house, fifty Hungarian soldiers, all very young, took possession of our main floor. They had come, they said, to defend our street. And it was typical of the general confusion and the disorganization of the military that just when these untrained students were being drafted to help defend Buda, Paul was ordered to withdraw his platoon of experienced troops from Buda and take them over to Pest, where the unit was disbanded. Late that night he came to say what he feared might be a final goodbye. The bridges were expected to be blown up at any moment.

Our unhappy young defenders were pathetic. Lost children. By some miracle our telephone was still working when they arrived, and they tried desperately, and for the most part vainly, to get in touch with their families while they still had a chance. Occasionally one of them would get through. And after the siege, the grieving mother would come to ask us if we knew what had happened to her son, who had spoken to her for the last time from our house.

Virtually without weapons, they didn't really know how to use the few rifles they had. And they were issued no rations; for three days and nights they got nothing whatever to eat. Their plight wrung my heart, and Marcsa's, to the point where we could stand it no longer and fed them ourselves from our precious store of Academy potatoes, depleting our own basic defense against starvation.

After skipping a day, Nina took up her diary again.

WEDNESDAY, DECEMBER 27
... This morning, G. Károly and I went down the hill to get bread. We stood for an hour in one queue with no result—and then in another for two hours, with a reward of four kilos of bread. Shells were falling all the while. ... We descended by a road that was intact, and when we came back up the same road—to the continual whirring and whistling of shrapnel and shells—it was covered with broken trees, fences, pieces of shrapnel, and scattered personal belongings. To make matters worse, poor G. had a very painful boil on the side of her foot, and fell into a tearful rage.

We have soldiers upstairs again. Fifty Hungarian boys. Very unhappy. They have only one rifle among five of them, and no food. They tell us that the Russians are only 400 meters distant from us.

There is no electric light. After some debate we have decided to sleep in the downstairs flat again, partially dressed.

There was more debate next morning. It was shared by Genevra and Károly, and covered the whole question of our relative safety. The danger was now too constant for the Airwarden's cellar to be of any use—we had given up going to it. But the folly of living on the top floor of a three-story house during an almost continuous bombardment was obvious. To move into the tiny, already-overcrowded, ground-floor flat would totally destroy whatever little comfort and privacy Genevra and Károly still enjoyed. But everyone agreed that it was the only sensible thing to do. And we did it just in time.

Nina's diary once more skips a day—the day of our move downstairs; no doubt the unexpected joy of having a bath put everything else out of her mind. Another joy was that Paul had returned from Pest.

FRIDAY, DECEMBER 29
To our joy, the water came on! We all had hot baths! I washed my hair and my underclothes, also.

Paul came this morning and pointed out to us just how the front lay. Budapest is still surrounded.

We have decided to restrict our use of candles—no candles after supper. István told us some of his adventures in Poland, and Károly played Cherubini's Symphony in D Major on the gramophone. We retired to bed, still dressed, to the continuous sound of machine-gun, rifle, and mortar fire.

SATURDAY, DECEMBER 30
This morning, at 11:00 AM, our house was hit by a shell for the first time. It shook under the impact. We were hit by two rockets, also. During the shelling we all crowded into the tiny downstairs hallway and drank *pálinkas*; and everyone talked at once. A soldier came in and we gave him a *pálinka*, too.

When things had quieted down, Károly and Genevra went upstairs to investigate. . . .

What they discovered was a huge, heavy artillery shell lying, unexploded, on the threshold of our top floor bathroom.

It had hurtled through three different rooms on its way to its final resting place. Needless to say it had shattered everything in its path; doors, glass panes, furniture, including a lovely antique chest containing all my best household linen, and two valuable cellos—K.'s second instrument and the one belonging to the student who had gone to a labor camp. By the wreckage it left in its wake, we were able to reconstruct the missile's extraordinary trajectory—though not what caused it to be so erratic. It had entered through the back window of the maid's room on the opposite side of the landing to the bathroom, and exited from it through a door at right angles to the window. It had then torn its way diagonally through the linen chest—which was in the nearest corner of the landing, gone on through the wide folding doors into the middle front room, made a U turn, and exited through another panel of the same doors, turning sharp right to the bathroom, where, its momentum spent, it landed—twenty feet away in a straight line from the door of the room it first entered.

That same afternoon, we moved most of our remaining household possessions, including my "big box," down to our ground floor hallway and stacked them in a recess under the stairs, protecting and concealing such valuables as pictures and oriental rugs behind the heaviest furniture. The grand piano had to be left on the second floor, along with whatever was needed by the soldiers. We asked them if they could remove the shell. A hundred pounds of explosive in the bathroom made us nervous. But they wouldn't touch it; it made them nervous, too, so much so that they decamped in the night for some other, safer ruin, taking all our mattresses with them, and, what was worse, our only stove. To have been afraid of a dud shell may have been irrational, but the instinct that told them to leave wasn't limited to the rational. Next day, a fully activated Stalin Organ tore a huge hole in the roof, blew out all the glass there was left in the windows, blew the balusters off the upper staircase, and narrowly missed killing Paul and Károly, who had gone up to assess the damage done earlier by a rocket.

In the midst of all this violence and danger, and the overriding determination to survive it that possessed our minds like a madness, we were, so to speak, brought up short; rebuked for putting our physical survival above everything else by a spiritual experience involving a moral decision for two of our honorary family members—István and Marcsa *néni*.

It happened on New Year's Eve, the day after our baptism of fire and the miracle of the unexploded shell, which, had it gone off, could have blown us all to "Kingdom Come."

In the superstitious moments that most of us succumb to in dangerous situations, I ascribed, only half in jest, our many narrow escapes from death to the magical properties of Ilona's bread and salt, and the symbolic sword of the French hairdresser's scissors.

A decade later, I would, in all seriousness ascribe our preservation to the presence among us of a saint.

Now, more than three decades later, I still believe that, though not in such a simplistic way. Suffice it to say that I still believe in the ultimate power of good to overcome evil. But precious few human beings are good enough to invoke this power and bring it into play. Marcsa *néni* was, I believe, one of those rare individuals.

During the almost three years that she had been with us, the quality of life had steadily deteriorated until it finally ceased to be a matter of "living," but only of staying alive.

Practically speaking, Marcsa *néni*'s long experience of procuring, preparing, and conserving food, her knowledge of all the possible markets—black and otherwise—and her peasant connections, were of immense value in keeping us alive. But the immeasurable quantity lay in the devotion with which she dedicated these skills—and under enormous difficulties—to people who were not her own flesh and blood. It was not the humble, and ultimately self-serving devotion of the paid servant, but a complex sentiment to which a religious concept of duty, an egalitarian sense of friendship, and the heroism born of spiritual strength all contributed. There was nothing in her of the servile dependant, or of its opposite, the warmhearted domestic tyrant. Nor did she ever play the martyr. She was a heroine and a saint unawares.

Physically, the lean years had stripped Marcsa *néni* of much of her peasant sturdiness and drawn the skin tighter over her sculptured features, accentuating the look of nervous sensibility that was part of her distinction.

Better educated than most peasant women—probably due to her own efforts—she was a thoughtful and intelligent reader; and not only of the newspapers, the Bible, and *The Imitation of Christ*, but of all kinds of books, including Hungarian translations of Dickens and other nineteenth-century novelists. All this had broadened her mind, but her view of life was, inevitably, influenced most strongly by her peasant upbringing and her religion. As a young country girl, one of the seven children of a prosperous peasant, she had seen Jewish people through the wary eyes of her elders, as clever, knowing, sharp, and usually on the side of the great landowners, whose wealth they often managed. Like everyone not fully understood, they were regarded with a certain amount of fear and mistrust. As a mature woman, working for wealthy employers in Budapest, she had come in contact with Jewish doctors, lawyers, and artists, and her attitude had changed. But, paradoxically, it was only through the prism of her deep Catholic faith that she was able to perceive them not as a race apart, not better or worse than anyone else, but as fellow human beings traversing the vale of tears along with everyone else, but for some obscure reason called upon to endure the maximum amount of human suffering on the way.

It was through this illuminating prism that she saw her co-honorary member of the family, István.

Ever since Christmas and the start of the battle for Buda, with its savage assaults on the Vár and the Rózsadomb, the rhythm of our day to day, or, rather, our moment to moment existence, was determined by two factors: the varying intensity of the battle and the absence of electricity, or any other form of artificial light except home-dipped candles made out of any kind of waxy substance that we could scrape up, including remnants of floor polish. Daylight saving became an imperative. We rose in the morning as soon as it was light, happily surprised to find ourselves still alive, and retired to our mattresses again very soon after our less-than-frugal evening meal, when the one candle we allowed ourselves was religiously blown out—anticipating the time when we might not have any candles left to blow out.

But on New Year's Eve, a combination of tradition and superstition impelled us to stay up until midnight.

The children were put to bed, and Edit and Oléna lay down with them. Marcsa sat up with us in the dark. Linked with the absence of light was the absence of the sound that ever since my marriage to K. had been for me the natural accompaniment of living and breathing; the voice of his cello, which he had kept by him and played every day as usual up until the day when the house was shelled and his second cello reduced to matchwood. He could not afford to lose his Italian instrument in the same manner, so he packed it, padded with soft rags, into its traveling case and put it into the most protected corner of the Airwarden's cellar.

Music in some form, however, was a spiritual necessity for us all, and luckily, though the cello was gone, the piano upstairs in an icy danger zone, and the radio silent, we still had Károly's windup phonograph and some classical records—scratchy from over-use, but speaking the "language of the gods" just the same. Almost wholly overwhelmed by the noise of the inferno outside, these other-worldly voices, of Mozart, Beethoven, and Bach, came through like whispered messages over a crackly telephone line, telling us not to despair.

The peculiar, hypnotic mood induced by the effort to hear these superhuman whispers above the noise of battle by shutting it out of our consciousness, was suddenly broken into by an imperative knocking on the outside door—and no sound could have been more threatening.

Károly stopped the phonograph. The knocking grew louder. Károly asked through the locked door, "Who is there?"

"An officer in the Hungarian army. Open, please."

Károly unbolted the door. Genevra lighted the candle, and István moved away from the circle of light.

The officer, who had two soldiers with him, said, "Captain X. . . ." and Károly automatically responded with his own name and rank. This exchange of formalities was reassuring. Then the captain said, "I have come for the priest who is living in this house. Please bring him to me."

An instant of paralyzing panic. Then István stepped forward and said very calmly, "I am here, Captain."

"Good. You are urgently needed, Father. Twenty of my men were killed in today's fighting, and I want to give them a Christian burial before we change our position. But there is no time to lose. Are you willing to come with me right now?"

After a barely perceptible hesitation, István said, very low, "Of course I am willing. But I need a little time . . . to prepare myself. . . ."

"All right," the captain said, "I'll give you ten minutes. We will wait for you outside."

When the door had closed on them, István said in English, "I can't do it."

"Of course you can do it," Genevra said.

"But I don't know what to do! I don't know what to say!"

As non-Catholics, we didn't know either. Only Marcsa *néni* could tell him, and she alone among us could fully understand his dilemma and the question of conscience it involved. But she went out of the room without saying anything. I supposed that her conscience forbade her to participate in what must seem to her a sacrilegious deception.

I had underestimated her. A moment later she came back with her missal, open at the *Prayers for the Burial of the Dead*, and handed it to István. Putting me to shame, and forcibly reminding me that I had in my possession an object that would undoubtedly be of help to him. After my mother's death, I had found among her things a silver-and-ebony crucifix, of the kind that nuns and monks wear dangling from their girdles. For her sake, and in memory of her, I had taken it with me from country to country, and hung it above my bed. Since moving downstairs I had kept it on me by day and under my pillow by night. Now, with an inward wrench, I took it out and gave it to István, surprised to find parting with it so painful. I did not realize then how small a sacrifice I had made compared with Marcsa's stupendous act of faith in giving to a Jew the sacred words of requiem for the souls of the unsuspecting Christian dead.

Edit and Oléna, neither of whom understood English, looked on, full of admiration for the handsome young priest who was not afraid to perform his office under fire.

The captain opened the door and looked in, "Hurry up, Father!" We said, "See you later." Then we blew out the candle again and sat silent; as if with our unspoken thoughts we could draw a miraculous circle of safety around him. For me, estranged from the religious beliefs of my girlhood but still influenced by them, this exercise of the will was a bizarre mixture of magic and prayer; an invocation of Divine Sorcery. But wasn't that just what Marcsa was doing as she fingered her rosary?

Whether or not our invocations, holy or unholy, had anything to do with it, István came safely through his ordeal. He was obviously moved, and deeply, by the experience, but he didn't want to talk about it. He told us only that a shallow grave had been dug in the garden of a bombed-out villa down the road, and that the bodies laid in it side by side were of mere boys—some of the lost children, no doubt, who had said goodbye to their mothers from our house. "I don't really remember what happened after I looked down into the grave—I went through it all in a dream."

Just before midnight, Károly surprised us by bringing out a bottle of champagne that he had secretly stashed away to celebrate whichever came first, the end of the war or the New Year. Then he and K. went to the door and opened it wide to let the New Year in.

II

As I get deeper and deeper into the "war experience," I find myself more and more frequently using the first person plural—saying *we* rather than *I*.

First and foremost, *we* stands for myself and K., brought so close to each other by the reduction of life to its fundamentals that to all intents and purposes we were one person. I never thought of myself apart from him. All my actions and reactions were connected in some way to him, and influenced by my love for him.

But the same forces that eliminated all distance between me and K. also welded together the disparate group of which we were the center, creating a larger *we*; the extended "family" born of the exigencies of war and confined for weeks on end in what amounted to a "dugout"—one of those sandbagged chambers in the trenches of the 1914 war.

The interval between the day we opened our door to let in the

New Year and the day we opened it to the rifle butts of the Russians, was exactly one month. But in it there was no sense of time passing; we seemed to be trapped in an interminable present moment, where events, experiences, and discoveries tumbled over one another like the snowflakes in a glass paperweight—as they still tumble over one another in my memory, defying me to arrange them in chronological order.

Discoveries were both emotional and practical. I found out, for example, that it takes a bucketful of snow to produce a teacupful of water. And early one morning, when I ventured out into the yard to look for some clean snow to heat up for our breakfast "tea" (a concoction of dried blackberry leaves), it was revealed to me in a flash how much I could love a city, how much I identified this particular city with K., and what pain the sight of its physical destruction could cause me.

Going outdoors, a risk we all have to take for various reasons, is like "going over the top," and has to be carefully timed to coincide with lulls in the fighting, which, like everything else in the universe, has its own rhythms and dynamics, including pauses of unpredictable duration on which one gambles one's life.

On this bitter morning, the stillness, coming after a series of reverberating explosions, is uncanny. It could be a cease-fire, were it not for the intermittent crack of rifles sharp and clear across the snow—though whether from near or far is impossible to judge, with the concert-hall acoustics of our hill.

As I round the corner of the house, and the frozen river comes into view—the whole wide sweep of it, thanks to bomb-flattened buildings and leafless trees, I feel a shock like a physical blow in the region of the heart. It stops my breath and brings tears to my eyes.

The bridges, the lovely bridges, so graceful and strong, so integral a part of the landscape, linking the plain to the hills, now hang half in and half out of the ice floes below, hideously twisted, like noble birds with their necks broken.

The retreat of the German army from Pest to Buda, and ultimately to the catacombs under the Vár (once used as a refuge against the Turks), where they made their final stand against the Russians, signaled the start of a devastating, unremitting bombardment of the Vár and its surroundings by small Russian planes that were based close enough to allow them to come and go in a series of overlapping attacks that foiled any successful intervention. They approached their target from the southwest, in mini-squadrons of three or four planes at a time. Their bombs dropped, they would turn and fly northwest, grazing the crest of the Rózsadomb, and leaving a trail of machine-gun bullets in the gardens of the villas, including ours. Day after day, hour after hour, this deadly small rain of bombs was kept up, enveloping the Vár in a permanent cloud of smoke, dust, and flame.

Our less strategically important hill was left to the heavy artillery to demolish at their leisure; shelling us at close range from the neighboring hillsides whenever they felt like it; while the gentle northeasterly slope overlooked by the Margaret Island—the little pleasure island in the middle of the river—was swept with the same ease by the rifles and machine guns of the Russians already encamped there.

A memory comes up now, bizarrely linked with one of Old Rotterdam, recorded more than twenty years earlier.

It must be some time in the second half of January, for our food is running very low, and there is no more to be had for love or money—even the meager ration of sour rye bread has come to a stop. Water, gas, electricity, even candles, are memories of a past civilization, and warmth will soon join them.

We are hungry, thirsty, cold, unwashed, and on edge, when the Airwarden, who has appointed himself town crier for his bailiwick, bursts in with some good news for once—good news with a catch to it. He tells us that the *Nyilas* are distributing small quantities of dried beans and meat... *"Meat?"* ... first come first serve to holders of unredeemed coupons, of which we have whole books. The catch is that the *Nyilas* headquarters for our district, where the food is being given out, is located on the slope facing the Margaret Island, and getting there involves running the gauntlet of Russian fire over a good half-mile of exposed road.

Károly says he will go, and István offers to go with him. But

Károly says there's no point in both of them risking their skins.

Genevra starts pulling on her snowboots. "Don't waste time arguing. *I* am going with Károly. And it's no use trying to stop me."

Genevra's reckless courage is a constant challenge to those of us who are more timid, or more cautious. In general, I am more cautious, but now I am wholly on her side. In a like situation nothing would stop me from going with my husband. We have all developed a certain degree of fatalism as a defense against fear. For Marcsa, it simply means absolute trust in God and acceptance of His will. But her God is a wise and compassionate Father, and Fate is a dispassionate force, with which it pays to use guile.

Deprived by Genevra's action of an easy opportunity to separate husband and wife, Fate chooses instead to protect them, and though shells burst all around them and machine guns spray the road as they run from cover to cover, they come triumphantly home with the prize for which they have risked their lives; a couple of pounds of dried beans and a slab of dark red meat wrapped in newspaper.

We regard it with awe and delight, as if it were a great work of art. "*Beef!*" Next to roast goose, boiled beef is K.'s favorite food.

"No," said Genevra. "Horse."

Simmering, with the last remaining onion and a half-frozen carrot, on top of the iron stove, it fills the close air with gulyás dreams, that dissolve to a tough reality of boiled leather and string that no amount of chewing will soften. But instead of spitting them out like pieces of chewed gum, I swallow these lumps of fibrous residue whole—not to lose an iota of nourishment.

I have come a long way since the day when I shuddered squeamishly at the mere sight of the dark red meat in the back-alley shops of Old Rotterdam, and was told mildly by Ferson, in his Russian accented French, "They eat that here—and it's not bad."

Pursuing the links between then and now, I revisit the Rembrandtesque house in which Genevra was born, and I see how clearly her impetuous entry into the world foreshadowed her flouting of danger now. Did Ferson, too, foreshadow the present? Was the gentle, bohemian Ferson, the first, and only, Russian I

ever had as a friend, a prototype of the liberators we await now
with so much eagerness—and so much trepidation?

That surprise distribution of food by the *Nyilas* was never to be
repeated. It was in the nature of a valedictory; a final sop from a
failed regime to a betrayed citizenry. After that, real hunger
began to set in; not merely the undernourishment, the perpetually unsatisfied stomachs to which we had grown accustomed,
but the frightening hunger of famine; and the fear of starvation
that goes with the knowledge that there is simply no food to be
had, no possible way of obtaining any. In fact, while we were
eating our horse meat, several hundred people like us were facing
death by starvation in a cellar less than a mile away from us.

At the foot of the hill, on the corner of the main Körút, was a
small railed-in park, overlooked by a modern apartment building
six stories high. The Germans used the park as a storage place for
hundreds of containers of gasoline. The Russians bombed it, and
the apartment building collapsed in flaming ruins, burying alive
more than two hundred of its inhabitants who had taken more or
less permanent refuge in the cellars. There was, of course, no
question, no possibility of digging them out while the battle
raged, which it did for weeks.

The occupants of a whole city block of apartment buildings
farther down, on the river front, suffered the same fate when a
German munitions train running along the tram lines on the
embankment was hit by Russian bombs. We heard the tremendous roar of the explosion, or series of explosions, above all the
noise of battle. It seemed to shake the whole hill like an
earthquake.

It wasn't very long before our two walking newspapers found
out what had happened and passed the news on to us—Rubányi
with tears in his eyes, and the Airwarden with the dry comment
that there wasn't any hope that the people caught in the cellars
would come out alive.

Nor did they. It was well over a year before their living tomb
could be unsealed. One brilliantly sunny morning, I chanced to be
walking past the site when the bones of the dead were being
brought out in plain box-like coffins and loaded onto a truck. Not
much was said about it in the newspapers—after all, the damage

had been done by Russian bombs. But the workers told heart-breaking tales of names, goodbye messages, and expressions of hope and despair, rage and resignation, written on the walls as the means of life dwindled and no rescue came.

I happen to be one of those people who thrive best in an atmosphere of light, air, and space, and I have always preferred to live on a hill, or on the top floor of a house. But after this confrontation with the ashes of an agony almost past imagining, my natural preference for high, open spaces, became an obsessive flight from the various forms of living death symbolized by all underground places; cellars, caves, tunnels—even the subway.

Although our refuge during the siege was above ground, it began to feel, as the fighting intensified around it, like a front-line dugout.

In the beginning, as one explosion after another shattered the double windows—first the large inner panes and then, haphazardly, one here, one there, the smaller and more resistant outer ones—we patched them up with pieces of cardboard, sacking, Nina's old paintings, newspaper, anything we could find; which kept out the cold to a certain extent, but was no protection at all against stray bullets. From time to time we would find a pockmark warning on one of the inside walls, but it took more than that to cure us of our ostrichlike delusion of invulnerability—which sprang from confusing the opaque with the impenetrable.

The lowest point of our tedious but terrifying day was the time of the noonday devil; that languid interval in the early afternoon wisely dedicated in prewar Hungary to the recharging of energy with a good meal followed by a siesta, which had much the same effect as today's twenty minutes of transcendental meditation.

But now, with nothing in our stomachs, there could be neither restful siesta nor profitable meditation. Dreams and fantasies alike revolved around tantalizingly unattainable food, and the only mantra was *Bread.*

For most of us, the best defense against the noonday devil was reading. And the first contribution made by the A.'s collection of books was the natural one of providing us with something to read.

In perceiving the A.'s "library" as hopelessly incompatible with their unliterary personalities, I had failed to take into account the secret Walter Mitty in most mediocre men in mediocre positions, and the secret Emma Bovary in the frivolous, foolish women who sometimes marry such men for the very qualities that eventually bore them to death. It was clear to me now that the incompatibility lay between Mr. and Mrs. A., not between them and their respective means of escape from each other. No bookplates were needed to distinguish *his* from *hers*. The soberly bound biographies of great men, the accounts of their exploits and achievements—including *Mein Kampf*—and the gaudily jacketed Romances spoke for themselves and offered us, in Hungarian, of course, a choice of mental escapes from our present situation. But for me, as for Nina and Genevra, both avenues were blocked—wholly in my case—by my old enemy, the language barrier. Luckily for us, however, there were a few German novels skulking behind the others, as if afraid of being found by the Russians. The only one among us for whom the library offered no relief, was Oléna, who was unable to read anything as complicated as a book in any language.

It is early afternoon on a bitterly cold day, with a northeast wind that cuts through our patched up windowpanes like a steel blade.

Károly is sick. He has some sort of virus and a high fever. He lies, covered with blankets, sweating and shivering by turns, on the double bed that almost entirely fills the third, and smallest, room.

Genevra, who is very anxious about him—cut off as we are from any kind of medical help—is trying to quiet the children, and keep them warm, by putting them down for a nap in the first room, which they share at night with me, and K., and Nina. Both communicating doors are wide open, to distribute what little warmth there is coming from the stove in the middle room. I am sitting as close to it as I can get, warming my feet and hands, while my back freezes in the draft from the windows.

K. and I are helping István to translate into Hungarian some English poems that he wants to set to music. Outside, it is relatively quiet; we seem to be in one of those coincidental intervals in the shelling and bombing that lull and deceive.

Suddenly, without any warning sound, I am stunned by what feels like a violent blow on my head, a terrific singing in my ears, and an icy blast of air—all at once.

Genevra gives a loud cry. I turn my head. The arctic wind is driving in through an empty window frame in Károly's room, and Károly has disappeared under a mound of white plaster from walls and ceiling. "Quick!" cries Genevra, trying to shovel it off with her hands, "Quick! Or he'll suffocate!"

The plaster was a lot heavier than the snow it resembled. But Károly emerged from the drift of debris still breathing and, miraculously, uninjured.

A soldier told us that a rocket had exploded up against the window, less than three feet from the end of Károly's bed. We had to admit, now, that the patched-up windows in all the rooms were weak points that needed to be strengthened. But with what? Mattresses would be good, but the only ones not in use were in the wrecked bedrooms on the top floor, buried under masses of debris, and uncomfortably close to the unexploded shell, which we preferred to leave undisturbed. Then someone, I think it was Nina, said, "Couldn't we use the books?"

As substitute sandbags, *hers* were just as efficient as *his*. Piled up two layers thick to within a few inches of the top window frames, they shut out most of the precious daylight, but they stopped the bullets bravely, and probably saved our lives many times over before they were taken down and put to a less heroic use by the Russian soldiers.

The new illusion of overall protection created by the book-barricades did not last long. Disillusionment, however, was accompanied by another miracle.

It is evening. Our main meal of the day—a handful of dried beans boiled in snow water and called "soup"—has been consumed; the sourdough bread that Marcsa bakes and rations, one slice per person per day, has been taken out of the oven, and Marcsa, Edit, and Oléna are sitting on low stools before its open door making the most of its dying warmth, while the rest of us hug the stove in the middle room. We are listening to the gramophone. Shelling is desultory, and in consequence, the music is less

fragmented than usual. The children are all ready for bed.
Genevra is holding the baby Elizabeth on her lap, cuddling a
little soft toy, a sort of mascot beloved by both children, and Peter,
sitting on the floor, is covertly trying to grab it. When the record
comes to an end, Genevra gets up. "Time to go to sleep now,
children."

On the threshold of the first room, where their brick-warmed
cot awaits them, the baby drops her toy. Genevra stoops to pick it
up and is frozen in the act by a crashing and splintering of plaster
and wood as some heavy object comes hurtling through the wall.
There are cries from the kitchen. Then Marcsa and the two girls
come stumbling out, covered in plaster from head to foot with
blood running down their faces.

They had heard no explosion. But a shell had exploded right
next to them, in the little room opening off the kitchen, wrecking
it and everything in it and sending pieces of metal in all directions. One such piece, weighing more than twenty pounds, had
passed over their heads, just barely grazing them, torn through
the top of the range and on through the wall, to land on the
children's still-empty cot.

That night, when a round of intensive shelling began at the
usual time just before dawn, and the Hungarian artillery—whose
big guns were sited not fifty yards away from us—started to
respond, I felt more than usually frightened. But K. put his arms
around me and held me to him so closely, so tightly, that Death
would have had a hard time taking either one of us without the
other. Nina, rolled up in her sleeping bag, covered her head with
a blanket, and I wished that her friend Paul were there to comfort
and support her. But the fighting had cut him off from us for the
time being, and she had the added anxiety of not knowing what
was happening to him.

We had got used, as one gets used to anything that goes on long
enough, to lying awake at night listening to the different sounds
made by the various types of shells, and guessing where each was
likely to land. Mortar shells and rockets had a peculiar clear,
smooth whine, and a sharp high-toned explosion. Other shells had
a long-drawn swooshing sound as they went over—and a loud,

deep explosion. Still others—they may have been Stalin Organs—hurtled through the air with the uneven, shunting noise of a freight train going full speed.

The rhythmic pattern of a shelling, its musical score so to speak, included pauses, moments of respite like those that follow an ear-splitting aria, giving the listener time to recover before the onslaught of the full chorus. I had been told often enough that you don't hear the shell that is going to kill you. But only now did I fully believe it. And it created a new fear; the fear of silences.

Measured against what would have happened if the kitchen stools had been an inch higher, or if Genevra had taken the children to bed a minute or two earlier, the miseries actually caused by what became known as "the kitchen shell" were petty. But in themselves they were maddening. Chief among them was the damage done to the range. The holes in the walls were mended by Károly and István with boards and mud. But there was no way of mending the battered range, which, though it could still be used—and had to be used—now filled the whole place with acrid smoke that burned our eyes and irritated our lungs.

The destruction of the room opening off the kitchen, and everything in it, caused, among other trials, the problematical loss of both beds and sleeping space for the two girls, and the irreparable loss of a slab of fat bacon and enough potatoes to keep us alive for a week—concealed there by Marcsa to protect them against pilferage by our chronically famished defenders. Luckily, her less-tempting "iron ration" of toasted bread crusts had been hidden elsewhere.

The damage to the range exacerbated the water problem. The stove had a small built-in tank in which we would boil melted snow for cooking and drinking purposes. Now, the tank had a hole in it, and the water had to be boiled on top of the range, which added the bitter taste of wood smoke to that of the various, unclassified, impurities to be found in snow shoveled up from a well-trodden battleground.

As long as the battle lasted, the lack of water was, like the lack of food, irremediable. With the mains gone, the only possible sources of water within walking distance of us were a private well, about half a mile distant, and the hot springs at the foot of the hill. Both were the scene of fierce fighting, including tank battles, and the well was frozen into the bargain. So were our drainpipes. Sanitation was virtually nonexistent. Ordinary decency was preserved only with great difficulty and at great risk. And with no soap and very little water, even minimum standards of cleanliness were unattainable. Only the babies were bathed, and even they got no more than a lick and a promise.

Mixed in with these mundane problems of everyday survival, are the spiritual problems created for István by the priestly role he has to sustain, for the sake of our safety as well as his own. The German Nazis have gone to ground, but the *Nyilas* are still among us, and so are the secret betrayers.

All the same, when István is asked once again, by the commanding officer of another company fighting on the hill, to officiate at the burial of the fallen, he declines, on the ground that he, as a seminarian, is not qualified to perform such an office except as a last resort—as the captain of a ship on the high seas is permitted to perform baptisms and burials. And he offers, rather rashly, to find a fully qualified priest to take his place.

The Franciscan church is less than a mile away, an easy walk— were it not that every step of it is exposed to enemy fire. But for István there are no safe roads. It is simply a matter of choosing which of two life-and-death risks to take, and he takes the one he believes to be morally right.

He comes triumphantly back with one of the Franciscan Fathers, a gentle, middle-aged monk who was once an army chaplain. He understands István's position, and exonerates him from all blame, both past and future—knowing that he will be faced with further unavoidable deception. As indeed he is. When a young woman living in a nearby cellar tries to kill herself and her child, and only the child dies, he cannot refuse to bury the child and absolve the mother. And when the Airwarden's house is hit and his old mother fatally injured, can the priest next door refuse to hear her confession?

The Czech baron, who is holed up with his wife and daughters in the cramped cellar of the villa in back of ours, has taken to looking in on us every now and then. He has made a gap in the fence between his yard and ours to make his visits easier. I suspect his wife, whose nose is long and pointed, of being a bit of a shrew as well as a snob. He escapes through the gap in the fence more and more often—rather too often for us. But he likes talking to K., who is too kind to discourage him, even when he goes on and on about his fears for his daughters, his "dear little girls," when the Russians capture the hill, and repeats horrendous rumors of raping and looting in Pest—already in Russian hands—though he knows that K.'s daughters are there, with no father to protect them.

The baron remarks, sometimes, on how cheerful we all are, how well we are bearing up. But are we? How much truth lies behind that impression? I know that K.'s calm demeanor reflects an indestructible inner serenity, but mine is very fragile. On the whole, I would say that the so-called "wild Hungarians" in the group are more even-tempered, less emotional, and less easily upset than the supposedly phlegmatic British, as represented by me and my daughters. True, Edit is given to tears, but she cries quietly, with her face buried in a metaphorical pillow, unwilling to admit that she is frightened.

Oléna is a being apart. She is unashamedly terrified of shells and spends much of her time under the table. But, unlike Edit and Nina, she is not in the least afraid of being raped by the Russians. Big-bosomed, big-hipped, bold-eyed, and cunning, she believes herself to be a match for any Russian soldier, and fully intends to choose her first lover freely. (And it will be her first; this earthy wench is virgin ground.)

Her attitude to us is rather flattering, in view of her revolutionary ideas. With the exception of Marcsa, we are all "enemies of the people," yet she can't help liking us—especially Nina, who is very nice to her. Nina, full of fears and anxieties that she bravely keeps to herself, is very nice to everyone.

The air is thick with rumors. Rubányi says that an independent Hungarian army no longer exists; that one Army Corps after another has gone over, generals and all, to the Russian side. The baron has secret information that a separate peace between the Hungarians and the Russians is imminent. The Airwarden, always grim, tells of treachery; of Russian emissaries of peace shot dead with white flags in their hands—"Those damned *Nyilas* will stick at nothing."

Showers of leaflets descend from the sky between bombings. Hungarian warnings of poisoned chocolate bars and explosive pens dropped by the enemy (Which enemy? Whose enemy?) to annihilate the civilian population—as if bombs and shells weren't enough. And from the Russians, promises of fair treatment in return for peaceful capitulation.

Why, in God's name, can't there be a peaceful capitulation— before we are all dead, and nothing is left on the hills of Buda but piles of stinking rubble?

If something doesn't happen very soon, we are going to starve. We are down to Marcsa's bread crusts. Ironically, now that our food has run out, our water supply is being replenished by a big new snowfall. How long can one last on moldy bread crusts and water colored with ersatz coffee—of which we still have a few ounces? Whatever the answer may be, our reaction to the snowfall is reflexive, and while it is still falling, and relatively unpolluted, we fill every possible receptacle, including, of course, the bathrub.

Late in the afternoon, three soldiers come stumbling in—the door is locked only at night—and stand on the threshold of our middle room staring at us as if struck dumb with amazement at finding us there.

In those few seconds of silent confrontation I see only the color of their uniforms. Then one of them says, "*Heil Hitler!*" To which K. replies with a simple "*Guten Abend.*"

They come shambling into the room and stand there swaying slightly, as if intoxicated. They look very young, very weary, and, I realize with something of a shock, very frightened. Were it not for their SS insignia, I would feel sorry for them.

The one who had given us the Hitler salutation and seems to be the oldest of the three—maybe nineteen or twenty—takes stock of our crowded quarters, the barricaded windows, the snow seeping in through the ceiling, the children playing on the floor, the priest seemingly absorbed in reading his office, and says, a bit suspiciously, "What are you doing up here? Why are you not in your cellar—like everyone else?"

"Because we have no cellar," K. says, and Genevra adds loftily, in her excellent *hoch Deutsch,* "We *prefer* to live above ground."

"Well," says the young German, "I advise you to go underground tonight, or you won't live long. The Russians are just around the corner, and they're getting ready to blitz this street— not a stone will be left standing."

They can hardly stand up themselves, and I feel obliged to ask them to sit. They collapse puppetlike, all three at once, on the nearest seat—which happens to be István's bed. A pot of the bitter, tasteless ersatz coffee is keeping warm on the stove top. I see them looking at it longingly, and once again I feel obliged to show them hospitality . . . Would they care for some?

"*Danke . . . Danke schön. . . .* We haven't eaten for days. Or slept. We need some place to sleep—a cellar, just for an hour or so, that's all—we don't intend to get caught by the Russians."

We have heard it said that the Russians never take the SS prisoner—they shoot them. Recalling this, I am seized by a panicky desire to get rid of these wretched boys before they fall asleep where they sit and are caught and shot by the Russians under our roof.

But where can we—where *should* we—send them? Rubányi, the baron, and the Airwarden all have cellars. Rubányi, whose young volunteers are in the thick of the fighting, will give these would-be deserters short shrift. The baron's "dear little girls" put his cellar out of the question. That leaves the Airwarden, whose hatred of the SS may be temporarily curbed by his fear of them— but they had better not sleep too deeply.

We tell them how to find the cellar—under the ruins of the little house next door—and advise them to go there at once, before all the space is taken.

They finish their coffee slowly, obviously reluctant to leave. They thank us and wish us well. They do not recognize us as the enemy. I watch them go with relief, clouded by a sense of having connived in their ultimate destruction; a nagging certainty that the Airwarden will somehow contrive to trap them.

Later in the evening, the baron comes over to give us the same news of a forthcoming Russian assault on the crest of the hill, and urges us to take refuge in his cellar. Which we may have to do, if we want to survive.

Meanwhile, we lie down fully dressed to await events. Strangely, the sounds of battle seem to be diminishing instead of increasing. Can it possibly be that a peaceful capitulation is under way? Listening to the unusual silence, letting our hopes rise, yet keeping alert for the first sign of an attack, we are startled by an unexpected sound; a dull, heavy thud just outside the door, as if a dead body had fallen, or been dropped, on our doorstep.

After a cautious interval, István tries to open the door. The object outside resists. But there is no noise. No outcry. We all push together, and the door slowly opens. Spread out on the snow, like a huge, many-petalled flower, is a pink nylon parachute.

But there is no dead body entangled in its folds, only a burst container. It is a German supply parachute that has fallen short of its target and scattered its tins of food among starving civilians, instead of the beleagured German troops holding the Vár. We get down on our knees and scrabble in the deep snow for the treasure trove. We find only tins of sardines—rich fare for starved stomachs.

Oléna covets the parachute itself. In its yards and yards of silky fabric she sees a fabulous trousseau in shocking pink. And she isn't the only one to have such ideas. We lug it into the house and decide to share it out equally when the time comes.

The snow has ceased falling, and the crystal-clear night is so still that it seems as if peace has already come. Tired out, and sated with sardines, we fall asleep, only to be awakened at dawn by a wildly excited Rubányi, wearing civilian clothes.

"The hill has been given up." he says, "I've sent all my boys over to the Vár and destroyed the remaining ammunition. . . ."

"Thank God!" We say it in chorus.

"What do you mean, *thank God*? Don't you realize that the Russians will be all over this hill in a few minutes?"

"Thank God! Thank God!" We repeat it over and over, laughing and crying at the same time.

"Well . . . I hope you're right. But take my advice and throw out any weapons you may have, and keep your door locked until they come—they're on the hunt for Germans. And for Heaven's sake, don't tell them that I was a soldier! Just a fellow musician, eh, Jenökém?"

III

Time starts moving again, and at an incredible pace—the pace of a hurricane.

Immensely tall figures in white cloaks and hoods come sweeping across the crest of the hill like a blizzard, storming every house, every ruin, every pile of rubble, with fixed bayonets; poking them into every closet, every cupboard, under every bed, anywhere a German soldier might be hidden. Finding none in our dwelling, they sweep out again. But from somewhere close by comes a throttled scream that freezes my blood.

More soldiers come pouring in. They have the same magnificent physique as the first contingent, and the same lofty air of avenging angels, but they are in less of a hurry. They respond to our words of welcome—translated by Oléna, whose Russian makes them laugh—with smiles and handshakes. Then they start to rummage through our drawers. They are searching, Oléna explains, for forbidden firearms—civilians are not permitted to have any weapons. They don't find any (thanks to Rubányi's timely advice), but numerous other, more innocent, objects are uncovered, joyfully exclaimed over, and shamelessly pocketed right under our noses. "Oléna! Please tell them. . . ."

But all Oléna tells them is how much we love them, how pleased we are to see them. And I try to persuade myself that the loss of a watch or a camera is a relatively small price to pay for liberation.

Next, two uncamouflaged Russian officers make their appearance; a major and a captain. The major is a very good-looking, and very polite, man. The captain is a not very good-looking, not very polite woman. She does all the talking. She is talking to the major when they enter, and with scarcely a break in the continuum of her sharp voice, she goes on to address us.

Oléna translates eagerly. "The Comrade Captain," she informs us with shining eyes, "wishes to billet ten staff officers here!"

There might, I think, be advantages to that. But how can we possibly squeeze ten high-ranking officers into our already overcrowded dugout? I am still naive enough to believe that we have some say in the matter, and Genevra is bold enough to say it, and in her loftiest tone, "Tell the captain that it's not possible. With eleven people living here already, we have absolutely no room."

Oléna's translation of this unqualified refusal is suspiciously lengthy and mellifluous. The captain pays no attention to it. She looks around the terrain as if assessing its elasticity, then she walks out, talking over her shoulder to the meekly following major, whose only utterance is the civil "goodbye" to us that she omitted to say.

"Well," says Genevra, "that's that."

Another naive belief, one that had helped to keep us going during the seige, was that as soon as the Russians captured the hill they would feed the starving civilian survivors.

Now, the Russians are here, they have been in and out all day, and they know that we are starving—Oléna keeps telling them so—but all they do is laugh and shake their heads. So we open a can of the German sardines—the only food we have—and reflect on the irony of fate.

A peculiar sound breaks into our sad reflections. A creaky, squeaky sound, accompanied by shouts and what sound like curses. I run to the barricades, remove a couple of books, and peep out.

Two peasant carts, each with a single skinny horse, and driven by what seem to be a couple of old peasants enveloped in army cloaks, are creaking and jolting over the twisted wire of the already broken-down fence and across the snow-covered garden, uprooting a young peach tree on the way. They are our first intimation of the wide use of horses, and horse-drawn carts in the Russian army, and they take me aback—they are so incongruous.

The drivers, or "coachmen" as they are called, are in a class of their own; transplants from the steppe; eternal peasants that no military equipment can disguise.

These two come tramping into our middle room—where we are all gathered together for mutual support—without ceremony; one with a friendly grin and the other with a scowl. We grin back at both of them, ask them to sit down, and offer them some of our so-called coffee. Since there is no question of our door being locked, or even closed, against our liberators at any time of the day or night, a warm welcome to all seems to be the best policy.

The older, and friendlier, of the two coachmen, a corporal, is the quintessential peasant; a weatherbeaten countenance, prematurely lined, a bushy mustache drooping over tobacco-stained teeth, bushy eyebrows beetling over shrewd, but not unkindly eyes, and a subterranean grumble underlying all his talk. He takes to Marcsa and tells her through Oléna that he is a married man, the father of a large family, and sick to death of the war that has kept him away from them for so many years that he won't recognize his children when he gets home—if he ever does.

His comrade, who is much younger, maintains a morose silence. A black, pointed beard and faunishly slanted eyebrows impart a satanic look to his face that does not inspire confidence.

After a while, Károly, whose temperature still rises in the evening, goes to lie down, and I, for one, would like to do the same. We are all tired out. But in the course of this, our first day of liberation, we have learned that our home, that is, our dugout, is no longer our castle.

I am wondering how we can get rid of the two coachmen without offending them, when four more Russians wander in; a young officer and three private soldiers, all slightly tight. The officer, a lieutenant, is the handsomest and most splendidly built example of Russian manhood that we have yet seen; but not the most pleasant. His smile is scornful, his manner insolent; he obviously doesn't think much of Hungarians.

He and his cohorts sit down and ask for drinks. Which makes us laugh. Sullen, they talk among themselves—evidently discussing whether to go or stay. They stay. The lieutenant brings out a pack of cigarettes, which he throws on the table for general use, and the soldiers start making up to Oléna and Edit, paying them crude compliments in a mixture of languages and generally trying to get off with them, but not forcing anything—yet. Edit, modest and scared, pretends not to understand what they are saying. Oléna verbally boxes their ears; she has eyes only for the lieutenant. But the lieutenant has eyes only for Nina, who assumes an air of goddess-like inaccessibility.

The lieutenant, who seems to be unaware of Károly's presence in the dark third room, orders K. and István to stand up and frisks them for weapons. A bad sign in the context. Now is the moment to produce the Russian version of Nina's letter of protection, an official document imposing in itself, which establishes her as a British subject, an ally, and implicitly, if not specifically, shelters the other members of her family under the same umbrella.

The lieutenant turns it over, examines the seal, then, holding it dangerously close to the candle flame, reads it out loud. The coachmen are visibly impressed—Mephisto's eyebrows shoot up almost to his hairline, but the other four seem uncertain of just how seriously to take it. Again they argue among themselves and evidently decide that of the three girls, Edit, neither brash nor officially protected, is likely to give them the least trouble.

One of the soldiers, who has found out that she is a dancer, demands that she dance with him. Trapped, she reluctantly complies, and her partner swiftly propels her out of the room; out of view, but not out of earshot. We can hear the tap of her dancing feet on the kitchen floor and her small sweet voice singing a folksong. So far so good. But it ends in a scuffle and stifled cries, and the door of the kitchen is slammed shut and bolted on the inside. "Oléna, please ask the lieutenant to stop this . . . tell him the *documente* applies to every one of us. . . ." The lieutenant merely laughs. Then Marcsa *néni* begins to cry and murmur white lies about Edit being her daughter. The lieutenant is unmoved. But not the old coachman, who gets up and goes out. We hear the hammering of a rifle butt on the kitchen door and a shouted order. Cries and curses come from inside. More hammering and shouting from the coachman. "What is he saying, Oléna?" "He says open the door or I'll smash it in and shoot you!"

That does it. The door is unbolted, and Edit comes running back to us trembling and in tears. Marcsa gives her a questioning look, and she shakes her head. Oléna watching, smiles a superior smile. The defeated Lothario takes himself off, shouting and cursing as he goes, and the other two follow. The lieutenant, looking a bit shamefaced—as well he may—offers a tacit apology in the form of a civil good night and a handshake for me and K., and the rest of the cigarettes.

Well . . . thank God that's over! Now for some sleep—but what about Edit's savior, the coachman, and his inscrutable comrade?

"They are going to stay and guard us while we sleep," Oléna says.

Mephisto beds down in the kitchen. The old peasant stations himself on the floor in the hallway, close to the entrance, and at intervals during the night we can hear him growling at would-be intruders like a bad-tempered watchdog.

At dawn, he and his comrade hitch up their horses, climb into

their creaky wagons, and drive away over the broken fence and
out of our lives.

Enter Staff Captain Friedman. Or is it really Eddie Cantor
impersonating a self-important adjutant in the Red Army? No
matter. This player is a natural comedian, who uses his enormous, melting brown eyes as props; rolling them, flashing them,
fixing them in a penetrating stare, even—but not today—
shedding real tears with them.

A little man, immaculately turned out, all spit and polish, no
battle stains, but a lot of decorations, quick-moving, quick-
witted, but a bit of a bully, Captain Friedman has, it seems the
authority to dispose of us and our living quarters as he sees fit. He
lines us all up and accuses us, one by one, in fluent ungrammatical German, of being Nazis, and one by one we vehemently deny
it. Nina produces her letter of protection, which he reads through
and hands back to her without comment. István declares himself
(to the open-mouthed astonishment of Edit and Oléna) as a Jewish
escapee from a labor camp, and is promptly sent off to labor for
the Russians with an assorted group of able-bodied civilians who
are clearing away rubble and corpses. K., whose grizzled beard,
grown during the siege, makes him look like an old man, and the
obviously ailing Károly are not forced to work, for which it is only
fair to give Captain Friedman a good mark.

The females in the party are ordered to get the place ready to
accommodate six staff officers, who will occupy the first room,
(thereby effectively blocking our only exit), and two army cooks,
who will occupy the kitchen. "Clear all your personal belongings
out of the staff room. Find a stove for it. Find another cooking
stove for the kitchen. Find beds and bedding for the officers. And
quick! Understood?"

He is like a ringmaster. Cracking the triple whips of his eyes,
voice, and dramatic talent, he keeps us all jumping; civilians and
soldiers jump through his hoops together. A battered kitchen
range is "liberated" from a half-ruined villa; a small, iron stove is
legitimately borrowed from the baron; four stalwart Russians
pick up the unexploded shell like a sack of potatoes and carry it
down the splintered stairway, laughing at our fears, while we
unearth beds and bedding, water-stained and torn, from the

wreckage of the top floor. Downstairs, in the kitchen, the miracle of the loaves and fishes is being re-enacted—but more about that later, and Nature is producing a timely miracle of her own, in the form of a thaw that unfreezes the drainpipe.

Clear of civilian possessions, and festooned with telephone wires, the first room now looks like a cross between a makeshift office and a makeshift dormitory. Our own newly constricted quarters need drastic rearrangement, but that will have to wait. The staff is about to hold a council of war in what is, theoretically, our territory. At Captain Friedman's behest, we have set six of the A.'s spindly chairs in a circle, center stage, that is, in the only available space, the middle room. Dissatisfied, he orders us to replace two of them with armchairs that are wider and a little more solid. Then ringmaster changes to adjutant, stations himself on the threshold, and holds up a warning hand.

Enter the staff.

Two colonels lead the procession. After gravely shaking hands with me and K., as heads of the household by virtue of age, they sit down side by side on the two armchairs, and they are so extraordinary, and the contrast between them is so melodramatic, that it is hard to believe they are real military men, and not a pair of extravagantly made-up actors in a play.

One of them brings to mind a Chinese Buddha. Squat, square, bulky, he sits absolutely motionless, his hands palm down on his knees. His flat-featured face is the color of copper faintly tinged with yellow. His eyes are half-closed, his expression remote. Were it not for his thick and curly white hair and his military dress, he might indeed be a bronze image of the Lord Buddha, and he seems to command an almost worshipful respect. Even to me, he is awesome.

His co-commander is his physical antithesis. Completely bald, with a pointed skull and a high domed forehead, he is all angles, sharp points, and movement. The ivory pallor of his skin is accentuated by the coal black of his brows, of his eyes—that sparkle like cut jet, of the tiny mustache on his upper lip, and the short, pointed beard on his chin. He has white, wolfish teeth, a long, thin, pointed nose, and long, thin, eloquent hands, which he waves as he talks.

A massive, bronze idol and a jet-and-ivory mobile placed side by side in a museum could not produce a more startling effect than does this fantastic pair.

Three lower-ranking officers take their places, with Captain Friedman, on either side of the two colonels. One of them, a major, who sits at the right hand of Buddha, seems to have more seniority than the others; he is addressed more frequently and has more to say. Watching him from the wings, I take an immediate liking to him. He has a kind face; I feel instinctively that he is a good human being. His junior comrades, including, surprisingly, the cocky Captain Friedman, are respectful listeners who contribute nothing but their assent. One, no doubt, keeps silent because of his youth; and one, I suspect, recognizing him as the woman billetting officer's silent partner, from sheer force of habit.

For a council of war, this meeting is strangely subdued, and its atmosphere strangely peaceful. At the foot of the hill, ten minutes walk away, fierce battles are still in progress, and the bombing of the Vár is still going on full tilt, but the planes are no longer machine-gunning us on their way back to their bases. We are in a charmed circle of peace in the midst of war; listening to the almost inaudible voice of a bronze Buddha issuing the orders of the day.

The conference ended, the jet-and-ivory colonel takes his leave—he is billetted elsewhere. Buddha remains seated, as though the act of rising from his chair is a greater effort than he can make, and the other officers remain seated with him. A heavy silence descends.

Nina lightens it ever so slightly by an offer of gramophone music. Ah! Music! She has, it seems, rung the right bell. Hoping to please, she puts on a record of Mussorgsky's *Pictures at an Exhibition*. It is the wrong choice. "The colonel would rather hear some dance music," Captain Friedman says. Nina stops Mussorgsky in mid-exhibit and puts on *The Umbrella Man*.

Now Buddha stirs. It is as if the rhythm of the dance tune has entered his torpid bloodstream and set it coursing. Slowly, he gets to his feet. The other officers rise with him. For a moment, he and the senior major stand solemnly facing each other. Then, with equal solemnity, as though performing a set ritual, they start fox-trotting together.

They call up from my past an image of stately, stiff-jointed

Royals opening a court ball. And the aristocratic dignity that these two Red Army officers share with those overthrown monarchs, whether they know it or not, is what saves them from absurdity.

After three or four turns, Buddha relinquishes his partner, and bows ceremoniously to Nina, who accepts the courtly invitation with matching grace.

They make an odd pair, the war-weary old man, half-soldier, half-god, and the war-bedraggled young girl, half-nymph, half-captive, as they sway back and forth within the small circle of chairs to a lilting tune that demands the length and breadth of a ballroom.

When the record winds down, they go on dancing without any music, and after a moment or two the adjutant restarts it, rolling his histrionic eyes as though humoring, against his better judgment, an over-tired little boy who refuses to go to bed without one last tune.

Suddenly, Buddha staggers, and his copper-colored face turns purple. The watchful adjutant and the very young officer rush to catch him before he collapses. Between them they carry Buddha into the "staff room" and lay him on one of the beds. "A heart attack," says the adjutant. "He had one a couple of weeks ago—he is not a well man." But no army doctor comes near him. He is tended only by Annushka, the woman billeting officer, who redeems her rudeness to us by her gentleness to him.

His inert presence in what we now call "the Russian room," increases our embarrassment at having to pass through it a hundred times a day, as we must. To me it is outrageous that so remarkable a personage should be left to die in what amounts to a public right of way—for Buddha is dying, no doubt about that. Annushka knows it, I can hear her knowledge of it in the softening of her sharp voice as she attends to his needs. The very young officer knows it too—I have seen tears in his eyes, and so does the senior major, whose kind face betrays his sorrow as he takes down the sick man's whispered commands. And what of the officers and men of all ranks who stream in and out of the room all day on various errands? Do they know it, too? Are they saying goodbye to a great soldier in their own way? And is that, perhaps, the way he wants it?

The miracle of the loaves and fishes that is being re-enacted hourly in the kitchen does not extend to us, or any civilians. "Supplies are insufficient," says Captain Friedman, shamelessly voicing official policy in the face of what looks like an overstocked supermarket. But the two cooks, one a big, black-mustachioed Turk, and the other a beady-eyed little man from the Caucasus, have an unofficial and more truly communistic policy of their own: never stated, just tacitly "understood," it boils down to, *If you work for us you can take your payment in kind when we are not looking.*

Working for the cooks is sheer slavery. Driving themselves far beyond ordinary human endurance, they drive their hapless civilian helpers far beyond the limits of theirs. And the chancy rewards are worth the effort only in relation to our extreme need. To people who have come to the end of their resources after living for weeks on the edge of starvation, anything edible is a feast.

The work goes on night and day. It involves not only the constant preparation of vast amounts of food under nearly impossible conditions, but also the gathering of kindling, splitting of logs, bringing in of endless buckets of snow, and, as soon as the well is unfrozen and accessible, the hauling back of water over half a mile of rough ground that conceals danger in the form of unexploded land mines, and horror in the form of rotting corpses.

By day, the cooks and their two constantly smoking stoves—that take up a full third of the minute kitchen—are kept busy turning out hearty hot meals, on request, for a couple of dozen staff officers (both resident and nonresident), their orderlies, and anyone else attached to H.Q., including the indispensable coachmen. By night they work frenetically to produce hot food for the troops fighting at the foot of the hill, and elsewhere in the neighborhood. Around daybreak, containers of cabbage soup are loaded onto horse-drawn carts, and delivered to points just behind the front line.

Only when the last cart has rumbled away can the cooks catch an hour's sleep, stretched out on top of their cooling stoves.

The same carts that deliver the food to the front-line troops deliver the supplies for the cooks to work with. A phantasmagoria of luxuries; hams, chickens, sides of beef, bacon, eggs, butter, red and green cabbages, potatoes by the ton. . . . The mere sight of it all makes my head swim. Most of it has been commandeered from peasants in Russian-occupied zones. Some of it has been "liberated" from hoarders and would-be black marketeers who managed to escape the depredations of the Nazis. And some of it, mostly canned goods, is of German origin—provisions left behind by the army as it retreated.

Our spoils from this first, dizzying display of plenty are modest; two loaves of black bread snitched by Oléna from a pile of several dozen before the cooks had time to miss them. The tacit system of self-payment in kind for work done has not yet been established, and we are very nervous. We don't know what's going on, what we are expected to do, which, or how many, of the officers milling around are to occupy the Russian room at night. Only two beds have been set up there—on one of which lies the sick colonel. The tattered mattresses from the top floor are stacked against the wall.

The Russians keep the folding doors between our territory and theirs wide open all the time; creating a shared life; a bizarre mixture of domestic hearthside and military campfire, which may help to assuage in them the soldier's yearning for home, but from which the only benefit we derive is light—the fitful, dramatic light provided by bowls of melted fat with floating wicks made from a twisted stocking.

While Genevra gets her two babies ready for bed, half-a-dozen officers lounge around our stove, unhooked, bootless, and very much at ease. Their wet riding boots are lined up in back of the stove to dry out gradually, and their topcoats and white cloaks hang steaming over it on an improvised clothesline, adding the animal smell of hot leather and damp wool to the emanations of unbathed humanity, and, floating in from the kitchen, the tantalizing aroma of unshared cabbage soup.

The officers talk among themselves in Russian, and we talk among ourselves in English. Captain Friedman is not present, and neither is Oléna—she is cutting up the cabbages for the soup. In the absence of our interpreters, a new language is born; a spontaneous Esperanto made up of Russian, Hungarian, German, English, and mime. Trying it out with a sheepish grin, the very young officer, whom we nickname the Little Major—although he is six feet tall, makes us understand that he and his comrades are weary, and want to sleep. Fine! So do we! Then it dawns on us that they plan to sleep there with us.

After half an hour of frantic reorganization, we arrive at a jigsaw arrangement of beds and bodies that covers all the available floor space and offers the most protection to the most vulnerable; the three unmarried girls, and, though for different reasons, the two children. The small double bed in the third room is exchanged for two divans placed very close together, on which K. and I, Marcsa, Nina, and Edit can all fit, if we lie as rigid as mummies in a sarcophagus. Oléna, who is not sure that she wants to be protected, chooses the floor. The children's cot is wedged in between the foot of the bed and the barricaded window.

In the middle room, Genevra and Károly lie marooned on their own bed, as on a private island surrounded by hostile waters, while Annushka harangues her major, half on and half off the narrow reclining chair that she insists on sharing with him. The Little Major and three other young officers roll themselves up in their topcoats—still damp—and anything else they can find in the way of covering. They spread themselves out on the floor, where István, returning late from his labors, has a hard time finding enough room for his own long body.

Captain Friedman also returns late—from a woman hunt. But he has assigned himself to the Russian room.

When we pass through it, one by one, on a final visit to the toilet—or the outdoors—it is occupied only by Buddha, still and silent, with his eyes cast up to the ceiling as though in a trance, and the senior major, sitting at the table poring over a map by the tiny flame from a saucer of fat.

Whether out of politeness or indifference—probably the latter, the major takes no notice whatever of our unavoidable intrusion. Yet, however indifferent to us he may be, his presence there gives me a sense of security, a feeling of being protected, that I believe is not wholly illusory.

When Marcsa creeps into her strip of divan, after working in the kitchen half the night, she tells us of the adjutant's braggart return from the chase. She reports that he has taken the second bed in the Russian room for himself, leaving the senior major to sleep on one of the torn mattresses on the floor.

The movement of time, resumed and accelerated, is an irresistible onward rush through the unknown into the unpredictable. And it seems to carry us with it all the faster because we have no way of measuring it. Our watches have all disappeared into Russian pockets. Church clocks, less easily plundered, have long since ceased to chime the hours. We have no new calendar for 1945, on which to tick off the passing days. Even day and night have become confused—since the Russians draw no distinct boundary between them.

We live in a state of turmoil whose pattern is constantly changing, like the patterns in a kaleidoscope, but remains chaotic.

The cramped apartment that we had once thought unbearably overcrowded with our own "family" of eleven persons, now hums with a moving population of upwards of thirty Russians of all ranks, who swirl around the nucleus of the six staff officers originally assigned to us and penetrate into every corner of what we used to think of as our private lives. The inescapable presence of all these alien strangers, to whom we represent a vanquished enemy with no claims on their consideration, has the effect of making our resident officers seem like friends. Theirs are the only familiar faces in the crowd, and it is by their faces and personalities that we know them. With the exception of Captain Friedman, their names elude us. We never see them written, and our efforts to learn them by ear are frustrated by the confusing variations—the diminutives, the patronymics—that make it so hard to identify the characters in Russian novels.

We solve the problem by addressing "our" officers simply as Major, or Captain—whatever the rank may be (to which Oléna adds the prefix *Comrade*)—and referring to them among ourselves by nicknames. Even Captain Friedman becomes *Eddie Cantor* when we don't want him to know that we are talking about him. We call the senior major *The Poet*, not because he writes poetry, but because he loves it, and in some indefinable way, embodies it. The half-sardonic, half-affectionate title of *Little Major* sticks to the youngest of the group even when we know he is just a lieutenant. Only the silent major, poor man, never achieves an identity of his own; he is always Annushka's Major, and K. and I privately call the pair of them *Worm* and *Worm's*

wife—after the characters in a British cartoon about a henpecked
husband.

On the second evening after his collapse, Buddha is put on a
stretcher and taken to the field hospital. The Little Major goes
along with him. After they have gone, a deep gloom descends on
the Russians, and its shadow darkens us all. Annushka, who
keeps a private store of looted liquor hidden among our things,
consumes a whole bottle of vodka during the night, and nags her
major nonstop. We none of us get any sleep.

Early in the morning, the Little Major returns, weeping incon-
solably. His "Little Colonel" is dead.

"A hero! A great soldier and a great man! Beloved by us all!"
Captain Friedman says, grandiloquent even in grief. But the
tears in his eyes are the real thing.

He banishes grief by the classic method of plunging headlong
into action; in this case, the harsh and pitiless action of interrogat-
ing German prisoners of war, which exorcises Buddha's benign
ghost from the Russian room as nothing else could.

We are sternly forbidden to pass through the Russian room
during the proceedings, and Captain Friedman closes the communicating doors—a purely symbolic gesture; we can see and
hear everything through the broken glass panes.

The prisoners are brought in one at a time and questioned in
German by Captain Friedman, who translates both his questions
and their answers into Russian for the benefit of the other officers
present. The questions are on matters of no interest to me. What
fascinates me is the relationship between the interrogator and the
interrogated; the ironic shift of power and its effect on both
parties, but especially on the man who wields it—the Ukrainian
Jew who now has the whip hand over the sullen, defeated men
representing not only his country's enemy, but the archdestroyer
of his race.

He shouts, bullies, pounces; his timing is perfect. He makes
brilliant use of every trick in the repertory of intimidation without resorting to physical violence, or any verbal threat of it; he
knows the rules pertaining to prisoners of war, and he sticks to
them—in letter, if not in spirit. Yet to me it all seems like acting;
all part of a histrionic *persona* that has been his lifelong shield

against unendurable humiliations, and will continue to protect a soft, sentimental spot at the core of his braggadocio's being long after this moment of spurious power is over.

But in my eyes, his saving grace is his sense of humor, not his sentimentality; though at times the two qualities come together to produce a *Petrushka*, a *Pagliacci*, or a *Pierrot*.

His reputation is that of a satyr. "He has every female in the neighborhood terrorized," says the baron, in a whisper, "for God's sake don't ever let him know about our dear little girls. They're hidden in the coal cellar—practically walled up—we feed them secretly, and so far the Russians don't know they exist."

Captain Friedman is in such a good mood after his bout with the prisoners, that K. and I take the opportunity to ask for his help in protecting our property; the unoccupied upper part of the house has been broken into and is being ransacked daily by bands of marauding soldiers.

He registers shock and surprise, and promises to look into the matter. It doesn't take him long. In less than half an hour he comes back, very stiff and formal, accompanied by an official interpreter. He lines us all up and makes a brief statement in Russian, which the interpreter translates into Hungarian. It is terse and categorical; "Ours is a civilized nation, as yours is a civilized nation; and the people of one civilized nation do not rob, or harm in any way, the people of another civilized nation. Understood?"

Perfectly understood. *What is happening cannot happen. Therefore it is not happening.* We are neatly trapped, and the ransacking of our home goes on, unhindered.

If that were all it would be bad enough. But vandalism and looting are not the only crimes to which the false syllogism can be applied, and the baron's fears for his dear little girls, substantiated by nightly screams from the Airwarden's cellar, are infectious.

The Airwarden is uncommunicative. He is ashamed to admit his powerlessness to prevent activities taking place in his shelter, right under his nose, that disgrace him—as a responsible official—as well as the perpetrators and the supposedly civilized nation to which they belong.

K., whose cello is as precious to him as any woman, fears for its safety in such uncontrollable surroundings; and there is no point in leaving it there in the Airwarden's cellar now that we are no longer being shelled. Joyfully, he retrieves it from its exile intact, but for two broken strings. He tucks it away in a corner of our tight-packed third room and sleeps all the better for knowing that it is there, under his protection—which happens to be a good deal more powerful than anyone else's. The combination of instrument and musician, like the combination of mother and child, generates respect in the Russian soul, and arouses emotions that exercise a restraining influence on lawlessness.

On a different level, it is art that breaks down the double barriers of language and ideology between us and the senior major, and discloses a kindred spirit.

Most of the officers eat their irregular meals in the Russian room. But the senior major takes his in the middle room, alone—except, of course, for our unavoidable presence. The first time his young orderly brings in the tray of food, I put a white cloth on the table, which the major says is not needed. I insist. To play hostess, even symbolically, salvages my pride.

"How *can* he," Genevra says with tears of rage in her eyes, "how *can* he sit there and guzzle a meal like that in our room, in our presence, without offering anything to us?"

The meal is breakfast; an odd but lavish breakfast of minced beef, pickled cabbage, fried eggs, and pancakes with jam. There is enough for six officers. The beady-eyed little Caucasian cook flutters in and out while the major eats . . . "Is it good? Is there anything else he would like?" Then, when the major gets up and leaves, he hastily shovels all the leftovers onto one plate and pushes it into my hands with his finger on his lips.

This happens again and again, and at first we give all the credit to the cook, who likes us, and who when Captain Friedman is not around, will often run in with a chicken leg or wing hidden under his apron and thrust it into our hands with the needless injunction to "eat it up quick!" But on closer acquaintance with the major, we realize that he is behind this subversion of "policy" in our favor and is just as anxious to keep it from the adjutant as the cook is.

Why he chooses to eat by himself in our room, instead of in the Russian room with his comrades, and seeks our company whenever he has any free time, is a mystery. Although he can express himself very well in the new Esperanto, there is hardly any verbal interchange between him and us. After greeting us politely, he sits among us in silence, either working with maps and papers at the table or relaxing in front of the stove with his boots off.

To begin with, his silent presence, and its frequency, worries me. War breeds mistrust of everyone and everything. Is he there to watch us? Does he suspect us of treachery? Apparently not. His occasional oblique questions betray only a mild curiosity as to what sort of people we are, what we do in normal life.

On discovering that K. is a cellist, István a composer, and Nina an artist (he finds this out when he catches her drawing him), he warms up a little, and tells us that in civil life he is a mechanic and has a job in a factory, to which he expects to return when the war is over. Then, as though fearful of going too far, he withdraws. But the first, crucial step has been taken toward communication; toward the ultimate breaking of a silence that is not mere taciturnity, but an attitude of mind.

When he finally breaks it, he does so in an unexpected manner. He bursts into song. Not the ubiquitous *Volga-Volga*, not any of the folksongs the soldiers used to sing around their campfires, but a lovely aria from *Eugene Onegin.*

His voice is untrained, but true; a low baritone with a timbre that brings out both the national sadness inherent in all Russian music, and the universal sadness that is in all human voices singing, regardless of what they sing, or in what language.

The aria is followed by a pause, in which nobody speaks or moves, as though the singer were a shy wild bird that the slightest movement could startle into flight.

Evidently satisfied that our silence is an invitation to continue, he says: "Pushkin," and launches into the recitation of a long poem of which we understand not a word. No matter. Pure sound is enough. Pure sound can soar above dictionaries, dogmas, ideologies, all the misunderstandings of the mind, and go straight to the heart.

In the few remaining days before the staff moves on to billets nearer the Vár—the last bastion of the Nazis, the major is metamorphosed into the *Poet*; the bard through whose voice the Russian soul speaks directly to us in the language of pure sound.

One afternoon, mail arrives from Russia. The Poet opens his in our room, and invites his orderly, an eighteen-year-old boy who admires and emulates him, to share some good news, look at some snaps of his children, and read a letter from his six-year-old son, which they laugh and exclaim over together. Do they come from the same home town? They might be father and son. There is no military stiffness between them, only the restraint of respect.

As I watch the little scene, I think that these two, the young soldier servant and the officer he serves, are truly equal, and both belong, like their dead colonel, to the aristocracy of the world.

But life with the staff is by no means all poetry, sweetness, and light from now on. The Russian body is much more in evidence than the Russian soul—though there will be situations in which the latter can be successfully appealed to or, less admirably, played up to. In the meantime, things are continually changing for better or worse, or both at once, and our sense of humor gets coarser every day.

One change concerns Oléna, who decides to give her virginity to the Little Major, thereby setting a precedent for herself of "officers only." It's a good first choice, and makes both of them happy. The Little Major is a decent, kindhearted young man, and such a naively idealistic Communist that sleeping with Oléna, half-Russian, and the only Communist in a bunch of bourgeois Westerners, must seem to him nothing less than his ideological duty.

A practical change that affects us physically is the replacement of the book barricades in the middle room with a clumsily carpentered wooden screen, that is moved aside during the day to let in the light. Some of the books, the lucky ones, regain the safety of their shelves intact; others are pockmarked with bullets. But many, very many of Mr. A.'s Great Men, including Hitler, get ruthlessly torn from their bindings to litter the floor of the toilet and clog the drains.

The wooden screen keeps out the drafts as efficiently as the books kept out the bullets. But now we want the air to come in; every night we nearly die of suffocation, and Genevra and Károly, on their island bed in a restless sea of heat-loving Russians, are the chief sufferers. A fresh supply of fuel has been obtained from somewhere, and Annushka, who must in a previous life have been a salamander, keeps the stove red-hot all night. In the third room, we still have our book barricades and our cold drafts, which have now become precious breaths of fresh air that we try to share with Károly and Genevra by keeping the door between the rooms open. But as soon as Annushka comes to bed she slams it shut. And as soon as she dozes off, Genevra opens it again. In this running battle, Annushka has the advantage; she has all the other Russians on her side. It can never be too hot, or too airless, for them.

Annushka, like most of her male comrades, drinks too much. And what makes drunken Russians so difficult to cope with is their stamina. No matter how drunk they get, they never pass mercifully out. They stay on their feet and get more and more intensively and uncontrollably themselves—dropping, like strippers, one inhibition after another, but never, never falling under the table.

Sobered up, the more sensitive are ashamed of their undisciplined selves and their goings-on. This is when Annushka's better side comes to the fore. She placates us with gifts from her store of looted trinkets, usually an odd gold cuff link or jeweled tiepin for István or Károly, for Annushka prefers men to women. Yet she is not the type of woman whom men usually prefer, and the bond between her and her handsome major piques our curiosity. What makes him put up so patiently with the shrewishness of a woman who is neither young nor pretty, and to whom he is not married? To us it seems that the answer can only lie in the irrational nature of sexual attraction. The possibility of political pressure having anything to do with it never enters my head.

What does become obvious in the area of relationships is Captain Friedman's growing interest in Nina, and the part played, consciously or unconsciously, by the Poet in protecting her.

The departure of the staff takes us by surprise. After all, why should they tell us that they are leaving—it's none of our business. All of a sudden, the soldiers start taking down the telephone installation and removing the officers' gear from the Russian room. I watch them with mixed feelings. Relief is uppermost, but I have a sense of loss, too. It is much the same complex reaction that one has after seeing a houseguest off at the airport; an eagerness to get back to one's usual daily routine, which is chilled on re-entering one's home by an emptiness that wasn't there before the guest came.

The departure of the cooks also involves both relief and loss—
the loss of our only source of food. Luckily the cooks turn their
backs long enough for Marcsa and Oléna to collect a little "sever-
ance pay" before the supplies are loaded onto the carts and all that
is left of the temporary supermarket is a huge, smelly pile of
garbage just outside the door—onto which the trash could be, and
was, thrown through the kitchen window.

Well . . . That's that. What next?

But that is not quite that. Not yet.

The beady-eyed cook has a bright idea. He is due for his first
night off duty since the taking of the hill, and where could he sleep
more peacefully than in our newly vacated Russian room? He has
been so good to us, that although we long to be alone, we tell him
that he is welcome. Does he want to use one of the beds? Oh no! All
he wants is a comfortable chair . . . Apparently cooks are not
entitled to beds, or even to normal sleep.

Within a few minutes, this one is dead to the world sitting
upright on one of the A.'s not-very-easy chairs. But even that
small comfort is denied him by Captain Friedman, who returns
unexpectedly, and is furious at finding him there with us, and
asleep! "Out with you! Out! OUT!"

And out the poor little fellow goes, staggering with sleep, dart-
ing murderous looks from his black boot-button eyes at his
tormentor—who goes out after him and stays away long enough
for our hopes of a night without Russians to revive.

We decide to go to bed while the going is good. But the process is
slower now that the bathroom is once more exclusively ours. K.
and I are still up when Captain Friedman walks in with the Little
Major, and an orderly laden with bottles of vodka, which they
propose to share with us. "A small party," says the Little Major in
English, with an accent disarmingly like Fersen's; he has picked
up more English than his comrades, and is proud of it. "A farewell party," says Captain Friedman in German, looking very sad.

A Russian invitation is virtually a command, to be refused only
at one's peril. But in this case, although we are all invited, only
Nina and Oléna are really wanted. Nina's company is not to be
had without mine and K.'s, and Captain Friedman is sharp
enough to realize that; but he is, I suspect, conceited enough to
believe that he can outwit our chaperonage, and that the less
outside support we have, the easier that will be. So Marcsa,

Edit, and István, who are all fast asleep, or pretending to be, are excused, and the well-simulated regrets of Károly and Genevra, the one pleading illness and the other maternal responsibilities, are accepted by Captain Friedman with equally well-simulated disappointment. Meanwhile, Nina and Oléna get dressed; Nina with great reluctance, and Oléna with joyful anticipation; and I prepare myself mentally for a battle of wits with Captain Friedman, who, in my judgment, is more likely to use guile than force in achieving his desire, which involves getting around the *documente* as well as the two guardians.

Captain Friedman ushers us into the Russian room as if it were his own private apartment, to which he is saying a last goodbye after the movers have left and all the utilities are turned off. Stripped of everything but a table, a few chairs, and one bed (we have taken the other one into the middle room for our own use, and the extra mattresses have simply disappeared), it is not exactly a convivial setting for a party. But for this one, it does have an eerie suitability.

Oléna is seated just where she wants to be, next to the Little Major, and Nina just where she doesn't want to be, next to Captain Friedman, who puts me on his other side, at the foot of the table, facing K. at its head; a host and hostess positioning that produces an illusion of being in control of the proceedings. An illusion that it won't be at all easy to preserve. Our stomachs are empty, as usual, but there is no food on the table, only bottles of vodka and brandy, and tall glasses—water glasses—from which we are expected to drink the fiery spirits straight, and bottoms up. Only the most cunning sleight of hand, coupled with equally cunning diplomacy, will keep us from losing with one toast the only real power we have—our wits.

To begin with, the atmosphere is almost comically formal, both manners and talk being on the high cultural level to which K. effortlessly raises any social occasion he takes part in. Culture, we have discovered, is our most valuable asset when dealing with our unpredictable liberators. It stands for something desirable, even to those who don't know exactly what it means; while those who do, are desperately eager to prove that their culture is just as good as ours. This leads to competitive litanies in praise of Russian composers, performers, poets, novelists—artists of all kinds, which K. usually wins through sheer breadth of knowledge, and wins hands down now by recounting his experience of playing Rachmaninoff's cello sonata at a concert with Rachmaninoff himself at the piano; an association that doubles, in Russian eyes, his already high prestige as an artist and a professor of music. After telling this story, he is humbly entreated to play for the present company; and I wish he could, it would help a lot, but he has no new strings with which to replace those that broke when his cello was in exile.

This is unfortunate. The desire for music, real music—that is to say *live* music—has been aroused, and failing K.'s Orphic tones, there is only one other available source; the Airwarden's teen-age nephew, a recent refugee in his cellar, who plays the concertina. A plebian instrument, earthy and emotional, under whose influence—combined with that of the vodka that the two Russians are drinking like water—the cultural level is bound to fall and the level of affection to rise.

Thus far, the affection displayed has been remarkably respectful. Even the acknowledged lovers, the Little Major and Oléna, have kept their embraces within bounds. And Captain Friedman has kept his hands off his "dear little English pigeon," and contented himself with hugging and kissing his "dear little English mother," to which I respond, playing up to him shamelessly, by hugging and kissing him, and calling him my "dear Russian son." K. looks amused and slightly surprised. Captain Friedman is quick to notice his quizzical expression and to misinterpret it. Embracing K. warmly on both cheeks, he tells him not to be jealous, "I love her only as a mother."

The concertina boy is sent for. Dragged from sleep, he comes in rubbing his eyes and looking very frightened. K. smiles at him reassuringly and tells him in Hungarian not to be nervous. Captain Friedman tells him in German to play something lively.

His repertoire is small. Except for *Volga-Volga*—now as familiar to us all as the national anthem—he knows only Hungarian folk tunes, most of them slow and sad. But the lively ones are galvanic. Very soon the table is pushed to one side and the two Russians are dancing cossack dances to czardas rhythms. The Little Major, loose-limbed and acrobatic, squats and kicks out his long legs in the tiny square of free space like a whirlwind in a sandbox; a *tour de force* that Captain Friedman cannot equal, but can, and does, parody—with devastingly comic effect.

Now the two girls are drawn in; whirled around, thrown up in the air, caught, whirled around . . . in a nonstop circular movement. The concertina boy loses speed. Captain Friedman urges him on. "Faster! Faster!" But he and his concertina can go no faster and no further. The music stops dead in mid-phrase, as it does in a game of musical chairs, and the dancers collapse in a heap like punctured balloons. Luckily for the concertina boy, Captain Friedman has danced himself into a very good temper.

While the dance was going on, I managed to upset my glass of vodka, and Nina's, without being observed. Now the empty glasses are noticed and refilled to the brim, and the problem of how to make the vodka disappear without getting blind drunk on it begins all over again.

I venture a timid wish for something to eat, and Captain Friedman calls, surprisingly, for food. Official policy, it seems, is no longer in effect. But neither, as his orderly reminds him, is the staff kitchen. Captain Friedman utters what must be the Russian equivalent of "so what?" and the hapless orderly is sent out into the night to find food of some kind somewhere—and quick!

One order begets another. The concertina boy, who was quietly falling asleep, is told to start playing again. He looks questioningly at K., who hums the first bar of *Volga-Volga*, the epic folkballad about a river pirate, with dozens of verses and an irresistible tune—to which the two Russians and Oléna sing the story, while we non Russians sing "*Volga, Volga, Mother river,* Tum ti *tum. . . . Ti tum ti tum*," ad infinitum.

After half a dozen stanzas, K. gets up and leaves the room, presumably on a visit to the toilet. A moment or two later, the Little Major and Oléna go out in the same direction.

Alone with me and Nina, Captain Friedman stops singing and empties his pockets of miscellaneous treasures acquired while prowling the neighborhood in search of amorous adventure; fountain pens, bracelets, rings, a pair of elbow-length, white kid gloves, and a dainty little revolver inlaid with mother-of-pearl. He wants to give us both presents—anything we like, except, of course, the revolver. He fingers it almost tenderly. "A young lady, not very far from here, tried to kill me with this."

I risk teasing him. "Really? Why on earth would she want to kill you?"

"Because she was a *Nyilas*." The dark look in his eyes makes the past tense sinister, and the other trinkets less tempting. But refusal of them is difficult, and has to be done with great tact. "The gloves are lovely, so fine and soft! What a pity they are not the right size!" The rings are not the right size, either, with the exception of one little circlet of pearls, which he slips onto Nina's finger, holding her hand in his while he searches her face with a look of intense longing. "How beautiful you are, my little English pigeon! How sweet!" Then, as though on an irresistible impulse, he turns to me, "Mother! Give me the little girl!"

My thoughts must be written on my face, for he beats his forehead with his fists, "Ah God! No! Not like *that!* I want to marry her!"

"But, Captain Friedman, you can't marry her now—you are in the middle of taking a city!"

"When will you give her to me? When?"

"I can't *give* her to you—that's not the way we do things. She must decide for herself whether or not she wants to marry you."

"Well . . . my dear little English pigeon, what do you say?"

"Perhaps . . ." Nina says cautiously, "one day, when I know you better . . . After the war."

"After the war . . . ," he repeats her words as sadly as if she had said, "In another life."

Sighing, he kisses her hands, putting his lips to the pulsating veins on the inside of her wrists. I sense her inner shrinking, and so does he. "Don't be afraid," he says, "I am not going to hurt you. I love you. I can sleep with a dozen different women every night, and it means nothing to me—less than nothing. But you! You I *love.*"

Drawing her to him for a moment, he kisses her chastely on the forehead, then lets her go, and expends his frustrated ardor by lavishing filial embraces on me, which I return as before. But what had been an innocent gambit, now feels like a cruel deception; all the more shaming because Captain Friedman is not deceived. Searching my face for something that isn't there, he says, "My dear, dear little English mother . . . *you* are not beautiful . . . no . . . but you are clever. Very, very clever."

I wish K. would come back. I miss his moral support, and I am getting a bit worried about him. But while I am thinking this, the

Little Major and Oléna come back, looking flushed and frazzled, and K. follows. He comes over to me and kisses me lightly on the cheek—it is his way of saying he is sorry to have left me unsupported for so long. I press his hand. It is icy cold. "Are you all right?"

"Yes. I'm just cold, that's all."

"Where were you all this time?"

"In the W.C. I couldn't get out. Those two were blocking the door—and I had to let them finish."

The concertina boy, who has had his share of vodka, is falling asleep again, which makes Captain Friedman angry. Half-drunk, the boy picks up his concertina and gropes for the notes of a mournful song about exile and loss, a lament in a minor key whose yearning melody alone is enough to dissolve Captain Friedman's anger and turn the party into a wake.

Rivers of tears begin to flow. The Little Major weeps bitterly for his lost idol. "My good, good, good Little Colonel! Oh, my God! My God!" Captain Friedman remembers how, in his birthplace, the city of Kiev, the Germans threw little Jewish children and frail old men and women out of windows five stories high, and he too weeps bitterly. "Oh, my God! My God! My people! My people! I am so lonely, so unhappy. Oh, my God! So lonely. . . . So unhappy. . . ."

Sobbing, he covers his face with his hands and lays his head on my breast. And I, too, feel like weeping; both for and with this complex, unhappy man from whom the truth has been finally wrung... by what? By a mournful tune? By too much vodka? Or by an illusion born of his own deep need—a mirage of love in a desert of war?

Again the mood changes. Ashamed, no doubt, of his momentary display of weakness, Captain Friedman shouts at the concertina boy to play something lively. But K. intercedes for him, and he is allowed to go home.

The orderly sent off in search of food is not very successful. All he brings back is a slab of "quince cheese," a solid preserve made of quinces, and a bottle of raspberry syrup. "All for you," says Captain Friedman. We consume the preserve in two minutes. The bottle of raspberry syrup is put aside to be shared with the

rest of the family. "Children will like," says the Little Major, who
likes the children. Then he and Oléna go into the middle room,
leaving the door open. Its occupants, István, Károly, and Genevra,
appear to be fast asleep—which is not very likely, but helps me to
take a risky plunge. "I think it is time, now, for us all to get some
sleep, Captain Friedman."

"Ah yes! Sleep! Where will you sleep?"

"In the inner room—as usual."

"And I?"

"Here, in this room—I'll get a blanket for your bed."

"And the little girl?"

"In the inner room, with us."

"No! The little girl with me! Not so, Nina? You sleep with me?"

"No, not tonight," says Nina, gently, but firmly. "After the war,
in Russia, when we are married."

His face clouds. I feel the storm coming. Still perfectly coher-
ent, still perfectly steady on his feet, he is nevertheless very
drunk, and therefore dangerous. I go up close to him and take
both his hands, imprisoning them in mine. "Tell me, am I really
your English mother?"

"Yes, yes. My dear little English mother. . . ."

"And are you my Russian son?"

"Ah yes! My God, yes!"

His big brown eyes, those instruments that he uses so effectively when he is sober, have a helpless monkey-pathos in them
now, that is closer to truth.

"Then be a good son, and listen to me. Look at that boy on the
floor with Oléna. He is a nice lad, but he has no culture. You, my
dear Russian son, *do* have culture. And a cultured man doesn't
sleep with his bride before the wedding."

I hold him with my eyes as well as with my hands. Everything
hangs in the balance for a moment, then he says curtly, "All right.
Go to sleep."

Nina and K. say goodnight and retire while the going is good. I
fix up Captain Friedman's bed and go after them. He catches me
by the arm. "Give me the little girl! Oh God, oh God! Mother! Give
me the little girl!"

But his plea is forlorn, like that of a little boy who knows very
well that his mother will not give him what he wants, and he lets
me go.

For a long time he paces restlessly in and out of the middle room. We can hear him muttering to himself, and swearing in a mixture of Russian and German at the Little Major and Oléna, whose mutual ectasies seem to be more than he can bear. As long as this goes on we are not safe. Suddenly the expected happens, and our door is thrown open. He doesn't come in, however. He stands on the threshold and turns the light of his torch full on Nina, who lies very still with her eyes closed. The tension becomes unbearable. It is as though we were all paralyzed by the glare of the flashlight. I am the first to break the spell. I look at him and smile. He switches off the light, and says very quietly, "I only wanted to see my little English pigeon once more—that's all. Good night."

There is not much of the night left. At daybreak, he and the Little Major mount their horses and ride away. When all seems to be quiet, I go on a pilgrimage to the bathroom. My precious bottle of raspberry syrup is nowhere to be seen.

"The soldier servant took it," Genevra says, "I saw him."

"Why didn't you stop him—it was given especially for the children!"

"How could I know that? Anyway, how does one stop a Russian from taking anything he wants?"

Later in the day, the Little Major comes riding back, to see Oléna, and invite her to visit him in his new quarters. With me, he is suitably shamefaced. "Last night not good. I drink and drink and not know what I do."

I realize that this is meant as an apology, and I don't undervalue it. I say, "*Nitchevo*—it is good to dance and drink and forget sometimes."

Oléna goes off with him, leaving us to spend a nervous night with a vacant Russian room, and no interpreter to help us cope with possible invaders. But we are left unmolested that night, and all the next day. The Airwarden tells us that heavy fighting has broken out between our hill and the Vár—which may explain the absence of idle soldiers.

Late that night, we hear horsemen dismounting outside our door, and the Poet comes limping in, helped along by his orderly. He is wounded in the leg, and unable to find the field hospital, which he thought was still in our district, but seems to have moved. Can he spend the night with us—he is too tired to go any farther.

No one could be more welcome. His unexpected reappearance is like the return of a good friend one never thought to see again, and it would give us the same joy, were it not for the wound that brings him back, the pain he is in, and the possible danger to his life, as he lies there like the dying Buddha, untended by any physician. Unable to sleep, he asks for music, and Nina puts records on the gramophone all through the night. At the crack of dawn, his devoted young soldier servant helps him out of bed and onto his horse, and they ride away—this time never to return.

We shall never see Captain Friedman again, either. When Oléna comes back from what seems to have been a highly profitable visit to the new staff quarters, she brings the news that during the same surprise action in which the Poet was wounded, Captain Friedman was killed.

IV

Once again, two horsemen come riding over the devastated garden, dismount at our symbolically wide-open door, and walk in on us.

The senior of the two is a rotund little man who introduces himself, in English, as an *intendant*—an officer in charge of supplies—and the young fellow with him as his assistant.

His manner is that of a casual visitor dropping by for a chat. He seems to know who we are—no doubt he was responsible for supplying the staff kitchen, though I don't recall having seen him before. Anyway, he is friendly and polite, which is more than can be said for his assistant, and eager to show off his English.

The conversation starts off with the usual cultural litany, into which he cleverly manages to insert his own personal claims. Unlike the Poet, whose culture was innate, the Intendant seems to have obtained his in a university; and although in civilian life he and the Poet were both employed in a factory, he was an executive, while the Poet was merely a mechanic. He shows us a snapshot of his wife, taken in their Moscow apartment; the young woman is unexpectedly pretty and well-dressed, and her surroundings are unexpectedly comfortable. All in all, he seems to

be typical of a class that we have always believed to be anathema
in the Soviet Union—the bourgeoisie.

His assistant, whose name is Vassili, though of higher rank
than the Poet's soldier servant, is a boorish lout in comparison to
that natural aristocrat. He sits disrespectfully sprawled in an
armchair, with his cap slightly askew, and stares steadily at Nina
through half-closed eyes. She ignores him, and taking up her
sketch block, she starts to draw a line here, a line there, as though
trying out an idea. But from where I sit I can see what she is up to,
watch her as she captures in a few bold strokes the quintessential
lout. Predictably curious, her involuntary model gets up to look
over her shoulder, and a broad grin, an incredibly fatuous grin,
stretches his pimply face. Nina's counteroffensive has misfired.

The Intendant begs Nina to draw him too. She is kinder to him,
and unwittingly makes a friend of him by presenting him with an
image of himself that is probably more consistent with his own
than the one he gets from his shaving mirror.

The delighted pair ride off in high good humor, and Genevra
predicts that we haven't seen the last of them. She thinks we were
too nice to them, that fraternizing is a mistake. An opinion that K.
counters with his concert agent's advice on programming, "You
catch more flies with honey."

As it turns out, Genevra and K. each score a point. We have not
by any means seen the last of the two self-satisfied supply officers,
but they prove to be flies worth catching. They decide to move in
with us; but with them will come a cook and his assistant; our
barren premises will be transmogrified once again by that
wellspring of plenty, an army kitchen.

Sooner or later, in one way or another, good luck has to be paid
for, and the immediate price demanded of us for the magical
reappearance of vast quantities of food in our kitchen was that we
should be at the beck and call of our resident Russians at all hours
of the day and night—if one could sort out which was which—
either for hard work or hard drinking. Sleep was not on the
program, and the only way to get any was to drink oneself insensible, which the innocent Edit did so successfully at what might be
termed the "inauguration party," that she knocked herself out for
twenty-four hours.

In recounting these personal experiences of the piecemeal cap-

ture and occupation of Buda, I should emphasize that our particular position, on the occupied crest of a low hill, was rather like
being perched in the top branches of a not-very-tall tree with a
couple of tigers snarling around its foot. Intense street fighting
was still going on within a few hundred yards of us, bombers still
roared overhead on their way to attack the Vár, and all the
carousing that we were constrained to do was on an "eat, drink,
and be merry, for tomorrow we die" basis. And in addition to the
strain of that only too literal possibility, which we shared to some
extent with the Russians, we were prey to another kind of tension
all our own; the tension produced by the knowledge that only a
piece of paper, and our own personal ability to appeal to the better
side of individual Russians, stood between us and rape—in the
broadest meaning of the term as the comprehensive violation of
the dignity and rights of the civilian population by an occupying
army, which uses the physical rape of the women as a means of
subduing and humiliating the men, who are powerless to protect
them. And who only court worse disaster by attempting to do so.

The inaugural party begins in the morning of the day the
Intendant moves in, and is, in fact, the start of an on-going event,
like the non stop, no-sleep activity of the army kitchen; the only
difference being that the kitchen is run by an ex-engine driver,
and the party by a former executive, who continues as a supply
officer to be the master of his own work schedule, and allows himself an abundance of leisure time. As an officer he is obviously
more powerful than a cook, but the ex-engine driver is infinitely
more interesting, and equally useful to us in a different way.

His name is Ivan, and my first glimpse of him as I pass by the
kitchen is not reassuring. A tough looking character, dressed in a
dirty turtleneck jersey and khaki pants tucked into high boots,
with a red bandana tied around his head like a bandage, he looks
more like a pirate than a cook. And indeed, he and the Intendant
and their two good-for-nothing helpers are all engaged, both
singly and collectively, in a form of piracy known as "the just
redistribution of property," in which we tacitly connive—by
accepting its fruits—and will eventually practice ourselves,
along with everyone else.

Ivan will soon have all the women in the household working for
him; he is even harder pressed than the staff cooks were, since he

has to deliver hot meals to the front-line troops three times in the twenty-four hours; at noon, in the evening, and again in the early hours of the morning. But the only one of us available for work in the kitchen on "inauguration day" is Marcsa. Noblesse oblige that our cultured Intendant should grant the two mothers in the group, Genevra and myself, temporary exemption from "peeling potatoes" (a term that was soon to acquire a double meaning for the younger females conscripted for the chore). Nina and Edit are, of course, indispensable to the merrymaking—its raison d'etre in fact—and Oléna is still visiting the staff, which is work of another kind, yielding rich rewards of which we partake, for we are needy and Oléna is nothing if not generous.

Being Ivan's only female slave for the better part of a day and night, without any respite, is almost too much for Marcsa, worn out as she is by work for the staff cooks, her eyes inflamed by the smoke from the shell-damaged stove, her feet swollen from standing, every bone in her body aching. But despite all this, she accomplishes something above and beyond the preparation of food for the troops—she makes a devoted friend of Ivan, the pirate cook.

While she peels away at a mountain of potatoes, and he shapes innumerable meat balls between his dirt-ingrained palms, he talks about himself and she listens. They communicate in Hungarian, of which he has picked up enough during the campaign in Hungary to make himself understood. He can speak German, too, after a fashion. He picked that up, he tells Marcsa, before the war, as an engine driver on the Moscow-Berlin express, and it came in very handy when, on the outbreak of war, he became a partisan. After four years of guerrilla activity, which suited him down to the ground, he joined up as a regular Russian soldier, out of which all he got was an incapacitating wound that reduced him to serving his country by cooking for his comrades in arms. Driven more unremittingly than any express train, he keeps himself going on alcohol. He is never drunk, but he drinks anything he can lay hands on, from the finest French perfume to the raw spirits used in Primus stoves, and when Marcsa warns him that if he goes on like that he will burn out his insides, he says that he has no insides—only an engine. He and Marcsa are about the same age, both in their forties, but before the day is out he is calling her *Mama*.

For us, however, he is still an unknown quantity when he joins the second stage of the nonstop party after getting the evening meals carted off to the front lines.

The first stage of the party is relatively formal. The Intendant wants to show off his university education, and his ability to hold his own in the company of artists and intellectuals; an effort we encourage and challenge at the same time. Unfortunately, his ability to drink without getting drunk far exceeds ours, and we find it more and more difficult to keep up the level of intellectual challenge. Károly helps to sustain it by discoursing at length on agriculture—a subject on which the rest of us, including, I suspect, the Intendant, are abysmally ignorant. But after downing two obligatory toasts of straight vodka, he pales, and withdraws. Then Edit, whose glass has been kept filled with brandy by Vassili, shows signs of passing out, and Genevra, who stands in loco parentis to her, puts her to bed in the inner room and stays there with her and the children. From time to time, Nina escapes briefly on various pretexts, but she is always called back. The only unassailable refuge is the toilet, whose clogged drain makes it unendurable for any longer than one can hold one's breath.

At last, in the late afternoon, we are given a break. The Intendant and Vassili have to go out. In the vain hope that the party is at an end, we retire with deep sighs of relief and crashing headaches. Nina feels so ill that she takes to her bed—but with all her clothes on. Luckily.

For an hour or so we are left in peace. Then Vassili returns without the Intendant, bringing with him assorted comrades, two jars of wine, and a concertina. The party is on again.

We lie low. No good. Vassili calls for Nina. I tell him that she is sleeping, that she doesn't feel well. He comes in to see for himself, and yanks the covers off her. Faint, but furious, she gets up, and to get rid of Vassili, says she will join the party a little later, if she feels better. But there is no way of avoiding it; even to go to the toilet or bathroom she has to run the gauntlet of the assembled comrades. So she combs her long hair, ties it back with a bit of ribbon, takes a deep breath, and goes in. I go in with her. K. remains "on call," so to speak. For him to sit down and carouse with young cubs like Vassili and Andrei in the absence of their superior officer, would be to destroy his most valuable asset as a protector—his dignity.

Our other source of moral protection, the *documente*, should, we realize now, have been shown to the Intendant and Vassili when they first came to the house. But it hadn't seemed necessary then, and now it might even have an adverse effect; it could be taken as an admission of fear, fatal with all dangerous animals, human or otherwise.

Nina and I make, I think, a brave entrance, with our faces wreathed in false smiles. But my heart sinks as I look at the ruffianly faces around the table; their sinister qualities thrown into high relief by the bluish flames that rise from the bowl of fat in its center. Their strangeness is intimidating in itself. In this gallery of rogues, there are two (they turn out to be coachmen) with slit eyes and flat Mongol features who must be from Central Asia; alien, unreadable, and for that reason if for no other, threatening. Next to them, dwarfing them, sits an immensely tall soldier with very white teeth, who smiles all the time, but without the least warmth; he would go on smiling, I think, over our dead bodies. On the other side of the table is Vassili, and next to him is Ivan's assistant, Andrei; a young bruiser with a vicious, degenerate face, who makes the loutish Vassili seem like a fine gentleman. By himself at the end of the table is Ivan, playing the concertina.

He bends over it with the same concentration, the same detachment from his surroundings, that is characteristic of K. when he is playing his cello. But where K.'s detachment is due to his absorption in his art, Ivan's brooding expression is more likely due to sheer physical weariness.

When he does give us his attention, he looks straight at us with a pair of piercingly brilliant blue eyes; sea eyes, deep-set in his weathered face like the eyes of an old sailor, but too kind to be those of a pirate. He says in English, "Good night," puts his concertina down, and extends a hard, dirt-ingrained hand which seems to be made, like his face, of old leather. But his grip is firm—the grip of a man who can be trusted.

Vassili grabs Nina by the arm and pulls her down onto the chair next to him. I sit facing them across the table, a long table, liberated from someone else's kitchen. On its bare, wine-stained surface sits an incongruously delicate lacquer tray, piled high with hard-fried eggs. There are no plates or tableware, just a single two-pronged fork with which each man spears his own

eggs and pops them directly into his mouth. Nina and I follow
their example. Our desire for the eggs is stronger than our disgust, and to ask for a private fork would be an insult. The glasses,
the usual tall tumblers, are communal too. The smiling soldier
next to me drains the wine from the glass he has shared with the
coachman on his right, refills it to the brim, and holds it to my
lips.

Ivan plays *Volga-Volga*, and leads the company with his strong
bass voice through a dozen or more verses. Vassili gets bolder; it is
all Nina can do to fend off his exploring hands, but she does it with
a smile, and repeated promises to marry him in Moscow. I, too,
smile. And smiling, always smiling, I keep him trapped in a
steady stare. And it works. I sense uneasiness under his insolent
manner, a fear of incurring the Intendant's wrath by forcing
himself on the wrong girl, and in the wrong company—for the
hoodlum Andrei, and the two slit-eyed coachmen are only waiting for Vassili to make the first move in a terrible free-for-all, in
which the tall soldier will join, still smiling. But not Ivan. Of that I
feel sure; though I doubt whether he would, or could, do anything
to stop the pack from pouncing on Nina.

It takes me a while to realize that he is not really as detached as
he seems to be. I notice that whenever Vassili gets too bold, he
manages to create some sort of disturbance; he stops playing, or
announces a new song, or asks for more wine. And he asserts his
authority over Andrei by sending him off to the kitchen to fry
more eggs—of which the supply seems to be inexhaustible. And,
in fact, there are six hundred not-very-fresh eggs in our kitchen,
waiting to be eaten. They were found preserved in "water glass"
in a bakery cellar, and liberated by order of the Intendant.

Around midnight, when Nina, though still unravished and still
smiling, is on the verge of hysteria, the Intendant walks in, with a
jaunty, self-satisfied air that suggests time passed in the requisitioning of something other than food supplies. But he says just the
right thing. He says, "Where is the Professor? Bring in the
Professor!"

Thank God! We are safely back on the cultural heights again!

We find an opportunity to mention the *documente*, which we
bring out and show, casually but proudly, like a family photograph album. Vassili is inclined to jeer at it, but the Intendant
has a healthy respect for official documents, and this one works

wonders. It wins us a relatively early release from the party. Thanks to the respect it engenders in the Intendant, he allows us, with a fairly good grace, to retire at about 3:00 A.M.

We now have a means of telling the time of day, or night, without asking some Russian to look at one of the numerous liberated watches that he keeps on his person. Ivan has a clock; a large, loud, moon-faced clock looted from somebody else's kitchen, which no marauding soldier dares take from him. Ivan has another valuable possession, a small kerosene lamp—of which more later.

The party is still going on, or has been restarted, when we get up and pass through the room on our morning trip to the bathroom. And now there is something tempting on the table; two large cans of sliced pineapple—something that these particular Russians have never tasted before and don't much like. It doesn't take us long to eat it for them; slightly tart, it helps to counteract the nausea induced by a surfeit of fried eggs.

Today, the break comes early. The Intendant and Vassili have been wasting too much time, and they ride off on their requisitioning trip around noon, promising to be back by eight in the evening.

We talk matters over. Nina says that she can't take the strain of this sort of thing much longer—it's worse than the shelling, and I, too, am at the end of my tether. Finally we decide to test the power of the *documente* and risk passive resistance. When they come back, they will find us all in bed and asleep—except for Marcsa, who cannot, and will not, leave Ivan unaided. We instruct her to tell the Intendant and Vassili that we are all dead—from fatigue.

They were, it seems, furious. But the power of the *documente* was such that instead of routing us out, as Vassili had on the previous evening, they slammed out of the house in a rage, to look for greener pastures, which, apparently, they found.

The Intendant turned up next day in a sulky mood, but he accepted our humble, tongue-in-cheek apologies. The party, however, was over as far as we were concerned. With the Intendant were two little middle-aged men, stoop-shouldered and bespectacled, more like gnomes than soldiers, although they wore army uniforms. One was a tailor, and the other a shoemaker, and within an hour our Russian room had become a workshop for the mending and making of army boots and uniforms on two old-fashioned treadle machines operated by the feet of the gnomes; funny, decent, put-upon little men, who worked night and day, nonstop, save for occasional, brief, Napoleonic naps taken in relays on the single divan bed. They, too, had a kerosene lamp, but unlike Ivan's it had no subsequent history. When the gnomes disappeared, their lamp disappeared with them.

They took no notice of us. They were blind to everything but the task in hand. But their humming workshop protected us, and gave Ivan a valid excuse for keeping out strange soldiers. Despite his watchdog attitude, however, two soldiers bent on mischief caught sight of a small, shabby suitcase on top of a cupboard in the hallway, and made off with it before he could stop them. It belonged to Marcsa, and contained the only garments she possessed. Ivan ran after the thieving pair and tried to shame them into giving the suitcase back, but they merely laughed. Marcsa was in tears. Ivan told her gruffly to get on with her work, there was no use in crying over spilt milk—or the Russian equivalent of that annoying maxim. But when a bolt of fine woolen cloth fell into his hands, he gave it to *Mama* to replace what had been taken from her. She had qualms of conscience about accepting it. But we all told her not to feel guilty. This was a perfect example of a really *just* redistribution of property; moreover, she would not be the only one to benefit from it—there was enough material on the roll to clothe her sister and her nieces as well. So she took it, and hid it under the bed in the inner room.

A similar problem of conscience presented itself to the rest of us when Oléna returned from her visit to the staff, disillusioned with men, but laden with the liberated goods that she had cunningly extorted from them in exchange for her favors, and some of which she presented to us. Among them were two fine quality shirts in K.s size, which he desperately needed.

On the morning after Oléna's return, when the workshop had been in operation for two days and nights, the equilibrium produced by its unvarying tempo of activity was shattered.

The Intendant, who was always in and out, supervising, and who remained, rather surprisingly, friendly to us, suddenly had the machines pushed into a corner and the room filled up with bales and bales of textiles—beautiful materials that had not been obtainable for years. Some were in short lengths, others in whole bolts, and they all had to be parceled out into separate packages, weighed, then sewn up in sacking for shipment to Russia, for the families of the officers and men. The gnomes worked feverishly at this job all day, with several assistants. We were not conscripted to help—probably because the job was too specialized. Anyway, we were happy to be let off.

At about five o'clock in the afternoon, the Intendant came into our room with another officer, a stranger to us, and evidently his superior, for his manner to him was deferential to the point of being obsequious. When the two staff colonels had entered our room for the first time, Captain Friedman had introduced them to us. But apparently this glowering individual was a more important personage than even a staff colonel, for we were presented to him—as if he were visiting royalty. The Intendant, however, introduced K. as a "famous cellist," and professor at the Conservatory of Music, and he stressed the fact that Nina, Genevra, and I were all three English. Who was this man? And why was the Intendant so anxious to impress him with *our* credentials?

His name, like most of the Russian names, has got lost in time, I remember only that it started with an *L*. And it is under the forever anonymous designation of "Captain L," that his dark presence still haunts me. But time has altered my perception of him. I no longer see him as the personification of evil, but rather as its victim—the Devil's plaything.

My first impression of Captain L., as he shakes hands with each of us (Edit, Oléna, and Marcsa are working in the kitchen), and makes a clumsy attempt to pat the children on the head, is abstract; a combination of abstract qualities; darkness, power, danger . . . that set alarm bells ringing in a subterranean corner of my mind. Bells that evoke a childhood memory of a visit to a zoo, and my fear that a great, restless, black panther with yellow eyes would somehow get at me through the bars of his cage.

The introductions over, the two officers sit down at our little round table, the Poet's table, and a meal—which must have been previously ordered by the Intendant—is brought in by Andrei, together with a bottle of brandy. Captain L. then issues a curt invitation, with the ring of an order, to Nina, to come and share it with them, and the Intendant pulls up a chair for her with a great show of politeness, as though trying to warn Captain L. to go easy with this girl.

He drinks steadily and eats nothing. Like Buddha, he has the gift of immobility. Silent and motionless, he sits gazing at Nina as the panther I saw in the zoo might have watched a doe grazing within the range of its murderous leap. He has very strange eyes; the sort of eyes that seem to be looking inward even when they are fixed on some tangible object.

The Intendant tries, like a nervous hostess, to make conversation; encouraging Nina to show off her phrase-book Russian. But Captain L. is not inclined to show off his English. An impasse of this kind can usually be got over with German, but since the Intendant doesn't suggest it, we assume that Captain L. either cannot or will not speak the enemy's language.

His gloomy silence creates the stifling atmosphere that precedes a hurricane, and as the level of brandy in the bottle goes down like a rapidly sinking barometer, Captain L. starts to mutter to himself in Russian. Then, suddenly raising his head and addressing us all, he says, "You understand German—yes?" And without waiting for an answer, he launches into a ferocious accusatory tirade; spitting out in the German language a terrible hymn of hate for the German people; a litany of their crimes against the Russian people; the murder of his parents, his wife, his children; the burning of his home, the destruction of his village. Crimes that cry out for vengeance. He raises his hands aloft like some unholy chalice. "Look at these hands! Look at them! They have killed five hundred of the Fascist swine already!"

The children begin to cry, and the sound seems to bring him to his senses. He drops his hands with a little sardonic laugh. "Don't be afraid," he says, "they are not going to kill *you*."

Genevra takes the frightened children into the inner room, and Captain L. returns to his contemplation of Nina.

Now, the weight of his silence is crushing. I can think of nothing but his big, square, murderer's hands. He starts on a new bottle of brandy. He fills Nina's glass, but he does not press her to drink. For him, it seems, unlike the other Russians, drinking is a private, not a convivial act.

With his inward gaze still outwardly fixed on Nina, he says in German, to no one in particular, "Bring in the woman Olèna."

Oléna comes in perky and smiling, all set to please this important person. But he wipes the flirtatious smile from her face with a single shouted epithet. Then he fires questions at her like a machine gun. We understand enough Russian to get the gist of them.

"You left Ruthenia to come here with suspect people. "Why?"

"You did not accompany them further. Why?"

"You are living now with English bourgeois. Why?"

"You sleep with officers only. Why?"

"You have just spent several days at staff headquarters. Why?"

"Why? Why? Why?" (On a rapid crescendo.) *Why? Because you are a spy!*"

Two soldiers are called in. They take her forcibly away, screaming and protesting.

We are stunned. Oléna a spy! We refuse to believe it.

"You are fools," says Captain L.

After an interval of about fifteen minutes, during which no one speaks, and I imagine the worst, Oléna is brought back, subdued and sullen, and the rapid fire of accusations and questions begins all over again.

I am reminded of Captain Friedman's interrogation of German prisoners. But Captain Friedman was possessed, whether he knew it or not, by the spirit of comedy, and Captain L. is possessed by unmitigated hate; by a lust for vengeance that no longer discriminates between the innocent and the guilty, but embraces all humanity.

Once again, Oléna is taken away. Unresisting this time, but bitterly weeping.

I ask the Intendant in English what is going to happen to her, and Captain L. answers me in German, "She will be shot."

I stifle a cry, and the nervous Intendant gives me a warning look. We are trapped in a bad dream; one of those nightmares in which one cannot escape from some oncoming horror because of the quicksands that suck at one's legs. I find myself listening for the special sound of a firing squad—as if that would free me.

Then the incomprehensible happens—incomprehensible, that is, to us, for whom this is a first experience.

The convicted spy is brought in, white and trembling, but unharmed, and Captain L., instead of shouting at her, invites her to sit down and have a drink with him.

So now there are four at the Poet's table: Oléna and Nina, almost equally pale and frightened; and more sisterly than appears on the surface; the Intendant, who looks as though he is sitting on dynamite; and Captain L., the sturnine controller of the dream.

The Intendant makes a grab at normality by ordering fried eggs. And it isn't a bad idea. There is something of the peace pipe about a dish of fried eggs eaten with a communal fork. Even though Captain L. does not take part in the ritual, it eases the tension and revives Oléna's natural buoyancy. After half a dozen eggs washed down with a couple of straight brandies, she is making full use of the only defensive weapon she has; her earthy sexual appeal, and although Captain L. demonstrates later that he is impervious to it, he allows her to keep on trying, which works to Nina's advantage. All in all, his preoccupation with Oléna has had the effect of relaxing his preoccupation with Nina, and the wily Intendant, who, for obscure reasons of his own is more concerned with Nina's welfare than with Oléna's, takes advantage of it to remove Nina from his immediate proximity.

The work of packaging the textiles cannot, it seems, be completed on time without additional help, and he asks Nina and me to provide it. We understand his maneuver, and agree with alacrity. He puts us in the assembly line between the weighers and the labelers. Equipped with big, curved packing needles and string, our job is to sew up each parcel of goods in sacking as tautly and rapidly as we can, by the light of the tailor's little kerosene lamp.

From time to time, Captain L. comes in, and pressing up very close to Nina, growls, half as a question and half as an order, "*Du liebst mich, Nina.*" To which Nina replies, "I have work to do." Whereupon, he goes back to Oléna. His visits are followed by visits from the Intendant, ostensibly to see how the work is getting on. He, too, comes up close to Nina, and whispers in English, "Don't sleep with that officer, Nina." Nina replies that she has no intention of sleeping with any officer. But every time Captain L. makes his demand, the Intendant repeats his warning—and with more and more urgency. And I, thinking of these instruments of death, Captain L.'s hands, I grow more and more anxious as to how the night will end. It is not foreseeable; before the night is over, chance will have intervened twice to change its direction.

Around midnight, when the packaging work is almost finished, who should come running in, like a terrified hen, but the snobbish baroness from next door, with the two dear little girls.

She has never paid us a social call, but here she is, on her knees, metaphorically speaking, imploring sanctuary for her daughters at the most inopportune moment imaginable. I put my finger on my lips, but Captain L. and the Intendant have already heard the commotion, and they come in to see what it's all about.

Captain L. looks at the two fair-haired teenagers like a tiger licking its chops over a pair of tender, tethered goats. And a wicked gleam comes into the Intendant's small eyes that is not difficult to interpret. Chance has brought him the means of placating Captain L., enjoying himself, and saving Nina all at the same time. He speaks reassuringly to the two juicy morsels, and hustles them into the middle room, where K. and István try to calm their fears. Meanwhile, the naive baroness tells the tiger her story and begs for his assistance.

It seems that the only habitable room in their bomb-damaged villa is occupied by a lieutenant, who got wind of the two girls concealed in the cellar, but failed to find them—they were too securely walled up. So he told the baron that if they were not produced within half an hour, they would be "smoked out," and he meant that literally. Overhearing this, the baroness managed to sneak the girls out and through the gap in the hedge to us—and, ironically, into far more dangerous hands than those of the unfortunate lieutenant, whose hash was soon settled by Captain L.

Marcsa, who has been careful to keep Edit out of sight in the kitchen, takes advantage of Captain L.'s absence to slip with her into the inner room, which Genevra and Károly, who reoccupied it after the staff left, share not only with the children, Edit, and Marcsa, but with anyone who needs to be kept out of view and relatively safe from molestation. It amounts to a cul de sac, something that even the most amorous Russian is leery of entering. But the Intendant makes sure that the little girls don't take refuge there.

When Captain L. comes back from disciplining the lieutenant, he goes straight to the middle room, without reasserting his claim on Nina's love. Does that mean he has given her up for the easier prey? Or merely that he plans to enjoy them first? Either way, I am involved. The fact that the responsibility for the baron's dear little girls has been thrust upon me in no way lessens it.

Nina and I are just sewing up the last of our parcels, at about 1
A.M., when K. and István come into the workroom with the
Intendant. I tell him that the work is all done.

"Very good," he says. "Now you and Nina can go to bed."

K. gives me a look that I don't quite understand. "István and I
will be staying in here," he says.

"*In here!*" There is no place to sit, let alone lie down. Even the
gnomes' single cot is covered with packages—they are piled ceiling high.

The Intendant looks embarrassed. Up until now he has treated
K. with an almost exaggerated respect, yet here he is treating
him like a prisoner, turning him out of his own quarters and
putting him in the charge of a young soldier with a rifle. I open
my mouth to protest, but K. shakes his head, and says cheerfully,
"István and I will be all right in here. We will make ourselves
comfortable—after all, the packages are not filled with cast iron."

In the middle room, the two young girls and Oléna are sitting
around the Poet's table drinking, or pretending to drink, while
Captain L. repeats his hymn of hate and his litany of wrongs for
their benefit—which seems to be a strange way of courting them.
They look relieved to see me and Nina. But the Intendant
whispers to us urgently, in English, "Go to bed. Don't sit down. Go
to bed in the other room."

I know that he is trying to help us as well as himself by getting
us out of the way. But I cannot, I will not buy Nina's safety with
the bodies, and quite possibly the lives, of someone else's daughters. And I am certain that Nina, for all her horror of Captain L.,
wouldn't want that either. So we put on our smiling masks and
join the party.

Oléna is splendid; a champion of women's rights, if ever there
was one. She understands without being told why we can't and
won't leave the little girls to their fate; and although they belong
to a privileged class that she, as a Communist, wants to abolish,
she won't abandon them either, for the simple reason that they
are female—and as helpless as newborn kittens at that. (By her
standards.)

I have never in my life been as afraid of anyone as I am of
Captain L. Oléna is just as terrified of him as I am, but for reasons
quite different from mine. She knows that he still suspects her of
spying, and she believes, in her simplicity, that the best way to

avoid being shot by him is to sleep with him. And that if he enjoys
sleeping with her, he won't be interested in a pair of inexpe-
rienced schoolgirls, and Nina, difficult, English, and armed with
a letter of protection, may seem, after what Oléna has to offer
him, more trouble than she is worth. And so, in helping herself
she will be helping us, too.

This is a reasonable deduction, but Captain L. is not a reasonable man, or, in my judgment, even a sane one, and my fears are
centered on just how he will go about satisfying those sexual
desires once they are fully aroused. For the moment, he seems to
be half asleep; brooding on wrongs that have nothing to do with
us, but for which he is warped enough to avenge himself on the
innocent.

The Intendant, who regards Oléna as a whore, gets offensively
bold with her, and when I stare coldly at what he is doing, he
mutters, "Go to bed." But the Intendant is not Oléna's game—
getting off with him won't help her or anyone. Somehow she has to
pierce the dark cloud that envelopes Captain L. She thinks she
can do it with music. When Andrei comes in with more brandy,
she asks him for the loan of his concertina.

Its effect on Captain L. is immediate and alarming. After one
whining chord, he snatches the instrument out of her hands,
dashes it violently to the floor, and kicks it to pieces. All without
uttering a word.

But this physical burst of rage changes his mood. Like Captain
Friedman, in the course of the campaign he has helped himself to
numerous valuable objects. But where Captain Friedman's
choices were sentimental and indiscriminate, Captain L.'s have
the cold exclusiveness of the true collector.

One by one, he produces from his pockets twenty watches, of
varying shapes and sizes, but all made of gold or platinum, and
one or two set with diamonds; the luxury watches of the wealthy.
He lays them out in neat rows on the table, and sits gazing at them
with intense concentration, even with love—the love that he can
no longer feel for human beings. He touches them one after the
other with the square tips of his thick fingers, like a miser making sure that he still has all his money.

When, finally, he replaces them in his various pockets, he takes
care to display the two heavy service revolvers that he carries on
his person. And as if they were not enough to intimidate us, he

reaches into the back pocket of his riding breeches and brings out a short, tough, leather dog whip, and prowls up and down cracking it at a pack of imaginary dogs.

He is threatening me. I know that. I instinctively rise to my feet. Nina and the girls get up, too. Oléna has the wit to stay put and keep the Intendant's attention on herself.

Dog whip in hand, Captain L. comes up very close to me, and brutally orders me to get out. I refuse. "You can't order *me* around ... I am English!" He grabs me by the shoulders. I yell to Nina and the girls, "Run!" He lets me go and tries to stop them. But I am lighter and faster than he is. I intercept him. Enraged, he gives me a flying kick in the bottom that lands me face downward over the threshold of the cul de sac, just as his quarry vanishes into the dark interior. Rage animates. I am back on my feet in an instant, and in such a towering fury that I am no longer afraid of him, or his whip, or his revolvers—let him use them on me if he dare!

But he doesn't dare. We confront each other like David and Goliath at close range. (Though the simile doesn't occur to me until later.) I say nothing. I stand there staring him straight in the eyes in absolute silence, while he storms, raves, threatens, mocks. "I'll beat you within an inch of your life, you insolent English bitch! *'I am English.'* you say with your head in the air, *English... English... English...* I'll put your insolent head down for you!" And on, and on, and on he goes. But he does nothing. I never for an instant take my eyes from his, and in the end it is he who looks away. I have won, I think. Or have I? He suddenly slams the door shut in my face and turns the key, locking us all in. As fury cools, common sense returns—and fears for K.'s safety.

Now Oléna comes to the door with a whispered warning, "Don't try to escape through the window, the house is surrounded by an armed guard."

She is followed a moment or two later by Captain L., who, without unlocking the door, orders me to give the two little girls over to him. I refuse.

After an agonizing interval of silence, he says, clearly and loudly, so that everyone can hear, including K. and István, "If the two young girls are not produced *immediately*, the whole house will be destroyed."

This is the same threat that, made to the baron by the lieutenant, brought the girls to us in the first place, and the irony does not go unperceived by them. It makes them feel guilty. And they, in their turn, make us feel guilty, by saying that rather than bring destruction on our whole family, they will comply with Captain L.'s order. They tell him so themselves, through the door. They are frightened, but courageous. When the door is opened by Captain L., Oléna is there to assure us that she will do her best to help them. But Captain L. is having none of that. After roughly pulling the two girls over the threshold, he pushes Oléna in, and relocks the door. She tells us that K. and István are still under armed guard, but that so far no harm has come to them. We want to know why the house is surrounded by an armed guard. But she doesn't know that, either. She heard Captain L. give the order, but she didn't dare ask any questions.

I am shaking with cold and nerves. Genevra wraps my old fur coat around my shoulders and tells me that she is proud of the way I stood up to Captain L. But I feel defeated. I sit on the edge of the bed nearest to the door, listening. I think, "If I hear those girls scream I'll smash the door in and Captain L. can shoot me if he wants." But I hear only men's voices, Russian voices. Have they taken the girls away? There is a lot of coming and going on the other side of the door—what's happening?

Now, Captain L. comes to the door and says, "The Germans are in the next street. They will be in this house before morning—and they will shoot the whole damn lot of you!"

This announcement is followed by a stillness, a cessation of activity inside the house, that makes the constant background noise of battle outside seem suddenly closer and louder. What Captain L. said must be true—and in that case we probably will be shot. I start to pray silently, God help us. God help us. . . .

The key turns softly in the lock, the door is quietly opened, and the two little girls say in a whisper, "They've gone."

Warily, we investigate. K. and István are still in the workroom, safe and sound—probably thanks to the Intendant—but uncertain of whether it's safe to move. Everyone else has flitted. Cooks, tailor, shoemaker, sewing machines, packages, food—all have vanished. It seems that just after the two girls had put themselves at the mercy of Captain L., a patrol had come in and said that a unit of German troops had broken through the Russian defenses and were just around the corner, and everyone left in great excitement.

We all sit down in the middle room and wait to see what will happen next. We keep our voices very low. Oléna tells us what happened to her during her interrogation. When the soldiers had taken her away between grillings, they had blindfolded her, and frog-marched her back and forth in circles, at the barrel end of a rifle, telling her that they were taking her to headquarters, where she would be shot—by order of Captain L. She could save herself only by confession. The trouble was, she had nothing to confess— nothing, that is, of interest to Captain L. The soldiers in charge of her carried out these tactics with glee, according to István and K., who heard them laughing and talking about her—it served her right, they said, for being so choosy about whom she slept with. Well, chance had saved her, and us, from the tender mercies of Captain L. But what about the Germans?

As we talk, it begins to grow light, and the noise of battle recedes. The sound of a footstep in the hallway freezes us—is it the first German soldier?

It is Ivan, good old Ivan, dressed as a patrol and carrying a rifle—his dignity as a soldier momentarily restored. We are so pleased to see him we could hug him. And he seems equally pleased to find us all alive and intact. He sits down and offers us cigarettes, and smokes one with us. It was true, he said, that a pocket of Germans had managed to break through the Russian defenses at a point very close to us, but they had been driven back, and now there was no more danger. He was still on patrol duty, he said, not without pride, but later in the morning he would be back, with Andrei, to set up his kitchen again.

One more Russian night is over.

The Intendant avoided us after that night, and we never saw Captain L. again. But we learned from Oléna, who got it from one of her lovers on the staff, that he was a "political officer" (whatever that meant), and had the power not only to chastise a too-easy-going Intendant, but also to check up on the activities, or the inactivity, of a factory manager in civilian life, and get him sent off to learn the meaning of hard work in Siberia. And if that was true, the Intendant deserved more credit for his efforts to save Nina from a dangerous monomaniac than we gave him at the time.

Because Ivan was only marginally involved in our experiences with the Intendant and Captain L., I have allowed them to overshadow him. Yet his impact on our lives during his brief reign over our smoke-filled kitchen was greater than theirs, just as he himself was a greater human being than either of them. He ranks in my memory with the Poet. Though their juxtaposition in my gallery of Russian portraits provides just as wild a contrast as that afforded by our first two examples of Russian individualism —the bronze Buddha and the jet-and-ivory mobile.

Ivan's ambition was to have his portrait drawn by Nina; and she could hardly have found a more interesting subject; but he was so chronically weary, that he was unable to sit still for more than two minutes without falling asleep. Nina did make a few swift line drawings of him, and she may have given them to him; in any event, all I have to go on is my visual memory, and the images it comes up with. There was, of course, no way of taking any photographs. Our two cameras had been liberated from us by the first wave of Russians—as were everyone else's—and anyway, we had run out of film long before that.

It is impossible to separate Ivan's physical appearance from his personality. Tall and muscular, with a broad slavic face, he looked exactly what he was; a man born to hardship and labor; a man whose proudest achievement was to drive the engine of one of the fastest express trains in Europe; a man who enjoyed the dangers and risks of guerrilla warfare; and a man, finally, with enough sense of humor to salvage his pride by proclaiming himself, with a wink and a grin, as the best cook in the Red Army.

Like all good cooks, he was extravagant. His cabbage soup, and his borscht were based on pure essence of beef, and the meat from which it had been extracted would be thrown out of the kitchen window onto the ever-rising mountain of garbage—which was, fortunately for our health, still partially frozen. But after he saw Marcsa go out one day and retrieve the discarded soup meat for our supper, he would remove it from the pot sooner, while it still had some nourishment left in its fibers, and before putting it out on the garbage pile, he would carefully wrap it up in whatever paper he could get hold of, sometimes old newspaper, and sometimes the pages of Mr. A.'s books.

Circumventing official policy regarding the feeding of civilians was easier for Ivan than it had been for the little Caucasian staff cook; for one thing, Ivan was bolder, and for another, the Intendant was more careless and less authoritarian than Captain

Friedman. But although Marcsa could count on getting from
Ivan, one way or another, the wherewithal for our one daily meal,
she never knew when she would be allowed to cook it, since
feeding the troops was Ivan's first concern, and the two stove tops
were almost permanently covered with huge cooking pots liberated from some hotel kitchen.

There was one basic commodity that he and his kitchen lacked
in common with us, and that was soap. It had been unavailable for
a long time, but so had a lot of other items that had been
unearthed by the Russians. Was soap too precious to be squan-
dered on the troops—had it all been shipped off to Russia for
wives and families, like the textiles?

Anyway, Ivan didn't have any, and neither did we—even the
homemade lye soap with which we had washed our clothes before
the water stopped running had given out—and the lack of it was
a cause of mutual inconvenience, to put it politely. Only the
solitary hermit can go unwashed and wear the same penitential
sackcloth for weeks on end without offending. In this respect,
Ivan presented a curious anomaly. He could do without soap on
his body, a quick rubdown with icy water sufficed him, and he
always wore the same old turtleneck jersey—day and night. But
he liked the feel of a clean shirt next his skin and clean socks on his
feet; an oddly fastidious need that he met by the simple expedient
of liberating (or having Andrei liberate for him), clean, and often
brand new shirts and socks whenever he needed a change, and
throwing the soiled ones out on the garbage pile.

To me it was a measure of how far we had come in distinguish-
ing the essential from the nonessential, that we judged Ivan an
honest man and valued his friendship—for there is no other word
to describe his protective attitude toward us; his recognition of
us—strangers, foreigners, political and ideological aliens—as fellow human beings in need of help. And he helped us in every way
he could.

When the nearby private well fell into Russian hands, it
became the daily scene of an unequal struggle between hearty,
fur-hatted Russian soldiers and emaciated, thinly-clad civilians,
most of them women, vying for access to it. But we had the
advantage of being championed by Ivan.

As soon as it was light, Ivan would marshal his water

carriers—usually Marcsa, Nina, and István—and lead them across the treacherous, rubble and missile strewn half-mile to the site of the well. There, he would dispute violently with his compatriots for the right to fill his buckets first, and needless to say, *our* buckets were *his* buckets. But we got our fair share of the water, and Ivan's show of autocracy saved us both harassment and hours of waiting in line.

It was by the same cock-of-the-walk method that he saved us from graver trouble. The flitting of the gnomes, with their constantly humming machines, had left us wide open to intrusion at night, and to conscription as potato peelers for some subsidiary—or even wholly imaginary—kitchen. But Ivan would keep out these prowlers by telling them, in effect, "All the women in this house are *my* slaves, and don't you dare lay a finger on them!"

How much gratitude we owed him for this was brought home to me, and to all of us, very sharply one night, when a strange, distressful sound invaded my dreams, and finally woke me up. It came from the outer room. And it was weeping of a kind I had never heard before. Tears of grief, tears of mourning, evoke compassion. Tears of penitence, even tears of rage, can evoke respect. But the tears occasioned by defilement are a bitter distillation of shame that arouses a feeling of shame in others, and an instinctive recoil from its source. And I believe that the raped woman senses this, and that part of her agony and despair lies in the terrible realization that, through no fault of her own, she has become a pariah. A realization that must have been all the more devastating to this particular victim because she was newly married. Her husband, a young Hungarian soldier, who had deserted—along with hundreds of others—to avoid being sent to fight side by side with the Nazis on German soil, had been taken away by the Russians to work on a railway bridge. That night, his bride had been rounded up, with three or four older women, to peel potatoes. When the work was done, the older women had been let go, but the young one was forced to stay, to be brutally raped by half a dozen soldiers, over and over, until all she wanted was to die.

She had sought shelter with us because she knew Marcsa. But although we sheltered her, we could not console her. She lay on the bed in the inner room with the covers over her face, making little moaning sounds, even in her sleep. Then her husband came back, and learning that his wife was in hiding with us, and why, he presented himself at our door in a state of extreme agitation. But after Marcsa had talked with him, he grew calmer, and she took him into the inner room and left him alone with his wife.

He went in an outraged boy. An hour later, he came out a man; with his arm protectively around his wife's shoulders. They were both bravely smiling, but her smile was more uncertain than his. Perhaps, as a woman, she knew that the acceptance, even the forgiveness, of an irreversible wrong is easier than the long, slow business of forgetting it.

Shortly after the fall of Buda in mid-February, Ivan and the food left us for new quarters in another part of the city. And I don't know which was the most frightening; the loss of our only protector against molestation, or the loss of our only source of food—which last, Ivan tried to mitigate by turning a blind eye on a little minor redistribution of his supplies during the packing-up process—just enough to keep us going for a few days.

His farewell "thank you" to Marcsa for all her help was his kerosene lamp; and his legacy to us all was his clock. Simple objects of little intrinsic value, they were—at that time and place—infinitely precious. And to me they were symbolic. But their symbolism remained abstract, until, one night, the lamp was shot to pieces and the clock went on ticking.

5

After the Vortex, Limbo

*T*HE fall of Buda, which put the entire city of Budapest into Russian hands, eliminated the danger of being killed by an enemy missile, and, although it opened us up to many a lesser danger, set us free after weeks of virtual imprisonment in our dugout to explore the surrounding wilderness of death and devastation.

Terrible images come up in response to my recall of that desolating scene. Yet the echo that accompanies them is the echo, confused and elusive, of bird song and bells and the whirr of phoenix wings.

Let us go first, buckets in hand, to the thermal springs at the base of the hill in search of water. In normal times, with a shortcut down a steep cobbled street, the walk would have taken a scant twenty minutes. Now, we are not at all sure that we can accomplish it at all. The familiar streets are no longer recognizable. They are simply piles of rubble with nothing to distinguish them one from another. We can smell death everywhere. Under the rubble, frozen corpses are starting to rot in the first February thaw. We have to pick our way carefully to avoid stepping on them. As we scramble downward over the hills and valleys of rubble and enter the zone of the fiercest street battles, the stench and the horror are numbing. Dead soldiers, Russian and German and Hungarian, still lie where they fell, some of them stripped of their leather boots, some of them flattened by the wheels of passing vehicles, and they are all so young. So young. The thought of their mothers waiting and hoping in vain breaks my heart, and bursts open the lid of the box in which I have kept my own two sons locked away, shut out of my conscious mind, ever since the day when Hungary's entry into the war cut the lines of communication between us. And suddenly, here they are, lying dead in the blood-darkened snow, mutely demanding a requiem.

On the lower slopes of this nightmare landscape of rubble are grotesque barricades, ten feet high, made up of household belongings—tables, chairs, beds, gas stoves, pianos—dragged from the nearest ruins and piled up pell-mell one on top of the other.

Just beyond the first barricade is a disabled tank, still housing its dead crew; and an armored car with a dead man frozen at the wheel, awaiting his dissolution in the weak February sunshine, and close to the two vehicles, like part of the wrecked machinery, is the swollen carcass of a horse, with most of its flesh hacked away by the starving population.

They, the living, are no less pitiful. They emerge like gray ghosts from their cellars, stand for a moment dazzled by the light, and the unfamiliar contours of their once-familiar surroundings, and haltingly join the procession to the springs. The strange thing is that they all seem to be the same age—as if the weeks spent in darkness and danger and near-starvation had closed the gap between youth and age and made them all old.

Have we, too, aged, and become gray ghosts of ourselves? This is a sobering probability. But we soon find out that the older and grayer we look, the less likely we are to be picked up in the street and forced to work on rebuilding the bridges. Which is the way the Russians conscript unpaid labor. But the whole operation is so haphazard that escape at the end of a day is easy. They will catch someone else tomorrow. And tomorrow we shall see at least one of the blown-up bridges at close quarters, and watch the blood-stained river swirling up against the dam formed by the swollen bodies of corpses entangled in the wrecked pylons. And everywhere, everywhere, in the slush and rubble of unrecognizable streets and squares, we shall see in their hundreds the dead young men of three nations, sprawling alongside the half-eaten carcasses of their horses and the twisted skeletons of their tanks and armored cars.

The incongruous echo that accompanies these images like the tape of a happy, hopeful melody put on by mistake as background music for a Greek tragedy, is a shimmering, visionary, electronic piece entitled *Birds and Bells*. It is a hymn of renewal, finally realized by the composer, István Anhalt, and broadcast by Radio Canada, fifteen years after its inception on a February morning in 1945 amid all the wreckage and filth of the ransacked upper rooms of the house on the Rózsadomb.

Even after the cessation of hostilities, Pest remained a far country on the other side of a wide river with only two usable bridges—one ten kilometers upstream from where we lived, and the other about the same distance away in the opposite direction; both guarded by Russians, and for military use only.

István and Károly were the first of our group to make their way to that distant shore; István to rejoin his mother, and any of his relations who might have survived the Nazi persecution, and Károly to get news of various relatives and friends, among them K.'s two daughters. But before that, *we* had a visitor; not from the other side of the river, but from an almost equally far country on the other side of the Vár—the Kelenhegyi út, the scene of our early enchantment, now nothing but rubble.

The visitor was Paul. Desperately anxious about Nina, after having been completely cut off from us for weeks, he had made his way to her now over every conceivable obstacle, horror, and trap that can strew a recent battleground; bringing with him a priceless gift for us all, in the form of two immense turnips of the kind used to feed cattle.

His return to us, haggard, exhausted, twenty years older in appearance than when we saw him last, but uninjured, was the first truly joyful occasion we had had in a very long time, and we celebrated it by dining on one of the turnips—boiled until tender, and washed down by some bad wine filched from the Russians.

We exchanged experiences. His were more gruesome than ours, his survival, and that of his parents, more of a miracle.

Fifteen bombs and uncounted rockets and shells had rained down on their villa, which was on the front line, but he and his family had managed to keep alive in the cellar while the German troops fought from the ruins above them; Russian tanks on one side, German tanks on the other.

When the Germans entrenched in the ruins of the villa were finally forced to surrender, they fell on their knees before their Russian captors and begged for mercy. "They *yammered*," Paul said. "As long as I live I shall never forget the terrible yammering of those men."

But although that particular position had fallen to the Russians, the battle for the whole district was not yet over, and Paul and his father were no longer mute listeners in the dark to a battle being waged over their heads, but active participants, whether they liked it or not, in the Russian operation. They were ordered to crawl into a ruined garage in which fifty Russian soldiers were trapped, and bring them out one by one, the dead as well as the living. For twenty-four hours on end (at which point the older man collapsed), father and son picked up the wounded, the dying, and often the already dead, and carried them several hundred yards under heavy artillery fire to an area of relative safety.

Nina, who knew Paul better than any of us knew him, had discerned a change in him much earlier, when he was still an officer in the Hungarian army, and noted it in her diary. But it was only now, as I listened to his grimly laconic account of his life since we saw him last, and caught the irrepressible note of anger and bitterness in his voice when he spoke of the whimpering Nazis, that I recognized the irreparable aging that he had undergone; which was not physical—his body was young and resilient enough to renew itself under better conditions—but spiritual. In the sense that youth is a state of mind, he had, like all those, of whatever age, who have been betrayed by the powers of darkness and war, lost his youth forever.

Although Paul had heard more about what was going on politically and militarily than we had, most of it was still unverified rumor. One such rumor was that when the fall of Buda could be staved off no longer, the remaining German troops had tried to escape by way of some ancient underground passages leading from the catacombs of the Vár into a lonely meadow, where they had found the Russians waiting for them. This widespread and, it must be said, popular belief was not true, except perhaps for some of the SS who had good cause to fear Russian vengeance. But the facts were equally grim. The defeated Nazis had fled the city by night on their various motor vehicles, only to be ambushed by the Russians on both sides of that Cool Valley where K. and I had spent the night of an air raid, and annihilated.

The period that immediately followed the fall of Buda, which brought the battle of Budapest to an end, was chaotic. We had come through alive. But the struggle for survival was not yet over. It had simply moved to another level, on which it was up to us whether or not we went on living. For the second time in my life, a state of being in which the only possible action was a defensive reaction to forces beyond my control, was reversed by their removal. And in this case, a state of helpless dependence on Fate, which paralyzes initiative, was suddenly replaced by a state in which the only hope of survival lay in mounting an active offensive against the myriad forms of death stalking the rubble-strewn streets of a ruined city; a city without any of the safeguards of civilized life. No running water. (No *safe* water save that from the thermal springs.) No gas or electricity. No transport of any kind. No food, no medicines, no supplies of any kind. No functioning institutions of any kind. Nothing but miles and miles of stinking rubbish heaps—and unburied dead.

The Russian soldiers, many of whom had been fighting for years without respite, went wild, and the Russian military police, who were the only agents of law and order, were not disposed to curb them, still less to protect civilians against them. Only once did we get any help from a Russian MP, and that was thanks to Oléna and the magic word *documente* in combination. An obnoxious soldier had snatched Nina's letter of protection out of her hand and made off with it. Oléna ran down the road after him, yelling at him in Russian, and there, at the corner, was a military policeman, laughing his head off at the scene. But when Oléna told him in Russian that the man had stolen an important official document, he stopped laughing and made the man give it back.

Paul's reunion with us was the beginning of a change in the makeup of our "family," of which he became a semipermanent member. Both István and Edit were soon to leave us to rejoin their respective parents; but before that, our numbers were swelled by a new arrival, a wealthy Jewish lady for whom we had stored some treasured personal belongings when she went into hiding from the Nazis. Now, here she was in person, safe and sound, but homeless, and, as she put it, "without nourishment." We still had a roof—of sorts—over our heads, so we took her in, but we too were without nourishment. In fact, we were once again facing starvation. Forty per cent of the children in our part of Buda died of starvation during that terrible winter and spring, and Genevra's two babies were in danger of being among them, when Papa Waldbauer, the first violinist of the quartet, came to see whether or not we had survived. He himself was in a pretty bad way. Normally a robust man, weighing well over two hundred pounds, he was now a bag of bones. And that was not all. Over the cutting edges of extreme emaciation, sharpening them still further, hung the premonitory shadow of a serious illness— typhus—that was about to overtake him.

On his way to us, he had enountered a Russian soldier driving a truck loaded with sacks of flour, and offered to give him all the money he had in his pocket for a few kilos of it—as much as he could carry in his knapsack. But the soldier wouldn't sell it at any price, though he might, he said, exchange some for a gold watch, or a good pair of leather boots, or other articles of clothing. Waldbauer had only what he stood up in, and his watch had long since been taken from him by a Russian. But he told the man to come with him to our place, thinking that if we were still alive we would certainly need the flour, and might have something to barter for it.

During the siege, I had hidden the few pieces of jewelry I possessed, including two gold watches inherited from my grand-parents, where the Russians were least likely to find them—in a crevice of the shell-damaged wall of the inner room. And they were still there. But they represented our sole capital—to be parted with as a last resort only. Unfortunately, we had little else that the Russian wanted. Among the things I had stored for the old Jewish lady were some very good clothes made of prewar material, but she did not see fit to contribute them, and, perhaps because of this, the usually generous Oléna did not offer to add any of her "rewards" to the pile of odds and ends that failed to satisfy the Russian, who said in effect, "No deal," and got up to go. But Marcsa stopped him. And it was her contribution of all she had in the world—the bolt of cloth given to her by Ivan, that gave us all our daily bread for a little while longer. Needless to say, Papa's knapsack was filled.

So much for Ivan's first gift to Marcsa. Now for the second, the little kerosene lamp.

No longer under any military compulsion to keep perpetual open house, we have taken to barring our outer door after dark—a gesture whose value is more symbolic than actual. It serves to discourage the roving bands of soldiers who prowl the hill at night bent on mischief; but no Russian who really wants to get in can be kept out. The wild ones will shoot their way in, and those who are well-intentioned are more likely to remain so if they are invited in. For this reason, we still reserve the outer room as a "Russian room."

One evening at dusk, when the door is still unbarred, a horse and cart draws up, and in comes the coachman; a bumbling peasant, full of wine and good will. He shakes hands all around, and when Oléna tells him that three of us are English, he gives us affectionate pats on the back.

Invited to sit, he chooses the edge of the divan bed in the middle room, a point of vantage from which he proceeds to deliver a series of pronouncements, each punctuated by a spit on the worn-but-beautiful oriental rug that has suffered just about every indignity except that of being spat on. Oléna sits beside him, acting as interpreter at his bidding—he obviously thinks what he has to say is important. Oléna also leads the responses (imitated by us) in what amounts to a parody of Captain L.'s litany of hate for the Germans.

"The English and the Russians are friends." (Spit.)
Yes! Yes!
"The English and the Russians are good people." (Spit.)
Right!
"The Germans are pigs." (Spit.)
Right!
"They have killed my wife." (Spit.)
Groans.

"They have killed my child." (Spit.)
Deep groans.
"They have burned my home—like this!" (Sets fire to a kerchief.)
Cries of alarm.
"Don't be afraid." (He crushes the burning kerchief in his fist.)
Cries of relief.
"When I go to Germany I shall kill every German I see." (Spit.)
Noises of primitive approval tempered by civilized restraint.
"And now I sing!" (Spit.)
He sings in a hoarse voice, and badly off key, one Russian folksong after another—waiting between each for our applause, and finishes up with *Volga-Volga*, in which we all join.

Much clapping, handshaking, backpatting. "Goodbye! The English and the Russians are friends! Goodbye! Goodbye!"

Exit our Russian friend.

Enter three young soldiers, attracted, no doubt, by the rather raucous singing. They, too, are full of wine, and they have a bottle with them, which they want to share with Oléna. They are interested only in her. Too much so for her liking. But to get them off our hands, she invites them to sit and drink with her in the Russian room. Very soon, two of them leave, and the one who remains starts to press unwanted attentions on her—she never gives herself willingly to a common soldier. But this one is persistent, and judging by her cries, brutal. She screams for a light, for Marcsa *néni*, for me. Marcsa turns up the wick of her little treasure, the kerosene lamp, goes quietly in, and places it silently on the table. The soldier desists from whatever he is doing to the screaming Oléna long enough to pick up his rifle and put two shots through the lamp, and in those few seconds, Oléna escapes to the inner room, where he chooses not to follow her. Instead, he curses us all roundly, and slams out of the house, shooting his rifle into the air as he goes, like an angry child.

Oléna says, "I'm sorry about your lamp, Marcsa *néni*. But it saved my life—he was strangling me."

Maybe. Maybe he was only trying to shut her up. We bar the door and retire to bed.

First thing next morning, our friend the coachman turns up with a very long face. While he was with us last night, he says, somebody, *somebody* stole from his cart a pair of brand-new leather riding boots and a gramophone that he was taking to his captain. Could it have been one of us?

We are insulted. What does he think? We don't treat our friends like that! He can search the place if he doesn't believe us.

He does believe us. But he is very unhappy—he is going to get hell from his captain.

Oléna says, with a wicked gleam in her eye, "I bet I know who the thieves were—those three soldiers!" And she tells the coachman about them, how they looked, what their first names were.

"The scoundrels! The horse thieves! Just wait till I catch them!" And off he goes to find them, and give *them* hell.

"Good luck to you!" cries Oléna, delighted.

The fatal shooting of the kerosene lamp forced our return to daylight-saving in its most primitive form—once more we would go to bed when it got too dark to do anything else—and get up at first light. But by now, we had, to a certain extent, developed cat's eyes. And it was a combination of catlike skills that enabled Oléna to survive her next adventure.

It is early evening, cold, and very windy, but cloudless, and we are making the most of the longer-lasting daylight of clear skies to get some minor repairs done, when a rather nice soldier who is well known to us—he was one of the Intendant's men—drops by to see Marcsa *néni*, bringing with him an unknown officer, whose objective seems to be getting acquainted with Oléna. And he helps things along with a bottle of wine.

When darkness falls, Marcsa, who has the young soldier's respect, lets him know that the time has come for him and his officer to leave. But the officer says that he wants to lie down for an hour or two before leaving, and we have no alternative but to offer him the use of the bed in the Russian room.

It turns out that he wants Oléna to lie down with him, which she does—after we have discreetly retired for the night. Marcsa stays up, talking with the soldier in the dark kitchen, in case there is trouble.

At first, it sounds as though there might be trouble. But Oléna's cries and protests are not as desperate as they were last time; she is probably just being difficult. There is a short period of silence, after which her tone changes, and she and the officer seem to be having an amicable conversation. Now comes a long silence. Have they both gone to sleep?

We are dropping off to sleep ourselves, when loud cries of "Oléna! Oléna!" arouse us, and the doors are thrown open by the officer. "Where is Oléna?" Too angry to be cautious, he storms through the middle room and into the inner room, searching both under and in every bed, pulling the covers off all of us, including the terrified children, and failing to find Oléna, storms out again. We hear the voices of Marcsa and the soldier trying to calm him. There are sounds of a door being smashed in. Then shouts and cries of "Oléna! Oléna!" all over the garden, accompanied by the pleading, dissuading voice of the soldier. Now we hear them clattering up to the main floor of the house, and stamping around overhead. A confusion of crashing noises. A single revolver shot. More crashing noises, Two shots. Silence. Then a clattering descent, and more cries of "Oléna! Oléna! Olé . . . na!"

Where on earth has Oléna hidden herself? And why?

All Marcsa can tell us is that she heard Oléna go into the toilet and lock the door. But when, a few minutes later, the angry officer smashed it in, she was not there. Her escape through the tiny, high-set window was pure Houdini magic—believable only because there was no alternative.

The shouting and running outside stops. But the two men are still there; I can hear them talking, very low. If they think that Oléna will be deceived into showing herself, they are underestimating her intelligence. She is taking no chances.

It is getting light when we hear a tell-tale crash of falling masonry in the upper part of the house, followed by an equally tell-tale silence, like that of a burglar who fears he has awakened the household. But after that one stumble over the ruins, she moves so quietly that her whisper from outside asking if it is safe for her to come in, startles us.

Half-frozen, and shaking all over, she creeps into bed beside Marcsa, and as soon as her teeth have stopped chattering, she tells us that the officer wanted to take her away. But she knew what that meant—girls who were "taken away" never came back. Their bodies would be found in some isolated villa, discarded like used paper bags, and she wasn't going to let that happen to her. Aware that resistance was useless, that only cunning would save her, she agreed to go with him, and asked him to wait while she got ready. Locking herself in the toilet—to gain time—she managed, propelled by desperation, to wriggle out through the window, and sped on cat's feet to the upper part of the house, where she hid in one of the rooms on the main floor. But she didn't feel safe; the main floor was too easy of access, so she climbed the mountain of ruined stairs to the bedroom floor, and from there, spurred on by the sound of pursuing feet in the hall below, she hauled herself up to that end of the attic not destroyed by the Stalin Organ. The moonlight was shining through the huge hole the missile had made in the roof at the other end, and enabled her to see, quite close to where she stood, the short iron stair to the roof used by the chimney sweeps. So up she went, and out, closing the trapdoor behind her, and found herself standing on the chimney sweeps' narrow platform at the peak of the sloping roof. She threw her arms around a chimney pot to keep herself from being blown off by the wind, and she nearly fell off from shock when one of the bullets fired through the roof by her pursuer tore up the tiles within a yard of her.

She remained frozen to her chimney pot for as long as there were any Russian voices to be heard anywhere around; the moon was shining so brightly on the rooftop that the slightest movement could have betrayed her presence there. It was a couple of hours before she dared to lift the trapdoor and let herself down into the attic, where she waited until the continuing silence convinced her that it was safe to go on down.

In the end, Oléna, who obeyed only her instincts, was a more immediately triumphant survivor than any of us. She had made a bargain with herself regarding what she would and would not do, and she had stuck to it. Whether or not such a bargain was immoral, was strictly her own affair. She did not harm anyone; quite the contrary; she helped us immensely in every possible way, including the defense of Nina (and to some extent of Edit, too, though more grudgingly), against violation. Privately, I think, she considered chastity, as such, not worth making such a fuss about; but since they set so much store by it, and were not as well equipped as she was to deal with possible violence, she did what she could to divert the lightning to herself—even when she feared it.

She was not the cliché "prostitute with a heart of gold." She was not a prostitute. She was simply a shrewd peasant, a natural business woman who knew how to turn an unavoidable situation to her advantage. And having been sheltered, and treated as a friend by a group of total strangers, she had given her friendship and loyalty in return.

We could only admire her, and sincerely wish her well when she left us, some time in March, to go back to her native village, bearing with her a trousseau that would help her to find a good husband, to whom she would be a good and faithful wife.

Meanwhile, in a cellar on the other side of the river, two professional prostitutes, raddled army sluts of the lowest class, were helping my stepdaughter, Mari, to keep alive a severely wounded Hungarian soldier. His most serious injuries were internal; he had shrapnel in his lungs and his liver, but Mari could only guess at that, and give rough first aid to his surface wounds. She was helped by the whores, who brought water for him, and listened anxiously with her for each rasping breath that threatened to be his last.

As a deserter from the Hungarian army, openly wearing full battle dress, this twenty-year-old art student presented an anomaly peculiar to that time and place. A convinced pacifist, he was also a Hungarian patriot. Willing to fight in defense of his country, but not in defense of the Fascist cause, he was now in danger of death, not from a firing squad, but from wounds received while using his military uniform to facilitate his movements through the embattled city on errands of mercy for the civilian population.

Now, thirty-six years later, that obscure art student has achieved national fame as a sculptor. His name is Gyula Kiss-Kovács, and his sculptures can be seen in the parks and squares of Budapest, and of many other Hungarian cities, as well as in their museums.

In the years between, he married the girl who saved him (in more ways than one), gave her three beautiful children, and left her.

I have in my possession one of his early works; a life-size

woman's head carved from a block of yellow marble. Haunting, rather than beautiful, this powerful portrait of a Hungarian peasant girl dominates my workroom from the mantel of the gray marble fireplace. Unconsciously, as I wrote my novel *Arabesque* under her brooding gaze, I gave her blunt features, her high cheekbones, her slightly slanted eyes, her contemplative expression, to the tragic Rumanian princess, Lucréce. Adding to them only the subtle half-smile that always seemed to be hiding behind the grave marble lips of the sculpture, waiting for an opportunity to turn up their corners. And it seemed to me that in so doing I was merely carrying out in another medium what the sculptor had in mind, but could only suggest in marble. But once a character has been created, in any medium, it acquires a life, and a will, of its own. And between these two an exchange has taken place that was not envisioned by me. The tormented Lucréce has acquired the serenity of an old nun, and the sculpture now looks at me from the mantel with profound and unalterable melancholy.

The cellar in which the young sculptor almost died was under the apartment house in which K.'s ex-wife, Yoyo, lived with their two daughters. The house was situated on one of the main boulevards in a central part of the city, and overlooked an important intersection—the scene of fierce street fighting. All the buildings on this boulevard had extensive cellars, often on more than one level, and on the deepest they were connected by small openings in the walls between the buildings, holes about sixty centimeters square, just large enough for one person to crawl through at a time; a peculiarity of construction that enabled the Russians to take over Pest faster and more easily than Buda, with its hilly, irregular streets and its separate villas.

Later in the evening on the same day that Gyula had been brought, unconscious, into the cellar, a group of Hungarian soldiers had come in and marched its occupants off to another underground shelter—presumably on account of a Russian advance. But Mari, despite her mother's hysterical protests, had refused to leave the wounded man, who could not be moved. For reasons of their own, the two prostitutes also refused to be evacuated. They were keeping Gyula and Mari company in the deepest part of the cellar, where the cokes for the central heating used to be stored, when a faint light showed in the crawl space that connected it with the adjoining building.

"And then..." says Mari, recalling her particular moment, her particular grain of dust in the storm that changed the whole course of Hungarian history, "and then, a candle appeared, with a huge hand sheltering its flame, and above it a funny little round cap, that turned out to be on the head of a huge, very tall, broadly grinning young Russian. We begged him to leave his candle with us, but he refused, and hurried on through the cellar to find the hole that would take him into the next building. At last we were safely behind the line of siege!"

We in Buda had felt the same blessed euphoria when the Russians first appeared at our door in their white hooded cloaks. But safety, like everything else, is relative.

As apartment dwellers in Pest, my stepdaughters' experience, both during and after the siege, differed from ours in several important ways; one being the nature (not the degree) of the dangers peculiar to our respective situations. For as long as the siege lasted (which was almost three weeks longer in Buda than in Pest), we lived in continual, imminent danger of being killed either by a bomb or by one of the various explosives that were bursting all around us and blowing men to pieces under our eyes. And for me, at any rate, fear was a constant. It could be, and was, kept under control; but it never left me for a moment.

Mari, however, writing about that period, says: "I never felt fear, had no sense of danger, and the possibility of getting injured or killed never entered my mind. Perhaps because of Yoyo's hysteria, we [her sister and herself] were absolutely calm."

This may, of course, have been partly a matter of temperament. But I attribute it chiefly to the greater *visibility* of violent death in our case. And there was another fear-intensifying factor to be taken into account: noise. In the underground cellar of a tall city building, the sounds of battle are to some extent muffled. But our flimsy ground-floor shelter was shaken from all sides by a shattering volume of noise; magnified and prolonged by the echoing acoustics of our hill to a shrieking, nonstop assault on the whole nervous system.

On the other hand, until the Russians arrived, we had our flimsy shelter to ourselves. We were a tightly-packed family group, with all that implies of moral support, mutual trust, physical discomfort, and friction. But whatever internal bickering took place, we stood united against external threats. And for us, all threats came from outside; we had no enemy within to contend with—unlike the family in Pest, whose life in a communal cellar was fraught with internal dangers.

Most important difference of all, I had K. at my side; but his daughters, who loved him and needed him just as much as I did, had only their unstable mother with them.

By pure coincidence, we and they took up residence in the lower regions of our respective homes on the same day: Christmas day. But our descent was voluntary, whereas theirs was dictated by the Germans, who set up a defensive position in their apartment, whose front windows, with their strategic view over the intersection, provided an excellent range for rifle and machine-gun fire.

After making an abortive attempt to spend Christmas Eve as usual with their famous "Granny," and finding the Queen of the National Theater and First Lady of the National Cuisine barricaded in a building guarded by *Nyilas* who wouldn't let anyone in, the two girls and their mother returned home through the bomb-torn streets only to be evacuated from their flat at a moment's notice, and hurried down to the communal cellar. A purgatorial realm seething with mutually hostile elements—Fascist, anti-Fascist, Jewish, pacifist, Communist—held back from destroying one another only by their over-riding concern for their own safety.

The regular inhabitants of the building, together with the Jewish and other endangered friends and relatives they were hiding, formed a permanent civilian nucleus, surrounded by a floating, and often overlapping military and paramilitary population that included Arrow Cross men (*Nyilas*), off-duty German and Hungarian soldiers, a troop of so-called "Todt-men"—a forced labor company made up principally of soldiers being punished for various crimes, and a band of technical experts waiting to blow up the bridges. Serving them all impartially were the two hardworking whores.

"When the regular German soldiers finally left us," says Mari, ruefully, "they took with them my Christmas present to my mother; a pink quilt, for which I had bartered my only good sweater and all my savings. They draped it over the hood of their truck, to keep the engine warm."

It was about four weeks after that misappropriation of a pink quilt, that the last of the German "defenders" of Budapest went to meet their deaths in a Russian ambush at the far end of a cool, dark valley. And about two weeks after that, Károly made an epic journey across the river to Pest and back, bringing news to K. of his daughters, and their mother.

He had found them back in their ravaged apartment, with no quilts, no heat, no fuel, and nothing to eat but what the two girls could scavenge from under the rubble of ruined houses—a few grains of spilled rice, or a few dried beans—which they cooked over scraps of wood unearthed from the same rubble.

Yoyo was in a very bad way; seriously ill from prolonged vitamin starvation. A strongly built woman, there was hardly any flesh on her big frame, that weighed a scant ninety pounds.

But there was some food to be had in Pest—for those who had something of value to barter for it. There were no shops, or regular markets, but on one of the main *Körúts*, Károly came on a sort of free exchange. Anyone who had anything to sell stood niched in the arches of ruined buildings calling their wares at the top of their lungs, while others shouted their wants, and what they were willing to give in exchange; and bands of street urchins, and other, prowling ruffians, kicked over containers and stuffed their pockets with goods, running off before anyone could stop them. Things were offered for sale that had not been obtainable for years; things that must have been hoarded up from before the war, and miraculously preserved from robbery and destruction. Prices were fantastic; hundreds of *pengös* for one loaf of bread or a kilo of flour. Everyone who had a little flour made it into biscuits or pancakes, which they hawked on the streets to a ravenous populace willing to sell their souls, if need be, for a bite to eat.

Károly, who had crossed over to Pest by the bridge ten kilometers downstream, decided to try, with the help of some Hungarian soldiers, to return by way of the new bridge that the Russians were constructing near the Margaret Island. But in saving himself the long walk, he fell victim to forced labor, along with a bunch of other civilians, of both sexes and all ages. He had not yet fully recovered from the bone trouble that had kept him from active service, his hand was bandaged, and his arm was in a sling, but that did not save him, anymore than the age and weakness of some of the others saved them from being compelled to carry huge blocks of stone, weighing upwards of thirty pounds, for eleven hours, with one hour off, under armed guard, "for eating."

"*Eating!* Eating what?"

"Whatever you have with you," the guard says.

During this break for a nonexistent lunch, a woman came along with a trayful of biscuits for sale. But the guard said the price was outrageous and told the workers to take them without paying. Nobody touched them. So the guard took the tray from the women and tipped them into the river.

Later a shout went up from one of the workers, who pointed down at the water in great excitement. Entangled with the corpses floating downstream was a solitary unopened can of beef stew, recognizable by its size and shape as one of those issued to the army. A dozen pairs of eyes hungrily followed its bobbing course; a riveting sight, that aroused far stronger emotions than that of the sad, familiar dead, at which the Russian soldiers on the bank were taking pot shots with their rifles for fun.

Paul's father had won such a can of beef stew in a lottery, but when he brought it home his wife wouldn't touch it. She said it reeked of corpses. Paul and his father were less squeamish. After boiling the can for a full half-hour—to be on the safe side—they opened it up and devoured the contents between them with gusto, and had no ill effects. Luckily. For medical treatment was hard to get, and owing to the scarcity of the necessary serums, the organized innoculation of the populace against the diseases that spring from contaminated water and food did not get under way until much later.

The "limbo" period, in which we hung suspended between war and peace, with neither the dangers of the one nor the safeties of the other to sustain us, lasted through the spring. It was only in late May, when the government was finally re-established in Budapest, and the Allied Control Commission was in operation—and as a result, the Russian occupying troops were more tightly disciplined, that the structure of civic law and order could be rebuilt.

In the meantime, we all went a little crazy. The lawlessness that prevails immediately following a war, or any other major disaster that destroys the whole fabric of civilized life, is not confined to the criminal classes. It is an epidemic dementia that affects everyone. And in the case of a city long under siege, like Budapest, the common denominator is need. Need made scavengers of us all. Need tipped the scale between the permissible and the impermissible.

Piracy took new forms. And the Russians were not its only practitioners. Long after the new bridge was completed, crossing the river remained a difficult and hazardous undertaking. To get onto the bridge, you had first to stand in a queue half a mile long, from which the Russians could snatch you at any moment for unpaid work on some other bridge—even in some other city. But to cross by boat was equally risky, and expensive into the bargain; much too expensive for any of us—which was probably our good luck. The old ferries and rafts were now in dry dock for lack of motor fuel. But anyone who could lay hands on a rowboat was in business. Here, again, the line between honesty and dishonesty was extremely thin. The "honest" boatmen would ask an exhorbitant price to row a passenger over the river, but kept to it once it was agreed upon. The "New Pirates" would also ask an exhorbitant price, but would stop in midstream and give the passenger the choice of handing over double the agreed upon sum, or swimming the rest of the way.

Two forms of exclusively Russian piracy were not without their funny side—for everyone, that is, but their hapless victims.

One was a specialized form of highway robbery, directed at decently-clad civilians of both sexes. It might be described as "divestiture at gunpoint." And every musician in Budapest rocked with gleeful laughter when a pompous critic they all disliked was divested of everything but his underpants on a cold night while on his way home from a visit to his mother, who lived nearby. Thanks to the janitor of his building, who let him in, everyone knew next day what had happened.

The other was a special kind of forced labor, or "rape with a difference," the rapists being female—hefty amazons who had helped to man the Russian guns during the siege—and the victims civilian males, the weaker and the skinnier the better. The joke was to kidnap one of these poor debilitated creatures and put him to work. Beating him up and throwing him out would be his punishment for inadequate performance.

In retrospect I can see the funny side of an episode in which K. and I were the victims.

A few days before it happened, we had unearthed some unused cello strings from the wreckage upstairs, and the voice I had missed for so long began once again to sing. But only for short periods at a time, because during the weeks of no playing the protective calluses that form on the tips of a cellist's fingers had grown soft, making pressure on the strings very painful.

He is playing his morning scales when two Russian soldiers walk in. Nina has taken the children out for a little fresh air, and everyone else has gone down the hill to haul up the day's water supply. Amiably grinning, the two soldiers wander around, rummaging through our things like two women in a dime store searching for bargains. I tell them in my best Esperanto, that they are wasting their time—we have nothing of value left. I have forgotten, perhaps because it is so much a part of myself, the gold wedding band I have never taken off since K. first put it on my finger. Spotting it, one of the soldiers says, "*Davai!*"—the Hungarian version of a Russian imperative meaning "Give!" I say, "*Nyet.*" Again he says, "*Davai!*" Again I say, "*Nyet.*" His companion raises his rifle and presses its muzzle against my heart, "*DAVAI!*"

He is probably bluffing, but he might pull the trigger just for fun. I take off the ring and hurl it across the room as hard as I can. The soldiers laugh. One of them picks up the ring and pockets it. Then they both sit down, knees spread wide, rifles laid across them, and say, "Play, Old Father!"

K. is wiser than I was. He picks up his cello and plays the first thing that comes into his head, which happens to be Bach's Air for the G string. They like it. When it is finished, they say, "Go on, Old Father!" As he goes on from one classical piece to another, a beatific look comes over his listeners' rascally faces, while the set of his lips betrays his increasing pain.

Oléna's return, about half an hour later, brings the torture to an end. When I tell her about my ring, she tells the soldiers in plain Russian what she thinks of them. "And now," she says, "after listening to such a fine concert, the least you can do is give back the lady's ring."

"*Nyet*," says the soldier who has it in his pocket. "Goodbye, Old Father!" And off they go, laughing.

"Chicken catchers! Scoundrels!" Oléna shouts after them in Hungarian—adding a string of unprintables.

The loss of my wedding ring depressed me. I could not help seeing it as prophetic, not of the loss of K.'s love, but of K. himself. While the bombs and shells were falling, the danger of violent death overshadowed all other dangers; but now I became aware of his frail physical health, and the impossibility of protecting it.

In the little package of valuables hidden in the crevice of the wall, was my mother's wedding ring, which, on an impulse that I could not explain, even to myself, I had removed from her finger after her death. I did not wear it. It would have been as out of place on my hand then as her silver and ebony crucifix would have been at my waist. But I took both symbols with me from country to country and grief to grief, and in some strange way they sustained me through the "dark ages." Why this was so, and the nature of the subconscious urge that had prompted my taking of the ring in the first place, became clear to me only in the light of my relationship with K.

In a moment of great darkness, I had seized instinctively on an emblem of strength and unity, which my mother no longer needed, and, I believe, actually wanted me to have. Together, her wedding ring and her crucifix represented for my mother the two primary sources from which life springs; heavenly love, and earthly love, and the pain and sacrifice both demand for their fulfillment.

Despite her gentle Victorian absurdities, my mother was a remarkable woman; one of those rare women endowed with both spiritual strength and physical beauty. But the gap between our ages was so wide (she was past her mid-forties when I, her only child, was born) that I had to be middle-aged myself before I could really appreciate her—and by then she had been dead twenty years. Now, under circumstances undreamed of by her, I thought it would not be unfitting to replace my own stolen ring with the one that I had, in a sense, stolen from her. So I asked K. to put it on my finger, where no other ring will ever replace it.

The episode of the music-loving bandits is linked in my mind with the scene that confronted me when, shortly after the "liberation" of Buda, and the departure of the Russians from under our roof, I went upstairs to see who was playing the piano.

The room dedicated to music was the largest of the three rooms on the main floor—the one opening onto the terrace. I had not been up to that floor since asking Captain Friedman to put it out of bounds, and being told that "the people of one civilized nation etc. . . ."

Now, accustomed as I was to perpetual semidarkness, the cold brightness of the room dazzled me. Its bare white walls that reflected the sunlit snow beyond the glassless windows suggested the walls of an iceberg; under my feet, splinters of wood and glass, the broken spines of books, the delicate handles of china cups, and a thousand other cherished possessions, crunched like loose ice. The only thing not wrecked in that arctic palace was the beautiful, black, Bechstein grand piano, rising above the pitiful flotsam like a proud ship, its sail, the elongated triangle of its propped-up lid.

Sitting at the keyboard was István; oblivious of my entrance, absorbed in an effort to capture a fleeting glimpse of the future, to preserve in musical form the essence of resurrection.

The link between these two "musical episodes" was a paradox, one of the odd contradictions presented by what it is only fair to call "The Red Army" rather than "The Russians," since armies—like mobs—are independent entities with characteristics all their own. It was a paradox that became even more sharply defined when we started on the task of making the main floor habitable. And I pondered on it, with a mixture of psychological curiosity and physical disgust, as I scraped up dried human excrement from the floor with a knife (having no better means at hand). How was it possible that the same men who took care that a musical instrument should remain undamaged, free even from the wine spills and cigarette burns that marred everything else, should have defecated like animals all over the bathroom floor?

Cleaning up, both indoors and outdoors, was the first requisite for deliverance from limbo. The outdoor cleanup came first; and who should be the self-appointed organizer of the work parties but our Airwarden—now as fervently pro-Communist as he had been anti-Nazi. Day after day he lined up the able-bodied civilians in his bailiwick, with whatever tools they could lay their hands on, to break the lingering ice and clear streets and yards of debris—rubble, twisted bits of weapons, an occasional unexploded land mine, skeletons of horses, fragments of human bodies—and dump the lot in a nearby bomb crater. The garbage pile, formed and fed by the Russian army cooks, in our backyard, was four feet high and thirty feet long, and took several days to break up and cart away.

In the garden of a deserted, but not very badly damaged, villa were three fresh graves—emblems of an irony so bitter that the very thought of it evokes tears of rage. Rage and pity. The villa belonged to a Jewish family, of which three members, a middle-aged couple and a young girl, survived the Nazi persecution in hiding. Immediately after the fall of Buda, they came back to camp in the more or less habitable ground floor rooms of their villa, and welcomed as their saviors and friends the Russians who wandered in and out at all hours. But they were not as lucky as we were. The worst happened. A gang of drunken soldiers came in one night, tied up the two older people, and raped the girl under their eyes. After which, neither they nor the girl wanted to go on living.

In their suicide note, they spoke of the unendurable shame. But in Budapest at that time, the shame of being raped was a universal shame, shared by thousands of women and girls of all ages, and not insurmountable. What killed these three survivors of the Nazi persecution was, I believe, not so much the bitterness of their shame, as the bitterness of their disillusionment.

When March brought the heavy spring rains, and the ground became soft enough to work, we dug up our whole yard in preparation for the victory garden that would, if we could get seeds, help to feed us during the summer. And never was a garden so potently fertilized, thanks to the Russians who had stabled their horses in the unoccupied villas—both upstairs and downstairs, wherever possible. Recalling those glassless windows from which the gentle equine faces had peered out at us as we passed on our way to the well or the springs, Marcsa, Nina, and I went on a tour of inspection and found the parquet floors of half a dozen villas ankle deep in a rich mixture of horse droppings, straw, first editions of rare books, shards of pottery, tattered embroideries, oil paintings, arms and legs of sculptures—all the aesthetic debris of once-beautiful homes.

Separating the elements of this compost took time. But we managed to collect and bring back, barrowload by barrowload, at least a ton of relatively unmixed horse manure—to the envy and amazement of our less enterprising, or more fastidious, next-door neighbors, the baron and baroness.

Another cause for self-congratulation was our forethought in removing one set of the double casement windows on the main floor when we had to go and live on the bedroom floor to make room for the Germans. Carefully padded with rugs and heavy drapes, and packed away with the Big Box in the recess under the stairs, most of the panes had survived unbroken, or merely cracked, so we still had something to keep the cold out and let the light in.

It took us about three weeks to clean up the first floor, install the windows, patch up—with Paul's help—the worst of the holes in the walls and ceiling, and arrange the three rooms with a minimum of comfort. On the twenty-second of March, we slept there, in our own home, for the first time since Christmas. K. and I had the room with the piano, Marcsa and Nina shared the room next the kitchen, and Paul slept on a divan bed in the middle room, formerly the dining room, now our communal sitting room, and the warmest place in the house, since it faced south and had only one outside wall.

There was still no water, gas, or electricity, and our meager meals were cooked on the kitchen range fueled by scraps of damp wood collected from neighboring ruins—as were most of the materials we used to mend the holes in the walls, even the nails and screws, even the tools. Nothing that might be of use was too insignificant to pick up and bring home. Things we had had before, we had no longer; and in their place were things that didn't belong to us. The Russian redistribution of property had been quite far-reaching. People from all over the hill would come to see if by any chance we had their missing pots and pans. Even stoves, beds and other furniture had changed places, or vanished completely.

But it wasn't all the fault of the Russians; the "ragpicker syndrome" had affected the entire population. And even if I recognize one of my own long-lost garments on the stranger standing next to me in a crowd, what can I say, knowing that the shirt K. is wearing is monogrammed with some other stranger's initials?

We had had no news of my misguided English friend, Sybil, since Christmas. Now we got a message from her; an invitation to a Sunday morning celebration of survival. Her husband had added a postscript in Hungarian, *Greetings! Do come—there will be* bread and butter *to eat!*

In view of the pro–German sympathies hitherto so openly professed by them both, we felt a little uneasy about accepting. But bread-and-butter was an irresistible temptation. We hadn't tasted butter, or anything like it, for many months, and I was having recurring dreams of shops stocked with loaves of bread that would disappear when I stretched out my hand to take one.

We need not have worried. With a single exception, our fellow guests were Russians—clearly the source of the bread and butter. The exception was a middle-aged Hungarian woman, obviously Jewish, who was introduced to us by Sybil as her very good friend, Doctor X. . . . I could not recall ever having met her there before, but she seemed to be very much at home. The villa was small, little more than a cottage, and still-unrepaired shell damage had virtually reduced it to one room. Sybil apologized for the lack of chairs and the cramped space, and Doctor X. remarked that it was palatial compared to the space in which she had lived in hiding for more than three months. Asked by one of the Russians where that was, she said, "Up there," and pointed to an opening over the door leading to the bathroom.

Between the ceiling of the bathroom, (which was lower than the ceiling of the living room), and the roof, was a storage place for luggage, approximately five feet square by three feet high. Its opening looked like an upper panel of the door, and, as I remembered, had been effectively concealed by a picture.

The revelation that this Jewish woman had been doubled up in there, while German officers sat in the living room with her host, boasting about their efficiency in eliminating the Budapest Jews, was stunning. Not only, or even chiefly, because of its riskiness, or even the mental and physical torture it involved—she was not the only one whose concealment had involved agonizing positions— but because of the contradiction it exposed in the mind and heart of that unscrupulous opportunist, Sybil's husband. A flexible conscience, it seemed, could sometimes bend in the right direction.

As for Sybil herself, in the months ahead, she underwent a religious conversion that brought about her return, in body as well as in spirit, to her own country.

Toward the end of May, when the Allied Control Commission was established, a British journalist came to see me, and a flying saucer could not have excited more attention than his little British car parked by our broken-down fence. Only the gods had cars.

The young man, whose name has got lost—superceded in my memory by the two cakes of lavender-scented soap he presented me with—wanted my "story." Would I have lunch with him at the Control Commission's headquarters?

My reply was classic. "I can't possibly—I have nothing to wear, and I look awful."

"You look as if you could do with a good meal," he said. He was really rather a kind young man.

As usual, the offer of food was irresistible. I was only sorry that K. and Nina could not share it with me. Both were out; Nina trying to earn some money by giving English lessons, and K. at the Lizst Ferenc Academy, where classes were gradually getting under way.

I put on the only half-way presentable garment I possessed, a suit four years out of fashion and needing to be cleaned, and my only remaining pair of leather shoes, scuffed and down at heel from miles of walking. But I was lucky to have them; scores of women were walking around barefoot, or, at best, in wooden-soled sandals. My legs were bare. I had no stockings.

Yet, seated next to the neatly dressed journalist in his vehicle of the gods, it was not my shabbiness of which I felt ashamed, but my privileged position; my utterly false position.

The lunch in the elegant, soft-carpeted dining room of the mansion, or one of the mansions, that housed the officers of the Control Commission, was a success only insofar as it filled my chronically famished stomach. Questioned by the eager young journalist, I found that I had no "story"—at least, not the kind of story he wanted. Neither I nor my daughters had been put into a concentration camp. The Germans billeted in our villa had not been savage beasts. The Russians had not raped either me or my daughters. None of us had died of starvation. As for the bombs and shells and all that, it had been just as bad in London.

I don't remember what I ate, but whatever it was, all the time I was eating it and answering questions between mouthfuls, I was hating my surroundings and everyone there, including myself—for being there.

The other women in the room—assistants, secretaries, journalists—were well-dressed, well-groomed, self-assured. The ambiance was that of the dining room in a prewar London club, stiffened with some of the intimidating "correctness" of the Whitehall I had known as a young consular wife. It brought back memories of that long-ago journey from London to Bucharest in care of the young Irish king's messenger. I felt the same sense of an unbridgeable gulf between me and these people as I had felt between my younger self and the other *wagon-lit* passengers on the Orient Express.

Disappointed, but still polite, the journalist drove me down the Andrassy út (the Control Commission was located in a relatively undamaged quarter on the fringes of the park at the end of that long avenue) to the center of the town, from where, I assured him, I could easily make my own way home. He looked relieved. "Well . . . if you insist." Then, taking the two cakes of soap out of his pocket, he said, with a slightly embarrassed grin, "Perhaps you could find some use for these—I understand there's a shortage. . . ."

As I joined the stream of common humanity on the bridge—

people pushing handcarts with all their worldly goods piled up on them, people pushing the old or the sick along in wheelbarrows, people walking barefoot, people in ragged clothes, people in search of shelter, of food, of the bare necessities of life; people determined to live against all odds—I knew that this was where I belonged, that these disinherited people were my brothers and my sisters.

I had yet to learn how easy it is to forget such moments of truth.

Kinship with the crowds on the bridge was established in a more literal sense about two weeks later, when K., who had to undergo surgery, was brought home from the hospital on a two-wheeled handcart of the kind that has to be kept in balance or its load will slide off its flat top. Paul and Nina did the pulling, while Marcsa and I pushed from the back and tried to keep it steady.

The operation had been done by a friend of K.'s, in a small Catholic hospital in Buda, about five kilometers distant from where we lived. It was one of the first to open its doors to patients after the siege, thanks to the energy and determination of the nuns who staffed it and ran it as if it were an extension of their convent, subject to the same religious rules. An attitude that made K.'s brief sojourn there, in which I participated to some extent, spending as much time with him as I was allowed to, a funny, tender, and aggravating experience for him, and something of a revelation for me.

The men's ward, which K. shared with about a dozen other patients, some Catholic, some Protestant, some "nothing," was adorned with holy pictures and statues of the Virgin, before which all gifts of flowers were placed. It was connected with the chapel by folding doors (as was the women's ward on the other side of the building), which were opened wide for the main Offices of the day—Mass and Vespers—to allow the patients to take part in the devotions. Visitors were permitted to stay for Vespers if they wished, but non-Catholics, whether patients or visitors, were expected to maintain a respectful silence while the service was going on.

Vespers consisted mainly of a recitation of the rosary and a couple of hymns sung by the nuns to the accompaniment of a harmonium. And these hymns, with their combination of bad music, bad verse, and banal sentiments, were a cause of real anguish to K., destroying for him every evening the sense of respect for the Catholic religion generated in him every morning by the solemn ritual of the quietly whispered Latin mass that began the day, when the nuns' bent heads in their snowy coifs were like so many white birds preparing to unfold their wings at first light.

But each new day faced by these soft-spoken, iron-willed servants of God meant a renewed effort in the seemingly endless struggle for survival—their own as well as their patients'. And quite independent of medical care, survival meant having enough to eat. The nuns coped with this problem in two ways. First, by digging up the hospital grounds and planting every inch of them with vegetables, and later, when certain supplies became available in Pest, by turning themselves into beasts of burden. A team of the sturdiest among them would grasp the shafts of a farm wagon and drag it down to the river and over one of the temporary bridges to Pest. There, they would load it up with whatever was to be had—flour for bread, cornmeal, potatoes—and lug it back to the hospital, covering a distance of about seven kilometers each way.

Needless to say, I did not hear about this from the nuns themselves. It was K.'s doctor friend who told me.

Under such conditions, no patient was kept in the hospital for a minute longer than was necessary, which was why K. was discharged before he was able to walk. He had serious vascular problems that were later to threaten him with the loss of his legs. But in the meantime, this relatively minor surgery enabled him, after a few days of rest, to cope with the walking that he was obliged to do on his way to the academy, to the radio building (both in Pest), and to play in various parts of the city for the musical events, big and small, that were the earliest forms of artistic entertainment to be revived among the ruins. I would go with him to these events, with a knapsack on my back in which to bring home the musician's fee, that ranged from a jar of plum *lekvár* for one short piece, to ten kilos of potatoes for a whole recital.

Cello students who came to the house for private lessons also paid in kind. There was the Egg pupil whose mother kept two live hens in the kitchen of her fourth floor apartment; the Bacon pupil whose aunt in the country had killed a pig; and the Honey pupil, whose country relatives kept bees.

So music, always the food of love and of the soul, became a source of food for the body as well.

Along with the renewal of K.'s musical life came his reunion with his daughters, whose experiences during the siege had lessened their mother's psychological hold over them. Mari, in particular, had achieved during those few months a maturity that enabled her to give her mother the compassion she needed without succumbing to her emotional blackmail. The younger sister, Judit, whose health was frailer than ever, now clung more and more closely to her father, as if she foresaw a final parting still undreamed of by him—or by me.

6

Regeneration

I

NOW, time begins to move in wider arcs. We no longer exist from moment to moment, or even day to day, but rather from one stage in the quality and meaning of our lives to another; milestones of material and spiritual advance along the winding, obstacle-strewn road of regeneration, whose signposts are written in hieroglyphs that must be deciphered correctly before we can move on—like the fateful riddles of legend and fairy tale. The reductions of war acquire in retrospect a nostalgic simplicity compared to the choices and complexities of an incomplete peace.

Early in July, 1945, the consular branch of the British "element" of the Allied Control Commission transmitted to me a message received from my uncle in England, asking for news of us, and requesting that I be informed that both my sons were alive and well; Peter in India, and Eldon in America. Ordinary lines of communication between England and Hungary were still closed, and would remain so for some time, even after the war was ended. Inquiries concerning individuals, and messages to them, were handled by the Red Cross in conjunction with the consulate; from which terse, impersonal replies would go back. But my uncle's military rank, and his string of decorations, had caught the consul's attention, and, combined with Nina's well-known family name, had prompted him to talk with me personally, with the result that he offered to do me a special favor. He was willing, he said, in view of my "rather unusual circumstances" to get a personal letter from me back to my uncle—presumably in the diplomatic pouch, though that was left unsaid. But the letter, or letters (I could write more than one if I liked, provided I used thin paper and put them all in the same envelope), must be brief, and discreet. Which last meant, of course, "be careful what you say about the Russians"—a limitation that affected all my correspondence for as.long as I was in Hungary.

Seated at a desk in the consul's office, with two sheets of tissue-thin paper before me, I found myself at a loss. Deep gulfs of unshared, and as yet untold, experience lay between me and my sons, once so close to me. Separated for six years, and incommunicado for the last four of them, we were facing one another now from opposites sides of a war. And, in British eyes, I was on the wrong side.

My letter to Peter was a nervous, bare-bones summary of what had happened to us as a family in the past four years, and the pivotal changes in our lives; our move to the Rózsadomb, Genevra's marriage to a Hungarian, and the birth of her two children— new ties to Hungary that could only increase, in his mind, the distance between him and us already created by the war. Eventually, his two sisters would deal, each in her own way, with this rift in time and space. My concern was the distance between him and me. For although my feelings toward him were unchanged, although I loved him as much as ever, I was no longer the same person. And the war that had changed me, must, inevitably, have changed him, too. When the time of reunion came, we would meet as strangers, in the sense that his father and I had met as strangers when we were reunited at the end of the last war.

My relationship with Eldon was less complex, and although my letter to him was a continuation of my letter to Peter—the second half of a joint communication that would also be read by my uncle, in addressing Eldon, whom I knew to be in the United States, I felt free to go against the tide of British disdain for my adopted country and defend its victimized people, as distinct from its misguided rulers and politicians.

Re-reading now what I wrote thirty-six years ago, I am struck by its vehemence and emotional intensity, and I am not very proud of the moderation that has, with age, replaced it. That hastily written letter, with no paragraphs and not much punctuation, disorganized, and melodramatically phrased, burns with a flame too fierce to last, a shining truth impossible to live up to. But true nonetheless. And just as true now as it was then. Every day, somewhere in the world the same essential scene is being repeated, the same essential agony endured as that which aroused my pity and indignation in Budapest after the siege.

> The real people of this country are fighting with every nerve to live, to work, to rebuild. They have, most of them, lost everything—their families, their money and possessions, their homes, and in many cases, their health.... But on top of this bottomless pool of ruin and misery and unhappiness, an unhealthy foam of life is going on. The newly rich, food speculators, cocottes, crooks of all kinds, create an extraordinary atmosphere of false gaiety that goes ill with the ruined streets and the white faces of the half-starved children. When I see these people spending hundreds of pengös in an hour on sweet cream cakes and I know that the children are dying for want of milk, and of everything else, I long to whip them out of their sidewalk cafés as Christ whipped the usurers out of the temple.... I am one with the poor and the hungry and all desperately unhappy people.... I can understand the thief and even the murderer, because now I know, deep inside me I know what they feel. All my values have changed. I know that one can do without nearly everything. ... The only things that matter are food and drink, warmth, sleep, and liberty. And if you deny these things to people, especially to one section of the community only, you are going to get criminals and anarchists—and by God I am with them!

The trouble is that prosperity is an anesthetic. Although I learned then, once and for all, that a thief and a murderer sleeps within every human being, I no longer *feel* the presence of mine. Realizing that Eldon might think this a funny sort of letter for me to be writing to him after four years of enforced silence, I tried to excuse my rhetorical tone,

> I cannot express myself as well as I used to, I am out of practice—I cannot write smoothly anymore. And I don't think smoothly, either. I think violently. . . .

But, I assured him, I could still laugh, at myself and at life.

> Actually, I laughed an enormous amount right through the siege, especially after our liberators came in—our strange, wild, dangerous, lovable devils of liberators. When I was not afraid I was simply bound to laugh—things were so fantastic. And indeed, I often laughed even when I was afraid.

Would the consul consider that reference to the Russians indiscreet? Or was it too discreet to be sincere?

A little of both, perhaps, at the time. But from my present perspective, I see it as a pretty accurate characterization of those Russians with whom we came in contact.

At about the same time that I was writing these first awkward missives to Peter and Eldon, Peter was writing to me from India, on the off chance that my uncle could get the letter through to me. Which he did, thanks to the consul, who gave it to me with a strong hint not to regard the consulate as a post office. It was brief, and discreet to the point of obscurity, but contained one calmly irrational statement that revealed the dichotomy between the nature of my son and the role that he had to play as an officer in British Military Intelligence. He said:

> I know that you and Nina have come through safely. I had a vision, in which I saw you both walking down a wide stairway, and smiling. But it was not the stairway of the Kelenhegyi villa—you must have taken refuge somewhere else.

At the time he wrote that, he knew nothing about our move to the Rózsadomb. Both he and Nina had more than a touch of the psychic in their makeup, and both were prophetic dreamers. But

during his long sojourn in India, Peter had gone a step further
into mysticism, and had learned how to conjure visions.

The news that Peter and Eldon were safe coincided with other
forms of relief; a general upward turn toward a normal existence,
which came more slowly in Buda than in Pest, on account of the
longer lasting siege and greater devastation. When running
water, gas, and electricity were one by one restored to us with the
coming of summer, we had been without them for approximately
five months—long enough to appreciate them as luxuries, and not
to be taken for granted. Food was still difficult to obtain and still
more difficult to pay for—a runaway inflation was setting in, and
the peasants were leery of money and preferred barter. But for
us, the danger of actual starvation was over, thanks partly to the
distribution of Red Cross and CARE parcels, partly to the har-
vest from my well-manured garden, and partly to Marcsa *néni*'s
peasant connections and the renewed possibility of contacting
them.

It was after one of her trips to the country in late summer that
we invited two of our good friends to share with us a feast of
poppyseed noodles. A plebian dish, unthinkable at a prewar
dinner party, its status had been raised to Lucullan heights by
privation, and our two guests, Ede Zathureczky and Gustav Oláh,
exclaimed in delight when Marcsa proudly produced a mountain
of homemade noodles tossed in butter, sugar, and ground poppyseed. It was neither side dish nor dessert; it was the whole meal.

We ate at a round table in our all-purpose sitting room, once our
formal dining room, where my efforts to revive some vestiges of a
past elegance were simultaneously supported and derided by the
sun. Pouring in at the wide-open casements, it gilded the folds of
the satiny, apple green curtains (retrieved undamaged from my
Big Box), threw into cruel relief the brownish stains of damp and
the patches of peeling plaster on walls and ceiling, and left a
candid photograph of the whole scene imprinted on my memory.

In the still vivid image of that war-scarred, sun-flooded room,
and three of the most respected figures in Budapest's musical life
devouring poppyseed noodles with all the gusto of schoolboys
enjoying a special treat, I see reflected both the guilelessness of
those for whom art is synonymous with life, and the naive hope

that many of them still cherished in that first summer after the war; the hope of a Hungary reborn—free.

Imre Waldbauer was more skeptical. He was preparing to take up an offer of a teaching position in America, and he tried to enlist my help in persuading K. to follow his example, to leave while the going was good. But K.'s ties to Hungary, both musical and emotional, were extremely strong, and he was not yet ready to break them. And neither was I ready to retrace the difficult step I had taken eight years earlier and embark on another new life, in a world unfamiliar to both of us, and an ocean away from all our children, except Eldon.

We all agreed, however, that Nina should go back to England as soon as the opportunity arose. Even Paul, who was devastated by the mere thought of losing her, believed that she would now be better off in her own country. But he and I both hoped that the opportunity would not arise too soon. And I think Nina felt the same way; she had so many unresolved anxieties concerning her friends, so many reunions to achieve before she could leave with her mind at rest.

One by one, soldiers, prisoners of war, and other survivors, were coming home. A few—very few, and mostly women and girls—bore the stigmata of Auschwitz and other concentration camps. (And they did not always consist only of tattooed numbers.) Many more were young men from the rather less lethal forced labor companies, who had somehow avoided being shot, or taken to Germany, when the disintegration of defeat began to set in. Most of these escapees had, like István a few months earlier, made their way back to their homes on foot, often to find nothing left of their former lives.

Among these lone survivors was K.'s student, the young cellist who had left his instrument and his winter coat in our keeping. He had gone first to his parents' place in the country, to learn there from neighbors that his entire family had been taken away to the death camps.

He came to see us in Budapest, in the hope of retrieving his cello, which was not only the symbol of the new life that he had to reconstruct for himself on the ashes of the old, but also, quite literally, the instrument through which he could achieve it. The news of its loss—which K. had difficulty in breaking to him without tears—must have seemed like the final blow from a fate inexplicably determined to strip him down to the bone.

Unconsciously linking the metaphor to a pragmatic fact, I said, "Your winter coat is undamaged—I kept it safe in my Big Box. . . ." and the moment I had said it, I thought what a stupid, frivolous thing it was to say to a man who has just lost everyone and everything in the world that he cared about. But his face lit up. "Thank God!" he cried, "Somewhere, somehow, I'll get another cello—if I have to beg, borrow, or steal one, but I couldn't get another winter coat."

Another survivor who made his way back from Hell on foot to find only desolation, an empty house, in each shuttered room a ghost—his mother, his father, his sister—was Nina's friend, Péter.

His first impulse was to get away from this haunted shell of his childhood and youth, get away from Rumania with its all-too-familiar associations. Go to Budapest. Find Nina. Reassure himself that one person, at least, whom he loved was still in the land of the living. And there was just a possibility of finding a living relative there; an aunt of his by marriage, a widow whose home was in Budapest, might conceivably have survived.

Crossing the frontier without papers was risky. But Péter managed to pass the border undiscovered, lying flat on top of a train. His courage was rewarded. He found both Nina and his aunt alive and well and under the same roof. It was she who had come to us after the fall of Buda, homeless and "without nourishment." When we moved upstairs, she had gone elsewhere, but as soon as part of our top floor had been made habitable, and the stairway repaired, she had collected her scattered belongings and moved in. The housing shortage was such that people were still existing holed up in ruins, and every square yard of habitable space was inhabited. Rebuilding would take years. In the meantime, there were regulations as to how much living space each individual was entitled to. Theoretically, it was one room for one person. But a married couple without children, or with only a young baby, counted as one person; so a three-room flat might be occupied by three separate couples and three babies, all sharing the same bathroom and kitchen, and driving one another crazy, like the Russian families in the Greta Garbo comedy, *Ninotchka*. We kept our three rooms for ourselves by registering Marcsa *néni* as a relative and Paul as a lodger, and by taking advantage of a loophole that allowed extra space to anyone whose home also served as a "place of business," for which K. technically qualified —as a teacher of music who received private pupils.

Péter's aunt was dreaming of a new life in Australia, and wanted her nephew to emigrate with her. But he was dreaming a different dream, in which all that he had lost with the death of his family in Auschwitz would be restored to him by Nina. Unlike István, and the young cellist, Péter no longer saw art as the only cornerstone on which to build a new life—perhaps because painting had never been as all-important to him as music was to them, and his close acquaintance with death, and pain, and suffering had turned him away from the art of painting toward the art of healing. He was going to be a doctor, and his dream was to get his medical training in England, while Nina studied painting at his side; a touching equation of interchanging roles, in which she would practice his art as well as her own.

Every day of Péter's brief stay, he and Nina would go out into the garden after supper, spread a blanket on the ground under a tree, and sit there talking, long after darkness fell and the grass was drenched with dew; talking, talking . . . reweaving with words, both their own and those of the poets and philosophers dear to them, the strands of their interrupted friendship. K. and I, lying side by side in the peaceful night, with no more fear of death dropping out of the starry sky, could hear the rise and fall of their low-pitched voices against the high treble of shrilling cicadas— like two cellos playing a duet to an accompaniment of three notes repeated over and over by an orchestra of toy violins.

For the silent K., so much talking between two young people was hard to interpret, "What do you think, Tercsikém—is it love?"

They always sat under the same tree, which in retrospect seems to have a symbolic significance—though I doubt whether either of them, even the psychic Nina, thought of it at the time, any more than I did. A cherry tree, loaded every summer with the juicy morello cherries, dark and bitter, that make the best preserves, it was wounded during the siege when a rocket exploding near it tore a deep gash in its trunk. We thought it was going to die. In the spring, however, and every spring for as long as we were there, it put forth its usual fragrant cloud of blossom. But it never again bore fruit.

Another of Nina's close friends came back to Budapest while she was still there—Agnés.

Like István's, the story Agnés had to tell was an epic in which the Catholic Church played an important role. But so did a German guard—by one of those twists of fate that are not to be explained rationally. From her starred house in Budapest, she was taken by the *Nyilas* to a sort of "way-station" concentration camp, close to the Austrian border, where the inmates were "selected" for various destinations. It was one of the German guards who helped her to escape before that last, fatal, round-up. After her escape, she had found refuge in a Catholic convent, where the nuns kept her and many others in like danger, safely hidden in the cellars. This experience eventually led to her conversion to Catholicism.

In late September, a few British subjects who had stayed on in Hungary through the war for one reason or another, were repatriated in a British military plane, and Nina went with them. She took with her only two, rather shabby, suitcases, and a knapsack filled with her precious books. In the smaller of the two suitcases I had packed the Indian necklace I had given her for her birthday, and a few other little pieces of jewelry that I wanted her to have, and feared to lose, or be forced to sell, if I kept them with me in Hungary. But what I had successfully hidden from the Russians was taken from Nina by the Italians. The small suitcase was stolen from the back of a British army truck during a stopover in Naples, and never recovered.

Nina also took with her (but kept, luckily, on her person), a bulky envelope containing the account of our experiences during the siege and the Russian occupation of Buda that I had been writing, a little every day, over a period of weeks, for the benefit of my sons, my uncle, and any other relatives who might be interested. Closely handwritten with a fine-nibbed pen, without either paragraphs or margins, it covered both sides of twenty-two, legal-sized, brownish pulp paper obtained for me by Károly. Now, preserved by Eldon, this torn and faded document has

proved to be a gold mine of small but important details that might
otherwise have been blurred, or even completely lost by capricious memory.

At the bottom of the last page is a postscript, addressed to Peter
and Eldon:

> Nina is going today—and with her a big piece of my heart. I
> have not felt so unhappy since I said goodbye to you two one
> day in September six years ago. . . .

True. But there was a difference. When I parted with Peter and
Eldon in 1939, I had every reason to fear a long, and possibly
final, separation. Now, in 1945, with the war over, and the lines of
communication between one country and another opening up
instead of closing down, what I felt after seeing Nina off to
England was the kind of sadness a mother feels when her youngest daughter leaves home to go to college, or to get married; a
sense of brightness dimmed, of a light turned in another direction; but in no danger of being extinguished altogether. So I was
unprepared for the darkness and silence that swallowed Nina up.

She was staying in the home of Peter's mother-in-law. Peter,
just back from India, and awaiting new orders, had used his
interval of leave to marry the young woman doctor to whom he
had been engaged, dis-engaged, and re-engaged more than once
during the years of his absence. Her mother, now finally bereft of
her companionship, had offered to take Nina in while she found
her feet on the unfamiliar ground of her native land, in which she
had spent fewer than three years of her life—as a little girl in a
seaside boarding school. But helping Nina to adjust to postwar
life, and postwar sentiment in England after having spent the
war years in a dubiously neutral country that had ended up on the
enemy side, required more understanding of the whole situation
and more psychological expertise, than this well-meaning surro-
gate mother possessed.

She considered Nina a casualty—not only of the war, but of my
original sin in marrying a Hungarian, compounded by taking
Nina with me to Hungary, keeping her there with me instead of
sending her back to England with her brothers in 1939, and,

finally, letting the last train "home" leave without her. Behavior
that was little short of criminal in the eyes of this insular Englishwoman, who believed that Nina's only hope of living a normal
(the word is hers), happy life in her own country, lay in forgetting
the whole Hungarian experience. Which meant that she must be
weaned away from the only close friends she had, as well as from
me—her misguided mother.

Aside from the insensitivity of this judgment, and the wound-
ing implication that Nina's Hungarian experience had been
valueless right from the start, the idea of expunging from the
memory eight years of experience, whether good or bad, was
diametrically opposed to my own philosophy of accepting, assimi-
lating, and ultimately transcending all the experiences of one's
life.

But from where I stood then, there was nothing I could do to
combat this well-meant amateur brainwashing. My letters to
Nina went unanswered, and suspecting that they were being
intercepted, I ceased writing them, and wrote poems instead.
Most of the poems I wrote at that time were letters to a lost
daughter.

She would come back, after two years of attempted alienation,
both to me and to Hungary. In the end, it was I who had to leave
her. And the supreme irony was that she was caught and impaled
on a point of law between the same two democratic institutions
that had helped me and K. to forestall the descent of the Iron
Curtain; the British Foreign Office and the U.S. Department of
Immigration.

One summer Sunday morning, a few weeks before Nina left,
Mari brought Gyula to see us. K. and I were in the garden,
admiring my agricultural prowess, when we saw them coming
up the road hand in hand, looking at each other instead of where
they were going, and weaving from side to side as though intoxicated with their own happiness.

No need for K. to ask, "Is it love?" The question was, rather, "Is
it wise?" and the answer was, "No." But what have war and love to
do with wisdom?

Standing outside the gate, shyly smiling, while K. went to get the key, they were like two graceful, nervous colts hoping for sugar. And K. was not the man to withhold it, or even to rob it of its sweetness with a warning.

Gyula and Mari were married at the end of October, with no place of their own to live in, no household belongings, no possessions at all worth mentioning, and only one regular paycheck coming in—Mari's. Gyula relied on odd jobs; for him there was only one possible profession, only one goal in life—to become a sculptor, and a good one. His faith in his talent was unbounded, and so was Mari's.

A month or so after their marriage, they had a stroke of luck. The departure of Sybil and her husband created a small vacant space, which the newly married pair managed, with K.'s help, to inherit. Still unrepaired, cold, damp, comfortless, it had two advantages. It gave the young couple the privacy they needed, and it brought them geographically closer to us; close enough for Mari to leave her baby daughter—born at Easter time after an incredibly hard winter—in my care while she was at work.

The overriding memory of that winter is one of inescapable cold: of icy streets and no place in which to warm up, of unheated public buildings, theaters and concert halls so cold that the audience sat wrapped in blankets, and even at home in bed, of temperatures so low that we had to wear knitted gloves while we read ourselves to sleep, or we couldn't hold our books. Hell, I thought, is not fire, but ice with no fire to melt it.

No fire without and no fire within. Just as before the siege we had approached starvation by stages, advancing ineluctably from one degree of undernourishment to another, we were now retreating from it in the same manner, and that winter we were once again at the long-drawn-out stage when we had enough food to keep us alive but never enough to satisfy our hunger, or generate internal heat to combat the external chill.

But oases of warmth and plenty sprang into being like magic wherever a high-ranking Russian chose to go, and anyone lucky enough to be there at the same time shared its delights. It was our good luck that the Russians, whatever their rank, loved music.

So when K. was asked by the Minister of Culture, Dr. Dezsö Keresztüry, to play for a little musicale he was giving in his home for a few "distinguished guests," we knew pretty much what to expect. "Distinguished guests" meant high-ranking Russians, and Russians meant refreshments and warmth. This glowing prospect was somewhat dimmed for me by worry about my appearance. Not only were my clothes shabby and out of fashion, but I, too, looked the worse for wear. Due to a prolonged lack of vitamins, my clear "English rose" complexion was blotched and scaly; my hair had fallen out in handfuls, and what I had left was dull and brittle and turning gray; and my hands were covered with an itchy red rash, like measles, that had broken out all over my body; defects for which I had neither cure nor disguise, since medicines and makeup were equally hard to come by. All in all, my looking glass reflected such a sorry image that had it not been for my hunger I might have stayed at home. But hunger was stronger than vanity. And K., in whose eyes I was always perfect, or very nearly perfect, told me not to worry, I looked beautiful, and as for my clothes, everyone was in the same boat, and Keresztüry was the last man in the world to think less of a person for not being dressed in the latest fashion at any time, much less in times like these.

As soon as I entered the Keresztüry home, I realized how right K. was about our host. After shedding our coats and snowboots in the vestibule, we were ushered into a large, deliciously warm reception room, arranged to look like the music room in the Hubay Palace, with a grand piano at one end and rows of little gilt chairs facing it. In the middle of this elegant Biedermeyer drawing room, was a tall stepladder, and atop it, in his shirt-sleeves, was the Minister for Culture, struggling to repair the electric chandelier. He greeted K. with a wave of the hand and a friendly "*Servus*, Jenökem!" and apologized to me for not coming down to shake hands with me. "I have to get this thing fixed before they arrive, and they'll be here any minute now...."

I went with K. into a back room, where he could tune up his cello and practice a little without being heard, so I only found out who "they" were when I slipped into my seat just before the concert began.

In the middle of the front row sat the new "Royalty," Mátyás Rákosi, the Communist Party "Boss," and his Russian wife. I had never before seen Rákosi close up, in all his fleshiness, but his round, jowly face had stared at me from a hundred posters. A

burly man, his behind was too big by far for the fragile little chair
it sat on, and he brought to mind childhood pictures of Humpty
Dumpty before his great fall.

His wife had more natural dignity. Severely dressed in black,
stiff and unsmiling, with Asiatic features, and straight dark hair
strained back from her broad face, she had an air of aloofness that
somehow set her above her husband. They were flanked on either
side by bemedaled Russian generals. The Hungarian guests
were, for the most part, civilians, some of them high government
officials, but, whether in or out of uniform, they were distinguish-
able from the Russians by their lean look, and the famished-wolf
gleam in their eyes.

Although I can still see that audience as clearly as I saw it at the
time, there is a gap in my memory of the concert, of what was
played, and by whom, between K.'s opening performance of the
Bach suites, and the grand finale provided by a stranger, a young
Russian pianist who looked more like a soldier than an artist.

He entered the room by a side door, and marched up to the
piano with a brisk military step, and the grim, taut expression of
a guardsman on parade, which I attributed to nervousness of a
decidedly intimidating audience at uncomfortably close quarters. Muscular, square-shouldered, flat-featured, with short
bristly hair, he could have been one of the smiling bandits who
pocketed our watches and swallowed our eau de cologne in the
early days of the occupation, except that he did not smile; not once
did the faintest shadow of a smile cross that grim young face.

For a full minute, he sat absolutely still gazing down at the
keyboard, as pianists often do before starting to play; as though
their instrument were a human partner, to be asked "Are you
ready? Are you with me? Okay, let's go!" But this young Russian
seemed, rather, to be gauging the right moment to leap on and
subdue an unsuspecting enemy. And his attack, when it did come,
had the stunning force of an explosion.

Whatever it was that he played, it did not reach me as music,
only as a torrent of sound; a glittering display of virtuosity, that
for all its rushing brilliance left the heart and soul untouched, the
composer's deepest message undelivered.

He acknowledged the storm of applause with a series of little mechanical bows, from which I conceived the fantastic idea that he was not human, not a creature of flesh and blood, but a scientific phenomenon; the offspring of highly developed robots, a new species, capable of performing mechanical wonders, but not of engaging the human emotions.

When the applause had died down, I asked K., who was now seated beside me, who he was. "His name is Gillels," K. said, "Emil Gillels." The name meant nothing to either of us, it was still unknown outside the Soviet Union.

Any further discussion concerning this Communist prodigy was cut short by our host's announcement of supper. A word that drove everything else out of our minds, and might just as well have been *Abracadabra*, for at the same moment, the doors of the supper room were thrown open to reveal a sumptuous table loaded with now almost legendary delicacies that even in our dreams had been long since replaced by elusive loaves of bread.

The famished wolves piled their plates mountain high, which K. and I considered bad manners. "We can always come back for more," we said, serving ourselves modestly. But that was a miscalculation. A swarm of locusts could not have stripped that table faster or more completely than did our fellow guests. I felt cheated. "Never mind," said K., "we'll know better next time."

"Next time" was another musicale at which K. was asked to play; an afternoon affair given by the Nobel prize winner, Szent-Györgi, for various bigwigs, including the inevitable (and indispensable) Russian generals. After the concert, tea was served, and masses of little cream puffs, filled with real whipped cream. K. and I, not to be cheated a second time, took up a position near the door leading to the kitchen, and whenever a fresh supply of cream puffs was brought in, we each grabbed two.

They were light as air, but after the first half-dozen, they lay like stones on my conscience—wasn't I doing the very same thing that I had so righteously condemned in my letter to Eldon? K. was thinking of something else, something equally ironical. "Do you remember the greedy Duchess?"

I remembered her only too well—I could almost hear her laughing.

In such delayed sequels there is usually an element of poetic justice, and also of clarification; one way or another they set things straight. But the delay can be inordinately long, and the longer it is, the more purely coincidental the sequel appears to be.

But is there really such a thing as pure coincidence? I am asking myself that question in connection with the long-delayed sequel to that musical evening in Budapest just after the war, when I formed an impression so strong of Emil Gillels and his playing that it persisted for more than three decades, and kept me from buying his records despite his growing reputation as a great pianist.

This influence of a single past image on the ever-changing present was largely unconscious. Gillels returned to my conscious mind only when I was summoning up, for the purposes of this book, the entire scene in the home of the Minister for Culture, when by chance I found myself in the alien company of two very diverse products of Communism; a now-famous Russian pianist, and a never-anything-but-infamous Hungarian Party Boss.

Wearied by the effort to capture and put down on paper the images and echoes of that so-distant scene, I turned on the television, and there before me on the screen, where I had never before seen him, was Emil Gillels, playing the piano.

Thunderstruck by what seemed to be the reflection in a mirror of what was in my mind, I watched and listened as he finished the piece he was playing and accepted the applause and congratulations of what appeared to be a select group of people. It was clearly a special occasion, but I had missed the announcement of what it was and where it was taking place. No matter. In the minute or two of what I can only call his "materialization" in my living room, I learned something much more important. I was given the answer to a question I had never troubled to ask; how and in what manner had he changed in the thirty-six years since I last set eyes on him?

Physically, he had changed very little. Middle-age had rounded him out. The cut of his hair, though still short, was no longer militant. Success had replaced his youthful strut with the modestly dignified bearing of the man who knows that he has no more reason to be modest. Little things like that. The vital change in him, and by extension in his music, was fundamental. A spiritual metamorphosis. Something, or, more likely, someone, had brought the robot to life, given him a soul, and taught him how to smile.

II

I remember that chill and comfortless winter of 1945-46 as a period of extreme insecurity, affecting every aspect of our lives, and all the harder to accept because the war was over. Although reason, and history, told us that the signing of an armistice is no more than the official termination of legalized mass murder, whose effects can in no way be undone by the stroke of a pen, we felt let down. And I was constantly reminded that the removal of imminent physical danger is the removal of a certain kind of support; a stimulus; without which the problems, fears, and anxieties of life that have been temporarily eclipsed by the threat to life itself reassume all their termite power.

One of these was the growing fear of being coerced into living the rest of our miraculously preserved lives in a way that was not what we wanted for ourselves; a possibility that K. was reluctant to face; containing as it did the elements of a bitter emotional conflict. The kind of inner struggle that occurs when life with the person one loves more than anyone else in the world becomes intolerable on account of insanity, or the evil influence of some outside force, and one's friends advise one to break away, and one's heart, divided, leaps at the prospect of freedom, but murmurs, "not yet . . . not so long as there's any hope left."

István, determined to lead the rest of his life as he chose, took a risk, and won. Early in January, he slipped out of the country as quietly and successfully as he had slipped out of that sinister stable in Esztergom a year earlier. Next time we heard from him, he was studying composition in Paris.

A few weeks after István's unofficial departure from the country, Nina's Rumanian friend, Péter, unofficially entered it, for the second time, in the hope of finding her still with us. He had got his ankle nicked by a bullet while running away from a border guard. It was only a surface wound, but it caused him to limp, and had to be healed before he could "jump" back over the border. The emotional hurt he suffered at finding Nina gone was infinitely deeper, and played, I think, a bigger role in delaying his return to Rumania. As long as he was with us, in surroundings he associated with Nina, he felt closer to her, and was able to maintain the illusion that their separation was only temporary; that even if it was love on his side only, they would be reunited as friends just as soon as he could arrange to get to London. And in my desire to comfort and console him, I unwittingly encouraged this unrealizable dream by working with him for hours every day over his English; conversing with him, correcting his mistakes, setting him to write compositions, and helping him to translate his own poems and stories (for he was a gifted writer in his own language) into English.

There was, of course, no way in which I could make up for Nina's absence, but I was, in some sense, a living link between him and her; and when he left, very early one snowy morning, after having been with us for almost two weeks, I felt as if I were saying goodbye to a third son, and my intuition told me that in this case it would be final.

I never did see him again, and neither did Nina. But there was an epilogue. More than a decade later, when I was living and working in New England, I got a letter with a Rumanian postmark. I turned it over and over before opening it, in the futile way people often do with a letter addressed in an unfamiliar hand. That it might be from Péter never entered my mind—time had pushed him so far to the back of it.

We are apt to imagine ourselves forgotten by those whom we forget, but this letter demonstrated that Péter not only remembered me, he remembered what I had taught him. Short and bleak as the winter day on which I had last seen him, it informed me in faultless English that he had carried out his plan to study medicine, and for some years now had been a country doctor in Transylvania. He had married, but the marriage had ended in divorce, and he was alone.

Alone. Coming from him, the word was stark as a bony hand reaching up from under the sea.

He often thought of Nina. He wondered where she was, and whether she was still painting. He had got my address from my stepdaughter—he hoped I would forgive this intrusion from the past. He kissed my hands. ...

At the bottom of the page, his own carefully printed address mutely requested a response.

I responded with warmth, and news of Nina, who was living in London, and still painting, and would, I felt sure, be very happy to hear from him. ... But in giving him her address, I had to tell him that she was married.

He did not write to her. Nor did he ever again write to me. A dream that had stirred in its grave had lost all hope of resurrection.

This brief "intrusion of the past" brought with it the memory of another experience that was coincidentally linked with it in time.

It so happened that later on the same day that Péter set out in the snow to recross the border into Rumania "unofficially," K. set out to cross it officially, as a member of a cultural delegation to Bucharest sponsored by the Hungarian Government. The group, that consisted of a dozen or so representatives of Hungarian art and culture, would travel to Bucharest by train, in a special coach, and would spend two or three days there as the honored guests of the Rumanian Government. I would dearly have liked to go with them, to share with K. some scenes of my life before I knew him, and get high once again on that heady Rumanian champagne; but spouses were not invited.

The train was due to leave around six in the evening, and K., who had to go most of the way to the station on foot, set off at that melancholy hour of a winter afternoon when the light is beginning to fade and the shadows are long and blue.

It was our first real separation since our marriage. Aside from his brief stay in the hospital, we had never been parted overnight.

I went with him to the gate, where we kissed, and clung to each other as though for the last time. Then he urged me to go back indoors, out of the icy wind, and I said, "All right—but wait here until you see me at the window."

From the window I watched him walk down the road, his cello case in one hand, and his suitcase in the other, a strangely Gothic figure in his long winter coat and his wide-brimmed black felt hat. My heart swelled with love for him. There is no one like him in all the world, I thought—and at the same instant my whole being was flooded with the foreknowledge of a grief beyond all telling.

My anxiety concerning my two sons had moved at the end of the war from a physical to a psychological level.

Eldon had joined the Royal Canadian Air Force. Later, based in England, he had requested not to be sent on bombing missions to Hungary. Officially, no such exemption could be made, but a compassionate squadron commander had done his best to spare Eldon this anguish, and before very long ill health had rescued him from the whole predicament. He contracted a severe case of scarlet fever, which was followed by a long bout of rheumatic fever, which affected his heart, and after weeks of hospitalization, he was invalided out of the service altogether. When the war came to an end, he was back in Hollywood, striving to recover the lost years, and to make the difficult transition from juvenile roles to adult roles, and not succeeding very well.

To us he wrote cheerful letters, but his brother, who was in closer touch with him, having kept up a chess game with him by letter all through the war (in the superstitious hope that neither of them would get killed as long as it wasn't finished), told us that he was profoundly depressed regarding his interrupted career and a number of other things. And the sad fact was that his renewed contact with us in Hungary placed an added burden on his shoulders, since he was the only member of the family in a position to send us the food, clothing, and money that we so desperately needed.

Our critical lack of money was due in part to the general economic collapse that affected everyone. But K., in particular, suffered from the prolonged suspension of the country's musical life, of the concerts and the regular "live" performances over the radio, on which he depended for his personal income—since his salary as a professor at the Lizst Ferenc Academy went to support Yoyo and his daughters—for as long as they were dependent. In my case, the trouble stemmed, fundamentally, from the loss of my British citizenship when I married. The capital (an inheritance from a wealthy aunt) from which I derived my small private income was invested in England, where it was needed at that time for the living expenses and education of my two older children. The advent of the war made its transfer to some neutral country advisable, and it ended up in the United States—in Eldon's account. I had had no direct access to it for years. But now, as the result of what is known as "human error" during the period of Eldon's absence, it had got entangled in the American wartime currency laws, and was threatened with unjust confiscation. The responsibility of saving it fell on Eldon; a crushing responsibility for a boy of twenty-three, involving a long-drawn-out lawsuit against the United States government, which he ended by winning. But it was largely a Pyrrhic victory. Most of the disputed money was swallowed up by the legal expenses of the case, and the toll it took of Eldon himself was incalculable.

At the time, we were too out of touch with normal reality, and too far away, to realize fully what poor Eldon was up against. Our own immediate condition was so primitive; our wants so simple. And when he sent us a banker's draft for fifty dollars, it seemed like a fortune—in more ways than one.

The inflation had already reached the point where the paper pengös one got in exchange for a fifty-dollar check would fill a fair-sized suitcase, but if they were not immediately exchanged for either gold, food, or clothing, you might just as well have put the check down the drain instead of cashing it.

With this in mind, K., Marcsa néni, and I set off for the bank with two suitcases. The notes were handed out to us in rubber-banded packages—that we had no time to count. We stashed half of them in one suitcase, with which K. rushed to the nearest black market dealer in gold, and half in the other, with which Marcsa and I rushed to the nearest food market. At strategic points, and especially near markets, loudspeakers were set up over which the galloping devaluation of the pengö would be announced from time to time. Marketing was no longer a leisurely bargaining with the peasants for good value, and the best quality produce; one does not haggle over the size of an egg whose price is tripling by the minute.

These insane conditions turned every transaction into a nightmarish, unwinnable race against the loudspeakers. When our absentee landlord finally agreed to repair the shellhole in our roof, he told us airily to have the job done and deduct the cost from the rent. But the workmen demanded each day's wages in advance every morning, and would dash off to spend the money while it would still buy something. A procedure that put us in a double bind. First we had to catch the falling pengö in mid-air first thing every morning, and then calculate what the rent money would be, according to the gospel of the loudspeaker—at that particular moment in time. An absurd undertaking, whose results the landlord did not want to accept—and small wonder!

By midsummer, this monstrous inflation had reached astronomical figures that might have made even today's computers feel dizzy. Something had to be done, some drastic step had to be taken. And at what was, for some, disastrously short notice, the pengö was let fall into the equivalent of a black hole, and replaced with the forint.

But it was against the perpetually shifting background of the inflation, and all the other uncertainties of the immediate postwar period, that the delicate process of mending, or reconstructing, human relationships broken off or damaged by the war had to be undertaken.

After his marriage, and a period of home leave, my son Peter was assigned to the Allied Control Commission in Vienna. This was wonderful news—Vienna was practically next door. But when I wrote to tell him how eagerly we were looking forward to seeing him, he replied rather guardedly that he would have to wait a few weeks before he could ask for more leave. Which was probably quite true, but not the whole truth; which was, he eventually had to admit, that he had decided not to come.

This sudden manifestation of the gulf that I had dreaded on the very threshold of my expected reunion with him, was a stunning emotional shock.

I wept, and sought comfort from K., who, as always, restored my emotional balance. And with that, I recovered my fighting spirit, and the most important defensive weapon in my armory—my sense of humor.

I refused to accept Peter's decision, and challenged him to justify it. He took up the challenge, and very soon we were engaged in a fierce epistolary duel over whether a painful situation was better faced or avoided. We were both expert duelists with the pen, and thoroughly enjoyed a battle of wits over abstract ideas. But this one had to do with the affections rather than the mind. It stemmed from the bond that was forged between me and him during the first sixteen months of his life, and later strengthened by suffering from the same circumstances. And now we were testing its strength.

It proved unbreakable, and we laid down our arms. The gulf of war and separation still yawned between us, but out of the letters that flew back and forth above it week after week, a fragile bridge of words had been constructed that would help us to cross it when he came to Budapest in the spring, as he promised to do.

He kept his promise. But, after all the frantic preparations made by me and Marcsa—the saving up of food, the rearranging of rooms—to give him a warm welcome, his arrival was marred by a misunderstanding as to where K. and I would meet him. While he was waiting for us at the airport, we were waiting for him at the inner city terminal. When he did not arrive in the only limousine of the afternoon, I thought he had changed his mind about coming, and, bitterly disappointed, K. and I trudged home, to find him, standing forlornly outside the locked garden gate. He had taken a taxi all the way from the airport, to find no one at home. Which, as I realized later, was the worst thing that could have happened to Peter at that moment in time.

He had changed hardly at all in the six and a half years since I had last seen him. Still extremely slender, he looked very young for his age, which was just twenty-eight, and his military rank of major. Only his manner was different, more withdrawn, and the look in his eyes. As a boy, his eyes had gone cloudy when he was hurt, and the cloud now seemed to be permanent.

He had two suitcases, both very large—especially for a brief visit. I picked one of them up while K. was unlocking the gate. It might have been filled with lead. "What on earth is in it?" I asked, and he said, "It's the fatted calf. I thought I'd better bring it with me."

Can after can of *Spam* came out of the heaviest suitcase. What had felt to me like lead turned out to be gold.

The spring sunshine made it seem warmer out of doors than in the unheated house, where the chill of winter still lingered. So every day after breakfast, when K. had gone to the academy,

Peter and I went for long rambling walks over the Buda hills. We both had the English addiction to long walks, which had often been, in the past, our means of escape from a difficult situation at home, and, in a wider sense, from reality.

"Do you remember, Mother . . ." (most of our conversations began with that phrase), "do you remember walking with me along the Chausea in Bucharest—oh! ages ago, I must have been about ten years old—and telling me the stories of the operas that you and father went to see every week? How the hunchback court jester, Rigoletto, who cared for no one but his daughter, found her dead in a sack? You called that poetic justice. And how the fickle gypsy, Carmen, was stabbed at a bullfight by her discarded lover—poetic justice again. Do you remember?"

I remembered. And I still believed that poetic justice, the justice of cause and effect, was God's justice—slow, but sure, and impossible to evade.

Now, traversing recent battlefields with my grown-up son, it was my turn to listen, while he told me bit by bit, day after day, the story of his life since the war parted us. And listening, I began to understand the reasons, conscious and subconscious, for his earlier reluctance to revive the mother-son relationship with me that time and circumstance had forced into abeyance.

He was torn by an inner conflict unconnected with me, but in which I was unwittingly involved: first by exemplifying in my own life the dangers of marrying on the eve of an indefinite separation, and later by not being in the right place at the right time.

As soon as Peter had got his degree in German language and literature from London University, he reported once again for service in the British Armed Forces. His qualifications earned him a commission, and he was assigned to a branch of Military Intelligence based, for some obscure reason, in New Delhi; which put him and his girl in exactly the same position that his father and I had been in twenty-four years earlier, and faced with the same choice; whether to get married before parting, or wait for the unpredictable end of the war.

They decided to wait. Peter was less impetuous than his father, and his girl was less romantic than his mother. But waiting has its own classic dangers, and they did not fail to crop up.

Peter's response to the mystery and mysticism of India was not that of the usual Englishman. He made Indian friends, learned their ways, and preferred their company to that of his brother officers. And as time and distance gradually cooled the relationship between him and his English fiancée, he was more and more drawn to the strikingly handsome and remarkably intelligent daughter of a high-caste Indian family with which he was friendly. The girl in England, tired of waiting, took up with another man, leaving Peter free to ask his Indian love to be his wife. But he had to have her parents' consent, and they absolutely refused it. Not that they did not like him, but at that time, for an Indian girl of good family to marry a British officer was a step down; a step into social limbo—to become an outsider vis-à-vis her own people, without becoming an insider in her husband's social circle. So in the end it was Peter who found himself in limbo—with one love lost and the other forbidden, and his family far out of reach.

When he arrived back in London, blitzed and grim, at the end of the war, with no home to go to, no member of his family there to welcome him, his sense of isolation and sheer physical loneliness were more than he could bear, and he went to his ex-fiancée's flat as if nothing had come between them.

The Indian girl would never re-enter his life as anything more than a friend, but her dark beauty and brilliant mind continued to haunt his imagination, and his unfilfilled love for this unattainable Indian goddess subtly undermined, and ultimately destroyed, whatever happiness he might otherwise have achieved with his down-to-earth English wife.

In the spring of 1947, when he had been demobilized, and was teaching at London University, his inner conflict resulted in a breakdown. Luckily, it happened near the start of the long vacation, and all concerned, including Nina—who had escaped from Peter's mother-in-law and was living on her own in London—and Peter himself, thought that the best cure for him would be to spend the vacation with us, in Budapest; that a return to the past might help him to sort out his life.

We were no longer at war, but peace was not yet established, and all kinds of permissions had to be obtained before such a trip could be made. Everything at the English end went smoothly, but despite British approval, on compassionate grounds, of Peter's projected visit to us, backed up by medical certificates and letters from influential persons, the necessary entry permit from the Allied Control Commission in Budapest was not forthcoming. I went to see them about it, and was put off with excuses, and bidden to be patient. I went again and again. Still no visa. Desperate, I cried, "But why? *Why?* I don't understand why!" And the equally exasperated British official hissed under his breath, "I'll tell you why! This whole bloody show is run by the Russians—that's why!"

Light dawned. And with it came an apprehension that went far beyond the immediate situation. If the Russian general who was the chairman for this tri-lateral body had the power to withhold from a British subject an entry visa already approved by both the British and the Americans, the outlook for the future was grim indeed.

Peter's visa was eventually granted, but our minds had been finally turned toward the idea of departure. And once the mind changes its direction, the body is not slow to follow.

The seemingly sudden decision triggered by the British official's illuminating outburst was actually the culmination of a very slow process indeed; the process of relinquishment. A progressive "letting go," begun in the villa on the Kelenhegyi út in 1939.

The period between Peter's first visit, in the spring of 1946, and his second and longer stay in the summer and fall of 1947, was one of kaleidoscopic changes, interior and exterior, visible and invisible. On the invisible level, everything was moving irrevocably away from prewar normality. Everyone; those who, like us, would leave; those who would stay, by choice or from necessity; those who had been away in some other hell and had come back for good; all, without exception, were subconsciously preparing themselves for life in a new world. Meanwhile, on the visible level, everyday life was gradually returning to the semblance, at least, of prewar normality, as the streets were cleared of rubble, utilities and basic services restored, and civilian law and order reestablished. Equally important was the full revival of the city's artistic life; concerts, plays, opera, ballet, not to mention British and American films (not shown for years), offered temporary

forgetfulness of fears and anxieties that were better left unspoken; it was safer to weep over *Waterloo Bridge*, or *Mrs.
Miniver*, than over one's own forebodings.

One of the great achievements of that resurrection of the performing arts amid the ruins of Budapest, was a splendid production of Bartók's ballet *The Miraculous Mandarin*, banned for
decades as immoral, and now triumphantly performed for the
first time. An event that seemed to signify a new era of artistic
freedom oddly at variance with the threatened Soviet domination.

In that brilliant "world premiere" of Bartok's *Mandarin*,
which took place soon enough after his death in America to be his
Hungarian requiem, everything—the extraordinary music, the
powerful theme, the mimetic genius of the dancer in the principal
role, and the visual genius of Oláh's staging—combined to create
an image of immortality. It evoked a sense of Bartók's presence
among us in the darkly magical form of the Mandarin, who, in
turn, was the incarnation of his music.

The haunting experience would be granted to me again; given
to me, on the invisible level, as a remembrance.

III

Among those who went away of their own accord, the first to
come back were the "Mettys." In leaving Budapest before the
siege to avoid being raped by the Russians, K.'s timid sister and
her two timid daughters had only exchanged the possibility of one
ordeal for the certainty of another; the terrible homelessness, the
outlawry of the refugee on the road to nowhere.

The problems they came back to were nothing compared to
what they had been through, and Big Metty conceded that perhaps we had been right to stay where we were. Yet it was on that
bleak road to nowhere that the older of the two girls, the spinsterish one, whose chances of finding love had seemed nonexistent,
encountered it head-on. Big Metty told us the story—the kind of
tale from which ballets are made, and folk operas. The tale of a
young Hungarian captain, billeted with his men in a village
where a group of refugees have found a temporary shelter; of a
little human tenderness, simply offered and simply accepted,
that suddenly burst into flame and ignited the fiercest of all love's

fires—the overwhelming, unconditional, all-consuming passion of those who have only the present moment in which to condense the whole of life. And then, the classic ending; the hurried wedding arranged with the village priest, the precipitate departure in the night before the advancing Russians—he to his death in battle, and she to the next stretch of the cold road she will walk for the rest of her life, taking with her, within her, the only memorial she will ever have of a fire that came and went like a dream.

It was sometimes difficult to determine whether the change that one perceived in others was in them or in oneself—in one's point of view. I felt like that about Little Metty, the lovely younger sister. Like everyone else, she had been physically aged by the war—though in her case "aged" is not quite the right word; "matured" is better. But neither word quite describes the subtle effect of the tightening of the skin over her high cheekbones, the slight hollowing beneath them, the sharpening of the jawline, and the wide strip of silver in her black hair. She was, I thought, even more beautiful now than she had been when I first knew her as a girl of eighteen. Yet now, her beauty, though deepened and enhanced by experience, no longer seemed wasted on the undistinguished but kindly man who was waiting for her, still constant, still loving, at the end of the circular road. I could see now that he was the right husband for her, and always had been; that in him lay the safety that this gentle, defenseless creature needed above all else in a world so demonstrably full of savage beasts in human form.

The return of Mr. and Mrs. A., after an absence of more than a year, had no such romantic overtones. They had, it seemed, found a safe haven somewhere deep in the German countryside, where neither the enemy's planes nor the smoke of Auschwitz darkened the skies. But Mr. A.'s unwilling awareness of the evils he had managed to avoid was implicit in his silent acceptance of things as he found them, both in the country as a whole, and in his own damaged home—he even took the conversion of his biographies of Great Men into sandbags and toilet paper with equanimity.

His wife, however, who gave the impression of having been enclosed in a dust-proof, sound-proof glass case for the duration, went around her once pretty little nest uttering cries of dismay and disbelief, and appeals to God in Hungarian (*"Istenem! Istenem!"*) and to the Holy Family ("Jesus Mary and Joseph!") in English; infuriating Genevra, who had worked hard to get the devastated apartment into some sort of order, and to salvage as many of Mrs. A.'s precious possessions as possible. But she kept her fury in check until Mrs. A. demanded that she replace a burnt-out electric iron. Whereupon she exploded and told Mrs. A. in three languages and unminced words how lucky she was— lucky to find a single stick of her wretched furniture intact, lucky *not* to find her living room floor knee-deep in horse manure and the broken bits and pieces of her precious possessions, lucky not to be scraping dried human excrement from her bathroom floor— as I had had to do upstairs, lucky to find the house still standing in the first place. . . .

The truth of all this was confirmed by everyone in the neighborhood. So Mrs. A. changed her tune; began to sing of her luck in having had people like us, people with letters of protection, occupying her apartment and taking care of her things while she was away.

The law that had deprived me of my British citizenship when I married K. was soon to be repealed. But my citizenship was given back to me in advance of that, chiefly on account of my sons having served in the British Armed Forces. And when Genevra went, with her two small children, on a pioneering visit to England, it was on a British passport.

Her reason for going was two-fold; to persuade the Home Office to admit Károly to the United Kingdom as a refugee, and to explore the possibilities for his employment. But although she pulled every possible string, she failed in both objectives. As far as the British were concerned, Károly's status was that of an ex-enemy alien of too recent vintage to be welcome, much less to be given a job that could be done just as well by a British ex-serviceman.

His future in Hungary was grim. As a dispossessed landowner he was on his way to becoming a nonperson. K.'s position, as a performing artist and a professor at the Academy of Music, was a relatively good one; but no one was absolutely safe, and the fact that K. was not permitted to vote in the so-called "free elections," was a straw in the wind worth noting.

Between the end of the war and the end of the *pengö*, Károly, who had lost everything, made a meager living as a salesman of imported cigarette paper for a firm with which he had friendly connections. When the collapse of the currency put a stop to that, he obtained work with the Society of Authors, Composers, and Publishers—probably thanks to his knowledge of languages. While his wife and children were in England, he stayed with one of the old aunts with whom he had lived before his marriage— people whose situation was even more desperate than his own, because of their age and frailty. But before Genevra's return, he found a makeshift apartment in a patched-up villa on our street.

Disappointed, disillusioned, but characteristically undefeated, Genevra helped out by riding the crest of a sudden demand for English lessons that reflected many a forlorn hope.

Meanwhile, the old Jewish lady who had the only two habitable rooms on our top floor, finally left for Australia, and her place was taken by Mari, Gyula, and their elfin child, whom I nicknamed, *Tinkerbell*. On the day before they moved in with their scant belongings, Mari came after work to clean up the empty rooms, and finished so late that she spent the night there, sleeping on the floor. When she came down to have breakfast with us, she was radiant. "Do you know what I saw when I woke up this morning and looked around me?"

We had no idea... A bird? A bat? Not—God forbid!—a bedbug? Laughing, she shook her head. "I saw *a home*," she said, bringing tears to her father's eyes.

My unhappy son, Peter, spent the best part of three months with us; reading, writing, thinking, listening to K. playing the cello, and taking long, discursive walks with me. When he went back to England at the end of September, to his wife and his teaching, he thanked me for having "tidied up his mind" for him. But I think that what really helped him to face reality was, paradoxically, his reimmersion in a past dream; the midsummer dream that we had all dreamed together in the villa on the Kelenhegyi út before the war. And I believe that what made this possible in circumstances that were so utterly different was an intangible; a kind of music; a constant that no cataclysm could destroy—the harmony of the relationship between K. and me.

The material conditions of our life were still very hard, and it was Eldon who kept us going with an unfailing stream of packages that were veritable treasure chests of unobtainable or unaffordable foods (the only milk the children had was the powdered milk he sent us in big cans), medicines, and clothing donated by his friends. He thought of everything, he even included reels of thread in the same colors as the garments, in case I had to alter them. That winter, he sent me the money to buy a Hungarian sheepskin coat for myself, so that the old fur coat that I had brought out from England in 1937 could be passed on to Marcsa *néni*, with whom I had been sharing it. Throughout the siege, this extraordinary woman had worked for us, under conditions of great hardship, without wages of any kind. And even now, her only reward was in the form of a woolen sweater or two from Eldon's parcels, and later a pair of leather shoes, also from him. She was, in everything except blood, a member of the family, sharing both our hardships and our blessings—and doubling the value of the latter by her genius for making a little go a very long way—as she did that Christmas, the Christmas of 1947, and the last one that K. would celebrate in Hungary, or with his daughters.

It was Eldon who gave us the idea of turning that Christmas into a family reunion. Worried by the slowness of our response to his urging that we emigrate to America, he decided to come and see us, and light a fire under us with his own hands, so to speak. He would fly first to England, to see Peter and Nina, and then come on to us in Budapest—that is, if a visitor's visa could be obtained.

Visitors' visas were now being handled by the Hungarian authorities, who were much more persuadable than the Russians. So K., who had fans of every political color, boldly asked for four visitors' visas—to allow all three of my absent children, and my new daughter-in-law, to unite with the Hungarian branch of the family for the holidays.

The response was typical. First, a flat "No." Then, on grasping who the petitioner was, a guarded, "Perhaps," followed by endless referrals from one official to another; all to create an impression of dealing with an unheard-of request, thereby making the eventual granting of it an unheard-of favor, when in fact letting foreigners in for brief visits afforded the Regime an opportunity to show off what it was doing to rehabilitate the city and its institutions. But the policy of making people wait, of never acceding to any request without a lot of fuss, was built into the philosophy of the Regime, the philosophy of power, as we would find out when we were awaiting our promised exit permits, and were told to come back tomorrow, and tomorrow, and tomorrow. . . .

The battle of the visas won, and the family reunion about to become a reality, we were faced with the problem of how we were going to feed four more persons when we didn't even have enough to feed ourselves, and we began saving up the canned meats from Eldon's packages for the great occasion. Even squeezing four more persons into our apartment would be hard; only Nina was used to such crowding. But Paul's absence in England on an official assignment left us a little extra space, which we were trying, rather fraudulently, to hold onto against his unlikely return—for if one of his motives for accepting the London assignment was his desire to be near Nina, as I felt sure that it was, he would stay there as long as possible. But although he was still Nina's closest friend, and had helped her to find and furnish a studio for herself in London, their friendship was approaching the climacteric of all such long-standing relationships; the moment of decision whether to draw the existing bonds still closer, or to cut loose from them altogether.

Marcsa *néni* who loved Nina very much, and had an uncanny understanding of her—that went back, perhaps, to some indecision in her own past that had kept her, beautiful as she must have been as a girl, from marrying—said to me many times that she did not think Nina would marry either of her two ardent suitors (Paul, and the desolate Péter, who would have followed her to the ends of the earth if he could), but someone quite different, someone still unknown to her.

Yet she loved them both, in her own way. Which was not the way they wanted.

Early in December, encountering Gustav Oláh at the house of a mutual friend, I told him how moved I had been by the splendid

performance of *The Miraculous Mandarin*, and how much I
wished that my visiting children could see it, but it did not seem to
be scheduled for the time that they would be with us. He smiled,
and said, no, it was not on the program for those two weeks... he
was sorry, perhaps if he had known sooner. ...

Creativity, particularly successful creativity, and concern for
other people do not always go together. But brilliance and kindness went hand in hand in the personality of this genie of the
Budapest Opera; which, together with his modesty, greatly
endeared him to K., who had the same traits.

Oláh's Christmas present to us—his parting present, for he
knew that we were leaving—was a special performance of *Mandarin* (with *Bluebeard's Castle* on the same program), and the
best seats in the house to see it from—the center box, usually
reserved for distinguished guests. He came to see us in the inter-
mission. Immensely tall, he bent almost double over my hand.
"Madame de Kerpely, this is your *Mandarin*," he told me. And I
felt that in all my life I had never received such a beautiful gift.

Eldon, who flew directly to Budapest, arrived a day or two
earlier than the contingent from England. It was our first meeting in eight years, and we needed a little time alone together.

There was no unhappy misunderstanding of where K. and I
would be waiting for him, as there had been with Peter on his
crucial first return. We were standing on the curb outside the
inner city terminal when the airport bus pulled up, and Eldon
emerged from it looking, to our eyes, like someone stepping out of
a bus in a Hollywood movie. In fact, he looked like any normal
Californian, except that his fashionable, square-shouldered,
tweed topcoat—bought especially for the Central European
"arctic"—didn't quite go with his wide-brimmed Stetson hat and
his dark suntan.

After years of total separation, the first shock of recognition lies
in the sound of the voice. However much the appearance may be
changed, there is in every adult human voice an individual reso-
nance, an identifying note that can be disguised only by deliberate falsification, or the ravages of disease. And it was this vocal
"fingerprint," discernible under all the acquired modulations of a
stage voice whose national inflections had been neutralized by

elocution lessons on both sides of the Atlantic, that divested the jaunty Californian of all his strangeness the moment he opened his mouth.

But the actor's habitual projection of success was an artificial barrier between him and us that he could not, or dared not, let down. He had to convince us that all was well with him; that he had both the material and the emotional resources to sponsor a massive family emigration to the land of the free. A rescue mission more important to him than anything he had undertaken while serving in the air force, and, in a sense, compensating for his blameless failure to die for his country, as most of his fellow flyers had done.

The *persona* he presented to us was so sunny and full of life that I only became aware of the darkness beneath the sparkling surface when I caught him one day in repose, believing himself unobserved, and I had another shock of recognition. I had seen that world-weary look on his father's face all too often, and I trembled now for the son of whom he had said, looking down at the bureau drawer in which he was laid, "Poor little bugger...." with so much pity and sadness that I had believed the child to be dead.

Since then, his life, prematurely begun, and sustained only by the ministrations of Old Terrible, had hung in the balance time after time; but each time his frail body had clung to its existence with amazing tenacity. Which seemed to refute the idea that a talent for acting was not his only inheritance from his father. I had yet to learn, from my own experience, that the will to live and the will to die can exist simultaneously in one and the same person, on two levels of consciousness.

An American friend who knew Eldon in Hollywood described him as "the most charming man I ever knew." Physically, he was slight, and small of stature—more like an adolescent than a grown man, but well proportioned, like the copy of a statue that is smaller than the original, but carefully constructed to scale. His good looks resided less in his regular features than in his wide, warm smile, and the contrast between his dark hair and brows, and his sea blue eyes. But the indefinable quality that people called his "charm," for want of a better word, çame from within. It was not put on to please. It was the natural expression of a nature too generous and expansive for its own good. In a world where the takers vastly outnumber the givers, Eldon was a giver.

His grand scheme for the family emigration was based less on his fear of political developments in Hungary under Soviet domination—something not very well understood by the average American—as on his great love for America, and for California in particular, and his desire to share its milk and honey and oranges with us, who had been deprived of them for so many years, both literally and figuratively. And deep down, perhaps, he wanted to establish a family for himself in his chosen country; not just a wife and children (he had fallen in love with a Hungarian girl), but a father and mother and siblings as well. In any case, whatever his motives, conscious and subconscious, he knew that now was the time to put these ideas into action. It was, in fact, the eleventh hour.

It was an Englishman who impressed that on me; a member of the British Council, a government-sponsored Society for the Propagation of the Gospel of British Culture, who sounded just like my friend the British consul had sounded back in 1939, when I wanted time to think over the question of whether my sons should go or stay. I encountered this common-sense missionary of culture at a musical gathering in a friend's house. When he heard that I had an actor son in California who wanted us both to go and live with him there, he stared at me, "Then why on earth are you still here? Surely you realize. . . ." I explained that we had dallied out of sentiment, that this was our home, K. had close ties to break. . . . But the machinery for our departure had now been set in motion. He said, lowering his voice (the habit of whispering was catching), "May I give you some advice? Get that machinery moving as fast as you possibly can if you don't want to find yourselves locked in, and probably locked up as well."

His words, and his earnestness, aroused deep anxieties in me, that manifested themselves in recurring dreams of the sea; of long sunlit beaches to which I could never gain access, frustrated by cliffs covered with impenetrable thickets, or dense fog, or a mirage-like disappearance of the goal just as I was about to reach it.

I worried over an incident that took place during Eldon's visit. The owners of the villa in which Genevra and Károly occupied the ground floor were Communists of the idealistic kind. Sincere reformers who, apparently, still cherished the hope that Hungary would eventually be able to evolve her own brand of Communism, or Socialism, independently of the Soviet Union. When they discussed it, we listened and said nothing. But I couldn't help recalling, with some embarrassment, my poor opinion of the A.'s silent neutrality when the boot was on the other leg. Wishing to please, these people gave a little party in honor of our visitors from England and America. The other invited guests were all Hungarian intellectuals, and Communists of one stripe or another.

Eldon, as a live Hollywood actor, was an object of interest to everyone, particularly to a young man who had something to do with producing movies himself, and who invited Eldon to visit the studio where he worked. They agreed to meet the next day at a coffeehouse in Pest. And why not? Peter's gynecologist wife had been taken to see every hospital in the city. All the same, I felt uneasy. But to break the appointment, fail to turn up at the agreed-upon meeting place, would cause grave offense, and giving offense had its dangers, too. So off Eldon went, telling me not to worry, he could take care of himself.

He came back thoroughly shaken. His friendliness of the night before had been misunderstood, his interest in Hungarian filmmaking had been mistaken for an interest in something quite different; in short, he had been "approached" with a view to his becoming a Communist agent in Hollywood. His quick wits and his acting ability had come to his rescue, enabled him to pretend successfully that he either hadn't heard, or hadn't grasped the import of what had been proposed; and once on his guard, he had managed to fend off any further attempt to suborn him.

IV

For all of us, including those who would have to stay behind, the first nine months of 1948 constituted a long drawn out period of preparation, both practical and emotional, for a journey of life-and-death significance that we could never, right up to the last minute, be sure would take place.

The political climate was darkening. The country would soon be completely overspread by Stalin's gigantic shadow, and its people drawn willy-nilly into the sphere of his sinister power—his black magic, that could prove the innocent guilty, and invent brand-new crimes for them to have committed, or, alternatively, to be contemplating. An unspoken wish to escape from it all, an untold dream of, say, America, was enough to land the dreamer in jail, and a cry in the night overheard by the listening walls and reported in the interests of self-preservation could explain that. But is not the exploitation of human weakness and fear a form of the blackest magic?

But the same forces, whether natural or supernatural, that had protected us thus far, continued to work for us. Though without the fire lighted under us by Eldon, and the man from the British Council, things might not have gone so well. K. was one of the last Hungarian citizens to be given an exit permit before the Iron Curtain came down. Only a few months later, Károly had to crawl across the Austrian border in the night, with guards and dogs at his heels.

The "machinery" of emigrating from Hungary to America at that time was complicated by a variety of traps on one side of the ocean, and cast-iron immigration laws on the other. With regard to the "quota," both K. and Károly were in luck. K. as a professor of music, and Károly as an agriculturist, were both in favored categories, qualified for nonquota visas. Otherwise, they would have had to wait years, since the quota for Eastern Europeans was small and the D. P. camps' waiting lists were enormous. Genevra and I, being British born, fell into the roomy British quota, though as Hungarian citizens by marriage we could not leave Hungary without exit permits.

Since one immigration project was quite enough for Eldon to undertake at one time, K. and I would be the first, and Károly and Genevra the next—if that was what they wanted. We still did not realize how close it was to the last minute.

Minor children were permitted to enter the United States on their parents' visas, and K.'s younger daughter, Judit, who was not yet twenty-one, was praying that her mother and the Hungarian authorities, both equally formidable, would permit her to go with her father.

Nina, twenty-three years old, and a free Briton, would join us later, when we were settled.

With K.'s eligibility for a nonquota visa established, and Eldon accepted as our sponsor, the next condition to be met was a firm offer of a teaching position for K., which was found for him by Eldon, with the help of Hungarian friends—musicians already settled in the United States. One was the composer Miklos Rozsa, who was living in Hollywood and became a good friend of us all, and another was the conductor Eugene Ormandy, who, though I never had an opportunity to meet him, won a place in my heart by saying of K., in a letter of recommendation, that he was "one of the truly great."

Next came the medical hurdles; blood tests and chest X rays— only T. B. and communicable diseases were a barrier; other ailments, such as the vascular problem that threatened to deprive K. of the use of his legs, and the general debility caused by the years of privation, didn't count. So we were all right. But the exclusion of anyone whose lungs were unsound destroyed at one stroke poor Judit's dream of coming with us. And it was the crushing of this hope, and the accompanying threat of a final separation from her father, that led her to spend more time with us in the last few months before our departure than in the whole preceding decade, when her frequent illnesses, her mother's possessiveness, and later the dangers of war, had kept her at a distance.

Before I bid her goodbye and go off to America, leaving her behind, I would like to add a few strokes to the sketch I made of her earlier in this book.

In recalling that prolonged period of farewell to Hungary, that was like waiting for an indefinitely delayed train with all one's bags packed and everything that one has to say already said, the image of my stepdaughter, Judit, that presents itself, is of her lying in her bath.

I have been helping her to shampoo her long, light brown hair, that floats around her now like pale fronds of seaweed. She lies there under my gaze with the open simplicity of a child. But she is a grown-up young woman, a gifted actress, and already under the spell of her fateful operatic love. Her slender body, half-veiled by the slightly soapy water, seems unreal, yet in its natural element, like the undulating body of a mermaid. As the water cools, she shivers, and allows me to wrap her up in a towel and rub her dry. Once dry, she lets the towel drop, goes to the mirror, and starts to make up her eyes.

There is no sequel to this. Perhaps it doesn't even add anything to what I wrote about her before. It is just a comment on the selectivity of that autonomous camera that we call "the mind's eye." Judit is now more than fifty years old, but when her sister writes to me about her, tells me how lonely she is, how deeply she mourns her singer, I don't see a middle-aged woman tending her late husband's grave. I see a lovely, languid girl lying in her bath amid the floating seaweed of her hair.

Nina, too, wore her hair rippling loose to below her waist.

That summer, a combination of dissatisfaction with elements of her life in London, restlessness engendered by her ripening decision to emigrate to America, and a nostalgic desire to recapture some of the early happiness she had known in Hungary, brought Nina back to us.

Her first serious art studies had been under the guidance of the Hungarian painter, Molnar. And now, at what she felt to be an important stage of her development as an artist, she wanted to go back to him for a time—while it was still possible.

As for her development as a person, her natural independence had been aggravated by the maternalism of Peter's mother-in-law to a permanent state of controlled rebellion against anyone who tried to run her life, not excluding her friend Paul. And against his entreaties, and the advice of her English relatives and friends, she applied for a six-month student visa to Hungary "for the purpose of studying art with the famous painter, Molnar C. Pál," and was granted it.

So a circle was completed. Once again, Nina and I and K. were all together again, as we had been at the start of our Hungarian odyssey in the villa on the Kelenhegyi út.

Toward the end of the summer, Nina made some inquiries at the American consulate in Budapest concerning her application for a permanent visa to the United States, and was startled to discover that although she was British in blood and bone, and a British subject into the bargain, the fact that she had been born in Bucharest put her into the Rumanian quota. "But my father was a career consul! He was posted to Bucharest by the Foreign Office!"

They were doubtful. "Well . . . we would need official confirmation of that. . . ."

I appealed personally to a good friend in the Foreign Office, now in a very high position. It was the same man I had been to see when I was embarrassingly pregnant with Nina, just before making that awful journey to Bucharest with my three other children. (How ironic! If only I had stayed on in England for another few weeks, there would be no problem now.)

My friend's reply was kind, but not encouraging. He would be only too happy to confirm the official status of Nina's father and the official nature of his presence in Rumania at the time of Nina's birth—in fact, he had been responsible for it. But, he said, that might not be enough. In those days, the Consular Corps and the Diplomatic Corps were two separate branches of the Foreign Service, and there were differences in the privileges enjoyed by each. Had Nina been born in the consulate, which was in the legation grounds, or even in the garden, she would have been, technically speaking, born on British soil. But a consul's private dwelling was not extra-territorial; Nina had entered the world on a shabby patch of Rumanian soil, which made her a Rumanian in the eyes of the U.S. Immigration Service. This was rather absurd, and it was just possible that the Americans might be persuaded to make an exception in Nina's favor. In any case, my friend would do everything he could to be of help.

It was so absurd, so illogical, that I felt fairly confident a way out of the dilemma would be found. I wrote to Eldon. He was born in Holland—did he enter the United States, back in 1939, on the Dutch quota? Yes, he did. But he had never given it a thought. For one thing, his uncle, and sponsor, had arranged everything; for another, the Dutch quota was just as good as the British quota, and anyway, once he was in the United States, his status was that of a Britisher living and working there on a permanent visa—a status that his absence in the air force had not changed. He advised Nina to take the matter up with the American Embassy in London, where our influential friend at the Foreign Office would carry some weight.

Nina, for whom every minute that she spent studying with Molnar was precious, stayed on in Budapest for several months after we left. So the battle of the quota, whose outcome would affect her whole future, was deferred in favor of a present, never-to-be-repeated, joy. And this despite an increasing awareness of risk, of the possibility of detainment even while possessing a

British passport; a possibility even more threatening to Genevra, for whom the British lion was less of a protection on account of her Hungarian marriage.

Nina went back to England at the end of January 1949, with the feeling that it wasn't a moment too soon. Genevra, who was pregnant, had moved sooner. On the strength of a medical certificate, issued by a highly reputable physician, at some risk to himself, she had asked for and obtained a permit to leave Budapest for three weeks in order to have her baby in Switzerland. Károly, then working as a translator in the American Legation, was, of course, the hostage.

Complications arose when the base upon which this escape plan rested was removed by the birth of the baby ahead of its time. But the doctor kept his mouth shut, and Genevra smuggled the newborn infant out in a tote bag.

I would like to skip over our last days in Hungary, with their leaden sense of finality—not yet replaced by the excitement of the new. But because of the esteem in which K. was held, and his own belief in the basic good will of his countrymen, I feel it only fair to record the manner of our leaving. It was not an "escape" (except in the sense that we left just in time to avoid the *necessity* of escaping), but an authorized departure, governed by regulations that were less restrictive than they might have been, given the existing political situation.

Once officialdom had decided to let us go, the procedures were accomplished in no time at all, prodded a bit, perhaps, by the loyal party member—with innumerable children—to whom our apartment had been promised after we left. (This was the prerogative of the government.) The agonizing uncertainties and delays were in the preceding months, and the "catch-22" lay in the synchronization of the date of K.'s passport with that of his exit permit. It worked like this. He could not apply for an exit permit before he was issued a passport—good only for a limited period. It would expire, or be on the point of expiring, by the time the exit permit was granted, necessitating a renewal, which would be held up until after the exit permit had expired. There was no knowing what lay behind this exasperating chain of missed connections. It could have been sheer bureaucratic inefficiency; or

the result of intervention on the part of someone whose interest it
was to prevent us from leaving—no one was without secret enemies, and the climate was favorable for the planting of false
information. And then again, it might have been a matter of
policy to keep us dangling until the last possible moment. In any
case, dangle we did, for weeks and months, until one day in
September, K.'s usually fruitless appeals at the altar of officialdom produced the miracle he was hoping for—a set of synchro-
nized papers. The mechanics of our move swung into action.

Surprisingly, we were permitted to take at least some of our
household possessions with us, particularly those things that I
had brought with me from England at the time of my marriage—
even the grand piano. We were instructed to collect in one room
everything that we wished to take out of the country, including
books and clothing. Next, an inspector appeared and, after examining everything minutely—shaking out books for concealed
paper money and reading, or pretending to read, papers and
letters—told us what we might and might not take with us. K.
could have his cello, his two bows, and his collection of sheet music
and scores, which represented his means of livelihood, but not his
collection of rare stamps, which represented currency. All but
one of my oriental rugs were allowed to go, but the inspector knew
his rugs, and the one we could not take was worth all the others
put together. A few pieces of antique furniture that had somehow
survived undamaged were also allowed to go—thank God—for
the sale of them at a later date saved my life. And Gyula was not
yet well enough known for his yellow marble head of a woman to
be considered a national asset, so they let me take that, too. When
the selections were all made, they were stamped, or tagged, and
locked up for the night.

Next day the packers came with their pads and cartons, but the
Big Box was packed by me. The operation was spot-checked from
time to time by the inspector, but any temptation I felt to smuggle
was checked by the suspicion that Big Brother was watching me
through the eyes of one of the packers. Finally, the only "dowry"
that we would take with us to the New World was loaded into a
very small lift-van, locked, sealed, and sent off to California by
rail and sea, to turn up there many months later, and be unsealed

and unpacked by U.S. Customs officials, of whom we were just as much in awe as we had been of the Communist Inspector—but with less justification.

My memory has completely wiped out the last goodbyes. I remember only sitting in the plane holding K.'s hand and thinking how odd it was that the sun remained in the same position all the way. Our first destination was Amsterdam, where K. went into the city, to an hotel, while I stayed at the airport waiting for the next flight to London, to see Peter. K. had hoped to go with me, but the British had refused his request for a transit visa. Which added another drop of bitterness to my already ambivalent feelings toward the country of my birth.

I arrived in London very late at night and was met at the terminal by Paul, who took me back to his own flat, where Peter, who lived at the end of a long bus ride, would pick me up in the morning. Physically and emotionally exhausted, I went straight to bed.

The following day may have been a Sunday, I don't remember. Anyway, Paul was free, and we sat for a long time over the polished oak breakfast table, talking of things that were safer to talk about in London than in Hungary—where for years now the only safety had lain in keeping silent. But whatever the subject of our conversation, at the center of Paul's thoughts, of his mind, of his whole world, was Nina. And behind everything he said was an unspoken appeal for answers to the questions that troubled him; why had she stayed on in Hungary although he had begged her not to? Why did she want to go to America? Why, in short, was she evading him?

I had never before seen Paul in surroundings that were completely his own. When I first knew him, it was against the elegant background of his parents' villa. Ever since then, the rubble and ruins of war and our own patched-up dwelling had been his setting. Now, in a country not his own, he was, for the first time in his life, in his own chosen ambiance, and very much at one with its well-bred simplicity. In that, I thought, might lie at least some of the answers he sought. Although he had been Nina's closest friend for years, there was an important aspect of her personality that had escaped him, or that he had not wanted to recognize. At some point in our conversation, that dangerous virtue, honesty, impelled me to tell him what it was. A wild bird, I told him, stops singing if it is caged, and may even die.

Peter's wife was absent on professional business of some kind, and I saw very little evidence of a woman's presence in the rather bleak North London flat. I was put into the biggest and brightest room, but it seemed too empty and tidy to have been temporarily vacated for me. I got the impression that Peter was living a semibachelor life between the kitchen, where we ate, and a small study spilling over with books and papers. We didn't talk much about his marriage; we talked about the past, sharing recollections of his childhood and early boyhood, and the storms that very nearly wrecked both our lives. As Nina's brother, he understood better than Paul why she wanted to go to America, but I knew that he wouldn't be sorry if she lost the battle of the quota.

When we parted, I felt very sad and somehow guilty. Though I loved him in a very special way, I seemed to be always leaving him. . . .

K. was waiting for me at the Amsterdam terminal, "Thank God you're safely back!" he said, "I was so afraid something might happen. . . ."

And I said, teasing him, "Well . . . now you know how I felt that time when you went off to Rumania without me."

We had dinner at the hotel, a luxurious meal paid for by Eldon. "This time tomorrow," K. said, "we'll be in America." And all of a sudden I felt young again.

BOOK THREE

The American
Experience

1

The Roller Coaster Ride

*J*UST how new the New World seemed to us can be fully appreciated only by those who came to it for the first time, as we did, from the still smoldering war zones of Europe. How new, and how exhilarating!

And in our case, how dizzying to be introduced within twenty-four hours to the two extremes of American city life; the Perpendicular in excelsis and the Horizontal ad infinitum.

Eldon had arranged for us to stay overnight in New York and to take an afternoon flight to Los Angeles on the following day. Too excited to recover the lost hours by sleeping late, we rose early and went out to see what Valhalla looked like by day. It could not have been more magical than it was in the light of that glittering fall morning, that gilded its soaring towers in high relief on a field of azure.

Our hotel was only a few steps from Fifth Avenue, up which we strolled arm in arm, window gazing, fascinated—and at the same time slightly shocked—by the luxury and variety of the merchandize offered, as if there had never been a war. We were on the lookout for some not-too-luxurious café in which to have breakfast. We chose a crowded place that recalled the old ABC tea-rooms in London—I think it was a Child's. When a harried waitress asked if we wanted a "regular," we said "yes," more for her sake than ours, since we had no idea what a "regular" was. It turned out to be much the same as a preausterity English breakfast, but with two unusual additions; syrup with the sausages and

big glasses of orange juice, a treat that we would soon come to
regard as a necessity of life—like water.

Replete, we strolled on up the avenue as far as Central Park.
There we turned in among the trees, some of them already
flecked with crimson and gold, and sat down on a bench to
contemplate the surrounding peaks while K. smoked a forbidden
cigarette—he had already used up his ration for one morning.
But this was no ordinary day. It was, in a sense, a birthday; with
all the ambivalent feelings that accompany middle-aged birthdays. But it partook of New Year's, too, with its wild hopes based
on the magical properties of a virgin calendar.

With the nervousness of the newly arrived immigrant, who has
none of the assurance of the tourist, we hurried back to the hotel,
to make sure of checking out before the noon deadline, and got to
the airport hours before our flight to the West Coast was due to
leave. We were not familiar with airports. Before the watershed
of the Second World War, most people traveled by train or boat.
K. had never flown, and my sole experience of the air was a trip
from Trieste to Venice, made for fun, in an open two-passenger
seaplane, that flew very close to the water and rose and fell on the
wind like a skimming gull. So our three-stage flight from the old
and tired to the newest of the new, was a fittingly novel experience for us both.

On the short, first stage of the trip, I had been conscious only of
keeping abreast of the westering sun. The transatlantic flight
above the clouds—the motion of the plane imperceptible with
nothing more than floating masses of cotton to measure it by—
had been pure science fiction. But this final, transcontinental
trip, made at a lower altitude most of the time, was a revelation.
To start with, looking down as the plane flew out from New York,
our attention was caught by a phenomenon that could only be
clearly perceived from above: the ubiquitous, multicolored mo-
saics formed by innumerable cars, bright as the tulip fields of
Holland, that added a new dimension to our definition of
"prosperity." And as we flew on over what amounted to a gigantic
relief map, their total absence from vast stretches of what
appeared to be primeval forest brought home to us the immensity
and the power of this land. This was a country that contained
within its borders the geographical characteristics of every coun-

try in Europe, as well as its own, on such a grand scale that the necessary scabs of industrialism seemed no more than pimples on the body of a dinosaur.

Dusk was falling when we entered the aura of Los Angeles, and descended in a long, gradual incline over an apparently limitless ocean of lights.

As we touched down on the runway, I experienced a moment of black panic. I felt the uncontrollable upsurge, like heartburn in the throat, of a deeply buried fear that usually surfaced only in a dream, a recurring nightmare in which I am stranded in a strange city, not knowing where I belong, or who I am.

The Californian scene is etched on my memory just as sharply as the Hungarian scene that preceded it, and for the same reason; its association with profoundly significant events and changes in my life. In the beginning, however, it was the absence of any associations whatever that made it the best possible place for us to have landed in—despite my moment of premonitory panic. Los Angeles, by which I mean the whole horizontal sprawl and everything it embraced, was unlike any place I had ever lived in before. It struck me as *sui generis*; a city without any past, whose future beyond the next day was hard to believe in. Yet it was precisely this "here today and gone tomorrow" quality of its streets and buildings—even the film stars' mansions—that rang a bell in me. A very distant bell. And the memory it awakened was that of my first ride on a roller coaster, when I was about twelve years old. The connection between that experience and my present surroundings was not immediately obvious. But memory, after a little prodding, supplied the link.

That roller coaster ride was, for me, the high point in a day's sight-seeing on one of my rare visits to London. There was a sort of "World's Fair" going on in a specially constructed location known as The White City. My parents must have thought it would be educational, though the world represented there was probably that of the British Empire. The facsimile "native" villages—African, East Indian, West Indian—all had an English history book familiarity. But they were no less exotic for that, and what they did for me was to stir up my longing for foreign travel, inherited from my poor mother, who was tied by poverty, duty,

and love to a remote country parsonage. A fate that I was determined to avoid. And did avoid. Though it took one war to liberate
me and another to blow me across the Atlantic to this large-scale
replica of a replica, the White City of Los Angeles.

We loved it. We accepted it on its own terms, which was,
indeed, the only way; that is, not uncritically, but as something
that had to be swallowed whole or not at all. And to Eldon's relief
and delight we swallowed it whole, thoroughly enjoying its invig-
orating effects. Looking back, I see that for us, for our particular
condition, its faults were, in fact, its virtues. Its rawness, its
brashness, its vulgarity (tempered by the unfailing amiability of
its citizens) were a drastic but effective cure for an unhealthy
attachment to a decadent past, whose values had to be set free
from their old forms before they could modify and civilize the
new.

At the time, however, we were not motivated by philosophy—
not consciously—but by a longing to recover a lost innocence, an
ability to be thrilled by the roller coaster ride of trivial amuse-
ments, small pleasures, and discoveries; to re-experience on a
completely different level, in a completely different world, an
emotional state akin to the bliss of our honeymoon in the Juliet-
balconied house on the cobbled street in Buda, pampered and
overfed by the French hairdresser's widow.

On the long, traffic-obstructed drive from the airport in
Eldon's little car, he was shy with us; uncertain, he confessed
later, of what our reaction would be to the city he so much wanted
us to love, afraid that we might be put off it in advance by the
shoddy environs of the airport.

He told us that he had decided to let us choose for ourselves just
where and in what sort of dwelling we wanted to live, after we
had had an opportunity to explore the possibilities. In the meantime, he was turning over to us the furnished duplex in which he
had lived for the past year. He had rented a studio apartment for
himself nearby. I asked, "What's a duplex?" Which made him
laugh. "It's what you would call a semidetached bungalow. Sometimes one is on top of the other, but here they are mostly side by
side."

It had two rooms, a kitchen big enough to eat in, and what

Eldon called a "half-bath"—whatever that might be. The front door opened directly into the living room, a rather disconcerting feature peculiar to American homes. Later, I would link it up with another peculiarity that I had never encountered elsewhere —unenclosed lawns on the residential streets—and perceive this combination of front doors that admitted one straight into some-one else's life, and front gardens open to the neighbors, their children, their dogs, and every passerby, as indicative of a singu-larly outgoing, friendly people.

Our first home in America was full of small surprises; one being the apparent absence of a bed, or of anything resembling one—no divan, no sofa. Puzzled, I said, "But . . . what do we sleep on?"

"I'll show you," said Eldon. "Just watch, it's quite simple." He opened a two-paneled door in the wall of the smaller room, pressed a button, and lo and behold a big double bed came slowly down, all made up for the night.

At the sight of my face, he burst out laughing. "Oh Mother dear!" he cried, hugging me, "You're so wonderfully surprise-able!"

The most touching surprise was what we discovered after he had gone. On the table in the living room was a bowl of red roses, and when we were not looking, he had tucked a little note in among them, addressed to both of us. "Everything is for you," it said, "Love, Eldon."

The meaning of this became clear only when we had unpacked and started to put away our personal possessions. Eldon had emptied the cupboards and shelves of his own things and replaced them with everything he could think of that we might need or enjoy. There were toiletries of all kinds; the French perfume and the English lavender soap I had always used in the civilized past; a new kind of shaving cream and the latest type of safety razor for K.; and for us both, the little daily indispensables, from aspirins to Bromo Seltzer and Band-Aids. There were writing materials in the living room, and a sewing basket for me, complete with a silver thimble. There were books and magazines to read and a brand-new table radio. None of the little amenities of a home had been forgotten.

"He hasn't really changed," I told K. "He's the same little boy who used to comfort me with violets when the postman failed to bring me a letter from you."

We stayed in the duplex for about two months; a period of intensive activity, in which the carefree exploration and assimilation of American life, California style, were combined with the carrying out of a kind of individual Marshall Plan, a postwar recovery program, in which all those aspects of our physical being that had been damaged or neglected during the war were brought up to standard. Doctors, dentists, oculists, beauticians, and kind friends, all took a hand in repairing and rebuilding us. But it was, of course, all planned and paid for by Eldon. With more strain than he allowed me to see.

He was, at the moment, what actors euphemistically call "resting," a misnomer for a state in which regular work is replaced by the feverish pursuit of every rumored possibility and the daily haunting of agents, auditions, and "casting." The last feature film that Eldon had acted in was a swashbuckler called *The Exiles*, in which Douglas Fairbanks, Jr., starred as Bonnie Prince Charlie, and Eldon played the most favored of the exiled prince's aristocratic young followers. But what had been an asset in that particular film, his cultivated voice with its British inflections—unmistakably British against the American tonal background—was a handicap when it came to young American roles. He found himself obliged to exploit it as a separate marketable skill; coaching American fellow-actors in how to speak English-accented lines, or anonymously promoting some British product over the radio. He made light of these frustrations to us, repeating his agent's optimistic assurance that the right vehicle for him would soon turn up, and that luck was with him in that he looked so much younger than his actual age—which was only twenty-six, anyway.

Meanwhile, aware that any such lucky break would take up all his time, he devoted his present involuntary leisure to us and our postwar recovery, which had to be accomplished, for all practical purposes, before the end of the year, when K. would be expected to start teaching.

K. had numerous Hungarian acquaintances and excolleagues

in the Los Angeles area. But except for Miklos Rozsa, who was expecting our arrival, he postponed contacting any of them. He needed to achieve a certain level of detachment from what he had left behind him forever, before he could risk entering the nostalgia-laden atmosphere of emigré society.

To many of those people, our behavior during the first weeks of our new life would have seemed unbelievably childish. And maybe it was. But the waters of Lethe can assume many different forms, and for us forgetfulness lay in allowing ourselves to be children again—for a little while.

There was something else, too. Though we were not then consciously aware of it, we were in a state of intoxication. We were high on freedom, that precious element, invisible as the air, whose value is fully appreciated only in its absence, and whose sudden restoration sets one reeling.

Below the fluttery images of those butterfly-winged days runs the straight line of an undeviating ritual; it is K.'s lifelong habit, broken only by the siege, of beginning each day with an act of homage to his art, as a monk begins each day with an act of homage to his God.

Almost unconsciously, I acquired the same habit—now an essential discipline of my writing life. But my writing life had barely begun then, and while K. so effortlessly practiced his consummate art, I was still struggling to master the ABCs of mine.

After our morning dedication to the arts came the household duties that were more of a pleasure than a chore because of their novelty for us, and because we shared them. Our daily walk to the supermarket, with a little shopping cart, was a walk straight into temptation; especially for K., who had gourmet tastes and, left to himself, would pick out all the most expensive delicacies. The laundromat, less romantic than the big washerwoman of yore, was just as efficient, and gave us an utterly fraudulent sense of personal accomplishment, though all we did was set the machines running and go to a nearby milk-bar (whoever heard of a *milk-bar*?) and get fat on milkshakes—one flavor for the washer and another for the dryer.

Eldon had persuaded us to adopt American meal times, and he

usually joined us in "grabbing a sandwich" for lunch, after which he would take us wherever we needed—or wanted—to go. I wanted to go to the ocean, which I thought was very much closer than it was—on account of the numerous young women who did their marketing in swimsuits. Eldon took us to Santa Monica by the longest and prettiest route—down Sunset Boulevard. (My stepdaughter, Mari, writes, *I still have a snapshot of you and Apuka standing together under the palms by the sea and looking so young and gay!*)

My favorite beach was several miles up the coast from Santa Monica; Zuma Beach, in those days a wild, unfrequented stretch of virgin sands and dunes. At one end of it, concealed by a barrier of rocks, and accessible only by clambering over them, was a solitary cove, where seals played, unalarmed, within twenty yards of the shore.

Trips to medical appointments were combined with shopping for badly needed new clothes. The only suit K. possessed, the one he had traveled in, though originally made to measure by a first-rate Budapest tailor, had since been turned and invisibly mended at elbows and knees. Unlike me, K. was easy to fit. He replaced his old suit with a new one straight from the rack. But he put it away in the closet, for formal occasions only. He had undergone a lightning conversion to Californianism. And if any of his old Hungarian friends had run across him strolling down Hollywood Boulevard, it is doubtful whether they would have recognized him, so transformed was he in his blue denim trousers and short-sleeved, open-necked, vividly patterned Hawaiian shirt.

Wherever we went with Eldon, he was constantly on the lookout for a possible home for us all, whether for rent or for sale. Eldon had big dreams. In that prehistoric age of innocence that K. and I were now, in some sort, re-living, we had harbored similar dreams. But fate had so thoroughly destroyed them, that I feared to tempt it again by daring to re-dream them.

We inspected some lovely houses that, according to Eldon, were reasonably priced. It was a period, especially in Southern California, when it was more economical to buy than to rent, even in the short run. But in our case there were too many uncertainties to be resolved before we could even decide on a location.

The teaching contract that had secured K. his nonquota visa had, in so doing, fulfilled its most valuable function. It provided him with a small income—just enough to tide us over the first months. But both K. and the administrators of the school realized that it was no more than a way station to something more in keeping with his abilities and his reputation, and that might well mean leaving the area. Another unresolved uncertainty was the future of Genevra, Károly, and their children. Their letters, like all the letters that we received from Hungary, were altogether too cheerful to be true, and set us poking around between the lines in search of hidden meanings. As to the Hungarian girl whom Eldon had hoped to bring to America, her letters to him grew cooler and cooler, until finally she told him that there could be no question of her coming. But here, too, the circumstances made her words ambiguous, though Eldon found it hard to believe that the private letters of ordinary citizens might be opened and read by the Hungarian secret police, and their contents used against the writers.

This break depressed Eldon. But his pain and disappointment were curiously impersonal—perhaps because his love for a girl whom he barely knew was symbolical, rather than actual, and his failure to hold her some sort of confirmation. In any case, it was clear that what hurt him most was not so much her rejection of his love as her rejection of his assistance (offered without strings attached) in bringing her to a free country. Young though he was, there was a patriarchal streak in him; a fatherly urge to help and protect, and a desire to lead those whom he loved into green pastures. A recognition, perhaps, that this was his true role in life.

He was less confiding than Peter; and although I felt the warmth of his love, both for me and for K., and encountered evidence of it at every turn, I had to find out for myself just what manner of man my youngest son had become.

It was only to be expected that his friends should know more about him than I did, but it was nonetheless disconcerting to see him through others' eyes. It was disturbing to learn indirectly that he was seeing a psychiatrist—which he made light of. "Everyone I know is in therapy of some kind," he said. "It's like keeping your teeth in order and your hair properly cut. I've told my therapist all about you and K., and he wants to meet you. I think you'll like him."

I said it was more important that he should like us, and Eldon laughed. "Don't worry, he will."

Eldon kept his professional life and his personal life separate. Most of the friends he introduced to us had nothing to do with the movie world, or were only marginally connected with it. There was one family into which he fitted like an adoptive son. But, knowing his need to invent a family for himself in the absence of his own, it was uncertain whether they had adopted him, or he them. At that time, the family was made up of a middle-aged couple and their married, or formerly married, daughter, then living at home. The father was the antithesis of Eldon's real father (though not unlike K.); a quiet, unobtrusively learned university professor, with whom Eldon discussed literature and played long, ruminative games of chess, one night a week. The professor's wife, the mother, was one of those American wonder-women, who combine elegance and femininity with the skills of a plumber, mechanic, housepainter, electrician, and general handyman, not to mention being gourmet cooks, good wives and mothers, and ever-ready friends.

Somewhat to my surprise, I felt no jealousy of this accomplished woman, so different from myself, whom Eldon regarded with so much affection and admiration. And if my appearance on the scene was upsetting to her, she did not show it. In fact, we trod too carefully. Delicacy made us too reticent with one another. She was afraid of hurting me by revealing how much she knew about Eldon, how often she had rescued him from despair, and I was too shy, too proud, to ask. We were both, I think, reluctant to form a generational alliance; even for the good of the young man who was, in the spiritual sense, son to us both.

Between me and Eldon's male friends there was no such tight-rope to walk. One of these was a writer who, though still in his early thirties, was partially crippled by the same type of circulatory problem that threatened to cripple K. He could walk with the aid of a cane, and he drove his own car, but bouts of intense pain obliged him to spend much of his time in a wheelchair. Of all Eldon's friends, he was the one I came closest to, the one who took

the initiative in establishing a relationship with us independent
of his friendship with Eldon. He was an intellectual Catholic
convert, and I shall call him Justin (which was not his real name),
after a Catholic saint with whom he had something in common; a
pagan philosopher living in Rome in the second century, who was
converted to Christianity, and thereafter devoted his brilliant
intellectual gifts to refuting the philosophy he had previously
expounded, and died a martyr.

Not that his unwitting namesake made any claim to holiness.
Quite the contrary, Eldon once said of him, "Poor old Justin. He
spends one half of his life committing what he calls sins and the
other half doing penance for them." But he respected goodness in
others, regardless of their beliefs, and Eldon was one of the
"pagans" in whom he discerned it. Yet although he loved his
friend all the more because of it, he could not help resenting what
he believed to be the moral superiority of a pagan.

Justin and I got along very well. We talked about writing and
books. I showed him some of my poems. He let me read the MS of
the novel he was working on, and he lent me Thomas Merton's
Seven Storey Mountain, the poems of Charles Peguy, and the
writings of Jacques Maritain. Like all converts, Justin was a
proselytizer.

The intellectual approach to Catholicism was new to me.
Brought up in the Church of England (my father was a clergy-
man), and with North Irish and French Huguenot blood min-
gling in my veins, I had learned to associate Catholics with the
cruelties of the Inquisition, the wickedness of the Borgias, and the
unreliability of the South Irish. Subsequently, life in various
Catholic countries introduced me to the aesthetics of Catholicism,
and its mystery, both of which attracted me, and, in some indefinable way, moved me. But it was only when I saw Catholics in
action, during the war, or, more precisely, when I perceived a
link between the actions of people like Marcsa *néni* and Pater
Antal, and their Catholic faith, that I reached the state of mind in
which I could respond without cynicism to the books that Justin
gave me to read; and to Justin himself, and his vain attempts to
remain in a state of grace for more than twenty-four hours at a
stretch.

Another of Eldon's good friends was a Catholic; but not, like

Justin, by choice, and he never mentioned the religion that had, so to speak, been thrust upon him in his cradle. All the same, I shall rechristen him, too, with the name of a Catholic saint; one Paulinus, who was born into the Faith, but had to be "touched by grace" before he set foot on the stony road to sainthood. The Paulinus I knew, and know better now than I did then, suffered from a lung ailment that laid him low for months at a stretch. His life was insecure from every point of view. Yet, like many who live on the precipice edge, he survived (and still survives), which Justin did not.

And then there was Douglas, the painter, younger than Justin and Paulinus, younger than Eldon, and in excellent physical health but insecure psychologically and not helped much by the pack he ran with.

What linked these three very disparate personalities was that each, in his own way, truly cared for Eldon.

The Christmas season took us by surprise, starting as it did three weeks ahead of the usual time. When we left the duplex at the end of November and moved with Eldon to a house on Laurel Canyon, the Hollywood streets were already festooned with Christmas lights. Santa was already in town—what's more, he had taken up residence in the house next door to the one we had rented.

Justin, on hearing this, said with a rather cryptic laugh, that some very peculiar people resided in Laurel Canyon.

It was at once bohemian and rustic; about a mile of narrow, upward-winding road, to whose upward-sloping sides clung dwellings of various shapes and sizes—some candid and glassy, some secretive and shabby, concealing themselves as best they could with the purple and gold of bougainvillea and trumpet vines. This misleadingly rural road flattened out and came to a dead end on a man-made plateau just below the wooded brow of the hill, where a few more assorted dwellings were haphazardly scattered. And among these was the split-level frame house in which, although we were renting it by the month so as not to be tied down, we would live for more than a year.

The rickety, multileveled house and its secluded location (that faintly echoed the villa on the Kelenhegyi út), appealed to me. It seemed to offer a propitious ambiance for the writing of the novel that was taking shape in my mind. But it had other, more practical advantages. Its lowest level was arranged as a separate, self-contained studio apartment, that Eldon could have to himself. And its "partly furnished" classification ensured the provision of basic necessities, but also promised plenty of room for our grand piano and other belongings that were due to arrive around Christmas time.

Our bedroom overlooked Santa's house, a little wooden box, with an only slightly smaller one beside it for his car. The lot on which these two boxes had been set up was still unlandscaped, and covered with thistles.

Every morning at eight, Santa would emerge from his box in full panoply, white beard and all, and drive off to his daily job of deceiving the very young. He would get back around six in the evening. The dead end was so quiet that even after dark we could tell which neighbor came home when, by the distinctive sound of each motor and the way each driver slammed the car door.

On Saturday, Santa came home early and brought a girlfriend with him. In the middle of the night, K. and I were awakened by sounds of female distress that made us think we were back among the Russians. I got up and went to the open window. A white wraith was stumbling around among the thistles plaintively wailing, "Let me in! Let me in!" like the ghost of some Gothic maiden haunting the castle of her shame.

"Well?" asked K.

"It's Santa's girlfriend. He seems to have locked her out. And she doesn't have anything on—at least, not much."

"Let me in! *Please!* Let me in!"

The temperature had dropped quite sharply, as it often did at night, and I shivered. K. put my robe around my shoulders. It made me feel guilty. "Shouldn't I offer to lend that girl my raincoat?" K. thought not. Just then, the wailing maiden turned into a fury, hammering on the locked door with both fists and screaming, "Let me in, you bastard!"

"Shut up, you bitch!" yelled Santa from inside. The ensuing duet, with all the known variations on four-letter insults, was a triumph for Santa. Reduced to what sounded like genuine tears, his girlfriend ceased hammering on his door, and wandering again among the thistles, she appealed to the deaf-mute neighbors. "Will somebody please help me? Will somebody *please* help me?"

I said to K., "I can't stand this. I have to do something. . . ." But Santa saved me from making a fool of myself. He suddenly threw open his door, rushed out—a powerfully built young man naked to the waist—picked up the girl, carried her to the garage, kicking and screaming, deposited her there like a sack of potatoes, and rolled down the door before she could stop him.

For a while she sobbed, the gulping, hiccuping sobs of a punished child. There was no response from Santa. The sobbing gradually ceased, and we fell asleep. But my sleep was fitful and uneasy. It was only after I heard Eldon, who had been to a Hollywood party, stop his car in the driveway and quietly enter the downstairs apartment, that I felt free of a nagging sense of responsibility for my neighbor's girlfriend.

Next day, Sunday, dawdling over a late breakfast in our sunporch, I saw her leaving; alone, on foot, and lugging her own suitcase.

The following weekend, Santa brought back a different girl; a domestic type, who didn't leave with him on Monday, but stayed on to take care of him, doing his laundry and hanging it out in the sun to dry, and clearing the front yard of its thistles.

On Christmas Eve, a dozen long-stemmed red roses were delivered to us by a florist. They came from István. We took them for a gesture of remembrance—a commemoration of Christmas 1944. But in fact, they were more than that. They were like the starting pearl in one of those necklaces to which one more pearl is added on each succeeding anniversary of a birth, or a wedding, or other important event, until the right length is achieved, and the two ends are joined with a golden clasp.

Between Christmas and New Year's, our household gods arrived. They were unpacked and franked by two amiable customs officials, who handled them with the indulgent care one bestows on the tattered treasures that children insist on taking with them to a new home. Installed, they looked out of place against the knotty-pine walls.

The irresponsible holiday was over. The roller coaster ride had come to a stop. The past had caught up with us in a lift-van.

2

The Mimosa Tree

I

*T*HE image that comes up now and fills the horizon is that of a tree. A tree like a feathery cascade, with slender, silvery leaves, and tiny, fluff-ball flowers of palest yellow. A golden mimosa tree in full bloom.

It spreads its delicate fragrance and scatters its powdery gold on a miniature garden, like a Japanese garden, with flagged steps, rock plants, and a fish pond, designed, and painstakingly carved out of the rocky soil by Douglas, the young painter. The garden is an outdoor extension of the studio he is building for himself on a hilltop that is only a few wingbeats, as the crow flies, from our house in Laurel Canyon, though it takes about twenty minutes to get from one to the other by car.

The life that Douglas leads in these idyllic surroundings is *la vie de Bohème*, California style. Carelessly inhabiting the unfinished building, he works on its construction, paints his pictures, and entertains male and female friends night and day.

K. and I are invited to tea on an afternoon when, by chance or design, Douglas is alone, and any telltale signs of riotous living have been tucked away out of sight. But the pseudo monastic atmosphere doesn't deceive K., who has lived his own, authentic, *vie de Bohème* in Paris. And he smiles indulgently at this modern staging of an old scene, with no heartless landlord, no tiny frozen hands—no way of turning off the heat. No winter.

The early months of the new year brought us mixed news.

375

From Hungary, Mari wrote that Marcsa *néni* had discovered that the bond forged between her and the de Kerpely family during the siege was too strong to break, and she was ready to give to K.'s daughter the same help and devotion that she had given to K. and me.

Genevra wrote from Switzerland telling us of the too-early arrival of her new baby (a daughter named Francesca) and the subsequent smuggling operation. She had, of course, no intention of returning to Hungary when her brief official leave of absence was up. Instead, the hostage, Károly, would try to make his escape. But when that would be, she had no way of knowing. They dared not correspond. All she could do was wait—and hope.

Finally, Nina wrote from London, *This morning I was summoned to the American Embassy to get their definitive answer about my visa. When they told me it could not be granted I burst into tears.*

They were sympathetic, she said, but the only consolation they could offer was a visitor's visa, or, possibly, a student visa. But both would be subject to strict limitations of time and scope, and what Nina wanted now was a stable foundation on which to build a life and a career—a future without any arbitrary limitations. No thank you. If they would not allow her to come to America for good on the British quota, in which she rightfully belonged, she would not come at all.

A stable foundation on which to rebuild his artistic life was what K. now needed, and the school that he was connected with could not provide it. But his prospects of finding a better position were darkened by his uncertain health. Troubled once more by severe pains, he consulted Justin's physician, whose prognosis was depressing in the extreme; precluding all possibility of concertizing, and even threatening his ability to play his instrument for his own satisfaction. This would not happen immediately; but he would go steadily down hill.

He took this blow which, for him, amounted to a sentence of death in life, with his usual gentle fortitude. But I refused to believe that his life had been preserved through every kind of physical danger only to be stripped of all its meaning. And in this, at least, I was right.

Justin, who felt somehow responsible for the devastating verdict delivered by his physician, urged K. to get a second opinion, and he went to a lot of trouble to find out who might be the best man to consult. There was, he discovered, a completely new, surgical, treatment for K.'s condition; an arterial bypass operation, which had recently been performed, with success, on the King of England, and was now being done for less exalted patients in Los Angeles by a Doctor Marcus, who was reputed to be one of the best surgeons on the West Coast. But he commanded very high fees, and K., as a recently arrived refugee, had no insurance coverage; and Eldon had more than enough financial burdens already. Undeterred, Eldon made an appointment for K. with Doctor Marcus, and to be sure that K. kept it he went with us and waited with me while K. was being examined.

K. and the doctor came out of the office together. They were talking about Casals. Doctor Marcus, K. said, introducing him to us, was not only an ardent lover of music, but himself a musician—whose instrument happened to be the cello!

There was no doubt that this lucky coincidence played a role in bringing within K.'s reach the surgical treatment that gave him a new lease on life. But it was not the sole reason behind the doctor's response to K.'s predicament. Six years later, when I was lying ill in a hospital ward, I overheard another great surgeon (one of those who helped to restore the ruined visages of Hiroshima survivors) telling the woman in the next bed, the wife of a Mexican farm worker, not to worry about his fee; he would take only what her insurance was willing to pay, no matter how little it might be. And in the interval between these two incidents, I had already been given enough evidence of a national spirit of altruism, of kindness to the stranger within the gate, to come to the conclusion (which time has only strengthened) that Americans, by and large, are the kindest people on earth.

Our first year of American life was packed with key incidents; each one recognizable, in retrospect, as a vital cog in the wheel of change to which I seem to have been bound all my life.

One of these was, of course, the decision of the American Immigration authorities that effectively separated me from my youngest daughter. Another was Károly's dramatic, spy-thriller escape across the Hungarian border into Austria, where he and Genevra were reunited after four months of anguished waiting and silence; an event that set in motion the machinery of their emigration to America, which, in the long run, brought my eldest daughter closer—in more ways than one.

Then, in the midst of all these family responsibilities and preoccupations, chance brought Eldon the one real love of his life.

I shall call her *Jennifer.* Her real baptismal name is, like Justin's, irrelevant. What matters is not what she was called, but what she meant to Eldon. And the name of Jennifer, with its faintly old English cadence, fits the girl whom I remember; a girl like a hybrid flower, whose appearance and personality simultaneously evoked the wide-open California spaces and a sundialed English garden.

In the summer of 1949, pretty girls were still wearing pretty, feminine dresses, with well-defined waists and skirts that were full and frilly. When Eldon brought Jennifer to see us for the first time, she was wearing that kind of a dress, with a wide-brimmed straw hat on her blonde head.

Her manner to us was a disarming mixture of Californian breeziness and the respect that K. never failed to evoke, in which, as his wife, I automatically shared; although I had not earned it for myself, I felt so much one with K. that I had no difficulty in accepting it gracefully.

A combination of good looks and good manners, whether in a man or a woman, had an irresistible appeal for me, and on meeting a group of people for the first time, I would be initially drawn to those individuals who exhibited this all too-rare mix of attributes. But it did not take me long to find out what, if anything, lay below the attractive surface. That was one of the useful skills that I had acquired in embassy drawing rooms, where the wolves in sheep's clothing were not always the so-called "foreigners." So when Eldon asked me later what I thought of Jennifer, I could say without hesitation, "She rings true."

She was in her early twenties, no longer subject to parental prohibitions, but not a rebel. She was living with her parents, and it was important to her that they should like Eldon, and accept him as a possible son-in-law. And I think they did like him, but he had a long way to go before they would accept him as a son-in-law. They belonged to an upper middle-class social circle that revolved on an axis totally separate from that of the movie world. The space between the two could be crossed only by stars of the greatest magnitude, wealth, and respectability—qualifications of which Eldon had only one: respectability. His distinguished background and prominent family name, carried very little weight in a society that confuses aristocracy with wealth, and in which the aristocracy of wealth—acquired in the first place by enterprise and hard work—is at once more democratic and more powerful than the unearned and often poverty-stricken British aristocracy of birth.

I never met Jennifer's parents, but on one or two occasions I was in the car with Eldon when he picked her up at their house. A dignified residence in an exclusive district, set well back from the road amid emerald green lawns, rich and velvety as wall-to-wall carpeting, it told Eldon without any words what was expected of him. And what, in essence, he wanted; not only for Jennifer and himself, but for all of us. Jennifer put love above money. But then, she had never lacked for money. Eldon, who had worked for his living ever since he was twelve years old, recognized its importance. But his only hope of making it lay in the profession for which he had been trained since childhood. Acting, in one form or another, on stage or screen, was his life.

It was during that summer that Eldon persuaded me to try my hand at a screen play; a story of love and war based on fact. Jennifer typed it out for me, and Justin, who had done some script writing and had "connections," tried to market it for me. It was a hopelessly amateur effort, but one studio seriously considered buying the rights to the "story." Yet, although I had written it solely, as I thought, to make money, I felt more relieved than disappointed when it was finally rejected. I suddenly realized that it was not in me to write solely in order to make money, and that selling this or any other story that was rooted in my reality, as raw material to be used by strangers, and inevitably twisted by them to suit their purposes, was like selling one's own child to a circus.

This lightning recognition of the meaning of "artistic integrity," though revealed to me in connection with a work of little or no artistic merit, was the origin of my subsequent resistance as an experienced writer to the slightest tampering with my work by any other hands than mine; my determination that if revisions had to be made, I alone must make them, and in my own way. The author-editor relationship is a very delicate one, involving humility on both sides; the editor must not presume to usurp the author's role, and the author must guard against delusions of infallibility.

But in those early days I had no such delusions. I wanted help. I owned a gold mine of raw material, and I didn't know how to convert it into art; or even what form to give it. Should it perhaps be that of a memoir, rather than a novel? I was hoping to get some advice on that point from the only literary personage I knew at the time, Eldon's great uncle, the playwright Charles Rann Kennedy, who had brought Eldon to New York ten years earlier (and his father before him). He was now a "grand old man of letters" living in semiretirement with his wife in the Los Angeles area

But my visit to him, with K. and Eldon, produced only disappointment and disillusionment.

This humanistic writer, this passionate champion of the despised and rejected, and their exaltation in plays like *The Servant in the House* and *The Terrible Meek,* had become his own monument; too stratified in his literary *idea* of human suffering to be bothered with the reality of it. My burning desire to communicate what I had seen, felt, and learned during the war left him completely cold. The concept of evil had become more real to him than its results. His mind dealt in abstractions above and beyond my earth-bound vision of young men lying dead in the streets of Budapest.

A few months after this visit, the old man died. We went with Eldon to his funeral. His last drama was staged in accordance with his instructions, as a poetic embodiment of his life's philosophy. The ceremonial was simple and austere. The service was ecumenical. The pallbearers were carefully chosen to represent the spirit of equality—of race, religion, and social status. The eulogy, delivered by a well-known personage, praised the dead man's compassion, his love for all humanity, his dedication of his art to the cause of those whose dubious inheritance is the earth.

It was just in these terms that "Uncle Rann" had been represented to me by Eldon's unhappy father, for whom he had become the one and only true-burning light on an otherwise dark family horizon. But despite the love and admiration he inspired in father and son, in the last resort he failed them both; the one by a final rejection, and the other, perhaps, by mere forgetfulness. In his anxiety to leave a message to humanity in general, he had omitted to leave any message, or token of his love, for Eldon.

II

Memory, haunted by the image of the tree, drawn irresistibly into its treacherous shadow, is loath to linger by the way and tries to evade the step-by-step ascent to that miniature garden carved out of the rocky hillside. Yet carved on each step is a hieroglyph, part of a message that even the professional cryptographer failed to decipher. If the image of the tree and its ancient symbolic meaning are to be understood, they cannot be regarded as an isolated phenomenon, but rather as the shrine at the end of a pilgrimage, that derives its significance and power from the faith of each individual pilgrim.

Memory, reined in, its attempted Pegasus leap over the mundane and into the metaphysical frustrated, sulkily presents me with a jumbled series of scenes, conversations only half-understood, and flashes of insight allowed to escape unexamined, that add up to a record of incredible psychological blindness on everyone's part, including Eldon's.

The period covered by this cloud of "not-seeing" lay between the late summer of 1949—which was when Genevra came with her husband and children to join us in the New World—and early March 1950, when Nina tied herself more firmly to the old one, consolidating her just claim to British nationality by getting married to a Britisher. Two wholly unconnected events that seemed, when placed in context, to be the result of a malicious transposition of the cards by a mischievous hand; for each sister still longed in her heart of hearts for the land of promise to which fate had perversely led the other.

There is something profoundly touching about the arrival of refugees in this country. The pathos lies both within the new arrivals themselves and those who welcome them. Among the latter, it is most keenly felt by those who are themselves refugees, and are still close enough to the day of their arrival to remember

their mingled apprehension and euphoria, but already aware of
the long road that lies between the dream and its fulfillment.

I already knew that the smiling couple with the three small
children waving to us from behind the barrier at the Los Angeles
airport had come to the end of one long struggle for survival only
to start on another; less dangerous, but in some ways more difficult, in that its outcome would not depend on the blind chances of
war—bad luck in the form of an enemy bomb, or good in the form
of a Russian army cook—but almost wholly on their own
decisions.

I saw in the small, boyish figure of Genevra, dressed in a white
sleeveless blouse and a print skirt, and carrying the eight-month-
old Francesca in her arms, a pathos quite alien to her forceful
personality. It was as if my own emotions had given me the power
to pierce, like an X ray, her protective armor of courage and
self-assurance and see her hidden tenderness and vulnerability.
But our Englishness and the Magyar dignity of our respective
husbands kept our meeting outwardly unemotional, compared to
that of the other reunited families. The children, too, were
reserved, and almost preternaturally well-behaved; not shouting
and running about and getting lost in the crowd like the other
children, but quietly holding K.'s hand and looking up at him
with awe, as if his superior height had turned him into a god.

"Do you have much luggage?" Eldon asked, as we waited for it
to appear. "My car is not very large, I'm afraid. . . ."

"Don't worry," Genevra said, "everything we have will fit easily
into the trunk of any car, I assure you."

I thought of our lift-van, and felt guilty.

Károly, more literal than Genevra, said, "We have three
medium-sized suitcases—there's one of them now. . . ."

They fitted more easily into the trunk of the Chevy than the six
of us (not counting the baby) fitted into the car itself. Genevra sat
next to Eldon, in front, with the baby on her lap. I squeezed
myself in between Károly and K. on the back seat, and K. took a
child on each knee, keeping them amused by reading the neon
signs of Milk Bars, Quik Eats, Pancake Palaces, and all the other
unfamiliar wonders of the White City of the Angels; until, unable
to take it all in, they fell asleep.

Eldon was unusually quiet, and I knew why. He was weighed

down by his exaggerated sense of responsibility. Despite his achievement in bringing us all to the United States as permanent residents, and thereby saving us from the irrational persecutions and arrests of the Stalin era in Hungary, he reproached himself for his failure to carry out this "rescue" in the grand style that his lordly Leo temperament had envisaged.

At the end of the long drive back to Laurel Canyon lay disappointments and a lot of explanations that would probably sound to Genevra and Károly like excuses, and would seem to Eldon himself like humiliating admissions of defeat. Instead of the spacious home, many mansions under one roof, of which he had dreamed, all he could offer the newcomers were the same kind of cramped quarters that we had shared during the siege. And the job contract—an offer of regular work in a nursery garden—that had served to secure for Károly his nonquota visa, though genuine enough as far as it went, was no more than the means to an end, seized on in desperation when all attempts to find him a suitable position had failed. The influx of highly qualified European refugees had changed the job situation. Prospective employers were no longer so ready to engage applicants for responsible positions sight unseen. And there were fewer such positions waiting to be filled.

It took Károly almost three months to find even a half-way acceptable job in the so-called "field of agriculture," in which he was bound to stay for the first year. The position was that of gardener on a ranch in the Ojai Valley, owned by an elderly widower with a large visiting family. It was a job with no future, and it led nowhere, but it had some immediate advantages: accommodation for the family was included—a small cottage on the estate, too small, but the owner was willing to enlarge it—and the use of a pickup truck for their occasional private errands, which would save them from having to buy a car right away. A minor perquisite was a chicken run, with half a dozen chickens of egg-laying age to supply the breakfast table, and a few superannuated old hens for the Sunday soup pot. The trouble with these was that neither Genevra nor Károly could bring themselves to wring their scrawny necks, much less cut off their heads—as Hungarian peasants did—and watch them running around in search of their missing beaks. The impasse was overcome by

Genevra, who asked the head rancher to do the dirty work for them on the grounds that she was too tenderhearted to kill any living thing, and Károly belonged to a strict religious sect that forbade him to do so—which was no surprise to a native son of what must surely be the most fertile sect hatchery in the world.

It was not easy for the one-time master of his own country estate to be in a menial position on someone else's. But Károly's philosophical sense of humor combined with Genevra's British conviction that she was the equal, and more than the equal, of any of the old man's visiting daughters, or daughters-in-law, plus her ability to charm the old man himself, kept the flags of their own self-respect flying—which was all that mattered to them.

Their stay in Laurel Canyon had been uncomfortable but not unprofitable. It had given them time to get their bearings and make some friends. The two older children, the solemn, bespectacled Peter and his shy sister Elizabeth, of the sapphire blue eyes, had had their first experience of school and the company of rambunctious American children. Two of these playmates lived just across the road from us. The comradeship of the children brought about the acquaintanceship of the parents; and it was with these casually met neighbors that Genevra and Károly formed their first, lasting American friendship.

They left for Ojai in late November, and a week or two later Eldon, alerted by his ever-watchful agent, caught a glimpse of good luck for himself in the offing; only to have it disappear in a savage rainstorm a few hours later. It was one of Southern California's infrequent wet days—the first of the three or four heavy rainfalls that turn the dry river beds into foaming torrents, hillsides into mudslides, and highways into rivers. In the midst of this deluge, Eldon, always ready to be helpful, and never more so than when he was in good spirits, offered to drive a carless friend to the airport. On the way back in the treacherous early dusk, through sheets of rain, his car was run into from behind at a traffic stop, and he was thrown violently forward across the steering wheel.

He had told me that he would be home around six o'clock—well in time for dinner—and when, at seven-thirty, the phone rang, I expected to hear his voice explaining why he was late. But what I heard were the words "Police Officer...." which awoke an echo in me that galvanized every nerve in my body like an electric shock.

The voice of the law was kind, but noncommittal. It told me only that Eldon had been in an accident, a car accident, and gave me the name of the hospital to which he had been taken.

With K. close beside me, I called the hospital number, and, after an agonizing delay, I was informed in the unenlightening medical terms that seem to conceal the truth rather than tell it, that my son's injuries were not serious. I said, "I will be there as soon as I can—in about an hour." They told me to hold on. Another long wait—so long that I thought I had been disconnected. Then, just as I was about to hang up, I heard Eldon's voice at the other end of the line, telling me not to worry. He was okay. They had patched him up and now they were sending him home. The taxi was already there, waiting. "See you soon, Mother dear. Cheerio!"

Cheerio. It was a word from our long ago English past, from before the war. I had never heard Eldon use it since. And his use of it now conveyed a message; it said, "I am still your little 'Mannie,' no matter how patriarchal I may seem."

K. and I watched for his taxi from our glassed-in sun porch. But the glass was so blurred by the lashing rain that we kept on mistaking the headlights of homecoming neighbors for those that we awaited. When a car finally stopped before our house, I ran out into the rain, crying "Eldon! Eldon!"

"Get back inside!" he shouted in a reassuringly strong voice. After paying off the cabby, whose parting blessings betokened a lavish tip, he ran up the steep garden path as fleetly as ever. But as he came into the light, I saw that his head was bandaged and his face was extremely pale.

K. brought him a shot of brandy. And I said, like the typical over-solicitous mother, "What about something to eat? Supper's ready and waiting. . . ."

But he was not hungry. "A bit later, perhaps. I think I'll go down to my place and take a nap now. I've got a godawful headache."

After half an hour I went down to see how he was. He was wide-awake, lying on his bed staring up at the ceiling. He still wasn't hungry. "I'm trying to remember just what happened," he said, "but I can't. There's a gap between feeling an awful jolt and waking up on a hospital bed surrounded by gadgets."

I was curious to know what was under the bandage around his head. But since he avoided mentioning it, I thought I had better not ask. We talked for a while without saying much. All that mattered remained unsaid. He was glad to hear that I hadn't called Jennifer—"No point in alarming her. I'll call her myself tomorrow." He seemed to be very weary, but not at rest. He took a sleeping pill and set his alarm for eight-thirty. "But be a dear, Mother, and don't let me sleep through it."

I said, "I hope you're not planning to get up and go out first thing in the morning!"

"No," he said slowly. "No, I'm not. This has knocked the bottom out of my plans. But I do have to make a couple of early phone calls. I want to catch Jacob Chaitkin before he leaves for the courts. And I have to call my agent and tell him to cancel the appointment he made for me at the studio."

His eyes suddenly filled with tears. I took his hand. After a moment or two, he said, "Forgive me. It's just weakness. I'm all right now."

When I kissed him goodnight, he said, "Thank you."

Jacob Chaitkin was Eldon's attorney; a warmhearted, emotional Russian Jew who treated him more like a son than a client. He came to visit Eldon on the day following the accident, and when Eldon showed him the wound under the bandage—a deep semicircular gash right in the center of his forehead—the trained legal eye saw money in it; heavy compensation for damage to his client's career as an actor.

But the driver whose fault it was turned out to be a penniless young man who worked as a cook in a fast-food chain (he was trying to get to his job on time when he ran into Eldon), and had only the minimum accident insurance. "It's just my luck," Eldon said, "to get run into by a pauper."

The unsightly bandage was replaced by Eldon's doctor with an equally unsightly, and less romantic, taped-on square of gauze. He assured Eldon that as soon as the stitches were removed, the scar would gradually fade, and could easily be covered by makeup. But he must have known that a scar never fades from the mind, and that Eldon would continue to see it whenever he looked in the mirror, no matter how heavy his makeup. And that was not all. As the outward injury faded, an inward one made itself manifest. Eldon, formerly a "quick study" who could memorize an entire play in no time at all, now found himself unable to remember even a few lines for any length of time.

The brightest thing in his life at that low point was Jennifer, in whose presence he seemed to be almost childishly happy. It was as if he had made a conscious decision to detach their present from their future, and enjoy it for its own sake.

When Jennifer came into Eldon's life, she had edged the psychiatrist out. But he came back in again after the accident. I had made his acquaintance. He had come with his wife to have dinner with us, and, of course, to appraise us—not so much as individuals, but as two elements of a classic triangle; mother, son, and stepfather. My awareness of this had made me uncomfortable with him. But according to Eldon, he had approved of both me and K., though he thought that Eldon should not remain permanently under the same roof with us; there was danger for all three of us in such interdependency, which he called "an over-compensation for the separations brought about by the war."

Eldon's young painter friend, Douglas, played the role of *deus ex machina* in resolving this situation to the satisfaction of the psychiatrist. He had been invited to live and work in New York for a few months, and he offered Eldon the use of his hilltop studio during his absence.

The immediate impact on our lives of Eldon's departure from the ground floor flat was drastic, but wholly unconnected with him. No sooner had he moved out, than a circus moved in. Basically, it consisted of three young airline hostesses; a giddy triumverate banded together to make the most of their staggered schedules, which allowed each girl the exclusive use of the jointly rented flat at regular intervals, when each could enjoy the company of her current boyfriend undisturbed. A near-seamless arrangement that left only a few vacant hours here and there in which K. and I could enjoy each other's company undisturbed. Eldon's classical records and quiet conversations were replaced night and day with perpetual pop music overlaid with laughter, shouting matches, and squeals, all the noisy apparatus of love that isn't enough in itself; and at the end of each shift, usually around six o'clock in the morning, the thin walls would vibrate with the angry buzz of a vacuum cleaner furiously wielded. It must have been part of the arrangement that each girl should leave the place clean for the next party.

Apart from this unexpected side effect, the splitting in two of our single household made very little difference in our daily life. But it did give Eldon more space, both literally and figuratively, in which to pursue his.

One of his more chimerical objectives at that time was to turn what had been an occasional bit of fun into a regular source of income. He had remarkably few vices—his overwhelming sense of responsibility for other people left very little room for self-indulgence—but a gambling streak had come down to him from my sporty Irish ancestors on my father's side, and it was brought out when a friend took him (this was before we came to America) to the horse races at Santa Anita, and he bet on a horse for the first time in his life. He put a small sum of money on a longshot, simply because it was called *Stepfather*. Stepfather won, and Eldon made, as they say, "a packet." Agreeably surprised, but still too cautious to risk his shirt on anything so uncertain, he embarked on a semiscientific study of horse racing, and came to believe that picking a winner was largely a matter of properly applied mathematics. Now, with his fortunes at such a low ebb that he grasped at every straw, he was trying to work out the unattainable formula that would make him a long-term winner at the race track.

Under these circumstances, his acquisition of a new car seemed like an unjustifiable extravagance. But I already knew enough about Hollywood and the acting profession to realize the importance of preserving an "affluent image," especially at a time when the affluence is nonexistent. And his trusty little "Chevy" had been prematurely aged by the accident.

K. and I had learned how to get about the city in buses, but Eldon would arrange to pick us up at the corner of Sunset and the entrance to Laurel Canyon, to save K. the long climb. We saw one another every day, even though we didn't live under the same roof. We went to the latest movies together, drove up the coast on Sundays, and once a week we went to the supermarket—all in the "affluent" car.

Except when he was otherwise engaged, Eldon took his evening meal with us. He would come over around six-thirty, when K. was finishing up his evening practice, and I was preparing the dinner. He would mix brandy alexanders (his favorite predinner drink) for all three of us, and sit down at the kitchen table to drink his and watch me at my cooking. The combination of the first drink of the day and the fragrant coziness of a kitchen at suppertime brings out confidences as nothing else can. And it drew from the usually secretive Eldon odd, isolated remarks that seemed to be nonsequiturs, but were actually the tail ends of his unspoken thoughts.

One evening, he said apropos of nothing, "You're a saint, Mother, if ever there was one." A statement so absurd and so embarrassing that I clattered my pots and pans and pretended not to have heard him. Another time, he said, with the same abruptness, "Jennifer and I will never be married." And when, startled, I asked him why, he said, "I just know it, that's all."

And once he said, "You ought not to be doing this. You ought to be writing. You're wasted in the kitchen."

I *was* writing. Every morning, immediately after breakfast, I would sit in the sun on the porch steps, with an exercise book and a pencil, and compose a page or two of what would be my first novel. And if ever a novel was written spontaneously, unhampered by preconceived notions of how to write a novel, or by rules pertaining to form and structure and "point of view," it was this one. All I had was an acquired ability to write a clear English sentence, and a natural gift for telling a story. But I was not so self-confident that I did not fear the effect of adverse criticism. If I was to keep going, I had to believe in what I was doing. So I kept it a secret from everyone except K., from whom I had no secrets of any kind.

Now, in response to Eldon's concern, and implied belief in my powers, I told him about the novel, and said he should see it soon—I would value his opinion. He was obviously pleased. So pleased that I very nearly showed him my exercise books there and then. But I didn't. I wish I had.

One lovely spring evening in early March, I was making crêpes—Eldon's favorite dessert—when the phone rang. I asked K. to pick it up, "I hope it's not Eldon saying he can't come. . . ."

It was Justin, asking for me. He said, in a voice so low it was barely audible over the background chatter of what sounded like a cocktail party. "Can you hear me? This is important. I want you to call Eldon *immediately*. If he doesn't answer, go on ringing until he does. Then call me back." And he rang off.

Alarmed, I dialed Eldon's number. We had a private signal, two rings, stop, redial, two rings. . . . I used it now. But after redialing over and over again and getting no answer, I let the bell go on ringing until I could no longer bear the echoing emptiness of the unanswered summons.

While I stood listening to that echo of an absence first sounded years ago in the villa on the Kelenhegyi út, K. whispered, "What is it, Tércsikem? What's wrong?" and I said, "I wish to God I knew."

Justin answered my call at first ring. "Well?"

"He's not there. I rang and rang. Justin . . . what happened? Please explain. . . ."

In his momentary silence, I felt concealment. Then he said, "I'm sorry to have left you in the dark, but there was no time for explanation. I was afraid that he might . . . leave before you could reach him."

"Leave?"

"Go out. I had just had a call from him. He was very upset. . . ."

"Upset? What about?"

"I don't know. He didn't say. I couldn't talk to him freely—there were other people in the room—they've gone now—and he hung up on me. That's all."

I was quite sure that was not all, merely all that he wanted to tell me. "Look," he said, "why don't we drive up to the studio. I'll pick you up outside your house in about twenty minutes. Be ready. I'll sound my horn."

His words were casual, but his tone was urgent—frighteningly urgent.

I said to K., "What could possibly have happened to upset Eldon so much and so suddenly?"

"He could have had a quarrel with Jennifer. After what he said to you the other evening, they may even have broken up."

I decided to call Jennifer. Trying my best to sound casual, I asked her if she happened to know where Eldon was. The question obviously surprised her. "I don't understand," she said. "When I saw him this afternoon, he said he would be spending the evening with you. . . ."

"That's right, but he didn't come, and he didn't call me—which isn't like him."

"Have you called the studio?"

"Yes, several times. He's not there. Jennifer . . . forgive me for asking, but, this afternoon, did you have any kind of disagreement—or lovers' quarrel?"

"Absolutely not!"

"And you didn't get the impression that he was in any way upset?"

"Not at all; in fact, he seemed to be more than usually relaxed . . . I really don't understand. . . ."

The mixture of bewilderment and anxiety in her voice checked me. I was doing to her what Justin had done to me, but with less reason. So I stopped pretending and told her what little I knew. When she heard that Justin was driving me up to the studio, she said she would meet us there, but I asked her to stay by her phone, as K. would stay by ours, in case Eldon called.

We were still talking when Justin's horn sounded. For a moment I clung to K., then I ran down to the car just as I was and got in beside Justin.

For a long time neither of us spoke. All talk seemed futile. But I finally brought myself to ask one of the many questions that were troubling me: "If Eldon was so upset, why didn't he call *me*?"

"He couldn't call you," Justin said, "he loved you too much," adding, after a pause, "He only called me to keep a promise—a solemn promise that he gave me a long time ago."

Justin did not say what the promise was. And I could not ask. Friendship, I thought, like love, has a right to its secrets.

The winding road up the hill, a cutting between high banks, was extremely dark. But the night was exceptionally clear, and the view from the summit was a sparkling sea of lights, unveiled by smog, just as it was on the day of our arrival.

Eldon's car was parked in its usual place, and I thought, Thank God there hasn't been any accident. Justin parked near it, and limping over to it, he looked in, as if he were half expecting to find

Eldon sitting there at the wheel, or asleep in the back. It was quiet enough for sleep, so quiet that the sound of water trickling from a garden hose left running was a noise.

The lights were on in the studio, and the door was wide open. A stream of light came through it and silvered the edge of the tree, the mimosa tree, that grew a few feet away from it, slightly to the side. It was in full bloom, drooping like a willow under its fluffy burden of blossoms, that filled the air with their subtle fragrance. It was all I could do not to leap up the flagstone path to that open door, leaving poor Justin, sixteen years younger than I, to limp after me. But I knew that was something that Eldon would never have done, he was much too kind, so I let Justin lead the way, one step at a time, planting his rubber-tipped cane like an anchor on each successive step.

At the door, he stood aside to let me go in first, but I felt that he did so reluctantly. Eldon was nowhere to be seen, and, except for the shower, this easy living space, with its open alcoves for cooking and sleeping, offered no concealment. But although there was no one there, it was still inhabited; like a room whose occupant has stepped out only for a moment, to stretch his legs and get a breath of air. The desk, which belonged to Eldon, was strewn with papers and open books, his typewriter was uncovered, his jacket hung over the back of a chair, and on a low table between two wicker chairs were the teacups used by him and Jennifer in the afternoon. I said, "He's gone out for a walk—as a boy he often went out for a walk when he was upset." But my sense that he was within calling distance was so strong that I went to the door and stood on the step calling his name as loudly as I could, as I used to call the children in from the garden or the beach when they were small.

Now, only echoes answered me. But deep inside me I felt the vibrations of an inaudible voice saying, "I'm here, Mother." And it seemed to me that a little breeze sprang up from nowhere and ruffled the light-silvered branches of the tree, telling me where he was.

III

From my present perspective—at a distance of thirty-two years—I can see the images of that night more clearly than I could when I was closer to them. They have become, in a sense, stylized; like historical events depicted on canvas by the Old Masters.

I see a slender figure in blue jeans stretched out on the ground like a tired boy who has lain down under a tree to rest and has fallen asleep. His face, illumined by his friend's flashlight, is smooth and serene as a sleeping child's. Death, invited, has treated him gently. So small is the mortal wound, so thin the trickle of blood from a temple miraculously unshattered, that the ugly German Luger that has dropped from the boy's hand seems too brutal an instrument to have done such precise and delicate work.

I see Justin kneeling beside his friend, weeping, and praying aloud, *Hail Mary full of grace*. . . . And while he implores the Mother of God to pray for us *Now and at the hour of our death*, I lay my cheek against the cold cheek of my son and beg him to forgive me for my blindness.

Now Justin is speaking to me, "Theresa. . . Theresa. . . ." And again, as though trying to bring me back from some distant place, "Theresa. . . ."

I feel his hand on my arm, raising me up, and together, the halt and the blind, we climb the steps, few but steep, from the vaulted shadows of the tree to the lighted archway of the door, and re-enter the land of the living. There to put on our masks and begin the inescapable rites, the ritual dances prescribed for the Death of a Young Man in Time of Peace, which, even when not self-inflicted, is harder to accept than the death of a whole generation of young men in Time of War—when all the dead are heroes.

Now the images blur, lost in a confusion of echoes; some soft as the whisper of summer rain, some discordant as the cries of jungle birds. The heartbreaking voice of a young girl's first great grief. The cold, questioning voice of the Law doing its duty. The hushed, hypocritical voices of those whose living depends on the death of others. And, muted by distance, Genevra's anguished cry of disbelief, and the almost unbearable eloquence of K.'s tears.

Now the echoes die away, one by one. The preliminary rites have been accomplished. The grieving girl has been tenderly embraced by the grieving mother and friend, and has gone reluctantly home to the cold comfort of her own family. Justin and I are

once more physically alone. It is almost midnight, and there is
nothing more to be done that cannot be done tomorrow, or the day
after, or the day after that. Yet something keeps us there; some
ancient fear, perhaps, of curtailing the last farewells of a briefly
lingering soul.

Justin said, "I could do with a drink, and I think you could do
with one, too. There must be a bottle of brandy somewhere
around."

He found it and poured out two fingers for each of us. I had
eaten nothing since noon, and the alcohol raced through my veins
like fire; breaking down the barriers between me and Justin.

Glass in hand, he moved about the room restlessly, touching
Eldon's things with a curious tenderness, as if through them he
could touch Eldon himself. Then he poured himself another two
fingers of brandy and sat down in the wicker chair opposite mine.

"I loved him," he said. "But what he felt for me was friendship,
not love. Friendship based on a common bond. That was why he
was able to call me and tell me what he was going to do. But not
you."

"His father always gave me a chance to stop him."

"I know that—Eldon told me. He called it emotional blackmail,
and he despised it."

"It was motivated by love . . . by the need for love—the need to
know that I still loved him enough to want to stop him."

"Eldon's love for you was more selfless. And his death wish was
stronger. His father *wanted* to be stopped, but he did not."

"I was blind. Blind! How could I have not seen this night
coming?"

"Because he did all he could to conceal it from you. He didn't
want you to see it. The guilt is mine, not yours. I could have opened
your eyes. . . . But I chose not to."

"Why, Justin? Why?"

"I loved him," he said.

"I too loved him, Justin." But Justin went on as though he had
not heard me (or had he?). "That is what kept me from warning
you—until it was too late. I knew that I could rely on him to keep
his promise to me, and I wanted—God forgive me—to be the one
who stopped him. *Mea culpa—mea maxima culpa.* . . ." He

covered his face with his hands, and for a long time we were both silent.

Too late. Justin's use of that saddest of all word combinations in any language awoke a buried recollection; recalled something said to me by Peter at the time of my departure for America, but pushed out of my conscious mind by the emotion of the moment. Now, echoed by Justin, Peter's words came back to haunt me: "I'm glad you're going to be with Eldon, Mother. He needs you... I only hope it isn't too late."

When Justin spoke again, it was to say in a matter-of-fact tone, "I'm hungry—what about you? I'll see if I can find something to eat."

He found a loaf of brown bread and some cheese, and he brought me a sandwich. I was ravenous, but I pushed the plate away so violently that the sandwich fell on the floor. Justin picked it up and put it back on the plate. "A little dust won't hurt you."

"I don't mind the dust," I said. "It's the idea of eating here . . . now . . . of not being able to watch for an hour in Gethsemane without being overcome by one's bodily needs."

"Eating is no worse than drinking and a good deal better than getting drunk—which will happen to you if you don't eat something. And anyway, people eat and drink and even get drunk at wakes, and the dead don't mind. Come on, eat."

I wolfed down the sandwich with the same mixture of hunger and shame that I had felt years ago, when, watching beside my mother's deathbed, and pregnant with Eldon, I had devoured the hospital food pressed on me by the nurse. The memory was so vivid, the past so much part of the present, that I felt myself growing faint under its impact. There was still some brandy in my glass, and Justin held it to my lips. "Drink up," he said.

Once again the alcohol quickened my heart, and this time it affected my perceptions; enlarging and expanding my surroundings, producing a sense of space, transforming the studio into a lofty cathedral. Justin assumed the mien of a celebrant priest, and the food and drink of which we had partaken took on the nature of a sacrament in a private requiem for Eldon, that had to be completed for the sake of his soul and ours, and in which we had thus far reached only the confiteor.

The passage of time, that has cleared and sharpened my visual

images of that night, has, on the other hand, made it more difficult to distinguish between what Justin and I actually said to one
another during the course of that midnight requiem, and what
was communicated without any words between our two minds,
united as they were in contemplation of the same human enigma
and the same eternal mystery.

My thoughts went wandering back down the corridors of my
dead son's childhood in search of the beginnings of tonight's
ending; and found only contradictions. Time and time again his
death had touched him, and each time he had gamely fought it off;
and the pathos of my funny-sad memories of little "Mannie" lay in
the contrast between his bright, valiant spirit and his frail body.

Justin wanted to know how much Eldon had suffered from
his father's manic-depression, and I told him, "Eldon was the
court jester. Of all the children, he was the only one who could
make his father laugh, and who knew how to be impudent without making him angry."

The streak of inherited melancholy that I had sensed in the
adolescent Eldon, had seemed, when he came to visit us ten years
later in Budapest, to be under control, and I had felt less anxious
on his account than I had on Peter's. Yet what Eldon had successfully hidden from me must have been perceptible to his older
brother. And now Justin was telling me that long before that,
when Eldon returned to Hollywood after having been invalided
out of the war, and he and Justin met for the first time, the
"common bond" on which their subsequent friendship was based
was already firmly embedded in Eldon's psyche. Under his
sunny, sparkling, life-enhancing outer personality, that drew
everyone to him, lay the darkness of a powerful death wish,
growing stronger every day, like a monstrous fetus.

"I recognized it," Justin said, "in the way that secret sufferers
from a mortal disease recognize one another, by symptoms invisible to those who do not have it."

"The psychiatrist must have recognized it . . . he should have
been of some help."

"He should have. For myself, I have found the confessional
more helpful than any psychiatrist."

Although I had long ceased to practice the Anglican faith in
which I had been brought up, and my attitude to the Catholic

faith was still that of an onlooker—attracted, but fearful—I was
by no means irreligious. I believed in God and in the immortality
of the soul, which involved the question of punishment and
reward, and the generally accepted Christian tenet that to take
one's own life was to forfeit God's mercy, and exile one's soul from
Him forever. Every crossroad in England is believed to be
haunted by the unquiet spirits of those pariahs who, by refusing
to live out their earthly lives, offended both God and their neighbor, who in turn refused to contaminate consecrated ground with
their sad, unblessed remains.

"Justin, tell me honestly, do you, as a Catholic—not as Eldon's
friend, but as a Catholic—really believe that his soul will automatically be cast into Hell forever because of a single impulsive
act?"

"No, I do not!"

"But doesn't the Catholic Church teach that suicide is the ultimate mortal sin that shuts the door on all hope of forgiveness?"

"Yes . . . but it holds the door open until the last breath and
beyond. Catholicism is the sinners' religion. Even at the moment
of death it gives the sinner the benefit of the doubt. An act of
contrition does not have to be heard by a priest to be heard by
God."

"What did Eldon know about 'acts of contrition'! And what were
his 'mortal' sins? He never did anyone any harm, he never willingly hurt anyone, he did everything he could to help other people, and at great cost to himself . . . he was filled with love!"

"An act of contrition *in extremis* is a turning of the soul toward
God in the act of dying," Justin said. "And we are all sinners."

No one knew that better than I did. As I wrote to Eldon after
the siege, I had learned in the war that a thief and a murderer
sleep within every human being. Which seemed to me to be all the
more reason why he, who had managed to remain full of love and
compassion in a world that was seething with hatred, should be
given some credit for it.

A shared grief can, at the height of its intensity, open doors that
we usually keep closed. Jealously guarded personal secrets and
cherished perceptions that we believe to be ours alone emerge to
startle us with their similarity. Yet they are never quite the same,
for our limited field of vision allows each one of us to see only

certain facets of the beloved being we have lost, as well as of ourselves. And so it was with me and Justin on that dark night of search and revelation. I could cast a long backward beam of light on the first seventeen years of Eldon's life for Justin, and Justin could illumine for me the last seven. The few years in between, when I was still cut off from him, and Justin had not yet met him, had to be reconstructed in the context of the past and the present, like a missing chapter three parts of the way through a book.

Little by little, out of combined memories and perceptions of him, and the self-revelation inseparable from all intimate recollection, there emerged a four-dimensional image of the being we both loved from such widely differing angles. The duality of his nature, the heritage of a father and mother temperamentally poles apart, that was so clear to Justin, had never been fully recognized by me. Only now, when it was over, did I realize that the whole of his short life had been an heroic struggle to reconcile irreconcilables; and achieve a tolerable balance between the forces of life and death.

What had made him give up the struggle—and so suddenly?

Even as Justin and I asked ourselves this question, we both knew that only the final act was sudden. The decision to give up had been arrived at step by step, with each successive failure—or what he believed to be a failure. And the reaching of this decision had been manifested in his apparent relinquishment of his anxieties concerning his future with Jennifer, and acceptance of the happiness offered by the present; a happiness whose culmination was the serenity of his last hours with her—that he must have wished to be unmarred for her by any foreboding. Yet we who loved him had all, with the possible exception of Justin, who had kept his insights to himself, failed to interpret these signs correctly. And Eldon himself had been blind; with the blindness peculiar to the suicide, who sees nothing beyond the moment of his own longed-for annihilation. A blindness that may seem wilfull, but which is, I believe, an unsolicited mercy conferred by death in advance on all those who capitulate willingly.

Now Justin told me of the pact between him and Eldon, the promise each had made not to commit the irrevocable act without getting in touch with the other to say goodbye, and thus giving him a chance for dissuasion. "It was my idea," Justin said, "and at first it was just as much to help myself as to help him. Later, I had the restraints and deterrants of the Catholic faith to keep me in line. But Eldon didn't believe that suicide was a sin in itself, though for him, at that time, it would have been an unpardonable act of desertion; the desertion of those whom he loved, and knew to be in a dangerous situation from which they might not escape alive, and whose hopes for the future, should they survive, lay in his hands. How many young men in their early twenties are faced with that kind of responsibility? And how many would have shouldered it so bravely?"

This semi-rhetorical question filled me with mingled pride and guilt.

"And those packages that he sent off to you so regularly after the war.... Did he ever show you the garage he rented as a base for what he called his 'Operation Lifesaver'? No? Well, he was good at carpentry, and he fitted it up with a long trestle table to work on, and shelves for the food supplies that he got in whenever he could—some of them, like sugar, were his own rations—and stacked there, and all the clothes donated by his friends. It was like a commercial packing house, with dozens of cartons, rolls of waterproof packing paper, gummed tape, string—his packages, he said, had to be practically indestructible, they had such a long, rough journey ahead of them."

"And they were, Justin. They took four months to reach us, by land and sea, and nothing was ever damaged or lost—except for the time when a four-pound can of honey burst... God! What a mess that was!"

"He was working most of that year, which meant he had to get up very early to be on the set on time, and he still had the lawsuit on his hands, so his packing had to be done at night or on weekends. He would never let me help him—except to put my thumb on a knot, or type a label. He had his own way of doing things and he was a virtuoso packer, fitting everything together like a jigsaw puzzle. Sometimes, watching him, I used to wonder whether you, and the others who were at the receiving end of the operation, realized just what a tremendous undertaking it was. . . ." He broke off, "Forgive me, I shouldn't have said that."

But there was some truth in it; the myth of America as an inexhaustible source of plenty, and relatively untouched by the war, made all the help coming from there seem more effortless than it actually was.

Justin reached out and gripped my hand. "For God's sake don't imagine that I was reproaching you, or suspecting you of ingratitude! It was simply that until Eldon let me read your account of the siege, I had no conception of what life was like over there, of what you had been through, and were still going through. It is very hard for Americans to imagine something so totally outside the framework of their own lives. They even have difficulty in believing it—you must have noticed that."

I had noticed it, and I had already accepted it as an insurmountable barrier to perfect understanding between me and my new friends. But I was wiser and less demanding (and less alone) than I had been in my dark ages, when I had raged against what was fundamentally the same, very human trait; the unwillingness to confront, and much less to rub shoulders with, misfortune, suffering, death—and by so doing, admit a vulnerability they prefer to deny.

"They don't want to believe it," I said. "Which is natural enough, but terribly dangerous."

"Which is why you should keep on telling them. Better still, write about it—people are more inclined to believe what they read in a book than what someone tells them."

The night was almost over. Physically and emotionally exhausted, full of tears that I could not shed, I wanted to go home; I longed for the haven of K.'s arms. But first, I had to ask Justin for something that was now in his sole possession, but to which I thought I had an equal right. The intensity of my feelings made me brusque. I said, "Justin, I have tried to be wholly honest with you tonight, and I think you have tried to be the same, but you have kept back something very important to me . . . what Eldon said when he called you to tell you goodbye, in fulfillment of his promise."

"He didn't say very much."

"I want his words, his exact words. I want to keep them—they were the last he was ever to utter, and he left no other message."

I felt, or imagined I felt, a reluctance on Justin's part to give me what I asked, but he said, "Very well. You shall have our entire conversation. When I picked up the phone there was a lot of chatter going on in the room, and he said, 'Justin?' as if he didn't recognize my voice—or wanted to be quite sure that he was speaking to me. Then he said, 'Listen, Justin. This is goodbye. I have made up my mind to go.' There was no mistaking what he meant, and I said, 'For Christ's sake don't go without saying goodbye to your mother!'"

Justin's voice broke. I gave him time, and after a minute or two he continued. "He said, 'I can't do that. She would stop me. And it's better that I should go. They will all be better off without me. Goodbye and God Bless.' Then he hung up, and I called you."

"Is that all? Did he say nothing else?"

"Nothing. I only wish to God he had said something else! Something for *me* to keep. But he did leave another message. I saw it on his desk when we first came in here looking for him. I didn't want you to see it then, so I pushed it under some loose papers—I'll get it for you."

It was a sheet of ruled paper torn from a spiral exercise book. Scrawled on it in pencil, in Eldon's rounded hand, were the words, *I leave everything I possess to my mother and stepfather.* Under them were his signature and that day's date. He must have written it just before he went out into the garden.

Justin turned off the lights, and we left. Our private requiem was ended; but it was only five years later, by earthly time, that the final requiescat was pronounced. It came from the lips of a deeply spiritual Carmelite monk. Believing him to be very close to God, I told him the story of Eldon's life and death; hoping for some sort of assurance of absolution from him more consoling than the simple recommendation to trust in God's mercy given to me by Justin, and other Catholics—some of them priests. And I was not disappointed. After listening to my story with the stillness and attention that were characteristic of him, he gave me an answer that was at once simple and comprehensive. He said, "The soul that God has already seen fit to fill with His love can never be exiled from Him."

When Justin left me off at the house in Laurel Canyon, a new day had already begun. K., who had waited up for me all night, was in the sun porch. He came down the path to meet me with outstretched arms, and clasped me to him without any words.

The self-control that had kept me outwardly calm and strong and my tears frozen inside me broke now, and he had to guide me up the path and into the house as if the unexpected brilliance of the sunrise had blinded me. He laid me gently down on the unslept-in bed, and knelt to take off my sandals. Then he lay down beside me, and taking my hand in his he gripped it tightly, as Mr. Fitch-Keane had done years ago when I was in labor with my first son.

Little by little, the storm abated, and the terrible pain that encompassed my whole being slowly relaxed its hold. It was finally overcome by the sleep of total exhaustion. But not for long. Merciful nature was defeated by human efficiency, in the form of Western Union, briskly determined to deliver a joyful message to us, whose world had been emptied of joy overnight.

The message was a cablegram from London, bearing the same date as Eldon's penciled will. It said: *Married to Philip Selby this afternoon. Stop. Tremendously happy. Stop. Love to all from us both. Stop. Letter follows. Stop. Nina.*

Death is followed by a Greek Chorus of voices that echo through the emptiness without ever filling it.

The voices reach me in various ways: by telephone, telegram, letter, or across the small space between two chairs. And whether the speakers are young or old, women or men, they all have one thing in common; their love, in one form or another, for my son. There is beauty in that, but at the same time it seems, at least superficially, to demonstrate the futility of loving and the danger of giving (which was Eldon's form of loving) too much; more, that is, than the recipient is capable of giving in return.

The confiteor becomes general.

A young actress, later to be a star, who has been taking elocution lessons from Eldon, tells me in a letter that Eldon's life and death make her wish that her own life had been better, and that she had been a better person.

The psychiatrist faces me from the other side of the empty grate in what was once a living room, the same room in which he had politely, but nonetheless arrogantly, assessed my suitability as a parent, and admits to a humiliating professional failure where Eldon was concerned. "I had no idea, *absolutely no idea*, that this was likely to occur. Not once did he ever mention having any suicidal feelings. Not once! Please believe that!" (I do believe it.) "All the same, as his therapist, I should have seen it for myself." Which is what I think, too. But the blind are in no position to blame other people for failing to see.

Jacob Chaitkin, Eldon's fatherly attorney, sheds unabashed Russian tears, and blames himself for not having insisted that Eldon should draw up a proper will—especially after his automobile accident. But this sentimental man is as clever as he is goodhearted. He knows how to "get things done" and he gets them done for us with remarkable rapidity. For Eldon's sake, he takes charge of our unprofitable affairs, and remains our trusted friend until his own untimely death a few years later.

Douglas, the young painter, whose loan of his hilltop studio to Eldon had been so well-meant, now torments himself with the unanswerable question, *Would this terrible thing have happened if Eldon had continued to live in Laurel Canyon with his parents?* Douglas knows nothing about the ancient significance of the tree, the mimosa tree, and its relation to the dark, mysterious power that moved him to make the offer, and Eldon to accept it.

Jennifer, heartbroken, and bewildered by glimpses of depths beyond the scope of her experience, asks herself the question that torments all those whose human devotion has been defeated by Death's superior lure. *Why wasn't my love enough?* She is too romantic, and too fundamentally innocent, to realize that Eldon might have foreseen, dreaded, and decided to forestall the inevitable moment when his love would not—in itself alone—be enough for her.

Now, Eldon's other Catholic friend, Paulinus, who has always remained in the background, shyly assumes a more prominent place. His relative remoteness has been due less to physical distance (though he lives some way off, by the ocean), than to the rigid limitations imposed on him by the two, conflicting, factors that govern his existence; the need to work for a living, and the need for long periods of rest in order to stay alive. A balancing act that left him neither time nor energy for casual social contacts of the kind that we had with Justin, and with Douglas before he left for New York.

Paulinus had come to the house on only two or three more or less formal occasions, one being for Christmas dinner. Yet of all

Eldon's friends who were known to us during that period, Paulinus is the only one who has not vanished with time, but has become closer to me, though we live thousands of miles apart and have not seen one another in years. Every lasting relationship is based, like Eldon's relationship with Justin, on some common bond, or mutual need, usually psychological. And the special bond between Eldon and Paulinus was probably rooted in the latter's infirmities and his problems of living, which put Eldon in the position he liked best; that of helper and protector—even if only by way of small kindnesses and attentions when his friend was laid up. But the link between me and Paulinus was forged by our shared sense of humor. I liked his ability to laugh at himself and accept the tightrope walk to which he was permanently condemned as a little joke on the part of the Catechism Creator he had been instructed to love, as a small boy, and had tried to make less unlovable by endowing him with a sense of humor.

The image that comes up in my mind whenever I think of Paulinus, or receive a letter from him, is always the same. The scene is the lifeless living room of the house on Laurel Canyon. It is in the evening on the day of the funeral, or rather, of the brief funeral service performed in an anonymous chapel by an unknown Anglican priest before the cremation. K. and I and Genevra—who has come to be with me for a few days—are becalmed in the nightmarish limbo that follows on the final disappearance, the fiery sealing of the treaty with Death, after which we can never again look on the human face of the dead. In the same room with us, if not in the same nightmare, is Paulinus; a long-limbed, raw-boned, sandy-haired man of the type that never quite fits into any living room. And his awkward presence in this one relieves the gloom by challenging its supremacy.

We talk about Eldon, each constructing our own memorial myth from those aspects of him best known to each of us individually. And as Paulinus recalls the Eldon he knew in a disjointed series of touching, half-humorous anecdotes, I become aware of what he is doing for me, whether he knows it or not. He is painting for me a portrait of Eldon touched by the bright grace of laughter as by a ray of sunlight.

And this is not the only illumination to pierce my personal darkness. As a result of that night's conversation, in which the word, *failure* is implicit, if unuttered, I perceive quite clearly what I have to do. I see Eldon's death as the end of an arduous pilgrimage undertaken, from the beginning, for my sake; and that now it is up to me to justify it in my own life, and replace the word *failure* with its opposite—for his sake. Once again, this time in a different area of my life, I am being given a second chance.

Eldon had once said, in the casual manner in which one refers to such things, that if "anything happened" to him, he would want to be cremated and to have his ashes strewn from an airplane over the Californian landscape. Which last turned out to be against Californian law. But thanks to action taken by some of Eldon's friends, his ashes were laid to rest in Californian soil on Memorial Day, with military honors, beside those of other veterans of the war who had served in the Royal Canadian Air Force.

3

Of Money, Luck, and the
Nature of Love

*O*NE of the very few advantages of not having much money is that the lack of it forces one to rise above grief and loss, and get on with the job of living, whether one feels like it or not.

For me and K., that meant learning how to be self-sufficient in a country that was still new to us; learning, in late middle age, skills that Americans acquire almost as soon as they leave their cradles. A first requisite was to learn how to manage the finned monster that now lounged in our driveway idly eating up monthly payments. Jennifer offered to teach both of us to drive. But I was one of Nature's nondrivers; I couldn't control a bicycle, let alone an automobile. K., on the contrary, was eager to learn. He decided, however, to begin by taking lessons from a professional driving instructor in a car with dual controls and a notice on the back warning other drivers that a learner was loose on the road. A sensible decision considering the formidable practice terrain.

Every day for two weeks, K., who had never, in all his sixty-five years of life, driven a moving vehicle, or even ridden a bicycle, successfully navigated first the learner's car and then the monster around the sharp curves of the canyon road and into the stop-and-go torrent of traffic on Sunset Boulevard. After which tough apprenticeship, he easily passed his driver's tests, got his California license, and triumphantly took me out for a "joy ride."

This achievement meant infinitely more to him than the mere acquisition of a new technical skill. It restored his youth. It gave him a sense of power and personal freedom that under the long, successive tyrannies of an unhappy marriage, and two alien occupations of his homeland, had been provided only by his instrument—his cello, which released his spirit into spheres beyond the reach of any human tyranny. And now, with the affluent car Eldon had bequeathed to him a comparable talisman on another level. Skimming at seventy miles an hour along the open California highways (where in those days speed was limited only by the individual driver's concept of safety), all physical limitations were forgotten in an experience that was just as exhilarating to him as playing a cello concerto with a first-rate orchestra.

All the same, very long trips fatigued him. So it was Jennifer who drove us, in her own car, seventy miles or so inland, to the so-called "orange belt" to visit a Baptist university, where the Dean of the Music Department, who had heard K. play back in Europe, was trying to persuade a Philistine president that, although there was little or no demand for cello lessons, K.'s presence on the music faculty would have prestige value. And, since they already had an excellent pianist and were just about to hire an excellent violinist, the addition of a cellist, particularly a cellist of K.'s caliber and reputation, would make possible the formation of a faculty trio, which could not fail to enhance the university's musical image. The Philistine president, more concerned with raising funds for his university than enhancing its musical image, grudgingly gave in, and K. was offered a part-time position ("affiliation" is a more accurate word) at a ridiculously low salary.

Our reasons (all our major decisions were made jointly) for accepting this paltry offer were complex; but we were influenced in the first place by its timing. It acquired a somewhat meretricious desirability by coming, as it did, when we were standing, uncertainly, at a very dark crossroads; and our overwhelming desire to get away from surroundings that reminded us of Eldon at every turn, coincided with the urgent necessity to cut our living expenses down to a minimum. Which could be done more easily in a small country town than in Los Angeles.

The niggardliness of the salary offered by this prosperous private university bothered K. less than it bothered me. He was notoriously unpractical—even in Hungary I was the one who managed the family resources—and the prospect of forming a chamber music ensemble that would help to fill the empty place left in his life by the unavoidable breakup of the Waldbauer-Kerpely quartet, after thirty-five years, had more appeal for him than any amount of teaching. It would give him something more valuable than anything money could buy; and despite my necessary practicality, he and I were of one mind in placing spiritual values above material ones. All his life he had been a contemplative musician, whose naturally introverted temperament led him to seek perfection in his art for its own sake, regardless of public acclaim. And now, more than ever before, this inner satisfaction would be his greatest reward.

As for me, I saw in the neat little town, set in the midst of the citrus groves that provided its sole industry, an ideal location in which to "recollect emotion in tranquility" and finish my novel about the war. After which I would start another one—already taking shape at the back of my mind; in short, I believed that I had, by a happy chance, found my birthplace as a writer, and I was naive enough to imagine that the publication of my first novel would more than make up for the stinginess of the university. This first visit must have taken place in the spring vacation, for the university campus had that misleading air of monastic serenity that college campuses assume in the absence of their students. And this one, not venerable, not ivied, but all fresh white stucco, banked with scarlet cannas against a backdrop of blue sky, orange trees, palms, and blue mountains—with just a hint of white on their peaks—had a strong resemblance to a Spanish Mission. A resemblance that was heightened for me, somewhat irrationally, by the exquisite, bridal scent of orange blossom, that filled the air for miles around with the fragrance of Eden.

Some time in June, when everything was settled with the university, we revisited Eden in search of a place to live, but the very things that made the little town so attractive—the absence of citified streets, tall buildings, blocks of apartment houses—made rentals hard to find. And we were late. The best places had already been snapped up by earlier birds; newcomers to the university in fields of more practical importance than music. We had seen only one possibility; but it wouldn't be available until the first of September, and we had already given our Laurel Canyon landlady notice. Besides, the rent was too high for us. We were standing outside the real estate office on Main Street, trying to come to a decision, when the glass door next to it—with a painted sign saying *Notary Public* and below that a cardboard sign saying *Out to Lunch*—opened and a little man in shirt sleeves came out, locking the door behind him. After walking past us, and giving us an interested glance, he stopped and came back.

"Pardon me, but I couldn't help overhearing what you were saying, and I thought that my sister's place might suit. I am the Notary Public," he added, as though that guaranteed his sister's respectability.

K. offered proof of his respectability by identifying himself as a professor in the department of music at the university. After which exchange of guarantees, the notary told us that his sister's place was in a country village about five miles from the university, on a street named Onyx, or Agate, or something equally unlikely—all the streets in this village had the names of semiprecious stones—"It's right opposite the trout hatchery. You can't miss it."

The street proved hard to locate, because it was not what is usually called a street; merely a dusty strip of dirt road leading to the trout hatchery. But once that landmark was discovered, there was no missing the place we had come to see. An ungainly, two-storied, gray frame house, its ungraceful contours partially concealed by a trio of eucalyptus and one emerald green pepper, it stood in the middle of nowhere like an old wooden vessel marooned on the dry bed of what was once an inland sea. A pair of low white cottages in back of it, surrounded by flowers, combined, however, with the vivid green of the pepper tree and a gleam of blue from the trout hatchery's small, rectangular substitute for a lake, to suggest the pleasanter metaphor of an oasis in the desert. And how often in the future would we long to join the young trout in their azure swimming pool!

The landlord and his wife, the notary's sister, came out from one of the white cottages to greet us. The vacant apartment was, as I had guessed, in the big house, which had that orphaned air that distinguishes rented houses from those occupied by their owners. It was up on the second floor, under the roof, and had all the bohemian charm of a rather rickety attic, and all its disadvantages as well, of which the biggest would be heat. When we mentioned that, the landlord offered to put in a "desert cooler," but omitted to tell us that in July and August the temperature could go up as high as one hundred and fifteen degrees in the shade, and there was precious little shade over that roof.

On the other hand, it would be extremely quiet—the first floor tenants were away at work all day and K. could play as much as he pleased; it commanded a beautiful, unobstructed view of the distant mountains; the landlord and his wife were obviously decent people and anxious to have us as tenants, and most important of all at that particular juncture, the rent was low, only fifty dollars a month, and we could rent by the month, so that if we were too uncomfortable we would be free to move at a month's notice.

Such were the rationalizations that led us, hot, tired, and discouraged, to settle then and there for the ramshackle dwelling (that was almost shamefully unsuitable in the opinion of the university), in which we would spend three mild blue winters and red-hot summers, until the publication of my novel made a move possible, and a doctor's warning that K.'s heart could not be counted on to carry him safely up a steep flight of stairs several times a day made a move imperative.

Since money played—though mostly in absentia—such a big role in determining the nature of my American experience, perhaps this is the appropriate place for a brief digression on the subject.

Money, like Luck, with which it is closely (but mistakenly) connected in most people's minds, seems to have a selective will of its own, and is more inclined to favor those who love it than those who merely need it.

My feelings with regard to it were ambivalent; the result, no doubt, of being taught by my parents when I was young that money was the root of all evil, and at the same time suffering— and watching my parents suffer, physically and emotionally— from the lack of it. And Money seemed to be aware of the ambivalence sown in me by this contradiction, and treated me accordingly. It would never come to live with me, but neither would it wholly desert me; one way or another it would always turn up in time to save me from total disaster. Luck, working independently of Money, displayed much the same attitude.

The only unearned money I ever possessed, the money that the lawsuit with the U.S. government was about, is a case in point, and the manner in which it came to me is a Gothic tale in itself. I have used parts of it in a novel. But here is the complete story, unmodified by the exigencies of a fiction whose theme was not Money, but Love.

It begins way back in the mid-nineteenth century, and that part of it is, of course, hearsay. But it came from two impeccably truthful sources; my mother, who regarded lying as a grave sin, and my aunt, who regarded it as not only wrong, but unnecessary—even in the interests of ordinary civility.

My maternal grandmother was of aristocratic French Huguenot descent, and took just as much pride in her inherited aura of martyrdom as she did in her inherited halo of aristocracy. Her husband, my grandfather, had neither. He was simply an English gentleman, who had lowered the standards of his class—that of the country squirearchy—by becoming a sugar planter on the island of Mauritious, where my mother was born. She was the youngest of three daughters, and dispersed among the girls, and very near to them in age, were three sons.

The languid, sheltered life led by my grandmother on that perfumed isle, must have been rather like that of the mistress of a Southern plantation in this country at the same period; though more isolated, linked with the rest of the world only by the irregular visits of trading vessels from England, the small white community was more turned in on itself socially; the principal diversions between ships being the begetting of children, for the men, and the less entertaining bearing of them for the women. But young as my mother was when she left the island, she took with her a lifelong yearning to recover a lost paradise.

It was lost when my mother was five years old, and my grandfather died suddenly. True to type, this English country gentleman, with his inborn disdain of "trade," had left the financial side of his venture entirely in the hands of a trusted business partner. His trust was misplaced. After his death, his widow and his six fatherless children, were packed off to England on the next trading vessel with barely enough money to keep them for a few months. And that was that. It should not be forgotten that a Victorian wife had no "rights," and any money brought by her to her marriage automatically became the property of her husband. Which facilitated the untrustworthy partner's skulduggery.

How this benighted family managed to survive is not part of my story. Only the plight of the three girls is relevant. In those days, an impoverished young gentlewoman had only two acceptable options: marriage, or the genteel subservience of a governess in a "nice" family. The oldest girl, a delicate beauty, married for love at sixteen and died of it in her twenties. The youngest, my mother, also married for love, but only after years of domestic subjugation, first at home, caring for her mother and her younger brother who died of tuberculosis, and then in other people's homes, as governess and companion. The spirited middle girl, the aunt of this story—determined to avoid both fates, married a good, but dull man purely for his money. That was when Money took the first step in my direction.

The man my aunt married was the second son of a landed family who would inherit a large country estate on the death of his mother. In the meantime, he occupied a gentlemanly Civil Service position in India. When he met my aunt, he was in England on leave and looking for a suitable wife to take back with him. He was lonely.

At first, my aunt found life in India, with a different servant for every chore, reminiscent of life on the island. But after she lost her first two children, both sons, from unnatural causes (one by poison), she grew to hate it, and when her daughter was born, she made her husband relinquish his post and return to England for good. Luckily for him, this coincided closely with the realization of his inheritance, but it was an act of surrender from which he would never recover. From then on, he became more and more of a nonentity in his own household; a mere signer of checks at his wife's behest, a silently resentful provider of luxuries for their nymphomaniac daughter, who was detested by him and spoiled and adored by her mother, and who hated them both.

She was six years older than I, and she took full advantage of my school-girlish adoration to use me as an ally in deceiving her mother. But even I, naive and sexually unaware as I was at twelve years old, sensed something disturbing about her and her behavior. My uncle saw it and turned his back. But my aunt was blinded by an excess of maternal love, and it took a major crisis to open her eyes. From emotional instability my cousin progressed by way of an illegitimate pregnancy passed in the secrecy of an expensive private mental institution, to paranoia and schizophrenia, and ended up a screaming madwoman, fat and repulsive, all her transient beauty gone with her mind.

After vainly scouring Europe for someone, anyone—whether a psychiatrist, a spiritualist, or a faith healer—who might be able to cure my cousin, my aunt finally accepted the verdict of a well-known London brain specialist, that my cousin was suffering from incurable and progressive Dementia Praecox, but disregarded his recommendation that she be placed in an institution. No! Never again!

Unaware that the doctor's advice had been largely based on his conviction that my cousin's virulent hatred of both her parents was an aggravating element in her illness, my aunt and uncle shut themselves up in their country home with their mad daughter. I went to see them there before I left England to live in one distant country after another. They were still presenting a brave false front to their increasingly rare visitors from the outside world. But I knew them too well to be deceived, and I was appalled by the deterioration that had already set in, both in them and their surroundings—from the unkempt lawns and weed-filled flowerbeds to the flush of too much brandy on my aunt's florid face and the vacancy in my uncle's pale blue eyes. Before I left, I asked to see my cousin. "Better not," my aunt said, "she won't recognize you." My uncle suddenly gave a cackle of laughter, "*You* won't recognize *her*," he said, with a malice I would never have thought him capable of. He was right. I insisted on seeing her, but I wished afterwards that I hadn't.

The image left on my mind by my visit to the disintegrating scene of so many happy summer holidays in my childhood, is that of a black comedy with three characters, each nailed down alive in a separate coffin, but tied to the others by knotted ropes of love and hate breakable only by death.

The first of the three to die was my uncle. He left his entire estate to my aunt, unconditionally. Marriage had not lessened his loneliness. But Money had fulfilled its promise to my aunt, and in the process had come a step nearer to me.

My aunt was now in a position to make a will of her own. And the occasion of its signing was the last one on which the family solicitor, an adviser and friend of long standing, was invited to come to the house. From then on, all business between him and my aunt was conducted by correspondence, which made him uneasy, but there was nothing he could do about it.

When my aunt died, I was in South America. I was notified of her death in a briefly worded cable, followed by a letter from the solicitor informing me that she had "succumbed to an internal disease," and enclosing a copy of her will. It stipulated that her daughter should never be placed in an institution, but be allowed to live out her life in her present surroundings, and that the income from the estates should be wholly devoted to keeping them up, and to providing her with the best of care and comfort. At my cousin's death, everything—the lands, the house, and everything in it—were to be sold at auction, and the resulting monies, after duties and taxes had been paid, were to be divided into three equal portions, one of which would be mine—absolutely.

A couple of years later, back from South America and vacationing in the South of England before going to a new post, I went to see the solicitor. He seemed pleased to see me. Apparently, I was the only one of the beneficiaries of my aunt's will whom he had laid eyes on ("Poor lady! So generous and kind, and so quickly forgotten!"), and the only one to show any interest in what was happening to my cousin. All the same, he was very reserved when I asked for details of my aunt's death. "It was very sad," he said, "very sad indeed. It is painful to think of, even now. But I suppose that you do have a right to know how it was. . . . Will you come and have lunch with me?"

A bottle of wine made the telling easier—and the listening.

One day, he told me, after not having seen my aunt for several years, he suddenly got a call from the physician who had attended my uncle in his last illness, telling him that my aunt was dying and the situation was desperate, and asking him to come to the house as quickly as possible.

He was met at the door by the old couple, my uncle's former

coachman and his decrepit wife, who had stayed on to care for their mistress as best they could when everyone else had fled a house they believed to be under a curse. The old couple, alarmed by my aunt's condition, had called the doctor in without her permission—they hoped they had done right.

The solicitor, who knew the geography of the house, expected to be taken to my aunt's big bedroom upstairs. But the old man led him to a sitting room on the ground floor known as the "morning room," which, when my uncle was alive, had formed part of a suite of three communicating rooms—the plush-lined coffins—in which father, mother, and daughter, had spent their long, useless days, unable ever to open the communicating doors.

The old man knocked, and the doctor came out, and took the solicitor aside to tell him, hurriedly, to be prepared for a shock. The last time, the doctor said, that he had attended my aunt was after my cousin had attacked her and nearly killed her. And even then, he said, she had received him in the main drawing room, attired as if for a teaparty. But that was almost two years ago.... And what had happened since then was shocking... Shocking!

And shocked the solicitor was—almost to the point of throwing up. The room stank, he said, like an animal house at the zoo. On a small iron bed in one corner of the otherwise richly furnished room, lay the bloated figure of my aunt, unconscious, and breathing the rasping breaths of the dying. Crouched on the floor in another corner and whimpering like a sick animal was my cousin, surrounded by piles of shredded newspaper. Empty bottles were piled up everywhere; no trash had been thrown out, no sweeping or dusting done, the beautiful Aubusson carpet was covered with ugly stains, the bathroom was incredibly filthy, and the earth in the cat boxes hadn't been changed for weeks. And the woman who lay dying in the midst of all this had been one of the proudest hostesses in the whole county, famous for the epicurean elegance of her dinner parties.

She was too ill to be moved—she did not last through the night—so a trained nurse was brought in, and now, this same nurse ("A very efficient young woman, with the highest credentials") was in full charge of my cousin, "Would you care to go and see for yourself how the terms of your aunt's will are being carried out?"

Sitting in that same "morning room," eating an excellent lunch deftly served by a maid in white cap and apron, it was hard to believe what the solicitor had told me. But my hostess, the chatelaine-nurse, corroborated everything he had said, and filled in some details that he had omitted; one being the source of the shredded paper, "Cutting up old newspapers into little pieces was what your cousin did all day—when she wasn't . . . doing something else." "Something else? What?" "Bad habits," said the nurse.

After lunch, we toured the house. It was like taking a tour back into my childhood.

"You can't imagine what this place was like when I first got here. It was the sort of thing you read about in one of those horror stories. The house was falling to pieces, the damp had got in and the paper was peeling off the walls. Cobwebs were hanging all over the place like curtains, the dust was inches deep, the bedroom floors were covered with the droppings of bats that lived in the chimneys, the drains were clogged up, and heaven only knows how long it had been since your aunt had been able to wash herself, or her daughter. And then, of course, there were the cats, about twenty of them; they'd gone on having kittens. . . . The smell was something awful! It took weeks, and a whole army of workers, inside and outside, to clean things up and make the place habitable. But it looks nice now, doesn't it?"

The drawing rooms were ghostly in dust sheets, but the long table in the dining room, that used to seat twenty guests, was uncovered and smelled agreeably of beeswax.

Upstairs, my aunt's big bedroom had been taken by the nurse for herself, and smelled of her soap and perfume—she was young and pretty enough to take an interest in her appearance, and, as she explained with a smile, she had her social life. She could have a friend to stay whenever she liked, and whenever she wanted a weekend off a substitute was provided. Her patient occupied what had once been my uncle's dressingroom, and a larger room beyond it, both with communicating doors to the nurse's room. I wondered aloud if she kept them locked at night. "You bet I do!" she said. "Not that the poor creature's likely to do me any harm— she's stopped being violent now that her mother's gone, but you never know."

We talked about the patient. "She never speaks. But she's

docile. She lets me bathe her and dress her, and aside from her bad habit she does what she's told. But you can't keep her from masturbating anymore than you can keep her from breathing."

I didn't want to see her, but I thought it was my duty to make quite sure that she was getting the proper care. The nurse unlocked the door slowly, and called her name before opening it, as one might on entering the cage of some shy and unpredictable animal. There she was, my once charming, coquettish cousin, enormously fat, vacant-eyed, sitting in a rocking chair rocking back and forth with her hand on her crotch.

She was neat and clean, and so was the room, but behind the fragrance of jonquils in a bowl on the table, I detected the curious odor that emanates from the mentally ill, as if their illness was physical in origin.

The grave illness of my husband had brought us back to England, and we were living in London, when I got one of the solicitor's rare communications. He thought it right to inform me, he said, that my cousin was in "poor health," and might have to undergo surgery. But compared to my husband's condition, and its devastating effect on our lives, the state of my cousin's health seemed academic, and soon slipped from my mind. So a telegram announcing her death came as a surprise. It informed me of when and where the funeral was scheduled to take place—clearly the solicitor expected me to be there. That would mean spending a night away, and missing my usual afternoon visit to my husband, who was in a sanatorium at the time. But I thought I owed it to my aunt to pay a last tribute to her poor, lost child. So I ordered a wreath of white flowers, and took it down to the country with me on the Devon and Cornwall express.

The solicitor met me at the station and drove me out to the village church; he and I, and the nurse, were the only mourners, and mine were the only flowers. As my cousin's coffin was lowered into the place reserved for it next to her mother and father, I wept; not for them—their troubles were over—but for myself.

It was only on the train back to London that I fully realized what had happened. Money had reached the end of its tortuous journey toward me. Money had arrived—just in time to save me from the same fate as my unfortunate French grandmother.

My aunt's legacy, invested for me in gilt-edged securities by a prudent friend, would, in the normal course of events, have provided me with a modest income for the rest of my life. But the course of events had been anything but normal. True, I was responsible for making the first erratic move, but the foreseeable risks of my marriage to a Hungarian, and even the consequent loss of my British citizenship, were negligible. There had been no reason to suppose that in less than two years a world war would immeasurably complicate every aspect of my situation, and eventually, aided by the human error mentioned earlier, lead to the wrongful confiscation of our ill-starred but impeccably British family funds by the U.S. Government. An action that it would take a long and costly lawsuit to reverse. And what mysterious power decreed that the money should be released just in time to save us from being shut in behind an Iron Curtain?

Now, Money—my aunt's money—exhausted by so much last-minute rescuing, is getting ready to leave me.

Jacob Chaitkin, appointed executor of Eldon's estate, warns us, sadly, that when taxes, legal expenses, medical expenses, and other obligations—most of them incurred on our behalf—have been met, very little will remain. Aside from a few hundred dollars in cash, all we are likely to inherit is the still un-repaid principal of a long-term unsecured loan made by Eldon to help out a friend who was getting married. It will come to us in the form of monthly payments of principal and interest, which will not amount to very much. But combined with the equally small monthly check from the university, it will just be enough to keep us alive from one month to the next—if we don't get sick.

So until I publish my novel, and K. is able to establish a viable chamber music group, our existence will virtually depend on the honesty and goodwill of a stranger.

II

Money was on its way out, but Luck was on its way in, though so inconspicuously that I did not recognize it. In fact, it disclosed its identity only in retrospect; like the luck that causes a motorist lost in an unfamiliar landscape to take the one, unmarked, turn in the road that leads to the desired destination.

Although I hoped to make money by my writing, I had regarded it first and foremost as an art, to be practiced and perfected in my own sweet time. But under the goad of necessity I completed in a few months a work that without that imperative would have taken me three times as long—and been all the better for that. I was helped by K., as I was in everything I did. And, in this case, practical assistance was added to advice and encouragement. He taught himself to type on Eldon's old portable, and every evening he typed out for me what I had written in long hand during the day. Typed, its flaws would be more apparent, and K. would make innumerable drafts. But he did it willingly. He was fascinated by the similarity between the way I worked to express my ideas in words, and the way he worked to express his in music; and not merely in his own occasional compositions, but in his playing; in his performances of the works of the great composers, and his individual interpretations of them.

He would read and comment on what I had written, but his suggestions would be on substance rather than style, since English was not his native language, though as a musician, he had a more highly developed sense of form and structure than I had at that time. But most important of all, he had a profound and sympathetic understanding of *me*, and of what I was trying to say in my book. Which enabled me to share with him, and gain by sharing with him, a process that I have never been able to share with anyone else.

K.'s loving understanding was being called into play by another process that was going on in me simultaneously with the creative, and allied to it, though on a different level. It had started with the faintest of tremors deep within my being one summer's night on a hill overlooking the river Danube; a process of spiritual growth, nourished in darkness on the truths laid bare by the fires of war and persecution, and brought to fruition more than a decade later on a hill overlooking the city of Los Angeles.

I was being drawn back to the God from whom I had strayed; but along an unknown road, and through a more ancient gateway than the one through which I had fled; the strait and narrow gate of the Catholic Church.

Inevitably, these two creative processes, the literary and the religious, got entangled with one another, to the detriment of my novel, fervor of any kind being incompatible with objectivity.

The final chapter of my novel was an epilogue, and I had just begun writing it, when Justin told me about a contest sponsored by a Catholic group called The Christophers, who offered a prize of fifteen thousand dollars for the best MS submitted on a Catholic theme, either fiction, or nonfiction. And as my novel was set in a Catholic country, and central to its love story was the attitude of the Church, and of individual Catholics, to members of the persecuted Jewish population, he thought it might qualify. But the deadline for entries was very close, and they had to be submitted by either a publisher or a literary agent.

Justin knew of two literary agents who might possibly be of help; one was Paul Reynolds, who had worked hard, if unsuccessfully, to place Justin's own first novel, and the other was a newly established agent, who was unknown to him personally, but had been highly recommended by a friend, for whose book he had found a publisher almost immediately.

I had never heard of either of them. But instinctively I leaned toward the man who had taken so much trouble over a not very "saleable" MS. "Actually," Justin said, "it was not Paul Reynolds himself who handled my stuff, but one of his associates, a man named Oliver Swan. It's a bit late in the day to expect . . . but I suppose there's no harm in trying."

Totally ignorant of what I might reasonably expect of Mr. Swan, or any other literary agent, I packed up my MS, minus the epilogue, which I said would follow by the next day's mail, and sent it off to Mr. Swan with the brash request that he read it, and, if he deemed it worthy, enter it into the Christopher Contest for me—all within the space of a few days. And I was less surprised than I should have been when he did just that.

My entry got into the finals and was described, flatteringly, as "important." But the prize went to a nonfiction book, and a more accomplished book than mine, on a related subject; *Pillar of Fire* by Karl Stern.

Although I had to admit, on reading that excellent book, that the judges' choice of it over mine had been fair, I still bore a grudge against Luck for not putting in an appearance on my behalf. It might not have taken much to tip the scale in my favor—after all, my book *was* in the finals.

What I had yet to discover was that Luck had indeed put in an appearance—even before the judging began. But instead of obstructing justice on my behalf, it had helped me in a more impartial, if less spectacular way, by introducing into my writing life one of those rare individuals who, once they take you up never let you down.

When Mr. Swan got my MS back from The Christophers, he sent me a copy of their letter, in which the words, "important entry" softened the blow of losing, and said in his cautious way that, with my permission, he would send it out to "at least a few publishers." He realized of course, as I did not, that it was rather too Catholic in tone to please ordinary secular publishing firms. And so I entered joyfully, and all unawares, that zone of acute suffering specially reserved for neophyte authors with tender skins.

It is, I believe, in a first novel that an author most rashly exposes his, or her innermost self to the careless cruelty of others; which is often unintentional, or stupid, or both—but no less painful on that account. I once heard my friend Leonard Wibberly, urge a group of would-be fiction writers to "cultivate a tough hide." And I tried to tell the same group how to utilize criticism constructively. But a first book is like a first baby; the smallest suggestion that it is not absolutely perfect is unendurable to the mother.

It was a good thing for me that running concurrently with that nerve-racking cycle of high hopes, waiting, suspense, disappointment, and hope renewed—a bit weaker each time—was the comedy of our adjustment to our new ambiance, the Baptist University, to which we could not have been more temperamentally unsuited.

The academic year began with a "Retreat," a mandatory gathering of faculty and administration in a nearby mountain resort; one of those artificially contrived occasions of "fellowship in a beautiful natural setting"—to quote the retreat program—that resemble nothing so much as a Sunday School outing. Every minute of the day, and it went on for two days, was rigorously programmed with an interlocking schedule of business and "relaxation" (organized games), with only the briefest intervals for going to the bathroom. As for snatching a cigarette, smoking, drinking, and dancing were moral offenses that no faculty member, or faculty wife or child, could commit with impunity either on or off campus. And here, even solitude, or the desire for a few moments of it, was regarded as an offense against fellowship. And the fellowship offered very little stimulation—its collective wit and intelligence having been rendered temporarily inactive by an overdose of ill-timed piety.

All through the deadly tedium of our compulsory orientation into a way of life and thought essentially foreign to us, I was wondering why it should seem so familiar. When, and where, had I heard these complacent hymns before, encountered this same decent banality, this reduction of God to a friendly business associate, this whiff of hypocrisy in the studied decorum?

Button. The word jumped into my vacant mind as I sat half asleep in the middle of a long row of male and female Buttons being lectured on the duty of the faculty family to set the student body a good example.

Button! Of course! How could I have forgotten? Miss Jane Button—spiritual mother of the American Baptist Missionaries vainly toiling in the unfruitful Rumanian field. Their spotless apartment on the Calea Victoria, and the final singing of hymns in the entrance hall that would shortly—just as soon as the unregenerate British vice-consul moved in—vibrate to the sinful rhythms of the dance, and the clink of glasses filled with that wicked Rumanian champagne. Did Miss Button foresee this desecration? Was that why she failed to mention the cockroaches living their night-lives in the kitchen and the bedbugs concealed in the puritanical furniture she had fobbed off on us? Was it her idea of poetic justice?

I nudged K. and whispered to him, "I have been here before." His eyebrows went up. "Ages ago—in another life," I said. And the female Button next to me said, "Shh. . . ."

For newcomers like us, the general assumption that everyone attending the Retreat was a true believer (or ought to be), created the nervous atmosphere of a Party-rally in a totalitarian country where everyone is afraid of everyone else. But once released from the oppressive concentration of supposedly true-blue Buttons all in one place, the dissidents soon discovered one another.

The core of our small but vital circle of kindred spirits was the newly established Trio, and its auxiliary members, the Trio wives, that is to say, myself and the wife of the violinist. The pianist was not married. The ruling passion of each member of the Trio was, undoubtedly, music. In K., the oldest of the three by half a lifetime, music had already absorbed all other passions into itself—even his love for me was a form of harmonics. John, the twenty–five–year–old violinist, was still too young and too newly married for that. He also had a lively, though temporarily thwarted, passion for horses. The pianist, known affectionately as "Herbie," was only a few years older than John, but still uninvolved in married love and its accompanying expenses, he could afford to indulge two secondary passions; one for the desert, and the other for the car (as loved and cherished and expensive as any woman), that took him there whenever he felt the need to escape from the university. And it was a measure of his friendship for us that he was always willing and ready to take us with him.

As a worshipper of the ocean, I found the aridity and the deathly stillnesses of the desert oppressive, both physically and psychologically. At the same time, I was visually enchanted by its magical colors; the burning blue of its midday skies, the purple and gold of its royal sunsets, and—resplendent under their slanting light—the chocolate brown and old rose, verdigris green, chalk white and sulphur yellow of the purgatorial mountains that encircle the parched floor of Death Valley.

One night, my need to resolve the conflict between the forces of attraction and repulsion symbolized by the desert, manifested itself in a strange and vivid dream. I recounted it to K. immediately on awakening. K. said, "You should turn it into a short story." And I said, "Before I can do that, I have to dream the ending."

I did not dream the ending. I lived it. And I called the story, *Ocean in the Desert.*

Our daily lives quietly settled into our accustomed, and satisfying, pattern of music making and writing, plus a few hours of teaching for K. Reading was our principal diversion, or listening to records on Herbie's stereo system (we did not possess one), or an occasional bridge game. Pleasures that cost money were limited by our almost invisible income. But the war years had proved that so long as we were together we could live on little or nothing and still be happy, in the deepest sense of the word. And I had not forgotten another lesson of the war; that material possessions burden and endanger the freedom of the spirit. But it was hard not to envy the careless possessors of the stereos, television sets, washing machines, air conditioners, and many other desirable luxuries that they regarded as necessities. But, thanks to Eldon's extravagance, we did have one big luxury that for K. really was a necessity—the car.

One Sunday morning, soon after we moved into our new home, I asked K. to drive me into the town for High Mass at the Catholic church. We had not been to a Catholic Mass since we left Hungary, but K. said, "Yes, of course," as if it were the most natural request in the world. I said, "I don't suppose the music will be up to much." "Neither do I," he said. "I'll wait for you in the car; I can read the Sunday paper and do the crossword puzzle."

I sat up near the front, just behind a row of black-winged nuns. The celebrant, who also preached the sermon, which was short and very simple, had a marked foreign accent that was vaguely familiar to me—could it be Dutch? Short and plump, there was nothing ascetic in his appearance, but there was something about him, and the reverent, unhurried way in which he performed the beautiful age-old ritual, that impressed and moved me.

When the Mass was over, I remained in my seat until the rest of the congregation had filed out. Then I went and knocked on the sacristy door. It was opened by one of the altar boys. I asked if I might have a few words with the priest. "Someone to see you, Father," said the boy, and the priest, who was still wearing his cassock—the usual garb of Catholic priests in Hungary—came over and asked me what he could do for me. I had acted on impulse, and impulse answered for me, "I want to become a Catholic."

His response was unexpectedly cautious. "That is a wonderful thing," he said, looking at me very hard, though not unkindly. "But first we will have to talk—let me get my appointment book."

He suggested a date more than two weeks ahead. I must have

looked disappointed, for he said, "I want that you should have
time to think, and to pray, before taking even the first step in so
serious a matter."

I did not want to wait so long, now that I had already taken
what I thought was the first step. But I respected him for being
perceptive enough to recognize an impulsive act when he saw one,
and for not taking advantage of it to gain a convert.

K. was waiting for me on the church steps, and looking rather
worried. "Where have you been?" he asked, "When you didn't
come out with the others, I looked inside the church and I couldn't
see you anywhere."

"I was in the sacristy. I went to see the priest. I'm going to
become a Catholic—if they'll have me."

The car was parked under a tree on the other side of the road.
We walked over to it in silence, arm in arm, hand in hand. But I
sensed in him an unspoken apprehension, and before he started
the car, he leaned over and kissed me very tenderly—almost as
though he were bidding me goodbye.

During the fallow period when uncertainty over the fate of my
first novel kept me from starting a new one, I wrote a long poem
on the theme of death and atonement, which I called *The Mimosa
Tree*. It came straight from the depths of my subconscious mind
and contained pagan symbolism and imagery that were not part
of my conscious intellectual equipment. I set it down just as it was
"given" to me. Its rhythms had a kind of incantatory magic, that
was immediately diminished by any attempts to remove what
seemed to me to be flaws. I found a similar resistance to being
polished, or revised, in another long poem I wrote during the
same period; a savage, undisciplined poem based on a dreamed
vision of Hell as a modern apartment house; a luxury dwelling
filled with the living dead.

Rereading these two poems now, I perceive their meaning
more clearly than I did when I wrote them; and they provide a key
to my state of mind when I knocked on the sacristy door and
announced without premeditation that I wanted to be a Catholic.
I see this impulsive act as part of a much larger pattern, an
infinite pattern "with no beginning and no ending," on which I

wrote another poem, much calmer and more accepting, called *The Sleepers*.

The Luck (Fate? Providence?), that had put the MS of my first novel into the best possible hands, now did the same for my troubled spirit. Had I searched the entire State of California for the priest best qualified to lead me into the Catholic Church, I doubt if I could have found anyone better suited to the task than the unassuming little Dutchman, a humble curate, who had had the good sense to make me wait and examine my motives.

Not that waiting weakened or changed my resolve. But reflection gave me an inkling that becoming a Catholic might be less easy, less simple a matter than I had imagined. And looking back, I believe that had my instructor and guide been an average Irish-American parish priest, I would have found it impossible.

What immediately broke down all barriers between me and the total stranger who told me to call him Father was our common experience of the war in Europe, not only of its dangers and privations, but of living in a country occupied by the Nazis; and the revelation that afforded of the myriad ways in which humanity responds to inhumanity. We had both seen human nature, including our own, stripped of its civilized outer skin, and had come face-to-face in broad daylight with evils that a priest usually confronts only in the veiled security of the dark confessional box. This all-encompassing moral and physical experience that I and my instructor had in common provided a point of departure for our discussions on good and evil, sin and redemption, and made the process of conversion more like a process of reconciliation between two points of view on agreed upon truths.

We met twice a week, facing each other across a large desk in the dreary rectory parlor. A crucifix hung on the wall above my instructor's head, and behind me, on the opposite wall, was a tasteless representation of Christ with a bleeding heart—which I was grateful not to have to look at. Our sessions were supposed to last for one hour, but they frequently lasted for two, or even three.

Father John (which was what most people called him, for his last name was hard to pronounce), was a highly intelligent, highly literate man, and I think he found me as interesting as I found him. Our conversations were sometimes heated, but never dull. And little by little, he elicited from me the story of my life with all its follies and failures, before and after that central experience which needed no explaining. He led me as cleverly as any psychiatrist back through the dark ages that I wanted to forget, and out into the early morning sunlight of my country parsonage childhood. He ended up knowing more about me and my interior life than anyone alive, except K.

It was only when all troublesome problems of doctrine had been overcome (in some instances by my willingness to accept as holy mysteries what I could not accept as rational facts), that my instructor warned me that my marriage to K., a divorced man whose former wife was still living, could be a serious impediment to my reception into the Catholic Church.

This possibility had never entered my mind; the idea that our fourteen years of legal, harmonious, and absolutely faithful married life could be condemned by God, or anyone else, as "living in sin," was too utterly preposterous.

My reaction to Father John's last-minute raising of this unforeseen obstacle, that resembled the unexpected last-minute withholding of a long-promised passport, was a furious outburst of indignation, of which Father John, as the bearer of the bad news, had to take the brunt. I reproached him bitterly for not having brought up such an important matter sooner—he had known almost from the beginning that K. had been divorced. Why then had he wasted his time and mine in hours of useless preparation for an end that he believed to be unattainable—at least on my terms.

Obviously hurt, but patient, he heard me out. Then he said quietly, "I think you know that whatever happens our time was not wasted. Now, if you have to make a choice you will not make it blindly."

"If you mean a choice between my husband and the Church," I said, "I think you know that there never has been and never will be any question as to which I would choose."

"It may not come to that. Canon Law, like any other legal code, has its exceptions, its technical loopholes."

This well-meant effort to reassure me only made me angrier. "Technical loopholes! Don't talk to me about technical loopholes! If I enter the Church it won't be through a loophole! It will be through the front door or not at all."

Although I regarded him as a friend as well as a mentor, I had always treated him with the utmost respect. And here I was shouting at him. He said nothing, but he looked so sad, so distressed, that I felt as if I had shouted at Christ Himself. I said, "I'm sorry, Father. I lost my temper. Please forgive me. But you do see, don't you, that this is a matter of principle, of not degrading something beautiful, something of great value?"

"Yes," he said, "I know that. But let us not talk about it now. Instead, I suggest that you go into the church and meditate for a while, and ask the Blessed Mother to help you. I will see you next week at the usual time."

I did as he suggested and went into the church, which I probably would have done anyway. As a young girl engaged in the inevitable, if only temporary, warfare that goes on between adolescent girls and their mothers, I had found the chill and musty interior of my father's tiny, eleventh-century church to be both a refuge and a good cooling-off place. It also fostered the religiosity that is often mixed up with, and sometimes replaces, the developing sexuality of strictly brought up young girls. Later, when the conflicts of adolescence had been superceded by the far more deadly conflicts of an incompatible marriage, the old habit had revived, and I had sought similar oases of calm in other churches, most of them being the great Roman Catholic cathedrals of Europe; in which I found a synthesis of the mystical, the sensuous, and the aesthetic.

Later still, widowed, and living in London, I found the same indescribable consolation in the plainer and less mysterious Brompton Oratory—the only Roman Catholic church within easy reach of where I lived. I did not go there to hear Mass, or the solemnly chanted litanies; I preferred to drop in when nothing was going on, and the comforting silence was unbroken. I would kneel down facing a plaster statue of the Virgin Mary surrounded by flickering candles and votive lights, to which I would add my own little flame. The petition it carried up to Heaven was always that K. and I would some day come together. Believing, as I so fervently did, in the spirit rather than the letter of the law, I could see no reason why the "Virgin most merciful, Mirror of justice" should not intercede on our behalf. And on that miraculous morning when I sat on the grass in Green Park and read the letter from K. in which he said that his wife had agreed to set him free, the first thing I did on my way home was to thank the Virgin Mary for her help and lay flowers at her feet.

And now? Now I was being asked to believe that the justice she mirrored was only the rigid human translation of God's living poetry. Had I been deceiving myself all along? Had I allowed myself to be drawn back to God by my faith in the poetry of His justice, only to have the door of His Church shut in my face by His official translators?

I could not and would not believe it.

Pleading my cause with my patient instructor, I gave him a hard time, that was all the harder because in his heart he too believed in a Heavenly justice that transcended the narrow confines of the law that he, as a priest, was bound to uphold.

"If God is love," I argued, "then He must be the source of love. And how can He condemn what is part of His own nature?"

"That depends on your definition of *love*."

"I can no more define love, Father, than you can define God. Like God, love *is*, or *is not*. And the love that *is* between me and K., and the manner in which it has evolved over fourteen difficult years, comes as close to perfection as any human love can."

"That," my instructor said, with a little smile, "is visible to the naked eye."

"And as far as I am concerned, Father, you know what lies in the invisible background; you know the state of despair I was in when K. first entered my life. But I did not tell you what *his* life was like; what despair he was in. We saved each other, Father. We were *both* drowning."

This conversation took place around New Year's 1951, and was followed by many more; most of them on the nature of love and the point at which sacred and profane love can unite and become one. They were not fruitless discussions. Six weeks later, on the seventeenth of February (the twenty-ninth anniversary of my mother's death), I was baptized into the Roman Catholic Church, and given the name of *Mary*. K. was there with me, and so were a few of our closest friends. When the ceremony was over, K. embraced me and kissed me, just as he had on our wedding day, and we walked down the aisle arm in arm, hand in hand.

4

Celebrations

I am deeply distressed, my dear Theresa, by the step you have taken. That you should have seen fit to desert the faith in which you were baptised and confirmed, and in which both your father and your grandfather were ordained priests, to become a Roman Catholic(!), is, I frankly confess, beyond my comprehension. . . .

First Hungary, then America, and now Rome. Of all these steps I had taken beyond the pale—as my dear old military-minded uncle defined that nebulous frontier, the last was, for him—as for my numerous other paternal relatives (my father had eleven brothers and two sisters)—the least forgivable. Nothing could cause that staunchly Protestant North Irish family clan more embarrassment than a defection to Rome.

This bachelor uncle, who had done what he could to replace his older brother, the father I had lost when I was still young enough to need one, was the only member of the clan with whom I was still in close touch. So the others had left it to him to express the collective disapproval. But once he had said what he felt it his duty to say, he never brought up the subject again, and continued to send his heretical niece the family news and a regular monthly package of Twining's Earl Grey tea, until he died at the age of eighty-six.

I encountered a less rational, because less politically justifiable, hostility to "Rome" in the Baptist University. Warned by an

431

unbigoted colleague that my conversion to Catholicism might have an adverse effect on K.'s position, I tried to avoid any mention of religion. But one of the similarities between a religious conversion and a great human love is the urge, in each case, to proclaim it from the housetops. And concealment of it, for whatever reason, dims its glory at best, and at worst, can turn it into a shameful secret.

A little scene comes to mind. The stage is the kitchen of a building being used by the Faculty Wives' Club for a special occasion; a talk given by a prominent preacher from out of town. A tea will follow the talk, and the members of the refreshment committee, of which I am one, are busy preparing it in advance. My fellow-workers are nice, friendly women with whom I have almost nothing in common; least of all the subject that they are discussing while they work, which is, not surprisingly, preachers, and the respective talents of those who can be heard every Sunday in the God-fearing little town's inordinate number of churches. All but three of them fall into the general category that my Anglican family dubbed "Nonconformists," and as such are, apparently, acceptable to one another, which Catholics, and even Episcopalians, are not. What I don't yet realize is the nature and the extent of the difference between the Church of Rome and the Church of England in the eyes of those who are outside both folds.

What do *I* think of the various preachers? Trapped, I have to admit I have never heard any of them preach. One of the women comes, unintentionally, to my rescue, "But of course, you're English—you must be Episcopalian."

Discretion whispers, "Leave it at that," and is thrown to the winds. "No. I'm a Roman Catholic." (There! I've said it, I've shocked them, and I'm glad!)

They can't quite believe it. After a moment of stunned silence, I am given a chance to retract, or at least to modify my bald statement.

"You don't mean, do you, that you are actually a *practicing* Catholic?" The speaker is a Dean's wife, and the head of our committee.

"Yes. That's exactly what I mean—in fact, I'm a recent convert."

From the change of expression on the nice, hitherto friendly faces, I see that I might just as well have confessed to being a practicing witch.

Someone looks in, "How are things going? The talk is due to begin in five minutes."

"Come on, girls!" says the Dean's wife, "It's time to start the coffee machine."

I offer to do it.

"Thank you. But don't bother. If you're all finished with the sandwiches, why don't you go in and sit down?"

The lady is very polite, but the message is clear. I am no longer "one of the girls."

"Do you mind?" asks K. on the way home.

"Not in the least—so long as it doesn't rebound on *your* head."

"Don't worry. It's much less dangerous for you to be caught going to Mass than for me to be caught smoking on campus."

But the cigarette ends in the coffee tin that he uses in the rehearsal room as a "silent butler" represent a far more serious threat than any university sanctions. He knows what I am thinking. "Don't be cross," he says, "I've been very good. I've only smoked two in three hours. I cut each of them into three pieces, to spread out the pleasure. That Tchaikowsky Trio we're doing may be effective, but it's altogether too long. . . ."

Effective is a key word in programming, and subject to many different interpretations. For K. it is not entirely free from a taint of concession, of lowering artistic standards to please an audience. Which is what the Philistine president wants him to do when he asks the trio to play for convocation. "But what the occasion calls for," he tells K., "is something *heartwarming*—for heavens' sake don't try to *educate* the students!"

Aside from K. whose happiness was bound up with mine (as mine was with his), the one person who truly rejoiced over my conversion to Catholicism, and understood it, was Justin. He knew, of course, that he had had a hand in it; he had given me the right books to read at the right time, books that introduced me to the thinking of intellectual Catholics, which helped me to overcome my own intellectual doubts of what I had already accepted emotionally. And he knew that our shared requiem for Eldon had been a climacteric, but he could not know how precise that turning point was, that it hinged on a single utterance, an exact moment; the moment when Justin said, "Catholicism is the sinner's religion."

He drove down from Los Angeles one weekend to tell me how happy he was on my account, and to give us some good news of his own.

He had been undergoing a new kind of physiotherapy that had done away with his need for a wheel chair, and as a result of his new-found mobility, he had landed a long-sought-after writing assignment in Europe. His flight to London was already booked, and he was jubilant. But he was so vague about his ultimate destination, and the details of his assignment—"A series of articles... possibly a book...."—that K. and I, plot-conscious, like all postwar arrivals from Eastern Europe, thought we detected a sulphorous whiff of cloak and dagger in the air. Be that as it may (we never found out for sure), Justin did not return from that assignment alive. Less than three years after his friend's death on a Hollywood hill, Justin encountered his own in a troubled European city. And his requiem was a Solemn Memorial Mass, celebrated, most fittingly, in the Los Angeles church to which he had gone so often to confession in the past.

I told my children about my conversion only when it was a *fait accompli*. Not that they would have offered any opposition; for one thing they knew that trying to stop me from doing anything that I had made up my mind to do was a waste of time, and for another, they had experienced enough tyranny, both domestic and political, to set a high value on personal freedom, and believed that parents as well as children should be allowed to live their own lives in their own way. But that did not mean that they were indifferent to this step that I had, to use my uncle's phrase, "seen fit" to take without consulting them.

Genevra was skeptical; not of my sincerity, but of religious experiences in general. Despite her ecumenical christening on board the British merchant ship docked in Rotterdam, she was against all organized religions; but she was not intolerant. Other people could worship whatever gods they chose—so long as they did not attempt to impose their religious beliefs on her, or worse still, on her children. By the same token, she did not try to foist her own unbelief on me; even though she considered the consolation that I had turned to (as she believed) in my pain over Eldon's death to be a mere placebo. All this was understood, but left unspoken. We had no opportunity for a face-to-face talk at that time. Lured by the promises of an over-optimistic entrepreneur, she and Károly had left Ojai to chase a rainbow in the desert. An experience that was almost literally searing. Coping with the heat and the various plagues that went with it, including a plague of grasshoppers, with not enough money to pay for the necessary defenses, was wearing out even Genevra's energy and determination. To make matters more difficult, she was pregnant.

Peter was having his troubles, too, but of a different kind. Genevra's marriage was her Rock of Gibraltar, but Peter's was a quicksand, from which he would painfully free himself only to fall headlong into another.

His attitude to life was defensive rather than aggressive (though he had an aptitude for planting occasional darts—mostly verbal—into his antagonist's vitals), and irony was his principal weapon of defense. He would disarm criticism and deflect threatened attacks in advance, by self-mockery. And by the same means he did his best to de-Christianize the religious sense that he had inherited from me. But although he proclaimed himself to be anti-Christian, he was certainly no rationalist—and he was positively irrational when it came to dreams and visions. So behind the gentle fun that he poked at my unexpected embrace of what he regarded as the least rational branch of Christianity, I detected more interest than disapproval, and even a private satisfaction. Whatever my shortcomings as a mother, I could be relied upon never to bore him. And he never bored me, either. We kept up a regular, discursive correspondence, that was like a perpetual fencing match between friends, in which the foils touch now one and now the other, and there is no winner.

Nina, who, as a young girl in besieged Budapest had written in her diary, after reading philosophy all day to the sound of the Russian guns, "I find that I cannot accept Christianity . . ." now accepted my belated return to it via the Catholic Church without question; perceiving it, no doubt, as a manifestation of the personal freedom that she, perhaps more than anyone in the family, so ardently cherished. I had accepted her unheralded marriage in the same spirit. Yet in essence, both her marriage and my entry into the Church were acts of submission to forces stronger than ourselves; and the freedom lay only in the choosing, in the voluntary decision to relinquish certain freedoms.

Seen in the light of its uncanny juxtaposition with Eldon's death, Nina's marriage was an emblem of renewal. But in the long shadow of retrospect, I see that it was also an impetuous leap into an arena, a duelling ground for the two conflicting sides of her personality; the passionate woman, needing to love and to be loved, dreaming of flesh and blood children, and the equally passionate artist, needing solitude and silence in which to create her children of the mind.

For the moment, however, these combatant forces had not yet emerged from the honeymoon fog, and the young couple's main concern was how to make ends meet. They had met (about six months before their marriage) as fellow students at the Hammersmith School of Art, where Philip was completing a course in commercial art, and Nina, who had been awarded a major merit scholarship, was working for her Fine Arts diploma. Dependent on Philip's earnings as a free-lance graphic artist, they had started their married life in squalid surroundings. But when Philip landed a permanent job with an advertising agency, they moved away from their slum to the relative luxury of one large room, partitioned off into three small areas, in a converted Georgian house near Regent's Park. The house was tenanted by various bohemians like themselves, plus an office or two and a hairdressing establishment on the ground floor. And, said Nina, only one toilet for the whole building! A bit of information that called up an image of the apartment on the Calea Victoria in which she was born, and its locked toilets out on the landing. Otherwise, their new dwelling sounded rather like our Californian attic, except that we had more privacy, and, of course, London roofs didn't suffer from too much sun, but too little.

More closely bound up with our immediate existence was Jennifer, who for more than a year had well and truly filled the role of my "American daughter."

In the not-so-distant past, a girl in her sad position would have been expected to live out the rest of her life in a cloister, and later, in the Victorian era, to settle for permanent spinsterhood, good works, and the care of aged parents. And one weekend, when Jennifer drove down to see us, wind-blown and bare-headed in her jaunty convertible, my eyes were suddenly opened, and I saw what my own state of mind had prevented me from seeing up until then; namely, that this vital, emancipated Californian girl was actually in danger of succumbing to the same romantic fallacy of perpetual mourning that had stunted the lives of her nineteenth-century counterparts.

What shook the dust out of my eyes on that particular occasion, I don't know. But I realized for the first time that the aura of general well-being that surrounded her, and acted on us like a tonic whenever she came to visit us, did not come from within, from the spirit, but was a purely physical phenomenon, created and conveyed by the simplest of visual impressions; the excited movement of her arm when she waved to us from a distance, the complementary lines of her long slender body and her sleek, slender-bodied chariot, the flying gold of her hair, even the shape of her sunglasses; and that behind all this flurry of movement and light, was a stopped clock.

That afternoon, when K. was taking his siesta, Jennifer and I had a long talk about life, and what I believed to be its fundamental inescapability—like a task that must be completed, if not by the one to whom it was allotted, then by someone else.

"There is only one tribute that we who loved Eldon can offer him," I told her, "and that is to finish his life for him. To fulfill as far as possible in our own lives what he dreamed for us, which was nothing more or less than the fulfillment of our own dreams for ourselves."

She was quick to draw the right conclusions; to realize that I was obliquely urging her to reopen doors she had closed when Eldon came into her life; to renew her former friendships and activities, and if love, marriage, and children were what she ultimately wanted, not to refuse them in the name of fidelity to the dead.

My attitude upset her, and even made her angry—which may have been a good thing, given the curative power of anger—but even though I had rudely destroyed the Niobe image of me that she cherished, it must have been, at least subconsciously, a relief to her to discover that I did not expect her to remain faithful to my son's memory in any conventional sense. Quite the contrary.

A long period of apparent estrangement followed this visit; a continued silence on Jennifer's part that made me uneasy. Had I made a mistake? Been tactless? Spoken too soon—pushed away from me someone who still needed me? Then, one day, I got a letter from her. I had not made a mistake. She wrote in the warmest and most affectionate terms to thank me for what I had done, and to tell me how right I had been. She had found love again.

Writing the story of one's life, if one does it honestly, is more difficult than writing a novel, if only because one is not in control of either the characters or the events, but only of the words in which one clothes them.

The characters come and go as they please; some to vanish forever after one brief appearance, others merely to wait in the wings for their next scene—out of view but not out of touch. Among these last is István, who has been out of view for about six years (and a couple of hundred pages), but by no means incommunicado.

His link with me is his ritual gift of a dozen long-stemmed red roses, which never fails to arrive in time to commemorate his own Christmas-tide arrival at our gate in 1944. His link with K. is music. But since music plays just as great a role in István's life as it does in K.'s, the long letters he writes to K. in Hungarian are inevitably autobiographical. He is living in Montreal, and although, like the rest of us, he has problems making ends meet, he is standing on the threshold of a long and successful career as a composer and teacher. But it took luck as well as talent to get there.

Less than a year after leaving our battered refuge at the end of the siege, to seek out surviving members of his family in Pest, István had left the country (clandestinely), and had made his way to Paris, where, as that product of war, a "displaced person," he had contrived to pick up once again the musical studies that the labor camp had interrupted. He entered the Conservatoire, and among his notable teachers were Nadia Boulanger for composition, and Forestier for conducting. His problem was lack of money, and the impossibility of getting any from his family in Hungary, on account of the strict currency regulations. Even correspondence between them was unreliable. However, a dependable link was provided by that practical saint, Pater Antal, who had saved István from the Nazis in 1944.

In a letter to István dated January 11, 1948, Pater Antal, who was still presiding over the monastery in Rákospalota, thanks him for his postcards from Paris, but hopes that "they do not represent a financial strain." He goes on to tell of a recent visit to István's family, and how he and István's father and a neighbor, "an old lady with a sweet smile," drank a glass of wine together, and although they did not see eye to eye on everything, had a "peaceful discussion."

The last two paragraphs of this letter (in a literal translation from the Hungarian made for me by István, who has kept all Pater Antal's letters to him), are illuminating; reflecting as they do the attitude of the Catholic Church to the persecuted members of a different religion, even after the threat of death has been removed. Here they are:

> I promised to your father, when he visited us [in the Monastery], that one way or another I shall try to get some help to you. I have to admit though, that I cannot find a way for this right now. I would not like to be put in prison, and you would not accept that from me anyway. Should I find a legal and nonperilous way for sending money to you, it would cause us much pleasure. If this should prove to be impossible, we shall be sad, and you will tighten your belt just once more.
>
> Be prudent, dear Pista,* lead carefully your steps in the world, in a manner that avoids dangers, especially the dangers of the soul. I am wishing for you a blessed New Year, excellent health, unperishable cheerfulness, and in your studies constant success, and all other good things.

---

*The diminutive for István.

Some of Pater Antal's New Year's wishes for István were fulfilled, thanks to a foundation that was set up after the war to locate thirty European intellectuals among the displaced persons stranded in Paris without any money and bring them to Canada. Hearing of this through a Jewish organization, István put in an application, and was the only artist in the group of thirty recipients of a Lady Davis Fellowship (all the others were scientists), which took him to McGill University in Montreal, on a grant that would be paid to him as a monthly subsistence stipend over a period of two years. When his two years were up, he stayed on in the music department as a part-time instructor, and eked out his earnings by giving private lessons; and all the time he was composing. One of the compositions he was working on was a piano trio for K., which he dedicated to us both.

But Pater Antal's wishes for him had included all "good things," and one of these unspecified blessings—and a very important one at that—materialized in the form of a young woman aptly named, *Beata.*

So that was where K. and I, and the principal characters in my story, stood, when a telegram came for me from Oliver Swan, telling me that Bruce wanted my novel, "subject to considerable cutting."

Shaken simultaneously by tremors of delight and alarm, I wired in reply: *Hurrah! But I do the cutting.*

It was my first, instinctive, declaration of literary independence; an assertion of my right as an author to deal with my literary offspring, however fractious, in my own way. How far I would have gone, at that time, in defense of the principle, had it been put to the test, I don't know. The author of a first novel, especially one with a kitetail of rejection slips attached, is very susceptible to editorial pressure. Luckily, I encountered an editor who correctly interpreted my mixed signals of *Help!* and *Hands off!* and dealt with me accordingly; that is, with extraordinary tact and persuasiveness. His name was Bernard Wirth, and he brought the double gifts of a good teacher and a good psychologist to his editorial work. He gave me a sound reason for every change or deletion that he suggested, but at the end of five typewritten pages of what he called "sketchy suggestions," he wrote:

> Do what you can by way of following them, at whatever
> speed you work best, and without worrying that you might
> not please an editor. You are the author, who has already
> done a fine job of work in this manuscript, and you are the
> one to decide finally what revisions you can make. . . .

Even allowed this freedom, I did not enjoy picking stretches of
finished work to pieces and rearranging them in a different
manner. I must admit, however, that in most cases the new
configurations were more *effective*. Cutting, whose principal
object was not to improve the text but merely to shorten it,
threatened to ruin it altogether until I remembered how, in the
days of my youth, I had learned the deceitful art of cutting
flowers for my room without disturbing the symmetry of the
flower bed from which I had filched them.

The whole process took me less than three months, and my kind
editor congratulated me both on the "thorough-going way" in
which I had acted on his suggestions, and also on the amount of
retyping I had done—for which last, of course, K. was wholly
responsible!

My working title for the book had been *Beauty for Ashes*, which
came from the Bible, from the Book of Isaiah, in the King James
version, whose cadences, heard every day throughout my childhood, were part of the language in which I thought. But at the
publisher's request, I changed it to conform with the Douay
translation: *A Crown for Ashes*—more familiar to Catholics. I
asked one of our kindred spirits on the university faculty, the
painter Richard Beaman, if he would design the jacket for it;
which he did, after reading the galleys, and deciding that it was
"Not a *Catholic* novel, but a *humanitarian* one!" Although I knew
that this was intended as a compliment, I was tempted to ask him
what the difference was. But I thought better of it.

The last few weeks before publication date—filled with excitement, fear, and a kind of anguish—were comparable in my
experience with the last few weeks of my first pregnancy, during
World War I. And when my advance copy of *A Crown for Ashes*
arrived, wearing its striking jacket, I felt the same pride of
achievement, the same sense of the miraculous, that I had felt on

that March morning in England, thirty-four years earlier, when my first flesh-and-blood child was placed in my arms.

II

Success, like *Effective*, is a word with so many subjective meanings that in itself it is virtually meaningless. When I started to write that flawed first novel into which I poured my undistilled emotions so lavishly that they all but drowned the tiny seeds of art trying to germinate, I defined success as critical recognition, of which, I imagined, financial gain would be the automatic, though slightly discreditable, accompaniment. By the time my manuscript was completed, however, financial gain had become an urgent necessity. And the royalty check that followed publication, small though it was by today's standards, meant so much to us that at first I failed to notice the lopsided nature of the recognition that the money represented, and its significance to me as a writer.

But as the press clippings came in, my delight at the rave reviews from the Catholic press all over the country was tempered by the puzzling absence of any reviews, good or bad, from the secular press. One of the few non-Catholic notices came from *Jewish Bookland*, whose reviewer, Alexander Steinbach, said— among other complimentary things—that *A Crown for Ashes* combined "the poetry of tenderness and terror in a chronicle which should be classed among the finest novels centering around World War II."

Why, then, was it being ignored by the secular press?

I had to ferret out the answer for myself, since nobody, on either side of the fence, cared to admit that any novel issued under the imprint of a strictly Catholic publishing house would almost certainly be ignored by the regular literary reviews on the assumption that religious fiction is, by definition, bad fiction. This was a disturbing discovery. As a newly converted Catholic, I was happy that my book should be so favorably received by Catholics everywhere. As a new and impoverished author, I profoundly appreciated what Bruce had done to promote my work; no publisher could have launched it more enthusiastically. But my religious conversion had not, it seemed, purged me of ambition. I wanted a wider audience for what I had to say, and I was determined to get it—with Oliver Swan's help, which in my unregenerate pride, I took for granted, but did not undervalue, then or ever.

My total earnings from *A Crown for Ashes* amounted to a little over three thousand dollars. To us, living on a shoestring as we were, and a frayed one at that, this represented a small fortune; for spending, not for saving. Life had taught me to make the most of what I had while I had it; to live for today, not for an unpredictable tomorrow.

The bulk of this manna from heaven fell into my lap about seven months after my book came out, and just at the start of what would have been our third purgatorial summer in our oven of an attic. Now, at last, we had the means to escape! When we told the notary public's good sister that we would be leaving, she and her husband were so distressed (and bewildered, because we had never complained) that we tried to soften the blow by giving them only the most acceptable of our reasons. We told them the truth— that K.'s doctor had warned him against climbing stairs, but not the whole truth—that one more summer in their oven could reduce us both to ashes, and now, thank God, we didn't have to take that risk.

We found a suitable home, without stairs—at a much higher rent, of course, but the manna would cover that—and two years from now at the most, I thought, my new novel would be finished and more manna would be forthcoming.

The little house that we had leased was still under construction, and we were told at the end of June, when we were hoping to move in, that it would not be ready for occupation until the beginning of August. So K. and I decided to spend some of our newly acquired riches on a month's holiday by the sea. We drove down to Laguna Beach to look for a cottage to rent. So late in the season there wasn't much choice, and the sum we had set aside for this extravagant project turned out to be not enough for the sort of place that we had in mind. The real estate agent, after ascertaining what she called our "price range," showed us a few run-down shacks, nowhere near the ocean, that she described as "desirable." But they aroused no desires in us, so we thanked her for her trouble, and were about to go off to her rival across the street, when she said, "Wait a minute! I have an idea...."

After making a brief phone call, she said, "One of my most

desirable rentals just happens to be available, and I'd like to have you see it. It's the lower part of a lovely English lady's split-level home. Fully furnished. Contemporary decor. Big, glass-fronted living room. Fine ocean view. High efficiency kitchenette—everything you could ask for, even a garbage disposal!"

"It sounds ideal. But is it within our price range?" (Her classified ad style was catching.)

"I'd say that the rent was ... negotiable. Why don't we go see it first and talk business later? There might be some flexibility for desirable tenants—like yourselves."

Aha! So we too had negotiable assets. K. cocked a questioning eyebrow at me, and I let myself be led into temptation. On the way there, we learned that this ultra-desirable residence was available only because the people who had rented it for July and August had backed out at the last minute. Light dawned. At least one month's rent would certainly have been paid in advance, and would be forfeit, so whatever the lovely English landlady got from us would be a bonanza.

Lovely was one of those words whose American usage could still mislead me. But the brisk owner of the ultra-desirable, split-level home was indubitably English, and a lady—in the British sense of *that* versatile word. Clipped as a well-kept yew hedge in manner and speech, she said "How d'you do" in an upper-class British accent that sounded foreign, and even a bit ridiculous, to my already Americanized ear.

The apartment, all bamboo-shaded sunlight and fresh sea breeze, lived nobly up to its classified ad description. It was well worth its high rental—which the agent had finally admitted to be more than a hundred dollars above our top limit—and as K. and I looked around it we fell deeper and deeper into temptation.

Meanwhile, the real estate lady was whispering conspiratorially to the landlady, who replied without lowering her cool, clear English voice one iota, "Oh dear no! I couldn't possibly. It's quite out of the question." The incisive tone, the arrogant cutoff of all discussion, even the quality of the voice itself, with its rising inflections, challenged me like a flung gauntlet.

Our well-mannered duel ended in a draw, or rather, a stalemate. But the gage was not really money. It was pride. We parted with handshakes, and polite expressions of regret on both sides, as if each was bound by some unbreakable rule. The real loser was K., like all peacelovers in all wars.

The real-estate lady was clearly baffled by such intransigence on the part of two lovely English ladies. She had no more suggestions, but she took down our phone number just in case something should turn up. Her rival across the street had no suggestions either, so we drove home feeling disappointed and depressed, and, in my case, guilty. Why had I allowed the antagonisms of a long-dead past—stirred up by the tone of an upper-class English voice—to spoil the happiness of the present?

I said to K., "I'm sorry. I should have let you do the talking. There was something about that woman's way of speaking, and her hoity-toity British accent, that put my back up."

K., always philosophical, said that he thought it was probably just as well. We couldn't really afford to spend so much, and Laguna Beach wasn't the only place to go, only the most expensive. Tomorrow we would try somewhere else.

Next morning, when we were just about to leave on another voyage of exploration, the phone rang. K. hated to talk on the phone, so I picked it up. "Long distance calling for Mr. or Mrs. Deekerpelly." It was from Laguna Beach, from the real-estate lady, whose message was rendered semi-incoherent by crackles, "... It's yours ... on your terms ... isn't that just wonderful? You can move in right away if you want ... but bring rent with you in greenbacks. ..."

"In *what?*"

"Greenbacks—CASH! Okay?"

We loaded the car and drove down to Laguna that same afternoon, cash in hand. When we turned it over to the agent in exchange for a set of keys, I asked her how she had managed to change the landlady's mind, and so quickly. "I'll be honest with you," she said. "It wasn't me that did it. It was your lovely accent that got to her. She called just as soon as my office opened this morning to say she'd been doing some thinking, and if you still wanted her place you could have it. Summer tenants being what they were—and they're always a risk—she had made a mistake in turning down your offer. It would be worth dropping the price a bit, she said, to have someone downstairs who speaks the same language ... and you do talk just like she does, Mrs. Deekerpelly—I guess you must both be from the same part of England. . . ."

K. smiled his enigmatic little smile. In the car, I said, "I don't really talk like that, do I?"

"A little bit, but only a little bit—and I love it. It makes every word you say sound interesting."

Fortunately, the landlady and I shared two other British characteristics: standoffishness and the national ability to laugh at what nobody else finds funny. On the day we moved in, she inducted us into those minor mysteries—idiosyncratic lights, locks, faucets, and what-not—that bestow individuality even on mass-produced dwellings, and showed me how to work the disposal, a luxury gadget not yet in general use, of which she was as proud as I was nervous.

"It gets rid of all kitchen scraps in a jiffy," she said. "You just scrape your plates straight into it."

"Even bones?"

"Even bones. Though I wouldn't advise you to give it a whole lamb leg at one go—it might balk at that."

Did we want the phone connected? No . . . we wanted to be on a desert island. She looked doubtful. "Oh well . . . I suppose you could use my phone in an emergency. . . ." And, rather to my surprise, she took us outside and up a rickety flight of steps, almost wholly concealed by bougainvillea, to her deck, which looked like an illustration from *Better Homes and Gardens* and provided our living room with a decorative roof. Both her kitchen and her living room had glass doors opening onto the deck, and she showed us under which pot of geraniums we could find the keys if she was not at home; a mark of confidence in us that made me like her much better.

"And now that you know all the ins and outs," she said, "I shall leave you to yourselves." Which she did, and not merely for the moment. She would pass the time of day with us if we chanced to meet coming or going, which was seldom, since we had separate entrances. But she never invaded our desert island, and we deeply appreciated it. Even on holiday, K. and I maintained the discipline—the regular, if modified, working routine that keeps creativity alive even when dormant, and artistic performance up to scratch. We wanted no uninvited company to upset the delicate balance of work and relaxation—during which the work is quietly carried on in the realm of the subconscious.

We would rise early and work until noon. Then we would eat a light lunch and take an hour's siesta. When the dangerous sun was safely past its burning meridian, we would drive to an unfrequented beach and bathe body and soul in the white surf and the grayish, glistening sand. On our way home, at about five o'clock, we would stop at the supermarket to buy something for supper, and a copy of *The Los Angeles Times*—our daily dose of reality, to be shared and discussed over a pot of soothing Earl Grey tea, thanks to my faithful uncle. The murder and mayhem digested, and the crossword puzzle solved, K. would sit down at the typewriter, to type out what I had written in longhand during the morning, and I would prepare our supper. Later, when the dishes were done and I had signed off from domestic duties for the day by turning on the disposal, we would slide back the screens from the tall windows and sit in the fresh, unobstructed evening air watching the sun fall into the sea, and sipping the sweet, strong, powdery black coffee that K. liked. The tinkle of glasses, laughter, and English voices would drift down from above, like the cool summer rain of England, to deliver the all-too-familiar accusation of being in the wrong garden.

On one such tranquil evening, I had just turned on the disposal and was waiting for it to finish its work before I joined K. at the window, when a muted conversational buzz on the upper deck abruptly changed to hysterical shrieks, and frantic calls for me from the landlady. What on earth . . . ? I rushed out and ran up the rickety stair to the deck, two steps at a time, to be slapped on the face at the top by something cold and slimy. An exhaust pipe at the corner of the house was spewing liquified garbage all over the gaily-striped cushions and chairs, the tray of cocktail tidbits, and the guests—two prim spinsters who ran a tea shoppe in town . . . it was pure slapstick farce. . . .

"Don't laugh," the landlady said, "it's *your* garbage."

"But it's *your* disposal!"

K. must have turned it off, for it suddenly stopped erupting. The landlady and I looked at each other, grinned, and fell into fits of helpless laughter—in which the tea shoppe ladies did not join.

While they were in the bathroom washing my garbage out of

their hair, I helped the landlady hose down the deck. "Well," she said, in her crisp, matter of fact way, "it's a jolly good thing that I wasn't entertaining the Duke and Duchess of Windsor."

The plumber who came next morning to see what the trouble was admitted that it was in the installation, absolving me of all blame. The faulty job had been done, he said, by a careless assistant who was no longer working for him.

"That has nothing to do with me," the landlady told him. "It is your responsibility to put it right."

When he sent her a bill for forty dollars (I was with her at the mailbox when she got it), she said, "Well! Of all the bloody cheek! *He* owes *me* forty dollars! His incompetent work has already cost me that much in cleaner's bills!"

Her words pressed a memory button in me, and I laughed. She looked at me coldly. "I'm sorry, but I fail to see the joke."

"That's because you haven't heard it yet," I told her. "I was laughing at something I suddenly remembered—it's about a man called Archibald Clark Kerr."

"*Ambassador* Clark Kerr?" Like many British expatriates who can never quite cut the umbilical cord, she had a wide but superficial acquaintance with members of the British Diplomatic Corps; no matter where she lived or how far she traveled, she always "kept in touch." And I mentally placed her in the category of visiting British subjects in foreign capitals whose letters of introduction rate an invitation to lunch, but not to dinner.

"Yes," I said, "that's the one. But when I knew him he was only a minister. He was in charge of the British Legation in Santiago de Chile, and everyone called him *Archie*."

"Oh ... Yes ... He had a young Chilean wife, didn't he, who ran off with an attaché, or something of that sort?"

I could have told her a lot about Archie's *coup de foudre*, about his whirlwind courtship of a Chilean girl almost thirty years younger than himself—a girl who looked like a rare and exquisite variety of orchid—and about their romantic, stormy, but ultimately enduring love for one another. But I didn't want to, and anyway, it was irrelevant. The memory evoked by the plumber's outrageous bill was not about Archie's beautiful wife, but about his dog.

When Archie took up his post in Santiago, he was in his mid-

forties; a charming, witty man who wryly proclaimed himself to
be a "confirmed old bachelor"—partly, no doubt, as a way of
defending himself against wily British matrons with marriageable daughters. But he was more than half in earnest. Aside from
the dinners and receptions that he was obliged to give on a lavish
scale, his way of life was simple and ascetic to the point of
eccentricity—for a man in his position. He was not cut out of the
usual diplomatic cloth, which endeared him to my husband, his
vice-consul, who wasn't cut out of it either, but offended those who
expected His Britannic Majesty's representative abroad to
be as close a replica of His Majesty himself as possible. Archie
was nobody's replica. He was a great human being in his own
right.

"Before he got married," I said, "his closest companions were
his two dogs—a pair of Alsatians. . . ."

One of them was a sneaky, ankle-nipping female who treated
every legation visitor as a potential burglar. The other was a
bounding, good-tempered male named Hodge, whose absolute
trust in the human species made him no good as a watchdog. So on
weekends, when Archie, and everyone who was anyone, went to
the Country Club to play tennis and swim and throw dice for
drinks, he would leave Mrs. Smith at home to deal with the
burglars, and take Hodge with him. The club rule was that dogs
must be kept on a leash, which Archie thought was absurd—at
least where Hodge was concerned. What harm could he do? He
had never bitten anyone in his life! So when Hodge got bored with
being tied up, Archie would let him loose for a run, and the club
manager, who didn't have the nerve to challenge Archie head on,
put up a lot of new notices in conspicuous places, like, MEM-
BERS ARE REMINDED THAT DOGS MUST BE KEPT ON
A LEASH AT ALL TIMES. Or, ABSOLUTELY NO DOGS IN
THE POOL!

Although Hodge was a bit spoiled, he was intelligent, and
Archie had made it quite clear to him that the pool was taboo. But
one pantingly hot afternoon he decided to chance it, and plunged
in when Archie was not looking.

"It was just like the other evening, up on your deck. Everyone
started to shriek—you'd have thought that Hodge was a crocodile.
. . ."

The landlady waited for me to stop giggling. (I never could tell a funny story without laughing all the time.) Then she said, "Well?"

"Well . . . Archie hauled Hodge out of the pool, cuffed him, put him on the leash, and apologized to everyone on his behalf—and that was that."

"How amusing," the landlady said in a tone that conveyed just the opposite. "Well, I'm afraid I have to go now."

"Just a minute," I said, "let me finish the story." As I gave her the relevant bits in a few words, her bored look changed to a wicked grin. "Thanks for the tip," she said.

By plunging into the sacred pool, Hodge had delivered his master into the hands of the club manager; given him the power to punish Archie for his arrogant disregard of the club rules without having to confront him man to man. The country club management sent an enormous bill to The British Legation for "the unscheduled emptying, cleaning, and disinfecting of the club swimming pool after its prohibited use by a dog belonging to His Britannic Majesty's Minister."

Archie responded, of course, with a personal check. But not for the total amount claimed. He deducted the cost of disinfecting and shampooing his dog after its "insalubrious immersion in the club swimming pool." After which he proceeded to tell the story to all his friends (and enemies) as a joke against himself; a diversionary tactic that he used with great skill in a variety of awkward situations, and particularly in forestalling malicious gossip about his personal life—and like all outstanding individuals, Archie had more than his share of venomous snakes to defang.

Our extravagant month at Laguna Beach was a transatlantic echo (transposed to a minor key by the intervening years) of our prewar, prewedding honeymoon on one of the Channel Islands. And even at a time, not so very far in the future, when the money that we had so recklessly expended on it would have saved me from a state of humiliating penury, I never for an instant regretted it. The value of a genuine idyll (as obsolete today as chivalry, courtly love, and Camelot), is not to be measured in what our good angel the real estate lady referred to as "greenbacks—CASH, Mrs. Deekerpelly!"

III

Earlier in this book, I remarked on the intimate relationship between emotional experiences and their physical settings, which are often wildly incongruous, but nonetheless inseparable; welded together by the strength and intensity of the feelings involved. And if ever a place was simultaneously at variance with and inseparable from the wide range of emotional experience of which it was the scene, it was the new house that we moved into on our return from Laguna Beach.

An unromantic white stucco bungalow, it squatted in the middle of a square half-acre lot enclosed by a wire fence. No landscaping had been done. In an uncleared corner of the lot behind the house, a few oleanders and a couple of moribund citrus trees had been left standing, otherwise it was a bare plot of newly ploughed land, that reeked of the fresh manure spread over it by the landlord (who believed in organic gardening) preparatory to seeding it with grass. A Scottish engineer, he had built the house for himself and his wife to live in after his retirement. In the meantime it would have to be rented. And he seemed to think that K. and I would be ideal tenants. We were always amazed by our apparent desirability as tenants, since we saw ourselves as undesirably impoverished bohemians. We had a few obvious assets—no children, no pets, and the university seal of propriety. But I think that our real attraction lay in something more nebulous; a combination of the prestige attached to performing artists and writers and the aura of mystery that surrounded all intellectual refugees from postwar Europe, particularly those from behind the Iron Curtain—a place of origin that in my case was rendered doubly mysterious by my British accent.

The Philistine President of the university expressed satisfaction that we had finally moved to a "better address," which I thought rather impertinent, since he had done nothing whatsoever to help bring it about, shown no practical recognition of the musical prestige that K., and the first-rate chamber music ensemble that he had formed, had brought to the university.

Certainly our new home was superior to the old one, but there was very little difference between their respective locations. The pious planners of this still rather primitive settlement on the edge of the orange groves, whose choice of names for its embryonic avenues—Jasper, Chrysolite, Onyx, Topaz—was clearly inspired by the Apocalypse, must have thought that to zone a budding new Jerusalem would be sacrilegious, for millennial equality prevailed. Well-kept homes on neatly landscaped grounds stood cheek by jowl with dilapidated cabins on overgrown lots with goats browsing among the weeds. And within easy smelling distance of our "good address" were the long, low-roofed sheds of a chicken farm, where befuddled hens labored night and day, not knowing which was which, under the false electric suns of a modern egg factory. I pitied these silly creatures but could not love them—such are the limitations of human compassion. A bad enough smell can cut it off at its source.

I defended myself against the odors of chicken and goat (and a hog or two) with a barricade of flowers—all the most fragrant flowers that I could find. What the neighbors called our "yard" and we called our "garden," remained the unmodified rectangle staked out by the engineer-owner, who had no affinity for decorative irregularities; but thanks to the sprinkler system that he installed, it was soon transformed from a muddy waste to an emerald sward, soft and unblemished as only a very young lawn in a state of predevilgrass innocence can be, and thanks to *me*, it was lavishly bordered on every side with that indiscriminate floral mix known as a "riot of color."

All I had to do to enliven the bare white interior of the bungalow was to hang up my pictures, arrange my books, strew around my bright homemade cushions, and adjust the length of my curtains to fit the windows—a job at which I was expert from constant practice.

But first we went out shopping for a gas range, a refrigerator, an air conditioner for the two front rooms, and a desert cooler for the bedroom, which faced south. This was a new experience for us, and great fun. Faced with a dazzling display of labor-saving and comfort-giving appliances in all sizes and shapes, we were irresistibly drawn to the latest and most expensive models. Luckily for our rapidly dwindling funds, one desired object, a washing machine, had been scratched from the list. A pair of kindred spirits with five children, having outgrown theirs, passed it on to us as a house-warming present.

This brand-new stucco box filled with brand-new appliances

could not have been more unlike the fairy tale villa on the Kelen-hegyi út, yet the echoes it evoked were of that time and place, or rather, of how I had felt at that time and in that place. I had the same sense of leaving grief behind me, of arriving at a new point of departure, of a future bright with promise unfolding before me, that I had had in the early days of our married life in Hungary; when the war that shattered the crystal was no more than a tone of voice, a threatening note in a hoarse voice heard over the radio.

When I was about fifteen years old, a gypsy woman at a fair read my palm for sixpence and told me that I would have an unusually long life. Since then, other palmists, astrologers, even a crystal gazer, have all told me the same thing, and I have always been pleased to hear it—even if life was hell for me at that particular time. I have never ceased to be curious as to what is over the next hill or around the next corner, and never ceased to hope for something pleasant.

At intervals on the long road of my life, there are lookout points from which the terrain already traversed can be seen, with all its ups and downs in correct proportion, as on a relief map. And looking back now at the period following the publication of my first novel, I see it in perpetual sunlight; an apex of happiness never to be duplicated. In all future joys, including the joy of achievement, one essential element would always be missing. The price one pays for a great love is that no one else will do.

My timid, and largely unnoticed, entry onto the literary scene coincided with K.'s final establishment of a place for himself in the musical life of the area to which circumstances had brought him, and to which his uncertain health and our shared lack of money, virtually confined him.

In the absence of any really talented students, he devoted himself to perfecting the Trio as an ensemble and developing the inherent musicality of its gifted, but less experienced younger members. Four of his young colleagues were involved at one time or another, owing to sabbaticals and departures. Such a lop-sided partnership between young and old could have been difficult had K.'s musical outlook not remained just as open and adventurous as it was when he and Imre Waldbauer, both in their twenties, had co-founded their famous string quartet, that would introduce Béla Bartók's revolutionary chamber works with brilliance and

understanding to audiences that were all too often outraged by
their disturbing genius. And now, K. was overjoyed when the
contemporary composer, Halsey Stevens (who was writing his
excellent life of Bartók at the time), became interested in the Trio
and composed a new work especially for them, which they pre-
miered in Los Angeles.

For some odd reason, "local talent" is expected to perform for
very much less than "imported talent"—if not for free. In that
part of California, "local" could mean anywhere within a fifty-
mile radius, so numerous small-town cultural organizations, to
which leaflets had been sent announcing the formation of the Trio
and its availability for concerts, were shocked to learn that this
new "local" group was not prepared to perform at cut rates; a
stand that simultaneously enhanced their reputation and limited
the number of their engagements. Which was fine with them—
they preferred quality to quantity.

But when *A Crown for Ashes* turned me into "local talent,"
quantity was what mattered. And as a little-known author in
search of readers, I was that godsend to program committees
with limited budgets, a speaker willing to speak in exchange for
publicity. Urged by my editor to grab all the publicity I could get,
I filled my calendar with engagements to "talk," and autograph
copies of my book, provided that my transport was taken care of.
Which was fair enough at that stage of my career, and might even
have been fun, but for one unforeseen factor—stage fright.

I had suffered from it in my adolescence—amateur theatricals,
even the game of charades had been torture to me—but after
years of living a form of charade, first in the interest of private
peace and public diplomacy, and later in the interest of physical
safety, I thought I had got over it. Yet less than an hour before I
was due to give my first talk, I was lying prone on my bed in a cold
sweat, overcome by nausea and faintness that were purely psy-
chosomatic. I begged K. to call and say that I was too ill to speak.
"I can't go," I said. "I can't possibly go!" But K. knew better. He
called to say that I might be a bit late. Then he brought me a
jigger of straight brandy, and reminded me of some seasoned
musicians we knew who had always swallowed a stiff schnapps
before going out to perform. "As soon as you start to speak," he
said, "your fear will leave you. And anyway, isn't it rather absurd

to be afraid of a few Catholic ladies, after standing up to the Nazis and the Russians?"

The group I was going to address was a chapter of the Catholic Daughters of America, of which I was myself a member, and a more inoffensive and receptive audience could not be imagined. K. dropped me at the back door of the parish hall, where the priest was on the lookout for me. He was not my Dutch instructor—who had suffered a serious illness—but his replacement, another Father John, of whom more later. He said, "What delayed you? Was anything wrong?"

"I felt ill. I still do—it's stage fright. I'm absolutely terrified, Father."

He was not the man to tell me that God would come to my rescue. All he said was, "Don't be silly."

K. was right; my nervousness vanished as soon as I started to speak. But even then, I was not in conscious control. I gave my talk in a kind of dream. It was as if someone else were using me as a mouthpiece. And when the applause at the end jolted me back to reality, I had only a hazy idea of what had been said in the dream. This peculiar experience was repeated, in a greater or lesser degree according to the size and makeup of my audience, every time I spoke in public; though I gradually lost my mistrust of the mechanism that "took over" and delivered my talk for me (not without additions of its own). Especially after being given convincing proof on two separate occasions that it hadn't done too badly.

In one case, an English professor in a Los Angeles college, who heard me give one of my more literary homilies to a group of aspiring authors, asked for a tape of it to play for her creative writing class, thereby conferring on me the seal of "academic approval." In the other case, reassurance came in the form of an ovation given me by a large audience of servicemen and their families at an air base. An ovation that was all the more gratifying because after I had told them, from my personal experience and observation, what it was like to live under the different but equally deadly tyrannies of Nazi fascism and Russian communism, I had gone on—or my independent mechanism had gone on—to warn them not to be too complacent, too quick to say of the Holocaust, "such a horror could never happen here," I told them not to forget that wherever racism is to be found, in whatever form, the seeds of genocide lie concealed within it, waiting for the right moment, the right climate, in which to germinate.

In view of the strong feelings aroused in me by the racial discrimination that I had been shocked to find in the land of the free (for to us, and most European immigrants at that time, America represented one all-encompassing good—freedom), it may seem strange that I have made no mention of the political situation in this country during the six probationary years that separated our initial step toward American citizenship—the taking out of "first papers" immediately after our arrival, and our final attainment of it. The omission is deliberate. We were not preparing to swear allegiance to any particular party or individual president, but to one central and virtually unalterable principle; the American Constitution. And American party politics, whose ins and outs were almost as unintelligible to us as the ins and outs of the ferocious American version of football, only confused the issue; in fact, a belief in their ultimate irrelevance was an essential article of the greater faith. And the same went for that other great institution that I had recently entered: the Roman Catholic Church. In order to recognize and accept its central truth, one had to believe in the irrelevancy of bad popes and unholy inquisitions.

Becoming an American citizen was, as I perceived it, a long, slow, adaptive process, of which the desired outcome was at once an end and a beginning; like the academic degree that crowns achievement, and at the same time launches the student on the far more difficult task of living up to it.

Our final, official, transformation into regular American citizens took place before a benevolent judge in the Superior Court of San Bernadino County on December 15, 1954, six years and ten weeks after eating our first regular American breakfast in the lower halls of Valhalla.

Both occasions were equally joyous, intimidating, and charged with emotion.

Later, at a celebration offered us by a group of kindred spirits, some of whom had been through the same experience themselves, and others whose forebears had been through it for them generations earlier, we discussed the lighter side of a unique rite that wraps up the emotions of a christening, a wedding, and a wake all in one package.

We had done our homework for it. We had read and digested the guidelines issued by the Immigration Service apprising us of what we would be expected to know about the American form of government. We were confident of our overall knowledge, and, of course, of our ability to express it in the English language. (Which, pathetically, some of our coapplicants for citizenship were not.) But we had done a lot of frantic last-minute cramming of forgettable details. We memorized the names of all the states in the Union, with their correct pronunciation (which revealed that linguistically Americans were just as erratic and illogical as the British), as well as the names, dates, and principal accomplishments of all the presidents from Washington to Ike. A feat that I found more difficult even than that bane of my childhood, the memorization of all the kings of England, whose accomplishments were more colorful. Wicked uncles who strangle their nephews, and fickle husbands who cut off their wives' heads, stand out more clearly in the memory than good, family men whose peccadilloes are less dramatic and less obvious.

We need not have bothered. The judge took our literacy and our intelligence for granted, and by the time we came face to face with him, we had already dealt with the only question that we had found difficult to answer: *Have you ever committed adultery?"* Luckily, it was part of a written questionnaire, which gave us time to think it over.

The mandatory six-year wait for citizenship, though irksome and in certain practical ways limiting, had, I believe, great psychological and spiritual value. It gave natural forces and environmental influences time to heal the wounds of exile, and subtly, little by little, to draw the immigrant's spirit away from the past, and into a state of mind in which the new can be embraced without guilt, with no sense of disloyalty to the old, but with, rather, a sense of amalgamation, of mutual enrichment.

That K., whose roots were so deeply embedded in the land of his birth, and who had told me when we were first in love that he could never live anywhere else, should have achieved this joyful acceptance of the new, was a measure of his greatness. But with me it was different. I had been uprooted and set on a wandering path so early in my life that I had never felt completely at home anywhere, least of all in my own country, on those rare occasions when I returned to it. And it occurred to me as I left the San Bernardino Courthouse with my certificate of naturalization in my hand, that I had at last found my rightful place in the world; a place in which people from every country that I had ever lived in, and loved, were to be found, and in which it was possible to retain one's most cherished national characteristics, and still become an American.

After seventeen years of married life, K. and I still had the habit of talking over the day's events—and sharing our most intimate thoughts—as we lay side by side in the dark before going to sleep. But on the night of our "transformation," K. said, as he lay down, "I'm tired . . . So tired . . ." and fell asleep even before I put out the light.

The tensions and emotions of that day's events had exhausted me, too, but I was not yet relaxed enough to sleep. I tried every trick I knew to make my mind a blank, yet it went on working against my will, insisting on examining and defending my theory that the best preparation for the final step we had just taken was, essentially, time. Time, and the daily contact over a long period with Americans of all sorts and conditions; whose effect, if one does not resist it, is like that of the sea on the rough surface of a rock.

If the six-year wait for citizenship, which had seemed to us when we first arrived to be quite unnecessarily long, had been suddenly cut down to three, we would not have been ready for it. No doubt, in the darkness and confusion into which we were plunged by Eldon's death, we would have welcomed the safety and stability that citizenship represented; but accepting it would have been a matter of expediency, not the heartfelt profession of faith that it was now—which had taken the remaining three years to arrive at, and two important milestones on the way; my reception into the Roman Catholic Church, and my debut as a published writer.

Of these two landmark events in my life, the first was the most instrumental in bringing K. into closer contact with ordinary people living ordinary lives unregulated by the university, and to most of whom the rarified musical atmosphere that was K.'s natural element was as unknown as the atmosphere of some distant planet. But there were exceptions to this, one being the Irishwoman who played the organ in my parish church.

In a small parish, where everyone knows everyone else, a new convert is an object of interest and curiosity, and comes in for a good deal of attention, of which I got rather more than my fair share, for various reasons. As an Englishwoman, and as the wife of a professor at the Baptist university, I was doubly a "brand snatched from the burning." And it soon got around that my well-known musician husband, though remaining unconverted himself, had been present at my baptismal ceremony, and had kissed me afterward, right there in the church, as if I were a bride. Moreover, he drove me in to Mass every Sunday morning, and waited for me in his car under the trees on the opposite side of the road. Tall, distinguished looking, shy and silent—but when he did say something in his engaging foreign accent, very polite—he was an object of considerable interest in his own right. But the members of the congregation who wished me good morning as I left the church after Mass, and watched me get into the car beside K. would never have got to know him any better if it hadn't been for the Irish organist. Her genuine love of music, which far exceeded her modest musical talent, won K.'s heart, as her love and understanding of poetry won mine. That and her generous spirit. The mother of a large, young family (her eldest was still in high school) and married to a kind business man who was a good father and husband, but intellectually limited as far as the arts were concerned, she was a poet and a musician *manqué*. K. and I both felt the pathos of it, though I don't think that she herself ever consciously regretted the choice she had made. She was hospitable, in the careless, lavish way of a woman who has so many people to cook for every day that a few more hardly make any difference. K. and I were often invited to her home and would meet there a wide assortment of people whom we would never have met otherwise, including visiting nuns and various parish priests from the area. And it was in her house that we first met the Carmelite Father who set my mind at rest concerning Eldon's soul, and who eventually became my spiritual director; influencing me not, as my instructor had done, through a common knowledge of the world and shared memories of the war, and not, as the second Father John had done, by his intellectual powers and a shared love of books, but by his personal holiness, that was never articulated, but shone from within him like a lamp.

Another acquaintance made, in the natural order of things, through the Irish organist, was the choirmaster, who had a fine tenor voice, and held the position of music therapist at the nearby state hospital, where he persuaded K. and members of his trio to give a free concert for the patients. He found it more difficult to persuade me to undertake a visiting project for friendless patients. "There are women shut up in there who haven't had a visit from a relative or a friend in years. They're tragically lonely; but the trouble is that even people who think it their Christian duty to visit the sick, don't want anything to do with the mentally ill. They're afraid of them."

I wasn't afraid of them. I was afraid of my own memories, of the ghost that would rise to haunt me the moment I set foot behind those locked doors. I said what I used to say to my children when they asked me for something that I didn't want to give them: "I'll think about it."

Unwittingly, the enthusiastic young therapist had set up a conflict of conscience in me, as well as reopened old psychological wounds. Next time he brought the subject up, I said, "You don't know what you are asking of me." Too literal-minded, or too young, even to guess at what I might mean, he said. "I'm not asking you to do anything on your own, I'm asking you to be the first volunteer, that's all—to set an example for others." "And what if there isn't any response?" "There will be a response—if only because no cradle Catholic likes to be outdone by a convert."

There were two other converts in the group of a dozen women who followed my lead, one of them recent, like me, and far more devout. But she was the first to give up. Gracefully aging herself, the animal sounds and smells of the old women's ward proved too much for her—which satisfactorily settled the question of convert superiority.

A mixture of pride and pity kept me going. Little by little I conquered my physical revulsion and began to develop personal relationships with "my" patients, thereby committing the "fatal error" that we had been warned against during our orientation. "Whatever you do," the psychiatrist had told us, "don't get emotionally involved." But that was asking the impossible from me, for whom the whole experience was a highly emotional one. And it soon became clear to me that a little emotional involvement was precisely what these forgotten women wanted—and the only thing that no member of the hospital staff could ever give them. Each one of them needed to believe that there was at least one other person in the world who cared for her as an individual; that I, or one of my companions, came to see her not in the line of duty, nor as an act of charity, but as one friend visiting another whose company she enjoyed. You can't make anyone believe that unless you feel it, and the moment you start to care, it breaks your heart. So as far as *we* were concerned, our mentors were right.

K. alone knew that my weekly visits to the hospital were a form of penance—of atonement—and he made a point of being at home when I got back, saddened and exhausted, to make me laugh at incidents of his day among the Baptists, and recharge my depleted vitality with his warmth and attention—and tea, hot or iced according to the weather. Which went to show, I thought, as I lay wakeful beside him, that no detail is too insignificant to be part of the tapestry of a marriage.

As if he were dreaming the same thought, K. stirred, and groping for my hand, drew it close against his heart; and fell asleep again.

The novel I was working on was about a marriage; but a very different marriage from ours. It was all about the destructive power of jealousy. When *A Crown for Ashes* came out, I had begun work on a projected long novel set in England, and unconnected with Catholicism. It did not appeal to *Bruce* (who had an option on my next book); *they* wanted something shorter and probably, though my editor did not say so, more Catholic. So I put my big project on ice. It would take a long time to write, anyway, and I needed to bring out another book soon. Our bank balance was at zero again, owing to the frequent failure of the mortgage payments on which we depended for our groceries. So I started to work on an idea I had for a short novel in which one of the characters was a Catholic priest.

The reception of *A Crown for Ashes* by the non-Catholic community was surprising. I actually found myself giving "talks" about it in both Baptist and Congregational churches, and expounding on "Writing a First Novel" for the University's "Writers' Week," in the company of established writers such as Joseph Wood Krutch, Wallace Stegner, Irving Fineman, and Leonard Wibberly, making K. very proud of me. The kindred spirit who had brought all this about was a professor of English at the University, who was also a lover of music and an amateur violinist, and the donor of the washing machine—which established a triple link between him and us.

The future bright with promise that I had envisioned when we moved into our new home seemed to be taking shape, and for K., as well as for me. His playing was more beautiful than ever, and our little stucco box resounded with the singing of his cello as he perfected his program for a solo recital; and after that, early in the new year, for some recordings.

His only distress came from Hungary, from his eldest daughter, Mari, whose sculptor husband, the wounded soldier whom she had kept alive in the cellar of their Pest apartment house during the siege, and whose art she had sustained through the lean years after the war by her own hard work, had left her and their three children for a young girl who had not worn herself out in caring for him, as Mari had done. The tragedy was that Mari still loved him.

My eldest daughter, Genevra, had had better luck. The bond between her and Károly was strong as ever. But their jointly faced trials were not over. Károly had had to undergo a life-and-death operation, and when he recovered, he abandoned the elusive rainbow in the desert, and settled down in San Bernadino, to pursue the more prosaic occupation of accounting and preparing income tax returns.

That Christmas was the tenth anniversary of the Christmas on which István had arrived in the honorary garb of a priest to become an honorary member of our family; and arranging his commemorative red roses in a bowl was as much of a ritual for us as the lighting of the tree on Christmas Eve.

On Christmas day, Károly and Genevra and the four children came over, and we all had dinner together on our patio; a Norman Rockwell image of peace and plenty superimposed on an image of war and starvation.

New Year's Eve, K. and I spent alone together, burning a ceremonial candle for each member of the family, and opening our door to the New Year at midnight. It slipped in very quietly, very softly—like sleep.

5

Mid-Winter Elegy

THE winter climate of our particular "orange belt" on the flanks of the San Bernadino Mountains was one of night and day extremes. At noon it could be hot enough to sunbathe, and at midnight on the same day the mercury could drop below freezing. Whenever that seemed likely to happen, the weather bureau would announce it over the radio in time for the growers to get their smudge pots ready, and for people who lived nearby to close their windows and doors, and put masking tape over every possible interstice—just as approaching air raids on Budapest had been announced over the radio in time for the people to seek shelter. But here the people were concerned only with sheltering the interior of their homes from the penetrating smoke of the smudge pots, that would, if given half a chance, sneak in through a loose-fitting sash and deposit an oily black film over every surface. And that, in its turn, evoked another echo, this time from the old country parsonage of my youth, and the paraffin lamps that were liable to smoke if their wicks were not evenly trimmed. It was a job for which I was responsible, and I remembered my mother's exasperation with me when, as a result of my carelessness, her white dimity curtains would have to be taken down and boiled clean in the big brick "copper."

But the scene in the groves was, like the scene in Budapest after the bombs had been dropped, a *Dantesque* vision of hell, to which, in this Californian version, the smudge pots squatting in the rides between the long rows of trees and belching forth smoke and flame like so many stage dragons gave a touch of grotesquerie; a theatrical motif repeated in the movements of the silhouetted workers, that became in the wavering light of the flames the contorted antics of demon stokers.

On one such threatening evening (it must have been between Christmas and New Year's), when a chill was descending with the dusk, I went out to bring in some laundry left hanging on the line. And there, perched on the back fence, was a huge bird, gray and forbidding in the half-light, and uncannily still. It took no notice of me, but remained as motionless as a stuffed bird in a museum. I called K. to come and see it. He said, "It's an owl—my family emblem." We stood there watching it with a sort of fascination, until slowly, deliberately, with an air of arrogant disregard for our presence, it spread its enormous wings and took off in majestic, unhurried flight across the neighboring lot and into a shadowy clump of eucalyptus trees.

I had never seen it before and would never see it again. It must have been taking a brief rest on its way to somewhere else. But it haunted my dreams that night in the form of an albatross. In that semiconscious state between sleeping and waking, in which we dream the only dreams that we remember, I dreamed that I was bound hand and foot by sleep to a bunk on a ship that the ill-omened bird was piloting into an oncoming storm.

About a week after that—five days into the new year to be precise, around six o'clock on another rapidly cooling evening, K. came back from the university tired after a long rehearsal for his forthcoming recital. "Well," I said, "How did it go?"

"Not bad."

This was the highest praise he would ever give his own playing. "I'm hungry," he said, "all I had for lunch was a hot dog. What's for supper—and how soon will it be ready?"

The dish that I was preparing happened to be one of his favorites, pancakes stuffed with spinach, "And there's mushroom soup to start with."

"Ah! That sounds very fine!"

"And I'll try to have it ready in half an hour."

"Good. And while you are doing that, I shall do some typing—how much do you have for me today?"

"About three pages—but they can wait. Why don't you lie down and rest until supper?"

"Because, sweet Tercsikém, I don't want to give you any excuse for not working tomorrow morning."

He was only half-teasing. Like many writers, I depended on certain rituals to get me started on my day's work. And for me, one of the most effective was to see what I had written in longhand the day before in the clearer form of typescript—which showed up its weak points—and to revise it.

So I gave him my exercise book, in which my first drafts were scrawled none too legibly in pencil, and a glass of sherry to sip between paragraphs; and he settled down at the typewriter in his study.

Listening to the click of the keys, as I packed the rolled-up pancakes into a fireproof dish, I thought for the thousandth time what a reassuring sound it was, and, produced by the slightly hesitant touch of those fingers whose particular magic lay in drawing forth heavenly music from the strings of a cello, how eloquent! Proclaiming in the simplest and most humble of terms his respect for my work, and his belief in its value.

The virtuoso cellist was by no means a virtuoso typist, but his lack of speed was more than made up for by his accuracy and his ability to read my handwriting, of which he was justly proud, since English was a foreign language for him even undisguised by my illegible script. Now, after typing for some twenty minutes, he came into the kitchen to show me a word that, for once, he was unable to decipher, and he was even more apologetic about it than he would have been for playing a wrong note.

I said, "Supper's just about ready—all I have to do now is fix the salad."

"And all I have to do now," he said, "is to type the last paragraph."

I was shaking the lettuce leaves dry in a wire basket when the click of the typewriter ceased, and I heard the slight scrape on the hardwood floor of the desk chair being pushed back. And then, a tremendous crash. No cry. No answer to my cry. I ran . . . I flew. . . .

He lay in a crumpled heap in between the desk and the easy chair beside it. He was unconscious, his breathing no more than the faintest flutter. I eased him into a lying position, and put a pillow under his head, and all the time I could hear my own voice murmuring endearments to him, reassuring him, soothing him, as if he could hear me, as if he were still there. I said, "I must leave you for a moment, my darling, to call the doctor."

The call took less than a minute. The doctor was at home—he would come at once. And then, out of my own need, I called Father John the second, who had a fast car and drove like the wind, and all I had to say to him was, "Please come at once."

When I returned to K., an expression of unclouded serenity lay like sunlight on his face. I opened his shirt and laid my cheek against his heart that wasn't beating anymore.

I had left the front door open for the doctor, but the priest was the first to arrive. He walked in unannounced and without asking any questions, he knelt down on the floor beside K. and, tracing the sign of the cross over his tranquil forehead and closed eyes, began to recite, very softly, the prayers for the dead.

The doctor said, "There was nothing that anyone could have done to save him. Death must have been almost instantaneous. But what a wonderful way for a great musician to go! With only a moment's pain, and still at the height of his musical powers!" He spoke as a family friend, a fellow Hungarian, and a great lover of music.

He and the priest went out of the room and closed the door, leaving me alone with my love for the last time. But his spirit had already taken flight across the ocean, to say goodbye to Peter in a dream, and deliver a message from me to my dreaming daughter Nina, and on, invisible as the wind, over the Iron Curtain and into the dreams of his own two daughters asleep in his native city. But his farewell to them, his last, winged message of love and consolation to them, remains their precious secret.

After a time that could have been minutes or hours, Father John opened the door and came in, to lead me gently away from death and into the muted life going on in the next room.

Genevra and Károly are there—Károly has to go back to be

with the children, but Genevra will stay with me. A few good friends are there, too. They embrace me in silence. I am calm and dry-eyed; thinking my pain rather than feeling it, as a surgical patient might whose mental and physical responses have been temporarily disunited by a local anesthetic. Which may account for the clarity of the images imprinted on my memory that first evening, compared with the confused glimpses that emerge from the anguish-ridden fog of the following days.

The doctor has found the bottle of sherry in the kitchen, and brings me some in a juice glass. "Drink it," he says, "it will help you to keep up your courage, and you're going to have to be very brave." An admonition echoed in one way or another by everyone in the room except Genevra, who knows that I need no urging to put on a brave show. Bravery is the armor that she and I have both worn for so long that it fits us like our own skins. But she wears hers undisguised, a constant, open challenge to battle, and I disguise mine with a series of masks, like the mask I assume now, of cool social politeness. "Will everyone join me in drinking a glass of sherry? Genevra . . . you know where the wine glasses are. . . ." The doctor follows her into the kitchen. Kind friend that he is, he is probably giving her instructions on how best to handle a grieving widow still in a state of shock, explaining to her the various stages of grief—with which she and I are both only too well acquainted. He comes back to take affectionate leave of me. He has to go to the hospital. He will keep in touch.

Under the influence of the sherry, the mourners relax; and I start up a conversation about the unusually cold nights we are having, and what they will do to the citrus crop, and whether tonight is going to be cold enough for the smudge pots.

Father John looks ill at ease. He says that he, too, must be going, but first he would like a word with me in private. So now he and I go into the kitchen.

He is wondering whether he can be of any help in making the necessary "arrangements." Do I know where to call, with whom to get in touch? He is apologetic about broaching this painful subject with me, but he thought that my daughter, who doesn't know him, who has never seen him before, might resent his interference in what is, strictly speaking, none of his business.

I understand what he means by "arrangements," and I appreciate his avoidance of that dreadful, two-edged word, *undertaker.* "No, Father. I have no idea of who would be the best . . . person to call."

"In the course of our pastoral work," he says, "we priests automatically acquire a lot of information about the various funeral homes in the area . . . how they do things, what they charge, and so on. One establishment that is always well spoken of by our parishioners happens to be owned by a Baptist. Which allows me," he adds with a faint smile, "to recommend him without prejudice."

He gives me the name and number to call, and I write it down on the pad that I use for my shopping lists.

"I will make the call for you, if that would help," he says.

I don't know what to say. He misinterprets my silence. He gives me a little pat on the shoulder. "You'd rather I didn't. Okay. I understand."

"No, Father. You don't understand. I would much rather have you make the call for me. But I don't want to embarrass you . . . to put you in an awkward position."

"Now, I really don't understand."

"The trouble is, Father, that I don't see how I am going to pay for the funeral."

He can't quite conceal his surprise, but he says, "That's a far more common predicament than you may think. It happens all the time. People don't like to put money aside for something they hope won't take place for a very long time, and can't enjoy when it does. Don't misunderstand me. I'm not talking about people like you and the professor. The survivors of wars have to rebuild their lives before they start providing for their funerals."

In the pause that follows this truism, I think of another reason why survivors are not concerned about their funerals. Those who have escaped death over and over again by the skin of their teeth are apt to develop delusions of immortality. Or a "charmed life" complex.

Father John is a practical man. He tells me not to worry. The installment plan extends to everything under the sun, and with only a little goodwill on one side and flexibility on the other, easy terms can be arranged, and down payments adjusted to fit the particular circumstances.

I am ashamed to tell him that no down payment could be small enough to fit my present circumstances.

After waiting in vain for me to volunteer something, he says apologetically, "The last thing I want to do is pry into the state of your finances. But if I am to help you solve this problem, I must have some idea of what you can afford—in the long run—and of how much money you have at your immediate disposal."

I gather up my courage. "I have a ten-dollar bill and some loose change, Father."

He explains patiently, as if speaking to a child, "I didn't mean in your purse, my dear, I meant in the bank—in your checking account, or your husband's checking account."

"It's a joint account. I have a savings account, too. But . . . just now . . . there isn't anything in either of them, Father."

He stares at me. "Do you mean to say that a ten-dollar bill is all. . . ."

I try to explain, which involves exposing the university's shabby treatment of its "artist in residence," and the shabbiness, amounting to dishonesty, of Eldon's so-called friend, who, though the son of a wealthy family, is constantly falling behind with the payments on which we depend. "He hasn't sent us anything for several months now, which has forced me to use up the last of my savings. . . ."

Father John raises his hand and lets it fall again in a weary gesture that says *enough.* The shabbiness and dishonesty of people who ought to know better is nothing new to him; he hears of it every Saturday night out of the mouths of the perpetrators themselves. Of all the priests whom I have got to know well since my entry into the Church, he is the most worldly wise, and the most cheerfully cynical with regard to human behavior—human behavior, that is, under ordinary, civilized circumstances; his experience of its startling contradictions under extraordinary and uncivilized circumstances having been, for the most part, limited to the fighting male. The closest that this Father John has been to the horrors of war was in the capacity of a wartime naval chaplain, a position that offers little opportunity to observe at close quarters, let alone share, the agony of bombed and persecuted civilians, and those arch sufferers among them, the women and children.

He regards me now with an unsentimental male compassion, and rallies me in the downright terms that he might have used to encourage a wounded Marine.

"You must have been in much tougher situations than this, and God helped you out of them, didn't He? It's thanks to Almighty God that you're still alive and kicking, isn't it? And has the Blessed Mother ever let you down? Well then . . . ? You say your Rosary, and I'll offer my early Mass for your intentions. And let us see you at the rectory some time tomorrow morning—say around ten-thirty, that's a good time for His Reverence. And now I really must be going, or he'll be thinking I've had an accident— he doesn't trust my car."

"What about that call, Father?"

"I'll make it from the rectory, and I'll ask them to let your daughter know just when to expect them. Meanwhile, my advice to you is, go to bed and take a sleeping pill and leave everything to your daughter. Now, where are my car keys . . . ?"

He finally brings them up from the depths of his trouser pocket along with his cigarettes, his lighter, a brightly colored handkerchief, and what looks like a crumpled wad of dollar bills—which last he holds out to me. "Take them," he says, "they may come in handy—you're going to need more than ten dollars during the next few days."

I push them away. "No, Father, thank you all the same, but I really can't. . . ."

"Don't be silly," he says, and with a quick, unexpected movement, he catches and pinions my wrists with one hand while with the other he stuffs the crumpled bills into the pocket of my cardigan. "There! Now they're in the right place—the place intended for them." He opens the back door. "Goodbye now, and God bless."

A moment or two later, I hear the unpriestly roar of his high-powered car as it takes off down the road like the racer he makes-believe it is.

Genevra hears it, too, and comes into the kitchen, where I stand appalled; a beggar on a street corner suddenly brought face to face with my own reflection in a plate-glass window.

My daughter asks as she enters, "Was that the priest who

converted you?" But without waiting for an answer, she puts her arms around my drooping shoulders. "Poor Mother. . . ."

Her embrace is comforting. We are too much alike to get along smoothly in day-to-day living; our very similarities are a cause of friction. But this grief, by subtly changing our roles, unites us. Now, she is the mother, and I am the child.

Out of the fog that envelops the no-man's-land between death and burial, through which I move like a sonambulist, only a few, isolated images, sensations, and echoes of spoken words emerge in recollection. For example, I recall the shock of my discovery that the crumpled bills in my cardigan pocket amounted to three hundred dollars, but the shock only, not the when and the how of it, nor whether Genevra was present to share my amazement.

I find myself in the rectory parlor without knowing how I got there. I am sitting in the same chair that I occupied hour after hour during the weeks of my instruction. But the priest who faces me over the desk now is the pastor of the parish—referred to with jocular affection by his assistant, Father John, as *His Reverence*.

The portrait of His Reverence filed away at the back of my mind is that of a long-faced Irishman; kindly, fond of a little joke, uncomplicated, unintellectual; a preacher of blessedly short sermons about the simpler sins and virtues. But now he is only a voice; a disembodied voice with an Irish accent, and I am striving to take in what it is saying to me through the fog that muffles all my senses.

He is talking about K. Describing him as a "scholar and a gentleman." Recalling the occasions on which he had "so generously" performed for charity functions, and one occasion in particular, when he had gone to the trouble of arranging the *Ave Verum,* and *Panus Angelicus* for voice, cello, and piano; and he and the Irish organist and the tenor-voiced choirmaster had performed them together, "Ah! But that was beautiful! Beautiful. . . ." The voice breaks ever so slightly.

Now, on a steadier note, the voice is commending K. for his ecumenical spirit in lending his time and talent to the causes of a religion that he did not himself profess—"Though anyone who is present at Holy Mass every Sunday already has one foot in the

Church." I cannot imagine what His Reverence means by that; it
was I who was present at Mass every Sunday, not K. But all
praise of K. uplifts and comforts me, like the bright sound of bells
proclaiming the Resurrection, despite the gloom of a cloud-
covered Easter morning.

A little silence falls. The puzzling words about hearing Holy
Mass every Sunday float back and forth in my mind, and finally
prompt me to ask a favor of His Reverence. "Would it be possible,
Father, for you to conduct his burial service . . . I mean a little
service at the graveside?"

One cannot ask a favor of a disembodied voice, and now, as I
look across the desk, the face of His Reverence comes into focus.
He is clearly startled by my request. He has never before been
asked to do such a thing . . . but he sees no reason why he shouldn't,
with reservations, of course—there are certain prayers that can
only be said for baptized Catholics. Yes, under those conditions he
would be willing . . . and, yes, the recitation of the Rosary on the
eve of the burial could be arranged too. "But are you quite sure,"
and he looks at me very intently, "are you quite sure that *he* would
have wanted these Catholic rituals? He was brought up in the
Lutheran faith, wasn't he?"

I can only say what I know to be true; that he would have
wanted whatever brought peace to *my* soul.

His Reverence bows his head as if in response to Divine command. "So be it," he says, and once again a little silence falls.

It is broken by one of those small, unnecessary coughs that
signal embarrassment. "As your pastor, I would like. . . ." His
Reverence hesitates, stops, and begins again, "I understand from
Father John that you have . . . that the suddenness of this sad
event has placed you in a difficult position. And as your pastor, I
would like to offer you a small token of our admiration for your
late husband, both as an artist and as a man. As a matter of fact,
it's in the nature of a farewell gift to him . . . I'm sorry, I'm not
being very clear, am I? Perhaps I'd better let this speak for itself."

He hands me a printed document. But the print is too fine for
me to be able to read it without my glasses. He waits in silence
while I take them out of my purse, put them on, and peruse the
official-looking paper. I read it through twice, very slowly. Not

because it is hard to understand, but because I feel myself on the verge of breaking down.

Of all the tokens of appreciation for his music that K. has received in the course of his career, including the payments in kind, the potatoes and bacon and homemade jam—for performances given in Budapest in the moneyless aftermath of the siege, this farewell gift of a final resting place in a Southern Californian burial ground must be the strangest.

Now, with the lightning displacement of dreams, I am in a large room full of open, silk-lined caskets, and an unknown man in a black suit is inviting me, in hushed, reverential tones, to choose the one I like best. As if I were furnishing a new home, and the objects on display were what they pretend to be—luxurious single beds pillowed with silks and satins, instead of the treacherous oubliettes they really are.

The black-suited stranger, who is evidently the owner of this emporium, draws my attention to one masterpiece of the coffin-maker's art after another, and to please him I duly admire each one, with an inward shudder. But when I finaly choose, as I must, the plainest and least expensive, he seems disappointed, and even a little hurt.

Once again, I hear the small unnecessary cough of embarrassment in the face of a delicate situation. This time it is followed by a little set speech: "The deceased, your late husband, was a great artist. We of this town were proud to have him among us. And now that he has been taken from us, it is my privilege to offer him, as a token of appreciation, a worthy funeral. And I most sincerely hope," he adds, like a spontaneous postscript, "that you, dear madam, will accept it on his behalf."

Now, an echo from my childhood makes itself heard; an echo of my mother's gently admonishing voice repeating one of the rather ambiguous maxims through which she sought to impress on me how to behave: *To refuse a gift is to reject the giver.*

True, says my own ironical inner voice, but don't try to make a virtue of necessity.

Someone, a member of the trio, perhaps, suggests that the

Philistine president of the university should be invited, pro
forma, to be one of the pallbearers, and I am too paralyzed by my
ever-increasing anguish to object. Not so Genevra. *"Mother!*
You're *not* going to let that man put his hypocritical hands. . . ."
The suggestion is dropped. More acceptable names are brought
up. K.'s coffin will be shouldered only by his true friends.

The ritual recitation of the Rosary takes place in the funeral
home on the eve of the burial. Genevra and Károly are there with
me, but not beside me in the kneeling group around the open
coffin. They stand at the back, with other non-Catholics who are
there, like them, out of love and respect for K., and for me, not as
active participants in a ceremony that they cannot believe in. An
appeal to grace and beauty of which I retain only one clear
image; that of K.'s waxen face, whose death-drawn features are
now as delicately carved as a fine intaglio—and as utterly remote.
Everything else is a blur, like a candle-lit scene watched from the
dark outside through a rain-washed window.

It is raining at the cemetery—or is it only the fog that sur-
rounds me finally dissolving in tears? I don't know. My memory of
the burial service is, like my memory of the previous evening, a
blur; with only one clear image; that of the coffin at the bottom of
the grave, awaiting the first handful of earth. An image accompanied by an almost physical sensation of being torn apart in a
life-and-death struggle between a primitive desire to lie down
next to him in the darkness of the grave, and my mystical conviction that he is not there; that his coffin houses only his discarded
and disintegrating chrysalis.

Once again, as in dreams, I find myself in another place, a place
filled with light and life and the warmth of the living, without any
recollection of how I got there. I am in the home of my good friend
the Hungarian doctor, whose Viennese wife has prepared a lavish
repast, with plenty of wine to induce forgetfulness.

I have no sense of time passing. It seems to be at a standstill—
like everything else. But it must be a day later, the day after the
funeral, that Károly comes to take Genevra home to her children.

It is evening—the loneliest time. I watch her getting ready to leave, with a feeling of utter panic, and my sense of abandonment after she has gone is overwhelming. But I tell myself that these, too, are primitive emotions. And the sooner I come to terms with my solitude, the better. Tonight, though, the silence in the house is more than I can bear. I take one of the sleeping pills given me by the doctor, get into my side of the cold, empty bed, and pull the covers up over my head like a child afraid of the dark.

The usual early-morning sounds of our semirural street awaken me at the usual time, and even before I open my eyes, the anesthetic of sleep gives way to an unspeakable anguish that pervades my whole being. My arms are stretched out across K.'s side of the bed as though to hold him. But the dream of his presence there beside me is already beyond recall.

I lie suspended between acceptance and refusal. The sleeping pills on my bedside table offer an indefinite prolongation of the night. But the impulses of morning are deep-rooted, and the voice of reason supports them. Sooner or later, it says, a new day has to be faced, the journey resumed, and delay will not bring back your lost companion.

I enlist the forces of habit, the power of the regular daily routine, the incantatory spell of simple actions performed in unvarying sequence. Showering. Dressing. Making up the bed. Opening the windows to let in the sharp morning air before the sun renders it sluggish, for the skies have cleared and the day is mockingly bright. Putting the kettle on to boil. Stepping out for a moment into the dew-drenched garden to see how the early-flowering bulbs are getting on in their sheltered bed against the south wall of the house.

Back indoors, I sit down, coffee cup in hand, and open the book that I had been reading before time stopped, but now it has absolutely no meaning for me. I put it down and pick up the typescript of the book that I had been writing before time stopped. Now, it is nothing but a bundle of dead leaves. Dead leaves. The metaphor is descriptive of everything that is in this dead house. My treasured possessions, the few objects of value saved from the devastation of the siege, the yellow marble head, the closed and silent grand piano, the cello standing forlorn in its corner, and in the kitchen, the new acquisitions, the labor-saving devices of the New World, all, all are dead. Even the plants, the tulips and hyacinths blooming in pots on the window sill, though manifestly alive in the literal sense, have been touched by death and deprived by it of their ability to communicate with me. Their beauty and their fragrance no longer reach me. Suddenly I am assailed by a terrible suspicion that the death that cuts me off from them is my own; that my essential being has not survived the loss of its other half.

The telephone rings. Suspended once again between acceptance and refusal, I let it ring and ring. Only the caller's extraordinary persistence overcomes my deadly inertia, coupled with a fear that it may be my daughter calling, and my failure to answer would alarm her. But the voice that responds to my reluctant "Hello," seems to come from another world. Which, in a sense, it does. It is coming from El Carmelo, the Carmelite Retreat House, and the voice is that of the rector, Father Patrick; a man who, by virtue of his monastic calling, and the Rule of the Order to which he belongs, is a remote and other-worldly figure compared with the secular priests who are part of the daily lives of their parishioners, and who, themselves, foregather at El Carmelo once or twice a year to recollect their "otherness" and renew their inspiration.

Father Patrick, who has the habit of silence, wastes no words in coming to the point of his call. He has just heard from one of the expected participants in his weekend retreat for women that she is unable to be there, and he is inviting me to replace her. Wisely, he takes my acceptance for granted—not that I want to refuse— but any decision is too much for me; the impulses of the morning have given way to a stifling noon lethargy. "If you can be ready to leave in an hour," he says, "one of the other retreatants will stop by your house on her way and drive you up to El Carmelo in her car. Will that be all right with you?" I am slow to answer. "Hello, are you there? Can you hear me?"

"Yes, Father. Yes. I shall be ready."

"God be with you," he says, very gently.

Time has begun to move again, and I have just made an unbreakable appointment to rejoin its relentless forward movement—and trust in God as to where that current shall carry me.

For the second time this day I enlist the forces of habit. I am going to be away overnight. So... Shut and lock all the windows and draw down the shades. Bolt the back door, after making the catch on the screen door secure. Water the plants. Exchange my house dress for a suit and my sandals for shoes, and don't forget to put my black lace mantilla in my pocket. Finally, pack what I need for the night. Toilet articles. Nightgown. Robe. Slippers. Nothing else. No books. No periodicals. No MS to consider and correct. No pencil. No exercise book. Figuratively speaking, those who go to El Carmelo in search of God's peace must go stripped; disencumbered of everything connected with their lives in the outside world, of everything, no matter how harmless, or even desirable it may be in itself, that can come between the searcher and the object of the search.

El Carmelo is a place of physical as well as spiritual beauty. And its location on the summit of a hill with a panoramic view of the town, the groves, the outlying "badlands" and the winding truck-traveled highway, symbolizes the belief on which its existence is based. The belief that the human spirit can rise above the material world, while still remaining a functioning inhabitant of it. But in order to accomplish this feat, the spirit must, so to speak, keep in practice, and an opportunity to do that is what El Carmelo offers.

It has only recently been opened, and Father Patrick is its founder. The main building was originally the home of a wealthy family, and it still retains something of the ambiance, as well as the physical characteristics, of a comfortable private house built earlier in the century—large rooms with high ceilings and a lot of wood paneling, parquet floors, wrought-iron candelabra, and a wide, graceful staircase with beautifully shaped and scrolled newel posts.

As I step from the sunlit patio into the cool, dim interior with my companion—a little late because picking me up took her farther out of her way than she had anticipated—Father Patrick is descending the noble stairway clad in the ivory habit of his Order, which both adds to his height (and he is a tall man) and distances him.

He comes over to shake hands with us and welcome us to El Carmelo. His manner is serious and a little remote. He is on his way to hear confessions. He makes no reference of any kind to my loss. But his silent pressure of my hand is more eloquent than any conventional phrases of condolence.

A young assistant priest—so young that it seems absurd to call him Father—is deputed to show us to our cells. The retreatants are housed at a little distance from the main building, in a newly constructed, and highly contemporary "cloister," whose sheltered walk overlooks an old orchard and the vegetable garden culti-vated by the Brothers. In the distance, glimpsed through the interlacing branches of the trees, are the mountains, now snow-capped. The town is on the other side of the hill; here, the only reminder of the world below is the sound of the big trucks chang-ing gears at an upward turn of the highway.

The cells are austere, but not uncomfortable. Each has its own "half-bath," and is furnished with a bed, a table, a chair, and a crucifix on the wall over the bed. On the table, I find the schedule that we are expected to follow, and the rules that we are expected to keep. We are all married women, and many of us are mothers, but for the next thirty-odd hours we shall be nuns, conforming voluntarily to the discipline without which nothing worthwhile can be achieved, whether in art or spirituality.

The rule that my fellow retreatants seem to find most difficult to keep is the rule of silence. Yet to me, it is the most basic discipline of all; a prerequisite for the difficult upward leap of the spirit, and in my case, the breaking away from a paralyzing grief, and achieving a sense of unity with a group of women whose individual lives have very little in common with mine, and to whom I can relate only in the larger context of the universal sisterhood of women. They all know who I am, and the nature of the grief I am in—though not its depth—and their emotional support is almost tangible, isolated as it is by the blessed silence. But talk, whether relevant or irrelevant, whether addressed to me, or among themselves, would diffuse it and nullify its value.

There is only one person with whom I feel able to communicate in words, and that is Father Patrick. But within the framework of a retreat, a private talk with him, or with any of the three officiating Fathers, comes under the heading of *Confessions*, which are heard, by appointment, at certain hours on the after-noon and evening of the first day. The structural limitations of this converted private residence determine the unusual settings of these "confessions" that are in fact, protracted conversations, bound by the secrecy of the confessional, but not limited by it to the subject of sins and shortcomings (the latter are taken for granted); they touch on all the woes of the human condition, for which the listening priest does his human best to offer, in his sacerdotal capacity as God's deputy, spiritual consolation and guidance, before bestowing the final grace of absolution.

So perhaps it is just as well that the chapel, an adaptation of what was originally the dining room, is not equipped with those stuffy little boxes in which one catalogues one's grievous faults as succinctly as possible, always mindful of the long lines of waiting penitents praying for patience.

The setting for my confessional-conversation with Father Patrick is the library; a cool and spacious room insulated against distractions, both actually and symbolically, by its lining of books, while a screen set up between the confessor's chair and the penitent's prie-dieu provides an illusion of anonymity that enables them to come spiritually closer to each other than they ever could face to face. And what I am confronting on the other side of that flimsy screen is a quintessential holiness, a flame of faith so pure that it speaks for the existence of God more powerfully than all the theological works on the library shelves put together.

I know, when I leave, with his blessing, that I have been touched by this flame, and strengthened by it. But I cannot foresee that from this half-hour of fundamental communication between me and this Carmelite Father will spring a friendship as undying as my marriage to K. That sixteen years after Father Patrick's death I shall still feel his gentle hold on my rebellious soul, just as twenty-eight years after K.'s death he will still hold his sovereign place in my heart.

They are closer to each other than one might think, these two, the saint and the musician. Their common bond is their dedication to the principle of perfection. K.'s belief that "all great music is holy," translates into Father Patrick's language as, "all true greatness, in music or anything else, is God's."

The fog that had numbed my senses and clouded my mind in the timeless interval after K.'s death, dispersed in the limpid air of El Carmelo, and I saw quite clearly where I stood, and what I had to do. I had crossed a frontier; I stood alone in a deep ravine on the other side of a border of no return. And my only way out of the ravine was to build a stairway for myself with the stones that littered its floor. A combination of landscape and situation that repeated itself in my life like a recurring nightmare. I had lost by death—which is, for good or ill, the only complete and irrevocable loss—my father, my mother, my first love, who was killed in World War I; my first husband, whose life was ruined by that same war; and my youngest son, whose life was ruined by World War II. And now I had lost the man who had comforted me, the man who by recognizing and loving my submerged self had given it back to me. Yet, although I was caught in the same recurring nightmare, the pain of this loss was like no other. It lay in wait for me everywhere, and in every innocent object. It stabbed me at every turn, piercing my heart. Yet in every fiery pang I felt a certain sweetness, as if he had touched me.

From where I stand now, looking back at my grieving self from a distance of almost three decades, I can see wherein that "certain sweetness" lay. I can see that the tears I shed for K. were unique in being the tears of pure loss, unmixed with relief for an end of suffering, unclouded by vain regrets for what might have been, unsullied by guilt—or even that self-indulgent remorse over little things left unsaid that acquire a false importance when the last chance to say them has been lost, and become hair shirts we cling to in expiation of greater wrongs. I know them all, these bitter emotions that muddy the tears of mourning. But in weeping for K., I was weeping solely for the loss of an irreplaceable being, and a voice stilled forever.

6

The Uncertainties of Spring

I

*T*HE loss of a life companion leaves the bereaved one dangerously vulnerable to kindness. Drawn irresistibly back into the mainstream of life, more by my instinct for survival than by any conscious desire to go on living, I found myself being impelled by that same instinct for survival to resist the solicitous hands that were being stretched out to help me. I was like those young people who fight against the parents whose help they need, precisely *because* they need it.

But again like the young, once I had affirmed my independence, at least to myself, my resistance to kindness became less sweeping, though I drew a fine line between what could and could not be safely accepted. At that crucial turning point in my life I had only one conscious incentive to keep going, and that was my writing. It was also my only means of making money. So I decided that whatever might further my writing career should be accepted. But anything that pandered to my weaknesses or fears must be rejected. Which was not always easy. For even unwanted kindnesses have their appeal when one is unhappy, if only because they testify to affection.

There was, for example, the problem of preserving my solitude, which was vital to my writing, while I was still suffering from acute physical loneliness, and being besieged by well-meant attempts to assuage it—offers to come and stay with me until I felt better, and offers from other single women to share their homes with me on a permanent basis.

I had never before lived completely alone. There had always been someone "coming home in the evening," and much of my adult life had been spent at the center of a large household—a circumstance that had been partly responsible for my late start as a prose writer. I realized that my natural genre was not the short story, anymore than it was poetry, but the long novel, and for that I needed long stretches of uninterrupted time. And a relatively free mind.

The solitude *à deux* that I had with K. while I was working on my first novel had been ideal. Each absorbed in our own demanding art, we had worked on parallel lines toward the same ultimate goal—to which he was a great deal nearer than I was. And our closeness fulfilled the human need for companionship without breaking the spell.

But that was a lost paradise. From now on, my working element would be solitude pure and simple; a state that by reason of its basic incompleteness is extremely difficult to keep inviolate, and in those emotion-filled early days it was next door to impossible. And all the more so because its raison d'être, the writing in which lay my psychological and financial salvation, was totally blocked. I would sit for hours with my exercise book open before me, and my mind would remain as blank as the pages. I would read the last pages that K. had typed, then the last chapter, and finally the whole MS from the beginning. But it was no use. The characters in my novel had turned to stone, and I had forgotten the words that would bring them to life again.

At such times I would let the telephone ring unanswered. And if a car stopped at the gate, I would quickly lock the doors and take refuge in my bedroom, and the privacy of its high, curtained windows, while the well-intentioned intruder circled the closed house like an anxious mother bird flapping her wings around an empty nest, and uttering plaintive cries of "Yoo-hoo . . . Yoo-hoo . . . Yoo-hoo . . ."

While this was going on, I would hold my breath. But as soon as the car door slammed and the motor started up, the dam of my pent-up emotions would burst, releasing a torrent of tears, imprecations, and cries of frustration, rage, grief, and rebellion against the fate that had taken away from me at one stroke my

two chief reasons for living; my only love, and what I believed to
be my only talent.

After one of these frantic outbursts, I was lying face down on
the floor in the state of utter exhaustion that followed in the wake
of such storms, when I seemed to hear a voice from very far away
saying something about a dream—and then the dream itself
came floating into my emptied mind; the strange and beautiful
dream whose mysterious beginning I had dreamed four years
earlier, and recounted to K., who had wanted me to turn it into a
short story. But I knew that I could not write it until the
undreamed ending had been revealed to me in some manner. And
now that I knew what it was, I "arose" like some biblical character moved by Divine revelation, and went into the living room,
and wrote as if from dictation my personal requiem for K., the
allegory of the beckoning blue ocean into which he had vanished.
A magical tale, it had magical powers, and the act of writing it
down was the key that released the spell-bound characters in my
novel, and brought them back to life.

The immediate problem of what I was going to live on for the
next two or three months, in which I hoped to complete my book
and get an advance on it, was settled by two letters from the
president of the university, each enclosing a check. One was for
three hundred and forty dollars, which represented K.'s "salary"
for two months (including the month in which he died), and one
hundred dollars extra, from the University Fellows, in token of
their gratitude for his playing at their meetings. The president's
covering letter was full of high-sounding phrases and expressions
of appreciation for K.'s contribution to the musical life of the
university, and how great a privilege it had been to have such an
eminent musician on the faculty. In which he may have been
sincere according to his lights, which were, however, too dim to
show him the discrepancy between his appreciative words and
the pitiful sum with which they were linked. The other, more
generous, check was the result of anonymous donations from
members of the faculty to a "de Kerpely fund" in lieu of flowers
for the funeral, and this he mercifully allowed to speak for itself
and its nameless donors. It said quite clearly: *Where there is*

justice there is no need for charity. But that utopia has not yet been achieved on this earth. So here, in tangible form, is our love.

When I offered, now that I had a little money, to give Father John back his three hundred dollars, he said once again, "Don't be silly. You're not out of the woods yet. You can repay me when Hollywood buys your book for the movies. Agreed?" An airily generous proposal that did not fit in with his circumstances. His stipend as an assistant pastor was barely enough to keep his winged horse in gas. So the relatively large sum that he had lent me on the spur of the moment must have come from some other source, and must, I thought, have been earmarked for some unusual and important expenditure. Yet when I said that I did not want to deprive him of it for any longer than was absolutely necessary, he told me not to worry, I wasn't depriving him. "Whether you give it back to me now or later," he said, "makes no difference to me. I wouldn't spend it on myself. I'd give it to someone else. And I don't know anyone else at the moment who needs it more than you do. So you may as well keep it."

When K., was alive, my contacts with the rectory and its inhabitants had been friendly but distant. I had been on close terms only with my instructor. His successor, the present Father John, was a totally different type of person, and I became interested in him for quite different reasons. My first impressions of him had been formed at Sunday Mass. He was at his best in the pulpit, where he reminded me of my own father, who had had the same gift for taking one of the more "difficult" biblical texts, and illuminating it, within the space of ten minutes, with a brilliant beam of light from an unexpected angle. But in the liturgical part of the Mass, which has many prayers and praises in common with the Anglican ritual, the cadenced chants, whose lineal purity was matched by that of my father's musical voice, were rendered excruciatingly flat by poor Father John, who could not for the life of him keep on key. This drove the musically and poetically sensitive Irish organist to distraction, but did not prevent her from inviting him to Sunday dinner afterward, and it was at her hospitable table that I met him socially for the first time—and found him remarkably entertaining.

He was that rarity among parish priests, an intellectual, with a broad and eclectic mind. But he was shrewd enough to realize that the average small-town Catholic congregation, and especially that indispensable auxiliary corps of devout ladies who keep the flowers fresh and the candles burning, can be suspicious of too broad a mind, and made to feel inferior by too much overt intellectuality. So he concealed his under an easy, bantering manner and a rather puckish humor. But he was always on the lookout for kindred spirits in the Catholic community, as K. and I had sought them among the Baptists. What caused him to recognize one in me, was my casual mention of Aldous Huxley's new book, *The Devils of Loudon.*

After that, whenever we encountered one another socially, he would teasingly ask me, "And what scandalous book are you reading now?" Which would lead us, if the occasion permitted, into a spirited discussion of a wide range of books that included Huxley's latest, *The Doors of Perception,* his earlier, *Grey Eminence* (inaccessible to me when it first came out), Simone Weil's *Waiting for God,* Teilhard de Chardin's challenging *Phenomenon of Man,* and on a less exalted plane, Waugh's *Brideshead Revisited.* And it was on this impersonal level that our acquaintance would probably have remained under ordinary circumstances. But his immediate, unquestioning response to my impulsive call when K. was dying, his respect for the fleeting soul that was not of his fold, his concern for me, and our subsequent conversation in the kitchen, had broken down a whole set of conventional barriers at one sweep, and generated an instant intimacy between us that paralleled on a down-to-earth level the spiritual friendship that sprang up between me and the other-worldly Father Patrick after my confessional conversation with him in the library of El Carmelo.

The pragmatic Father John believed that God helps those who help themselves, and on this premise, he gave me a lot of very sound advice. Although he thought that I was a good writer, he was not convinced that I would be able to support myself solely by my writing. But he knew that I had to try, so he did not discourage me. On the contrary, he backed me up in refusing to compromise my independence as long as I did not have to. And because of this, he became my confidant in everything that concerned my material welfare, and my writing life in particular. So when I got a

letter one Saturday morning telling me that *Ocean in the Desert*
had been accepted by *The Catholic World.* I immediately called
the rectory to give him the good news.

His Reverence answered the phone. "Ah, now, Mrs. de Kerpely!
And what can I be doing for you? Father John? No, I'm sorry to
disappoint you, but he's not here. He's never here on a Saturday—
it's his day off. He says his Mass at the crack of dawn and then he's
off like the wind in that noisy car of his to the Lord only knows
where. And I won't see hide nor hair of him until it's time for him
to hear the late confessions."

When I told Father John about this, he laughed. "His Reverence would give his eyeteeth to know where I go on my days off."

"Why don't you tell him?"

"It's more fun to keep him guessing."

I took the mischievous twinkle in his eyes as an invitation to
hazard my own guess. "Shall I tell you what *I* think?"

"Sure. Go ahead."

"Well, my guess is that you're writing a book, and you go once a
week to L.A., or to San Diego, to work on it, and do the necessary
research for it, in one of the university libraries. But you'd rather
His Reverence didn't get wind of it because he's so anti-intellec-
tual. Am I right?"

"You're plausible. It's just what I'd do if I actually were writing
a book. And you're right about His Reverence. But I'm not writing a book, and you couldn't be more wrong about where I go and
why. There's no money to be made in the carrels of a university
library."

"Money?"

"Yes. Money! Money with which to help people quickly, *when*
they need it—without going through all the rigmarole of a regular charity fund, people who don't fall into the category of 'the
poor' but who sometimes need help badly, people like you, for
example. What do you think I was doing with three hundred
dollars' worth of cash loose in my trouser pocket when I came over
in answer to your call? Haven't you wondered since where it came
from? You know how little we curates are paid . . ."

"Yes. I have wondered. . . ."

"But you haven't put two and two together. Okay. I'll do it for
you. On my days off I go to the races. To Santa Anita, or any other

track within reach where thoroughbred horses are running. And there, by the grace of God, and my own wits, I win. Not all the time, of course. But often enough to come out on top in the long run. And that's all I want—to be consistently a few hundred dollars to the good."

"You make it sound so simple—and so respectable."

"The way I go about it, it's perfectly respectable. And for me it's relatively simple, because I know what I'm doing. I was practically brought up in a racing stable—race horses are my brothers. But I'll tell you about that some other time. I must go now, or I'll be late for my appointment."

This conversation took place sometime in March. As he was leaving, he gave me a searching look. "Try not to grieve too much," he said. "I do hope that Huntington Hartford thing comes through—a complete change of scene would do you a world of good."

He was referring to my application for a three-month sojourn at a Shangri-la for creative artists in the vicinity of Pacific Palisades, founded, and generously endowed by a millionaire named Huntington Hartford; an ardent young man with the soul of an evangelist. His fortune derived from supplying, through a nationwide supermarket chain, reliable nourishment for the human body. But his moral-rearmament conscience told him that wasn't enough; his next step should be to nourish the human spirit, and that, in his opinion, was the primary function of Art— or should be. So, although he became as enthusiastic a patron of the arts as any Renaissance Pope, he was considerably less broadminded.

I bought my groceries at one of his chain stores, but I had never heard of him, or his Foundation, until a writer friend, Irving Fineman, came to see me on hearing of K.'s sudden death, and finding me in very low spirits, said, "What you need now is what I've been enjoying for the last couple of months—a spell at the Huntington Hartford Foundation."

He smiled when I asked him "What's that? And where is it?"

"It's a sort of 'game preserve' for artists, and it's in a deep canyon north of L.A.' it's just the place for you at this moment in your life, when you're having a hard time getting back to work."

He went on to catalog its virtues: "Beautiful surroundings.

Peace and quiet in which to work. Stimulating company when
you need it. Cross-fertilization of ideas among artists in different
mediums. Comfortable living quarters. Absolute privacy. Excellent food—the cook's a Hungarian, by the way—and all for free!
They'll even pay for your writing materials. You'll need only
enough money to buy your own toothpaste, or cigarettes, or
Scotch, or whatever your particular vice happens to be—but it
had better not be a disruptive one or you won't get invited a
second time."

"How does one get in for the first time?"

"If you're unknown, talent. Promise. Good recommendations.
And a convincing reason—like having to finish a book under
stressful conditions."

In the depths of my depression, I felt a faint stirring of renewed
interest in life, which he must have sensed, for he said, "Look, why
don't you send for an application form right away? I'll give you
the address, and mail the letter—why wait?"

When he left, he took with him not only my letter, but also a
carbon copy of my novel-in-progress, and a few other examples of
my work that would help him, he said, to write his letter of
recommendation for me.

Just now, I referred to him as a "friend," which he certainly
was, though not in the ordinary sense of the word. Our only
common bond was that we were both engaged in writing what is
known as "serious fiction," and even in that we were separated by
race and religion. Our day-to-day lives were totally unconnected,
and our points of contact were few and far between. His home was
in New England, and even when he came to the West Coast, as he
did from time to time, to be near his son, a young man of coruscat-
ing brilliance who was a student at "Caltech," he was still seventy
miles distant from my gemstone village. So our relationship had
nothing whatever to do with propinquity. It rested on something
more fundamental; a reciprocal goodwill that was impersonal in
origin. My friendly feelings toward him were called into being by
his generous attitude to me and my work, which sprang in its
turn, I believe, from the genuine empathy with the Jewish outlook that he sensed in me. In any event, he was one of those
individuals whose brief appearance on the periphery of one's life
is beneficial, and goes on being beneficial long after they have

gone—like a shower on a hot day that continues to cool the air for hours after the rain has ceased to fall.

I met him for the first time at a PEN club dinner in Los Angeles, at which he was the after-dinner speaker, and I was an after-thought—invited, I found out later, at his suggestion. Apparently, he had read the glowing review of *A Crown for Ashes* in *Jewish Bookland*, and later, the book itself. When somebody told him who I was and where I was living, he was interested enough to want to make my acquaintance. The first thing he said to me when we met was, "Why on earth do you use a pen name when your real name is so much more interesting and attractive?"

I explained that the name *de Kerpely* was so well known in Hungary that its use on a book that was uncomplimentary to the Russians might have placed the members of K.'s family who were still there in serious jeopardy, at a time when any excuse was enough to put innocent people in jail.

He was scheduled to speak on the influence of the Holocaust on postwar Jewish-American writing. It was a subject of particular interest to me, but when I mentioned that to him, he said, "Don't be surprised if I talk about something quite different. After-dinner speeches should be spontaneous, suggested by whatever comes into the speaker's head during dinner, and by the mood of the audience."

On that occasion, he began with the Jewish-American writers, and their response to the horrors that had taken place in Europe, but he soon moved into the broader field of all writers in America who were concerned, like John Hersey, for example, with the Jewish experience. And much to my surprise he included me among them, placing me with a few carefully chosen words on the same literary level. Writers are more sensitive than most people to the subtle nuances of words, whether written or spoken. Words alone, without any accompanying action, can have a tremendous psychological and emotional impact on a writer; and where I was concerned, this virtual stranger, named Irving Fineman, chose just the right ones, both then and a couple of years later, when he estimated my talent and my literary potential for the Huntington Hartford Foundation. Words that would come back into my mind, and keep me going at times when excellence seemed to be a mirage, and the struggle to attain it a fool's errand. Though I should have known, after eighteen years with K., that excellence lies in the pursuit, the unfaltering pursuit, of an unattainable perfection.

It was close to the deadline for spring applications to the Foundation, so I had to get mine off in a hurry; which was just as well, for the pressure helped me to combat the powerful undertow whose current ran counter to the slowly rising tide of life in me.

I had taught myself to type, after a fashion, but I was still very inexpert, and producing a legibly typed statement of my reasons for requesting a fellowship, a description of my project, and a sample chapter of my novel-in-progress, took time and perseverence. Other requirements were three references in my field, two character references, a clean bill of health—to be certified by a physician if, and when, my fellowship was granted, and, finally, a one-page, handwritten letter addressed to Mr. Huntington Hartford personally, which Leonard Wibberly, who was familiar with the selection procedures, called "the Founder's veto." Huntington Hartford was, it seemed, an amateur graphologist, and these handwritten missives supplied the fingerprints that helped him to keep undesirables out of his elysium.

Leonard Wibberly was one of my literary references, along with my staunch friend and kindred spirit, the English lit. professor at the university—who had introduced me to him in the first place—and, of course, Irving Fineman. I left the defense of my character in the hands of Father John and the Irish organist, sure that both of them would be charitable.

When I finally mailed the whole package, I felt very much as if I had just bought a ticket in a sweepstake, not really expecting it to win, not even sure that I wanted it to win, yet, by the mere act of buying it, revealing, as much to myself as to anyone else, the renewed presence of hope.

The weeks of waiting for an answer had the virtue of temporarily limiting my horizons; postponing the need to make long-term decisions about my future. But it was an uneasy respite, in which I tried to reestablish as normal a pattern of life for myself as I could—with an all-important element missing.

I resumed my visits to the state hospital, and the welcome back given me by "my patients" was touching—all the more so because I was conscious of coming back to them empty-handed. In the past I had brought my happiness with me, but now I brought only my loss. I went to see the Catholic chaplain, an elderly Scot with a bluff manner and a vast reservoir of compassion for his afflicted flock. "I have nothing to give them, Father. I am too unhappy myself to be able to help them."

"Don't give up," he said. "Those women may be crazy, but they're not fools. They know what has happened to you, and the chances are that it's brought you closer to them, made them feel that for once *they* can do something for *you.* Whether they can or they can't doesn't matter. Just *feeling* needed is enough for people who aren't needed anywhere on this earth."

Grief is so self-centered an emotion, and the pain of it so blinding while it lasts, that it is only when looking back at it from a distance that the sufferer can clearly perceive the role played by others in alleviating it. And it was only in retrospect that I recognized the seemingly casual weekend invitations from my daughter and my friends as lifelines cunningly extended to rescue me from the added sadness that Sundays and holidays hold for all those who are lonely or unhappy. The families that took me to their hearts differed widely in every way but one; they all had one revivifying element in common—children, and remarkable children at that. Bright and beautiful children with eloquent, evocative names like *Deidre,* and *Cormac, Corinth,* and *Thrace, Arabella,* and *Francesca....*

One of these child-garlanded households was that of the gentle satirist of *The Mouse that Roared,* Leonard Wibberly, and his wise and beautiful wife, Hazel—the center of his universe. "Every author," he told me once, "should have a wife like Hazel." To which I replied, "Every author should have a husband like K."

And in fact, Hazel was to Leonard, the well-known writer, what K. had been to me, a still unknown one; a combination of muse, interested listener, and intelligent critic, and an ever-ready typist into the bargain. Hazel's equivalent of K.'s own demanding art was her motherhood—giving birth to and raising four sons and two daughters. It was in the warm and noisy bosom of his family that Leonard was best able to work.

> There are times (he wrote me once) when the six of them almost roar me down—but not quite. That's because I'm Irish and when the Irish die they have to do so with a great shout of farewell to the world and greeting to God. At least that's my plan.

And I had no doubt at all that when the time came he would carry it out. He was Irish through and through. He had made a happy home for himself on the sunlit shores of the New World, and there he would probably remain. But his soul belonged in the mists of that land so loaded down with antiquities that "you cannot feel the wind for the crying of the bones"—as they say in Dublin.

Blue-eyed, bearded, and jolly, there was something of the sea-faring man, even the buccaneer, about him that contrasted oddly with the understated humor and subtly ironic wit that character-ized his writing, or what I knew of it, which was less than I thought I knew. For this single-hearted husband and father (who whenever he went on a trip to England, or Ireland, or Europe, took part of his family with him, and the whole lot if possible), lived a quadruple writing life; producing an incredible number of books in every literary form, each one expressing a different facet of his versatile personality, using four different names, his own and three pseudonyms. Yet so capricious is fame that the name of Leonard Wibberly is more firmly linked in the public mind with the film of *The Mouse that Roared* than it is with the little gem of a book from which the movie was made, or any other of the excellent books that he published under his own name.

Unlike most of my other memories, my recollection of the two enchanted weekends that I spent at the Wibberlys' home in Her-mosa Beach are not visual. The impression they left on my mind was sensory—in the way that the blind must apprehend their surroundings; a sense of the familiar, of the past revisited, of a well-known, well-loved air replayed in a different key. This is what I mean; when Leonard gets up without a word, takes a book from the shelf, and starts to read poetry aloud, a hush falls on the room; even the children put down their games and listen, and I am uncertain where I am, and whose voice it is that is filling the air with music.

It was on one of these visits that I made the acquaintance of another gentle satirist, Robert Nathan, whose verbal magic was temporarily eclipsed, as Leonard's would be, by a single impressive example of its translation into the visual language of the screen. Inevitably, perhaps, some of the subtlety and the mystery of his haunting novel, *Portrait of Jennie*, was lost in the film version, which was on too grand a scale for such an essentially gossamer theme, and the faintly menacing atmospherics that glimmer and whisper between the pages of the book sent more cold shivers up my spine than the raging storm at sea that ends the movie.

Soft-voiced and courtly, Robert Nathan's outward personality seemed to be all of a piece with his writings (a more rare occurrence among writers than I realized at that time), and I took an instant liking to him, which I hoped was reciprocated, for I learned later that he was on the selection committee for the Foundation, and had voted in my favor on the strength of my work, and I would not have wanted my personality to have made him regret having done so.

I expected to get a decision from the Foundation, one way or another, soon after Easter, which fell that year on the seventh of April. Just at the time when Southern California's brief spring would merge with its early summer to form a fifth season; the season of Paradise. When the air is mild, and sweet with the fragrance of violets and narcissi, orange blossoms and red roses all at the same time. And as it drew nearer, I found myself looking forward to it with a strange kind of joy, perceiving it in a new light. As someone brought back from the brink of hell might perceive the living world that was almost lost.

II

It is Palm Sunday; the day that ushers in for Christians the universal drama of death and resurrection. I have spent it with my own family, for whom its significance is traditional rather than religious. But for the two youngest children it signals the approach of a festival second only to Christmas; the only Saturday night in the whole year on which a miraculous rabbit lays miraculous eggs all over the garden, to be hunted for by the children on Sunday morning.

The two older ones—Peter, who is rising thirteen, and Elizabeth, who has just turned eleven—no longer believe in miraculous rabbits, but they do believe in tradition. Perhaps because they were both born within the maelstrom of war, and exposed to its terrors and privations during their early childhood, they are more sedate, and take life more seriously than their American friends of the same age. And half-Hungarian as they are, and old enough to understand what is going on in Hungary, they share their parents' concern for those they have left behind.

My day with them has been happy and relaxing, but now that Károly has brought me home, I feel deadly tired, as I often do these days for no apparent reason; so tired that, although it is barely nine o'clock, I decide to take a shower and go to bed.

After my shower, I knot a towel around my waist, and stand bare-breasted before the mirror to braid my hair, as I do every night, without really seeing myself. But tonight, something my daughter said earlier in the day about my being too thin, comes back to my mind, and makes me look more closely at my mirrored self. She is right, I think. I am thin to the point of being skinny, and it gives me a haggard look. With a couple of hairpins between my lips, I raise both arms to pin my braids on the top of my head, and suddenly I see something else that I haven't noticed before—a bluish shadow, like a bruise, on the underside of my right breast, and all at once my heart starts beating very fast. My hair pinned up and out of the way, I feel the blue shadow, pressing it lightly with the tips of my fingers, and finding it not in the least tender, but hard, and resistant to my touch. Hard and smooth, like an avocado pit under the skin, but smaller.

There is no doubt in my mind as to what it is. No doubt at all. This inner certainty of its evil nature is so strong that it makes me feel faint. A cold sweat breaks out on my forehead. I stumble into the bedroom, and manage to lie down on the bed before passing out.

When I come to, the last streaks of light in the sky have faded, and the room is completely dark. I may have slept for a while—I don't know. As always with me after an emotional shock, the realization of what stunned me comes back very slowly, reinvading me little by little, like a pain as an anesthetic wears off. I feel for the lump in my breast. It was no illusion. It is still there, growing. And something has to be done to stop it. But what? And when? Our Hungarian family doctor is in Europe, attending some medical convention, and won't be back for another three weeks. Should I wait for him? And if not, to whom shall I go? I can't think clearly. I take a sleeping pill, and eventually drift into the restless, superficial sleep in which the mind goes on working over its problems.

I awaken suddenly. The luminous dial of my clock says it is four o'clock in the morning, and while I slept, my never sleeping subconscious pushed up from the depths the memory of an incident in the recent past—let go, perhaps, because it had no relevance for me at the time. Now, summoned back to the surface to answer a question, it unfolds before me in a series of visual images, for which my reawakened memory supplies the unspoken dialog, in much the same way that the mind fills in the omitted details in the movie version of a book.

This miniature drama takes place soon after the publication of my novel, *A Crown for Ashes*. It begins with a fan letter, so devoutly Catholic in tone that it might have been written by a nun. But the writer identifies herself as a lay teacher of English in a Catholic school in Los Angeles. Her appreciation of my book, though rather over-emotional, has the ring of sincerity, which is ever so slightly compromised by not being her sole reason for writing to me; she wants to send me the partial MS of a novel that she is writing. My literary friends have warned me that aspiring writers will try to take advantage of me in this way, and urged me not to let them do it. But in this woman's timid request, tacked on at the end of her letter like an apologetic postscript, I sense a note, or rather, an undertone of pleading, that I feel it would be cruel to ignore.

So she sends me the first two chapters of her novel—a story about an old Catholic priest and his poverty-stricken flock in a Mexican village. It rings true, and it is not badly written, but it is only a beginning. I send it back to her with a few comments that I think may be helpful, and as much encouragement as I can honestly give her, and receive in return an emotional letter of thanks, in which she invokes the blessing of the literary Saint Teresa (my patron Saint) on me and all my works.

But that is not the end of it. A couple of weeks later, I get a letter from a woman of the same name, who says that she is the writer's sister, begging for one more favor—may she bring her to see me? They would not take up more than half an hour of my time, and it would mean so much to her sister to meet me personally— "More than you can possibly imagine. . . ." These last words are heavily underlined.

I am touched, and, I must confess, a little flattered that anyone should be willing to make a trip of seventy miles each way for the pleasure of spending half an hour in my company, so I ask them to lunch on one of the days that K. spends at the university.

When I hear their car stop in front of the house, I run downstairs to meet them. They are formally attired, as if for church, with hats, gloves, and high-heeled pumps—making me feel uncomfortable in my simple cotton sundress and barefoot sandals, and I fear that the attic may be a further shock. I ask which of them is the writer, and the younger of the two blushingly admits to it. My guess is that she is about ten years younger than her sister—probably in her late twenties—but she takes the steep flight of stairs slowly, with frequent pauses, like an old woman short of breath.

I suggest that they take off their hats, and make themselves comfortable after the long, hot drive. The writer's curly blonde hair, freed from a rather silly hat, is fashionably styled, and makes her look even younger than I had thought her at first. She is pretty in a delicate, rather childish way, but from time to time I see a peculiar look, almost a contortion, pass like a sinister shadow over her candid face, transforming it for a fraction of a second into the wizened mask of the old woman climbing the stairs.

Far from being shocked by the attic, she seems to find it enchanting. She looks around the awkwardly shaped, slope-ceilinged living room, almost cut in two by the disproportionate bulk of the grand piano, and exclaims with delight over its "interesting contours." She is fascinated by the yellow marble head, and by a strip of very old Hungarian peasant embroidery hanging on the wall, and examines with interest a photograph of K. playing the cello. She is like an eager child, full of questions.

The older woman is self-effacing. Her attitude to her sister is an odd mixture of pridefulness, indulgence, and the covert watchfulness of a nanny keeping an eye on what her charge is up to while pretending not to notice.

Over lunch, I bring up the subject that I know the writer both wants and fears to discuss; her book. It is a conflict common to most beginning writers, that although they feel the need of an objective opinion on their work, they instinctively dread the blight that the slightest adverse criticism can cast on the whole, still-tender, project.

Sensing a more-than-ordinary vulnerability in this timid creature, I am more than ordinarily careful in what I say, and she trustingly responds by outlining for me in detail the plot, characters, and scenes of her still unwritten novel as she has conceived them in her imagination—a concept as clear and precise as an architect's blueprint. The blueprint of a dream.

She grows suddenly pale. "It is time for us to leave," her sister says. "Why don't you lie down on the couch for a few minutes, while I help Mrs. de Kerpely with the dishes?"

In the kitchen, she says, "My poor sister will never finish her book. She is dying of cancer. It began in one breast, but she didn't see it in time to prevent it spreading—she is convent-bred, and the nuns taught her to be modest. . . . First one breast was removed, then the other. Then they tried chemotherapy—that's why she wears a wig, all her hair fell out. Such lovely hair, it reached below her waist. But nothing has been of any use, and now she has only a few weeks to live—or at best, a few months. She is not afraid of dying. Her faith is very strong. All she asks is that God should allow her to finish her book before He takes her."

I have my answer. It comes from beyond the grave. And it says, *Don't wait. Act at once. Every moment is precious.*

But what reputable physician will give a new patient an immediate appointment? I can think of only one possibility— short of enlisting the help of friends, which I don't want to do, and that is the young doctor who has recently come to live in the village, and wants to build up a local practice. He is reported to be

bright, but not as bright as he thinks he is. And he hasn't yet
learned that would-be patients don't like being told that there's
nothing the matter with them.

He is younger and brasher, than I expected. The mere thought
of being examined by him is embarrassing. But I cannot fault
him. He is businesslike and thorough. His brashness is only verbal; his breezy substitute for an obsolete "bedside manner."

My clothes and my dignity restored, I ask him with assumed
British phlegm, "Well . . . what is your opinion?" And he answers
without hesitation, "I advise you to have a biopsy done just as soon
as it can be arranged."

I have no idea of what it entails, but I want to get it over.

"That's fine with me—the sooner the better. What about
tomorrow?"

He smiles. "It's not quite as simple as that. It has to be done in a
hospital, and preferably by a surgeon with experience in . . . that
particular field."

His avoidance of the word that is in both our minds recalls
Father John's avoidance of the word *undertaker*, and stresses
their relation to each other. But I manage to keep my imperturbable mask in place. "Can you suggest anyone?"

He thinks about this long and seriously enough to confirm my
guess that he views the biopsy as only the first move in a long, and
probably losing, game with death. Finally, he says, "There are
two excellent surgeons in town, both with the right experience.
But the one I would choose for you is not easy to get. He's probably
the best on the whole West Coast, and he's in a position to limit his
commitments, to take on only special cases—and he has his own
ideas about what makes a case special."

I realize that my case is special only to me. From the medical
point of view it is routine. The young doctor looks searchingly at
me as though trying to find in me some other likely qualification.
His scrutiny prompts me to make a sarcastic suggestion, "Perhaps my British accent will recommend me." His face brightens,
as if I had given him an idea. "Look," he says, "why don't you take
a seat in the waiting room while I make a phone call?"

There are no other patients in the waiting room. From another
part of the house comes the sound of a baby crying, and a woman's
voice trying to soothe it. I feel like crying myself. But this doctor is

still too young to handle tears—except, perhaps, those of his own child. After about ten minutes, he comes into the room looking very pleased with himself. He has had a little talk with his revered colleague, who has agreed to see me—and as soon as tomorrow afternoon. "You're all set. From now on you'll be in the best possible hands," he assures me, beaming. I would love to know how he achieved this happy result, but he doesn't volunteer the information, and I can't very well ask him. "As to a hospital bed," he says, "you don't have to worry about that. The community hospital always manages to find room for *his* patients." He speaks with admiration, but I think I detect a touch of bitterness, too. He still has a long way to go.

I soon find out that what makes me "special" for this idiosyncratic surgeon, no matter how simple my case, is being K.'s widow. During the friendly talk that we have before I get ready to be examined, he tells me that he is an amateur violinist, and as one of the first violins in the local community orchestra, he had the "great privilege," as he puts it, of playing in a couple of concerts for which K. was the guest soloist.

I learned while in Hungary to equate the practice of medicine with a love of the arts, and of music in particular. (In Budapest at that period there existed a "doctors' orchestra" entirely composed of members of the medical profession.) So I find it only mildly coincidental that the Los Angeles surgeon who helped to prolong K.'s life, and this one, who will, I hope, help to prolong mine, should both be string players. And, however irrationally, it increases my confidence in the man who may soon be holding my life in his sensitive surgeon's hands to know that he also uses them to make music. It encourages me to tell him about my writing: How it brought me out of the depths of despair and restored my will to live, and about the Foundation, and what it would mean to me to go there, and what a blow it would be to have to turn down an invitation on account of my health.

"So time is of the essence in more ways than one," he says.

The examination over, I wait for him to speak. He says (though I don't think he believes it any more than I do), that the growth in my breast may well turn out to be benign. But—in the interest of saving precious time—he would like to have my permission to go straight ahead with whatever surgery may be necessary should the biopsy reveal it to be malignant.

He consults his calendar, and instructs the nurse to call the community hospital, and find out how soon they can admit me. She comes back to say that they will have a bed free in a semiprivate ward on Thursday. Today is Tuesday. "Will that be all right with you?" the doctor asks. "If so, we will operate early on Friday morning."

It is all right with me. I want to get it over. But this coming Friday is not just an ordinary weekday. It is Good Friday—the most solemn Holy Day of the Christian year; and for me, as a Catholic, the symbolic significance of its fortuitous choice as the day of my personal ordeal is too awesome to contemplate.

Now that everything is settled and there can be no turning back, I call my daughter. She is upset. Why didn't I call her as soon as I made the discovery? And wouldn't it have been wiser to wait for our own doctor? Rational questions for which I have no rational answers.

My news startles Father John into an unclerical expletive. "You are like Job," he says.

As for Father Patrick, when I tell him that my operation will take place on Good Friday, he says simply, "What a tremendous privilege!"

I have never before entered a hospital as a patient. And everything in me rebels at the surrender of one's own will—not to mention one's body—that it involves. I resent being made to undress and get into bed at five o'clock in the afternoon, whether I feel like it or not. I particularly resent the mandatory enema (bane of my early childhood), and I see no reason why I should submit to being sponged all over like a baby when I have just had a hot bath at home. But the middle-aged nurse's aide who does the job is a low comedian, who, as she works, keeps up a patter of slightly vulgar jokes, making me laugh in spite of myself, and conducts each disagreeable procedure with the brisk authority of a gym teacher; "Don't *clench* your bottom—relax! . . . Up with your arm . . . Now up with the other one . . . Now roll over on your stomach. . . ." And then, like the connoisseur of the female form that she must have become after countless rubdowns, "You certainly do have a beautiful back." Which is something that I have been told before, more than once, but never, until now, as an effort to console me in advance for the almost certain loss of my beautiful front.

A carefully timed succession of sedative pills and injections reduces me overnight to a suitable state of passive cooperation. As an orderly trundles me down the corridor to the operating room and into the hands of the white-masked doctors, I couldn't care less what they do to that alien object I call my body, with which my mind seems to have severed its connection.

The two do not reunite easily. Once freed from its physical burden, whether by drugs, or an anesthetic, or even a deep sleep, the mind is reluctant to reassume it. There seems to be an invisible frontier that, once crossed, discourages the traveler from returning.

For me, the way back to the conscious world lies through a vast field of pain that I try not to enter, using every possible subterfuge, retreating behind closed eyes, deliberately dropping down to the bottom of the sea, only to be irresistibly brought up to the surface again by the incantatory power of my own name repeated over and over, soft but insistent—a telephone bell in a distant room that no one can answer but me.

"Theresa... Theresa...." I know that voice. Very slowly, I open my eyes, my unwilling lids feel like lead. Father John and my daughter Genevra stand smiling down at me. Father John cries joyfully, "Happy Easter!" and Genevra says, "Hello, Mother!" as if I had just arrived on a visit.

My eyes close again of their own accord. Next time I open them, Father John has gone, but Genevra is still there, sitting beside my bed. "How do you feel?" she asks.

"Like hell. It hurts like hell. . . ."

A nurse says, "It won't hurt so much when the pressure bandage comes off."

I haven't yet got my bearings. "What time is it? What day is it?"

Genevra looks at her watch, "It's almost four o'clock, and it's Saturday afternoon—tomorrow is Easter Day."

Saturday? Where have I been all this time? Talking hurts. But I have another question. "It's gone, hasn't it?"

She knows what I mean. "Yes. It had to go. The doctor will tell you why—he'll be in to see you very soon."

Ridiculous tears fill my eyes, and trickle down each side of my nose, and I am helpless to stop them. Genevra wipes them away for me with a piece of tissue. "It's just weakness," she says, "you'll feel better tomorrow."

Once again, my pain has brought us closer. Once again, though she may not know it, we have exchanged roles.

Very early next morning, Father John comes to bring me the Blessed Sacrament. And around midday, when the Easter Mass has been celebrated in the chapel of El Carmelo, Father Patrick slips away for a while, to bestow on me the serenity of his presence.

In the afternoon, during regular visiting hours, the Irish organist comes, bringing flowers, and home-decorated eggs, and affectionate attempts at consolation for a loss that only another woman can fully understand. "There's a place in L.A. where they make the most wonderful falsies . . . specially designed . . . a woman I know has one, and you just can't tell the difference. . . ."

When the visitors leave, the comic aide comes on duty, after having had two days off. Finding a third of my beautiful back obscured by the pressure bandage, she tells me now that I "certainly do have a beautiful bottom." And on Monday, the surgeon offers me his special brand of consolation; the scar, he says, that is now a burning streak of pain running from just below my collar bone almost to my waist, will eventually disappear altogether. And because I now know that he helped to restore the ruined faces of Hiroshima, I believe him. He explains in layman's terms just what is meant by the operation known as a radical mastectomy, which in my case was just as radical as he could possibly make it, in order to eliminate, if possible, any necessity to follow it up with the slow and painful process of chemotherapy. "If all goes well," he says, "as I hope and believe that it will, you will keep your hair on your head, and probably live to be ninety."

My immediate recovery is slow. My temperature goes up every night, and I am plagued by a minor but annoying complication, that calls for some disagreeable treatments—administered by two cheerful young nurses who have no idea of how they are making me suffer. I tell them jokingly that they are a pair of sadists, at which they laugh merrily. But next day they are glum and sulky. "What's the matter? Is anything wrong?"

They look at each other. "Well, if you want to know, it's that word you called us yesterday. We looked it up in the dictionary."

"But that was only a joke! Of course you're not really sadists—you're ministering angels!"

They look at me suspiciously. "Is that a joke, too?"

It's hopeless, I think. Nobody understands my British sense of humor.

It was only after my emergence from the protective cocoon of the hospital world, in which the welfare of the body was predominent, that I felt the full psychological impact of my physical mutilation.

My emergence had been reluctant. In less than two weeks, the dependency, the forced regression into childhood, that I had at first so bitterly resented, had become a security that I feared to leave; unsure of my readiness to take up, on a second front, so to speak, another battle in the on-going war for survival. A struggle, this time, against sheer physical weakness.

A sneaky foe, it would catch me unawares in the middle of some ordinary activity, and bring me to a sudden dead stop, like a car whose gas has run out.

The slightest activity made me tired, and tasks that I used to perform with ease, such as digging in the garden, or washing the windows, were now wholly beyond me. My right arm had lost all its muscular power. Also its reach, and every movement of it was painful. Even when typing, even when lying in bed at night, I had to rest my forearm on a pillow to minimize the pain that ran up and down the nerves from my shoulder to my wrist, to the tips of my fingers.

A physical therapist who came in to work on me for an hour every day, assured me that in time I would get over these disabilities, "The body adapts itself," she said. "What you can't do with your right arm you will learn to do with your left. It's largely a matter of will—and the right exercises."

Maybe so. But nothing, I thought, neither will nor exercise, would ever bring back the lost wholeness of my body, or restore its lost grace.

My first reaction on seeing my mutilated self in my bathroom mirror, was, Thank God this didn't happen to me while K. was alive! But my reasons were purely aesthetic. As a worshipper of physical beauty, I had tried throughout my life to preserve whatever natural grace of form that I possessed. An effort set in motion by a worldly old aunt, who told me when I was twelve years old, that since I would never be a "beauty" in the Edwardian tradition of Lily Langtry and her like (I was much too small, for one thing), I had better sharpen my wits—brains being the next best thing to beauty—and take good care of my skeleton, which was not at all bad, and my complexion, which was unusually good. An effort for which I was rewarded at age nineteen by my first husband's beautiful mother, when she bestowed on me the flattering sobriquet of "Pocket Venus."

My Catholic conscience suggested that perhaps I was being punished for putting too high a value on physical beauty; for being too ready to equate outward with inward grace, and, conversely, to allow an unprepossessing exterior to come between me and the shining soul behind it.

But the more deeply I considered the spiritual significance of what I can only call my "benign disfigurement," the more clearly I perceived it as a mark of ratification rather than a punishment, the final seal on a covenant concerning the nature of love for which I had fought so hard at the time of my conversion. A symbolic taking of the veil.

I had been at home, struggling to recover my strength, for about a week when I heard from the Foundation. They offered me a fellowship for the months of July, August, and September. But what would have been a message of pure joy only a few weeks earlier, now put me into a fever of uncertainty as to what I ought to do. In the end, I did what I thought was right. I wrote them a letter of conditional acceptance, in which I told them about my recent operation, and expressed my hope that it would not disqualify me.

But in my heart, I was terribly afraid that it would. Afraid that by telling the truth I had thrown away what might be my last hope of finishing my novel; for however optimistic my doctor professed to be, cancer was a hydra-headed monster whose destruction could never be counted upon.

A week of agonizing suspense followed. And then came a kind and charming letter from the director of the Foundation, the composer John Vincent, saying that the fact of my having undergone recent surgery would present no obstacle to my acceptance provided the general state of my health was good.

The next problem to overcome was the old, familiar one of my permanently shaky finances. Medical expenses above and beyond what my insurance would pay for had wiped out my small reserves, and the monthly payments from Eldon's false friend had once again come to a stop.

A letter explaining the straits I was in brought no response from him. But his wife, whom I had never met, who must have read my letter, had more conscience—or more compassion. She sent me her personal check for the payments her husband owed me up to that point—it had no accompanying message—and I got the feeling that she did not want her husband to know that she had sent it. Now I could settle my rent, ensuring a home to come back to at the end of my stay at the Foundation. But I still did not have the money to pay for what Irving Fineman had described as "toothpaste" while I was there, and it looked as if I should have to pawn the few trinkets that I had managed to save from the Russians, when, just as before, when I was in urgent need, the magical sum of three hundred dollars appeared out of the blue. But not from the same source. Not as the result of Father John's luck, but of my own. It came from the *Los Angeles Times*—my prize for correctly solving their weekly crossword puzzle.

7

The Enchanted Gates

*T*HE Huntington Hartford Foundation, and everything that it meant to me, was symbolically contained in its immense, double-winged, wrought-iron gates, that were opened and closed by remote control in response to the correct password.

This imposing old-world symbol of privileged privacy appeared, with startling incongruity, just around the last and steepest bend in a dirt road that had wound up the side of a sagebrush hill for miles without any sign of human habitation. A road so narrow that the Foundation car, a heavy, broad-beamed station wagon that met newcomers at their varying points of arrival, had to hug the hillside to keep from falling over the outer edge. The driver, who had told me as soon as he heard me speak, that he was a fellow Britisher ("The name is Lewcox"), stopped before the magnificent gates, and got out, leaving the motor running while he announced our arrival to someone at the other end of a telephone concealed in a niche of the stone wall; then jumped back in again as the gates slowly opened to let us pass through.

We were now on a smooth, paved driveway, heavily bordered by trees and shrubs, that descended by long, easy curves to the floor of a deep canyon, glimpsed now and then through the trees, but fully disclosed only at the last downward turn; a sun-dappled scene of rustic simplicity, like a nineteenth-century landscape painting, with a promise of peace implicit in the total absence of people. Even its sole physical emblem of sophisticated living, a turquoise swimming pool in front of the main building, lay undisturbed in the mid-afternoon heat, its surface unruffled by human arms and legs.

The driver parked the car at the bottom of the hill and invited me to get out. It was like stepping into a spell—a Californian version of the Sleeping Beauty's enchanted forest. "Is it always as quiet as this, Mr. Lewcox?"

"Call me Lew—that's what everyone calls me."

"But where *is* everyone?"

"At this time of day the Fellows are all in their studios, working. Or," he added with the ghost of a grin, "sleeping. But Betty is in her office, and she wants a word with you before I take you to your studio."

He led me across a stretch of green lawn, across a little bridge over a running stream, and into a sprawling ranch house up against the opposite hillside.

Betty was the secretary: the official welcomer, and, when the time came to leave, the official dispatcher. And as I perceived her on that first meeting, cool and unruffled as the pool, pleasant, efficient, at once prim and girlish, young enough to be attractive, and old enough to put her foot down on an unruly artist if need be, she was the veritable prototype of the perfect secretary. But I soon discovered that she was much more than that. Indispensable to, and beloved by, everyone, she was the human lynchpin supporting the fragile structure of day-by-day human relations in a fluid and constantly re-forming group of wildly disparate personalities.

Yet I remember her now with all the more affection because, secretarial paragon though she was, she didn't know how to change her own typewriter ribbon—an endearing shortcoming revealed when I asked her to show me how to change mine.

She said now, "I hope you will like your studio—it's one of the loveliest. . . ."

And it was. It was so lovely, so perfectly in harmony with its idyllic setting, that it gave me pangs of conscience for ever having made fun of Mr. Huntington Hartford's reputed taste in art, and evangelistic notions about its mission. For whether or not he had had any say in the physical design of this beautiful place that would be my refuge from mundane cares for the next three months, he *had* provided the money for it, and that in itself was a gallant thing to do, given his mistrust of modern painting, music, and literature. And many of the current recipients of his hospitality were living proof of his implicit acknowledgment of the creative artist's right to freedom of expression, regardless of what he, or any other benefactor, might think of the results.

But these were conclusions come to later, as I got to know the other members of the group, and became aware of the protective framework for our cherished freedom of expression, afforded, paradoxically, by a paternalistic structure in which every member of the staff, beginning with the director himself, played a vital role, important not only in fulfilling a particular function, but in the manner of its performance. And in this regard, I think that the choice of two creative artists, a composer and a print-maker, as the director and his assistant respectively, was a brilliant one, linking as it did the dream with the reality.

The studios, scattered among the trees at varying distances from the community house and one another, were actually self-contained cottages, in which, thanks to the provision of a hot plate and a miniature refrigerator, a misanthropic Fellow could exist without making any contact with the others. But while I was there, misanthropy was limited to a forgivable preference on the part of a seventy-year-old sculptress for having her breakfast alone. We had lunch alone, anyway—Lew brought it to each of us, sandwiches and fruit in a basket, around noon every day. Dinner was a communal meal for which, Betty told me tactfully, "We all try to be very punctual—actually, you may want to come over early this evening. It would give you a chance to meet some of the Fellows before going in to dinner."

The last phrase suggested a social occasion. "What should I wear?"

"Oh, nothing formal—just any summer dress. The idea is that people shouldn't come to dinner in their work clothes, that's all. The only dress-up occasions are the director's cocktail parties—and they don't happen very often."

It was a good thing they didn't, I thought, as I unpacked the one and only "dressy" dress that I had brought with me—just to be on the safe side. With no expectation of social events in a colony devoted to work, I had brought very little in the way of personal adornment, giving preference to material I needed for my writing, a few books, and, of course, my typewriter. Besides, I didn't know how much room there would be in my quarters. But everything I had brought with me virtually vanished in a two-roomed studio big enough to contain everything I possessed in the world, twice over.

It was one of a pair of stone Siamese twins, joined end to end by the wall between their respective bedrooms; thus ensuring the quiet of the working-living area at each outer end, whose spaciousness was doubled by the illusion of bringing the outside in through one whole wall, and half of another one, made entirely of sliding glass panels. The outside in this case was a flagged patio open to the woods, and at one end of it a little green lawn, on which a trusting doe and her fawn would come to graze, undeterred by my presence on the other side of the glass, as long as I kept still.

But not all my animal visitors were as inoffensive as the deer. Raccoons were a pest, on account of their ingenuity and persistence in getting the lid off my trash can, no matter how securely I tied it on. I made their acquaintance one night when I came back late after spending the evening with two new friends, and was greeted by five pairs of headlamp eyes glowing in the dark around my door. I knew they belonged to raccoons, but I didn't know how far raccoons could be trusted not to bite. Feeling very bold, I walked between them to my door and let myself in. Clearly, they were not afraid of me. They had remained absolutely motionless as I walked past them. But a few moments later I heard them playing football with my trash can.

There was a lot of wild life in the canyon. At night, the woods beyond my open windows were alive with the sounds of nocturnal creatures out hunting; owls and their squeaking prey; skunks and porcupines lumbering through the undergrowth; a fox barking; and now and then, the distant yowl of a bobcat prowling the higher slopes, along with the mountain lion. There were also a variety of snakes, most of them harmless, but some as venomous as they were beautiful. The Foundation waged war against only one species, the one most likely to harm an unwary city-bred Fellow out for a walk in the woods—the rattler. A bounty of five dollars was offered for every dead rattlesnake brought in, and I had a chance to earn it when I came back from breakfast one morning to find one coiled in the middle of my lawn, enjoying the sun. But killing a rattlesnake was beyond me. I didn't know how. I had no weapon handy. I had no strength in my right arm. And I was afraid. Let someone else have it! I turned tail and ran back to the community house—about a quarter of a mile—as fast as I could, and bumped into just the right person coming through the door, Charlie Rogers, the director's assistant. "What's the hurry?" he asked.

"There's a rattlesnake on my lawn! Do you want it?"

"You bet!"

I was out of breath, so he went on ahead of me, picking up a stout stick on the way. By the time I reached the scene, the snake was dead. "It's a beauty," Charlie said, slinging it over his shoulder. "I'll take it in and collect the bounty for you."

I said, "It's your snake—you killed it."

"But *you* found it."

We ended up splitting the bounty.

Anxious not to offend on my first evening, I overdid the punctuality. There was no one in the lounge when I walked in, half an hour early. But I was rather glad. It made me uncomfortable to walk into a room filled with people unknown to me, but well known to one another. I had never been able to follow the advice given to me as a young wife by my socially adept mother-in-law; "Always be the last to arrive at a party—that way you'll make sure of being noticed; and the first to leave—that way you'll make sure of being talked about."

Now, I sat down in a corner opposite the door, and picked up an art magazine big enough to hide behind as I watched people come in. The first person to arrive was a tall man with a music case in his hand, who seemed to be on his way to somewhere else—and in a hurry to get there. Half-way across the room, he noticed me, stopped, and came over to me. "I'm John Vincent," he said, "and you must be our new Fellow—Theresa de Kerpely ... Welcome!" After which he dashed off again. He needed, he said, a shower before dinner.

It didn't occur to me that I might have something to do with his presence there for dinner that night, and it may well have been

simply chance that his subsequent appearances on a weekday
evening usually coincided with the arrival of a new Fellow. But if
it was intentional, it was characteristic of the tact and geniality
that he brought to his position.

The Vincents had a beautiful home in the vicinity of U.C.L.A.,
where Dr. Vincent taught, and, as a general rule, they occupied
the director's apartment on the second floor of the community
house only on weekends and holidays. Mrs. Vincent, petite, elegant, and younger than her husband, brought to her position as
the director's wife social graces that recalled those of the
"embassy wives" of my diplomatic past, and preserved us from
the danger of losing touch with the world outside the enchanted
gates, where a different set of values prevailed, and to which we
all had to return sooner or later.

The simple dining room, with its one long table, reminded me
of the refectory at El Carmelo—a mental association that might
or might not have pleased Mr. Huntington Hartford. But the fare
was by no means monastic. It was prewar Hungarian cooking at
its best. And my introduction by John Vincent to the assembled
company elicited a spontaneous cry of delighted recognition from
the middle-aged man in a white jacket who was serving the meal.

His name was André Székely, and he was one of the many
highly educated, but no longer young, professional men who had
left Hungary after the war to start a new life in the United States.
And there discovered that the price of their coveted freedom in a
democratic society was the relinquishment of the social and professional status enjoyed by them in what had been a fundamentally feudal society, before the war stood it on its head.

Now, this doctor of philosophy and law was, together with his
wife, responsible for the Foundation meals and everything connected with them. A position that in itself was certainly a come-
down. But André and Ida Székely were not just a cook and a
butler; they were, like all the other members of the staff, an
integral part of a benevolent conspiracy to make life a little bit
easier for those whose work goes all too often unrecognized, and
unrecompensed during their lifetime. Which was surely something worth doing. And they had their own measure of the privacy, and security, provided by the gates. They had their own
pretty cottage among the trees, to which, when the day's work

was done and the kitchen locked up for the night, they invited Hungarian friends to sip Hungarian wine and listen to records of Hungarian music. I was their guest on more than one occasion at a patio party that might have been taking place on the terrace of a villa in Buda that no longer existed.

Getting to know the Fellows was rather like getting to know one's fellow passengers on a ship, without any passenger list. No doubt Betty had one in her office, but I felt that to ask her to let me see it would be a breach of the right to anonymity, and would also interfere with my intuitive first impressions, in which I had a lot of faith—too much. So for two dinners and two breakfasts I played a game with myself of sorting out the visual artists from the writers and composers, simply by listening to their talk.

The composers were easy to identify. There were only two of them, and they managed to convey an impression of being an elite minority with a language all their own. The painters were easily recognizable, too. An open, convivial lot, they formed an extended family group with the printmakers and sculptors, that like any other family group was at once comradely and contentious; critical of one another's work, but united against attack from the outside. The writers, on the other hand, were loners, who appeared to be wary, and even suspicious of one another—and of me. I felt myself being tested for my potential as an enemy or a disciple. But I was still too unfamiliar with the literary scene to know why. I had yet to learn that writers, generally speaking, were the most self-centered of artists, and the least generous with their praise of one another's work—unless they belonged to the same clique, which rendered it suspect. All of which, combined with the power, and the dangerous properties of words as compared with silent images and pure sound, justified their mistrust of their own kind.

We occupied the same seats around the refectory table every day, morning and evening; and seated directly across from me were three singular individuals. One, a painter, and a native American, with the high cheekbones and slightly acquiline nose of her race, was remarkable for her aura of tranquility, and her listening silence. The other two, both writers, were remarkable for the wit and brilliance of what they said whenever they broke theirs. They and the Indian painter who sat beside them were obviously worlds apart; yet they shared some indefinable quality that set all three of them aside from the rest of the company.

The distinctive physical appearance of the two writers added to the impact of their original personalities. They were husband and wife. But I didn't know that on my first evening—I had been misled by John Vincent's reference to them as "Horace Gregory and Marya Zaturenska," names that to anyone who knew anything about the American literati of the day, would have immediately identified them as distinguished members of an intellectual elite, and important poets. But my first impressions of them were uninfluenced by any awareness of their literary status and achievements.

For me, the name *Gregory* sounded an Irish note that went very well with his reddish hair, his slight, leprechaun physique, and the good-natured humor written all over his mobile face. While the unmistakably Russian patronymic, *Zaturenska*, triggered in me a bizarre mental leap backward in time from its handsome, witty owner with the deep chuckling laugh, to the enigmatic Ukrainian colonel, so beloved and admired by all his men, whom I had christened, *Buddha.*

Seeking for points of resemblance between the living woman facing me and the inscrutable image of the long-dead hero of the Red Army, I found one in her dark, sleepy eyes, and another in the mask of passivity she assumed when the conversation bored her. I did not know then that their elusive similarity was racial; that she, too, came from the Ukraine.

I had, I still have, a photographic memory—which can be an embarrassment, like the snapshot albums of one's childhood. But it does preserve intact much that would otherwise be modified, and even obliterated, by time's inevitable changes in the eye of the beholder, in the object beheld, and in the distance between them. Even so, the truth of the indestructible image is relative; dependent on the atmosphere, the light, and the state of the photographer's mind at a given moment.

In my indestructible images of Horace and Marya Gregory, they are always together. Like me and K., they are inseparable in the most profound sense. It is impossible to imagine either of them married to anyone else. Yet each has a strongly separate identity—all the more carefully preserved, perhaps, because they both practice the same art.

I see them walking back to their rose-trellised cottage after breakfast; two strikingly dissimilar figures who, in conjunction, are recognizable from a considerable distance. Marya's measured pace and erect bearing suggest a much taller woman, possibly with a water jar or a basket balanced on her head. But Horace's spare and angular figure appears to be smaller than it actually is, on account of his uncertain gait and his lowered head as he concentrates on the path before him as if it were a tightrope. Despite the inconsonance of their individual movements, however, the two figures keep abreast of one another, and the distance between them always remains the same; wide enough to symbolize independence, and narrow enough to be covered in an instant if ever the tightrope walker should slip. But he never does. He has perfect balance in the way that some people have perfect pitch.

They kept very much to themselves. In the evening, when most of us foregathered in the lounge for ten minutes or so before going in to dinner, the Gregorys would arrive like royalty—punctual to the minute—just as the dining room doors were being opened; charm and amuse the company during the meal; and afterward, instead of sitting around in the lounge for a while, talking with the rest of us, they would depart, with murmurs of regret (for they were extremely courteous) that I was pretty sure they did not feel.

I had learned from one of the other writers that Horace was working on a translation of Ovid's *Metamorphoses*, that was very near completion, and that Marya was a lyric poet, who had won a Pulitzer Prize for her first volume of poems. Someone else told me that together they had written a "somewhat controversial" history of American poetry. Those of their works that were in the Foundation library, which was very small, had been signed out by other interested Fellows, when I went to look for them. But aside from their literary achievements, Horace and Marya Gregory fascinated me as people, and I very much wanted to get to know them better. Which did not seem likely, given their exclusiveness, and the fact that they would have to take the first step.

A basic principle of life at the Foundation was privacy; uninterrupted privacy for the group as a whole, and for the individual

Fellows. The gates kept out strangers and visitors alike. No outsider could be invited to dinner at the community house without special permission from the director or his assistant, and the right qualifications—namely, some standing in, or connection with, the arts. Within the gates, each individual studio was the proverbial Englishman's castle. No Fellow might visit another uninvited. There were no telephones, and only a message of life and death urgency would be transmitted—by hand—from Betty's office. These, and a few other minor rules, were unwritten laws that nobody wanted to transgress, because they were not so much restrictive as protective.

I could, of course, have invited the Gregorys to visit me in my studio. But my life in British diplomatic, and European, society had given me a sense of hierarchic values; of what was, and was not, as the British say, "done." And I had resigned myself to remaining at a distance from the two most interesting people then at the Foundation, when Marya took me aside one morning after breakfast, and invited me over to their cottage at nine o'clock on the following evening ("Horace always works until nine . . ."), for a glass of Dubonnet.

The precision of time and day—more than thirty-six hours ahead—struck an oddly formal note. The required "invitations" were usually no more than casual suggestions made on the spur of the moment.

A photographic memory locks subject and setting together so firmly that never again can the one be recalled without the other. The little white-painted cottage to which I am making my way through the fading midsummer twilight will be, for as long as I live, inseparable from its present, transitory occupants, and is about to be memorialized by my mental camera as the birthplace of an unlikely friendship that will have an enormous influence on my future.

Although it is made of wood, which English country cottages rarely are, this charming retreat has an Old English air; derived, perhaps, from its diamond-trellis trim, and the small glass panes of the white-curtained bay window, and the tall tree-roses—the pride of Mr. MacKenzie, the Scottish gardener—that stand sentinel around it, though their out-size blooms are pure Californian exaggeration.

The interior is less cozy. . . . "More like New England," Marya says, taking me into a prudish little room, the one with the bay window, where Horace sits reading, his angular frame fitted awkwardly into the unyielding embrace of a puritanically un-cushioned armchair. I am offered a low upholstered seat without any arms, and known as a "sewing chair" for precisely that rea-son. It fits me nicely. Marya, after serving the Dubonnet, reclines on a scroll-back Victorian sofa that resembles the one in the vicarage dining-room of my youth, on which my mother would lie down for an hour every afternoon, while I read aloud to her the poems of Christina Rossetti and Elizabeth Barrett Browning. Between my memory image of my fragile, gray-haired mother, with her fading eyesight and her unfulfilled dreams, and the living subject of this evening's mental photography, there are only two points of physical resemblance. They both have the finely turned ankles and small, delicately shaped feet with high arched insteps that were held to be a mark of aristocracy in women of the Victorian era—along with the "tiny" hands immor-talized by Puccini. But Marya's hands are smaller and livelier than my mother's, which lie motionless on her lap, blue-veined and thin, like the hands of the dead.

Horace talks about books. Marya talks about writers. I listen—alternately fascinated, startled, and amused. But, unlike most brilliant talkers, they are not monologists. They give me plenty of chances to contribute my opinions. They do not, however, suffer bores gladly—I have observed that at the dinner table—and my fear of boring them with my relative lack of literary sophistica-tion makes me diffident.

But literature grows out of life itself. And where real-life expe-rience is concerned, I can speak with some authority. My tales of the Red Army, my descriptions of life under siege, and the tyranny of successive totalitarian regimes, amuse and interest my hosts, and earn me a second invitation. Very soon they are asking me over almost every evening, and in exchange for what they teach me about poetry and poets, I give them some of the bitter raw material of which poetry is the purest distillation.

Pure is the word used by Horace to define Baida, the serenely silent Indian painter and her paintings, that depict in limpid colors, in symbols, and abstractions, the ancient beliefs, rituals, and ceremonial dances of her people. A word that links them in

my mind with those musical compositions in which Bartók simultaneously enshrines and ennobles the ancient, unwritten folk
songs of the Hungarian people. And, finally, a word that, like all
well-chosen adjectives, tells me a lot about the user.

I became good friends with several of the painters simply as a
result of meeting them every evening at dinner. But with Baida,
who seldom took part in these dinner-table conversations, it was
different. She deliberately chose me for her friend. Though what
uncanny sixth sense it was that guided her choice is still a mystery to me. Finding me alone on the community house patio one
evening after dinner, she sat down on the wicker chair next to
mine, and said, shyly but abruptly, "May I talk to you?" And I
could not have been more surprised and touched if a unicorn had
stepped out from the shelter of the trees and approached,
unafraid, to nuzzle my hand.

The metaphor is not as far-fetched as it may seem. Horace's
word for her had been very well chosen indeed. What a less
perceptive person might have taken for naiveté, was a kind of
primeval innocence. She moved among the pitfalls of the present
as if she had never completely emerged from the mists of her
racial past—or had, for the sake of her art, returned to them in
spirit.

I should say at this point that she was not a young girl. It is
difficult to assess the age of those whose racial physiognomy
differs from one's own, especially when they spring from an
ancient civilization. But I judged Baida to be in her middle
thirties.

Having asked permission to talk to me, she was silent for a long
time, and her silence now lent depth and weight in advance to
whatever it was that she felt the need to speak of to me, a virtual
stranger.

When, finally, she did open the conversation that she had
sought, she very nearly ended it there and then, with one word.

"A few months before I came here," she said, "my sister died.
And for months before that I had been staying with her in her
home, taking care of her. And the home. Near the end she couldn't
do anything for herself. She was in such terrible pain. She had
cancer. . . ."

The light on the patio was already too dim for Baida to see the expression on my face as she uttered the last word. But she must have sensed my inward recoil—or perhaps she was expecting it. Anyway, she broke off, as if waiting for me to say something before she went any further. After a while, when I didn't speak, she said rather timidly, "Shall I go on?" And I said, "Yes. Of course." But it took an effort of will. Poor Baida had unwittingly opened a door that I was trying to keep closed, and had let an angel in; a dark, pursuing angel, bent on reminding me that I cannot escape him. That escape is not possible—only postponement.

Baida was used to communicating in colors, not words. And what she went on to tell me was halting and fragmented, and seemed to add up to an old story; the familiar story of sacrifice taken for granted, or not even recognized as a sacrifice, but seen as a family obligation that she, as a single woman without any regular job (for Art can be picked up and put down at will), was the obvious person to assume.

So Baida had put her art down, and picked up the burden of nursing her dying sister, taking care of her pretty home, and feeding the good, kind, unhappy husband who went out to work every day to pay for it all. But when, at last, her sister's death set her free to pick up her art again, she could not find it. She had been away too long. She had lost the key to the world of the unicorns.

Then providence, in the form of an artist friend, did for her what Irving Fineman did for me. And the lost key was found again. So? "It's wonderful being here," Baida said. "I'm painting like crazy—and better than ever before."

So? I did not ask. I waited for her to tell me what still remained to be solved. Meanwhile, two painters, with whom Baida was friendly, finished the chess game that they had been playing in the lounge and came out to join us, which gave me a chance to say goodnight and leave Baida in their company. "See you tomorrow," they said, and Baida added, with a question mark, "After breakfast?"

I usually went straight back to my studio after breakfast. I, too, was working "like crazy," and I did my best work in the morning. But when Baida asked if she might walk part of the way with me, I said once again, "Yes, of course."

"I won't keep you," she said, "I just want to tell you what I would have told you last night if we hadn't been interrupted." A moment of silence, then, in a rush, "I'm going to get married. To my brother-in-law. The wedding is set for the weekend after next."

This was the last thing that I had expected to hear. I was speechless with surprise, and a little horrified, which Baida must have sensed, for she tried to explain. "He has been so lonely since my sister died—he needs someone to take her place in his life— and in many ways I resemble her. . . ."

I thought, "Beware of pity." I said, "What about your Fellowship?" She still had almost three months left of an enviable five-month Fellowship. "Surely you're not going to throw that away?"

Oh no, she said, she planned to stay on at the Foundation after she was married. But her husband would pick her up every Saturday afternoon, and bring her back on Sunday. Which would mean several hours of driving in exchange for a weekly night of love, but in California distance was one of the facts of life.

"And when your Fellowship comes to an end, and you go home with him for good, will he give you the time and the freedom to go on with your painting?"

Oh yes, she said, he had promised never to stand between her and her art. He understood what it meant to her. He really was a very nice man—she was sure that I would like him.

But for all her protestations, she did not succeed in convincing me that she herself was convinced that the step she was taking was right. She had secret misgivings, I thought, and consciously or unconsciously, she was seeking reassurance from me as a fellow artist—albeit in a different medium—who was also a woman, who had been twice married, and who understood the conflicts involved. As indeed I did. But I knew too much to risk advising her either one way or the other. I knew both the light and the dark possibilities of the situation, and although the odds were against the triumph of the light, I knew that it *could* happen, because it had happened to me.

So I wished her the best of luck, and the Foundation gave her and her bridegroom a lavish wedding reception, at which every-one there was present to wish her well, and after a brief honeymoon, she began the precarious double life of painting "like crazy" on one level of enchantment, while cleaning house, cooking, and, presumably, making love on another.

When the time came for me to return to the real world, Baida said, looking very sad, "I shall miss you." But her sadness was not entirely on account of my departure. Taking her dead sister's place in her husband's life was proving more difficult than she had anticipated. The trouble was, she told me, that her sister was still there.

I knew what she meant. I knew what it was to be haunted. "It might help," I said, "if you and your husband were to move—start a new life together in fresh surroundings, unconnected with the past."

But she didn't think that would make any difference. Her sister would move with them.

"We all have our private ghosts," I told her, "My artist daughter exorcises hers by embodying them in new forms on canvas. And I do the same with mine, on paper."

The look on Baida's face as I gave her this bit of oblique advice, reminded me that the exorcism of this particular ghost did not lie in her hands alone. She needed some advice on how to loosen the grip of the living on the dead. But the means that a more sophisticated woman would have used to bring this about were not in Baida's nature. All her power was in her art, and in what it signified. "Just keep on painting," I told her. "No matter what happens, *keep on painting!*"

When the Gregorys left the Foundation, about two weeks before I did, they had already become my literary mentors. Marya had read my first novel, and, pronouncing it to be "very lyrical," was indulgent with its flaws, but not blind to them. Horace read the MS of my short story, *Ocean in the Desert,* praised it, and made a couple of valuable suggestions as to how I could strengthen it, which I still had time to carry out before it went to press. They told me all about Yaddo, one of the two older "refuges" for creative artists, on which Huntington Hartford had partially modeled his Foundation (the other was the MacDowell Colony, in New Hampshire), and offered to back my application to either place, or to both, if I wanted to go there. They

invited me to stay with them at their Riverside Drive apartment
in New York. All these gestures of good will implied a belief in
my potential as a writer, which, especially coming from two such
dedicated artists, meant a great deal to me at that point, when
there were no certainties in my life—only hope.

There remains one incident to relate in connection with this
early stage of my acquaintance with these two poets who had so
unexpectedly befriended me. A personal experience so strange
that even now I can find no rational explanation for it, except,
possibly, that my grief over K.'s death, my ensuing illness, and
my psychological struggle against death as a way out, had rendered me abnormally sensitive to the supranatural.

Books were the Gregorys' constant companions; as indispensable to their well-being as K.'s cello was to his. Marya worked at a
little secretary in the bedroom, but she did her afternoon reading,
like my mother, on the scroll-back sofa in the sitting room. Left
alone there for a few minutes, while Horace helped Marya to
remove a stubborn cork from a new bottle of Dubonnet—it must
have been on my third or fourth after-dinner visit to them—I
wandered over to look at the little pile of books lying on the table
next to the sofa, along with Marya's eyeglasses; the poems of St.
John of the Cross, the *Imitation of Christ* (both of which surprised
me), a Penguin copy of *Mediaeval Latin Lyrics* translated by
Helen Waddell, and, to my delight, a thin, black volume on whose
slender spine was written in gold, *Selected Poems of Marya Zaturenska*. I picked it up, and was leafing through it with a sense of
excitement and discovery when Horace and Marya re-entered
the room, and I hastily put it down, feeling as uncomfortable as if
I had been surprised with a private letter in my hand.

"Grove Press brought that out last year," Marya said. "It's
rather elegant, don't you think?"

I asked if I might borrow it, and Horace's *Selected Poems*, too, if
he had a copy with him—the library copies seemed to be permanently signed out. They smiled indulgently at this oblique
admission of my unflattering ignorance of their work, but they
seemed reluctant to remedy it themselves; as if lending their own
works was a form of self-advertisement that went against their
grain. But I ended up taking the *Selected Poems of Marya Zaturenska* back with me to my studio (Horace promised to lend me

his later), and I settled down to read them, without paying any heed to the warning implicit in the title of the first poem in the book: *Thou Knowest Not Into What Dreams Thou Wanderest.*

Marya gave me the book as a parting present, after writing the last two stanzas of her poem, *Terraces of Light,* on the fly leaf in her flowing, "musical" hand. And Horace gave me his *Selected Poems,* inscribed to me with words of encouragement and affection. In the course of writing this chapter, I have reread both of them, moved, as always, by the distinctive music of each voice, whose spell, like that of the great classical compositions, remains undiminished by time or repetition.

Tucked in between the pages of Marya's book is a letter written by me to my daughter Nina at the time of my rash wanderings into the unknown territory of a poet's dreams. The more hallucinatory an experience seems to be, the more one feels the need to tell someone else about it, if only to verify one's own sanity— though the opposite is more likely to result. Life had taught me to be wary of confiding my innermost thoughts to anyone, and the only person I knew who was capable of accepting a hallucinatory experience as authentic, was the visionary Nina, who had had strange dreams herself. Even so, I was cautious, fearful of not being understood, so instead of putting my letter into the mailbox, I put it into the book of dreams that had caused me to write it in the first place, and there it has remained for twenty-eight years.

> . . . As I read one poem after another, I experienced an uncanny sense of recognition, as if I were being shown the deepest recesses of my own soul mirrored in another's luminous sensibility. As if all the chaotic elements of my inner life—the loves and sorrows, the dreams, the mystical lights, the backward and forward visions of my mind, the unvoiceable love of God and sense of the nearness of the angels, the music of nature and of words—had been gathered up by this sorcerer-poet and fitted together into a gleaming mosaic in which everything, light and dark, is in its appointed place. . . .
>
> Yet, face to face with the poet herself, I found it impossible

to identify her with her own magic. Was the night's revelation some sort of lunacy?

I read the poems again by the common-sense light of day, and exactly the same thing happened. I took to reading one or two of the poems every day before starting work, finding inspiration in their assurance (or was it an illusion?), that the poet's fire also burned in me, waiting for me to learn how to use it. And little by little, the poems became both the poet's and mine, and it seemed to me that I had been privileged, through the alchemy of words and their mysterious subconscious associations, to pass the ultimate barrier that separates one individual soul from another, and I thought that this visibility in the light that emanates from God, was what life in the Beatific Vision, promised to the Saints, might mean to those who attain it.

I replaced this unposted letter to Nina with another one, written from the other side of the gates. It was less romantic, less spontaneous, and less real—if only because perspective subtly alters every view.

II

It was one of Mr. Hungtington Hartford's supermarkets that jolted me back into the reality of life outside his enchanted forest.

On the day when Betty the welcomer turned into Betty the dispatcher, my good friend and kindred spirit the English lit. professor took time off from the university to come and drive me home, and his company did a lot to alleviate the pangs of withdrawal. But the real break took place only when we stopped, at his suggestion, for me to pick up some groceries at the A & P store a few miles from my village. It was such an obviously sensible idea that he must have wondered why I had not suggested it myself, since there was no food in my refrigerator, and the only way I could get to the supermarket was in some kind friend's car. But I was subconsciously resisting my return to the world of material values (of which the supermarket was a prime symbol), as opposed to the immaterial world of the imagination, in which I had been a carefree sojourner for the past three months; thanks, in the final analysis, to that same supermarket. An ironical example of the convoluted manner in which every aspect of life is tied to its opposite.

And deeper down, on the level of hidden emotions, I dreaded going back to my desolate home, haunted by echoes of joy and love departed, and dark with the lingering shadows of death.

My friend offered to come into the store with me. As a family man with five children to feed, he was, he said, an experienced, not-to-say expert grocery shopper. But this was no ordinary marketing, and I had to do it on my own. So he stayed in the car and read the evening paper while I re-entered what passed for the real world through doors that opened of themselves at my approach and closed behind me, as though eager to draw me in, and unwilling ever again to let me out. It was almost closing time, and the store was crowded with last-minute shoppers. I took a basket and pushed it slowly down one aisle and up another, stopping every now and then to stare at the laden shelves as if they were enigmatic paintings on the walls of an art gallery. My inner resistence, defeated by a suggestion that I could not reasonably turn down, and a pair of automatic doors, had now taken the form of a mental blackout. My mind refused to tell me what items I needed to buy, or where to find them. It was like one of those nightmares in which one is lost in a foreign city without a passport, searching for a hotel whose name and location one has forgotten, along with one's own name.

A glimpse of my friend standing on the other side of the cash registers and waving to me, brought me to my senses. My mind suddenly came up with a shopping list. Bread. Butter. Eggs. Meat. Fruit. . . . I scurried around picking them up at random; white bread or brown, apples or oranges, pork or beef, it made no difference. They filled only one bag. "Is this all?" asked my friend. "You were in here so long that I thought you were shopping for the next six months!"

I said, "I'm sorry I was so slow. . . ." and left it at that. I didn't want him to think me crazy.

As I picked up the threads of my pre-Foundation existence, I realized more and more every day how much my stay there had done for me. How valuable to me as a writer had been the suspension of all my preoccupations but one—the completion of my book, combined with the exclusive society of people who believed in the importance of art. And how much the physical rest, the good meals, the general pampering and protecting had done for me as a physical and emotional convalescent. I still tired easily, my right arm was still painful to use, I still had trouble sleeping, but my nervous energy had come back to me; the driving force that had carried me forward thus far on my obstacle-strewn journey through life, now dispersed the shadows of death and brightened the little house with renewed hope. And the echoes of joy departed were replaced by the echo of K.'s voice saying *Bravo!* from whatever shining sphere he now inhabited, as I typed out the final page of my new novel.

In view of what Oliver Swan had done for my first novel, I took his approval of this new MS as a virtual guarantee that sooner or later he would find a congenial home for it—which he did, and remarkably soon, with Appleton-Century-Crofts. Bruce had the usual option on my next novel. But since they had not been interested in the one I had started to write after *A Crown for Ashes*, their claim on this one was more of a "gentleman's agreement" than anything else. William Bruce, who headed the publishing firm and set its tone, was a gentleman of the old school; so when Oliver Swan, a gentleman of great tact, explained that I wanted, with this book, to reach out to a wider, and more secular audience than their readership provided, I was let go with the utmost grace. My religion meant a lot to me, and I strove to live up to its precepts. But I had embraced it relatively late in a very un-Catholic life. And since life—as a writer has lived it or observed it—is the seedbed of all serious fiction, I felt that I could not be tied down to the limited subjects and strictly Catholic point of view to which such a specifically religious publishing house was committed. In some ways I was very sorry to leave this dignified firm, which had given me such a good start, and the editor, Bernard Wirth, who had treated my tender susceptibilities so gently; a little too gently, perhaps. Rereading that first effort now, I think that in his place I would have been more exacting.

My editor at Appleton-Century-Crofts had relatively few revisions to suggest, and most of them called for expansion rather than cutting. But it had to be done very fast, and I wrote slowly.

So I gave the job of retyping the revised chapters to a young woman, herself an aspiring author, who had been one of my protegés at the state hospital, and was now trying to make it on her own in the outside world.

We worked together in feverish haste at my house. She typing at top speed (she had worked as a secretary in the past), while I proofread each finished page, and made last-minute corrections on those still to be typed. In this streamlined manner we finished the job just in time to meet the publisher's deadline. But more than that had been accomplished; the book had, in a manner of speaking, acquired a co-author. A dream had assumed the aspect of a reality, and become a possibility in the errant mind of the dreamer.

It was now early in January 1956—the first anniversary of K.'s death—and my new book was scheduled to come out in late May. It had also been accepted for publication in England. On the strength of this evidence that I had put my stay at the Foundation to good use, I applied for a second term, to work on two new projects I had in mind. The advances that I had received from Appleton-Century-Crofts, and from Hodder & Stoughton in London, though modest, were enough to keep me going for the next few months, if I was careful. But I was not yet "out of the woods," as Father John cautioned me once again when I made another attempt to give him back his three hundred dollars, "I want you to keep it," he said, "until you are rich enough to give it to me without missing it." The kindness and wisdom of this soon became apparent. The fitful monthly repayments to me on the unsecured loan that Eldon had made to people he believed to be his friends, came to a final stop when they went to live in another state, leaving upwards of seven thousand dollars of the principal still owing, and irrecoverable. Even the illusion of a safety net is a source of moral support—though it could be defined as a dangerous psychological crutch better thrown away. However that may be, mine had been rudely taken away; leaving me face to face with the fact that from now on my survival would depend entirely on my own skill.

My second novel, a short book whose title, *The Burning Jewel*, derived from a poem by Marya Zaturenska, called *The Visitation of Angels*, got an ambiguous reception that puzzled me at the time, but seems in retrospect to have been, at least partly, the result of the book's ambiguous identity. As far as the secular press was concerned, it was to all intents and purposes a first novel, written by an unknown woman, and of no particular significance, or timeliness; all good reasons for neglect. To the Catholic press, on the other hand, it was that embarrassing product, the second novel that fails to live up to an over-praised first, putting fair-minded reviewers into a dilemma of their own making. Most of them steered a middle course between moderate praise and those minor, but maddeningly diverse reservations that in the aggregate can ravage a whole work, as a swarm of tiny caterpillars can defoliate an entire tree. But the fiction reviewers of the two Catholic journals that I most respected intellectually, *Commonweal*, and *The Catholic World*, pronounced such conflicting judgments that it was hard to believe they were writing about the same book. The *Catholic World* review called it a "significant achievement," praised, among other things, its "stylistic sophistication," and said that it placed me in "the front rank of American Catholic writers." But *Commonweal* devoted a whole page to poking malicious fun at what the reviewer described as "religious claptrap" without any literary value whatever. Both these reviewers were men. Leonard Wibberly said of these two critiques that they should be an object lesson to me not to swallow anything whole; too much praise and too much blame are equally bad for a writer's stomach. Leonard was good for me; he could make me laugh when I felt like crying with rage.

Once again, I was invited to the Huntington Hartford Foundation for the months of July, August, and September, but this time I went there in a very different frame of mind. After eighteen months without K., I had finally succeeded in making the emotional and intellectual transition from one stage of my life to another. The creative energy generated by love, and sustained by love's constant encouragement, was fueled now by ambition, necessity, and the finally attained (if still-shaky) belief in myself that K. had so patiently nurtured throughout our years together, and that was, in a sense, his legacy to me.

Emotionally, having put romantic and sexual love (inextricably linked in my philosophy), behind me, I was entering an area of human relationships of which I had little or no previous experience; the area of personal friendships; the most selfless and pure of all human relationships, according to the ascetic Simone Weil's beautiful but uncompromising essay on the subject. My concept of friendship was simpler and less lofty, but still too idealistic, as one's concept of any yearned-for, but untried, relationship tends to be.

As a solitary child living in a remote country village, educated privately, and over-protected by my mother, I had none of the usual opportunities to make friends of my own age, and I turned to books as companions. My wartime marriage and motherhood, when I was barely out of my adolescence, only widened the already existing gap between me and my contemporaries. And when my husband came back from the war, the irrational jealousy that was the reverse side of his love for me precluded anything approaching an autonomous friendship between me and anyone else, whether man, woman, or child (including my own). As time went on, and his progressive "sickness of the soul" that was wrecking our family life threatened to wreck his professional life as well, the need to conceal it was another barrier between me and potential friends. So perhaps it was only to be expected that when everything came out in the open and I was in desperate need of a friend, none was forthcoming. But according to Simone Weil's stern philosophy, in reaching out for help *de profundis* I had been looking for charity and compassion, which have nothing to do with friendship as she defines it.

In any event, my lifelong yearning for a close friend was rendered obsolete by my marriage to K.

Ever since K.'s death, I have been the recipient of unlimited charity and compassion, which have to be transformed into friendship if they are not to end up tasting bitter. But, and here I have to agree with Simone Weil, there can be no friendship where there is inequality. At some point, on some level, there must be reciprocity. But what have I left to give—now that the music has stopped? I try to analyze myself, to determine what desirable attributes I possess in my own right, if any. The result is not encouraging. What I see is a woman of what the French call *un certain âge* (in other words, half over the hill). A widow with none

of a widow's appealing prefixes—not *merry*, not *wealthy*, not even
plump. A late-blooming writer, still in dubious bud with winter
just around the corner. My thoughts go back to my worldly and
far-sighted aunt, who told me when I was twelve to sharpen my
wits, because they were my chief asset—aside from a moderately
well-formed skeleton. Time, and misadventure, have somewhat
diminished the skeleton's supple grace, but not entirely destroyed
it. As for the wits, they are getting sharper every day. Age has its
compensations.

Last summer's bosky refuge amid the grazing deer was given
to someone else this time, and I was assigned to less romantic and
less isolated quarters; a sunny two-roomed cottage with a view of
the corral, the wishing well, and the community house. Next to it,
within hailing distance, was an old barn that had been partially
converted into a painter's studio. A vast, unfinished space, with
shadowy rafters, that rendered its present occupant, a very small,
neat, Japanese painter named Mitsu, as inconspicuous as a mouse
in a cathedral. But Mitsu was no mouse. She embodied in her
compact little person traces of all the baffling elements of the
Japanese national character as it is portrayed in their literature
and their films; where extremes of delicacy and restraint go
hand-in-hand with extremes of blood-curdling violence. Years
ago, in some forgotten European capital, I had encountered, and
admired at various social functions, the exquisitely beautiful
young wife of a Japanese diplomat. But Mitsu was the first
Japanese woman with whom I had come in everyday, informal
contact. And she fascinated me.
    On the evening of my arrival, she had emerged from her barn
door—by accident or design—just as I was passing it on my way
to the community house for dinner. She said, "Hello! I am Mitsu. I
paint." To which I replied, "Hello! I am Theresa. I write."
    "Poems?"
    "No. Novels."
After which terse exchange we strolled along side by side in
silence, sizing each other up, and in my case, wondering whether
the proximity of our living quarters would turn out to be an
advantage or a nuisance. I need not have worried. Mitsu was far

too sensitive, and well-mannered, ever to be intrusive. And by tacit agreement, we formed the habit of walking together to and from the community house every evening—and sometimes in the morning as well—though Mitsu rose earlier than I did.

We enjoyed each other's company, largely, I think, because it was so free of outside associations. And again, as if by mutual agreement, we each followed the golden rule that those who meet and make friends beyond the frontiers of their normal daily existence, do well to keep them there. This protective discretion kept our spontaneous mutual liking independent of those impersonal exterior forces—national origin, religion, social and economic status, what have you—that are just as powerful in keeping compatible individuals apart as they are in uniting the incompatible into artificial groups. And for me, it turned our little téte à tétes into voyages of discovery; not into Mitsu's life outside the gates, but into her mind. Into that mentality of irreconcilable extremes that was so alien to my own inherited British mentality of compromise.

One thing that Mitsu and I had in common was our passionate involvement in the never-ending conflict between art and bread and butter. Our circumstances were different, but the intensity of the struggle was the same for us both. And it was through our preoccupation with this subject, to which our discussions on art, and women's position in the world of the arts, always ended by leading us, that I got some idea of what Mitsu's circumstances were. And just what her stay at the Foundation meant to her. She was married, with at least one young child, though when she spoke of having a "family" to care for, I was never quite sure what she meant. One Sunday afternoon, a whole carload of people came to visit her in her barn (we could entertain guests in our own studios provided that we notified Betty of their coming), and later she referred to them as her "family." Her husband, also Japanese, was a gifted artist, whose work had already brought him some recognition, but not, as yet, very much money. So to make ends meet, Mitsu had put her own artistic ambition aside, to work for a porcelain factory handpainting floral designs on expensive cups and saucers. This was her first visit to the Foundation. She had been there a month when I arrived, and still had one month to go.

She was there, I gathered, with the full agreement of her "family." Yet behind the joy of her liberation from uncreative drudgery, and the resuscitation of her own aspirations as a painter, I sensed the presence of guilt—that pathetic guilt that is felt only by the innocent.

One evening, taking a circular route back to our studios after supper, we passed by the Ping-Pong table, that was set up on a patch of level ground sheltered by trees from the wind. Net, balls, and paddles could be obtained from Betty. The table was dusty with disuse. Mitsu asked me if I played. "I know how to play," I said, "but I was never very much good, and now I have lost the muscular strength of my playing arm."

Mitsu laughed. She laughed a lot, and when she wasn't laughing she was smiling. "Excuse me, please," she said, "but I think that you do *not* know how to play. And if you wish, I will teach you. A strong arm is not needed—only a strong wrist."

Mitsu at the other end of a Ping-Pong table was a revelation. Self-effacing, soft-voiced, polite to the point of exaggeration, she changed as soon as she had a Ping-Pong paddle in her hand to a female warrior of startling ferocity. But her rage was not directed against me, I knew that. She was battling an intangible enemy for which I was merely the stand-in. And I don't think I was far wrong in identifying her antagonist as the code of traditional values that accused her; the same rigid code that compels a Japanese soldier to do his Emperor's will, even when it involves his own suicide.

We played almost every evening. Mitsu won nine times out of ten, and she probably gave me the odd game out of politeness. But in the process of losing to her, I learned how to win (mostly by guile) against other, less-expert players. And the modest skill I achieved proved a useful asset in future situations.

When Mitsu left the Foundation at the end of July, to return, presumably, to what she believed to be her duty, I missed her. I never saw her again, but we kept in touch for as long as I remained in California. From time to time, she would send me little decorated cards of her own designing, inscribed with wistful messages in her charmingly stilted English. And for Christmas she sent me an ingenious plastic gadget for washing dishes under a running faucet, that she hoped would give me more time for writing what she called my "important works."

Sometimes my Ping-Pong battles with Mitsu would be watched, briefly, by the seventy-year-old poet, Jean Starr Untermeyer, who would smile at us indulgently (though not without a touch of condescension), as though humoring the antics of a pair of competitive children.

Mrs. Untermeyer, which was what she liked to be called, was lodged in what I still thought of as the Gregorys' cottage (for me, all its subsequent occupants were usurpers), and I never got used to finding her ensconced in the austere little sitting room, where her stylish, grande-dame appearance seemed as out of place as a spray of orchids in a jam jar. She had beautiful clothes, and believed in looking her best at all times. Clothes played an important part in her life. They were, so to speak, her "colors," the banners that proclaimed her a devotee of beauty, in all its manifestations. But where deeper values were concerned, these bright banners only served to conceal them; to make her worship of beauty seem superficial, even frivolous. And one of her early poems included in her last published collection attests to her melancholy realization that her clothes do not convey her "true image." But notwithstanding this epiphany, she continued to fly her brave colors—she was flying them still—while baring the depths of her soul in her later poems; heartrending lamentations in which the accumulated weight of her own personal sufferings (and she *had* suffered atrociously) and those of the whole Jewish race, was almost too great for a reader to bear. Music might have made the burden less intolerable. But strangely, for such a musical person (a trained lieder singer, a pianist, and an ardent music lover), there is almost no music in her poetry. This places her poetically at the opposite extreme from Horace and Marya, whose poems—especially Horace's—are two-thirds pure music. In other ways, too, they were poles apart. Yet both sides befriended me; which testifies to their fair-mindedness, and also, I like to think, to the depth of their affection for me—perched precariously on the apex of the triangle.

Although these were the most lasting and influential friend-

ships to spring from my two sojourns at the Huntington Hartford
Foundation, there were others, whose inevitable transience did
not make them any the less stimulating; and reassuring, in that
they demonstrated my ability to communicate on both an intellectual and emotional level with creative people of all ages, whose
backgrounds were totally different from my own. This was a
valuable discovery for me, and within it was another one, namely
that my "certain age" was just the right age to qualify me as a
desirable confidante. I was old enough to remain impersonal, but
not too old to be tolerant. And as for experience, I could always
say, "I know! I know!" with conviction, and if anyone doubted it, I
could prove it. Yet though all this was gratifying, it was also
inimical to my writing. It gave me interesting glimpses into
human nature, but it also invaded my mental solitude and used
up a lot of my creative energy. In allowing myself to be cast in the
role of confidante, I had unwittingly aggravated the novelist's
classic dilemma: how to combine the antithetical means required
to bring about the desired end; how to balance the need to mingle
with all kinds of people, and learn at firsthand what makes them
tick, with the need for long periods of solitude, in which to convert
this raw material into art—or at least into a good story. A
dilemma already aggravated in my case by the dichotomy in my
own temperament, inherited from an outgoing, charismatic
father, and a withdrawn, visionary mother, whose sentiments
toward people could be aptly summed up in four lines from one of
her favorite hymns, which lauds the beauty of the world. . . . *From
Greenland's icy mountains/to India's coral strand.* . . . A world in
which, it concludes misanthropically . . . *every prospect pleases/
and only man is vile.*

8

Renewal Begins with a Whirlybird Ride

*T*HE Hungarian uprising of 1956 and its tragic defeat by the Soviet tanks, that took place shortly after my return home from the Foundation in October, challenged my faith in the moral greatness of my newly adopted country as it would never again be challenged. Because never again would I be so naive as to imagine that any head of state, even the president of the most democratic country in the world, would put an unwritten moral obligation ahead of expediency.

In retrospect, there are rational explanations for President Eisenhower's seemingly callous disregard for Hungary's desperate cries for help; to intervene militarily would have been to risk another war for the sake of a country which had fought, however unwillingly, on the enemy's side in the last one; and this crisis had come up at a bad moment, just when another one was brewing—fanned by the British—around the Suez Canal, a competitive event that was also taking up the attention of that nominal source of help, the United Nations. But at the time, to all those who were emotionally involved in Hungary's fate, President Eisenhower's failure to take any positive action to save her, looked like a shabby betrayal.

Among those who were psychologically injured by this traumatic disillusionment, were the teen-age sons and daughters of postwar Hungarian immigrants to the U.S.A., the contemporaries of the gallant young revolutionaries who had died fighting Soviet tanks with homemade hand grenades. These innocent boys and girls who had had the luck to be taken out of harm's way, and transplanted while still very young into the free soil of America, were now prey to the indefinable guilt that haunts all those who escape, or manage to survive a situation in which others like them perish. And mixed up with this unjustified sense of guilt may well have been a romantic, youthful regret for glory missed.

One such young product of war and dislocation was the eldest of Genevra's four children, the fourteen-year-old Peter. As the son of a dispossessed Hungarian father and a staunchly British mother, born in Hungary during the war on the country estate that should have been his inheritance, but became a battlefield instead, and now growing up in America, this rather frail boy found himself pulled three ways, by three separate loyalties that would eventually have to be synthesized if he was to become a whole man. Normally shy and diffident, his immediate response to this emotional pressure was to stand up in school and challenge his political science teacher in front of the whole class to reconcile America's abandonment of Hungary to the Soviets with the grand principles of democracy and freedom of which America was supposed to be the defender.

The young seem able to recover from traumatic experiences, whether physical or emotional, more easily than their elders. And the tragedy of the failed Hungarian uprising left no visible scars on my grandson's personality. He went through the various maddening phases of adolescence like any other teenager, and if he differed from his American peers, it was in his tendency to be secretive, to keep his ideas and opinions to himself. It was there, in the secret places of the heart, that the trauma of 1956 had left its deadly seeds.

As for my own divided loyalties, I was used to them. I had lived with them for years, and had come to regard them as part of the human condition. With disillusionment, too, I was familiar. Which did not make it any the less painful. But this time the pain, that was mixed with anger, was mitigated by the overwhelming proof I received that even a government that is for and by the people does not necessarily reflect the people's thinking.

When the Hungarian revolution became front-page news, vying for space with the Suez Canal crisis, the local newspaper sent a reporter to interview me. Next day, an article appeared in the paper reminding its readers of K., and the contribution that he, a Hungarian refugee, had made to the musical life of the town; and then, after mentioning my first novel, that was set in wartime Hungary, spoke of my present anxiety concerning the safety of K.'s two daughters and three grandchildren living in Budapest. The response to this article amounted to an apology, a collective atonement on the part of the people for their government's sins of omission.

During the see-saw period between the first hopeful stage of the uprising and its despairing final stages, when the Iron Curtain was lowered once more between Hungary and the West, nervous Hungarians took the opportunity to cross the Austrian border in droves, and on reading about this, a well-to-do citizen, who had been one of K.'s admirers, offered to sponsor Mari's immigration to the United States with her three children. The offer was conveyed to her through the Red Cross, and she let us know by the same means that she could not accept it. It was only much later, when it was possible for her to communicate with me more freely, that I pieced together her reasons for deciding to stay in Hungary, come what might; and I think I am safe in saying that what held her back was a mixture of love, pity, and fear of the unknown—but mostly love. Love for her frail younger sister; compassion for her mother; pity, and a few stubborn vestiges of love for her faithless husband, who was critically ill at the time; and finally, love for her native land, which only a stronger, more personal attachment on this side of the Atlantic could have outweighed. Had her father been still alive, she would, I believe, have taken the leap into the unknown that was all the more frightening because it was so sudden and so final. As it was, she succumbed to the gravitational pull of the city in which she had lived all her life, and the outstretched hands of those who needed her there.

According to all reports, living conditions in Budapest were little better at this point than they had been immediately after the war, and many of the basic necessities of life, particularly clothing, were in such short supply that for a long time after the revolution was over, individual "care" packages (limited to a certain number per person per month), were allowed into the country duty free. And very soon my living room was piled high with gifts of clothing of all kinds and sizes, donated not only by my personal friends, but also by people I scarcely knew, who had read my books, or heard me speak, or heard K. play. And along with these tangible testimonials of sympathy came the money to pay for their postage to Hungary—which was high. In the face of such love and generosity, how could resentment live? In spite of myself, I began to think more kindly of President Eisenhower.

As I sorted out all these things according to size and suitability, packed them into cartons, which had to be very securely packaged, and lugged them one at a time to the post office, I thought of Eldon, and his "Operation Lifesaver," and of how I had promised after his death to requite his devotion by making a success of my life in the New World to which he had brought me. And that meant, could only mean, making a success of my life as a writer. But what constituted success? My definition of it was changing, and the steps leading up to it were becoming more and more difficult to climb. I had written my first novel in less than a year, for the simple reason that I had no idea of what the problems were that I was so rashly tackling. I had a story to tell, and I went ahead and told it in the straightforward narrative style that came to me naturally, without any awareness of novelistic techniques. But since then, I had lost my innocence, and now it would take me five years, or more, to write a novel of the same length.

During my second summer at the Foundation, I had been invited to speak at Mount Saint Mary's College in Los Angeles, and afterward to autograph copies of my recently published second novel, as well as a few copies of my first. The scholarly nun who was in charge of the event congratulated me warmly on having learned so much in such a short time about how to write a novel. A backhanded compliment that delighted me because it was so honest. I still had a lot to learn. But I knew the difference now between a good story and a good novel. I also knew that the good story was likely to make the most money. But I saw no reason why popularity and literary worth should be mutually exclusive. Wouldn't real success be a combination of the two?

To Horace and Marya Gregory, success meant first and foremost excellence, and its recognition by those whose opinion they respected. Money, though they were often in need of it, like most poets, was incidental. This would have been a dangerous philosophy to preach to a penniless middle-aged neophyte like me, had I not been exposed to it before. Not long ago, the Gregory's son, Patrick, told me that his parents had feared that they might have done me a disservice by raising such lofty standards for me to emulate, and communicating to me their disdain for mediocrity. Never having known K., they could not know that they were only restating, and reinforcing for me, the artistic creed that K. had lived by all his life.

Luckily for my base material welfare, these high and heady principles were kept in balance with reality by the practical-minded Oliver Swan, who discouraged any attempts on my part to indulge in literary flights for which my wings were inadequate. When I sent him the tentative MS of an "experimental" novella, he responded sternly, "How often must I impress on you, Theresa, that the first function of a novel is to be entertaining." Which besides being undeniably true, strengthened my resolve to succeed one day in writing an entertaining novel that had literary merit as well, and would make some money for me (and him) into the bargain.

But what was I going to live on in the meantime? By the winter of 1956 this problem was becoming acute. It was momentarily solved by the sale of the grand piano to a new member of the university music faculty, who fell in love with its rich, prewar Bechstein tone. It was going, like a loved pet, to a "good home," where it would be played on for hours every day, instead of sitting unopened and untouched in a corner of my living room, going quietly out of tune. But the parting was sad. It had been my wedding gift to K. It had come through the siege unscathed. It was part of my life that the movers were carrying out the door.

I was getting advice on my situation from all sides. Those of my friends who considered the writing of books to be a hobby rather than a profession, urged me to find a job, "There must be all sorts of opportunities open to you, with your languages and experience . . . and you can always write on the weekends." My literary friends, who knew how important it was for me to put all of my limited energy (and what might be my limited time) into my writing, advised me to try for Fellowships at the two artists' colonies in the East: Yaddo, and the MacDowell Colony, for both of which the Gregorys and Mrs. Untermeyer said they would recommend me. Father John, more intellectual than the first group, and more practical than the second, advised me to do both; apply for the Fellowships, and during the waiting period, look around for a job, in case I didn't get them. I followed this advice. But the jobs I turned up, he was the first to turn down. A wealthy old man, confined to a wheelchair, wanted a live-in secretary/companion. An elderly Catholic couple in San Diego offered a comfortable room and full board in return for a little "light housekeeping." . . . "You don't want to be a housekeeper! Or the slave of some crotchety old man!" "Of course I don't, Father—but what else can you suggest?"

Mrs. Untermeyer had a suggestion. Her wide circle of friends and literary acquaintances was nothing if not ecumenical. And among them was the Catholic poet-nun, Sister Madeleva, who was then president of Saint Mary's College for women, in South Bend, Indiana. She would certainly be interested in me as a new Catholic writer, and might possibly have some part-time position to offer me. So Mrs. Untermeyer wrote to Sister Madeleva about me, and she agreed to meet with me when she came to Los Angeles to give some readings. The Irish organist, who was thrilled by the idea of meeting the famous poet-nun, drove me up to Los Angeles in her car. We arrived at the convent where Sister Madeleva was staying a few minutes before the appointed time. But it was only after a long wait in one of those chilly convent parlors that condemn the sin of luxury *in absentia*, that a fluttery young nun ushered us into what I can only call "the presence."

Pale and remote in her nun's habit and coif, the poet sat on a hard, straight-backed armchair (of the kind found in church sanctuaries), with the dignity of a queen giving an audience. I presented the Irish organist to her as an ardent admirer of her work, and herself a poet and occasional contributer to Catholic magazines. Sister Madeleva accepted the compliment with a faint, self-deprecating smile, but expressed no interest in the Irish organist's versifying. Instead, she asked her if she would care to see the Convent Chapel, and thus politely dismissed, my friend went off with the young nun and left me there feeling like an unsatisfactory novice about to be reprimanded by the Mother Superior.

She asked me a few questions about myself, as if to confirm what Mrs. Untermeyer had told her about me. Then she said, "There are many fine writers who are unable to live solely by their writing. It is unfortunate." Then, after a little silence, "What do you want me to do for you?"

What I wanted her to do at that moment was to show me a little human warmth—something that was not, as I knew from Father Patrick, incompatible with holiness. But it did imply a certain degree of spiritual freedom, of achieved self-mastery, and looking back, I think that this poet-nun may still have been engaged in the struggle to purge herself of the human emotions that her poems unwittingly betrayed.

I said, in answer to her question, that seemed to be more than half rhetorical, "Mrs. Untermeyer thought that you might be able to offer me a part-time position of some sort. . . ."

She considered this for a moment or two. Then she said, "Would you be willing to live in one of our dormitories? They are rather noisy. . . ."

A noisy dormitory was the last place I wanted to live in, but I knew that I had to say "Yes" without hesitation.

She held out her hand. "I will look into the matter when I get back, and let you know if something can be found—but in any case, it would not be until the fall semester."

The interview was over.

"What a beautiful woman!" the Irish organist said, as we drove away. "So spiritual! Just like her poems. Is she going to give you a job?"

"I don't know. I don't even know if I want her to. It would mean leaving all my friends."

"You would soon make new ones. You're the sort that makes friends wherever they are . . . good grief! What an awful sentence! But you know what I mean."

"The older that sort get the more difficult it becomes," I said, and we both laughed; a little hysterically in my case, to cover my disappointment.

Waiting, and uncertainty, blocked my writing. There was nothing I could do to hasten the decisions from Yaddo and the MacDowell Colony. But I could, and did, end the uncertainty created by my interview with Sister Madeleva. When it became clear to me that its cause was not only my reluctance to leave the friends who had buoyed me up through so many bad times, but my fear of once again losing my independence as a writer; of coming under the domination of the "snow queen" whose icy lure had both fascinated and terrified me in the fairy-tale world of my childhood. Guided by intuition, I wrote to Sister Madeleva, thanking her for giving me her time and attention, but telling her only half the truth, namely that I did not feel ready yet to leave California, my family, my friends, and all the memories that it held for me. She did not answer this letter. And perhaps she was right not to. For only a few months later, I did precisely what I had told her that I was not ready to do.

When I got a letter from Yaddo inviting me to go there for the months of June and July, and one from the MacDowell Colony, inviting me for the months of August and September and offering me a "free scholarship," (Yaddo was free, but the Mac-Dowell Colony, less well-endowed, asked for a modest weekly fee from those who could afford it), I could scarcely believe my good fortune; which was, I knew, less the result of my qualifications, than of the belief in my talent and the efforts on behalf of it of all my literary friends, old and new, and of the Gregorys in particular. Not to mention the prayers offered up by my friends Father Patrick and Father John, who believed in me as a person.

The invitations arrived in April, which gave me about six weeks in which to make up my mind about a number of things before flying to New York, where I would stay for a few days with the Gregorys before going on by train to Yaddo, in Saratoga Springs. But it took me less than one week to make a second intuitive decision. I gave my good Scots landlord a month's notice, as of the first of June—much to his dismay. He had hoped that I would go on living in his house until he was ready to live in it himself, and he suggested that I should sublet it furnished during my four-month absence. But my intuition told me that the California phase of my life was at an end, and it was only as a concession to well-meant advice that I kept enough things to furnish a studio apartment, in case my intuition was wrong. These things, with some cartons of books, my pictures, and the Big Box packed with my small personal possessions, were stored for me by the English lit. professor, who had a large house, and by Károly and Genevra in their garage. The yellow marble head found a temporary home with a friend who had fallen in love with its melancholy half-smile. My oriental rugs went (all but one) to Father John, as a more fitting repayment of his kindness than money, and of more value to him, since he had been moved to a new position, with uncarpeted living quarters. The cello I shipped to a well-known dealer in old instruments, recommended to me by Mrs. Untermeyer, for appraisal and eventual sale—if he could find a good buyer. Quite apart from the money, I wanted it to be played on once again. Everything else I sold. Which left me, when all my obligations were taken care of, with an airline ticket to New York in my pocket and four hundred dollars in the bank.

The last objects to be sold were my gas refrigerator and stove. I had put a notice on the want-ads board in the village post office, offering them for sale at twenty-five and fifteen dollars, respectively. On the last day but one, a tall, old man with a long, white beard that made him look like a prophet, came to look at the refrigerator, and finding it in good working order, offered to buy it for twenty dollars cash. "Done," I said. "You can pick it up tomorrow."

As he took the notes from his wallet, he gave me a penetrating look, as if he doubted my honesty. "Are you saved?" he said.

Surprised, and a bit embarrassed, I said, "I hope so."

"You *hope* so? What sort of answer is that? *Are you, or are you not saved?*"

The Catholic spirit in me gave the wrong answer. "Whether or not I am saved," I said, "depends on the mercy of God."

He put his wallet back in his pocket. "Good day to you," he said. "I do business only with the saved."

Next day, I let the refrigerator and the stove and a couple of other household items go for five–dollars–the–lot to a dealer in junk who didn't care whether I was saved or damned so long as he got a good bargain.

Genevra came every day to help me pack. She was sad. "This

isn't just another move," she said, "it's the breakup of a home." And she knew me well enough to realize that it would not be put together again in California.

I spent my last night in California at the home of the English lit. professor and his wife, who would drive me next day to an open field a few miles distant, from which a helicopter shuttle would take me to the Los Angeles airport. Earlier in the evening, I went to say goodbye to the Irish organist, and to Father Patrick, who would be at her house to give me his blessing. He was late in arriving, and we were still talking when she had to leave for a choir practice.

"I wish I didn't have to go," she said, hugging me, "but it isn't as if you were leaving forever—we'll be seeing each other again in a few months' time. . . ."

But I would never see her again. Or Father Patrick.

The day of my departure was cloudless. I climbed into the whirlybird with a sense of excitement and anticipation. It was my first helicopter ride ever, which seemed an appropriate beginning for a new chapter in the on-going adventure of my life.

On the previous evening, I had called Marya Gregory to confirm the time of my arrival at the Riverside Drive apartment, which, since I was taking the more economical night flight to New York, would be about eight o'clock in the morning. Would that be too early for her and Horace?

"We are usually up and about by eight," Marya said, "but if we are still asleep when you get here, just walk in. We will leave the door unlocked."

"Aren't you afraid of being robbed while you sleep?"

She laughed; her wonderfully amused laugh that set one laughing too, without even knowing what the joke was. "The only valuable things we possess," she said, "are our books, and thieves have no use for books. There's no market for them—you know that."

DATE DUE

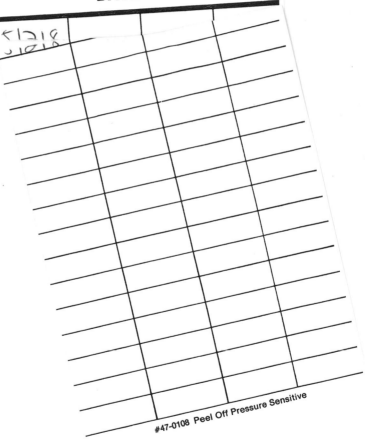

#47-0108 Peel Off Pressure Sensitive